MW01169999

The Essential Sternberg

Essays on
Intelligence,
Psychology,
and Education

About the Editors

James C. Kaufman, PhD, is an Associate Professor at the California State University at San Bernardino, where he is also the director of the Learning Research Institute. He received his PhD from Yale University in Cognitive Psychology, where his mentor was Robert J. Sternberg. Kaufman has authored more than 100 articles and written or edited 12 books. Kaufman was recently named a co-editor of the official journal for APA's Division 10, *Psychology, Aesthetics, and the Arts*. He received the 2003 Daniel E. Berlyne Award from Division 10 of the American Psychological Association for outstanding research by a junior scholar, and the 2008 E. Paul Torrance Award from the Creativity Division of National Association of Gifted Children.

Elena L. Grigorenko, PhD, received a doctorate in general psychology from Moscow State University, Russia, in 1990, and a doctorate in developmental psychology and genetics from Yale University, USA, in 1996. Currently, Dr. Grigorenko is Associate Professor of Child Studies and Psychology at Yale and Associate Professor of Psychology at Moscow State University. Dr. Grigorenko has published more than 200 peer-reviewed articles, book chapters, and books. She has received awards for her work from five different divisions of the American Psychological Association. In 2004, she won the APA Distinguished Award for an Early Career Contribution to Developmental Psychology.

The Essential Sternberg

Essays on Intelligence, Psychology, and Education

Editors
James C. Kaufman, PhD
Elena L. Grigorenko, PhD

SPRINGER PUBLISHING COMPANY

New York

Springer Publishing Company, LLC
11 West 42nd Street
New York, NY 10036
www.springerpub.com

Acquisitions Editor: Philip Laughlin
Production Editor: Pamela Lankas
Cover design: David Levy
Composition: International Graphic Services

Ebook ISBN: 978-0-8261-3838-5

09 10 11 12 13 / 5 4 3 2 1

Library of Congress Cataloging-in-Publication Data

Sternberg, Robert J.
   [Essays. Selections]
   The essential Sternberg : essays on intelligence, psychology, and education / editors, James C. Kaufman, Elena L. Grigorenko.
        p. cm.
   Includes bibliographical references and index.
   ISBN 978-0-8261-3837-8
   1. Intellect. 2. Intelligence tests. 3. Educational psychology. 4. Learning, Psychology of. 5. Sternberg, Robert J.   I. Kaufman, James C.   II. Grigorenko, Elena L.   III. Title.
   BF431.S84 2009
   153.9—dc22   2008045857

Printed in the United States of America by Bang Printing

Contents

Robert J. Sternberg (Bob Sternberg) is the foremost psychological and educational theorist, researcher, and reformer of his time. He left an endowed professorship at Yale University to become the Dean of the School of Arts and Sciences and Professor of Psychology and Education at Tufts University to bring his ideas to a hands-on, real-life situation. He is changing the admissions process at Tufts in ways that have been called "bold," "innovative," and "exciting."

About This Book

The goal of this book is to compile a "best of" Sternberg's work. As his research is being applied more and more and the impact of his writing extends to thousands of people, a new audience for his work and writings is developing. This book provides a core collection of what he and his colleagues think are his best papers, tracing the evolution of his popular theory of successful intelligence and his thoughts on the educational process.

We have selected, in consultation with Bob and our colleagues, what we believe to be some of the best writing, research, and theoretical contributions by Sternberg. In Section I, we've selected three different articles, from 1980, 1984, and 1999, that show the development and progression of Sternberg's theory of successful intelligence. In Section II, we include articles on each one of the three components of Sternberg's theory: creativity, practical intelligence, and analytic reasoning. Section III describes Sternberg's theory as it relates to the classroom, with a theoretical piece and two empirical articles that focus on how the theory of successful intelligence can be used to improve student performance and supplement traditional exams. Section IV includes two recent essays that directly test the theory in college admission settings. Section V presents two articles about Sternberg's most recent theory, the WICS (wisdom, intelligence, and creativity, synthesized) model, with its new focus on wisdom. Finally, Section VI offers brief writings by Sternberg that yield insight into his opinions on different questions in psychology.

We hope that this collection provides a comprehensive yet convenient overview of Sternberg's work. For those familiar with Sternberg's theories and research, this book represents a chance to read his original articles. For those unfamiliar with Sternberg's legacy, this book offers a rare treat—the chance to see the evolution of one of the great thinkers of our time.

James C. Kaufman, PhD, San Bernardino, CA
Elena L. Grigorenko, PhD, New Haven, CT

Acknowledgments

The editors would like to especially thank Phil Laughlin for his efforts in making this volume come together. We also thank Stacy Brooks, Pamela Lankas, Samaneh Pourja-lali, and Cheri Stahl for their help in preparing the manuscript and obtaining permissions.

Permissions

Cianciolo, A. T., Grigorenko, E., Jarvin, L., Gil, G., Drebot, M. E., & Sternberg, R. J. (2006). Practical intelligence and tacit knowledge: Advancements in measurement and construct validity. *Learning and Individual Differences, 16*, 235–253. Reprinted with the permission of Elsevier Ltd.

Hedlund, J., Wilt, J. M., Nebel, K. R., Ashford, S. J., & Sternberg, R. J. (2006). Assessing practical intelligence in business school admissions: A supplement to the Graduate Management Admissions Test. *Learning and Individual Differences, 16*, 101–127. Copyright Elsevier (2005). Reprinted with the permission of Elsevier Ltd.

Stemler, S. E., Grigorenko, E. L., Jarvin, L., & Sternberg, R. J. (2006). Using the theory of successful intelligence as a basis for augmenting AP exams in psychology and statistics. *Contemporary Educational Psychology, 31*, 344–376. Reprinted with the permission of Elsevier Ltd.

Sternberg, R. J. (1977). Component processes in analogical reasoning. *Psychological Review, 84*, 353–378. Copyright (1977) by the American Psychological Association. Reprinted with permission.

Sternberg, R. J. (1980). Sketch of a componential subtheory of human intelligence. *Behavioral and Brain Sciences, 3*, 573–584. Reprinted with the permission of Cambridge University Press.

Sternberg, R. J. (1984). Toward a triarchic theory of human intelligence. *Behavioral and Brain Sciences, 7*, 269–287. Reprinted with the permission of Cambridge University Press.

Sternberg, R. J. (1997). Fads in psychology: What we can do. *APA Monitor, 28*(7). Copyright (1997) by the American Psychological Association. Reprinted with permission.

Sternberg, R. J. (1998). A balance theory of wisdom. *Review of General Psychology,* *2*, 347–365. Copyright (1998) by the American Psychological Association. Reprinted with permission.

Sternberg, R. J. (1999). The theory of successful intelligence. *Review of General Psychology,* *3*, 292–316. Copyright (1999) by the American Psychological Association. Reprinted with permission.

Sternberg, R. J. (2003). APA is a diamond in the rough. *APA Monitor, 34*(1), 5. Copyright (2003) by the American Psychological Association. Reprinted with permission.

Sternberg, R. J. (2003). It all started with those darn IQ tests: Half a career spent defying the crowd. In R. J. Sternberg (Ed.), *Psychologists defying the crowd* (pp. 256–270). Copyright (2003) by the American Psychological Association. Reprinted with permission.

Sternberg, R. J. (2003). Teaching for successful intelligence: Principles, practices, and outcomes. *Educational and Child Psychology, 20*(2), 6–18. Reprinted with permission of the British Psychological Society.

Sternberg, R. J. (2004). Good intentions, bad results: A dozen reasons why the No Child Left Behind (NCLB) Act is failing our nation's schools. *Education Week, 24*(9), 42, 56.

Sternberg, R. J. (2005). Producing tomorrow's leaders—in psychology and everything else. *Eye on Psi Chi, (10)*1, 14–15, 32–33. Copyright (2005) by the National Honor Society in Psychology. Reprinted with permission.

Sternberg, R. J. (2005). WICS: A model of positive educational leadership comprising wisdom, intelligence, and creativity synthesized. *Educational Psychology Review, 17*(3), 191–262. Reprinted with the permission of Springer Science + Business Media.

Sternberg, R. J. (2006). The nature of creativity. *Creativity Research Journal, 18*, 87–99.

Sternberg, R. J., & Grigorenko, E. L. (2001). Unified psychology. *American Psychologist, 56*(12), 1069–1079. Copyright (2001) by the American Psychological Association. Reprinted with permission.

Sternberg, R. J., Grigorenko, E. L., Ferrari, M., & Clinkenbeard, P. (1999). A triarchic analysis of an aptitude–treatment interaction. *European Journal of Psychological Assessment, 15*, 1–11. Reprinted with the permission of Hogrefe & Huber Publishers.

Sternberg, R. J., & The Rainbow Project Collaborators. (2006). The Rainbow Project: Enhancing the SAT through assessments of analytical, practical and creative skills. *Intelligence, 34*, 321–350. Reprinted with the permission of Elsevier Ltd.

Sternberg, R. J., Torff, B., & Grigorenko, E. L. (1998). Teaching triarchically improves school achievement. *Journal of Educational Psychology, 90*, 374–384. Copyright (1998) by the American Psychological Association. Reprinted with permission.

Section I

An Introduction to the Theory of Successful Intelligence

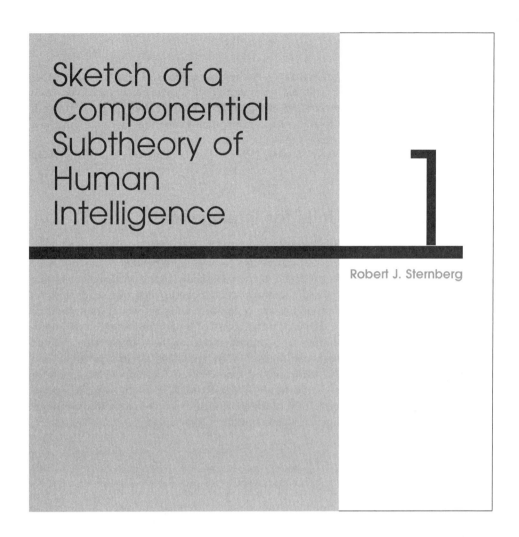

Sketch of a Componential Subtheory of Human Intelligence

1

Robert J. Sternberg

This chapter presents a sketch of a componential subtheory of human intelligence. This theory attempts to account for many of the empirical phenomena reported in the literature on human abilities. In view of the obvious ambitiousness of this attempt, I wish to make explicit two caveats implicit in the title of the chapter.

First, the chapter presents a sketch, not a finished product. Some of the proposals are clear and reasonably well articulated; others are fuzzy and in need of further articulation. Some of the proposals have solid empirical backing from my own laboratory or the laboratories of others; others have only the most meager empirical backing, or none at all. These last proposals are intended as stimuli for future research, rather than as generalizations from the results of past research. It will be many years before the theory as a whole will have been subjected to thorough empirical testing. In the meantime, it suggests possible directions for empirical research. As time goes by, the outline should become sharper and the shading better articulated.

Second, the chapter presents a limited subtheory, not a comprehensive, full theory of intelligence. Even if the proposals were close to their final form, they would still constitute a subtheory, because there is almost certainly much more to intelligence than is covered by the scope of the present proposals. They do not deal at all with issues of motivation, initiative, and social competence, and they deal only minimally with issues of creativity and generativity (see Sternberg, 1981a). There are many other issues that are dealt with only minimally, or not at all. The subtheory evolved from research on reasoning, problem solving, and their acquisition. Hence, its most immediate applicability is probably to those aspects of intelligence that derive from these domains; and even here, the coverage of the theory is certainly incomplete.

Having expressed these two caveats, I proceed to a consideration of the theory's predecessors.

Alternative Basic Units for Intelligence

Theories of human intelligence have traditionally relied on some basic unit of analysis for explaining sources of individual differences in intelligent behavior. Theories have differed in terms of (a) what is proposed as the basic unit; (b) the particular instantiations of this unit that are proposed somehow to be locked inside our heads; and (c) the way in which these instantiations are organized with respect to one another. Differences in basic units have defined "paradigms" of theory and research on intelligence; differences in instantiations and organizations of these units have defined particular theories within these paradigms. What are these alternative units, and what are the theories that have incorporated them? Three alternative basic units for intelligence will be considered: the factor, the S-R bond, and the component (or elementary information process). Each of these basic units leads to a somewhat different conception of what intelligence is and how it is constituted.

The Factor

In most traditional investigations of intelligence, the basic unit of analysis has been the factor. The paradigm in which this unit has been defined and used is referred to as the "differential," "psychometric," or "factorial" paradigm. Factors are obtained by "factor analyzing" a matrix of intercorrelations (or covariances) between scores on tests of measures of ability. Factor analysis tends to group into single factors observable sources of individual-difference variation that are highly correlated with each other, and to group into different factors observable sources of variation that are only modestly correlated or not at all correlated with each other. These new groupings are each proposed to represent unitary, latent sources of individual differences at some level of analysis. Theorists generally agree that other levels of analysis, in which factors would either be further subdivided or further combined, would be possible as well.

What, exactly, is a factor? There is no single, agreed-upon answer to this question. Thurstone (1947) noted that "factors may be called by different names, such as 'causes,' 'faculties,' 'parameters,' 'functional unities,' 'abilities,' or 'independent measurements' " (p. 56). Royce (1963) added to this list "dimensions, determinants, . . . and taxonomic categories" (p. 522), and Cattell (1971) has referred to factors as "source traits."

Factor theorists have differed with respect to the particular factors purported to be basic to intelligence. (See Brody & Brody, 1976; Butcher, 1970; Cronbach, 1970 for reviews.) Spearman (1927) suggested that intelligence comprises one general factor that is common to all of the tasks that are used in the assessment of intelligence, and as many specific factors as there are tasks. Holzinger (1938) suggested the need for a third kind of factor, a group factor common to some but not all of the tasks used to assess intelligence. Thurstone (1938) proposed that intelligence is best understood in terms of multiple factors, or primary mental abilities, as he called them. He tentatively identified seven such factors, leaving open the possibility that more would be discovered later: verbal comprehension, word fluency, number, reasoning, spatial visualization, perceptual speed, and memory. Guilford (1967) has proposed a theory encompassing 120 factors formed by crossing five operations, six products, and four contents. The concept of a hierarchical theory can be traced back at least to Burt (1940), and more sophisticated hierarchical factor theories have been proposed by Jensen (1970), who reviews a variety of hierarchical theories, and by Vernon (1971). In Jensen's theory, intelligence is viewed as comprising two levels: associative learning ability (called Level I) and conceptual learning and problem solving (called Level II). Spearman's general factor is seen as corresponding to Level II intelligence. In Vernon's theory, factors are proposed to be of four kinds: (1) a general factor, encompassing all tasks; (2) major group factors, including a verbal-educational factor and a practical-mechanical factor; (3) minor group factors; and (4) specific factors. Humphreys (1962) has proposed a sophisticated hierarchical theory that combines aspects of the Burt-Vernon tradition of hierarchical factor analysis with aspects of Guttman's (1954) facet analysis, in which intelligence is subdivided in terms of logical dimensions. Cattell (1971) and Horn (1968) have proposed a theory according to which the general factor noted by Spearman (1927) is alleged to comprise two subfactors: crystallized ability, measured by tests such *as* vocabulary and general information; and fluid ability, measured by tests such as abstract analogies and abstract series completions. Horn and Cattell (1966) also extracted subfactors representing visualization and cognitive-speed abilities.

The S–R Bond

Stimulus-response (S–R) theorizing has had less influence on theory and research in intelligence than have the other units we are considering, and hence will be treated more briefly. The role of the S–R bond concept in theorizing about intelligence can be traced back to Thorndike (1911; Thorndike, Bregman, Cobb, & Woodyard, 1928) who, like subsequent S–R theorists, viewed intelligence primarily in terms of the ability to learn. In early S–R theorizing, intelligence was understood in terms of the buildup of simple S–R bonds. A more sophisticated and variegated view has been proposed by Gagne (1970), who has suggested that there are eight kinds of learning, which differ among themselves in both the quantity and quality of S–R bonds involved. From simplest to most complex, these are signal learning (Pavlovian conditioning), stimulus-response learning (operant conditioning), chaining (complex operant conditioning), verbal association, discrimination learning, concept learning, rule learning, and problem solving.

The Component

A component is an elementary information process that operates on internal representations of objects or symbols (Sternberg, 1977; see also Nevell & Simon, 1972). The component may translate a sensory input into a conceptual representation, transform one conceptual representation into another, or translate a conceptual representation into a motor output. What is considered elementary enough to be labeled a component depends on the desired level of theorizing. Just as factors can be split into successively finer subfactors, so components can be split into successively finer subcomponents. Thus, no claim is made that any of the components referred to later in this chapter are elementary at all levels of analysis. Rather, they are elementary at a convenient level of analysis. The same caveat applies to the proposed typology of components. Other typologies could doubtless be proposed that would serve this or other theoretical purposes as well or better. The particular typology proposed, however, has proved to be convenient in at least certain theoretical and experimental contexts.

A number of theories have been proposed during the past decade that might be labeled, at least loosely, as componential. Hunt (1978; Hunt, Frost, & Lunneborg, 1973; Hunt, Lunneborg, & Lewis, 1975) has proposed that individual differences in the efficacy of execution of information-processing components such as those found in simple tasks studied in the cognitive psychologist's laboratory are a significant source of individual differences in higher-order verbal ability as measured by standard tests of intelligence. For example, Hunt has found that in the matching task of Posner and Mitchell (1967), the difference in response latency between a name match ("Aa" match in name but not in physical appearance) and a physical match ("AA" match in physical appearance as well as in name) is moderately correlated across subjects (about −.30) with scores on a verbal ability test. Carroll (1976) has done a compelling armchair analysis of a number of factors from standard psychometric ability tests in terms of some of the information-processing components that might be sources of individual differences in these factors. Jensen (1979; Jensen & Munro, 1979) has found that simple reaction time and movement time in an elegant choice reaction time paradigm are moderately correlated with scores on the Raven (1965) Progressive Matrices. Pellegrino and Glaser (1979) have found that certain components of information processing seem to be common across inductive reasoning tests such as verbal analogies, geometric analogies, and letter series extrapolations. Snow (1979) has suggested that individual differences in intelligence can be understood in part in terms of differences in latencies of component execution, as well as in terms of differences in choices of components, in strategies for combining components, and in global aspects of information processing. Campione and Brown (1979) and Butterfield and Belmont (1977) have shown that mental retardation can be understood at least in part in terms of the retarded individual's tendency to select strategies that are nonoptimal for task performance.

Interrelations Among Units

The alternative units discussed previously are not mutually exclusive; on the contrary, they are complementary. Stimulus–response theorizing concentrates on the external or environmental contingencies that lead to various kinds of responses, whereas factorial and componential theorizing concentrate on the internal effects of these contingencies. Factorial models tend to be structural ones, although they often contain clear implications for understanding information processing; componential models tend to be process ones, although they often contain clear implications for understanding how information is structured. I propose, along with Carroll (1976) and others, that factors can be understood in terms of components. But components should not be viewed as superseding factors in that for at least some educational purposes (such as predicting performance), factors are probably still the preferred unit of analysis. For other educational purposes (such as training performance), components are probably the preferred unit of analysis (see Sternberg, 1981).

Certain of the theories noted earlier help place interrelations among alternative units of analysis into sharper perspective. Spearman's (1927) general factor, for example, has often been understood in terms of individual differences in people's abilities to implement Spearman's (1923) three principles of cognition—apprehension of experience (encoding stimuli), eduction of relations (inferring rules), and eduction of correlates (applying rules). Guilford's (1967) theory has clear process implications, in that one of the three facets in Guilford's structure-of-intellect cube isolates processes as factors. And in Jensen's (1970) theory, Level I intelligence can be understood in terms of the relatively simple kinds of associative learning studied by early S–R theorists, whereas Level II intelligence can be understood in terms of the more complex kinds of conceptual learning studied only by later S–R theorists (such as Gagne, 1970). In sum, then, the various units are compatible, not contradictory. They highlight different aspects of the global and ill-defined concept of intelligence. The emphasis in this chapter on the component as the unit of analysis reflects my view that the component is a particularly useful unit for understanding the nature and functioning of human intelligence.

The remainder of this chapter will be devoted to the elaboration of my own particular componential subtheory of human intelligence.[1] This subtheory is not necessarily representative of all theories of this kind, and it is still primitive in many respects. But unrepresentative and primitive as it may be, it is probably one of the more fully developed componential subtheories of intelligence. It thus suggests one direction in which this kind of theory can proceed. The subsequent discussion will be divided into four sections. The first will deal with properties of components, the second with kinds of components, the third with interrelations among kinds of components, and the fourth with how the subtheory accounts for various empirical findings in the literature on human intelligence.

A Componential Subtheory of Human Intelligence

Properties of Components

Each component has three important properties associated with it: duration, difficulty (that is, error probability), and probability of execution. Methods for estimating these properties of components are described in Sternberg (1978) (see also Sternberg, 1977, 1980b; Sternberg & Rifkin, 1979). The three properties are, at least in principle, independent. For example, a given component may take a rather long time to execute, but may be rather easy to execute, in the sense that its execution rarely leads to an error

---

[1]Useful recent reviews of other componential types of theories can be found in Carroll and Maxwell (1979), Pellegrino and Glaser (1979), Snow (1979), and Sternberg (1979b). The heavy emphasis on "metacomponential" functioning that characterizes my own perspective is consistent with and has been influenced by such metacognitive (but not necessarily componential) theorists as Brown (1978; Brown & DeLoache, 1978; Campione & Brown, 1979) and Flavell (Flavell & Wellman, 1977).

in the solution; or the component may be executed quite rapidly, and yet be rather difficult to execute, in the sense that its execution often leads to an error in the solution (see Sternberg, 1977, 1980b). Consider "mapping," one component used in solving analogies such as LAWYER is to CLIENT as DOCTOR is to (a) PATIENT or (b) MEDICINE. Mapping calls for the discovery of the higher-order relation between the first and second halves of the analogy. The component has a certain probability of being executed in solving an analogy. If executed, it has a certain duration and a certain probability of being executed correctly (Sternberg, 1977).

Kinds of Components

Components can be classified by function and by level of generality.

Function

Components perform (at least) five kinds of functions. *Metacomponents* are higher-order control processes used for executive planning and decision making in problem solving. *Performance components* are processes used in the execution of a problem-solving strategy. *Acquisition components* are processes used in learning new information. *Retention components* are processes used in retrieving previously stored knowledge. *Transfer components* are processes used in generalization, that is, in carrying over knowledge from one task or task context to another.

Metacomponents

Metacomponents[2] are specific realizations of control processes that are sometimes collectively (and loosely) referred to as the "executive" or the "homunculus." I have identified six metacomponents that I believe are quite common in intellectual functioning.

   1. *Decision as to just what the problem is that needs to be solved.* Anyone who has done research with young children knows that half the battle is getting them to understand what is being asked of them. Their difficulty often lies not in actually solving a problem, but in figuring out just what the problem is that needs to be solved (see, for example, Flavell, 1977; Sternberg & Rifkin, 1979). A major feature distinguishing retarded persons from normal ones is the retardates' need to be instructed explicitly and completely as to the nature of the particular task he or she is solving and how it should be performed (Butterfield, Wambold, & Belmont, 1973; Campione & Brown, 1977, 1979). The importance of figuring out the nature of the problem is not limited to children and retarded persons. Resnick and Glaser (1976) have argued that intelligence is the ability to learn in the absence of direct or complete instruction. Indeed, distractors on intelligence tests are frequently chosen so as to be the right answers to the wrong problems. In my own research, I have found that the sheer novelty of a task, defined in terms of subjects' unfamiliarity with what they are being asked to do, is an important determinant of the task's correlation with measured intelligence (Sternberg, 1981b).

---

[2]Research on the isolation of metacomponents from task performance is being pursued in collaboration with Bill Salter, and is summarized in Sternberg (1979d).

2. *Selection of lower-order components.* An individual must select a set of lower-order (performance, acquisition, retention, or transfer) components to use in the solution of a given task. Selecting a nonoptimal set of components can result in incorrect or inefficient task performance. In some instances, the choice of components will be partially attributable to differential availability or accessibility of various components. For example, young children may lack certain components that are necessary or desirable for the accomplishment of particular tasks, or they may not yet execute these components in a way that is efficient enough to facilitate task solution. Sternberg and Rifkin (1979), for example, tested children in grades 2, 4, and 6, as well as adults, in their abilities to solve simple analogy problems. They found that the performance component used to form the higher-order relation between the two halves of the analogy (mapping) was used by adults and by children in the fourth and sixth grades. The authors suggested that the second graders might not yet have acquired the capacity to discern higher-order relations (that is, relations between relations). The unavailability or inaccessibility of this mapping component necessitated a rather radical shift in the way the youngest children solved the analogy problems. Sometimes the failure to execute the components needed for solving a task can be traced to a deficiency in the knowledge necessary for the execution of those components. Sternberg (1979a), for example, found that failures in reasoning with logical connectives were due, for the most part, to incorrect encodings of these connectives. Had the meanings of these connectives been available to the subjects (and especially the younger ones), the components of reasoning might well have been correctly executed.

3. *Selection of one or more representations or organizations for information.* A given component can often operate on any one of a number of different possible representations or organizations for information. The choice of representation or organization can facilitate or impede the efficacy with which the component operates. Sternberg and Rifkin (1979), for example, found that second graders organized information about analogies differently from older children and adults, but that this idiosyncratic organization enabled them to solve the analogies in a way that compensated for limitations in their working memories and mapping abilities. Sternberg and Weil (1980) found that the efficacy of various representations for information (linguistic, spatial, linguistic and spatial) in the linear-syllogisms task (for example, John is taller than Bill; Bill is taller than Peter; who is tallest?) depended upon individual subjects' patterns of verbal and spatial abilities. In problem solving, the optimal form of representation for information may depend upon item content. In some cases (for example, geometric analogies), an attribute-value representation may be best. In other cases (for example, animal-name analogies), a spatial representation may be best (Sternberg & Gardner, 1979). Thus, the efficacy of a form of representation can be determined by either subject variables or task variables, or by the interaction between them.

4. *Selection of a strategy for combining lower-order components.* In itself, a list of components is insufficient to perform a task. One must also sequence these components in a way that facilitates task performance, decide how exhaustively each component will be used, and decide which components to execute serially and which to execute in parallel. In an analogies task, for example, alternative strategies for problem solving differ in terms of which components are exhaustive and which are self-terminating. The exhaustively executed components result in the comparison of all possible encoded attributes or dimensions linking a pair of terms (such as LAWYER and CLIENT, or DOCTOR and PATIENT). The components executed with self-termination result in the comparison of only a subset of the attributes that have been encoded. The individual

must decide which comparisons are to be done exhaustively, and which are to be done with self-termination (Sternberg, 1977). An incorrect decision can drastically affect performance. Overuse of self-terminating components can result in a considerable increase in error (Sternberg, 1977; Sternberg & Rifkin, 1979). Overuse of exhaustive components can result in a considerable increase in solution latency (Sternberg, Ketron, & Powell, 1982).

5. *Decision regarding speed–accuracy tradeoff.* All tasks and components used in performing tasks can be allotted only limited amounts of time, and greater restrictions on the time allotted to a given task or task component may result in a reduction in the quality of performance. One must therefore decide how much time to allot to each component of a task, and how much the time restriction will affect the quality of performance for that particular component. One tries to allot time across the various components of task performance in a way that maximizes the quality of the entire product. Even small changes in error rate can result in sizable changes in solution latency (Pachella, 1974). I have found in the linear-syllogisms task, for example, that a decrease in solution latency of just one second (from a mean of about seven seconds to a mean of about six seconds) results in a seven-fold increase in error rate (from about 1% to about 7%; Sternberg, 1980a).

6. *Solution monitoring.* As individuals proceed through a problem, they must keep track of what they have already done, what they are currently doing, and what they still need to do. The relative importance of these three items of information differs across problems. If things are not progressing as expected, an accounting of one's progress may be needed, and one may even have to consider the possibility of changing goals. Often, new, more realistic goals need to be formulated as a person realizes that the old goals cannot be reached. In solving problems, individuals sometimes find that none of the available options provides a satisfactory answer. The individual must then decide whether to reperform certain processes that might have been performed erroneously, or to choose the best of the available answers (Sternberg, 1977). In the solution of linear syllogisms, the best strategy for most subjects *is* a rather nonobvious one, and hence subjects not trained in this strategy are unlikely to realize its existence until they have had at least some experience solving such problems (Quinton & Fellows, 1975; Sternberg & Weil, 1980).

A full discussion of methods for isolating metacomponents from composite task performance is outside the scope of this chapter (but see Sternberg, 1979d). Generally, metacomponents cannot be isolated on the basis of performance in standard information-processing paradigms, because latencies of higher-order planning and decision operations are usually constant across item types. As a result, metacomponential latencies are confounded with the constant response component or regression intercept. This confounding, in turn, can result in the seemingly inexplicable correlation of the response constant with scores on tests of intelligence (Hunt, Lunneborg, & Lewis, 1975; Pellegrino & Glaser, 1980; Sternberg, 1977, 1979c). One or more metacomponents can be isolated if planning and decision times are manipulated. We have developed paradigms in which items vary in the amount of strategy planning they require, and these paradigms have enabled us to extract metacomponential latencies from latencies for standard performance components (Sternberg, 1979d; Sternberg & Salter, 1980). For example, an analogy of the form A is to B as C is to X (where a series of X represents multiple answer options) requires less strategy planning than an analogy of the form A is to X, as Y is to D, where both X and Y represent multiple options. Strategy planning time and difficulty are manipulated by varying the number and placement of the variable terms.

Performance Components[3]

Performance components are used in the execution of various strategies for task performance. Although the number of possible performance components is quite large, many probably apply only to small or uninteresting subsets of tasks, and hence deserve little attention. As examples of performance components, consider some components that are quite broad in applicability, those used in analogical and other kinds of inductive reasoning and problem-solving tasks. Examples of other kinds of inductive reasoning tasks include classification and series completion problems (Sternberg, 1977; Sternberg & Gardner, 1979).

Encoding. In any problem-solving situation, a person must encode the terms of the problem, storing them in working memory and retrieving them from long-term memory information relating to these problem terms. Consider, for, example, the analogy cited earlier, LAWYER is to CLIENT as DOCTOR is to (a) PATIENT or (b) MEDICINE. From long-term memory the person must retrieve attributes of LAWYER such as "professional person," "law-school graduate," and "member of the bar," and place these attributes in working memory.

Inference. In inference, a person detects one or more relations between two objects, both of which may be either concrete or abstract. In the analogy, the person detects relations between LAWYER and CLIENT, such as that a lawyer provides professional services to a client.

Mapping. In mapping, a person relates aspects of a previous situation to aspects of a present one. In an analogy, the person seeks the higher-order relationship between the first half of the analogy (the previous situation) and the second half of the analogy (the present situation). In the example, both halves of the analogy deal with professional persons.

Application. In application, individuals use the relations between past elements of the situation and the decision made about them in the past to help them make current decisions. In the example, the person seeks to find an option that is related to DOCTOR in the same way that CLIENT was related to LAWYER.

Justification. In justification, the individual seeks to verify the better or best of the available options. In the example, PATIENT may not be viewed as a perfect analogue to CLIENT, because a patient may be viewed as a type of client, but not vice versa; but PATIENT is clearly the better of the two options.

Response. In response, the person communicates a solution to the problem. In the present example, the person communicates selection of the option PATIENT.

Methods for isolating performance components in a large variety of reasoning and problem-solving tasks have been described elsewhere (Guyote & Sternberg, 1978;

---

[3]In most of my earlier writings, I referred to performance components simply as "components."

Schustack & Sternberg, 1979; Sternberg, 1977, 1978, 1980b; Sternberg & Nigro, 1980; Sternberg & Rifkin, 1979). Similar methods have been used by others in a broad range of cognitive tasks (for example, Clark & Chase, 1972; Posner & Mitchell,1967; Shepard & Metzler, 1971; S. Sternberg, 1969). These methods have in common their manipulation of stimulus characteristics such that each particular kind of manipulation results in prolonging the latency of one particular performance component. Taken together, the various manipulations permit the simultaneous isolation of multiple performance components, either through analysis of variance or multiple regression techniques.

Acquisition, Retention, and Transfer Components[4]

Acquisition components are skills involved in learning new information; retention components are skills involved in retrieving previously acquired information; transfer components are skills involved in generalizing retained information from one situational context to another. Our research has not yet enabled us to specify what these components are; at present, we are still trying to identify the variables that affect acquisition, retention, and transfer of information in real-world contexts. What are some of the variables that might be involved in these three aspects of information processing? I shall address this question in the context of a person's trying to acquire, retain, and transfer information about unfamiliar words embedded in familiar contexts, such as newspapers and magazines.

Number of Occurrences of Target Information. Certain aspects of a situation will recur in virtually every instance of that kind of situation; others will occur only rarely. Higher acquisition, retention, and transfer of information would be expected from those aspects that recur with greater regularity. In the example, the more times a new and originally unfamiliar word is seen, the more likely an able person is to, acquire, retain, or transfer its meaning.

Variability in Contexts for Presenting Target Information. Some kinds of information about a given kind of situation will be available in multiple contexts, whereas other kinds may be available only in single or very limited contexts. Higher acquisition, retention, and transfer of information would be expected from aspects of a situation that are presented in more variable contexts. For example, the more variable the contexts are in which a previously unfamiliar word is presented, the more likely one is to acquire, retain, or transfer the word's meaning.

Importance of Target Information to Overall Situation. Some kinds of information about a given kind of situation will be central to that situation and decisions made about it; other kinds will be peripheral, and will have only a minor impact on subsequent decisions. Higher acquisition, retention, and transfer of information would be expected from those aspects that are central to that kind of situation. For example, the more important the meaning of a previously unfamiliar word is to understanding the passage in which it occurs, the better the context is for acquiring, retaining, and transferring the word's meaning.

---

[4]Research on the identification and isolation of acquisition, retention, and transfer components in everyday reading is being pursued in collaboration with Janet Powell, and is summarized in Sternberg (1979d).

Recency of Target Information. Certain information about a situation may have occurred more recently in one's experience, whereas other information may have occurred in the more distant past. Higher retention would be expected from those aspects of a kind of situation that have occurred in one's more recent experience. If, for example, a previously unfamiliar word has been recently encountered, one is more likely to retain its meaning.

Helpfulness of Context to Understanding Target Information. Certain kinds of information may be presented in contexts that facilitate their acquisition, retention, and transfer; other kinds may be presented in less facilitative contexts. Better acquisition, retention, and transfer would be expected when the context is more facilitating. For example, the more clues a new word's context provides as to its meaning, the more likely one is to acquire, retain, and transfer the word's meaning.

Helpfulness of Stored Information for Understanding Target Information. Previously stored information can facilitate acquisition, retention, and transfer of new information. Higher learning, retention, and transfer would be expected in cases where information learned in the past can be brought to bear on the present information, providing a context that may not be contained in the new learning situation itself. For example, if one recognizes a Latin root in an unfamiliar word, one is more likely to acquire, retain, and transfer the meaning of that word.

Because I have dealt only minimally with acquisition, retention, and transfer components in my previous writings, it may be useful if I describe in some detail the experimental paradigm we are using to isolate the effects of the variables believed to affect these components (see also Sternberg, 1979d). In our current research paradigm, we present subjects with a series of narrative passages of the kind found in newspapers, textbooks, magazines, and other everyday sources of information. The passages are typical in every respect except that they contain embedded within them one or more words of extremely low frequency in the English language. A given low-frequency word can occur one or more times within a given passage, or many times across passages. After reading each passage, subjects indicate what they believe to be the gist of the passage; they also define each of the low-frequency words. Structural variables in the narrative passages are used to predict the relative difficulties of learning, transferring, or retaining the various words. At the end of the experiment, subjects are again asked to define all the words, this time only in the context of the complete set of low-frequency words they have seen.

The first possible test of the meaning of a given word is at the end of the passage in which the word first occurs. At this time, the subject can look back at the passage to try to figure out what the word means. Results from this test are used to estimate the difficulty of acquisition variables. The second possible test of the meaning of a given word is at the end of a passage in which that word occurs for the second time in a second and new context. In this test, as in the preceding one, the subject is allowed to look back for help in defining the word in the passage that was just read. The subject is not allowed to look back at the preceding passage in which the word occurred, however. Improvement in the quality of this second definition relative to the quality of the first serves as the basis for estimating the difficulty of transfer variables. The same procedure applies to the third and fourth possible tests. The last possible test of the meaning of a given word is in the final definitions test. In this test, the only supporting context is provided by the other low-frequency words.

Subjects are not allowed to look back at the previous passages. Definition quality in this final test is used as the basis for estimating the difficulty of retention variables.

Level of Generality

Components can be classified in terms of three levels of generality. *General components* are required to perform all tasks within a given task universe; *class components* are required to perform a proper subset of tasks that includes at least two within the task universe; and *specific components* are required to perform single tasks within the task universe. Tasks calling for intelligent performance differ in the numbers of components they require for completion and in the number of each kind of component they require.

Consider, again, the example of an analogy. "Encoding" seems to be a general component, in that it is needed in the solution of problems of all kinds—a problem cannot be solved unless its terms are encoded in some manner. "Mapping" seems to be a class component, in that it is required for the solution of certain kinds of induction problems. But it is certainly not needed in problems of all kinds. No task-specific components have been identified in analogical reasoning, which is perhaps one reason why analogies serve so well in tests of general intellectual functioning.

Two points need to be emphasized with regard to the level of generality of components. First, whereas components with different functions are qualitatively different from each other, components at different levels of generality are not. Function inheres in a given component; level of generality inheres in the range of the tasks into which a given component enters. Second, whereas a given component serves only a single function, it may serve at any level of generality, with the level depending on the scope of the set of tasks being considered. A component may be general in a very narrow range of tasks, for example, but class-related in a very broad range of tasks. Levels of generality will prove useful in understanding certain task interrelationships and factorial findings; their primary purpose is to provide a convenient descriptive language that is useful for conceptualizing certain kinds of phenomena in componential terms.

Interrelations Among Kinds of Components

Components are interrelated in various ways. I shall discuss first how components serving different functions are interrelated, and then how components of different levels of generality are interrelated. Because levels of generality and functions are completely crossed, the interrelations among components of differing levels of generality apply to all of the functionally different kinds of components, and the interrelations among the functionally different kinds of components apply at all levels of generality.

Function

My speculations regarding the interrelations among the functionally different kinds of components are shown in Figure 1.1. The various kinds of components are closely related, as would be expected in an integrated, intelligent system. Four kinds of interrelations need to be considered: Direct activation of one kind of component by another is represented by double solid arrows. Indirect activation of one kind by another is represented by single solid arrows. Direct feedback from one kind to another

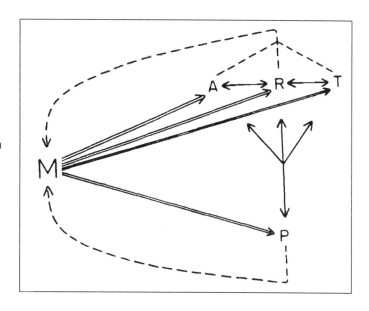

1.1

Interrelations among components serving different functions. In the figure, "M" refers to a set of metacomponents, "A" to a set of acquisition components, "R" to a set of retention components,"T" to a set of transfer components, and "P" to a
set of performance components. Direct activation of one kind of component by another is represented by solid double arrows. Indirect activation of one kind of component by another is represented by single solid arrows. Direct feedback from one kind of component to another is represented by single broken arrows. Indirect feedback from one kind of component to another proceeds from and to the same components as does indirect activation, and so is shown by the single solid arrows.

is represented by single broken arrows. Indirect feedback proceeds from and to the same components as does indirect activation, and so is shown by the single solid arrows. Direct activation or feedback refers to the immediate passage of control or information from one kind of component to another. Indirect activation or feedback refers to the mediated passage of control or information from one kind of component to another via a third kind of component.

In the proposed system, only metacomponents can directly activate and receive feedback from each other kind of component. Thus, all control passes directly from the metacomponents to the system, and all information passes directly from the system to the metacomponents. The other kinds of components can activate each other indirectly, and receive information from each other indirectly; in every case, mediation must be supplied by the metacomponents. For example, the acquisition of information affects the retention of information and various kinds of transformations (performances) on that information, but only via the link of the three kinds of components to the metacomponents. Information from the acquisition components is filtered to the other kinds of components through the metacomponents.

Consider some examples of how the system might function in the solution of a word puzzle, such as an anagram (scrambled word). As soon as one decides on a certain tentative strategy for unscrambling the letters of the word, activation of that strategy can pass directly from the metacomponent responsible for deciding on a strategy to the performance component responsible for executing the first step of the strategy, and subsequently, activation can pass to the successive performance components needed to execute the strategy. Feedback will return from the performance components indicating how successful the strategy is turning out to be. If the monitoring of this feedback signals lack of success, control may pass to the metacomponent that is "empowered" to change strategy; if no successful change in strategy can be realized, the solution-monitoring metacomponent may change the goal altogether.

As a given strategy is being executed, new information is being acquired about how to solve anagrams in general. This information is also fed back to the metacomponents, which may act on or ignore this information. New information that seems useful is more likely to be directed back from the relevant metacomponents to the relevant retention components for retention in long-term memory. What is acquired does not directly influence what is retained, however, so that "practice does not necessarily make perfect." Some people may be unable to profit from their experience because of inadequacies in metacomponential information processing. Similarly, what is retained does not directly influence what is later transferred. The chances of information being transferred to a later context will largely depend on the form in which the metacomponents have decided to store the information for later access. Acquired information also does not directly affect transformations (performances) on that information. The results of acquisition (or retention or transfer) must first be fed back into the metacomponents, which in effect decide what information will filter back indirectly from one type of component to another.

The metacomponents are able to process only a limited amount of information at a given time. In a difficult task, and especially a new and different one, the amount of information being fed back to the metacomponents may exceed their capacity to act on the information. In this case, the metacomponents become overloaded, and valuable information that cannot be processed may simply be wasted. The total information-handling capacity of the metacomponents of a given system will thus be an important limiting aspect of that system. Similarly, the capacity to allocate attentional resources so as to minimize the probability of bottlenecks will be part of what determines the effective capacity of the system (see also Hunt et al., 1973, 1975).

Figure 1.1 does not show interrelations among various individual members of each single functional kind of component. These interrelations can be easily described in words, however. Metacomponents are able to communicate with each other directly, and to activate each other directly. It seems likely that there exists at least one metacomponent (other than those described earlier in the chapter) that controls communication and activation among the other metacomponents, and there is a certain sense in which this particular metacomponent might be viewed as a "meta-metacomponent." Other kinds of components are not able to communicate directly with each other, however, or to activate each other. But components of a given kind can communicate indirectly with other components of the same kind, and can activate them indirectly. Indirect communication and activation proceed through the metacomponents, which can direct information or activation from one component to another of the same kind.

Level of Generality

Components of varying levels of generality are related to each other through the ways in which they enter into the performance of tasks (Sternberg, 1979c, 1980c). Figure 1.2 shows the nature of this hierarchical relationship. Each node of the hierarchy contains a task, which is designated by a roman or arabic numeral or by a letter. Each

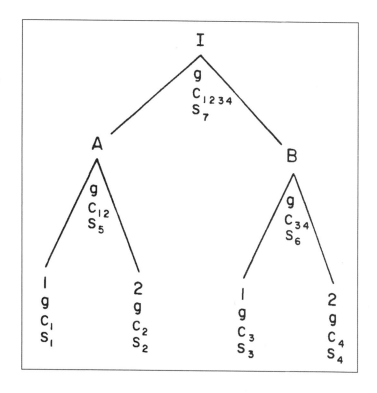

1.2

Interrelations among components of different levels of generality. Each node of the hierarchy contains a task, which is designated by a roman or arabic numeral or by a letter. Each task comprises a set of components at the general (g), class (c), and specific (s) levels. In the figure, "g" refers to a set of general components; "c_i" and "c_j" each refer to a set of class components, and "c_{ij}" refers to a concatenated set of class components that includes the class components from both c_i and c_j; "s_1" refers to a set of specific components.

task comprises a set of components at the general (g), class (c), and specific (s) levels. In the figure, "g" refers to a set of general components; "c_i" and "c_j" each refer to a set of class components, whereas "c_{ij}" refers to a concatenated set of class components that includes the class components from both c_i and c_j, and "s_i" refers to a set of specific components. The levels of the hierarchy differ in terms of the complexity of the tasks assigned to them. More complex tasks occupy higher levels of the hierarchy; simpler tasks occupy lower levels. Relative complexity is defined here in terms of the number and identities of the class components contained in the task: the more sets of class components concatenated in a particular task, the more complex the task is.

At the bottom of the hierarchy are very simple tasks (IA1, IA2, IB1, IB2), each of which requires a set of general, class and specific components for its execution. At one extreme, the general components are the same in all four tasks (and in all of the tasks in the hierarchy), in that a general component is by definition one that is involved in the performance of every task in the universe (here expressed as a hierarchy) of interest. At the other extreme, the specific components are unique to each task at this (and every other) level, in that a specific component is by definition one that is only relevant to a single task. The class components are also not shared across tasks at this level: Task IA1 has one set of class components; Task IA2 another; Task IB1 another; and Task IB2 yet another. As examples, Task IA1 might be series completions (such as 2, 4, 6, 8, ?), Task IA2 metaphorical ratings (How good a metaphor is "The moon is a ghostly galleon?"), Task IB1 linear syllogisms (N is higher than P; P is higher than L; which is highest?), and Task IB2 categorical syllogisms (All C are B; some B are A; can one conclude that some C are A?) (see Sternberg, 1980c).

Consider next the middle level of the hierarchy, containing Tasks IA and IB. Tasks IA and IB both share with the lower-order tasks, and with each other, all of their general components but none of their specific components. What distinguishes Tasks IA and IB from each other, however, and what places them in their respective positions in the hierarchy, is the particular set of class components that they each contain. The class components involved in the performance of Task IA represent a concatenation of the class components involved in the performance of Tasks IA1 and IA2; the class components involved in the performance of Task IB represent a concatenation of the class components involved in the performance of Tasks IB1 and IB2. Tasks IA and IB contain no common class components, however. For example, Task IA might be analogies, which require a concatenation of the class components from series completions and metaphorical ratings. Task IB might be the higher-order task of quantified linear syllogisms (for example, all H are higher than all Q; some Q are higher than all Z; can one conclude that some H are higher than some Z?), which requires a concatenation of class components from linear and categorical syllogisms (see Sternberg, 1980c).

Finally, consider the task at the top level of the hierarchy, Task I. Like all tasks in the hierarchy, it shares general components with all other tasks in the hierarchy, but it shares specific components with none of these tasks (again, because these components are, by definition, task-specific). Performance on this task is related to performance on Tasks IA and IB through the concatenation of class components from these two tasks. In the present example, Task I might be inductive syllogisms, which require a person to induce the premises of a syllogism and then to solve the syllogism. Scientific reasoning is often of this kind: one must induce regularities from empirical data, and then deduce properties of these regularities (see Sternberg, 1980e).

According to the present view, many kinds of tasks are hierarchically interrelated to each other via components of information processing. The proposed hierarchical model shows the nature of these interrelations. It should be made clear just what is arbitrary in this hierarchical arrangement and what is not. The arrangement does not prespecify the degrees of differentiation between the top and bottom levels of the hierarchy, nor where the hierarchy should start and stop. As was stated earlier, the level that is defined as "elementary" and thus suitable for specification of components is arbitrary: what is a component in one theory might be two components in another, or a task in still another. The level of specification depends on the purpose of the theory. Theories at different levels serve different purposes, and must be justified in their own right. But certain important aspects of the arrangement are not arbitrary. The vertical order of tasks in the hierarchy, for example, is not subject to permutation, and although whole branches of the hierarchy (from top to bottom) can be permuted (the left side becoming the right side and vice versa), individual portions of those branches cannot be permuted. For example, IA and IB cannot be switched unless the tasks below them are switched as well. In other words, horizontal reflection of the whole hierarchy is possible, but horizontal reflection of selected vertical portions is not possible. These nonarbitrary elements of the hierarchy make disconfirmation of a given theory both possible and feasible. A given hierarchy can be found to be inadequate if the various constraints outlined here are not met. In many instances, the hierarchy may simply be found to be incomplete, in that branches or nodes of branches may be missing and thus need to be filled in.

The interrelational schemes described above are intended to provide a framework for explaining empirical phenomena, rather than to provide an actual explanation. This framework will be used below to provide a unified perspective for understanding empirical findings in the literature on intelligence.

Relations Between Components and Human Intelligence

On the componential view, components account causally for a part of what we consider to be human intelligence. If one takes a broad view of general intelligence as capturing those aspects of behavior that contribute to the effectiveness of adaptation to everyday living, there will certainly be major parts of intelligence that are not accounted for within the componential framework. Nevertheless, components are perhaps able to account at one level for an interesting portion of what we call "intelligent behavior." Consider some of the key phenomena described in the textbook literature on intelligence (for example, Brody & Brody, 1976; Butcher, 1970; Cronbach, 1970; Vernon, 1979), and how they would be explained within the componential framework. Some of these phenomena have actually appeared to be mutually incompatible, but no longer appear so when viewed through the "lens" of the componential framework. None of these phenomena has been established beyond a doubt; indeed, some of them are subject to considerable controversy. Nevertheless, they are about as solid as any phenomena reported in the literature on intelligence, and they are ones I, at least, am willing to accept tentatively until the evidence sways me to believe otherwise.

1. *There appears to be a factor of "general intelligence."* Various sorts of evidence have been adduced in support of the existence of a general intelligence factor (see Humphreys, 1979; McNemar, 1964). Perhaps the most persuasive evidence is everyday experience: Casual observation in everyday life suggests that some people are "generally" more intelligent than others. People's rank orderings of each other may differ according to how they define intelligence, but some rank ordering is usually possible. Historically, the evidence that has been offered most often in favor of the existence of general intelligence is the appearance of a general factor in unrotated factor solutions from factor analyses of tests of intelligence (for example, Spearman, 1927). In itself, this evidence is not persuasive, because factor analysis of any battery of measures will yield a general factor if the factors are not rotated: This is a mathematical rather than a psychological outcome of factor analysis. However, the psychological status of this outcome is bolstered by the fact that an analogous outcome appears in information-processing research as well: Information-processing analyses of a variety of tasks have revealed that the "regression constant" is often the individual-differences parameter most highly correlated with scores on general intelligence tests (see Sternberg, 1979c). This parameter measures what is constant across all of the item or task manipulations that are analyzed via multiple regression. The regression constant seems to have at least some parallels with the general factor.

The strongest evidence that has been offered against the existence of general intelligence is that some rotations of factors fail to yield a general factor. But this failure to find a general factor in certain kinds of rotated solutions is as much determined by mathematical properties of the factorial algorithm as is the success in finding a general factor in an unrotated solution. Moreover, if the multiple factors are correlated, and if they are themselves factored, they will often yield a "second-order" general factor.

In componential analysis, individual differences in general intelligence are attributed to individual differences in the effectiveness with which general components are used. Because these components are common to all of the tasks in a given task universe, factor analyses will tend to lump these general sources of individual-difference variance into a single general factor. As it happens, the metacomponents have a much higher proportion of general components among them than do any of the other kinds of components, presumably because the executive routines needed to plan, monitor, and possibly replan performance are highly overlapping across widely differing tasks. Thus, individual differences in metacomponential functioning are largely responsible for the persistent appearance of a general factor.

Metacomponents are probably not solely responsible for "g," however. Most behavior, and probably all of the behavior exhibited on intelligence tests, is learned. Certain acquisition components may be general to a wide variety of learning situations, which also enter into the general factor. Similarly, components of retention and transfer may also be common to large numbers of tasks. Finally, certain aspects of performance —such as encoding and response—are common to virtually all tasks, and they, too, may enter into the general factor. Therefore, although the metacomponents are primarily responsible for individual differences in general intelligence, they are probably not solely responsible.

2. *Intelligence comprises a set of "primary mental abilities."* When a factorial solution is rotated to a Thurstonian (1947) "simple structure," a set of primary mental abilities usually appears. The concept of simple structure is complexly defined, but basically involves a factorial solution in which factors tend to have some variables loading highly on them, some variables loading only modestly on them, and few variables having intermediate loadings on them. As noted previously, the appearance of one or another kind of factor set is largely a mathematical property of factor analysis and the kind of rotation used (see also Sternberg, 1977). If one views factors as causal entities, as do many adherents to the traditional psychometric approach to intelligence, then one may become involved in a seemingly unresolvable debate regarding which is the "correct" rotation of factors. Mathematically, all rigid rotations of a set of factor axes are permissible, and there seems to be no agreed-upon psychological criterion for choosing a "correct" rotation. In componential analysis, the choice of a criterion for rotation is arbitrary—a matter of convenience. Different rotations serve different purposes. The unrotated solution considered earlier, for example, is probably ideal for isolating a composite measure of individual differences in the effectiveness of the performance of general components.

Consider next what is probably the most popular orientation of factorial axes among American psychometricians, that obtained by Thurstonian rotation to simple structure. In such rotations, primary mental abilities such as verbal comprehension, word fluency, number, spatial visualization, perceptual speed, memory, and reasoning may appear (see Thurstone, 1938). The simple-structure rotation, like the unrotated solution, has somehow seemed special to psychometricians for many years, and I believe that it may well be, in a sense, special. Whereas the unrotated solution seems to provide the best composite measure of general components, my inspections of various rotated solutions have led me to believe that simple-structure rotations tend to provide the "best" measures of class components—best in the sense that there is minimal overlap across factors in the appearances of class components. A simple-structure rotation distributes the general components throughout the set of factors so that the same general components may appear in multiple factors: Such factors, therefore, will necessarily be correlated. But I believe the low to moderate correlations are due for the most part to overlap among general components: The class components found at a fairly high level of generality seem to be rather well restricted to individual factors. Given that the factorial model of primary mental abilities originally proposed by Thurstone was nonhierarchical, there will have to be some overlap across factors in class components; but for theoretical and practical purposes, this overlap seems to be minimized. Thus, neither the unrotated solution of Spearman (1927) and others, nor the simple-structure solution of Thurstone (1938) and others, is "correct" to the exclusion of the other. Each serves a different theoretical purpose and possibly a different practical purpose as well: The factorial theory of Spearman is useful when one desires the most general, all-purpose predictor possible; the factorial theory of Thurstone is useful when one desires differential prediction, for example, between verbal and spatial performance.

3. *In hierarchical factor analyses, there seem to be two very broad group factors (or general subfactors), sometimes referred to as crystallized ability and fluid ability.* The crystallized-fluid distinction has been proposed by Cattell (1971) and Horn (1968), and a similar distinction has been proposed by Vernon (1971). Crystallized ability is best measured by tests that measure the products of enculturation: vocabulary, reading comprehension, general information, and the like. Fluid ability is best measured by tests of abstract reasoning: abstract analogies, classifications, series completions, and the like. (Verbal items are also useful for this purpose if their vocabulary level is kept low.) Once again, I believe that there is something special about this hierarchical solution. Crystallized ability tests seem best able to separate the products of acquisition, retention, and transfer components. I say "products," because crystallized ability tests measure outcomes of these component processes, rather than the operations as they are actually executed. The vocabulary that is measured by a vocabulary test, for example, may have been acquired years ago. Fluid ability tests, on the other hand, seem most suitable for separating the execution of performance components. These tests seem heavily dependent on a rather small set of performance components (Sternberg, 1979c; Sternberg & Gardner, 1979), in particular, those mentioned earlier in this chapter. Thus, dividing factors along the crystallized-fluid dimension seems to provide a good distinction between the products of acquisition, retention, and transfer components on the one hand, and the current functioning of performance components on the other. Crystallized and fluid factors will be correlated, however, because of shared metacomponents.

Horn (1968) has found that crystallized ability generally continues to increase throughout one's lifetime, whereas fluid ability first increases, then levels off, and finally decreases. I would like to suggest that the contrast between the continued increase in crystallized ability with age and the increase followed by decrease in fluid ability with increasing age is due less to the kinds of abilities measured than to the ways in which they are measured. Crystallized ability tests primarily measure accumulated products of components; fluid ability tests primarily measure current functioning of components. I think it likely that current functioning decreases after a certain age level, whereas the accumulated products of these components are likely to continue to increase (at least until senility sets in). Were one to measure current functioning of acquisition, retention, and transfer components—by, for example, tests of acquisition of knowledge presented in context—rather than the products of these components, I suspect the ability curve would show a pattern of rise and fall similar to that shown on standard fluid ability tests.

4. *Procrustean rotation of a factorial solution can result in the appearance of a large number of "structure-of-intellect" factors.* Procrustean rotation of a factorial solution involves rotation of a set of axes into maximum correspondence with a predetermined theory regarding where the axes should be placed. Guilford (1967; Guilford & Hoepfner, 1971) has used procrustean rotation to support his "structure-of-intellect" theory. According to this theory, intelligence comprises 120 distinct intellectual aptitudes, each represented by an independent factor. Horn and Knapp (1973) have shown that comparable levels of support can be obtained via procrustean rotation to randomly determined theories. The viability of Guilford's theory is therefore open to at least some question (see also Cronbach & Snow, 1977). Nevertheless, I believe that there is probably a psychological basis for at least some aspects of Guilford's theory, and that these aspects of the theory can be interpreted in componential terms.

A given component must act on a particular form of representation for information, and on a particular type of information (content). The representation, for example, might be spatial or linguistic; the type of information (content) might be, for example, an abstract geometric design, a picture, a symbol, or a word. Forms of representations and contents, like components, can serve as sources of individual differences: A given individual might be quite competent when applying a particular component to one kind of content, but not when applying it to another. Representation, content, and process have been largely confounded in most factorial theories, probably because certain components tend more often to operate on certain kinds of representations and contents, and other components tend more often to operate on different kinds of representations and contents. This confounding serves a practical purpose, that of keeping to a manageable number the factors appearing in a given theory or test. But it does obscure the probably partially separable effects of process, representation, and content. Guilford's theory provides some separation, at least between process and content. I doubt the product dimension has much validity, other than through the fact that different kinds of products probably involve slightly different mixes of components. On the one hand, the theory points out the potential separability of process and content. On the other hand, it does so at the expense of manageability. Moreover, it seems highly unlikely that the 120 factors are independent, as they will, at a minimum, share metacomponents.

The distinction among process, content, and representation is an important one to keep in mind, because it is in part responsible for the low intercorrelations that are often obtained between seemingly highly related tasks. Two tasks (such as verbal analogies and geometric analogies) may share the same information-processing components, and yet show only moderate correlations because of content and representational differences. Guilford's finding of generally low intercorrelations between ability tests is probably due in part to the wide variation in the processes, contents, and representations required for solution of his various test items.

5. *One of the best single measures of overall intelligence (as measured by intelligence tests) is vocabulary.* This result (see, for example, Matarazzo, 1972) has seemed rather surprising to some, because vocabulary tests seem to measure acquired knowledge rather than intelligent functioning. But the preceding discussion should adumbrate why vocabulary is such a good measure of overall intelligence. Vocabulary is acquired incidentally throughout one's life as a result of acquisition components; the vocabulary

that is retained long enough to be of use on a vocabulary test has also been successfully processed by a set of retention components. And for the vocabulary to be retained and recognized in the particular context of the vocabulary test, it probably also had to be processed successfully by transfer components. Moreover, to operate effectively, all these kinds of components must have been under the control of metacomponents. Thus, vocabulary provides a very good, although indirect, measure of the lifetime operations of these various kinds of components. Vocabulary has an advantage over many kinds of performance tests, which measure the functioning of performance components only at the time of testing. The latter kinds of tests are more susceptible to the day-to-day fluctuations in performance that create unreliability and, ultimately, invalidity in tests. Because performance components are not particularly critical to individual differences in scores on vocabulary tests, one would expect vocabulary test scores to be less highly correlated with performance types of tests than with other verbal tests, and this is in fact the case (see Matarazzo, 1972).

It was noted earlier that in some instances lack of knowledge can block successful execution of the performance components needed for intelligent functioning. For example, it is impossible to reason with logical connectives if one does not know what they mean (Sternberg, 1979a), or to solve verbal analogies if the meanings of words constituting the analogies are unknown. Thus, vocabulary is not only affected by operations of components, it affects their operations as well. If one grows up in a household that encourages exposure to words (which is one of the variables cited earlier as affecting acquisition, transfer, and retention components), then one's vocabulary may well be greater, which in turn may lead to superior learning and performance on other kinds of tasks that require vocabulary. This is one way in which early rearing can have a substantial effect on vocabulary and the behaviors it affects.

This view of the nature of vocabulary tests in particular, and of tests of verbal ability in general, differs from that of Hunt, Lunneborg, and Lewis (1975). These authors have sought to understand individual differences in verbal ability in terms of individual differences in performance components involved in relatively simple information-processing tasks used in laboratories of experimental psychologists. They suggest, for example, that a major element of verbal ability is the speed of accessing simple verbal codes in short-term memory. This framework is not incompatible with that presented here: The two views may highlight different aspects of verbal comprehension.

6. *The absolute level of intelligence in children increases with age.* Why do children grow smarter as they grow older? The system of interrelations among components depicted in Figure 1.1 seems to contain a dynamic mechanism whereby cognitive growth can occur.

First, the components of acquisition, retention, and transfer provide the mechanisms for a steadily developing knowledge base. Increments in the knowledge base, in turn, allow for more sophisticated forms of acquisition, retention, and transfer, and possibly for greater ease in executing performance components. For example, some transfer components may act by relating new knowledge to old knowledge. As the base of old knowledge becomes deeper and broader, the possibilities for relating new knowledge to old knowledge, and thus for incorporating that new knowledge into the existing knowledge base, increase. There is thus the possibility of an unending feedback loop: The components lead to an increased knowledge base, which leads to more effective use of the components, which leads to further increases in the knowledge base, and so on.

Second, the self-monitoring metacomponents can, in effect, learn from their own mistakes. Early on, allocation of metacomponential resources to varying tasks or kinds of components may be less than optimal, with a resulting loss of valuable feedback information. Self-monitoring should eventually result in improved allocations of meta-componential resources, in particular, to the self-monitoring of the metacomponents. Thus, self-monitoring by the metacomponents results in improved allocation of meta-componential resources to the self-monitoring of the metacomponents, which in turn leads to improved self-monitoring, and so on. Here, too, there exists the possibility of an unending feedback loop, one that is internal to the metacomponents themselves.

Finally, indirect feedback from components other than metacomponents to each other, and direct feedback to the metacomponents, should result in improved effective-ness of performance. Acquisition components, for example, can provide valuable information to performance components (via the metacomponents) concerning how to perform a task, and the performance components, in turn, can provide feedback to the acquisition components (via the metacomponents) concerning what else needs to be learned to perform the task optimally. Thus, other kinds of components, too, can generate unending feedback loops in which performance improves as a result of interactions between different kinds of components, or between multiple components of the same kind.

There can be no doubt that the major variables in the individual-differences equation will be those deriving from the metacomponents. All feedback is filtered through those elements, and if they do not perform their function well, then it won't matter very much what the other kinds of components can do. It is for this reason that the metacomponents are viewed as truly central in understanding the nature of general intelligence.

7. *Intelligence tests provide imperfect, but quite good, prediction of academic achievement.* A good intelligence test such as the Stanford-Binet will sample widely from the range of intellectual tasks that can reasonably be used in a testing situation. The wider this sampling, and the more closely the particular mix of components sampled resembles the mix of components required in academic achievement, the better the prediction will be. A vocabulary test, for example, will provide quite a good predictor of academic achievement, because academic achievement is so strongly dependent on acquisition, transfer, and retention components, and on the metacomponents that control them. A spatial test will probably not be as good a predictor of general academic performance, because the performance components sampled in such a test will not be particularly relevant to general academic achievement, such as that required in English or history courses. An abstract reasoning test will probably be better than a spatial test, because the particular performance components involved in these tasks seem to be so general across tasks requiring inductive reasoning, including those found in academic learning environments. All intelligence tests will necessarily be imperfect predictors of academic achievement, however, because there is more to intelligence than is measured by intelligence tests, and because there is more to school achievement than intelligence.

8. *Occasionally, people are quite good at one aspect of intellectual functioning, but quite poor at another.* Everyone knows of people who exhibit unusual and sometimes bizarre discrepancies in intellectual functioning. A person who is mathematically gifted may have trouble writing a sentence, or an accomplished novelist may have trouble adding simple columns of numbers. In the componential framework, the discrepancy can be accounted for in either of two ways. First, there may be inadequate functioning of or inadequate feedback from particular class components. The discrepancy cannot be in

the general components, because they are common to all tasks, nor can it be in the specific components, because they apply only to single tasks. Hence, the discrepancy must be found in those class components that permeate performance of a given set of tasks, such as mathematical tasks, verbal tasks, spatial tasks, or any of the other tasks that constitute measures of the "primary mental abilities." Note that in contrast, someone whose intellectual performance is generally depressed is more likely to be suffering from inadequacies in the execution of or feedback from general components (and possibly, class components as well). Second, the discrepancy can be accounted for by difficulty in operating on a particular form of representation. Different kinds of information are probably represented in different ways, at least at some level of information processing. For example, there is good reason to believe that linguistic and spatial representations differ in at least some respects from each other (MacLeod, Hunt, & Mathews, 1978; Paivio, 1971; Sternberg, 1980b). A given component may operate successfully upon one form of representation but not on another, as discussed earlier.

9. *Intelligence is a necessary but not sufficient condition for creativity.* Creativity, on the componential view, is due largely to the occurrence of transfer between items of knowledge (facts or ideas) that are not related to each other in an obvious way. In terms of the conceptualization in Figure 1.1, creative ideas derive from extremely sensitive feedback to and from transfer components. Such feedback is more likely to occur if, in acquisition, knowledge has been organized in a serviceable and richly interconnected way. But for interesting creative behavior to occur, there must be a rather substantial knowledge base so that there is something to and from which transfer can occur. Thus, for creativity to be shown, a high level of functioning in the acquisition, retention, and transfer components would seem necessary. These high levels of functioning are not in themselves sufficient for creativity to occur, however, because a sophisticated knowledge base does not in itself guarantee that the knowledge base will be used in sophisticated feedback to and from the transfer components. This mechanism is not intended to account for all creative behavior, nor even to give a full account of the creative behavior to which it can be applied. It does seem a start toward a more detailed account, however.

This componential view is consistent with recent research on expert-novice distinctions that suggests that a major part of what distinguishes experts from novices is differences in the knowledge base and its organization (for example, Chase & Simon, 1973; Glaser & Chi, 1979; Larkin, 1979). The view is also consistent with that of Horn (1980), who has suggested that creativity may be better understood by investigating crystallized ability rather than fluid ability. Our previous failures to isolate loci of creative behavior may derive from our almost exclusive emphasis on fluid abilities. The creativity tests that have resulted from this emphasis have measured what I believe to be rather trivial forms of creativity having little in common with the forms shown by creative novelists, artists, scientists, and the like. Research on transfer may be more productive.

10. *Speed and accuracy (or quality) of intelligent performance may be positively correlated, negatively correlated, or uncorrelated.* The results of the "new wave" of intelligence research (for example, Hunt et al., 1975; Mulholland, Pellegrino, & Glaser, 1980; Sternberg, 1977) make it clear that speed and quality of performance bear no unique relation to each other. In the analogies task, for example, faster inference, mapping, application, and response component times are associated with higher intelligence test scores, but slower encoding is also associated with higher test scores. This finding

can be understood at a metacomponential level: Individuals who encode stimuli more slowly are later able to operate on their encodings more rapidly and accurately than are individuals who encode stimuli more rapidly. Faster encoding can thus actually slow down and impair the quality of overall performance (Sternberg, 1979c). Similarly, individuals with higher intelligence tend to spend more time implementing the planning metacomponent, so as to spend less time in executing the performance components whose execution needs to be planned (Sternberg & Salter, 1980).

Findings such as these emphasize the importance of decomposing overall response time and response accuracy into their constituent components, as different components may show different relations with intelligent performance. These findings also show the importance of seeking explanations for behavior at the metacomponential level. As important as it is to know what individuals are doing, it is even more important to know why they are doing it.

11. *Training of intelligent performance is most successful when it is at both the metacomponential and performance-componential levels.* Research on the training of intelligent performance has shown that the most successful approach addresses metacomponential or metacognitive as well as specific performance components or strategies (Borkowski & Cavanaugh, 1979; Brown & DeLoache, 1978; Butterfield & Belmont, 1977; Feuerstein, 1979a, 1979b; Sternberg, 1981a). This finding is consistent with the kind of framework proposed in Figure 1.1. The interaction of metacomponents and performance components is such that training of just the one or the other kind of component will be fruitless unless there is at least some spillover into the other kind. The two kinds of components work in tandem, and hence are most successfully trained in tandem. To obtain generalizability as well as durability of training, it may also be necessary to train transfer components.

12. *Intelligence can mean somewhat different things in different cultures.* Cross-cultural research suggests that intelligence can mean somewhat different things in different cultures (Berry, 1974; Cole, Gay, Glick, & Sharp, 1971; Goodnow, 1976; Wober, 1974; see also Neisser, 1976, 1979). This view is consistent with the componential framework presented here. I interpret the available evidence as providing no support for the notion that the components of human intelligence or the ways in which these components are organized differ across cultures; but the evidence provides considerable support for the notion that the relative importance of the various components differs across cultures, as does the importance of components as distinguished from other aspects of adaptive functioning. In some cultures, the kinds of behaviors that matter to successful adaptation may be heavily influenced by the kinds of components that have been discussed in this chapter; in other cultures, behaviors that matter may be only minimally influenced by these components. In a hunting culture, for example, cleverness in tracking down an animal may be influenced by various kinds of information-processing components, but the bottom line is whether the hunter can kill the animal being tracked down. If hunters have poor aim with a stone, bow and arrow, or whatever, it doesn't matter how clever they have been in stalking the animal: there won't be any food on the table. The previous discussion in this chapter is most definitely biased toward the kinds of things that tend to matter in our own culture.

The 12 findings on intelligence just discussed provide only a very partial list of empirical generalizations in the literature on intelligence, but they cover sufficient ground to convey some sense of how the componential view accounts for various phenomena involving intelligence. As noted earlier, none of these generalizations is fully established; and the accounts provided here are certainly simplifications of the undoubtedly complex factors that lead to the phenomena covered by the generalizations. The componential view can account for a number of other findings as well, but it is worth emphasizing again that it does not account for or even deal with all phenomena involving intelligence, broadly defined. Although the various kinds of components form the core of the proposed intelligence system, they are by no means the only sources of individual differences (Sternberg, 1981b). First, components act on different informational contents, and the informational content can be expected to influence the efficacy with which components function in different individuals (Sternberg, 1977). Second, information can be presented in a variety of modalities (visually, orally, kinesthetically), and the modality of presentation can be expected to influence the efficacy of information processing (Horn, 1974, 1979). Finally, information processing will be affected by a host of motivational variables, each of which can have a substantial effect on performance (Zigler, 1971). Thus, the functioning of various kinds of components can be adequately understood only in the whole context in which they operate.

The componential framework sketched in this chapter is intended to furnish one possible start toward providing a unified outlook on a number of different aspects of intelligent functioning. In particular, it suggests (a) a classification scheme for various kinds of information-processing components, (b) ways in which these components might be interrelated, and (c) how the components and their interrelations can be used to account for various empirical phenomena that have been reported in the literature on human intelligence. The present framework is certainly not the only one that can provide suggestions of these kinds. But it seems like a useful supplement to existing frameworks that attempt to understand the cognitive bases of human intelligence and its manifestations.

References

Berry, J. W. (1974). Radical cultural relativism and the concept of intelligence. In J. W. Berry & P. R. Dasen (Eds.), *Culture and cognition: Readings in cross-cultural psychology.* London: Methuen.

Borkowski, J. G., & Cavanaugh, J. C. (1979). Maintenance and generalization of skills and strategies by the retarded. In N. R. Ellis (Ed.), *Handbook of mental deficiency* (2nd ed.). Hillsdale, NJ: Erlbaum.

Brody, E. B., & Brody, N. (1976). *Intelligence: Nature, determinants, and consequences.* New York: Academic Press.

Brown, A. L. (1978). Knowing when, where, and how to remember: A problem of metacognition. In R. Glaser (Ed.), *Advances in instructional psychology,* vol 1. Hillsdale, NJ: Erlbaum.

Brown, A. L., & DeLoache, J. S. (1978). Skills, plans, and self-regulation. In R. Siegler (Ed.), *Children's thinking: What develops?* Hillsdale, NJ: Erlbaum.

Burt, C. (1940). *The factors of the mind.* London: University of London Press.

Butcher, H. J. (1970). *Human intelligence: Its nature and assessment.* London: Methuen.

Butterfield, E. C., & Belmont, J. M. (1977). Assessing and improving the cognition of mentally retarded people. In I. Bialer & M. Sternlicht (Eds.), *Psychology of mental retardation: Issues and approaches.* New York: Psychological Dimensions.

Butterfield, E. C., Wambold, C., & Belmont, J. M. (1973). On the theory and practice of improving short-term memory. *American Journal of Mental Deficiency, 77,* 654–669.

Campione, J. C., & Brown, A. L. (1977). Memory and metamemory development in educable retarded children. In R. V. Kail, Jr., & J. W. Hagen (Eds.), *Perspectives on the development of memory and cognition.* Hillsdale, NJ: Erlbaum.

Campione, J. C., & Brown, A. L. (1979). Toward a theory of intelligence: Contributions from research with retarded children. In R. J. Sternberg & D. K. Detterman (Eds.), *Human intelligence: Perspectives on its theory and measurement.* Norwood, NJ: Ablex.

Carroll, J. B. (1976). Psychometric tests as cognitive tasks: A new "structure of intellect." In. L. B. Resnick (Ed.), *The nature of intelligence*. Hillsdale, NJ: Erlbaum.

Carroll, J. B., & Maxwell, S. E. (1979). Individual differences in cognitive abilities. *Annual Review of Psychology, 30*, 603–640.

Cattell, R. B. (1971). *Abilities: Their structure, growth, and action*. Boston: Houghton-Mifflin.

Chase, W. G., & Simon, H. A. (1973). The mind's eye in chess. In W. G. Chase (Ed.), *Visual information processing*. New York: Academic Press.

Clark, H. H., & Chase, W. G. (1972). On the process of comparing sentences against pictures. *Cognitive Psychology, 3*, 472–517.

Cole, M., Gay, J., Glick, J. A., & Sharp, D. W. (1971). *The cultural context of learning and thinking*. New York: Basic Books.

Cole, M., & Scribner, S. (1974). *Culture and thought: A psychological introduction*. New York: Wiley.

Cronbach, L. J. (1970). *Essentials of psychological testing* (3rd ed.). New York: Harper & Row.

Cronbach, L. J., & Snow, R. E. (1977). *Aptitudes and instructional methods*. New York: Irvington.

Darlington, R. B. (1968). Multiple regression in psychological research and practice. *Psychological Bulletin, 69*, 161–182.

Feuerstein, R. (1979a). *The dynamic assessment of retarded performers: The learning potential assessment device, theory, instruments, and techniques*. Baltimore: University Park Press.

Feuerstein, R. (1979b). *Instrumental enrichment: An intervention program for cognitive modifiability*. Baltimore: University Park Press.

Flavell, J. H. (1977). *Cognitive development*. Englewood Cliffs, NJ: Prentice-Hall.

Flavell, J. H., & Wellman, H. M. (1977). Metamemory. In R. V. Kail, Jr., & J. W. Hagen (Eds.), *Perspectives on the development of memory and cognition*. Hillsdale, NJ: Erlbaum.

Frederiksen, J. R. (1980). Component skills in reading: Measurement of individual differences through chronometric analysis. In R. E. Snow, P.-A. Federico, & W. E. Montague (Eds.), *Aptitude, learning, and instruction: Cognitive process analysis*. Hillsdale, NJ: Erlbaum.

Gagne, R. M. (1970). *The conditions of learning* (2nd ed.). New York: Holt, Rinehart, & Winston.

Glaser, R., & Chi, M. (1979). *Progress report presented at ONR Contractors meeting*. New Orleans.

Goodnow, J. J. (1976). The nature of intelligent behavior: Questions raised by cross-cultural studies. In L. B. Resnick (Ed.), *The nature of intelligence*. Hillsdale, NJ: Erlbaum.

Gorsuch, R. L. (1974). *Factor analysis*. Philadelphia: W. B. Saunders.

Guilford, J. P. (1967). *The nature of human intelligence*. New York: McGraw-Hill.

Guilford, J. P., & Hoepfner, R. (1971). *The analysis of intelligence*. New York: McGraw-Hill.

Guttman, L. (1954). A new approach to factor analysis: The radex. In P. E. Lazarsfeld (Ed.), *Mathematical thinking in the social sciences*. Glencoe, IL: Free Press.

Guyote, M. J., & Sternberg, R. J. (1978). *A transitive-chain theory of syllogistic reasoning*. NR 150-412 ONR Technical Report no. 5. New Haven, CT: Department of Psychology, Yale University.

Harman, H. H. (1967). *Modern factor analysis* (2nd ed. rev.). Chicago: University of Chicago Press.

Holzinger, K. J. (1938). Relationships between three multiple orthogonal factors and four bifactors. *Journal of Educational Psychology, 29*, 513–519.

Horn, J. L. (1967). On subjectivity in factor analysis. *Educational and Psychological Measurement, 27*, 811–820.

Horn, J. L. (1968). Organization of abilities and the development of intelligence. *Psychological Review, 75*, 242–259.

Horn, J. L. (1974). Theory of functions represented among auditory and visual test performances. In J. R. Royce (Ed.), *Multivariate analysis and psychological theory*. New York: Academic Press.

Horn, J. L. (1979). Trends in the measurement of intelligence. In R. J. Sternberg & D. K. Detterman (Eds.), *Human intelligence: Perspectives on its theory and measurement*. Norwood, NJ: Ablex.

Horn, J. L. (1980). Concepts of intellect in relation to learning and adult development. *Intelligence, 4*, 285–317.

Horn, J. L., & Cattell, R. B. (1966). Refinement and test of the theory of fluid and crystallized general intelligences. *Journal of Educational Psychology, 57*, 253–270.

Horn, J. L., & Knapp, J. R. (1973). On the subjective character of the empirical base of Guilford's structure-of-intellect model. *Psychological Bulletin, 80*, 33–43.

Humphreys, L. G. (1962). The organization of human abilities. *American Psychologist, 17*, 475–483.

Humphreys, L. G. (1979). The construct of general intelligence. *Intelligence, 3*, 105–120.

Hunt, E. B. (1978). Mechanics of verbal ability. *Psychological Review, 85*, 109–130.

Hunt, E. B. (1979). *Intelligence as an information-processing construct*. NR 154-398 ONR Technical Report no. 5. Seattle: Department of Psychology, University of Washington.

Hunt, E. B., Frost, N., & Lunneborg, C. (1973). Individual differences in cognition: A new approach to intelligence. In G. Bower (Ed.), *The psychology of learning and motivation,* vol. 7. New York: Academic Press.

Hunt, E. B., Lunneborg, C., & Lewis, J. (1975). What does it mean to be high verbal? *Cognitive Psychology,* 7, 194–227.

Jensen, A. R. (1970). Hierarchical theories of mental ability. In W. B. Dockrell (Ed.), *On intelligence.* Toronto: The Ontario Institute for Studies in Education.

Jensen, A. R., & Munro, E. (1979). Reaction time, movement time, and intelligence. *Intelligence, 3,* 121–126.

Kerlinger, F. N., & Pedhazur, E. J. (1973). *Multiple regression in behavioral research.* New York: Holt, Rinehart & Winston.

Larkin, J. H. (1979). Processing information for effective problem solving. *Engineering Education, 70,* 285–288.

MacLeod, C. M., Hunt, E. B., & Mathews, N. N. (1978). Individual differences in the verification of sentence-picture relationships. *Journal of Verbal Learning and Verbal Behavior, 17,* 493–507.

McNemar, Q. (1964). Lost: Our intelligence? Why? *American Psychologist, 19,* 871–882.

Matarazzo, J. D. (1972). *Wechsler's measurement and appraisal of adult intelligence* (5th ed.). Baltimore: Williams & Wilkins.

Mulholland, T. M., Pellegrino, J. W., & Glaser, R. (1980). Components of geometric analogy solution. *Cognitive Psychology, 12,* 252–284.

Neisser, U. (1976). *Cognition and reality: Principles and implications of cognitive psychology.* San Francisco: Freeman.

Neisser, U. (1979). The concept of intelligence. In R. J. Sternberg & D. K. Detterman (Eds.), *Human intelligence: Perspectives on its theory and measurement.* Norwood, NJ: Ablex.

Newell, A., & Simon, H. (1972). *Human problem solving.* Englewood Cliffs, NJ: Prentice-Hall.

Pachella, R. G. (1974). The interpretation of reaction time in information-processing research. In B. H. Kantowitz (Ed.), *Human information processing: Tutorials in performance and cognition.* Hillsdale, NJ: Erlbaum.

Paivio, A. (1971). *Imagery and verbal processes.* New York: Holt, Rinehart, & Winston.

Pellegrino, J. W., & Glaser, R. (1979). Cognitive correlates and components in the analysis of individual differences. In R. J. Sternberg & D. K. Detterman (Eds.), *Human intelligence: Perspectives on its theory and measurement.* Norwood, NJ: Ablex

Pellegrino, J. W., & Glaser, R. (1980). Components of inductive reasoning. In R. E. Snow, P.-A. Federico, & W. Montague (Eds.), *Aptitude, learning, and instruction: Cognitive process analysis.* Hillsdale, NJ: Erlbaum.

Pellegrino, J. W., & Lyon, D. R. (1979). The components of a componential analysis. *Intelligence, 3,* 169–186.

Posner, M. I., & Mitchell, R. (1967). Chronometric analysis of classification. *Psychological Review, 74,* 392–409.

Quinton, G., & Fellows, B. (1975). "Perceptual" strategies in the solving of three-term series problems. *British Journal of Psychology, 66,* 69–78.

Raven, J. C. (1965). *Advanced progressive matrices, sets I and II.* London: Lewis.

Resnick, L. B., & Glaser, R. (1976). Problem solving and intelligence. In L. B. Resnick (Ed.), *The nature of intelligence.* Hillsdale, NJ: Erlbaum.

Royce, J. R. (1963). Factors as theoretical constructs. *American Psychologist, 18,* 522–527.

Royce, J. R. (1979). Toward a viable theory of individual differences. *Journal of Personality and Social Psychology, 37,* 1927–1931.

Royce, J. R. (1980). Factor analysis is alive and well. *American Psychologist, 35,* 390–392.

Rumelhart, D. E. (1977). Toward an interactive model of reading. In S. Dornic (Ed.), *Attention and performance,* Vol. 6. Hillsdale, NJ: Erlbaum.

Schustack, M. W., & Sternberg, R. J. (1981). Evaluation of evidence in causal inference. *Journal of Experimental Psychology: General, 110,* 101–120.

Shepard, R. N., & Metzler, J. (1971). Mental rotation of three-dimensional objects. *Science, 171,* 701–703.

Snow, R. E. (1979). Theory and method for research on aptitude processes. In R. J. Sternberg & D. K. Detterman (Eds.), *Human intelligence: Perspectives on its theory and measurement.* Norwood, NJ: Ablex.

Spearman, C. (1923). *The nature of "intelligence" and the principles of cognition.* London: Macmillan.

Spearman, C. (1927). *The abilities of man.* New York: Macmillan.

Sternberg, R. J. (1977). *Intelligence, information processing, and analogical reasoning: The componential analysis of human abilities.* Hillsdale, NJ: Erlbaum.

Sternberg, R. J. (1978). Isolating the components of intelligence. *Intelligence, 2,* 117–128.

Sternberg, R. J. (1978a). Intelligence research at the interface between differential and cognitive psychology. *Intelligence, 2,* 195–222.

Sternberg, R. J. (1979a). Developmental patterns in the encoding and combination of logical connections. *Journal of Experimental Child Psychology, 28,* 469–498.

Sternberg, R. J. (1979b). Intelligence research at the interface between differential and cognitive psychology: Prospects and proposals. In R. J. Sternberg & D. K. Detterman (Eds.), *Human intelligence: Perspectives on its theory and measurements,* Norwood, NJ: Ablex.

Sternberg, R. J. (1979c). The nature of mental abilities. *American Psychologist, 34,* 214–230.

Sternberg, R. J. (1979d). A review of "Six authors in search of a character": A play about intelligence tests in the year 2000. In R. J. Sternberg & D. K. Detterman (Eds.), *Human intelligence: Perspectives on its theory and measurement.* Norwood, NJ: Ablex.

Sternberg, R. J. (1979e). Six authors in search of a character: A play about intelligence tests in the year 2000. *Intelligence, 3,* 281–291.

Sternberg, R. J. (1980a). A proposed resolution of curious conflicts in the literature on linear syllogisms. In R. Nickerson (Ed.), *Attention and performance VIII.* Hillsdale, NJ: Erlbaum.

Sternberg, R. J. (1980b). Representation and process in linear syllogistic reasoning. *Journal of Experimental Psychology: General, 109,* 119–159.

Sternberg, R. J. (1980c). Toward a unified componential theory of human intelligence: 1. Fluid ability. In M. Friedman, J. Das, & N. O'Connor (Eds.), *Intelligence and learning.* New York: Plenum.

Sternberg, R. J. (1980d). Componentman as vice-president: A reply to Pellegrino and Lyon's analysis of "The components of a componential analysis." *Intelligence, 4,* 83–95.

Sternberg, R. J. (1980e). The development of linear syllogistic reasoning. *Journal of Experimental Child Psychology, 29,* 340–356.

Sternberg, R. J. (1980f). Factor theories of intelligence are all right almost. *Educational Researcher, 9,* 6–13, 18.

Sternberg, R. J. (1981a). Cognitive-behavioral approaches to the training of intelligence in the retarded. *Journal of Special Education, 15, 165–183.*

Sternberg, R. J. (1981b). Intelligence and nonentrenchment. *Journal of Educational Psychology, 73,* 1–16.

Sternberg, R. J. (1982). Reasoning, problem solving, and intelligence. In R. J. Sternberg (Ed.), *Handbook of human intelligence* (pp. 225–307). New York: Cambridge University Press.

Sternberg, R. J., & Gardner, M. K. (1979). *Unities in inductive reasoning.* NR 150-412 ONR Technical Report no. 18. New Haven, CT: Department of Psychology, Yale University.

Sternberg, R. J., Guyote, M. J., & Turner, M. E. (1980). Deductive reasoning. In R. E. Snow, P.-A. Federico, & W. Montague (Eds.), *Aptitude, learning, and instruction: Cognitive process analysis.* Hillsdale, NJ: Erlbaum.

Sternberg, R. J., Ketron, J. L., & Powell, J. S. (1982). Componential approaches to the training of intelligent performance. In D. K. Detterman & R. J. Sternberg (Eds.), *How and how much can intelligence be increased* (pp. 155–172)? Norwood, NJ: Ablex.

Sternberg, R. J., & Nigro, G. (1980). Developmental patterns in the solution of verbal analogies. *Child Development, 51,* 27–38.

Sternberg, R. J., & Powell, J. S. (1983). The development of intelligence. In P. Mussen (Series Ed.), J. Flavell & E. Markman (Volume Eds.), *Handbook of child psychology* (Vol. 3, 3rd ed., pp. 341–419). New York: Wiley.

Sternberg, R. J., & Rifkin, B. (1979). The development of analogical reasoning processes. *Journal of Experimental Child Psychology, 27,* 195–232.

Sternberg, R. J., & Salter, W. (1980). *Stalking the elusive homunculus: Isolating the metacomponents of intelligence.* Manuscript in preparation.

Sternberg, R. J., Tourangeau, R., & Nigro, G. (1979). Metaphor, induction, and social policy: The convergence of macroscopic and microscopic views. In A. Ortony (Ed.), *Metaphor and thought.* New York: Cambridge University Press.

Sternberg, R. J., & Turner, M. E. (1981). Components of syllogistic reasoning. *Acta Psychologica, 47,* 245–265.

Sternberg, R. J., & Weil, E. M. (1980). An aptitude-strategy interaction in linear syllogistic reasoning. *Journal of Educational Psychology, 72,* 226–234.

Sternberg, S. (1969). The discovery of processing stages: Extensions of Donders' method. *Acta Psychologica, 30,* 276–315.

Thorndike, E. L. (1911). *Animal intelligence: Experimental studies.* New York: Macmillan.

Thurstone, L. L. (1938). *Primary mental abilities.* Chicago: University of Chicago Press.

Thurstone, L. L. (1947). *Multiple factor analysis.* Chicago: University of Chicago Press.

Tourangeau, R., & Sternberg, R. J. (1981). Aptness in metaphor. *Cognitive Psychology, 13,* 27–55.

Vernon, P. E. (1971). *The structure of human abilities.* London: Methuen.

Vernon, P. E. (1979). *Intelligence: Heredity and environment.* San Francisco: Freeman.

Whitely, S. E. (1980). Latent trait models in the study of intelligence. *Intelligence, 4,* 97–132.

Wober, M. (1974). Towards an understanding of the Kiganda concept of intelligence. In J. W. Berry & P. R. Dasen (Eds.), *Culture and cognition: Readings in cross-cultural psychology.* London: Methuen.

Zigler, E. (1971). The retarded child as a whole person. In H. E. Adams & W. K. Boardman III (Eds.), *Advances in experimental clinical psychology,* vol. 1. New York: Pergamon.

Toward a Triarchic Theory of Human Intelligence

2

Robert J. Sternberg

A Triarchic Theory of Human Intelligence

The goal of this chapter is to present a synopsis of a new "triarchic" theory of human intelligence. The theory is "triarchic" in the sense that it comprises three subtheories that serve as the governing bases for specific models of intelligent human behavior. The theory is believed to go beyond many previous theories in its scope, and to answer a broader array of questions about intelligence than has been answered in the past by single theories. The chapter cannot present all details of the theory, which requires a book-length presentation (Sternberg, 1985). Nevertheless, sufficient detail will be presented to convey the scope of the theory and a sense of the kinds of questions it can (and cannot) handle.

The triarchic theory of human intelligence comprises three subtheories. The first subtheory relates intelligence to the external world of the individual, specifying three classes of acts—environmental adaptation, selection, and shaping—that characterize intelligent behavior in the everyday world. This subtheory is thus one of a set of contextual theories of intelligence that emphasize the role of environmental context in determining what constitutes intelligent behavior in a given milieu (see, e.g., Berry, 1981; Charlesworth, 1979a, 1979b; Dewey, 1957; Laboratory of Comparative Human

Cognition, 1982; Neisser, 1976). The second subtheory specifies those points along the continuum of one's experience with tasks or situations that most critically involve the use of intelligence. In particular, the account emphasizes the roles of novelty (see also Cattell, 1971; Fagan & McGrath, 1981; Guilford, 1967, 1982; Horn, 1968; Kaufman & Kaufman, 1983; Raaheim, 1974; Snow, 1981) and of automatization (see also Lansman, Donaldson, Hunt, & Yantis, 1982; Perfetti, 1984) in intelligence. The third subtheory relates intelligence to the internal world of the individual, specifying the mental mechanisms that lead to more and less intelligent behavior. This subtheory specifies three kinds of information-processing components (processes) that are instrumental in (a) learning how to do things, (b) planning what things to do and how to do them, and (c) actually doing the things. This subtheory is thus compatible in many respects with other current cognitive theories that emphasize the role of information processing in intelligence (e.g., Campione & Brown, 1979; Carroll, 1981; Hunt, 1980; Jensen, 1979; Pellegrino & Glaser, 1980; Snow, 1979).

The three subtheories in combination provide a rather broad basis for characterizing the nature of intelligent behavior in the world and for specifying the kinds of tasks that are more and less appropriate for the measurement of intelligence. The contextual subtheory specifies the potential set of *contents* for behaviors that can be characterized as intelligent. It addresses the question of which behaviors are intelligent for whom, and where these behaviors are intelligent. The two-facet subtheory specifies the relation between intelligence as exhibited on a task or in a situation, on the one hand, and the *amount of experience* with the task or situation, on the other. It addresses the question of when behaviors are intelligent for a given individual. The componential subtheory specifies the potential set of *mental mechanisms* that underlies intelligent behavior, regardless of the particular behavioral contents. It addresses the question of how behaviors are intelligent in any given setting.

The first subtheory is "relativistic" with respect to both individuals and the sociocultural settings in which they live. What constitutes an intelligent act may differ from one person to another, although the needs for adaptation, selection, and shaping of environments do not. The second subtheory is relativistic only with respect to the points at which novelty and automatization are relevant for a given individual. But the relevance of the two facets to intelligence is perceived to be universal. The third subtheory is universal: Although individuals may differ in which mental mechanisms they apply to a given task or situation, the potential set of mental mechanisms underlying intelligence is viewed to be the same across all individuals and sociocultural settings. Thus, the vehicles by which one might wish to measure intelligence (test contents, modes of presentation, formats for test items, etc.) will probably need to differ across sociocultural groups, and possibly even within such groups: but the underlying mechanisms to be measured and their functions in dealing with novelty and in becoming automatized do not differ across individuals or groups.

The Context of Intelligence

Although many of us act as though intelligence is what intelligence tests measure (Boring, 1923; Jensen, 1969), few of us believe it. But if intelligence is not identical to what tests measure, then what is it? The approach taken here is that of first conceiving of intelligence in terms of the context in which it occurs.

Consideration of the nature of intelligence will be limited in this chapter to *individual* intelligence. Although the intellectual level of group accomplishments may be measurable in some sense, and has been shown to be important in a variety of contexts (see, e.g., Laboratory of Comparative Human Cognition, 1982), this issue would take the present discussion too far from its intended purpose. Hence, group intelligence is not dealt with here.

Why propose a contextual framework for understanding intelligence and even theories of intelligence? I believe there are at least three important reasons.

First, a contextual view offers an escape from the vicious circularity that has confronted much past research on intelligence, in which an attempt is made to escape from old conceptions of intelligence (such as the psychometric one that gave rise to IQ tests) by creating new conceptions (such as the information-processing one); the new conceptions are then validated (or invalidated!) against the old conceptions for lack of any better external criteria (see Neisser, 1979). There is a need to generate some kind of external standard that goes beyond the view, often subtly hidden, that intelligence is what IQ tests happen to measure. For, whatever its operational appeal, this view lacks substantive theoretical grounding, and when IQ test scores are used as the "external" criterion against which new theories and tests are validated, one is essentially accepting this operational view.

Second, a contextual view of intelligence provides a perspective on the nature of intelligence that is frequently neglected in contemporary theorizing. The bulk of the contemporary research deals with intelligence in relation to the internal world of the individual (see, e.g., Resnick, 1976; Sternberg, 1982a, 1982b; Sternberg & Powell, 1982). Such research provides a means for understanding intelligence in terms of the cognitive processes and structures that contribute to it but has little or nothing to say about intelligence in relation to the individual's external world. If one views intelligence at least in part in terms of adaptive behavior in the real-world environment (as even psychometric theorists, such as Binet & Simon, 1973, and Wechsler, 1958, have done), then it is impossible to understand fully the nature of intelligence without understanding how this environment shapes what constitutes intelligent behavior in a given sociocultural context. "Internal" analyses can elucidate the cognitive and other processes and structures that help form intelligent behavior, and external, contextual analyses can elucidate which behaviors or classes of behavior are intelligent in a given environment or class of environments. The two kinds of analyses thus complement each other.

Third, a contextual viewpoint is useful in countering the predictor–criterion confusion that is rampant in current thinking about intelligence on the part of both lay people and experts. This confusion—epitomized by the view that intelligence is what IQ tests test—results when the intelligence tests (whether they are called "intelligence tests," "mental ability tests," "scholastic aptitude tests," or whatever else) come to be viewed as better indicators of intelligence than the criterial, real-world intelligent behaviors they are supposed to predict. Many of us are familiar with admission and selection decisions where performance in tasks virtually identical to the criteria for such decisions is neglected in favor of test scores that have modest predictive validity, at best, for the criterial behaviors. Often, lower (or higher) test scores color the way all other information is perceived. There seems to be a need to study intelligence in relation to real-world behavior, if only as a reminder that it is this behavior, and not behavior in taking tests that are highly imperfect simulations and predictors of such behavior, which should be of central interest to psychologists and others seeking to understand intelligence.

Contextualist approaches to intelligence are nothing new, and the views presented here draw on or are compatible with the views of many others who have chosen to view intelligence in a contextual perspective, for example, Berry (1972/1974, 1980, 1981), Charlesworth (1976, 1979a, 1979b), Cole (1979–1980) and his colleagues (Laboratory of Comparative Human Cognition, 1982, 1983), Dewey (1957), Ford and Miura (1983), Gordon and Terrell (1981), Keating (1984), and Neisser (1976, 1979). My purpose is to present a contextualist view in one place and, especially, to consider it in light of objections that have been or might be raised against it. Although my own views derive from and draw on the views of others, I of course make no claim to represent anyone else's position: Contextualist views, like other views, are subject to considerable variation and disagreement (see Sternberg & Salter, 1982).

A Contextualist Subtheory of Intelligence

Although it is not possible to summarize all of the various contextualist views in detail, it seems to be fair to describe contextualist theories as representing regions on a continuum of the purported cultural specificity of intelligence. These theories, then, vary in the degree to which they view intelligence as a culturally specific entity. Consider four such theories, each of which is successively less extreme in the degree of cultural specificity it asserts.

At one extreme, Berry (1972/1974) has taken a position he refers to as radical cultural relativism. This "position requires that indigenous notions of cognitive competence be the sole basis for the generation of cross-culturally valid descriptions and assessments of cognitive capacity" (p. 225). According to this view, then, intelligence must be defined in a way that is appropriate to the contexts in which the people of each particular culture reside.

The members of the Laboratory of Comparative Human Cognition (1982) have asserted that the radical cultural relativist position does not take into account the fact that cultures interact. According to their view, it is possible to make a kind of "conditional comparison," in which the investigator sees how different cultures have organized experience to deal with a single domain of activity. This comparison is possible, however, only if the investigator is in a position to assert that performance of the task or tasks under investigation is a universal kind of achievement, and if the investigator has a developmental theory of performance in the task domain. This position thus asserts that certain conditional kinds of comparisons are possible in the domain of intelligence.

Still less "radical" is the position of Charlesworth (1979a, 1979b), whose "ethological" approach to studying intelligence has focused on "intelligent behavior as it occurs in everyday, rather than in test situations—and how these situations may be related to changes in it over ontogenesis" (Charlesworth, 1979a, p. 212). Charlesworth distinguishes between intelligence of the kind that has been studied by psychometricians and intelligence of the kind that is of particular survival or adaptive value. He believes it necessary to concentrate on the latter kind of intelligence, especially because "test psychologists generally view test performance as a way of indexing the individual's adaptive potential, but take virtually no cognizance of the environmental conditions which tap this potential and influence its expression over ontogenesis" (Charlesworth, 1979a, p. 212).

Least "radical" is the position taken by contextualists such as Keating (1984), and Baltes, Dittmann-Kohli, and Dixon (1982), who have combined contextual positions with more or less standard kinds of psychological research and experimentation. For example, Baltes has conducted fairly standard kinds of psychometric research (see, e.g., Baltes & Willis, 1979, 1982), but has combined this research with a contextual position on it. Of course, not all contextualists are as optimistic as Baltes regarding the reconcilability of contextual and psychometric kinds of theorizing (see Labouvie-Vief & Chandler, 1978).

To summarize, I have considered four (from among many) contextual positions that differ in their degree of radical contextual relativism. The positions range from one of extreme contextual relativism (Berry) to one in which contextualism is in some sense integrated with conventional kinds of psychometric theorizing (Baltes). In the next section of the chapter, I will present my own contextual view. Like Baltes and others, I believe an integration between standard kinds of theorizing—in my case, both psychometric and information-processing—is possible. My integration is rather different, however, from those previously proposed.

Contextual Definition of Intelligence and Some Constraints on It

I view intelligence in context as consisting of *purposive adaptation to, shaping of, and selection of real-world environments relevant to one's life*. This definition is, of course, extremely general, and further constraints will be placed on it later. Thus, this view is a starting point rather than a finishing point for a definition of intelligence. Consider what constraints this definition does have.

The Real World

First, I define intelligence in terms of behavior in real-world environments. I do so deliberately to exclude fantasy environments, such as might be invented in dreams or constructed by and for the minds of certain of the mentally ill. I would include in the domain of real-world environments those found in some laboratory settings and in certain testing situations that, no matter how artificial or trivial they may be, nevertheless exist in the real world. It is as much a mistake to exclude testlike behavior from one's view of intelligence, as it is to rely on it exclusively.

Relevance

Second, I define intelligence in terms of behavior in environments that are relevant to one's life. The intelligence of an African pygmy could not legitimately be assessed by placing the pygmy in a North American culture and using North American tests, unless it were relevant to test the pygmy for survival in a North American culture and one wished to assess the pygmy's intelligence for this culture (for example, if the pygmy happened to live in our culture and had to adapt to it). Similarly, a North American's intelligence could not be legitimately assessed in terms of adaptation to pygmy society unless adaptation to that society were relevant to the person's life. (See Cole, 1979–1980, and McClelland, 1973, for further perspectives on the importance of relevance to the understanding and assessment of intelligence.) There is one qualification of the relevance criterion, however. As will be discussed later, tasks and situations serve as particularly apt measures of intelligence when they involve some, but not excessive, novelty. Thus, a task requiring a North American to adapt to aspects of a pygmy environment might serve well to measure the North American's intelligence, but only in comparison with other North Americans for whom the task would be equally novel. Similarly, pygmies might be compared with respect to intelligence by their ability to adapt to certain aspects of North American culture. In this case, one is measuring ability to adapt to novelty, an important aspect of adaptation in any culture. A problem arises only when one attempts to compare individuals on the same task across cultures for whom the task is not equally novel. In this case, the task is not measuring the same thing for different individuals. Unfortunately, it is precisely this kind of cross-cultural comparison, which I believe to be invalid, that serves as the basis for much research seeking to compare the levels of intelligence of various individuals and groups from different cultures.

An implication of this view is that intelligence cannot be fully understood outside a sociocultural context, and that it may in fact differ for a given individual from one culture to the next. Our more intelligent individuals might be found to be much less intelligent in another culture, and some of our less intelligent individuals might be found more intelligent. Consider, for example, a person who is deficient in the ability to negotiate a large-scale spatial environment. Such people are often referred to as lacking a good "sense of direction." Although they can usually navigate through old, familiar terrain with little or no difficulty, they may find it difficult to navigate through new and unfamiliar terrains. To someone who comes from a sociocultural milieu in which people spend their lives in highly familiar environments, such as their hometown plus a few surrounding towns and cities, the idea of large-scale spatial navigation would never enter into the conception of intelligence, and such navigation would be an essentially unknown cognitive skill. Navigation in unfamiliar spatial terrains would simply be irrelevant to such people's lives, just as the ability to shoot accurately with a bow and arrow is irrelevant to our lives. Were such navigation to become relevant in the sociocultural milieu, then what is "intelligent" would change for that culture. In the Puluwat culture, for example, large-scale spatial navigational ability would be one of the most important indices of an individual's adaptive intelligence (Berry, 1980; Gladwin, 1970; Neisser, 1976).

One need not go to exotic cultures to find effective differences or changes in what constitutes intelligent behavior. As Horn (1979) has pointed out, the advent of the computer seems likely to change what constitutes intelligent performance in our society. For example, numerical calculation was an important part of some intelligence tests, such as Thurstone and Thurstone's (1962) Primary Mental Abilities Test. But with the advent of cheap calculators and ever-cheaper computers, the importance of numerical calculation skill in intelligent behavior seems to be declining. Certainly, using numerical calculation as one of five subtests measuring intelligence, or as the sole or main index of number skill, would seem inappropriate today, no matter how appropriate it may have seemed when the Thurstones devised their test—or even a few years ago when numerical calculation skill was a central part of people's lives in school and out (balancing checkbooks, keeping track of expenses, and so on). The importance of quantitative expertise to adaptive functioning has probably not changed; but what such expertise consists of may well have changed, at least with respect to the requirements of life in today's society. Thus, even in our own culture, we see changes over time, no matter how slow, in what constitutes intelligence. Businesses interested in assessing the intelligence of today's job applicants are much more likely to be concerned about skills in learning to use and in using electronic media, and much less concerned about calculational skills, than they were just a few years ago.

Purposiveness

Third, intelligence is purposive. It is directed toward goals, however vague or subconscious those goals may be. These goals need not be the attainment of the maxima of the goods most valued by society, for example, money, fame, or power. Rather, one may be willing to strive for less of one commodity in the hope of attaining more of another.

Adaptation

Fourth, intelligence is adaptive. Indeed, definitions of intelligence have traditionally viewed intelligence in terms of adaptation to one's environment (see, e.g., "Intelligence and Its Measurement," 1921). Adaptation consists of trying to achieve a good fit between oneself and one's environment. Such a fit will be obtainable in greater or lesser degree. But if the degree of fit is below what one considers satisfactory for one's life, then the adaptive route may be viewed, at a higher level, as maladaptive. For example, a partner in a marriage may be unable to attain satisfaction within the marriage; or an employee of a business concern may have values so different from those of the employer that a satisfactory fit does not seem possible; or one may find the situation one is in to be morally reprehensible (as in Nazi Germany). In such instances, adaptation to the present environment does not present a viable alternative to the individual, and the individual is obliged to try something other than adaptation to the given environment. Thus, it may be incorrect simply to equate intelligence with adaptation to the environment.

Shaping

Fifth, intelligence involves shaping the environment. Environmental shaping is used when one's attempts to adapt to the given environment fail. One then attempts to reshape it to increase one's fit with it. The marital partner may attempt to restructure the marriage; the employee may try to persuade an employer to see or do things differently; the citizen may try to change the government, through either violent or nonviolent means. In each case, however, the individual attempts to change the environment so as to result in a better fit rather than merely attempting to adapt to what is already there.

What this means is that there may be no one set of behaviors that is "intelligent" for everyone, because people can adjust to their environments in different ways. Whereas the components of intelligent behavior are probably universal, their use in the construction of environmentally appropriate behavior is likely to vary not only across groups, but also across individuals.

What does seem to be common among people mastering their environments is the ability to capitalize on strengths and to compensate for weaknesses (see Cronbach & Snow, 1977). Successful people are not only able to adapt well to their environments, but actually modify the environments they are in so as to maximize the fit between the environment and their adaptive skills.

Consider, for example, the "stars" in any given field of endeavor. What is it that distinguishes such persons from all the rest? Of course, this question, as phrased, is broad enough to be the topic of a book, and indeed, many books have been written about it. For present purposes, however, the distinguishing characteristics to which I would like to call attention are (a) at least one extraordinarily well-developed skill, and (b) an extraordinary ability to capitalize on that skill or skills in their work. For example, generate a short list of "stars" in your own field. Chances are that the stars do not seem to share any one ability, as traditionally defined, but rather share a tendency toward having some set of extraordinary talents that they make the most of in their work. My own list would include a person with extraordinary spatial visualization skills (if anyone can visualize in four dimensions, he can!), a person with a talent for coming up with highly counterintuitive findings that are of great theoretical importance, and a person who has a remarkable sense of where the field is going and repeatedly tends to be just one step ahead of it so as to time the publication of his work for maximum impact. These three particular persons (and others on my list) share little in terms of what sets them apart, aside from at least one extraordinary talent on which they capitalize fully in their work. Although they are also highly intelligent in the traditional sense, so are many others who never reach their heights of accomplishment.

Because what is adaptive differs at least to some degree, both across people and across situations, the present view suggests that intelligence is not quite the same thing for different people and in different situations. The higher-order skills of capitalization and compensation may be the same, but what is capitalized on and what is compensated for will vary. The differences across people and situations extend beyond different life paths within a given culture.

Selection

Sixth, intelligence involves the active selection of environments. When adaptation is not possible or desirable, and when shaping fails, one may attempt to select an alternative environment with which one is able, or potentially able, to attain a better contextual fit. In essence, the person recognizes that attempts to succeed within the given environment have not worked, and that attempts to mold that environment to one's values, abilities, or interests have also not worked; it is time to move out of that environment and find a new one that suits one better. For example, the partner may leave the marriage; the employee may seek another job; the resident of Nazi Germany might have attempted to emigrate. Under these circumstances, the individual considers the alternative environments available and attempts to select that environment, within the constraints of feasibility, with which maximal fit will be attained. Sometimes this option is not feasible, however. For example, members of certain religions may view themselves as utterly committed to their marriages, or an individual may decide to stay in a marriage on account of the children, despite its lack of appeal; or the employee may not be able to attain another job, either from lack of positions, lack of qualifications, or both; or the individual wishing to leave the country may lack permission or the resources to leave.

Consider how environmental selection can operate in career choices. A rather poignant set of real-world examples is provided in Feldman's (1982) account, *Whatever*

Happened to the Quiz Kids? The quiz kids were selected for the radio show, and later the television show, of the same name for a number of intellectual and personal traits. Existing records suggest that all or almost all of them had exceptionally high IQs, typically well over 140 and, in some cases, over 200. Yet, one cannot help but be struck by how much less distinguished their later lives have been than their earlier lives, often even by their own standards. There are undoubtedly many reasons for this lesser later success, including statistical regression effects. What is striking in biography after biography is that the ones who were most successful were those who found what they were interested in and good at and then pursued it relentlessly. The less successful ones had difficulty in finding any one thing that interested them, and in a number of cases floundered while trying to find a niche for themselves.

We have made several attempts to measure intelligence as it applies to real-world contexts. I will describe two of these approaches here.

Measurement of Contextually Directed Intelligence

One approach we have taken to understanding intelligence as it operates in the everyday world is that underlying successful performance in many real-world tasks is a set of judgmental skills based on tacit understanding of a kind that is never explicitly taught, and, in many instances, never even verbalized. Interviews with prominent business executives and academic psychologists—the two populations that served as the bases for our initial studies—revealed a striking level of agreement that a major factor underlying success in each occupation is a knowledge and understanding of the ins and outs of the occupation. These ins and outs are generally learned on the job rather than in any preparatory academic or other work. To measure potential for occupational success, therefore, one might wish to go beyond conventional ability and achievement tests to the measurement of individuals' understanding of and judgment in using the hidden agenda of their field of endeavor.

In particular, we have found three kinds of tacit understanding to be particularly important for success, namely, understanding regarding managing (a) oneself, (b) others, and (c) one's career (Wagner & Sternberg, 1995). These understandings and the judgments based on them were measured by items drawing on decisions of the kinds one typically has to make in the everyday professional or business world. Separate questionnaires were constructed for the business executives and academic psychologists. For example, one item on each questionnaire presented the situation of a relatively inexperienced person in the field who had to decide which tasks were more or less urgent. Subjects rated the priorities of the various tasks. Another item presented various criteria that could be used in judging the success of an executive or an academic psychologist, and subjects had to rate how important each criterion was. Yet another item presented various considerations in deciding which projects to work on; subjects had to decide how important each of the various considerations was in deciding which project to work on. Subjects receiving the psychology questionnaire were a national sample of university psychology faculty and graduate students as well as a sample of Yale undergraduates; subjects receiving the business questionnaire were national samples of business executives and business graduate students, executives at a local bank, and Yale undergraduates. Scores on the questionnaires were correlated at about the .4 level with measures of success among members of each occupation, such as number of articles published in a year or published rating of the university with which a subject was affiliated for academics, and merit salary increases and performance ratings for the business executives. The subscale most highly correlated with successful performance was that for managing one's career. Moreover, at least for the undergraduates, performance on the two questionnaires was uncorrelated with scores on a standard verbal reasoning test, indicating that the correlations with external measures of success were not obtained via a measure that was nothing more than a proxy for an IQ.

A second approach we have used in measuring intelligence in the everyday world is based on the notion that intelligence can be measured with some accuracy by the degree of resemblance between a person's behavior and the behavior of the "ideally" intelligent individual (see Neisser, 1979). Sternberg, Conway, Ketron, and Bernstein (1981) had a group of individuals rate the extent to which each of 250 behaviors characterized their own behavioral repertoire. A second group of individuals rated the extent to which each of the 250 behaviors characterized the behavioral repertoire of an "ideally intelligent" person.

The behaviors that were rated had previously been listed by entirely different individuals as characterizing either "intelligent" or "unintelligent" persons. The intelligent behaviors were shown (by factor analysis) to fall into three general classes: problem-solving ability (e.g., "reasons logically and well," "identifies connections among ideas," and "sees all aspects of a problem"); verbal ability (e.g., "speaks clearly and articulately," "is verbally fluent," and "reads with high comprehension"); and social competence (e.g., "accepts others for what they are," "admits mistakes," and "displays interest in the world at large"). No attempt was made to classify the unintelligent behaviors, as they were not the objects of interest in the study.

We computed the correlation between each person's self-description and the description of the ideally intelligent person (as provided by the second group of individuals). The correlation provided a measure of the degree of resemblance between a real individual and the "ideally intelligent" individual. The claim was that this degree of resemblance is itself a measure of intelligence. The facts bore out this claim: The correlation between the resemblance measure and scores on a standard IQ test was .52, confirming that the measure did provide an index of intelligence as it is often operationally defined.

People's conceptions of intelligence can be used not only to predict their own scores on standard psychometric intelligence tests, but also to predict how people will evaluate the intelligence of others. We presented subjects with descriptions of persons in terms of the various intelligent and unintelligent behaviors that had been generated in our initial data collection. The subjects were asked to rate the intelligence of each person described on a 1-to-9 scale. We then attempted to predict people's ratings on the basis of the weights our theory assigned to each behavior in each description of a person. The correlation between predicted and observed ratings was .96.

In making their ratings, people weighted the two more academic factors—problem solving and verbal abilities—more heavily than social competence, but all three factors received significant weightings in people's judgments.

Criticisms of the Contextual View: Some Responses and Elaborations

I have outlined previously some of the main features of a contextual view of the nature of human intelligence. Contextual views have been criticized in the past on a number of grounds, among them, their relativism, their seeming reinforcement of the status quo and inability to accommodate cultural change, their vagueness and lack of empirical verification, and their seeming overinclusiveness, by which is meant their placing in the realm of intelligence mental and behavioral phenomena that many would place in other realms, such as those of personality and motivation. In this section I will describe and respond to each of these criticisms.

Relativism

It has been argued that contextualist views give up too much (Jonathan Baron, personal communication)—that they leave one essentially with no firm foundation for understanding the nature of intelligence, because "everything is relative." There are two bases for countering this argument.

First, I do not believe that everything is, in fact, relative. As I will discuss later, I believe that there are many aspects of intelligence that transcend cultural boundaries, and that are, in fact, universal. Moreover, I am aware of no evidence to suggest that either the hardware (anatomy and physiology) of cognitive functioning or the potential software (cognitive processes, strategies, mental representations, and so on) of such functioning differs from one culture or society to the next. What differ, however, are the weights, or importances, of various aspects of mental hardware and software as they apply to defining what constitutes intelligent behavior.

For example, the complex and interactive cognitive skills that are prerequisite for reading are to be found in varying degrees in all people in all sociocultural milieus, at least as far as we know. I include in such prerequisite skills not the knowledge that is taught to participants in literate cultures, but the skills such as pattern perception, articulatory ability, and comparison ability that can be developed but that exist in some amount in individuals whether or not they ever receive formal schooling. Whereas these skills may exist in some degree in members of every culture, however, their importance to intelligent behavior may differ radically from one culture to the next. The skills needed for reading, and especially those specifically relevant for reading but of little or no relevance for other tasks, will be much less important in a preliterate society than in a literate one. In contrast, coordination skills that may be essential to life in a preliterate society (e.g., those motor skills required for shooting a bow and arrow) may be all but irrelevant to intelligent behavior for most people in a literate and more "developed" society.

It is not probable that these skills exist in equal amounts across cultures: Some cultures are likely to put much more emphasis on developing certain kinds of skills than do others, which will in turn place their emphasis on developing other kinds of skills. As a result, two cultures may appear to show mean differences in levels of measured intelligence—but probably only when intelligence is measured in terms of the knowledge and skills required by one of the two (or more) cultures. Yet, it does not make sense to impose one culture's test on another culture, no matter how fair the test may be for the first culture, unless the adaptive requirements of the two cultures are essentially the same. And even if the requirements are the same, there is no guarantee that a given test will measure the same skills equally well in the two cultures: The within-culture validity of the test needs to be demonstrated independently for the two cultures. Such sameness is probably a rare event. This argument applies as well to multiple subcultures within a single culture. And even if one could find a set of test items that measured just those skills that are common to the adaptive requirements of members of the two cultures, the test would be incomplete because it failed to measure the aspects of adaptation that are specific to but nevertheless relevant in each of the individual cultures; moreover, the test would probably be scored incorrectly in a way that assumed that the weights of the common elements in adaptation were the same across the two cultures.

Stability and Change

One might—incorrectly, I believe—interpret the contextualist position as being unable to accommodate cultural change or as reinforcing the status quo. These objections are unfounded, however. In the contextualist view, the nature of intelligence can change within a single culture as well as between multiple cultures. In a rapidly developing culture, what constitutes intelligent performance may actually change over a relatively short span of time. As noted earlier, in our own culture it is likely that the logical skills needed for computer programming and management will become successively more important to intelligent performance in our society as calculational skills become successively less important.

There is, then, nothing in the contextualist view that either supports or vitiates the status quo. The contextualist view simply recognizes the changing nature over space and time of what constitutes intelligent behavior.

Vagueness and Lack of Empirical Verification

Contextual theories tend to be vague, general, and lacking in empirical verification. One of the reasons for this state of affairs, I believe, is that contextual theories cannot make a go of things on their own: They need supplementation. A contextual theory sets a perspective from which one can understand the nature of intelligence, but it accounts for only a limited aspect of intelligence, namely, its relation to the external world. Thus, whereas one could argue that intelligent behavior is adaptive, it would seem that not all adaptive behavior is intelligent, at least in the traditional senses of the word. For example, to know how to put a ribbon in one's typewriter may be adaptive, but the ability and knowledge needed to put the ribbon in are not usually seen as important aspects of intelligence. Hence, I would claim that the problem with contextual theories is not that they are wrong, but rather that they are incomplete. They do not, for example, specify the cognitive skills that underlie adaptation to the environment. In the triarchic theory, contextualism serves as the basis for just one of three subtheories, so that questions not raised by contextualism can be addressed by other aspects of the theory. These other questions include those concerning what, more exactly, (a) are the relationships between amount of experience with a task or situation and the amount of intelligence required to perform the task or in the situation, and (b) what are the mental mechanisms by which intelligent behaviors are accomplished.

Overinclusiveness

The contextualist view presented here is certainly highly inclusive in the sense that it includes within the realm of intelligence things that might typically be placed in the realms of personality or motivation (see also Baron, 1982). For example, motivational phenomena relevant to purposive adaptive behavior—such as motivation to perform well in one's career—would be considered to be part of intelligence, broadly defined (see also Scarr, 1981; Zigler, 1971).

Another element included in the present view of intelligence is environmental selection. Obviously, one's choice of environment will be limited by many factors of luck over which one has no control. Indeed, the role in life of chance factors such as time and place is almost always passed over lightly in analyses of intelligence (but see Jencks, 1972). One can scarcely be faulted for circumstances beyond one's control. The only circumstances relevant to the evaluation of intelligence are those in which one has some behavioral control and in which one has an adequate opportunity to express one's intelligence. The more control one has and the greater the opportunity for expressing intelligence, the more relevant the circumstances are for evaluating one's intelligence. It should be emphasized that I speak here of the control an individual *could* have: People often fail to realize the full extent to which they can control or at least influence their environments.

I would like to say, in closing this section, that the contextualist view is in no meaningful sense warmed-over Social Darwinism. The Social Darwinist viewpoint has never seemed to be well suited to taking into account life circumstances that are beyond one's control. The present view, on the other hand, is "conditionalized" upon such circumstances. What is adaptive for the ghetto-dweller may be different from what is adaptive for the wealthy suburbanite. They are from two distinct subcultures, which may differ as much as two national cultures, and comparing their adaptations may be inappropriate if the same behavioral criteria are used. Moreover, Social Darwinism usually becomes quite absolutist: The adaptive norm is set up as that of the dominant social class. The present view posits a pluralism of niches to which one may ultimately adapt, with the final niche partly determined by one's own choice and partly determined by life circumstances beyond one's control.

Facets of Intelligence

One needs more constraints in a full theory of intelligence than contextual views can provide. The two-facet subtheory proposed here provides one set of further constraints.

A Two-Facet Subtheory of Intelligence

The two-facet subtheory proposes that a task measures "intelligence" to the extent that it requires either or both of two skills (the nature of which will be specified in greater detail in the next section): the ability to deal with novel kinds of task and situational demands and the ability to automatize information processing. These two abilities apply to the interaction between individuals, on the one hand, and tasks or situations, on the other, precisely at those points where the relation between the individual and the task or situation is most rapidly changing. This fast rate of change makes these two points (or regions) of experience most relevant for assessing intelligence. Consider each of these abilities in turn.

Ability to Deal with Novel Task and Situational Demands

Novel Tasks

The idea that intelligence involves the ability to deal with novel task demands is itself far from novel (see, e.g., Cattell, 1971; Horn, 1968; Kaufman & Kaufman, 1983; Raaheim, 1974; Snow, 1981; Sternberg, 1981a, 1982b). Sternberg (1981a) has suggested, in fact, that intelligence is best measured by tasks that are "nonentrenched" in the sense of requiring information processing of kinds outside people's ordinary experience. The task may be nonentrenched in the kinds of operations it requires, or in the concepts it requires the subjects to use. According to this view, then, intelligence involves

> not merely the ability to learn and reason with new concepts but the ability to learn and reason with new kinds of concepts. Intelligence is not so much a person's ability to learn or think within conceptual systems that the person has already become familiar with as it is his or her ability to learn and think within new conceptual systems, which can then be brought to bear upon already existing knowledge structures. (Sternberg, 1981a, p. 4)

It is important to note that the usefulness of a task in measuring intelligence is not a linear function of task novelty. The task that is presented should be novel, but not totally outside the individual's past experience (Raaheim, 1974). If the task is too novel, then individuals will not have any cognitive structures to bring to bear on it, and as a result, the task will simply be outside their range of comprehension. Calculus, for example, would be a highly novel field of endeavor for most 5-year-olds, but the calculus tasks would be so far outside their range of experience that they would be worthless for the assessment of 5-year-olds' intelligence. In Piagetian (1972) terms, the task should primarily require accommodation, but it must require some assimilation as well.

Implicit in the preceding discussion is the notion that novelty can be of two kinds, either or both of which may be involved in task performance. The two kinds of novelty might be characterized as involving (a) comprehension of the task and (b) acting on one's comprehension of the task. Consider the meaning of each of these two kinds of novelty.

Novelty in comprehension of the task refers to the novelty that inheres in understanding the task confronting one. Once one understands the task, acting on it may or may not be challenging. In essence, the novelty is in learning how to do the task rather than in actually doing it. Novelty in acting on one's comprehension of the task refers to novelty in acting on a problem rather than in learning about the problem or how to solve it. The genre of task is familiar, but the parameters of the particular task are not. It is possible, of course, to formulate problems involving novelty in both comprehension and execution of a particular kind of task and problems that involve novelty in neither. The present account would suggest that problems of these two kinds might be less satisfactory measures of intelligence than problems involving novelty in either comprehension or execution, but not both, because the former problems might be too novel, whereas the latter problems might not be novel enough to provide optimal measures of intelligence.

Novel Situations

The notion that intelligence is particularly aptly measured in situations that require adaptation to new and challenging environmental demands inheres both in expert and lay notions of the nature of intelligence (Intelligence and Its Measurement, 1921; Sternberg et al., 1981). The idea is that one's intelligence is not best shown in run-of-the-mill situations that are encountered regularly in everyday life, but rather in extraordinary situations that challenge one's ability to cope with the environment to which one must adapt. Almost everyone knows someone who performs well when confronted with tasks that are presented in a familiar milieu, but who falls apart when presented with similar or even identical tasks in an unfamiliar milieu. For example, a person who performs well in the everyday environment might find it difficult to function in a foreign country, even one that is similar in many respects to the home environment. In general, some people can perform well only under situational circum-stances that are highly favorable to their getting their work done. When the environ-ment is less supportive, their efficacy is greatly reduced.

Essentially the same constraints that apply to task novelty apply to situational novelty as well. First, too much novelty can render the situation nondiagnostic of intellectual level. Moreover, there may exist situations in which no one could function effectively (perhaps as epitomized by the situation confronted by the protagonist in Sartre's [1976] *No Exit*). Second, situational novelty can inhere either in understanding the nature of the situation or in performing within the context of that situation. In some instances, it is figuring out just what the situation is that is difficult; in others, it is operating in that situation once one has figured out what it is.

Measurement of the Ability to Deal with Novelty

I have attempted directly to measure individuals' skills in dealing with novel tasks using two different paradigms of research and measurement. (As I have not yet attempted directly to measure automatization, I will discuss only the issue of novelty here.) The first paradigm involved novelty primarily in task *comprehension.* The second paradigm involved novelty primarily in task *solution.*

The first paradigm involved presenting individuals with variants of a "concept projection" task. Consider just one of the five variants that were used (Sternberg, 1982b). Individuals were presented with a description of the color of an object in the present day and in the year 2000. The description could be either physical—a green dot or a blue dot—or verbal—one of four color words, namely, *green, blue, grue,* or *bleen.* An object was defined as green if it appeared physically green both in the present and in the year 2000. An object was defined as blue if it appeared physically blue both in the present and in the year 2000. An object was defined as grue if it appeared physically green in the present but physically blue in the year 2000 (i.e., it appeared physically green until the year 2000 and physically blue thereafter). An object was defined as bleen if it appeared physically blue in the present but physically green in the year 2000 (i.e., it appeared physically blue until the year 2000 and physically green thereafter). (The terminology is based on Goodman, 1955.)

Because each of the 2 descriptions (one in the present and one in the year 2000) could take one of either 2 physical forms or 4 verbal forms, there were 36 (6 x 6) different item types. The individual's task was to describe the object in the year 2000. If the given description for the year 2000 was a physical one, the subject had to indicate the correct verbal description of the object; if the given description for the year 2000 was a verbal one, the subject had to indicate the correct physical description of the object. There were always three choices from which the subject had to choose the correct answer. There were many complexities in the task, which cannot be described here, that rendered the problems quite challenging for the subjects. For example, certain types of items presented inconsistencies, and other types presented, information that was only partially valid.

Performance on the task was modeled by an information-processing model of task performance. The model accounted for an average of 92% of the variance in the response-time data (averaged over five variants of the task and five sets of subjects). The median correlation between task performance and scores on a battery of inductive reasoning tests (taken from standard intelligence measures) was −.62 (with the correlation negative because response times were being correlated with the number of correct answers on the reasoning tests). Most important, however, was that when individual processing-component scores were correlated with the reasoning measures, it was precisely those components that measured ability to deal with novelty (e.g., time spent in switching from one conceptual system to another, and time spent in recognizing physical transformations from one time period to another) that correlated with the induction tests. The results therefore suggested that it was ability to deal with novelty, rather than more conventional aspects of test performance, that were critical to measuring subjects' reasoning skills.

The second type of novel task involved "insight" problems of the kinds found in puzzle books at any bookstore. Consider some examples of the insight problems we used (Sternberg & Davidson, 1983):

1. If you have black socks and brown socks in your drawer, mixed in the ratio of 4 to 5, how many socks will you have to take out to make sure of having a pair the same color?
2. Water lilies double in area every 24 hours. At the beginning of the summer there is one water lily on a lake. It takes 60 days for the lake to become covered with water lilies. On what day is the lake half-covered?

We theorized that three kinds of insights are involved in problems such as these. The first kind of insight, *selective encoding*, involves recognizing those elements of a problem that are relevant for task solution, and those elements that are not. For example, Fleming's discovery of penicillin involved an insight of selective encoding, in that Fleming recognized that the mold that had ruined his experiment had done so by killing off the bacteria in a Petri dish. Thus was born the first of the modern antibiotics through a selective encoding of information that would have escaped most scientists. The second kind of insight, *selective combination*, involves figuring out how to combine information that has been selectively encoded. Such information can typically be combined in many ways, only one of which is optimal. For example, Darwin's formulation of the theory of evolution hinged on his recognizing how the multitudinous facts he and others had collected about species could be combined to yield an account of the transition between species over the course of time. The third kind of insight, *selective comparison*, involves figuring out how new information can be related to old information. For example, Kekulé's discovery of the structure of the benzene ring hinged on his recognizing that a dream he had had of a snake reaching back and biting its tail provided the basis for the geometric structure of the ring.

We used these problems to test our theory of insight (Davidson & Sternberg, 1983; Sternberg & Davidson, 1982, 1983). The main question we addressed was whether we could isolate selective encoding, selective combination, and selective comparison in subjects' performance. We were in fact able to isolate all three processes by manipulating the amount of information given to subjects solving problems. In particular, subjects would receive the insight problems either with or without pre-cuing by one of the three kinds of insights. Providing subjects with each of the three kinds of insights substantially improved performance, especially for less able subjects who were less likely to have the insights on their own.

We also sought to determine whether the ability to deal with these novel problems provided a good measure of intelligence. Note that the novelty in these problems is not in understanding the instructions (which are straightforward—namely, to solve the problems), but rather in coming up with a strategy for task solution. Although some of the problems can be solved by conventional algorithms, the problems typically could be solved more easily by shortcuts or heuristics that are not normally taught in mathematics classes. Solution of problems such as these requires a fair amount of insight, but very little in the way of prior mathematical knowledge. And performance on such problems is correlated about .6 to .7 with IQ. Thus, insight problems measure something related but not identical to what IQ tests measure. What they add to IQ test measurement, however, would seem to be an important part of intelligence, broadly defined.

Ability to Automatize Information Processing

The proposed model of automatization of information processing proposes that controlled information processing is under the conscious direction of the individual and is hierarchical in nature, with executive processes (processes used to plan, monitor, and revise strategies of information processing) directing nonexecutive processes (processes used actually to carry out the strategies that the executive processes select, monitor, and revise). Automatic information processing is preconscious, not under the conscious direction of the individual, and nonhierarchical in nature: There is no functional distinction between executive and nonexecutive processes. Instead, production is in the mode of a production system, where all kinds of processes function at a single level of analysis. In processing information from new domains (and especially novel ones of the kind considered earlier), the individual relies primarily on controlled, global processing. A central executive directly activates nonexecutive processes, and receives direct feedback from them. Information processing is of strictly limited capacity, and attention is focused on the task at hand. The total knowledge base stored in long-term memory is available for access by the processes used in the given task and situation.

In processing information from old domains or domains that are entrenched by nature, the individual relies primarily on automatic, local processing. A central executive initially activates a system consisting of locally applicable processes and a locally applicable knowledge base. Multiple local systems can operate in parallel. Performance in these systems is automatic and of almost unlimited capacity; attention is not focused on the task at hand. Only knowledge that has been transferred to the local knowledge base is available for access by the processes used in a given task and situation. A critical point is that activation is by executive processes in the global system to the local system as a whole. The executive processes can instantiate themselves as part of this local system; when used in this instantiation, they do not differ functionally from processes of any other kind.

The domains in which one has little expertise have processing that is largely focused in the global processing and knowledge system. As expertise develops, greater and greater proportions of processing are transferred to (or packed into) a given local processing system. The advantage of using the local system is that the system as a whole is activated, rather than individual processes within the system, so that the amount of attention that needs to be devoted to use of the domain is much less than it is under global control. Indeed, attention allocation for a whole local system is comparable to that for a single lower-order process activated by the global system as part of the global system's functioning. The disadvantages of using the local system are that it is able to call on only a limited knowledge base, in particular, that base that has been packed into that local system, and that the local system is able to call on only those processes that have been packed into the local system. Experts are able to handle a wide variety of situations through the use of the local system, because they have packed tremendous amounts of information into it. Novices can hardly use local systems at all, because these systems have as yet acquired relatively few processes and relatively little knowledge.

Control passes to a local processing system when an executive process recognizes a given situation as one for which a local system is potentially relevant. The local system is presumed to be of the nature of a production system, with a set of productions ready to act on the problem at hand. The productions comprise functions that are executive in nature, as well as functions that are not. But all of these functions are integrated into a single, nonhierarchical system. Control is passed back to the global processing system when, during task performance, none of the productions in a system is able to satisfy a given presented condition. When the bottom of the production list is reached and no given condition is satisfied, global processing is necessary to decide how to handle the new task or situation. Once this task or situation is successfully handled, it is possible to pack what has been learned from global processing of the new experience into a given local processing system, so that the next time such a situation is encountered, there will be no need to exit from the local processing system. According to this view, the extent to which one develops expertise in a given domain largely depends on the ability of the individual to pack new information, in a usable way, into a given local processing system and on the ability to gain access to this information as needed.

The experts are at an advantage in their domain of expertise, because their ability to stay for longer periods of time in the better-developed local processing system enables them to free global processing resources for what, to them, are new situations. Novices are overwhelmed with new information, and must engage global resources so frequently that most of the new information encountered is quickly lost. Therefore, the experts are more competent in handling familiar tasks within the domain of expertise. They are also more proficient at learning new tasks, because global processing resources are more readily available for the intricacies of the task or situation confronted. In essence, a loop is set up whereby packing more information and processes into the local system enables them to automate more processing, and thus to have global resources more available for what is new in a given task or situation. Experts are also able to perform more distinct kinds of tasks in parallel, because whereas the global processing system is conscious and serial in its processing, multiple local processing systems can operate in parallel. For novices, for example, driving a car consumes almost all of their available global resources. For experts, driving a car consumes local resources and leaves central resources available for other tasks, unless a new situation (such as a roadblock) is confronted that requires redirection of control to their global resources.

To summarize, the present view essentially combines hierarchical and nonhierarchical viewpoints by suggesting that information processing is hierarchical and controlled in a global processing mode, and nonhierarchical and automatic in local processing modes. Expertise develops largely from the successively greater assumption of information processing by local resources. When these local resources are engaged, parallel processing of multiple kinds of tasks becomes possible. Global resources, however, are serial and of very limited capacity in their problem-solving capabilities.

Automatization as a Function of Task

Many kinds of tasks requiring complex information processing seem so intricate that it is a wonder we can perform them at all. Consider reading, for example. The number and complexity of operations involved in reading is staggering, and what is more staggering is the rate at which these operations are performed (e.g., Crowder, 1982; Just & Carpenter, 1980). Performance of tasks as complex as reading would seem to be possible only because a substantial proportion of the operations required in reading are automatized and thus require minimal mental effort (see Schneider & Shiffrin, 1977, and Shiffrin & Schneider, 1977, for a discussion of the mental requirements of tasks involving controlled and automatized information processing). Deficiencies in reading have been theorized to result in large part from failures in automatization of operations that in normal readers have been automatized (LaBerge & Samuels, 1974; Sternberg & Wagner, 1982).

The proposal being made here is that complex verbal, mathematical, and other tasks can be executed only because many of the operations involved in their performance have been automatized. Failure to automatize such operations, whether fully or in part, results in a breakdown of information processing and hence less intelligent task performance. Intellectual operations that can be performed smoothly and automatically by more-intelligent individuals are performed only haltingly and under conscious control by less-intelligent individuals.

As in the case of novelty, automatization can occur either in task comprehension, task execution, or both. Consider how each of these kinds of automatization operates in various tasks.

The standard synonyms test used to measure vocabulary is highly familiar to most middle-class students at or above the secondary-school level. Indeed, when confronted with a multiple-choice synonyms test, about the only things the students need to check are whether the test is in fact one of synonyms (as opposed to, say, antonyms, which has a similar surface structure) and whether there is a penalty for guessing. Examinees can usually read the directions to such a test cursorily, and could probably skip them altogether if only they were told the name of the task; comprehension of what is required is essentially automatic. But the solution of individual test items may be far from automatic, especially if the test requires discriminating relatively fine shades of meaning. Students may find they have to give a fair amount of thought to the individual items, either because they need to discriminate shades of meaning or because they are unsure of particular words' meanings and have to use strategies to guess the best answers for very difficult items. In the standard synonyms task, comprehension of task instructions is essentially automatic (or nearly so), but solution of test items (beyond the simplest ones) probably is not.

In contrast, experimental tasks used in the cognitive psychologist's laboratory seem to present the opposite situation, in at least one respect. Tasks such as the Posner and Mitchell (1967) letter-matching task and the fixed-set (S. Sternberg, 1969) memory-scanning task are probably unfamiliar to most subjects when they enter the cognitive psychologist's laboratory. The subjects do not automatically know what is expected of them in task performance and have to listen reasonably carefully to the instructions. But after the task is explained and the subjects have had some practice in performing the tasks, it is likely that task performance rapidly becomes automatized. The tasks come to be executed almost effortlessly and with little conscious thought.

It is possible, of course, for task performance to be fully automatized, or not to be automatized at all. When one gets hold of a mystery story to read, one knows essentially automatically what one is going to do and how one is going to do it. Comprehension of the task and then performance of it are both quite automatized. In contrast, learning how to solve a new kind of mathematics problem, such as a time–rate–distance problem, is probably not automatized with respect to either comprehension or task execution.

Automatization as a Function of Situation

Very little is known about how situations affect automatization of task performance. Clearly, one wishes to provide as much practice as possible on the task to be automatized, and to use a fixed-set rather than a varied-set mode of presentation (Shiffrin & Schneider, 1977). Presumably, one might wish to minimize distraction from the task in order to allow the individual to concentrate on learning and eventually on automatizing it.

Relations Between Abilities to Deal with Novelty and to Automatize Processing

For many (but probably not all) kinds of tasks, the ability to deal with novelty and to automatize information processing may occur along an experiential continuum. When one first encounters a task or kind of situation, ability to deal with novelty comes into play. More-intelligent people will be more rapidly and fully able to cope with the novel demands being made on them. Moreover, the fewer the resources that need to be devoted to processing the novelty of a given task or situation, the more the resources that are left over for automatized performance; conversely, more efficient automatization of performance leaves additional processing resources for dealing with novel tasks and situations. As a result, novelty and automatization trade off, and the more efficient the individual is at the one, the more resources are left over for the other. As experience with the kind of task or situation increases, novelty decreases, and the task or situation will become less apt in its measurement of intelligence from the standpoint of processing of novelty. However, after some amount of practice with the task or in the situation, automatization skills may come into play, in which case the task will become a better measure of automatization skills. According to this view, the most interesting points on the experiential continuum, from the standpoint of measuring intelligence, are those (a) when the task or situation is first encountered and (b) when novelty wears off and automatization begins to set in. Measuring task performance at other times will be less informative with regard to a person's intellectual level. Note that a given task or situation may continue to provide apt measurement of intelligence over practice, but for different reasons at different points in practice: Early in the person's experience, the ability to deal with novelty is assessed; later in the person's experience, the ability to automatize information processing is assessed.

What Tasks Measure Intelligence and Why?

The proposed two-facet subtheory suggests some properties of tasks and situations that make them more or less useful measures of intelligence. Consider some of the tasks most frequently used, and the implications of the subtheory for understanding why these tasks are more or less successful.

Laboratory Tasks

A variety of laboratory tasks have been claimed to measure intelligence. According to the present view, the simpler tasks, such as simple reaction time, choice reaction time, and letter identification, have some validity as measures of intelligence because they primarily measure automatization of various kinds. For example, simple reaction-time tasks measure in part the extent to which an individual can automatize rapid responses to a single stimulus, and letter-identification tasks measure in part the extent to which access to highly overlearned codes stored in long-term memory is automatized. Speed is a reasonable measure of intellectual performance because it is presumably highly correlated with degree of automatization; but it is only an indirect measure of this degree of automatization, and hence an imperfect one. One might expect some increase in correlation of task latencies with measured intelligence as task complexity increases, even at these very simple levels, because of the increased element of novelty in the higher levels of even simple tasks. Thus, choice reaction time introduces an element of uncertainty that is absent in simple reaction time, and the amount of uncertainty, and hence of novelty, increases as the number of response choices increases.

The more complex laboratory tasks, such as analogies, classifications, syllogisms, and the like, probably measure both degree of automatization and response to novelty. To the extent that subjects have had practice on these item formats (such as taking intelligence and aptitude tests, as well as participating in experiments), their selection and implementation of strategies will be partially automatized when they start the tasks. But even if they have had little or no experience with certain item formats, the formats tend to be repetitive, and in the large numbers of trials typical of cognitive-psychological experiments, subjects are likely to automatize their performance to some degree while performing the tasks. The more complex items also measure response to novelty, in that the relations subjects have to recognize and reason with will usually be at least somewhat unfamiliar.

Psychometric Tasks

The psychometric tasks found in ability tests are likely to measure intelligence for the same reasons as the complex laboratory tasks, in that they contain essentially the same kinds of contents. They are apt to be slightly better measures than the laboratory tasks for three reasons. First, the pencil-and-paper psychometric items tend to be harder, because laboratory tasks are often simplified in order to reduce error rates. Harder tasks will, on the average, involve greater amounts of novelty. Second, psychometric test items are usually presented en masse (subjects are given a fixed amount of time to solve all of them) rather than individually (subjects are given a fixed or free amount of time to solve each separate item). Presenting the items en masse requires individuals to plan an interitem as well as an intraitem strategy, and hence requires more "executive" kinds of behaviors. Such behaviors may have been previously automatized in part, but are also necessarily responses to whatever novelty inheres in the particular testing situation confronted (content, difficulty, time limits, etc.). Third, the psychometric test items found in most test batteries have been extensively validated, whereas the items used in laboratory experiments seldom have been.

Implications for Task Selection

The proposed theory carries with it certain implications for the selection of tasks to measure intelligence. In particular, one wishes to select tasks that involve some blend of automatized behaviors and behaviors in response to novelty. This blending is probably best achieved within test items, but may also be achieved by items that specialize in measuring either the one skill or the other. The blending may be achieved by presenting subjects with a novel task, and then giving them enough practice so that performance becomes differentially automatized (across subjects) over the length of the practice period. Such a task will thereby measure both response to novelty and degree of automatization, although at different times during the course of testing.

The two-facet view suggests one reason it is so exceedingly difficult to compare levels of intelligence fairly across members of different sociocultural groups. Even if a given test requires the same components of performance for members of the various groups, it is extremely unlikely to be equivalent for the groups in terms of its novelty and the degree to which performance has been automatized prior to the examinees' taking the test. Consider, for example, the by-now well-known finding that nonverbal reasoning tests, such as the Raven Progressive Matrices or the Cattell Culture-Fair Test of g, actually yield greater differences between members of different sociocultural groups than do the verbal tests they were designed to replace (Jensen, 1982). The nonverbal tests, contrary to the claims that have often been made for them, are *not* culture-fair (and they are certainly not culture-free). Individuals who have been brought up in a test-taking culture are likely to have had much more experience with these kinds of items than individuals not brought up in such a culture. Thus, the items will be less novel and performance on them more automatized for members of the standard U.S. culture than for nonmembers. Even if the processes of solution are the same, the degrees of novelty and automatization will be different, and hence the tests will not be measuring the same skills across populations. As useful as the tests may be for within-group comparisons, between-group comparisons may be deceptive and unfair. A fair comparison between groups would require comparable degrees of novelty and automatization in test items as well as comparable processes and strategies.

In sum, it has been proposed that behavior is intelligent when it involves either or both of two sets of skills: adaptation to novelty and automatization of performance.

This proposal has been used to explain why so many tasks seem to measure "intelligence" in greater or lesser degree. Most important, the subtheory provides an a priori specification of what a task or situation must measure in order to assess intelligence. It is distinctive in that it is not linked to any arbitrary choice of tasks or situations. These follow from the subtheory, rather than the other way around.

Components of Intelligence

A theory of intelligence ought to specify the mechanisms by which intelligent performance is generated. The purpose of this section is to specify the mechanisms proposed by the triarchic theory. An earlier version of this subtheory was presented in more detail in Sternberg (1980b).

A number of theories have been proposed during the past decade that might be labeled, at least loosely, as "componential" (e.g., Butterfield & Belmont, 1977; Campione & Brown, 1979; Carroll, 1976, 1981; Hunt, 1978, 1980; Jensen, 1979; Pellegrino & Glaser, 1979; Snow, 1979). These theories share the cognitive focus of the present view, but differ in some details. Jensen (1979) has suggested that individual differences in intelligence can be understood in terms of speed of functioning in choice–reaction time tasks. Hunt (1978) and Keating and Bobbitt (1978) have proposed that individual differences in intelligence can be understood at a somewhat higher level of processing, in particular, in terms of differences among individuals in speed of access to lexical information stored in long-term memory. Butterfield and Belmont (1977) and Campione and Brown (1979) have emphasized individual differences in cognitive and metacognitive processes and strategies as bases for understanding individual differences in intelligence; and Pellegrino and Glaser (1979), Snow (1979), and Sternberg (1977a) have studied individual differences in intelligence in terms of the still higher-level reasoning processes measured by problems such as analogies, series completions, and classifications. At a still higher level of processing, Simon (1976; see also Newell & Simon, 1972) has sought to understand individual differences in intelligence in terms of individuals' component abilities in complex problem solving, such as that used in solving cryptarithmetic, logical, and chess problems. Thus, one way of characterizing differences in emphasis in these cognitive accounts is in terms of the level of processing on which they concentrate: At one extreme, Jensen looks at speed of functioning at very low levels of processing; at the other extreme, Simon looks at accuracy and strategy of functioning at very high levels of processing.

Although all of these theorists look at components of intellectual functioning at various levels of processing, it is important to emphasize that most of the theorists do not place the emphasis on information-processing "components" that I do, nor do the theorists differ solely in terms of the level of processing they emphasize. Another major difference among theorists occurs in their emphasis on speed of functioning. In general, theorists studying lower levels of processing tend to place greater emphasis on speed, whereas theorists studying higher levels of processing tend to place less emphasis on speed; the correlation is not perfect, however. Moreover, the theorists differ greatly in their preferred methods for studying mental processing: Some, like Jensen, place a heavy emphasis on reaction-time methodology; others, like Simon, emphasize computer simulation; and still others, like Hunt, use both of these methodologies. A more detailed analysis of some of these positions can be found in Sternberg (1985).

A Componential Subtheory of Intelligence

The Unit of Analysis

Theories of human intelligence have traditionally relied on some basic unit of analysis for explaining sources of individual differences in intelligent behavior (see Sternberg, 1980b, 1982b). Theories have differed in terms of (a) what is proposed as the basic unit; (b) the particular instantiations of this unit that are proposed somehow to be locked inside our heads; and (c) the way in which these instantiations are organized with respect to each other. Differences in basic units have defined "paradigms" of theory and research on intelligence; differences in instantiations and organizations of these units have defined particular theories within these paradigms. Some of the units that have been considered have been the factor, the S–R bond, and the TOTE (test-operate-test-exit). The present subtheory designates the information-processing component as the basic unit of analysis. (See Sternberg, 1977b, 1980b, for details regarding this unit and the theory developed around it.)

What Is a Component?

A component is an elementary information process that operates on internal representations of objects or symbols (Sternberg, 1977b, 1980b; see also Newell & Simon, 1972). The component may translate a sensory input into a conceptual representation, transform one conceptual representation into another, or translate a conceptual representation into a motor output. What is considered elementary enough to be labeled a component depends on the desired level of theorizing. Just as factors can be split into successively finer subfactors, so components can be split into successively finer subcomponents. Thus, no claim is made that any of the components referred to here are elementary at all levels of analysis. Rather, they are elementary at a convenient level of analysis. The same caveat applies to the proposed typology of components. Other typologies could doubtless be proposed that would serve this or other theoretical purposes as well or better. The particular typology proposed, however, has proved to be convenient in certain theoretical and experimental contexts at least.

Properties of Components

Each component has three important properties associated with it: *duration, difficulty* (that is, probability of being executed erroneously), and *probability of execution*. Methods for estimating these properties of components are described in Sternberg (1978; see also Sternberg, 1977b, 1985; Sternberg & Rifkin, 1979). The three properties are, at least in principle, independent. For example, a given component may take a rather long time to execute, but may be rather easy to execute, in the sense that its execution rarely leads to an error in solution; or the component may be executed quite rapidly, and yet be rather difficult to execute, in the sense that its execution often leads to an error in solution (see Sternberg, 1977b, 1980b). Consider "mapping," one component used in solving analogies such as LAWYER is to CLIENT as DOCTOR is to (a) PATIENT, (b) MEDICINE. Mapping calls for the discovery of the higher-order relation between the first and second halves of the analogy. The component has a certain probability of being executed in solving an analogy. If executed, it has a certain duration and a certain probability of being executed correctly.

Kinds of Components

Components perform (at least) three kinds of functions. *Metacomponents* are higher-order processes used in planning, monitoring, and decision making in task performance. *Performance components* are processes used in the execution of a task. *Knowledge-acquisition components* are processes used in learning new things. It is essential to understand the nature of these components, because they form the mental bases for adapting to, shaping, and selecting environments, for dealing with novel kinds of tasks and situations, and for automatizing performance. In this section, I will consider measurement issues simultaneously with the consideration of each of the kinds of components.

Metacomponents

Metacomponents are specific realizations of control processes that are sometimes collectively (and loosely) referred to as the "executive" or the "homunculus" (although, as discussed earlier, they lose their executive character during automatic processing). I have identified seven metacomponents that I believe are quite prevalent in intellectual functioning.

1. *Decision as to what the problem is that needs to be solved.* To solve a problem the individual must first figure out just what the nature of the problem is.

2. *Selection of lower-order components.* An individual must select a set of lower-order components to use in the solution of a given task. Selecting a nonoptimal set of components can result in incorrect or inefficient task performance. In some instances, the choice of components will be partially attributable to differential availability or accessibility of various components.

3. *Selection of one or more representations or organizations for information.* A given component can often operate on any one of a number of different possible representations or organizations for information. The choice of representation or organization can facilitate or impede the efficacy with which the component operates.

4. *Selection of a strategy for combining lower-order components.* In itself, a list of components is insufficient to perform a task. One must also sequence these components in a way that facilitates task performance, decide how exhaustively each component will be used, and decide which components to execute serially and which to execute in parallel.

5. *Decision regarding allocation of attentional resources.* All tasks and components used in performing tasks can be allocated only a limited proportion of the individual's total attentional resources. Greater limitations may result in reduced quality of performance. In particular, one must decide how much time to allocate to each task component, and how much the time restriction will affect the quality of performance of the particular component. One tries to allocate time across the various components of task performance in a way that maximizes the quality of the entire product. Even small changes in error rate can result in sizable changes in solution latency (Pachella, 1974).

6. *Solution monitoring.* As individuals proceed through a problem, they must keep track of what they have already done, what they are currently doing, and what they

still need to do. The relative importance of these three items of information differs across problems. If things are not progressing as expected, an accounting of one's progress may be needed, and one may even have to consider the possibility of changing goals. Often, new, more realistic goals need to be formulated as a person realizes that the old goals cannot be reached. In solving problems, individuals sometimes find that none of the available options provides a satisfactory answer. The individual must then decide whether to reperform certain processes that might have been performed erroneously, or to choose the best of the available options.

7. *Sensitivity to external feedback.* External feedback provides a valuable means for improving one's task performance. The ability to understand feedback, to recognize its implications, and then to act on it is a key skill in task performance.

Although my own view emphasizes the role of metacomponents in intelligence, not all investigators share this view (e.g., Detterman, 1980, 1982; Egan, 1982; Hunt, 1980; Jensen, 1979). Consider, though, why I believe that accounts such as these alternative ones that emphasize performance components at the expense of metacomponents are inadequate as accounts of intelligence, and indeed, may miss its essence. I will take as an example the importance of the metacomponent of allocation of resources, and how ignoring it leads to erroneous conclusions about the nature of intelligence.

The assumption that "smart is fast" permeates our entire society. When we refer to people as "quick," we are endowing them with one of the primary attributes of what we perceive an intelligent person to be. The pervasiveness of this assumption can be seen in a recent study of people's conceptions of intelligence, in which we asked people to list behaviors characteristic of intelligent persons. Behaviors such as "learns rapidly," "acts quickly," "talks quickly," and "makes judgments quickly" were commonly listed (Sternberg et al., 1981). It is not only the person in the street who believes that speed is associated with intellect: Several prominent contemporary theorists of intelligence base their theories in large part on individual differences in the speed with which people process information (Brand & Deary, 1982; Eysenck, 1982; Jensen, 1979).

The assumption that more-intelligent people are rapid information processors also underlies the overwhelming majority of tests used in identification of the gifted, including creativity as well as intelligence tests. It is rare to find a group test that is not timed, or a timed test that virtually all examinees are able to finish by working at a comfortable rate of problem solving. I would argue that this assumption is a gross overgeneralization: It is true for some people and for some mental operations, but not for all people or all mental operations. What is critical is not speed per se, but rather, speed selection—knowing when to perform at what rate and being able to function rapidly or slowly depending on task or situational demands. Thus, it is resource allocation, rather than the resource itself, that is central to general intelligence.

Many of us know people who, although often slow in performing tasks, perform the tasks at a superior level of accomplishment. Moreover, we know that snap judgments are often poor ones. Indeed, in our study of people's conceptions of intelligence, "does not make snap judgments" was listed as an important attribute of intelligent performance. Moreover, there are theoretical reasons for believing that to be quick is not always to be smart. In his classic but little-known book on the nature of intelligence, Thurstone (1924) proposed that a critical element of intelligent performance is the ability to withhold rapid, instinctive responses, and to substitute for them more rational, well-thought-out responses. According to this view, the automatic responses one makes to problems are often not the optimal ones for problem solution, and the ability to inhibit acting on these responses and to consider more rational forms of response is a critical one for high levels of task performance. More recently, Stenhouse (1973) has arrived at the same conclusion by a comparative analysis of intelligence across different species. Interestingly, his conclusion appears to be wholly independent of Thurstone's; there is no evidence that Stenhouse was aware of Thurstone's book.

A number of findings from psychological research—both my own and others'—undermine the validity of the assumption that smart is always fast. I will cite several of the findings that indicate the fallacy of this view.

First, it is well known that, in general, a *reflective* rather than an *impulsive* cognitive style tends to be associated with more intelligent problem-solving performance (see Baron, 1981, 1982, for reviews of this literature). Jumping into problems without adequate reflection is likely to lead to false starts and erroneous conclusions. Yet timed tests often force the examinee to solve problems impulsively. It is often claimed that the strict timing of such tests merely mirrors the requirements of our highly pressured and productive society, but, for most of us, there are few significant problems encountered in work or personal life that allow no more than the 5 to 50 seconds of time spent on a typical problem in a standardized test. Of course, there are some people, such as air traffic controllers, who must make consequential split-second decisions as an integral part of their work lives. But such people seem to be the exception rather than the rule.

Second, in a study of planning behavior in problem solving (Sternberg, 1981a), we found that more-intelligent persons tend to spend relatively more time than less-intelligent persons on global (higher-order) planning, and relatively less time on local (lower-order) planning. In contrast, less-intelligent persons seem to emphasize local rather than global planning (relative to the more-intelligent persons). The point is that what matters is not total time spent, but rather distribution of this time across the various kinds of planning one can do. Although for the problems we used (complex forms of analogies), quicker problem solving was associated, on the average, with higher intelligence, looking simply at total time masked the compensating relations for the two kinds of planning.

Third, in studies of reasoning behavior in children and adults, it has been found that although greater intelligence is associated with more rapid execution of most components of information processing, problem encoding is a notable exception to this trend. The more-intelligent individual tends to spend relatively more time encoding the terms of the problem, presumably in order to facilitate subsequent operations on these encodings (see Mulholland, Pellegrino, & Glaser, 1980; Sternberg, 1977b; Sternberg & Rifkin, 1979). Similar outcomes have been observed in comparisons of expert and novice problem solvers confronted with difficult physics problems (Chi, Glaser, & Rees, 1982; Larkin, McDermott, Simon, & Simon, 1980). Siegler (1981) has also found that intellectually more advanced children are distinguished especially by their superior ability to encode fully the nature of the problem being presented to them. The point, again, is that what matters is not total time spent, but rather distribution of this time across the various kinds of processing one can do.

Fourth, in a study of people's performance in solving insight problems (arithmetical and logical problems whose difficulty resided in the need for a nonobvious insight for problem solution rather than in the need for arithmetical or logical knowledge), a correlation of .75 was found between the amount of time people spent on the problems and measured IQ. The correlation between time spent and score on the insight problems was .62 (Sternberg & Davidson,1982). Note that in these tests, individuals could take as long as they liked solving the problems. Persistence and involvement in the problems were highly correlated with success in solution: The more able individuals did not give up, nor did they fall for the obvious, but often incorrect, solutions.

Fifth, in a study of executive processes in reading (Wagner & Sternberg, 1983), we found that although faster readers, on the average, tended to have higher comprehension and to score higher on a variety of external ability measures, simply looking at overall reading time masked important differences between more and less skilled readers. In the study, which involved reading standard texts of the kinds found in newspapers and textbooks, we found that relative to less skilled readers, the more skilled readers tended to allocate more time to reading passages for which they would be tested in greater detail, and less time to reading passages for which they would be tested in lesser detail.

Obviously, it would be foolish to argue that speed is never important. For air traffic controllers, it is crucially important, and in dangerous situations occurring in driving a car, slow reflexes or thinking can result in an accident. In many other situations, too, speed is essential. But many, if not most, of the consequential tasks one faces in life do not require problem solving or decision making in the small numbers of seconds typically allotted for the solution of IQ test problems. Instead, they require an intelligent allocation of one's time to the various subproblems or problems at hand. Ideally, IQ tests would stress allocation of time rather than time or speed in solving various kinds of problems.

To the extent that simple tasks, such as those used by Hunt (1978), Jensen (1982), and others, correlate with IQ, it may be in part because of the shared but ecologically unrealistic time stress imposed on performance in both kinds of tasks. I doubt, however, that the speed-demand is the only source of the correlation. What remaining correlation is left after sheer shared-speed requirements are taken into account may well be accounted for in part by metacomponential processing. A finding in Jensen's (1982) research, for example, is that the correlation between choice reaction time and IQ increases as the number of choices in the reaction-time task increases. This result suggests that the more metacomponential decision making required in selecting from among alternative choices, the higher the correlation obtained with tested intelligence. A finding in the Hunt (1978) research paradigm, which is based on the Posner and Mitchell (1967) letter-comparison task (in which the subject has to decide whether both members of a pair of letters, such as *Aa*, represent either the same physical appearance or the same letter name), is that as the complexity of the comparison to be made increases, so does the correlation between performance on the comparison task and measured intelligence (Goldberg, Schwartz, & Stewart, 1977). Again, the result suggests that it is higher-level decision making, rather than sheer speed of simple functioning, that is responsible for correlations obtained between performance on cognitive tasks and performance on psychometric tests. And cognitive tasks such as these may well become automatized over the large number of trials they require for subject performance, and thus will measure efficacy of automatization as well, another key ingredient of intelligent performance.

Performance Components

Performance components are used in the execution of various strategies for task performance. Although the number of possible performance components is quite large, many probably apply only to small or uninteresting subsets of tasks, and hence deserve little attention.

Performance components tend to organize themselves into stages of task solution that seem to be fairly general across tasks. These stages include (a) encoding of stimuli, (b) combination of or comparison between stimuli, and (c) response. In the analogies task, for example, I have separated encoding and response components (each of which may be viewed as constituting its own stage) and inference, mapping, application, comparison, and justification components (each of which requires some kind of comparison between stimuli). Why is it important to decompose global performance on intellectual tasks and tests into its underlying performance components? I believe there are several reasons.

First, studies of mental test performance have shown that one set of performance components, the performance components of inductive reasoning—such as inferring relations between terms, mapping relations between relations, and applying old relations to new situations—are quite general across formats typically found in intelligence tests. Sternberg and Gardner (1983) showed that high correlations (with magnitudes as high as .7 and .8) can be obtained between component scores and performance on psychometric tests of inductive reasoning, and high correlations are also obtained between corresponding component scores on the various inductive tasks. Thus, at least these performance components seem to be quite generalizable across both cognitive tasks of theoretical interest and psychometric tests of practical (and for many, theoretical) interest.

Second, decomposition of task performance into performance components is important because there is evidence that different components behave in various ways. Consider three instances of such differences.

One kind of difference, discussed previously, is in terms of speed allocation. For most performance components, greater speed of processing is associated with superior overall task performance. But for at least one component, encoding, the opposite pattern holds.

A second kind of difference is in the kinds of representations on which the various components act. Consider syllogistic-reasoning tasks, for example. Some of the components of syllogistic reasoning operate on a linguistic representation, and others on a spatial representation (Sternberg, 1980a; Sternberg & Weil, 1980). Overall scores on syllogistic-reasoning tests, whether expressed in terms of latencies or errors, are therefore confounded with respect to the linguistic and spatial abilities involved. An individual could achieve a given score through different combinations of componential efficacies, and even through the use of different strategies. For example, Sternberg and Weil (1980) found that untrained subjects spontaneously use at least four different strategies for solving linear syllogisms. To the extent one wishes to understand the cognitive bases of task performance, componential decomposition of task performance is desirable and even necessary.

A third kind of difference is in the centrality of the components of the task to what it is the examiner actually wishes to measure. Most tasks contain components that are of greater and lesser interest for measuring a particular construct. By separating out component scores, it is possible to obtain purer measures of the construct of interest. In the case of inductive reasoning, for example, one would probably wish to separate out the reasoning components (inference, mapping, application, justification) from the others.

Such separation becomes especially important for purposes of diagnosis and remediation. Consider, for example, the possibility of a very bright person who does poorly on tests of abstract reasoning ability. It may be that the person is a very good reasoner, but has a perceptual difficulty that leads to poor encoding of the terms of the problem. Because encoding is necessary for reasoning on the problem terms as encoded, the overall score is reduced, not by faulty reasoning, but by faulty encoding of the terms of the problem. Decomposition of scores into performance components enables one to separate, say, reasoning difficulties from perceptual difficulties. For purposes of remediation, such separation is essential. Different remediation programs would be indicated for people who perform poorly on reasoning items because of flawed reasoning, on the one hand, or perceptual processing, on the other.

Finally, componential decomposition can be important if the individual's problem is not in the components at all, but rather in the strategy for combining them. A person might be able to execute the performance components quite well, but still do poorly on a task because of nonoptimal strategies for combining the components. By modeling the examinee's task performance, it is possible to determine whether the person's difficulty is in the performance components per se, or rather in the way the person combines those performance components.

Knowledge-Acquisition Components

Knowledge-acquisition components are processes used in gaining new knowledge. It is proposed that three components are relevant to the acquisition of declarative and procedural knowledge in virtually all domains of knowledge. These components were considered earlier in the context of insight.

1. *Selective encoding.* Selective encoding involves sifting out relevant from irrelevant information. When new information is presented in natural contexts, relevant information for one's given purposes is embedded in the midst of large amounts of purpose-irrelevant information. A critical task for the learner is that of sifting the "wheat from the chaff": recognizing just what information among all the pieces of information presented is relevant for one's purposes (see Schank, 1980).

2. *Selective combination.* Selective combination involves combining selectively encoded information in such a way as to form an integrated, plausible whole. Simply shifting out relevant from irrelevant information is not enough to generate a new knowledge structure: One must know how to combine the pieces of information into an internally connected whole (see Mayer & Greeno, 1972).

3. *Selective comparison.* Selective comparison involves relating newly acquired information to information acquired in the past. Deciding what information to encode and how to combine it does not occur in a vacuum. Rather, encoding and combination of new knowledge are guided by retrieval of old information. New information will be all but useless if it cannot somehow be related to old knowledge so as to form an externally connected whole (see Mayer & Greeno, 1972).

The emphasis on knowledge-acquisition components in the present theory contrasts with certain other views regarding what should be emphasized in intelligence. Consider some of these other views.

If one examines the contents of the major intelligence tests currently in use, one will find that most of them measure intelligence as last year's (or the year before's, or the year before that's) achievement. What is an intelligence test for children of a given age would be an achievement test for children a few years younger. In some test items, like vocabulary, the achievement loading is obvious. In others, it is disguised; for example, verbal analogies or arithmetic problems. But virtually all tests commonly used for the assessment of intelligence place heavy achievement demands on the individuals tested.

The emphasis on knowledge is consistent with some current views of differences in expert versus novice performance that stress the role of knowledge in performance differences (e.g., Chase & Simon, 1973; Chi et al., 1982; Keil, 1984; Larkin et al., 1980). And indeed, there can be no doubt that differences in knowledge are critical to differential performance between more- and less-skilled individuals in a variety of domains. But it seems to me that the critical question for a theorist of intelligence to ask is that of how those differences in knowledge came to be. Certainly, sheer differences in amount of experience are not perfectly correlated with levels of expertise. Many individuals play the piano for many years, but do not become concert-level pianists; chess buffs do not all become grandmasters, no matter what the frequency of their play may be. And simply reading a lot does not guarantee a large vocabulary. What seems to be critical is not the sheer amount of experience, but rather, what one has been able to learn from that experience. According to this view, then, individual differences in knowledge acquisition have priority over individual differences in knowledge. To understand expertise, one must understand first how current individual differences in knowledge evolved from individual differences in knowledge acquisition.

Consider vocabulary, for example. It is well known that vocabulary is one of the best, if not the best single predictor, of overall IQ score (Jensen, 1980; Matarazzo, 1972). Yet, few tests have higher achievement loadings than do vocabulary tests. Can one measure the latent ability tapped by vocabulary tests without presenting children with what is essentially an achievement test? In other words, can one go beyond current individual differences in knowledge to the source of those individual differences, that of differences in knowledge acquisition?

There is reason to believe that vocabulary is such a good measure of intelligence because it measures, albeit indirectly, children's ability to acquire information in context (Jensen, 1980; Sternberg & Powell, 1983; Werner & Kaplan, 1952). Most vocabulary is learned in everyday contexts rather than through direct instruction. Thus, new words are usually encountered for the first time (and subsequently) in textbooks, novels, newspapers, lectures, and the like. More-intelligent people are better able to use surrounding context to figure out the words' meanings. As the years go by, the better decontextualizers acquire the larger vocabularies. Because so much of one's learning (including learning beside vocabulary) is contextually determined, the ability to use context to add to one's knowledge base is an important skill in intelligent behavior. We have attempted to measure these skills directly by presenting high school children with paragraphs written at a level well below their grade level (Sternberg & Powell, 1983). Embedded within the paragraphs are one or more unknown words. The children's task is to use the surrounding context to figure out the meanings of the unknown words. Our theory of task performance attempts to specify exactly how children accomplish this decontextualization (see Sternberg & Powell, 1983). We found high correlations between the predictions of the theory, which specifies the cues people use in decontextualizing word meanings (e.g., spatial, temporal, and class membership cues) and the actual ease with which people can figure out word meanings. Correlations between predicted and observed values were .92 for literary passages, .74 for newspaper passages, .85 for science passages, and .77 for history passages. Note that in this testing paradigm, differential effects of past achievements are reduced by using reading passages that are easy for everyone, but target vocabulary words that are unknown to everyone. We have found that the quality of children's definitions of the unknown words is highly correlated with overall verbal intelligence, reading comprehension, and vocabulary test scores at about .6 in each case (Sternberg & Powell, 1983). Thus, one can measure an important aspect of intelligence—knowledge acquisition—directly and without heavy reliance on past achievement.

Conclusions

I have proposed in this chapter a synopsis of a triarchic theory of human intelligence. The theory comprises three subtheories: a contextual subtheory, which relates intelligence to the external world of the individual; a componential subtheory, which relates intelligence to the internal world of the individual; and a two-facet subtheory, which relates intelligence to both the external and internal worlds of the individual. The contextual subtheory defines as intelligent behavior that which involves purposive adaptation to, selection of, and shaping of real-world environments relevant to one's life. The two-facet subtheory further constrains this definition by regarding as most relevant to the demonstration of intelligence contextually intelligent behavior that involves either adaptation to novelty, automatization of information processing, or both. The componential subtheory specifies the mental mechanisms responsible for the planning, execution, and evaluation of intelligent behavior.

The theory has clear implications for the evaluation of people's intelligence. First, one should test people on behavior that is relevant to, or predictive of, contextually appropriate behavior in their real-world environments. But not every contextually appropriate behavior is equally informative with respect to individual differences in intelligence (e.g., eating). Hence, one should assess behaviors in response to novelty or in the development of automatization. But even here, not all behaviors are equally informative: Response to novelty, for example, would seem to have more to do with intelligence if it involves solving a new kind of complex problem, such as learning calculus, than if it involves solving a new kind of simple problem, such as what to do if a staple falls out of a set of collated pages. Hence, the behaviors most relevant to evaluation are those that more heavily involve components and particularly metacomponents of intelligence. In sum, all three subtheories of the triarchic theory are relevant to the evaluation or assessment of intelligence.

The triarchic theory is able to answer a rather wide range of questions regarding the nature and measurement of intelligence. For example, it can account for many of the results obtained by factor analysts in terms of the mixes of components that enter into different factorial solutions: A general factor tends to be obtained when the factor emphasizes individual-differences variance from metacomponents; group factors tend to be obtained when the factors emphasize individual-differences variance from performance components (see Sternberg, 1980a, 1980b). Similarly, the theory can account for many of the results obtained by cognitive theorists: The extent to which cognitive tasks have succeeded in capturing important aspects of intelligence is viewed as depending on the extent to which the tasks have measured individuals' skills in adapting to novelty and in automatizing information processing.

The theory attempts to capitalize on people's intuitions that the nature of intelligence is determined at least in part by the contexts in which it is exercised, at the same time that not all aspects of intelligence are contextually determined and hence relative. Thus, intelligent behavior can always be understood in terms of fits to environments, but what fits may differ from one environment to another. Moreover, the extent to which the given adaptive behavior will be viewed as intelligent—as opposed, merely, to adaptive—will be determined by the extent to which that behavior involves adaptation to novelty, automatization of information processing, or both. Finally, the mental mechanisms underlying that behavior can be understood componentially. Although I would argue that the metacomponents, performance components, and knowledge-acquisition components described in this chapter underlie intelligent behavior in all cultures, the tasks in which they would appropriately be measured will vary from one culture to the next, and the importance of the various components to intelligent behavior may likewise vary.

An important issue concerns the combination rule for the abilities specified by the three subtheories. How does the intelligence of a person who is average in the abilities specified by all three theories compare, say, to the intelligence of a person who is high in some abilities but low in others? Or what can one say of the intelligence of people whose environmental opportunities are so restricted that they are unable to adapt to, shape, or select any environment? I am very reluctant to specify any general combination rule at all, in that I do not believe that a single index of intelligence is likely to be very useful. In the first case, the two individuals are quite different in their pattern of abilities, and an overall index will hide this fact. In the second case, it may not be possible to obtain any meaningful measurement at all from the person's functioning in the environment. Take as a further example the comparison between (a) a person who is very adept at componential functioning and thus likely to score well on standard IQ tests, but who is lacking in insight or, more generally, in the ability to cope well with nonentrenched kinds of tasks or situations, and (b) a person who is very insightful but not particularly adept at componential operations. The first individual might come across to people as "smart" but not terribly "creative"; the second individual might come across as creative but not terribly smart. Although it might well be possible to obtain some average score on componential abilities and abilities to deal with nonentrenched tasks and situations, such a composite would obscure the critical qualitative differences between the functioning of the two individuals. Or, consider a person who is both componentially adept and insightful, but who makes little effort to fit into the everyday environment. Certainly one would not want to take some overall average that hides the person's academic intelligence (or even brilliance) in a combined index that is lowered because of scant adaptive skills. The point to be made, then, is that intelligence is not a single thing: It comprises a very wide array of cognitive and other skills. Our goal in theory, research, and measurement ought to be to define these skills and learn how best to assess and possibly train them, not to figure out a way to combine them into a single, but possibly meaningless number.

The triarchic theory is empirically testable in many of its aspects, and indeed, a large number of tests of various aspects of the theory have been conducted and are reviewed elsewhere (Sternberg, 1985). Nevertheless, it is obviously not without limitations. First, the subtheories, and especially the contextual one, are in need of more detailed specification. Second, the connections among the subtheories, particularly with regard to how the components of information processing are used in adaptation, dealing with novelty, and attainment of automatization, need more detailed treatment. Third, although the componential subtheory has been empirically tested in some detail, only the part of the two-facet subtheory dealing with novelty has received any test, and the contextual subtheory has received only the most minimal empirical verification. Finally, the kinds of testing instruments generated by the theory (e.g., the tacit-knowledge questionnaires and the concept-projection task measure) have yet to be subjected to the kind of extensive empirical validation that earlier psychometric instruments have received.

The proposed theory is multifaceted and complex, and there are those who may say that it is just too complicated, or that it is grandiose. Nevertheless, I believe that an account of intelligence that strives for completeness will necessarily be complex in order to take into account a very wide range of theoretical and empirical questions. The triarchic theory is probably more nearly complete in the range of questions that it can address than are alternative theories that seek to understand all of intelligence within a single perspective, whether it be psychometric, Piagetian, cognitive, contextualist, or whatever. The triarchic theory draws from all of these in an attempt to center on the whole phenomenon of intelligence, rather than on any one particular paradigm for understanding it.

References

Baltes, P. B., Dittmann-Kohli, F., & Dixon, R. A. (1982). *Intellectual development during adulthood: General propositions towards theory and a dual-process conception.* Unpublished manuscript.

Baltes, P. B., & Willis, S. L. (1979.) The critical importance of appropriate methodology in the study of aging: The same case of psychometric intelligence. In F. Hoffmeister & C. Mueller (Eds.), *Brain function in old age.* Heidelberg: Springer.

Baltes, P. B., & Willis, S. L. (1982). Plasticity and enhancement of intellectual functioning in old age: Penn State's adult development and enrichment project (ADEPT). In F. I. M. Craik & S. E. Trehub (Eds.), *Aging* and *cognitive processes.* New York: Plenum.

Baron, J. (1981). Reflective thinking as a goal of education. *Intelligence, 5,* 291–309.

Baron, J. (1982). Personality and intelligence. In R. J. Sternberg (Ed.), *Handbook of human intelligence.* Cambridge: Cambridge University Press.

Berry, J. W. (1972). Radical cultural relativism and the concept of intelligence. In L. J. Cronbach & P. J. D. Drenth (Eds.), *Mental tests and cultural adaptation.* The Hague: Mouton. Condensed and reprinted in J. W. Berry & P. R. Dasen (Eds.), *Culture and cognition: Readings in cross-cultural psychology.* London: Methuen, 1974.

Berry, J. W. (1980). Cultural universality of any theory of human intelligence remains an open question. *Behavioral and Brain Sciences, 3,* 584–585.

Berry, J. W. (1981). Cultural systems and cognitive styles. In M. Friedman, J. P. Das, & N. O'Conner (Eds.), *Intelligence and learning.* New York: Plenum.

Binet, A., & Simon, T. (1973). *Classics in psychology: The development of intelligence in children.* New York: Arno.

Boring, E. G. (1923). Intelligence as the tests test it. *New Republic* (June 6), 35–37.

Brand, C. R., & Deary, I. J. (1982). Intelligence and "inspection time." In H. J. Eysenck (Ed.), A *model for intelligence.* New York: Springer-Verlag.

Butterfield, E. C., & Belmont, J. M. (1977). Assessing and improving the cognition of mentally retarded people. In I. Bialer & M. Sternlicht (Eds.), *Psychology of mental retardation: Issues and approaches.* New York: Psychological Dimensions.

Campione, J. C., & Brown, A. L. (1979). Toward a theory of intelligence: Contributions from research with retarded children. In R. J. Sternberg & D. K Detterman (Eds.), *Human intelligence: Perspectives on its theory and measurement.* Norwood, NJ: Ablex.

Carroll, J. B. (1976). Psychometric tests as cognitive tasks: A new "structure of intellect." In L. B. Resnick (Ed.), *The nature of intelligence*. Hillsdale, NJ: Erlbaum.

Carroll, J. B. (1981). Ability and task difficulty in cognitive psychology. *Educational Research, 10,* 11–21.

Cattell, R. B. (1971). *Abilities: Their structure, growth and action.* New York: Houghton Mifflin.

Charlesworth, W. R. (1976). Human intelligence as adaptation: An ethological approach. In L. B. Resnick (Ed.), *The nature of intelligence*. Hillsdale, NJ: Erlbaum.

Charlesworth, W. R. (1979a). An ethological approach to studying intelligence. *Human Development, 22,* 212–216.

Charlesworth, W. R. (1979b). Ethology: Understanding the other half of intelligence. In M. von Cranach, K. Koppa, W. Lepenies, & D. Ploog (Eds.), *Human ethology: Claims and limits of a new discipline.* Cambridge: Cambridge University Press.

Chase, W. G., & Simon, H. A. (1973). The mind's eye in chess. In W. G. Chase (Ed.), *Visual information processing*. New York: Academic Press.

Chi, M. T. H., Glaser, R., & Rees, E. (1982). Expertise in problem solving. In R. J. Sternberg (Ed.), *Advances in the psychology of human intelligence,* vol. 1. Hillsdale, NJ: Erlbaum.

Cole, M. (1979–1980). *Mind as a cultural achievement. Implications for IQ testing.* Annual report of the research and clinical center for child development. Sapporo, Japan: Hokkaido University, Faculty of Education.

Cole, M., & Means, B. (1981). *Comparative studies of how people think.* Cambridge: Harvard University Press.

Cronbach, L. J., & Snow, R. E. (1977). *Aptitudes and instructional methods.* Irvington, NY: Irvington.

Crowder, R. G. (1982). *The psychology of reading*: An *introduction*. Oxford: Oxford University Press.

Davidson, J. E., & Sternberg, R. J. (1983). *Insight in the gifted.* Paper presented at Annual Meeting of Society for Research in Child Development, Detroit.

Detterman, D. K. (1980). Understand cognitive components before postulating metacomponents. *Behavioral and Brain Sciences, 3,* 589.

Detterman, D. K. (1982). Does "g" exist? *Intelligence, 6,* 99–108.

Dewey, J. (1957). *Human nature and conduct.* New York: Modern Library.

Egan, D. E. (1982). A heuristic for componential analysis: "Try old goals." *Behavioral and Brain Sciences, 5,* 348–350.

Eysenck, H. J. (1982). Introduction. In H. J. Eysenck (Ed.), A *model for intelligence.* New York: Springer-Verlag.

Fagan, J. F. III, & McGrath, S. K. (1981). Infant recognition memory and later intelligence. *Intelligence, 5,* 121–130.

Feldman, R. D. (1982). *Whatever happened to the quiz kids?* Chicago: Chicago Review Press.

Ford, M. E., & Miura, I. (1983). *Children's and adults' conception of social competence.* Paper presented at the 93rd Annual Meeting of the American Psychological Association, Anaheim, CA.

Gladwin, T. (1970). *East is a big bird.* Cambridge: Harvard University Press.

Goldberg, R. A., Schwartz, S., & Stewart, M. (1977). Individual differences in cognitive processes. *Journal of Educational Psychology, 69,* 9–14.

Goodman, N. (1955). *Fact, fiction, and forecast.* Cambridge: Harvard University Press.

Gordon, E. W., & Terrell, M. D. (1981). The changed social context of testing. *American Psychologist, 36,* 1167–1171.

Guilford, J. P. (1967). *The nature of human intelligence.* New York: McGraw-Hill.

Guilford, J. P. (1982). Cognitive psychology's ambiguities: Some suggested remedies. *Psychological Review, 89,* 48–59.

Horn, J. L. (1968). Organization of abilities and the development of intelligence. *Psychological Review, 75,* 242–259.

Horn, J. L. (1979). Trends in the measurement of intelligence. In R. J. Sternberg & D. K. Detterman (Eds.), *Human intelligence: Perspectives on its theory and measurement.* Norwood, NJ: Ablex.

Hunt, E. B. (1978). Mechanics of verbal ability. *Psychological Review, 85,* 109–130.

Hunt, E. B. (1980). Intelligence as an information-processing concept. *British Journal of Psychology, 71,* 449–474.

Intelligence and its measurement. A symposium. (1921). *Journal of Educational Psychology, 12,* 123–147, 195–216, 271–275.

Jencks, C. (1972). *Inequality.* New York: Harper & Row.

Jensen, A. R. (1969). How much can we boost IQ and scholastic achievement? *Harvard Educational Review, 39,* 1–123.

Jensen, A. R. (1979). *g*: Outmoded theory or unconquered frontier? *Creative Science and Technology, 2,* 16–29.

Jensen, A. R. (1980). *Bias in mental testing.* New York: Free Press.

Jensen, A. R. (1982). Reaction time and psychometric *g*. In H. J. Eysenck (Ed.), *A model for intelligence.* New York: Springer-Verlag

Just, M. A., & Carpenter, P. A. (1980). A theory of reading: From eye fixations to comprehension. *Psychological Review, 87,* 329–354.

Kaufman, A. S., & Kaufman, N. L. (1983). *Kaufman assessment battery for children (K-ABC).* Circle Pines, MN: American Guidance Service.

Kaye, D. B., Brown, S. W., & Post, T. A. (1984). The emperor's new clothes: The "new look" in intelligence research. In R. J. Sternberg (Ed.), *Advances in the psychology of human intelligence,* vol. 2. Hillsdale, NJ: Erlbaum.

Keating, D. P., & Bobbitt, B. L. (1978). Individual and developmental differences in cognitive-processing components of mental ability. *Child Development, 49,* 155–167.

Keil, F. C. (1984). Mechanisms in cognitive development and the structure of knowledge. In R. J. Sternberg (Ed.), *Mechanisms of cognitive development.* New York: Freeman.

LaBerge, D., & Samuels, J. (1974). Toward a theory of automatic information processing in reading. *Cognitive Psychology, 6,* 293–323.

Laboratory of Comparative Human Cognition. (1982). Culture and intelligence. In R. J. Sternberg (Ed.), *Handbook of human intelligence.* Cambridge: Cambridge University Press.

Laboratory of Comparative Human Cognition. (1983). Culture and cognitive development. In P. Mussen (Ed.), *Handbook of child psychology:* vol. 1; J. H. Flavell & E. M. Markman (Eds.), *Cognitive development,* vol. 3. New York: Wiley.

Labouvie-Vief, G., & Chandler, M. (1978). Cognitive development and life-span developmental theories. Idealistic vs. contextual perspectives. In P. B. Baltes (Ed.), *Life-span development and behavior,* vol. 1. New York: Academic Press.

Lansman, M., Donaldson, G., Hunt, E., & Yantis, S. (1982). Ability factors and cognitive processes. *Intelligence, 6,* 331–345.

Larkin, J., McDermott, J., Simon, D. P., & Simon, H. A. (1980). Expert and novice performance in solving physics problems. *Science, 208,* 1335–1342.

Matarazzo, J. D. (1972). *Wechsler's measurement and appraisal of adult intelligence,* 5th ed. Baltimore: Williams & Wilkins.

Mayer, R., & Greeno, J. G. (1972). Structural differences between learning outcomes produced by different instructional methods. *Journal of Educational Psychology, 63,* 165–173.

McClelland, D. C. (1973). Testing for competence rather than for "intelligence." *American Psychologist, 28,* 1–14.

Mulholland, T. M., Pellegrino, J. W., & Glaser, R. (1980). Components of geometric analogy solution. *Cognitive Psychology, 12,* 252–284.

Neisser, U. (1976). *Cognition and reality: Principles and implications of cognitive psychology.* New York: Freeman.

Neisser, U. (1979). The concept of intelligence. *Intelligence, 3,* 217–227.

Newell, A., & Simon, H. (1972). *Human problem solving.* Englewood Cliffs, NJ: Prentice-Hall.

Pachella, R. G. (1974). The interpretation of reaction time in information-processing research. In B. H. Kantowitz (Ed.), *Human information processing: Tutorials in performance and cognition.* Hillsdale, NJ: Erlbaum.

Pellegrino, J. W., & Glaser, R. (1979). Cognitive correlates and components in the analysis of individual differences. In R. Sternberg & D. K. Detterman (Eds.), *Human intelligence: Perspectives on its theory and measurement.* Norwood, NJ: Ablex.

Pellegrino, J. W., & Glaser, R. (1980). Components of inductive reasoning. In R. Snow, P. A. Federico, & W. Montague (Eds.), *Aptitude, learning and instruction: Cognitive process analyses of aptitude,* vol. 1. Hillsdale, NJ: Erlbaum.

Perfetti, C. (1984). Reading ability. In. R. J. Sternberg (Ed.), *Human abilities: An information-processing approach* (pp. 59–81). New York: Freeman.

Piaget, J. (1972). *The psychology of intelligence.* Lanham, MD: Littlefield Adams.

Posner, M. I., & Mitchell, R. F. (1967). Chronometric analysis of classification. *Psychological Review, 74,* 392–409.

Raaheim, K. (1974). *Problem solving and intelligence.* Oslo: Universitetsforlaget.

Sartre, J. P. (1976). *No exit and three other plays.* New York: Vintage.

Scarr, S. (1981). Testing for children: Assessment and the many determinants of intellectual competence. *American Psychologist, 36,* 1159–1166.

Schank, R. (1980). How much intelligence is there in artificial intelligence? *Intelligence, 4,* 1–14.

Schneider, W., & Shiffrin, R. (1977). Controlled and automated human information processing: 1. Detection, search, and attention. *Psychological Review, 84,* 1–66.

Shiffrin, R. M., & Schneider, W. (1977). Controlled and automatic processing: 2. Perceptual learning, automatic attending, and a general theory. *Psychological Review, 84,* 127–190.

Siegler, R. S. (1981). Developmental sequences within and between concepts. *Monographs of the Society for Research in Child Development, 46* (Serial No. 189).

Simon, H. A. (1976). Identifying basic abilities underlying intelligent performance of complex tasks. In. L. B. Resnick (Ed.), *The nature of intelligence.* Hillsdale, NJ: Erlbaum.

Snow, R. E. (1979). Theory and method for research on aptitude process. In R. J. Sternberg & D. K. Detterman (Eds.), *Human intelligence: Perspectives on its theory and measurement.* Norwood, NJ: Ablex.

Snow, R. E. (1981). Toward a theory of aptitude for learning: 1. Fluid and crystallized abilities and their correlates. In M. Friedman, J. P. Das, & N. O'Conner (Eds.), *Intelligence and learning.* New York: Plenum.

Spearman, C. (1927). *The abilities of man.* New York: Macmillan.

Stenhouse, D. (1973). *The evolution of intelligence: A general theory and some of its implications.* New York: Harper & Row.

Sternberg, R. J. (1977a). Component processes in analogical reasoning. *Psychological Review, 84,* 353–378.

Sternberg, R. J. (1977b). *Intelligence, information processing, and analogical reasoning: The componential analysis of human abilities.* Hillsdale, NJ: Erlbaum.

Sternberg, R. J. (1978). Isolating the components of intelligence. *Intelligence, 2,* 117–128.

Sternberg, R. J. (1980a). Factor theories of intelligence are all right almost. *Educational Researcher, 9,* 6–13, 18.

Sternberg, R. J. (1980b). Sketch of a componential subtheory of human intelligence. *Behavioral and Brain Sciences, 3,* 573–384.

Sternberg, R. J. (1981a). Intelligence and nonentrenchment. *Journal of Educational Psychology, 73,* 1–16.

Sternberg, R. J. (1981b). Novelty-seeking, novelty-finding, and the developmental continuity of intelligence. *Intelligence, 5,* 149–156.

Sternberg, R. J. (1982a). A componential approach to intellectual development. In R. J. Sternberg (Ed.), *Advances in the psychology of human intelligence,* vol. 1. Hillsdale, NJ: Erlbaum.

Sternberg, R. J. (1982b). Natural, unnatural, and supernatural concepts. *Cognitive Psychology, 14,* 451–488.

Sternberg, R. J. (1985). *Beyond IQ: A triarchic theory of human intelligence.* Cambridge: Cambridge University Press.

Sternberg, R. J., Conway, B. E., Ketron, J. L., & Bernstein, M. (1981). People's conceptions of intelligence. *Journal of Personality and Social Psychology, 41,* 37–55.

Sternberg, R. J., & Davidson, J. E. (1982). The mind of the puzzler. *Psychology Today, 16* (June), 37–44.

Sternberg, R. J., & Davidson, J. E. (1983). Insight in the gifted. *Educational Psychologist, 18,* 51–57.

Sternberg, R. J., & Gardner, M. K. (1983). Unities in inductive reasoning. *Journal of Experimental Psychology: General, 112,* 80–116.

Sternberg, R. J., & Powell, J. S. (1982). Theories of intelligence. In R. J. Sternberg (Ed.), *Handbook of human intelligence.* Cambridge: Cambridge University Press.

Sternberg, R. J., & Powell, J. S. (1983). Comprehending verbal comprehension. *American Psychologist, 38,* 878–893.

Sternberg, R. J., & Rifkin, B. (1979). The development of analogical reasoning processes. *Journal of Experimental Child Psychology, 27,* 195–232.

Sternberg, R. J., & Salter, W. (1982). Conceptions of intelligence. In R. J. Sternberg (Ed.), *Handbook of human intelligence.* Cambridge: Cambridge University Press.

Sternberg, R. J., & Wagner, R. K. (1982, July). Automatization failure in learning disabilities. *Topics in Learning and Learning Disabilities, 2,* 111.

Sternberg, R. J., & Weil, E. M. (1980). An aptitude-strategy interaction in linear syllogistic reasoning. *Journal of Educational Psychology, 72,* 226–234.

Sternberg, S. (1969). The discovery of processing stages: Extensions of Donders' method. *Acta Psychologica, 30,* 276–315.

Thurstone, L. L. (1924). *The nature of intelligence.* New York: Harcourt, Brace.

Thurstone, L. L., & Thurstone, T. G. (1962). *Tests of primary mental abilities* (rev. ed.). Chicago: Science Research Associates.

Wagner, R. K., & Sternberg, R. J. (1983). *Executive control of reading.* Manuscript submitted for publication.

Wagner, R. K., & Sternberg, R. J. (1995). Practical intelligence in real-world pursuits: The role of tacit knowledge. *Journal of Personality and Social Psychology, 49,* 436–458.

Wechsler, D. (1958). *The measurement and appraisal of adult intelligence,* 4th ed. Baltimore: Williams & Wilkins.

Werner, H., & Kaplan, E. (1952). The acquisition of word meanings: A developmental study. *Monographs of the Society for Research in Child Development,* No. 51.

Zigler, E. (1971). The retarded child as a whole person. In H. E. Adams & W. K. Boardman (Eds.), *Advances in experimental clinical psychology,* vol. 1. New York: Pergamon Press.

The Theory of Successful Intelligence

3

Robert J. Sternberg

Many psychometric researchers studying intelligence believe there is overwhelming evidence for a conventional psychometric view, positing a general ability, or g, at the top of a hierarchy and then successively more narrow abilities below that. The thesis of this chapter is that conventional notions of intelligence are incomplete and hence inadequate. I argue further that a construct of *successful intelligence* better captures the fundamental nature of human abilities. If this new construct is taken into account in the laboratory, the schools, and the workplace, not only will science benefit, but so will individuals, organizations, and society, both in the short term and the long term.

Although many different definitions of intelligence have been proposed over the years (see, e.g., "Intelligence and Its Measurement," 1921; Sternberg & Detterman, 1986), the conventional notion of intelligence is built around a loosely consensual definition of intelligence in terms of generalized adaptation to the environment. Theories of intelligence extend this definition by suggesting that there is a general factor of intelligence, often labeled g, which underlies all adaptive behavior. As just mentioned, in many theories, including the theories most widely accepted today (e.g., Carroll, 1993; Gustafsson, 1994; Horn, 1994), other mental abilities are hierarchically nested under this general factor at successively greater levels of specificity. For example, Carroll suggested that three levels can nicely capture the hierarchy of abilities,

71

whereas Cattell (1971) and P. E. Vernon (1971) suggested that two levels were especially important. In the case of Cattell, nested under general ability are fluid abilities of the kind needed to solve abstract reasoning problems such as figural matrices or series completions and crystallized abilities of the kind needed to solve problems of vocabulary and general information. In the case of Vernon, the two levels corresponded to verbal–educational and practical–mechanical abilities. These theories and others like them, described in more detail elsewhere (Brody, 2000; Carroll, 1993; Embretson & McCollam, 2000; Jensen, 1998; Sternberg, 1994, 2000), are called into question in this chapter.

I argue here that the notion of intelligence as adaptation to the environment and as operationalized in narrowly based intelligence tests is incomplete. Rather, I argue for a concept of successful intelligence according to which intelligence is the ability to achieve success in life, given one's personal standards, within one's sociocultural context. One's ability to achieve success depends on one's capitalizing on one's strengths and correcting or compensating for one's weaknesses through a balance of analytical, creative, and practical abilities to adapt to, shape, and select environments.

The remainder of this chapter is divided into four main parts. First, I argue that conventional and some other notions of intelligence are, at best, incomplete and, at worst, wrong. Second, I suggest an alternative notion of successful intelligence that expands on conventional notions of intelligence. The formulation presented here goes beyond that in previous work (Sternberg, 1997). Third, I discuss how we have gotten to the point in psychology and society in which we draw heavily on theories and tests that are inadequate. Finally, I draw some conclusions about the nature of intelligence. This essay is not intended to provide a comprehensive review of theories and research on intelligence (but see Carroll, 1993; Jensen, 1998; Sternberg, 1990, 1994, 2000).

Notions of Intelligence That Are Inadequate

In this section, I argue that conventional notions of intelligence are incomplete. I argue that intelligence is not a unitary construct, and so theories based on notions of general intelligence, dating back to Spearman (1904) and up to the present (e.g., Brand, 1996; Carroll, 1993; Jensen, 1998), cannot be complete either.

Conventional Notions

There now has accumulated a substantial body of evidence suggesting that, contrary to conventional notions, intelligence is not a unitary construct. This evidence is a variety of different kinds, most of which suggest that the positive manifold (pattern of positive correlations) among ability tests is likely not to be a function of some inherent structure of intellect. Rather, it reflects interactions among the kinds of individuals tested, the kinds of tests used in the testing, and the situations in which the individuals are tested.

One kind of evidence suggests the power of situational contexts in testing (see also Ceci, 1996; Gardner, 1983; Lave, 1988; Nunes, Schliemann, & Carraher, 1993). For example, Carraher, Carraher, and Schliemann (1985; see also Ceci & Roazzi, 1994; Nunes, 1994) studied a group of children that is especially relevant for assessing intelligence as adaptation to the environment: Brazilian street children. Brazilian street children are under great contextual pressure to form a successful street business. If they do not, they risk death at the hands of so-called "death squads," which may murder children who, unable to earn money, resort to robbing stores (or who are suspected of resorting to robbing stores). The researchers found that the same children who are able to do the mathematics needed to run their street business are often little able or unable to do school mathematics. In fact, the more abstract and removed from real-world contexts the problems are in their form of presentation, the worse the children do on the problems. These results suggest that differences in context can have a powerful effect on performance.

Such differences are not limited to Brazilian street children. Lave (1988) showed that Berkeley housewives who successfully could do the mathematics needed for comparison shopping in the supermarket were unable to do the same mathematics when they were placed in a classroom and given isomorphic problems presented in an abstract form. In other words, their problem was not at the level of mental processes but at the level of applying the processes in specific environmental contexts.

Ceci and Liker (1986; see also Ceci, 1996) showed that, given tasks relevant to their lives, men would show the same kinds of effects shown by women in the Lave studies. These investigators studied men who successfully handicapped horse races. The complexity of their implicit mathematical formulas was unrelated to their IQ. Moreover, despite the complexity of these formulas, the mean IQ among these men was only at roughly the population average or slightly below. Ceci also subsequently found that the skills were really quite specific: The same men did not successfully apply their skills to computations involving securities in the stock market.

In our own research, my colleagues and I have found results consistent with those just described. These results have emanated from studies conducted both in the United States and in other countries. I describe here our international studies because I believe they especially call into question the straightforward interpretation of results from conventional tests of intelligence that suggest the existence of a general factor.

In a study in Usenge, Kenya, near the city of Kisumu, we were interested in school-aged children's ability to adapt to their indigenous environment. We devised a test of practical intelligence for adaptation to the environment (see Sternberg & Grigorenko, 1997; Sternberg, Nokes, et al., 2001). The test measured children's informal tacit knowledge of natural herbal medicines that the villagers believe can be used to fight various types of infections. At least some of these medicines appear to be effective, and most villagers certainly believe in their efficacy, as shown by the fact that children in the villages use their knowledge of these medicines an average of once a week in medicating themselves and others. Thus, tests of how to use these medicines constitute effective measures of one aspect of practical intelligence as defined by the villagers as well as their life circumstances in their environmental contexts. Middle-class Westerners might find it quite a challenge to thrive or even survive in these contexts or, for that matter, in the contexts of urban ghettos often not distant from their comfortable homes.

We measured the Kenyan children's ability to identify the medicines, where they come from, what they are used for, and how they are dosed. On the basis of work we had done elsewhere, we expected that scores on this test would not correlate with scores on conventional tests of intelligence. To test this hypothesis, we also administered to the 85 children the Raven Coloured Progressive Matrices Test (Raven, 1958), which is a measure of fluid or abstract-reasoning-based abilities, as well as the

Mill Hill Vocabulary Scale (Raven, Court, & Raven, 1992), which is a measure of crystallized or formal-knowledge-based abilities. In addition, we gave the children a comparable test of vocabulary in their own Dholuo language. The Dholuo language is spoken in the home, and English is spoken in the schools.

We did indeed find no correlation between the test of indigenous tacit knowledge and scores on the fluid-ability tests. But, to our surprise, we found statistically significant correlations of the tacit-knowledge tests with the tests of crystallized abilities. The correlations, however, were negative. In other words, the higher the children scored on the test of tacit knowledge, the lower they scored, on average, on the tests of crystallized abilities. This surprising result can be interpreted in various ways; however, on the basis of the ethnographic observations of the cultural anthropologists on our team, Geissler and Prince, we concluded that a plausible scenario takes into account the expectations of families for their children.

Children generally drop out of school before graduation, and most families in the village do not particularly value formal Western schooling. There is no reason they should; their children will, for the most part, spend their lives farming or engaged in other occupations that make little or no use of Western schooling. These families emphasize teaching their children the indigenous informal knowledge that will lead to successful adaptation in the environments in which they will actually live. Children who spend their time learning the indigenous practical knowledge of the community generally do not invest themselves heavily in doing well in school, whereas children who do well in school generally do not invest themselves as heavily in learning the indigenous knowledge: hence the negative correlations.

The Kenya study suggests that the identification of a general factor of human intelligence may reveal more about how abilities interact with patterns of schooling, and especially Western patterns of schooling, than it does about the structure of human abilities. In Western schooling, children typically study a variety of subject matters from an early age and thus develop skills in a variety of skill areas. This kind of schooling prepares the children to take a test of intelligence, which typically measures skills in a variety of areas. Often, intelligence tests measure skills that children were expected to acquire a few years before taking the intelligence test. But as Rogoff (1990) and others have noted, this pattern of schooling is not universal and has not even been common for much of the history of humankind. Throughout history and in many places still, schooling, especially for boys, takes the form of apprenticeships in which children learn a craft from an early age. They learn what they will need to know to succeed in a trade, but not much more. They are not simultaneously engaged in tasks that require the development of the particular blend of skills measured by conventional intelligence tests. Hence, it is less likely that one would observe a general factor in their scores, much as we discovered in Kenya. Some years back, P. E. Vernon (1971) pointed out that the axes of a factor analysis do not necessarily reveal a latent structure of the mind, but rather represent a convenient way of characterizing the organization of mental abilities. Vernon believed that there was no one "right" orientation of axes, and indeed, mathematically, an infinite number of orientations of axes can be fit to any solution in an exploratory factor analysis. Vernon's point seems perhaps to have been forgotten or at least ignored by later theorists.

The test of practical intelligence we developed for use in Kenya, as well as some of the other practically based tests described in this chapter, may seem more like tests of achievement or of developing expertise (see Ericsson, 1996; Howe, Davidson, & Sloboda, 1998) than of intelligence. But I have argued that intelligence is itself a form of developing expertise, that there is no clear-cut distinction between the two constructs. Indeed, all tests of intelligence, one might argue, measure a form of developing expertise. Crystallized-ability tests, such as tests of vocabulary and general information, certainly measure developing and developed knowledge bases. And available data suggest that fluid-ability tests, such as tests of abstract reasoning, measure developing and developed expertise even more strongly than do crystallized-ability tests. Probably the best evidence for this claim is that fluid-ability tests have shown much greater increases in scores over the last several generations than have crystallized-ability tests (Flynn, 1984, 1987; Neisser, 1998). The relatively brief period of time during which these increases have occurred (about 9 points of IQ per generation) suggests an environmental rather than a genetic cause of the increases. And the substantially greater increase for fluid than for crystallized tests suggests that fluid tests, like all other tests, actually measure an expertise acquired through interactions with the environment. This is not to say that genes do not influence intelligence: Almost certainly they do (Bouchard, 1997; Plomin, 1997; Scarr, 1997). Rather, the point is that the environment always mediates their influence, and tests of intelligence measure gene–environment interaction effects. The measurement of intelligence is by assessment of various forms of developing expertise.

The forms of developing expertise that are viewed as practically or otherwise intelligent may differ from one society to another or from one sector of a given society to another. For example, procedural knowledge about natural herbal medicines, on the one hand, or Western medicines, on the other, may be critical to survival in one society and irrelevant to survival in another (e.g., where one or the other type of medicine is not available). Whereas what constitutes components of intelligence is universal, the content that constitutes the application of these components to adaptation to, shaping of, and selection of environments is culturally and even subculturally variable.

The developing world provides a particularly interesting laboratory for testing theories of intelligence because many of the assumptions that are held as dear in the developed world simply do not apply. A study we have done in Tanzania (see Sternberg & Grigorenko, 1997; Sternberg, Grigorenko, Ngorosho, et al., 2002) points out the risks of giving tests, scoring them, and interpreting the results as measures of some latent intellectual ability or abilities. We administered to 358 young schoolchildren near Bagamoyo, Tanzania, tests including a form-board classification test, a linear syllogisms test, and a 20-questions test, which measure the kinds of skills required on conventional tests of intelligence. Of course, we obtained scores that we could analyze and evaluate, ranking the children in terms of their supposed general or other abilities. However, we administered the tests dynamically rather than statically (Brown & Ferrara, 1985; Budoff, 1968; Day, Engelhard, Maxwell, & Bolig, 1997; Feuerstein, 1979; Grigorenko & Sternberg, 1998; Guthke, 1993; Haywood & Tzuriel, 1992; Lidz, 1987, 1991; Tzuriel, 1995; Vygotsky, 1978). Dynamic testing is like conventional static testing in that individuals are tested and inferences about their abilities made. But dynamic tests differ in that children are given some kind of feedback to help them improve their scores.

Vygotsky (1978) suggested that children's ability to profit from the guided instruction received during the testing session could serve as a measure of children's zone of proximal development, or the difference between their developed abilities and their latent capacities. In other words, testing and instruction are treated as being of one piece rather than as being distinct processes. This integration makes sense in terms of traditional definitions of intelligence as the ability to learn ("Intelligence and Its Measurement," 1921; Sternberg & Detterman, 1986). What a dynamic test does is directly measure processes of learning in the context of testing rather than measuring these processes indirectly as the product of past learning. Such measurement is especially important when not all children have had equal opportunities to learn in the past.

In our assessments, children were first given the ability tests. Then they were given a brief period of instruction in which they were able to learn skills that would potentially enable them to improve their scores. Then they were tested again. Because the instruction for each test lasted only about 5–10 min, one would not expect dramatic gains. Yet, on average, the gains were statistically significant. More important, scores on the pretest showed only weak, although significant, correlations with scores on the posttest. These correlations, at about the .3 level, suggested that when tests are administered statically to children in developing countries, they may be rather unstable and easily subject to influences of training. The reason could be that the children are not accustomed to taking Western-style tests and so profit quickly even from small amounts of instruction as to what is expected from them. Of course, the more important question is not whether the scores changed or even correlated with each other but, rather, how they correlated with other cognitive measures. In other words, which was a better predictor of transfer to other cognitive performance, the pretest score or the posttest score? We found the posttest score to be the better predictor.

Modern Notions

Recognizing problems with general-ability theories, Gardner (1983, 1993, 1999) has proposed a model of multiple intelligences, according to which intelligence is viewed as comprising originally seven and now eight multiple intelligences: linguistic, logical–mathematical, spatial, musical, bodily–kinesthetic, interpersonal, intrapersonal, and now naturalistic. Gardner also has speculated that there may be existential and spiritual intelligences, which he has referred to as candidate intelligences. This theory has received widespread recognition and has been widely adopted in schools (see Gardner, 1993). The theory has made a valuable contribution to the literature on intelligence by suggesting an alternative to g theory. At the same time, there remains an apparent absence of predictive empirical data supporting or even testing the theory as a whole.

Other modern theories of intelligence also have been proposed (e.g., Baron, 1978; Ceci, 1990, 1996; Deary, 1988, 2000; Detterman, 1994; Kyllonen & Christal, 1990; Perkins, 1995; Snow, 1979; P. A. Vernon, Wickett, Bazana, & Stelmack, 2000). These theories, like Gardner's, provide plausible alternatives to the conception of successful intelligence presented here. Many of the modern theories overlap, however, in their claim that so-called general ability is less informative than it might first appear to be.

What, then, is intelligence? This question is addressed in the next section.

The Nature of Successful Intelligence

The theory of successful intelligence has four key elements (see also Sternberg, 1997). These elements are summarized in Figure 3.1.

Element 1: Intelligence is defined in terms of the ability to achieve success in life in terms of one's personal standards, within one's sociocultural context. The field of

3.1

The theory of successful intelligence.

Definition of Successful Intelligence

    The ability to achieve success in life

    According to one's personal standards

    Within one's sociocultural context

Types of Processing Skills Contributing to Successful Intelligence

    Analytical

    Creative

    Practical

Uses of Processing Skills for Successful Intelligence

    Adaptation to Environments

    Shaping of Environments

    Selection of Environments

Mechanisms for Utilization of Processing Skills in Successful Intelligence

    Capitalization on Strengths

    Correction of Weaknesses

    Compensation for Weaknesses

---

intelligence has at times tended to put "the cart before the horse," defining the construct conceptually on the basis of how it is operationalized rather than vice versa. This practice has resulted in tests that stress the academic aspect of intelligence, as one might expect, given the origins of modern intelligence testing in the work of Binet and Simon (1916) in designing an instrument that would distinguish children who would succeed from those who would fail in school. But the construct of intelligence needs to serve a broader purpose, accounting for the bases of success in all of one's life.

The use of societal criteria of success (e.g., school grades and personal income) can obscure the fact that these operationalizations often do not capture people's personal notions of success. Some people choose to concentrate on extracurricular activities such as athletics or music and pay less attention to grades in school; others may choose occupations that are personally meaningful to them but that never will yield the income they could gain doing work that is less personally meaningful. Although scientific analysis of some kinds requires nomothetic operationalizations, the definition of success for an individual is idiographic. In the theory of successful intelligence, however, the conceptualization of intelligence is always located within a sociocultural context. Although the processes of intelligence may be common across such contexts, what constitutes success is not. Being a successful member of the clergy of a particular religion may be highly rewarded in one society and viewed as a worthless pursuit in another culture.

Element 2: One's ability to achieve success depends on one's capitalizing on one's strengths and correcting or compensating for one's weaknesses. Theories of intelligence typically specify some relatively fixed set of abilities, whether one general factor and a number of specific factors (Spearman, 1904), seven multiple factors (Thurstone, 1938), or eight multiple intelligences (Gardner, 1999). Such a nomothetic specification is useful in establishing a common set of skills to be tested. But people achieve success, even within a given occupation, in many different ways. For example, successful teachers and researchers achieve success through many different blendings of skills rather than through any single formula that works for all of them.

Element 3: Success is attained through a balance of analytical, creative, and practical abilities. Analytical abilities are the abilities primarily measured by traditional tests of abilities. But success in life requires one not only to analyze one's own ideas as well as the ideas of others but also to generate ideas and to persuade other people of their value. This necessity occurs in the world of work, as when a subordinate tries to convince a superior of the value of his or her plan; in the world of personal relationships, as when a child attempts to convince a parent to do what he or she wants or when a spouse tries to convince the other spouse to do things his or her preferred way; and in the world of the school, as when a student writes an essay arguing for a point of view.

Element 4: Balancing of abilities is achieved to adapt to, shape, and select environments. Definitions of intelligence traditionally have emphasized the role of adaptation to the environment ("Intelligence and Its Measurement," 1921; Sternberg & Detterman, 1986). But intelligence involves not only modifying oneself to suit the environment (adaptation) but also modifying the environment to suit oneself (shaping) and, sometimes, finding a new environment that is a better match to one's skills, values, or desires (selection).

Not all people have equal opportunities to adapt to, shape, and select environments. In general, people of higher socioeconomic standing tend to have more opportunities, and people of lower socioeconomic standing have fewer. The economy or political situation of the society also can be a factor. Other variables that may affect such opportunities are education and especially literacy, political party, race, religion, and so forth. For example, someone with a college education typically has many more possible career options than does someone who has dropped out of high school to support a family. Thus, how and how well an individual adapts to, shapes, and selects environments must always be viewed in terms of the opportunities the individual has.

More details regarding the theory can be found in Sternberg (1985a, 1997). Because the theory comprises three subtheories—a componential subtheory dealing with the components of intelligence, an experiential subtheory dealing with the importance of coping with relative novelty and of automatization of information processing, and a contextual subtheory dealing with processes of adaptation, shaping, and selection—I have referred to the theory from time to time as *triarchic.*

Processes of Successful Intelligence

According to the proposed theory of human intelligence and its development (Sternberg, 1980b, 1984, 1985a, 1990, 1997), a common set of processes underlies all aspects of intelligence. These processes are hypothesized to be universal. For example, although the solutions to problems that are considered intelligent in one culture may be different from the solutions considered to be intelligent in another culture, the need to define problems and translate strategies to solve these problems exists in any culture.

Metacomponents, or executive processes, plan what to do, monitor things as they are being done, and evaluate things after they are done. Examples of metacomponents are recognizing the existence of a problem, defining the nature of the problem, deciding on a strategy for solving the problem, monitoring the solution of the problem, and evaluating the solution after the problem is solved.

Performance components execute the instructions of the metacomponents. For example, inference is used to decide how two stimuli are related, and application is used to apply what one has inferred (Sternberg, 1977). Other examples of performance components are comparison of stimuli, justification of a given response as adequate although not ideal, and actually making the response.

Knowledge-acquisition components are used to learn how to solve problems or simply to acquire declarative knowledge in the first place (Sternberg, 1985a). Selective encoding is used to decide what information is relevant in the context of one's learning. Selective comparison is used to bring old information to bear on new problems. And selective combination is used to put together the selectively encoded and compared information into a single and sometimes insightful solution to a problem.

Although the same processes are used for all three aspects of intelligence universally, these processes are applied to different kinds of tasks and situations depending on whether a given problem requires analytical thinking, creative thinking, practical thinking, or a combination of these kinds of thinking. Data supporting the theory cannot be presented fully here but are summoned elsewhere (Sternberg, 1977, 1985a; Sternberg, Forsythe, et al., 2000).

Analytical, Creative, and Practical Aspects of Intelligence

The Three Aspects of Intelligence Viewed in Combination

An important foundation of the theory of successful intelligence is the importance of analytical, creative, and practical abilities to intellectual functioning. A number of the studies described subsequently show both the internal validity and the external validity of these constructs.

Internal Validity. Three separate factor-analytic studies support the internal validity of the theory of successful intelligence. In one study (Sternberg, Grigorenko, Ferrari, & Clinkenbeard, 1999), we used the so-called Sternberg Triarchic Abilities Test (STAT; Sternberg, 1993) to investigate the internal validity of the theory. Three hundred twenty-six high school students, primarily from diverse parts of the United States, took the test, which comprised 12 subtests in all. There were 4 subtests each measuring analytical, creative, and practical abilities. For each type of ability, there were three multiple-choice tests and one essay test. The multiple-choice tests, in turn, involved, respectively, verbal, quantitative, and figural content. Consider the content of each test.

1. Analytical-Verbal: Figuring out meanings of neologisms (artificial words) from natural contexts. Students see a novel word embedded in a paragraph and have to infer its meaning from the context.
2. Analytical-Quantitative: Number series. Students have to say what number should come next in a series of numbers.
3. Analytical-Figural: Matrices. Students see a figural matrix with the lower right entry missing. They have to indicate which of the options fits into the missing space.
4. Practical-Verbal: Everyday reasoning. Students are presented with a set of everyday problems in the life of an adolescent and have to select the option that best solves each problem.
5. Practical-Quantitative: Everyday math. Students are presented with scenarios requiring the use of math in everyday life (e.g., buying tickets for a ballgame) and have to solve math problems based on the scenarios.
6. Practical-Figural: Route planning. Students are presented with a map of an area (e.g., an entertainment park) and have to answer questions about navigating effectively through the area depicted by the map.
7. Creative-Verbal: Novel analogies. Students are presented with verbal analogies preceded by counterfactual premises (e.g., money falls off trees). They have to solve the analogies as though the counterfactual premises were true.
8. Creative-Quantitative: Novel number operations. Students are presented with rules for novel number operations, for example, "flix," which involves numerical manipulations that differ as a function of whether the first of two operands is greater than, equal to, or less than the second. Participants have to use the novel number operations to solve presented math problems.
9. Creative-Figural: In each item, participants are first presented with a figural series that involves one or more transformations; they then have to apply the rule of the series to a new figure with a different appearance and complete the new series.

We found that a confirmatory factor analysis on the data was supportive of the triarchic theory of human intelligence, yielding separate and uncorrelated analytical, creative, and practical factors. The lack of correlation was due to the inclusion of essay as well as multiple-choice subtests. Although multiple-choice tests tended to correlate substantially with multiple-choice tests, their correlations with essay tests were much weaker. We found the multiple-choice analytical subtest to load most highly on the analytical factor, but the essay creative and performance subtests loaded most highly on their respective factors. Thus, measurement of creative and practical abilities probably ideally should be accomplished with other kinds of testing instruments that complement multiple-choice instruments.

In a second and separate study conducted with 240 freshman-year high school students in Murcia, Spain, we used the multiple-choice section of the STAT to compare five alternative models of intelligence, again via confirmatory factor analysis. A model featuring a general factor of intelligence fit the data relatively poorly. The triarchic model, allowing for intercorrelation among the analytic, creative, and practical factors, provided the best fit to the data (Sternberg, Castejón, Prieto, Hautamäki, & Grigorenko, 2001).

In a third study, we tested 511 Russian schoolchildren (ranging in age from 8 to 17 years) as well as 490 mothers and 328 fathers of these children. We used entirely distinct measures of analytical, creative, and practical intelligence. Consider, for example, the tests we used for adults. Similar tests were used for children (Grigorenko & Sternberg, 2001).

Fluid analytical intelligence was measured by two subtests of a test of nonverbal intelligence.

The Test of *g:* Culture Fair, Level 2 (Cattell & Cattell, 1973) is a test of fluid intelligence designed to reduce, as much as possible, the influence of verbal comprehension, culture, and educational level, although no test eliminates such influences. In the first subtest we used, Series, individuals were presented with an incomplete, progressive series of figures. The participants' task was to select, from among the choices provided, the answer that best continued the series. In the Matrices subtest, the task was to complete the matrix presented at the left of each row.

The test of crystallized intelligence was adapted from existing traditional tests of analogies and synonyms–antonyms used in Russia. We used adaptations of Russian rather than American tests because the vocabulary used in Russia differs from that used in the United States. The first part of the test included 20 verbal analogies (K-R 20 = 0.83). An example is *circle—ball = square—? (a) quadrangular, (b) figure, (c) rectangular, (d) solid, (e) cube.* The second part included 30 pairs of words, and the participants' task was to specify whether the words in the pair were synonyms or antonyms (K-R 20 = 0.74). Examples are *latent—hidden* and *systematic—chaotic.*

The measure of creative intelligence also comprised two parts. The first part asked the participants to describe the world through the eyes of insects. The second part asked participants to describe who might live and what might happen on a planet called "Priumliava."[1] No additional information on the nature of the planet was specified. Each part of the test was scored in three different ways to yield three different scores. The first score was for originality (novelty); the second was for the amount of development in the plot (quality); and the third was for creative use of prior knowledge in these relatively novel kinds of tasks (sophistication). The mean interstory reliabilities were .69, .75, and .75 for the three respective scores, all of which were statistically significant at the *p* < .001 level.

The measure of practical intelligence was self-report and also comprised two parts. The first part was designed as a 20-item, self-report instrument assessing practical skills in the social domain (e.g., effective and successful communication with other people), in the family domain (e.g., how to fix household items and how to run the family budget), and in the domain of effective resolution of sudden problems (e.g., organizing

---

[1]In Russian, the word *Priumliava* is a nonsense word. It does, however, contain the root *um,* which is similar to the English root *mind.* This feature of the word *Priumliava* was detected and played out by a few participants in the study. This accomplishment, however, was not incorporated in the rating scheme; those who capitalized in their writing on the presence of the root *um* in *Priumliava* were rated on the same bases as everybody else.

something that has become chaotic). For the subscales, internal-consistency estimates varied from .50 to .77. In this study, only the total practical intelligence self-report scale was used (Cronbach α = .71). The second part had four vignettes based on themes that appeared in popular Russian magazines in the context of discussion of adaptive skills in the current society. The four themes were how to maintain the value of one's savings, what to do when one makes a purchase and discovers that the item one has purchased is broken, how to locate medical assistance in a time of need, and how to manage a salary bonus one has received for outstanding work. Each vignette was accompanied by five choices, and participants had to select the best one. Obviously, there is no one "right" answer in this type of situation. Hence, we used the most frequently chosen response as the keyed answer. To the extent that this response was suboptimal, this suboptimality would work against us in subsequent analyses relating scores on this test to other predictor and criterion measures.

In this study, exploratory principal-components analysis for children and adults yielded very similar factor structures. Both varimax and oblimin rotations yielded clear-cut analytical, creative, and practical factors for the tests. Thus, with a sample of a different nationality (Russian), a different set of tests, and a different method of analysis (exploratory rather than confirmatory analysis), there was again support for the theory of successful intelligence. Now consider in more detail each of three major aspects of successful intelligence: analytical, creative, and practical.

External Validity.   We have done three studies examining simultaneously the external validity of analytical, creative, and practical abilities. In the first set of studies, we explored the question of whether conventional education in school systematically discriminates against children with creative and practical strengths (Sternberg & Clinkenbeard, 1995; Sternberg, Ferrari, Clinkenbeard, & Grigorenko, 1996; Sternberg, Grigorenko, Ferrari, & Clinkenbeard, 1999). Motivating this work was the belief that the systems in schools strongly tend to favor children with strengths in memory and analytical abilities.

We used the STAT, as described earlier. The test was administered to 326 children around the United States and in some other countries who were identified by their schools as gifted by any standard whatsoever. Children were selected for a summer program in (college-level) psychology if they fell into one of five ability groupings: high analytical, high creative, high practical, high balanced (high in all three abilities), or low balanced (low in all three abilities). Students who came to Yale were then divided into four instructional groups. Students in all four instructional groups used the same introductory psychology textbook (a preliminary version of Sternberg, 1995) and listened to the same psychology lectures. What differed among them was the type of afternoon discussion section to which they were assigned. They were assigned to an instructional condition that emphasized memory, analytical, creative, or practical instruction. For example, in the memory condition, they might be asked to describe the main tenets of a major theory of depression. In the analytical condition, they might be asked to compare and contrast two theories of depression. In the practical condition, they might be asked how they could use what they had learned about depression to help a friend who was depressed.

Students in all four instructional conditions were evaluated in terms of their performance on homework, a midterm exam, a final exam, and an independent project. Each type of work was evaluated for memory, analytical, creative, and practical quality. Thus, all students were evaluated in exactly the same way.

Our results suggested the utility of the theory of successful intelligence. First, we observed when the students arrived at Yale that the students in the high creative and high practical groups were much more diverse in terms of racial, ethnic, socioeconomic, and educational backgrounds than were the students in the high analytical group, suggesting that correlations of measured intelligence with status variables such as these may be reduced by using a broader conception of intelligence. Thus, the kinds of students identified as strong differed in terms of populations from which they were drawn in comparison with students identified as strong solely by analytical measures. More important, just by expanding the range of abilities we measured, we discovered intellectual strengths that might not have been apparent through a conventional test.

We found that all three ability tests—analytical, creative, and practical— significantly predicted course performance. When multiple regression analysis was used, at least two of these ability measures contributed significantly to the prediction of each of the measures of achievement. Perhaps as a reflection of the difficulty of deemphasizing the analytical way of teaching, one of the significant predictors was always the analytical score. (However, in an unpublished replication of our study with low-income African American students from New York, Deborah Coates [personal communication, December 7, 1998] of the City University of New York found a different pattern of results. Her data indicated that the practical tests were better predictors of course performance than were the analytical measures, suggesting that what ability test predicts what criterion depends on population as well as mode of teaching.) Most important, there was an aptitude–treatment interaction whereby students who were placed in instructional conditions that better matched their pattern of abilities outperformed students who were mismatched. In other words, when students are taught in a way that fits how they think, they do better in school. Children with creative and practical abilities, who are almost never taught or assessed in a way that matches their pattern of abilities, may be at a disadvantage in course after course, year after year.

In a follow-up study (Sternberg, Torff, & Grigorenko, 1998a, 1998b), we looked at learning of social studies and science by third graders and eighth graders. The 225 third graders were students in a very-low-income neighborhood in Raleigh, North Carolina. The 142 eighth graders were students who were largely middle to upper-middle class studying in Baltimore, Maryland, and Fresno, California. In this study, students were assigned to one of three instructional conditions. In the first condition, they were taught the course that basically they would have learned had we not intervened. The emphasis in the course was on memory. In a second condition, they were taught in a way that emphasized critical (analytical) thinking. In the third condition, they were taught in a way that emphasized analytical, creative, and practical thinking. All students' performance was assessed for memory learning (through multiple-choice assessments) as well as for analytical, creative, and practical learning (through performance assessments).

As expected, we found that students in the successful-intelligence (analytical, creative, and practical) condition outperformed the other students in terms of the performance assessments. One could argue that this result merely reflected the way they were taught. Nevertheless, the result suggested that teaching for these kinds of thinking succeeded. More important, however, was the result that children in the successful-intelligence condition outperformed the other children even on the multiple-choice memory tests. In other words, to the extent that one's goal is just to maximize children's memory for information, teaching for successful intelligence is still superior. It enables children to capitalize on their strengths and to correct or to compensate for their weaknesses, and it allows children to encode material in a variety of interesting ways.

In the third study—the Grigorenko–Sternberg (2001) study described earlier—the analytical, creative, and practical tests we employed were used to predict mental and physical health among the Russian adults. Mental health was measured by widely used paper-and-pencil tests of depression and anxiety, and physical health was measured by self-report. The best predictor of mental and physical health was the practical-intelligence measure, followed by analytical intelligence and then creative intelligence. All three contributed to prediction, however. Thus, we again concluded that a theory of intelligence encompassing all three elements provides better prediction of success in life than does a theory comprising just the analytical element.

Thus, the results of three sets of studies suggest that the theory of successful intelligence is valid as a whole. Moreover, the results suggest that the theory can make a difference not only in laboratory tests, but in school classrooms and even the everyday life of adults. Consider further the elements of the theory independently.

Analytical Intelligence

Analytical intelligence is involved when the components of intelligence (which are specified by the componential subtheory of the triarchic theory) are applied to analyze, evaluate, judge, or compare and contrast. It typically is involved when components are applied to relatively familiar kinds of problems in which the judgments to be made are of a fairly abstract nature.

In some of my early work, I showed how analytical kinds of problems, such as analogies or syllogisms, can be analyzed componentially (Guyote & Sternberg, 1981; Sternberg, 1977, 1980b, 1983; Sternberg & Gardner, 1983), with response times or error rates decomposed to yield their underlying information-processing components. The goal of this research was to understand the information-processing origins of individual differences in (the analytical aspect of) human intelligence. With componential analysis, one could specify sources of individual differences underlying a factor score such as that for "inductive reasoning." For example, response times on analogies (Sternberg, 1977) and linear syllogisms (Sternberg, 1980a) were decomposed into their elementary performance components so that it was possible to specify, in the solving of analogies or other kinds of problems, several sources of important individual or developmental differences: (a) What performance components are used? (b) How long does it takes to execute each component? (c) How susceptible is each component to error? (d) How are the components combined into strategies? and (e) What are the mental representations on which the components act?

Studies of reasoning need not use artificial formats. In a more recent study, we looked at predictions for everyday kinds of situations, such as when milk will spoil (Sternberg & Kalmar, 1997). In this study, we looked at both predictions and postdictions (hypotheses about the past in which information about the past is unknown) and found that postdictions took longer to make than did predictions.

Research on the components of human intelligence yielded some interesting results. For example, in a study of the development of figural analogical reasoning, we found that although children generally became quicker in information processing with age, not all components were executed more rapidly with age (Sternberg & Rifkin, 1979). The encoding component first showed a decrease in component time with age and then showed an increase. Apparently, older children realized that their best strategy was to spend more time in encoding the terms of a problem so that they later would be able to spend less time in operating on these encodings. A related finding was that better reasoners tend to spend relatively more time than do poorer reasoners in global, upfront metacomponential planning when they solve difficult reasoning problems. Poorer reasoners, on the other hand, tend to spend relatively more time in local planning (Sternberg, 1981). Presumably, the better reasoners recognize that it is better to invest more time up front so as to be able to process a problem more efficiently later on. We also found in a study of the development of verbal analogical reasoning that, as children grew older, their strategies shifted so that they relied on word association less and abstract relations more (Sternberg & Nigro, 1980).

Some of our studies concentrated on knowledge-acquisition components rather than performance components or metacomponents. For example, in one set of studies, we were interested in sources of individual differences in vocabulary (Sternberg & Powell, 1982; Sternberg, Powell, & Kaye, 1982; see also Sternberg, 1987b). We were not content just to view these as individual differences in declarative knowledge because we wanted to understand why it was that some people acquired this declarative knowledge and others did not. What we found is that there were multiple sources of individual and developmental differences. The three main sources were knowledge-acquisition components, use of context clues, and use of mediating variables. For example, in the sentence "The blen rises in the east and sets in the west," the knowledge-acquisition component of selective comparison is used to relate prior knowledge about a known concept, the sun, to the unknown word (neologism) in the sentence, "blen." Several context cues appear in the sentence, such as the fact that a blen rises, the fact that it sets, and the information about where it rises and sets. A mediating variable is that the information can occur after the presentation of the unknown word.

We did research such as that just described because we believed that conventional psychometric research sometimes incorrectly attributed individual and developmental differences. For example, a verbal analogies test that might appear on its surface to measure verbal reasoning might in fact measure primarily vocabulary and general information (Sternberg, 1977). In fact, in some populations, reasoning might hardly be a source of individual or developmental differences at all. And if we then look at the sources of the individual differences in vocabulary, we would need to understand that the differences in knowledge did not come from nowhere: Some children had much more frequent and better opportunities to learn word meanings than did others.

The kinds of analytical skills we studied in this research can be taught. For example, in one study, we tested whether it is possible to teach people better to decontextualize meanings of unknown words presented in context (Sternberg, 1987a). In one study, we gave 81 participants in five conditions a pretest on their ability to decontextualize word meanings. Then the participants were divided into five conditions, two of which were control conditions that lacked formal instruction. In one condition, participants were not given any instructional treatment. They were merely asked later to take a posttest. In a second condition, they were given practice as an instructional condition, but there was no formal instruction per se. In a third condition, they were taught knowledge-acquisition component processes that could be used to decontextualize word meanings. In a fourth condition, they were taught to use context cues. In a fifth condition, they were taught to use mediating variables. Participants in all three of the theory-based formal-instructional conditions outperformed participants in the two control conditions, whose performance did not differ. In other words, theory-based instruction was better than no instruction at all or just practice without formal instruction.

Research on the componential bases of intelligence was useful in understanding individual differences in performance on conventional tests of intelligence. But it became increasingly clear to me that this research basically served to partition the variation on conventional tests in a different way, rather than serving to uncover previously untapped sources of variation. Children develop intellectually in ways beyond just what conventional psychometric intelligence tests or even tests based on the theory of Piaget (1972) measure. So what might be some of these other sources of variation in intelligence? Creative intelligence seems to be one such source of variation, a source that is almost wholly untapped by conventional tests.

Creative Intelligence

Intelligence tests contain a range of problems, some of them more novel than others. In some of our work, we have shown that when one goes beyond the range of unconventionality of the tests, one starts to tap sources of individual differences measured little or not at all by the tests. According to the theory of successful intelligence, (creative) intelligence is particularly well measured by problems assessing how well an individual can cope with relative novelty. Thus, it is important to include in a battery of test problems that are relatively novel in nature. These problems can be either convergent or divergent in nature.

In work with convergent problems, we presented 80 individuals with novel kinds of reasoning problems that had a single best answer. For example, they might be told that some objects are green and others blue, but still other objects might be grue, meaning green until the year 2000 and blue thereafter, or bleen, meaning blue until the year 2000 and green thereafter. Or they might be told of four kinds of people on the planet Kyron: blens, who are born young and die young; kwefs, who are born old and die old; balts, who are born young and die old; and prosses, who are born old and die young (Sternberg, 1982; Tetewsky & Sternberg, 1986). Their task was to predict future states from past states, given incomplete information. In another set of studies, 60 people were given more conventional kinds of inductive reasoning problems, such as analogies, series completions, and classifications, but were told to solve them. However, the problems had premises preceding them that were either conventional (dancers wear shoes) or novel (dancers eat shoes). The participants had to solve the problems as though the counterfactuals were true (Sternberg & Gastel, 1989a, 1989b).

In these studies, we found that correlations with conventional kinds of tests depended on how novel or nonentrenched the conventional tests were. The more novel the items, the higher the correlations of our tests with scores on successively more novel conventional tests. Thus, the components isolated for relatively novel items would tend to correlate more highly with more unusual tests of fluid abilities (e.g., that of Cattell & Cattell, 1973) than with tests of crystallized abilities. We also found that when response times on the relatively novel problems were componentially analyzed, some components better measured the creative aspect of intelligence than did others. For example, in the "grue–bleen" task mentioned earlier, the information-processing component requiring people to switch from conventional green–blue thinking to grue–bleen thinking and then back to green–blue thinking again was a particularly good measure of the ability to cope with novelty.

In work with divergent reasoning problems having no one best answer, we asked 63 people to create various kinds of products (Lubart & Sternberg, 1995; Sternberg & Lubart, 1991, 1995, 1996) for which an infinite variety of responses were possible. Individuals were asked to create products in the realms of writing, art, advertising, and science. In writing, they would be asked to write very short stories for which we would give them a choice of titles, such as "Beyond the Edge" or "The Octopus's Sneakers." In art, they were asked to produce art compositions with titles such as "The Beginning of Time" or "Earth From an Insect's Point of View." In advertising, they were asked to produce advertisements for products such as a brand of bow tie or a brand of doorknob. In science, they were asked to solve problems such as one asking them how people might detect extraterrestrial aliens among us who are seeking to escape detection. Participants created two products in each domain.

We found that creativity is relatively, although not wholly, domain specific. Correlations of ratings of the creative quality of the products across domains were lower than correlations of ratings and generally were at about the .4 level. Thus, there was some degree of relation across domains, at the same time that there was plenty of room for someone to be strong in one or more domains but not in others. More important, perhaps, we found, as we had for the convergent problems, a range of correlations with conventional tests of abilities. As was the case for the correlations obtained with convergent problems, correlations were higher to the extent that problems on the conventional tests were nonentrenched. For example, correlations were higher with fluid-ability than with crystallized-ability tests, and correlations were higher the more novel the fluid test was. These results show that tests of creative intelligence have some overlap with conventional tests (e.g., in requiring verbal skills or the ability to analyze one's own ideas; Sternberg & Lubart, 1995) but also tap skills beyond those measured even by relatively novel kinds of items on the conventional tests of intelligence.

The work we did on creativity revealed a number of sources of individual and developmental differences. For example, to what extent was the thinking of the individual novel or nonentrenched? What was the quality of the individual's thinking? To what extent did the thinking of the individual meet the demands of the task?

We also found, though, that creativity, broadly defined, extends beyond the intellectual domain. Sources of individual and developmental differences in creative performance include not only process aspects but aspects of knowledge, thinking styles, personality, motivation, and the environmental context in which the individual operates (see Sternberg & Lubart, 1995, for details).

Creative-thinking skills can be taught, and we have devised a program for teaching them (Sternberg & Williams, 1996). In some of our work, we divided 86 gifted and nongifted fourth-grade children into experimental and control groups. All children took pretests on insightful thinking. Then some of the children received their regular school instruction, whereas others received instruction on insight skills. After the instruction of whichever kind, all children took a posttest on insight skills. We found that children taught how to solve the insight problems using knowledge-acquisition components gained more from pretest to posttest than did students who were not so taught (Davidson & Sternberg, 1984).

Tests of creative intelligence go beyond tests of analytical intelligence in measuring performance on tasks that require individuals to deal with relatively novel situations. At the same time, they probably measure creativity that is, for the most part, within existing paradigms (see Sternberg, 1999a). But how about situations that are relatively familiar, but in a practical rather than an academic domain? Can one measure intelligence in the practical domain, and, if so, what is its relation to intelligence in more academic kinds of domains?

Practical Intelligence

Practical intelligence involves individuals applying their abilities to the kinds of problems that confront them in daily life, such as on the job or in the home. Practical intelligence involves applying the components of intelligence to experience so as to (a) adapt to, (b) shape, and (c) select environments. Adaptation is involved when one changes oneself to suit the environment. Shaping is involved when one changes the environment to suit oneself. And selection is involved when one decides to seek out another environment that is a better match to one's needs, abilities, and desires. People differ in their balance of adaptation, shaping, and selection and in the competence with which they balance the three possible courses of action.

Much of our work on practical intelligence has centered on the concept of tacit knowledge. We define this construct, for our purposes, as what one needs to know to work effectively in an environment that one is not explicitly taught and that often is not even verbalized (Hedlund, Sternberg, Horvath, & Dennis, 1998; Sternberg, Forsythe, et al., 2000; Sternberg & Wagner, 1993; Sternberg, Wagner, & Okagaki, 1993; Sternberg, Wagner, Williams, & Horvath, 1995; Wagner, 1987; Wagner & Sternberg, 1986). We represent tacit knowledge in the form of production systems, or sequences of "if–then" statements that describe procedures one follows in various kinds of everyday situations.

We typically have measured tacit knowledge using work-related problems that one might encounter on the job. We have measured tacit knowledge for children and for adults in various occupations such as management, sales, academia, and the military. In a typical tacit-knowledge problem, people are asked to read a story about a problem someone faces and to rate, for each statement in a set of statements, how adequate a solution the statement represents. For example, in a paper-and-pencil measure of tacit knowledge for sales, one of the problems deals with sales of photocopy machines. A relatively inexpensive machine is not moving out of the show room and has become overstocked. The examinee is asked to rate the quality of various solutions for moving the particular model out of the show room. In a performance-based measure for salespeople, the test taker makes a telephone call to a supposed customer, who is actually the examiner. The test taker tries to sell advertising space over the phone. The examiner raises various objections to buying the advertising space. The test taker is evaluated for the quality, rapidity, and fluency of his or her responses on the telephone.

In our studies, we found that practical intelligence as embodied in tacit knowledge increases with experience, but it is profiting from experience, rather than experience per se, that results in increases in scores. Some people can have been in a job for years and still have acquired relatively little tacit knowledge. We also have found that subscores on tests of tacit knowledge—such as for managing oneself, managing others, and managing tasks—correlate significantly with each other. Moreover, scores on various tests of tacit knowledge, such as for academics and managers, are also correlated fairly substantially (at about the .5 level) with each other. Thus, tests of tacit knowledge may yield a general factor across these tests. However, scores on tacit-knowledge tests do not correlate with scores on conventional tests of intelligence, whether the measures used are single-score measures or multiple-ability batteries. Therefore, any general factor from the tacit-knowledge tests is not the same as any general factor from tests of academic abilities (suggesting that neither kind of g factor is truly general but, rather, general only across a limited range of measuring instruments). Despite the lack of correlation of practical intellectual with conventional measures, the scores on tacit-knowledge tests predict performance on the job as well as or better than do conventional psychometric intelligence tests.

In one study done at the Center for Creative Leadership, we further found that scores on our tests of tacit knowledge for management were the best single predictor of performance on a managerial simulation. In a hierarchical regression, scores on conventional tests of intelligence, personality, styles, and interpersonal orientation were entered first, and scores on the test of tacit knowledge were entered last. Scores on the test of tacit knowledge were the single best predictor of managerial simulation score.

Moreover, they also contributed significantly to the prediction even after everything else was entered first into the equation. In recent work on military leadership (Hedlund et al., 1998), we found that scores of 562 participants on tests of tacit knowledge for military leadership predicted ratings of leadership effectiveness, whereas scores on a conventional test of intelligence and on our tacit-knowledge test for managers did not significantly predict the ratings of effectiveness.

We also have done studies of social intelligence, which is viewed in the theory of successful intelligence as a part of practical intelligence. In these studies, 40 individuals were presented with photos and were asked to make judgments about the photos. In one kind of photo, they were asked to evaluate whether a male–female couple was a genuine couple (i.e., really involved in a romantic relationship) or a phony couple posed by the experimenters. In another kind of photo, they were asked to indicate which of two individuals was the other's supervisor (Barnes & Sternberg, 1989; Sternberg & Smith, 1985). We found female participants to be superior to male participants on these tasks. Scores on the two tasks did not correlate with scores on conventional ability tests, nor did they correlate with each other, suggesting a substantial degree of domain specificity in the task.

Practical-intelligence skills can be taught. We have developed a program for teaching practical intellectual skills, aimed at middle school students, that explicitly teaches students "practical intelligence for school" in the contexts of doing homework, taking tests, reading, and writing (Williams et al., 1996). We have evaluated the program in a variety of settings (Gardner, Krechevsky, Sternberg, & Okagaki, 1994; Sternberg, Okagaki, & Jackson, 1990) and found that students taught via the program outperform students in control groups that did not receive the instruction.

I would add that individuals' use of practical intelligence can be to their own gain in addition to or instead of the gain of others. People can be practically intelligent for themselves at the expense of others. It is for this reason that wisdom needs to be studied in its own right in addition to practical or even successful intelligence (Baltes, 2004; Sternberg, 1998a).

In sum, practical intelligence, like analytical intelligence, is an important antecedent of life success. Because measures of practical intelligence predict everyday behavior at about the same level as do measures of analytical intelligence (and sometimes even better), we believe that the sophisticated use of such tests roughly could double the explained variance in various kinds of criteria of success. Using measures of creative intelligence as well might increase prediction still more. Thus, tests based on the construct of successful intelligence might take us to new and higher levels of prediction. At the same time, expansions of conventional tests that stay within the conventional framework of analytical tests based on standard psychometric models do not seem likely greatly to expand our predictive capabilities (Schmidt & Hunter, 1998). But how did we get to where we are, both with respect to levels of prediction and with respect to the kinds of standard psychometric tests used to attain these levels of prediction?

How We Got to Where We Are

Academic Factors

Large numbers of psychologists, cited in books on the *g* factor, accept the conventional model and tests of intelligence (see Brand, 1996; Jensen, 1998). This support is understandable in view of the overwhelming evidence that (a) conventional tests of intelligence yield a general factor and (b) these tests predict a large variety of outcomes in school, in the workplace, and in other aspects of people's lives (Herrnstein & Murray, 1994). But the argument of this chapter is that the general factor is general only with respect to the academic or analytical aspect of intelligence. Once one includes in an assessment creative and practical abilities, the general factor is greatly diminished or disappears. Moreover, although the conventional tests do have predictive validity for a variety of types of situations, as almost all psychometricians have agreed, so do other types of measures (see Anastasi & Urbina, 1997; Cronbach, 1990). The argument of this essay is not that conventional tests are wrong or somehow inadequate but, rather, that they are incomplete. As Messick (1998) has pointed out, any problems with tests would have to be in the interpretation rather than in the tests themselves. In particular, it is the apparent overinterpretation and overgeneralization of test-score results that is most problematical.

I have argued elsewhere that, in the field of intelligence, it is possible to do more and more research and, in a sense, know less and less, or at least to become more and more confident about incorrect generalizations (Sternberg, 1999b). If we continue to limit the participant populations, material, and empirical methods we use in research on intelligence, we can continue to get support for conventional theories and measures of intelligence. As the earlier literature review should make clear, pointing out the limitations of traditional theories requires the use of broader participant populations, broader types of materials, and new types of measurement techniques.

Societal Factors

If conventional (and even some modern) theories of intelligence are inadequate, how have we gotten to where we are? The United States has developed a multimillion-dollar testing industry whose tests are based on conventional notions of intelligence. It is a curious industry, in many ways. Whereas the ideas generating most technologies have moved forward by leaps and bounds over the last few decades, the testing industry, like its tests, has remained largely (although not entirely) static. For example, the modern versions of the Stanford-Binet Intelligence Tests (Thorndike, Hagen, & Sattler, 1986) or the Wechsler Adult Intelligence Scales (Wechsler, 1997) look amazingly like the original tests, whether of Binet and Simon (1916) or of Wechsler (1939). Thus, whereas old computers and old VCRs and old telephones rapidly go out of date, old tests never seem to die, except for updating of norms and cosmetic changes. There are a few newer and innovative tests (e.g., Kaufman & Kaufman, 1983; Naglieri & Das, 1998), but these tests have not achieved the widespread use of the earlier ones.

Why have conventional tests held on so long? I believe there are several reasons, which I discuss in this section. These reasons are so powerful that they probably will lead to conventional tests holding onto their power into the indefinite future, no matter how inadequate they are.

First, the tests are there; their use is entrenched in the entire country, in testing for mental retardation, learning disabilities, private school admissions, college admissions, graduate school and professional school admissions, and other uses. Any change in the paradigm underlying testing would require a massive reeducation effort. It is not clear who would undertake such an effort or how it would be accomplished.

Second, training in the use of traditional tests is not going away. School psychologists still learn how to use much the same tests school psychologists have learned to use for several decades, with only the editions changing. They may also learn how to use more modern tests, but the testing industry has been rather reluctant to introduce highly innovative changes, so the number of newer options is strictly limited.

Third, not only students but teachers, principals, superintendents, and entire school districts are being judged on the basis of scores on conventional tests. The news magazine *U.S. News and World Report* did more to bolster traditional tests than perhaps has any other single source in the past several decades when it started publishing rankings of undergraduate and graduate institutions based in large part, although certainly not exclusively, on test scores. In consulting with admissions offices at the undergraduate and graduate levels, I have found that these best-selling issues of the magazine have resulted in schools placing even more emphasis on test scores to improve their rankings. Administrators may hate the ranking system, but they are subject to it nevertheless. The problem is not limited to the college and university level. Many states give conventional statewide mastery tests of achievement and publish the results district by district. This publication practice puts pressure on administrators, teachers, and parents to teach in ways that produce higher scores for their children, whether or not these ways of teaching are what the adults perceive as best educationally for the children.

Fourth, the kinds of skills measured by conventional tests do matter for school achievement and, to a lesser extent, for job success. Conventional tests predict roughly 25% of the individual-differences variation in school performance (Anastasi & Urbina, 1997) and perhaps 10% to 15% of the variation in job performance. Although that percentage leaves an extensive amount of variation unaccounted for, it is nevertheless impressive. Moreover, multiple scores from such tests may be useful clinically. As shown earlier, however, the percentage of variance accounted for would probably be substantially lower if instruction and assessment took into account a broader range of skills (Sternberg et al., 1996, 1998a, 1998b). Moreover, if we consider only straightforward memory skills, we need to recognize that these skills are essential antecedents of analytical, creative, and practical thinking. One cannot analyze information if one has no information to analyze. One cannot go beyond the given if one does not know what the given is. One cannot apply what is known if one does not know anything.

At the same time, one might be concerned that the use of tests has become blind. Studies of the validity of these tests for prediction to particular situations are conducted only fairly rarely. It is not enough just to go by studies conducted in another time or another place. For example, we conducted a study of the predictive validity of the Graduate Record Examination (GRE) for predicting graduate success at Yale (Sternberg & Williams, 1997). All matriculants into the graduate program over a 12-year period served as participants. As predictors, we used the verbal, quantitative, analytical, and subject-matter (psychology) tests. As criteria, we used 1st-year and 2nd-year grades; advisors' ratings of students' analytical, creative, and practical abilities; the same advisors' ratings of the students' research and teaching abilities; and the dissertation committee's averaged evaluation of the doctoral dissertation. We found that the GRE was a fairly good predictor of 1st-year grades, in line with what other studies have shown. However, we found that, for women, the GRE significantly predicted nothing else. For men, only the analytical section significantly predicted other criteria, and this prediction was relatively weak, at about the .3 level of correlation. Various corrections for restriction of range improved prediction of 1st-year grades but little else. The predictive validity obtained scarcely seems to justify the costs to students both in time and in money or the weight that universities often put on this test. Of course, results might be different elsewhere where there is a wider range of analytical abilities. But regardless of where the tests are used, closed systems, described next, make the tests look better than they are.

Closed Systems

According to Herrnstein and Murray (1994), conventional tests of intelligence account for about 10% of the variation, on average, in various kinds of real-world outcomes. Although this percentage is not trivial, it is not particularly large either, and one might wonder what all the fuss is about in the use of the tests. Of course, one might argue that Herrnstein and Murray have underestimated the percentage, but given their very enthusiastic support for conventional tests, it seems unlikely they would underestimate the value of the tests.

In fact, I would argue, they may overestimate the value of the tests for predictive purposes. Clearly, the tests have some value. But how much? In their book, Herrnstein and Murray referred to an "invisible hand of nature" guiding events such that people with high IQs tend to rise toward the top socioeconomic strata of a society and people with low IQs tend to fall toward the bottom strata. They present data to support their argument, and indeed it seems likely that although many aspects of their data may be arguable (Fraser, 1995; Jacoby & Glauberman, 1995), this one is not in U.S. society. Lawyers and doctors probably have higher IQs, on average, than do street cleaners, for example.

The problem is that although the data are probably correct, the story about the data probably is not. The United States and other societies have created societies in which test scores matter profoundly. High test scores are needed for placement in higher tracks in elementary and secondary school. They are needed for admission to selective undergraduate programs. They are needed again for admission to selective graduate and professional programs. It is really quite difficult to imagine how one could gain the access routes to many of the highest-paying and most prestigious jobs if one did not test well. Low GRE scores, for example, will tend to exclude one not only from one selective graduate school but from all of the others as well. To the extent that there is error of measurement, it will have comparable effects in many schools. Of course, test scores are not the only criteria used for admission to graduate and professional schools. But they count enough so that if one "bombs" one of the admissions tests, one can bid admission to many selective schools good-bye.

The 10% figure of Herrnstein and Murray implies that there are many able people who are disenfranchised because the kinds of abilities they have, although these abilities might be important for job performance, are not important for test performance. For example, the kinds of creative and practical skills that matter to success on the job typically are not measured on the tests used for admissions. At the same time, society may be overvaluing those who have a fairly narrow range of skills, and a range of skills that may not serve these individuals particularly well on the job, even if they do lead to success in school and on the tests.

It is scarcely surprising that ability tests predict school grades, because the tests originally were explicitly designed for this purpose (Binet & Simon, 1916). In effect, U.S. and other societies have created closed systems: Certain abilities are valued in instruction, such as, memory and analytical abilities. Ability tests are then created that measure these abilities and thus predict school performance. Then assessments of achievement are designed that also assess these abilities. Little wonder that ability tests are more predictive in school than in the workplace: Within the closed system of the school, a narrow range of abilities leads to success on ability tests, in instruction, and on achievement tests. But these same abilities are less important later on in life.

Closed systems can be and have been constructed to value almost any set of attributes at all. In some societies, caste is used. Members of certain castes are allowed to rise to the top; members of other castes have no chance. Of course, the members of the successful castes believe they are getting their due, much as did the nobility in the Middle Ages when they rose to the top and subjugated their serfs. Even in the United States, if one were born a slave in the early 1800s, one's IQ would make little difference: One would die a slave. Slave owners and others rationalized the system, as social Darwinists always have, by believing that the fittest were in the roles they rightfully belonged in.

The mechanism of a closed system can be illustrated by the fact that any attribute at all can be selected for. Suppose one wished to select for height. Only those with the greatest height would be admitted to the most prestigious undergraduate programs. Shorter people would have to enroll in less prestigious places. Elevator shoes, of course, would be forbidden in testing for height, in much the same way that cheating on tests currently is forbidden. Height standards for graduate admissions would be even more rigorous. Eventually one would find that people in the top socioeconomic strata tended to be very tall. In general, closed systems seal off individual options and distort society, depriving many individuals of opportunities they should have. Society is also deprived of their talents. Using conventional intelligence-based measures is probably better than using nose length or many other measures, but society probably can do better by expanding in what it tests.

Lest this all sound hypothetical, it is important to realize that society does, in fact, select for height. Chief executive officers, army generals, and the like tend to be taller than the people whom they supervise. The example of height points out that, regardless of the society, attributes other than intelligence are going to matter for success. These attributes may include height, ethnic group, and interpersonal attractiveness, as well as personal attributes including diverse aspects of personality, motivation, emotion, and so forth. Attributes that have nothing to do with intelligence (at least according to the present and most other definitions) can end up becoming conflated with intelligence. Consider an example.

When I was in Jamaica, I attended classes in a number of one-room elementary schools. In a typical school, there was no barrier separating the many classes in the single room, so the noise level was constantly high. I found myself asking what Binet might have put on his intelligence test if he had formulated his tests for these schools in Jamaica. I concluded that he might have decided to include in his test battery tests of hearing, the skill that seemed most important for hearing both the instruction and the test items, which typically were orally administered. People who heard better fared better, especially if they had the bad fortune to be anywhere but the front center of the classroom. Indeed, when I mentioned this observation in a colloquium, an individual from Guyana commented that she had grown up in similar schools and always wondered why the smartest children sat in the front of the class. In this case, sitting in the front of the class may well have made them appear smart. The teacher probably did not think that good auditory (sensory hearing) abilities were a component of intelligence but easily might have conflated the effects of such abilities with intelligence.

The experience in Jamaica also pointed out one other important fact, namely, that the assumption in much research on intelligence is that every child has an equal chance to succeed on ability tests and in school. In fact, they do not. In a study we did in Jamaica (Sternberg, Powell, McGrane, & Grantham-McGregor, 1997), we examined the effects of intestinal parasitic infections (most often whipworm) on children's cognitive functioning. We knew that children with moderate to high loads of intestinal parasites tended to perform more poorly in school, and we were interested in why. Our study revealed that infected children tended to do more poorly on tests of higher order cognitive abilities, even after controlling for possible confounding variables such as socioeconomic class. The data also revealed that although antiparasitic medication (albendazole) improved physical health, it had no effect on cognitive-ability test scores. Presumably, the deficits that were occurring had built up over many years and were not alleviated by a quick-fix pill. Children who are parasitically infected find it hard to concentrate on their schoolwork because they just do not feel well. Our data showed that the cumulative effect of missing much of what happens in school probably cannot be reversed quickly.

The general conclusion is that societies can and do choose a variety of criteria to sort people. Some societies use caste systems, whether explicit, as in India, or implicit, as in the United States. Others use or have used race, religion, or wealth of parents as bases for sorting. Many societies use a combination of criteria. Once a system is in place, those who gain access to the power structure, whether via their passage through elite education or elsewhere, are likely to look for others like themselves to enter into positions of power. The reason, quite simply, is that there probably is no more powerful basis of interpersonal attraction than similarity (see Sternberg, 1998b); thus, people in a power structure look for others similar to themselves. The result is a potentially endlessly looping closed system that keeps replicating itself.

Conclusions

The time has come to move beyond conventional theories of intelligence. In this chapter, I have provided data suggesting that conventional theories and tests of intelligence are incomplete. The general factor is an artifact of limitations in populations of individuals tested, types of materials with which they are tested, and types of methods used in testing. Indeed, our studies show that even when one wants to predict school performance, the conventional tests are somewhat limited in their predictive validity (Sternberg & Williams, 1997). I have proposed a theory of successful intelligence and its development that fares well in construct validations, whether one tests in the laboratory, in schools, or in the workplace. The greatest obstacle to our moving on is in vested interests, both in academia and in the world of tests, where testing companies are doing well financially with existing tests. We now have ways to move beyond conventional notions of intelligence; we need only the will.

What is especially interesting is that lay conceptions of intelligence are quite a bit broader than psychologists' professional ones (Berry, 1974; Sternberg & Kaufman, 1998). For example, in a study of people's conceptions of intelligence (Sternberg, Conway, Ketron, & Bernstein, 1981; see also Sternberg, 1985b), we found that layperson had a three-factor view of intelligence as comprising practical problem-solving, verbal, and social-competence abilities. Only the first of these abilities is measured by conventional tests. In a study of Taiwanese Chinese conceptions of intelligence (Yang & Sternberg, 1997a, 1997b), we found that although Taiwanese conceptions of intelligence included a cognitive factor, they also included factors of interpersonal competence, intrapersonal competence, intellectual self-assertion, and intellectual self-effacement. In a study of Kenyan conceptions of intelligence (Grigorenko et al., 2001), we found that four distinct terms constitute rural Kenyan conceptions of intelligence—*rieko* (knowledge and skills), *luoro* (respect), *winjo* (comprehension of how to handle real-life problems), and *paro* (initiative)—with only the first directly referring to knowledge-based skills (including but not limited to the academic). Even more important, perhaps, we discovered in a study among different ethnic groups in San Jose, California, that although the 359 parents had different conceptions of intelligence, the more closely their conception matched that of their children's teachers, the better the children did in school (Okagaki & Sternberg, 1993). In other words, teachers value students who do well on the kinds of attributes that the teachers associate with intelligence. The attributes they associate with intelligence are too limited.

In considering the results of implicit-theories research, it is important to remember that implicit theories provide a starting point, not an ending point, for explicit theories (Sternberg, 1985b; Sternberg et al., 1981). In other words, they can suggest directions in which to expand (or, in theory, contract) our notions about intelligence, but they do not directly test those notions per se. The reason, quite simply, is that people's implicit theories may be wrong. There are many historical illustrations of this fact. Implicit theories regarding the reality of phlogiston as the basis of fire provided the incentive for scientifically testing for the existence of phlogiston: These beliefs did not confirm or disconfirm the existence of this substance. Scientific testing of explicit theories was needed to provide such tests.

The time has perhaps come to expand our notion and everyone's notion of what it means to be intelligent. Exactly what kind of expansion should take place? I have suggested here an expansion of the conventional conception of intelligence to include not just memory and analytical abilities but creative and practical abilities as well. My original conceptualization of this expansion derived from personal experience working with students, but the confirmation of its feasibility came from psychometric and experimental studies of its internal and external validity. Other expansions are also possible. For example, research is ongoing with regard to emotional intelligence

(Davies, Stankov, & Roberts, 1998; Mayer, Caruso, & Salovey, 1999), with promising although as yet mixed results. Predictive empirical research, it is hoped, also will be forthcoming regarding the theory of multiple intelligences (Gardner, 1983). Ultimately, the answer to the question of how to expand our conception of intelligence will depend in part on the imagination of theorists, but more important, on the data showing incremental internal and external validity over the conventional notions that have dominated theory and research on intelligence to date. The memory and analytical abilities measured by these tests have been and likely will continue to matter for many forms of success in life. They never have been, and are unlikely ever to be, the only intellectual abilities that matter for success. It is for this reason that we have needed and will continue to need theories such as the theory of successful intelligence.

References

Anastasi, A., & Urbina, S. (1997). *Psychological testing* (7th ed.). Upper Saddle River, NJ: Prentice Hall.

Baltes, P. B. (2004). *Wisdom: The orchestration of mind and virtue.* Berlin: Max Planck Institute for Human Development.

Barnes, M. L., & Sternberg, R. J. (1989). Social intelligence and decoding of nonverbal cues. *Intelligence, 13,* 263–287.

Baron, J. (1978). Intelligence and general strategies. In G. Underwood (Ed.), *Strategies in information processing* (pp. 403–450). London: Academic Press.

Berry, J. W. (1974). Radical cultural relativism and the concept of intelligence. In J. W. Berry & P. R. Dasen (Eds.), *Culture and cognition: Readings in cross-cultural psychology* (pp. 225–229). London: Methuen.

Binet, A., & Simon, T. (1916). *The development of intelligence in children.* Baltimore: Williams & Wilkins.

Bouchard, T. J. (1997). IQ similarity in twins reared apart: Findings and responses to critics. In R. J. Sternberg & E. L. Grigorenko (Eds.), *Intelligence, heredity, and environment* (pp. 126–160). New York: Cambridge University Press.

Brand, C. (1996). *The g factor: General intelligence and its implications.* Chichester, England: Wiley.

Brody, N. (2000). History of theories and measurements of intelligence. In R. J. Sternberg (Ed.), *Handbook of intelligence.* New York: Cambridge University Press.

Brown, A. L., & Ferrara, R. A. (1985). Diagnosing zones of proximal development. In J. V. Wertsch (Ed.), *Culture, communication, and cognition: Vygotskian perspectives* (pp. 273–305). New York: Cambridge University Press.

Budoff, M. (1968). Learning potential as a supplementary assessment procedure. In J. Hellmuth (Ed.), *Learning disorders* (Vol. 3, pp. 295–343). Seattle, WA: Special Child.

Carraher, T. N., Carraher, D., & Schliemann, A. D. (1985). Mathematics in the streets and in schools. *British Journal of Developmental Psychology, 3,* 21–29.

Carroll, J. B. (1993). *Human cognitive abilities: A survey of factor-analytic studies.* New York: Cambridge University Press.

Cattell, R. B. (1971). *Abilities: Their structure, growth and action.* Boston: Houghton Mifflin.

Cattell, R. B., & Cattell, A. K. (1973). *Test of g: Culture Fair, Level 2.* Champaign, IL: Institute for Personality and Ability Testing.

Ceci, S. J. (1990). *On intelligence . . . more or less: A bioecological treatise on intellectual development.* Englewood Cliffs, NJ: Prentice Hall.

Ceci, S. J. (1996). *On intelligence: A bioecological treatise on intellectual development* (expanded ed.). Cambridge, MA: Harvard University Press.

Ceci, S. J., & Liker, J. (1986). Academic and nonacademic intelligence: An experimental separation. In R. J. Sternberg & R. K. Wagner (Eds.), *Practical intelligence: Nature and origins of competence in the everyday world* (pp. 119–142). New York: Cambridge University Press.

Ceci, S. J., & Roazzi, A. (1994). The effects of context on cognition: Postcards from Brazil. In R. J. Sternberg & R. K. Wagner (Eds.), *Mind in context: Interactionist perspectives on human intelligence* (pp. 74–101). New York: Cambridge University Press.

Cronbach, L. J. (1990). *Essentials of psychological testing.* New York: Harper & Row.

Davidson, J. E., & Sternberg, R. J. (1984). The role of insight in intellectual giftedness. *Gifted Child Quarterly, 28,* 58–64.

Davies, M., Stankov, L., & Roberts, R. D. (1998). Emotional intelligence: In search of an elusive construct. *Journal of Personality and Social Psychology, 75,* 985–1015.

Day, J. D., Engelhard, J. L., Maxwell, S. E., & Bolig, E. E. (1997). Comparison of static and dynamic assessment procedures and their relation to independent performance. *Journal of Educational Psychology, 89,* 358–368.

Deary, I. J. (1988). Intelligence and "inspection time." In H. J. Eysenck (Ed.), *A model for intelligence.* Berlin: Springer.

Deary, I. J. (2000). Simple information processing and intelligence. In R. J. Sternberg (Ed.), *Handbook of intelligence* (pp. 267–284). New York: Cambridge University Press.

Detterman, D. K. (1994). A system theory of intelligence. In D. K. Detterman (Ed.), *Current topics in human intelligence: Vol. 4. Theories of intelligence* (pp. 85–115). Norwood, NJ: Ablex.

Embretson, S., & McCollam, K. (2000). Psychometric approaches to the understanding and measurement of intelligence. In R. J. Sternberg (Ed.), *Handbook of intelligence.* New York: Cambridge University Press.

Ericsson, K. A. (Ed.). (1996). *The road to excellence.* Mahwah, NJ: Erlbaum.

Feuerstein, R. (1979). *The dynamic assessment of retarded performers: The learning potential assessment device, theory, instrument, and techniques.* Baltimore: University Park Press.

Flynn, J. R. (1984). The mean IQ of Americans: Massive gains 1932 to 1978. *Psychological Bulletin, 95,* 29–51.

Flynn, J. R. (1987). Massive IQ gains in 14 nations: What IQ tests really measure. *Psychological Bulletin, 101,* 171–191.

Fraser, S. (Ed.). (1995). *The bell curve wars: Race, intelligence and the future of America.* New York: Basic Books.

Gardner, H. (1983). *Frames of mind: The theory of multiple intelligences.* New York: Basic Books.

Gardner, H. (1993). *Multiple intelligences: The theory in practice.* New York: Basic Books.

Gardner, H. (1999). Are there additional intelligences? The case for naturalist, spiritual, and existential intelligences. In J. Kane (Ed.), *Education, information, and transformation* (pp. 111–131). Englewood Cliffs, NJ: Prentice Hall.

Gardner, H., Krechevsky, M., Sternberg, R. J., & Okagaki, L. (1994). Intelligence in context: Enhancing students' practical intelligence for school. In K. McGilly (Ed.), *Classroom lessons: Integrating cognitive theory and classroom practice* (pp. 105–127). Cambridge, MA: Bradford Books.

Grigorenko, E. L., Geissler, W., Prince, R., Okatcha, F., Nokes, C., Kenny, D., Bundy, D., & Sternberg, R. J. (2001). The organization of Luo conceptions of intelligence: A study of implicit theories in a Kenyan village. *International Journal of Behavioral Development, 25,* 367–378.

Grigorenko, E. L., & Sternberg, R. J. (1998). Dynamic assessment. *Psychological Bulletin, 124,* 75–111.

Grigorenko, E. L., & Sternberg, R. J. (2001). Analytical, creative, and practical intelligence as predictors of self-reported adaptive functioning: A case study in Russia. *Intelligence, 29,* 57–73.

Gustafsson, J. E. (1994). Hierarchical models of intelligence and educational achievement. In A. Demetriou & A. Efklides (Eds.), *Intelligence, mind and reasoning: Structure and development* (pp. 45–73). Amsterdam: North-Holland/Elsevier Science.

Guthke, J. (1993). Current trends in theories and assessment of intelligence. In J. H. M. Hamers, K. Sijtsma, & A. J. J. M. Ruijssenaars (Eds.), *Learning potential assessment* (pp. 13–20). Amsterdam: Swets & Zeitlinger.

Guyote, M., & Sternberg, R. J. (1981). A transitive-chain theory of syllogistic reasoning. *Cognitive Psychology, 13,* 461–525.

Haywood, H. C., & Tzuriel, D. (Eds.). (1992). *Interactive assessment.* New York: Springer-Verlag.

Hedlund, J., Sternberg, R. J., Horvath, J. A., & Dennis, M. (1998, April). *The acquisition of tacit knowledge for military leadership: Implications for training.* Paper presented at the Conference of the Society for Industrial and Organizational Psychology, Dallas, TX.

Herrnstein, R. J., & Murray, C. (1994). *The bell curve.* New York: Free Press.

Horn, J. L. (1994). Theory of fluid and crystallized intelligence. In R. J. Sternberg (Ed.), *The encyclopedia of human intelligence* (Vol. 1, pp. 443–451). New York: Macmillan.

Howe, M. J. A., Davidson, J. W., & Sloboda, J. A. (1998). Innate talents: Reality or myth? *Behavioral and Brain Sciences, 21,* 399–442.

Intelligence and its measurement: A symposium. (1921). *Journal of Educational Psychology, 12,* 123–147, 195–216, 271–275.

Jacoby, R., & Glauberman, N. (Eds.). (1995). *The bell curve debate.* New York: Times Books.

Jensen, A. R. (1998). *The g factor: The science of mental ability.* Westport, CT: Praeger/Greenwood.

Kaufman, A., & Kaufman, N. (1983). *Kaufman Assessment Battery for Children (K-ABC)*. Circle Pines, MN: American Guidance Systems.

Kyllonen, P., & Christal, R. (1990). Reasoning ability is (little more than) working-memory capacity?! *Intelligence, 14*, 389–433.

Lave, J. (1988). *Cognition in practice: Mind, mathematics, and culture in everyday life*. New York: Cambridge University Press.

Lidz, C. S. (Ed.). (1987). *Dynamic assessment: An interactional approach to evaluating learning potential.* New York: Guilford Press.

Lidz, C. S. (1991). *Practitioner's guide to dynamic assessment*. New York: Guilford Press.

Lubart, T. I., & Sternberg, R. J. (1995). An investment approach to creativity: Theory and data. In S. M. Smith, T. B. Ward, & R. A. Finke (Eds.), *The creative cognition approach* (pp. 269–302). Cambridge, MA: MIT Press.

Mayer, J. D., Caruso, D. R., & Salovey, P. (1999). Emotional intelligence meets traditional standards for an intelligence. *Intelligence, 27*, 267–298.

Messick, S. J. (1998). Alternative modes of assessment, uniform standards of validity. In M. D. Hakel (Ed.), *Beyond multiple choice* (pp. 59–74). Mahwah, NJ: Erlbaum.

Naglieri, J., & Das, J. P. (1998). *Das–Naglieri Cognitive Assessment System (CAS)*. Itasca, IL: Riverside.

Neisser, U. (Ed.). (1998). *The rising curve*. Washington, DC: American Psychological Association.

Nunes, T. (1994). Street intelligence. In R. J. Sternberg (Ed.), *Encyclopedia of human intelligence* (Vol. 2, pp. 1045–1049). New York: Macmillan.

Nunes, T., Schliemann, A. D., & Carraher, D. W. (1993). *Street mathematics and school mathematics*. New York: Cambridge University Press.

Okagaki, L., & Sternberg, R. J. (1993). Parental beliefs and children's school performance. *Child Development, 64*, 36–56.

Perkins, D. N. (1995). *Outsmarting IQ: The emerging science of learnable intelligence*. New York: Free Press.

Piaget, J. (1972). *The psychology of intelligence*. Totowa, NJ: Littlefield Adams.

Plomin, R. (1997). Identifying genes for cognitive abilities and disabilities. In R. J. Sternberg & E. L. Grigorenko (Eds.), *Intelligence, heredity, and environment* (pp. 89–104). New York: Cambridge University Press.

Raven, J. C. (1958). *Guide to using the Coloured Progressive Matrices*. London: H. R. Lewis.

Raven, J. C., Court, J. H., & Raven, J. (1992). *Manual for Raven's Progressive Matrices and Mill Hill Vocabulary Scale*. Oxford, England: Oxford Psychologists Press.

Rogoff, B. (1990). *Apprenticeship in thinking: Cognitive development in social context*. New York: Oxford University Press.

Scarr, S. (1997). Behavior-genetic and socialization theories of intelligence: Truce and reconciliation. In R. J. Sternberg & E. L. Grigorenko (Eds.), *Intelligence, heredity and environment* (pp. 3–41). New York: Cambridge University Press.

Schmidt, F., & Hunter, J. (1998). The validity and utility of selection methods in personnel psychology: Practical and theoretical implications of 85 years of research findings. *Psychological Bulletin, 124*, 262–274.

Snow, R. E. (1979). Theory and method for research on aptitude processes. In R. J. Sternberg & D. K. Detterman (Eds.), *Human intelligence: Perspectives on its theory and measurement* (pp. 105–137). Norwood, NJ: Ablex.

Spearman, C. E. (1904). "General intelligence" objectively determined and measured. *American Journal of Psychology, 15*, 201–293.

Sternberg, R. J. (1977). *Intelligence, information processing, and analogical reasoning: The componential analysis of human abilities*. Hillsdale, NJ: Erlbaum.

Sternberg, R. J. (1980a). Representation and process in linear syllogistic reasoning. *Journal of Experimental Psychology: General, 109*, 119–159.

Sternberg, R. J. (1980b). Sketch of a componential subtheory of human intelligence. *Behavioral and Brain Sciences, 3*, 573–584.

Sternberg, R. J. (1981). Intelligence and nonentrenchment. *Journal of Educational Psychology, 73*, 1–16.

Sternberg, R. J. (1982). Natural, unnatural, and supernatural concepts. *Cognitive Psychology, 14*, 451–488.

Sternberg, R. J. (1983). Components of human intelligence. *Cognition, 15*, 1–48.

Sternberg, R. J. (1984). Toward a triarchic theory of human intelligence. *Behavioral and Brain Sciences, 7*, 269–287.

Sternberg, R. J. (1985a). *Beyond IQ: A triarchic theory of human intelligence*. New York: Cambridge University Press.

Sternberg, R. J. (1985b). Implicit theories of intelligence, creativity, and wisdom. *Journal of Personality and Social Psychology, 49,* 607–627.

Sternberg, R. J. (1987a). Most vocabulary is learned from context. In M. G. McKeown & M. E. Curtis (Eds.), *The nature of vocabulary acquisition* (pp. 89–105). Hillsdale, NJ: Erlbaum.

Sternberg, R. J. (1987b). The psychology of verbal comprehension. In R. Glaser (Ed.), *Advances in instructional psychology* (Vol. 3, pp. 97–151). Hillsdale, NJ: Erlbaum.

Sternberg, R. J. (1990). *Metaphors of mind: Conceptions of the nature of intelligence.* New York: Cambridge University Press.

Sternberg, R. J. (1993). *Sternberg Triarchic Abilities Test (STAT).* Unpublished test.

Sternberg, R. J. (Ed.). (1994). *Encyclopedia of human intelligence.* New York: Macmillan.

Sternberg, R. J. (1995). *In search of the human mind.* Orlando, FL: Harcourt Brace.

Sternberg, R. J. (1997). *Successful intelligence.* New York: Plume.

Sternberg, R. J. (1998a). A balance theory of wisdom. *Review of General Psychology, 2,* 347–365.

Sternberg, R. J. (1998b). *Cupid's arrow.* New York: Cambridge University Press.

Sternberg, R. J. (1999a). A propulsion model of creative contributions. *Review of General Psychology, 3,* 83–100.

Sternberg, R. J. (1999b). Human intelligence: A case study of how more and more research can lead us to know less and less about a psychological phenomenon, until finally we know much less than we did before we started doing research. In E. Tulving (Ed.), *Memory, consciousness, and the brain. The Tallinn Conference* (pp. 363–373). Philadelphia: Psychology Press.

Sternberg, R. J. (Ed.). (2000). *Handbook of intelligence.* New York: Cambridge University Press.

Sternberg, R. J., Castejón, J. L., Prieto, M. D., Hautamäki, J., & Grigorenko, E. L. (2001). Confirmatory factor analysis of the Sternberg triarchic abilities test in three international samples: An empirical test of the triarchic theory of intelligence. *European Journal of Psychological Assessment, 17*(1), 1–16.

Sternberg, R. J., & Clinkenbeard, P. R. (1995). A triarchic model of identifying, teaching, and assessing gifted children. *Roeper Review, 17,* 255–260.

Sternberg, R. J., Conway, B. E., Ketron, J. L., & Bernstein, M. (1981). People's conceptions of intelligence. *Journal of Personality and Social Psychology, 41,* 37–55.

Sternberg, R. J., & Detterman, D. K. (Eds.). (1986). *What is intelligence? Contemporary viewpoints on its nature and definition.* Norwood, NJ: Ablex.

Sternberg, R. J., Ferrari, M., Clinkenbeard, P. R., & Grigorenko, E. L. (1996). Identification, instruction, and assessment of gifted children: A construct validation of a triarchic model. *Gifted Child Quarterly, 40,* 129–137.

Sternberg, R. J., Forsythe, G. B., Horvath, J., Hedlund, J., Snook, S., Williams, W. M., Wagner, R. K., & Grigorenko, E. L. (2000). *Practical intelligence in everyday life.* New York: Cambridge University Press.

Sternberg, R. J., & Gardner, M. K. (1983). Unities in inductive reasoning. *Journal of Experimental Psychology: General, 112,* 80–116.

Sternberg, R. J., & Gastel, J. (1989a). Coping with novelty in human intelligence: An empirical investigation. *Intelligence, 13,* 187–197.

Sternberg, R. J., & Gastel, J. (1989b). If dancers ate their shoes: Inductive reasoning with factual and counterfactual premises. *Memory & Cognition, 17,* 1–10.

Sternberg, R. J., & Grigorenko, E. L. (1997). The cognitive costs of physical and mental ill health: Applying the psychology of the developed world to the problems of the developing world. *Eye on Psi Chi, 2,* 20–27.

Sternberg, R. J., Grigorenko, E. L., Ferrari, M., & Clinkenbeard, P. (1999). A triarchic analysis of an aptitude interaction. *European Journal of Psychological Assessment, 15,* 1–11.

Sternberg, R. J., Grigorenko, E. L., Ngorosho, D., Tantubuye, E., Mbise, A., Nokes, C., Jukes, M., & Bundy, D. A. (2002). Assessing intellectual potential in rural Tanzanian school children. *Intelligence, 30,* 141–162.

Sternberg, R. J., & Kalmar, D. A. (1997). When will the milk spoil? Everyday induction in human intelligence. *Intelligence, 25,* 185–203.

Sternberg, R. J., & Kaufman, J. C. (1998). Human abilities. *Annual Review of Psychology, 49,* 479–502.

Sternberg, R. J., & Lubart, T. I. (1991). An investment theory of creativity and its development. *Human Development, 34,* 1–31.

Sternberg, R. J., & Lubart, T. I. (1995). *Defying the crowd: Cultivating creativity in a culture of conformity.* New York: Free Press.

Sternberg, R. J., & Lubart, T. I. (1996). Investing in creativity. *American Psychologist, 51,* 677–688.

Sternberg, R. J., & Nigro, G. (1980). Developmental patterns in the solution of verbal analogies. *Child Development, 51,* 27–38.

Sternberg, R. J., Nokes, K., Geissler, P. W., Prince, R., Okatcha, F., Bundy, D. A., & Grigorenko, E. L. (2001). The relationship between academic and practical intelligence: A case study in Kenya. *Intelligence, 29,* 401–418.

Sternberg, R. J., Okagaki, L., & Jackson, A. (1990). Practical intelligence for success in school. *Educational Leadership, 48,* 35–39.

Sternberg, R. J., & Powell, J. S. (1982). Theories of intelligence. In R. J. Sternberg (Ed.), *Handbook of human intelligence* (pp. 975–1005). New York: Cambridge University Press.

Sternberg, R. J., Powell, J. S., & Kaye, D. B. (1982). The nature of verbal comprehension. *Poetics, 11,* 155–187.

Sternberg, R. J., Powell, C., McGrane, P. A., & Grantham-McGregor, S. (1997). Effects of a parasitic infection on cognitive functioning. *Journal of Experimental Psychology: Applied, 3,* 67–76.

Sternberg, R. J., & Rifkin, B. (1979). The development of analogical reasoning processes. *Journal of Experimental Child Psychology, 27,* 195–232.

Sternberg, R. J., & Smith, C. (1985). Social intelligence and decoding skills in nonverbal communication. *Social Cognition, 2,* 168–192.

Sternberg, R. J., Torff, B., & Grigorenko, E. L. (1998a). Teaching for successful intelligence raises school achievement. *Phi Delta Kappan, 79,* 667–669.

Sternberg, R. J., Torff, B., & Grigorenko, E. L. (1998b). Teaching triarchically improves school achievement. *Journal of Educational Psychology, 90,* 374–384.

Sternberg, R. J., & Wagner, R. K. (1993). The geocentric view of intelligence and job performance is wrong. *Current Directions in Psychological Science, 2,* 1–4.

Sternberg, R. J., Wagner, R. K., & Okagaki, L. (1993). Practical intelligence: The nature and role of tacit knowledge in work and at school. In H. Reese & J. Puckett (Eds.), *Advances in lifespan development* (pp. 205–227). Hillsdale, NJ: Erlbaum.

Sternberg, R. J., Wagner, R. K., Williams, W. M., & Horvath, J. A. (1995). Testing common sense. *American Psychologist, 50,* 912–927.

Sternberg, R. J., & Williams, W. M. (1996). *How to develop student creativity.* Alexandria, VA: Association for Supervision and Curriculum Development.

Sternberg, R. J., & Williams, W. M. (1997). Does the Graduate Record Examination predict meaningful success in the graduate training of psychologists? A case study. *American Psychologist, 52,* 630–641.

Tetewsky, S. J., & Sternberg, R. J. (1986). Conceptual and lexical determinants of nonentrenched thinking. *Journal of Memory and Language, 25,* 202–225.

Thorndike, R. L., Hagen, E. P., & Sattler, J. M. (1986). *Technical manual for the Stanford-Binet Intelligence Scale: Fourth edition.* Chicago: Riverside.

Thurstone, L. L. (1938). *Primary mental abilities.* Chicago: University of Chicago Press.

Tzuriel, D. (1995). *Dynamic-interactive assessment: The legacy of L. S. Vygotsky and current developments.* Unpublished manuscript.

Vernon, P. A., Wickett, J., Bazana, P. G., & Stelmack, R. (2000). The neuropsychology and psychophysiology of intelligence. In R. J. Sternberg (Ed.), *Handbook of intelligence* (pp. 245–264). New York: Cambridge University Press.

Vernon, P. E. (1971). *The structure of human abilities.* London: Methuen.

Vygotsky, L. (1978). *Mind in society: The development of higher order processes.* Cambridge, MA: Harvard University Press.

Wagner, R. K. (1987). Tacit knowledge in everyday intelligent behavior. *Journal of Personality and Social Psychology, 52,* 1236–1247.

Wagner, R. K., & Sternberg, R. J. (1986). Tacit knowledge and intelligence in the everyday world. In R. J. Sternberg & R. K. Wagner (Eds.), *Practical intelligence: Nature and origins of competence in the everyday world* (pp. 51–83). New York: Cambridge University Press.

Wechsler, D. (1939). *The measurement of adult intelligence.* Baltimore: Williams & Wilkins.

Wechsler, D. (1997). *Manual for the Wechsler Adult Intelligence Scales (WAIS-III).* San Antonio, TX: Psychological Corporation.

Williams, W. M., Blythe, T., White, N., Li, J., Sternberg, R. J., & Gardner, H. I. (1996). *Practical intelligence for school: A handbook for teachers of Grades 5-8.* New York: HarperCollins.

Yang, S., & Sternberg, R. J. (1997a). Conceptions of intelligence in ancient Chinese philosophy. *Journal of Theoretical and Philosophical Psychology, 17,* 101–119.

Yang, S., & Sternberg, R. J. (1997b). Taiwanese Chinese people's conceptions of intelligence. *Intelligence, 25,* 21–36.

Components of Successful Intelligence: Creativity, Practical Intelligence, and Analytic Reasoning

The Nature of Creativity

4

Robert J. Sternberg

The field of creativity as it exists today emerged largely as a result of the pioneering efforts of J. P. Guilford (1950) and E. Paul Torrance (1962, 1974). It is wholly fitting to dedicate this essay to Torrance because of his seminal contributions to thinking about creativity. To this day, the Torrance Tests of Creative Thinking (Torrance, 1974) remain the most widely used assessments of creative talent.

Guilford and Torrance had many more agreements than disagreements about the nature of creativity and the ways to measure it. Both were basically psychometric theorists and conceived of and attempted to measure creativity from a psychometric standpoint. However, both were broad thinkers, and their conceptions were much more expansive than the operationalizations of these conceptions through their tests. Both concentrated on divergent thinking as the basis of creativity and devised tests that emphasized the assessment of divergent thinking. Both left behind numerous students and disciples to carry on their pioneering work. Torrance, in particular, was a warm, caring, and positive person. I met him only a few times, but I was enormously impressed with the modesty he displayed, given his preeminence in the field. He showed that the best people in the field have no need for the pretensions to which less-distinguished academics can be so susceptible.

There are a number of different approaches one can take to understanding creativity. Torrance preferred a psychometric approach to understanding creativity. My colleagues and I (e.g., Sternberg, Kaufman, & Pretz, 2002; Sternberg & Lubart, 1995, 1996) have chosen to use a confluence approach as a basis for our work on creativity. I will discuss two of the theories underlying our work and some of the empirical work we have done to test our ideas. These theories are part of a more general theory—WICS—of wisdom, intelligence, and creativity synthesized (Sternberg, 2003b).

The Investment Theory of Creativity

Our investment theory of creativity (Sternberg & Lubart, 1991, 1995) is a confluence theory according to which creative people are those who are willing and able to "buy low and sell high" in the realm of ideas (see also Rubenson & Runco, 1992, for the use of concepts from economic theory). Buying low means pursuing ideas that are unknown or out of favor but that have growth potential. Often, when these ideas are first presented, they encounter resistance. The creative individual persists in the face of this resistance and eventually sells high, moving on to the next new or unpopular idea.

Aspects of the Investment Theory

According to the investment theory, creativity requires a confluence of six distinct but interrelated resources: intellectual abilities, knowledge, styles of thinking, personality, motivation, and environment. Although levels of these resources are sources of individual differences, often the decision to use a resource is a more important source of individual differences. In the following sections, I discuss the resources and the role of decision making in each.

Intellectual Skills

Three intellectual skills are particularly important (Sternberg, 1985): (a) the synthetic skill to see problems in new ways and to escape the bounds of conventional thinking, (b) the analytic skill to recognize which of one's ideas are worth pursuing and which are not, and (c) the practical–contextual skill to know how to persuade others of—to sell other people on—the value of one's ideas. The confluence of these three skills is also important. Analytic skills used in the absence of the other two skills results in powerful critical, but not creative, thinking. Synthetic skill used in the absence of the other two skills results in new ideas that are not subjected to the scrutiny required to improve them and make them work. Practical–contextual skill in the absence of the other two skills may result in societal acceptance of ideas not because the ideas are good, but rather, because the ideas have been well and powerfully presented.

We tested the role of creative intelligence in creativity in several studies. In one study, we presented 80 people with novel kinds of reasoning problems that had a single best answer. For example, they might be told that some objects are green and others blue; but still other objects might be grue, meaning green until the year 2000 and blue thereafter, or bleen, meaning blue until the year 2000 and green thereafter. Or they might be told of four kinds of people on the planet Kyron—blens, who are born young and die young; kwefs, who are born old and die old; balts, who are born young and die old; and prosses, who are born old and die young (Sternberg, 1982; Tetewsky & Sternberg, 1986). Their task was to predict future states from past states, given incomplete information. In another set of studies, 60 people were given more conventional kinds of inductive reasoning problems, such as analogies, series completions, and classifications, but were told to solve them. However, the problems had premises preceding them that were either conventional (dancers wear shoes) or novel (dancers eat shoes). The participants had to solve the problems as though the counterfactuals were true (Sternberg & Gastel, 1989a, 1989b).

In these studies, we found that correlations with conventional kinds of tests depended on how novel or nonentrenched the conventional tests were. The more novel the items, the higher the correlations of our tests, with scores on successively more novel conventional tests. Thus, the components isolated for relatively novel items would tend to correlate more highly with more unusual tests of fluid abilities (e.g., that of Cattell & Cattell, 1973) than with tests of crystallized abilities. We also found that when response times on the relatively novel problems were componentially analyzed, some components better measured the creative aspect of intelligence than did others. For example, in the "grue–bleen" task mentioned earlier, the information-processing component requiring people to switch from conventional green–blue thinking to grue–bleen thinking and then back to green–blue thinking again was a particularly good measure of the ability to cope with novelty.

In another study, we looked at predictions for everyday kinds of situations, such as when milk will spoil (Sternberg & Kalmar, 1997). In this study, we looked at both predictions and postdictions (hypotheses about the past in which information about the past is unknown) and found that postdictions took longer to make than did predictions. Novel predictions and postdictions are more challenging and time-consuming than simpler ones.

Creativity and simply thinking in novel ways are facilitated when people are willing to put in up-front time to think in new ways. We found that better thinkers tend to spend relatively more time than do poorer reasoners in global, up-front metacomponential planning when they solve difficult, novel-reasoning problems. Poorer reasoners, conversely, tend to spend relatively more time in local planning (Sternberg, 1981). Presumably, the better thinkers recognize that it is better to invest more time up front so as to be able to process a problem more efficiently later on.

Knowledge

On the one hand, one needs to know enough about a field to move it forward. One cannot move beyond where a field is if one does not know where it is. On the other hand, knowledge about a field can result in a closed and entrenched perspective, resulting in a person's not moving beyond the way in which he or she has seen problems in the past. Knowledge thus can help, or it can hinder creativity.

In a study of expert and novice bridge players, for example (Frensch & Sternberg, 1989), we found that experts outperformed novices under regular circumstances. When a superficial change was made in the surface structure of the game, the experts and novices were both hurt slightly in their playing, but they quickly recovered. When a profound, deep-structural change was made in the structure of the game, the experts initially were hurt more than the novices, but the experts later recovered. The reason, presumably, is that experts make more and deeper use of the existing structure and hence have to reformulate their thinking more than novices do when there is a deep-structural change in the rules of the game. Thus, one needs to decide to use one's past knowledge.

Thinking Styles

Thinking styles are preferred ways of using one's skills. In essence, they are *decisions* about how to deploy the skills available to a person. With regard to thinking styles, a legislative style is particularly important for creativity (Sternberg, 1988, 1997a), that is, a preference for thinking and a decision to think in new ways. This preference needs to be distinguished from the ability to think creatively: Someone may like to think along new lines, but not think well, or vice versa. It also helps to become a major creative thinker, if one is able to think globally as well as locally, distinguishing the forest from the trees and thereby recognizing which questions are important and which ones are not.

In our research (Sternberg, 1997b; Sternberg & Grigorenko, 1995), we found that legislative people tend to be better students than less legislative people, if the schools in which they study value creativity. If the schools do not value or devalue creativity, they tend to be worse students. Students also were found to receive higher grades from teachers whose own styles of thinking matched their own.

Personality

Numerous research investigations (summarized in Lubart, 1994, and Sternberg & Lubart, 1991, 1995) have supported the importance of certain personality attributes for creative functioning. These attributes include, but are not limited to, willingness to overcome obstacles, willingness to take sensible risks, willingness to tolerate ambiguity, and self-efficacy. In particular, buying low and selling high typically means defying the crowd, so that one has to be willing to stand up to conventions if one wants to think and act in creative ways (Sternberg, 2003a; Sternberg & Lubart, 1995). Often creative people seek opposition; that is, they decide to think in ways that countervail how others think. Note that none of the attributes of creative thinking is fixed. One can *decide* to overcome obstacles, take sensible risks, and so forth.

In one study (Lubart & Sternberg, 1995), we found that greater risk-taking propensity was associated with creativity for artwork but not for essays. When we investigated why this was so, we found that some evaluators tended to mark down essays that took unpopular positions. We learned, therefore, that one of the risks people face when they are creative, even in an experiment on risk taking, is that the evaluators will not appreciate the risks if they go against their own beliefs!

Motivation

Intrinsic, task-focused motivation is also essential to creativity. The research of Amabile (1983) and others has shown the importance of such motivation for creative work and has suggested that people rarely do truly creative work in an area unless they really love what they are doing and focus on the work rather than the potential rewards. Motivation is not something inherent in a person: One *decides* to be motivated by one thing or another. Often, people who need to work in a certain area that does not particularly interest them will decide that, given the need to work in that area, they had better find a way to make it interest them. They will then look for some angle on the work they need to do that makes this work appeal to rather than bore them.

Environment

Finally, one needs an environment that is supportive and rewarding of creative ideas. One could have all of the internal resources needed to think creatively, but without some environmental support (such as a forum for proposing those ideas), the creativity that a person has within him or her might never be displayed.

Environments typically are not fully supportive of the use of one's creativity. The obstacles in a given environment may be minor, as when an individual receives negative feedback on his or her creative thinking, or major, as when one's well-being or even life are threatened if one thinks in a manner that defies convention. The individual therefore must *decide* how to respond in the face of the nearly omnipresent environmental challenges that exist. Some people let unfavorable forces in the environment block their creative output; others do not.

Part of the environment is determined by who is doing the evaluating. In our studies (Lubart & Sternberg, 1995), we had creative products of people of different ages rated for their creativity by raters of different age cohorts. We found informal evidence of cohort matching—that is, raters tended to rate as more creative products of creators of roughly their own age cohort. For example, people will often tend to prefer the popular music of the generation in which they grew up as early adolescents more than the popular music of the generation in which their parents or children grew up. Thus, part of what may determine growth patterns of creativity (Simonton, 1994) is in changing criteria for evaluations of creativity on the part of raters.

Confluence

Concerning the confluence of these six components, creativity is hypothesized to involve more than a simple sum of a person's level on each component. First, there may be thresholds for some components (e.g., knowledge) below which creativity is not possible regardless of the levels on other components. Second, partial compensation may occur in which a strength on one component (e.g., motivation) counteracts a weakness on another component (e.g., environment). Third, interactions may occur between components, such as intelligence and motivation, in which high levels on both components could multiplicatively enhance creativity.

Creative ideas are both novel and valuable. However, they are often rejected when the creative innovator stands up to vested interests and defies the crowd (cf. Csikszentmihalyi, 1988). The crowd does not maliciously or willfully reject creative notions. Rather, it does not realize, and often does not want to realize, that the proposed idea represents a valid and advanced way of thinking. Society often perceives opposition to the status quo as annoying, offensive, and reason enough to ignore innovative ideas.

Evidence abounds that creative ideas are often rejected (Sternberg & Lubart, 1995). Initial reviews of major works of literature and art are often negative. Toni Morrison's *Tar Baby* received negative reviews when it was first published, as did Sylvia Plath's *The Bell Jar*. The first exhibition in Munich of the work of Norwegian painter Edvard Munch opened and closed the same day because of the strong negative response from the critics. Some of the greatest scientific articles have been rejected not just by one but by several journals before being published. For example, John Garcia, a distinguished biopsychologist, was immediately denounced when he first proposed that a form of learning called classical conditioning could be produced in a single trial of learning (Garcia & Koelling, 1966).

From the investment view, then, the creative person buys low by presenting an idea that initially is not valued and then attempting to convince other people of its value. After convincing others that the idea is valuable, which increases the perceived value of the investment, the creative person sells high by leaving the idea to others and moving on to another idea. People typically want others to love their ideas, but immediate universal applause for an idea often indicates that it is not particularly creative.

The Role of Decision Making

Creativity, according to the investment theory, is in large part a decision. The view of creativity as a decision suggests that creativity can be developed. Simply requesting that students be more creative can render them more creative if they believe that the decision to be creative will be rewarded rather than punished (O'Hara & Sternberg, 2000–2001).

To be creative one must first *decide* to generate new ideas, analyze these ideas, and sell the ideas to others. In other words, a person may have synthetic, analytical, or practical skills but not apply them to problems that potentially involve creativity. For example, one may decide (a) to follow other people's ideas rather than synthesize one's own, (b) not to subject one's ideas to a careful evaluation, or (c) to expect other people to listen to one's ideas and therefore decide not to try to persuade other people of the value of these ideas. The skill is not enough: One first needs to make the decision to use the skill.

For example, ability to switch between conventional and unconventional modes of thinking is important to creativity. One aspect of switching between conventional and unconventional thinking is the decision that one is willing and able to think in unconventional ways—that one is willing to accept thinking in terms different from those to which one is accustomed and with which one feels comfortable. People show reliable individual differences in willingness to do so (Dweck, 1999). Some people (whom Dweck calls "entity theorists") prefer to operate primarily or even exclusively in domains that are relatively familiar to them. Other people (whom Dweck calls "incremental theorists") seek out new challenges and new conceptual domains within which to work. I have proposed a number of different decisions by which one can develop one's own creativity as a decision (Sternberg, 2001): (a) redefine problems, (b) question and analyze assumptions, (c) do not assume that creative ideas sell themselves: sell them, (d) encourage the generation of ideas, (e) recognize that knowledge can both help and hinder creativity, (f) identify and surmount obstacles, (g) take sensible risks, (h) tolerate ambiguity, (i) believe in oneself (self-efficacy), (j) find what one loves to do, (k) delay gratification, (l) role-model creativity, (m) cross-fertilize ideas, (n) reward creativity, (o) allow mistakes, (p) encourage collaboration, (q) see things from others' points of view, (r) take responsibility for successes and failures, (s) maximize person–environment fit, (t) continue to allow intellectual growth.

Evidence Regarding the Investment Theory

Assessment

Research within the investment framework has yielded support for this model (Lubart & Sternberg, 1995). This research has used tasks such as (a) writing short stories using unusual titles (e.g., the octopus' sneakers), (b) drawing pictures with unusual themes (e.g., the earth from an insect's point of view), (c) devising creative advertisements for boring products (e.g., cufflinks), and (d) solving unusual scientific problems (e.g., how could we tell if someone had been on the moon within the past month?). Our measures have the same goal as Torrance's do, but we attempt to use tasks that are more oriented toward what people do in school and in the real world when they think creatively. This research showed creative performance to be moderately domain specific and to be predicted by a combination of certain resources, as described as follows. The exact blend of resources and the success with which these resources are blended may vary from one culture to another. For example, Niu and Sternberg (2001) found that both American and Chinese evaluators rated two distinct artistic products (collages and science fiction characters) of American college students to be more creative than products of Chinese college students roughly matched for conventional intelligence (Niu & Sternberg, 2001). This finding held up regardless of whether the raters were American or Chinese.

One concern we have is whether creative skills can be measured in a way that is distinct from the way g-based analytical skills are measured, as well as the practical skills that, together with the analytical and creative ones, combine into my theory of successful intelligence.

In one study (Sternberg, Grigorenko, Ferrari, & Clinkenbeard, 1999), we used the so-called Sternberg Triarchic Abilities Test (STAT; Sternberg, 1993) to investigate the relations among the three abilities. Three hundred twenty-six high school students, primarily from diverse parts of the United States, took the test, which consisted of 12 subtests in all. There were four subtests, each measuring analytical, creative, and practical abilities. For each type of ability, there were three multiple-choice tests and one essay test. The multiple-choice tests, in turn, involved, respectively, verbal, quantitative, and figural content. Consider the content of each test:

1. Analytical–Verbal: Figuring out meanings of neologisms (artificial words) from natural contexts. Students see a novel word embedded in a paragraph and have to infer its meaning from the context.
2. Analytical–Quantitative: Number series. Students have to say what number should come next in a series of numbers.
3. Analytical–Figural: Matrices. Students see a figural matrix with the lower right entry missing. They have to say which of the options fits into the missing space.
4. Practical–Verbal: Everyday reasoning. Students are presented with a set of everyday problems in the life of an adolescent and have to select the option that best solves each problem.
5. Practical–Quantitative: Everyday math. Students are presented with scenarios requiring the use of math in everyday life (e.g., buying tickets for a ballgame) and have to solve math problems based on the scenarios.
6. Practical–Figural: Route planning. Students are presented with a map of an area (e.g., an entertainment park) and have to answer questions about navigating effectively through the area depicted by the map.

7. Creative–Verbal: Novel analogies. Students are presented with verbal analogies preceded by counterfactual premises (e.g., money falls off trees). They have to solve the analogies as though the counterfactual premises were true.
8. Creative–Quantitative: Novel number operations. Students are presented with rules for novel number operations, for example, "flix," which involves numerical manipulations that differ as a function of whether the first of two operands is greater than, equal to, or less than the second. Participants have to use the novel number operations to solve presented math problems.
9. Creative–Figural: In each item, participants are first presented with a figural series that involves one or more transformations; they then have to apply the rule of the series to a new figure with a different appearance, and complete the new series.

We found that a confirmatory factor analysis on the data was supportive of the triarchic theory of human intelligence, yielding separate and uncorrelated analytical, creative, and practical factors. The lack of correlation was caused by the inclusion of essay as well as multiple-choice subtests. Although multiple-choice tests tended to correlate substantially with multiple-choice tests, their correlations with essay tests were much weaker. We found the multiple-choice analytical subtest to load most highly on the analytical factor, but the essay creative and performance subtests loaded most highly on their respective factors. Thus, measurement of creative and practical abilities probably should be accomplished with other kinds of testing instruments that complement multiple-choice instruments. In sum, creative skills could be measured separately from analytical and practical ones.

In a second and separate study, conducted with 240 freshman-year high school students in the United States, Finland, and Spain, we used the multiple-choice section of that STAT to compare five alternative models of intelligence, again via confirmatory factor analysis. A model featuring a general factor of intelligence fit the data relatively poorly. The triarchic model, allowing for intercorrelation among the analytic, creative, and practical factors, provided the best fit to the data (Sternberg, Castejón, Prieto, Hautamäki, & Grigorenko, 2001).

In a third study, we tested 511 Russian schoolchildren (ranging in age from 8 to 17 years) as well as 490 mothers and 328 fathers of these children (Grigorenko & Sternberg, 2001). We used entirely distinct measures of analytical, creative, and practical intelligence. Consider, for example, the tests we used for adults. Similar tests were used for children.

We measured fluid intelligence using standard measures. The measure of creative intelligence also consisted of two parts. The first part asked the participants to describe the world through the eyes of insects. The second part asked participants to describe who might live and what might happen on a planet called "Priumliava." No additional information on the nature of the planet was specified. Each part of the test was scored in three different ways to yield three different scores. The first score was for originality (novelty), the second was for the amount of development in the plot (quality), and the third score was for creative use of prior knowledge in these relatively novel kinds of tasks (sophistication). The measure of practical intelligence was self-report and also comprised two parts. The first part was designed as a 20-item, self-report instrument, assessing practical skills in the social domain (e.g., effective and successful communication with other people), in the family domain (e.g., how to fix household items, how to run the family budget), and in the domain of effective resolution of sudden problems (e.g., organizing something that has become chaotic).

In this study, exploratory principal component analysis for both children and adults yielded very similar factor structures. Both varimax and oblimin rotations yielded clear-cut analytical, creative, and practical factors for the tests. Thus, a sample of a different nationality (Russian), a different set of tests, and a different method of analysis (exploratory rather than confirmatory analysis) again supported the theory of successful intelligence. Now consider in more detail each of three major aspects of successful intelligence: analytical, creative, and practical.

In a recent study, creativity was measured using open-ended, performance-based measures (Sternberg & the Rainbow Project Collaborators, 2006) to assess creativity. These performance tasks were expected to tap an important part of creativity that might not be measured using multiple-choice items alone, because open-ended measures require more spontaneous and free-form responses.

For each of the tasks, participants were given a choice of topic or stimuli on which to base their creative stories or cartoon captions. Although these different topics or stimuli varied in terms of their difficulty for inventing creative stories and captions, these differences are accounted for in the derivation of item response theory ability estimates. Each of the creativity performance tasks were rated on criteria that were determined a priori as indicators of creativity.

1. Cartoons. Participants were given five cartoons purchased from the archives of the *New Yorker*; however, the captions were removed. The participants' task was to choose three cartoons and to provide a caption for each cartoon. Two trained judges rated all the cartoons for cleverness, humor, originality, and task appropriateness on 5-point scales. A combined creativity score was formed by summing the individual ratings on each dimension, except task appropriateness, which theoretically is not a measure of creativity per se.

2. Written stories. Participants were asked to write two stories, spending approximately 15 min. on each, choosing from the following titles: "A Fifth Chance," "2983," "Beyond the Edge," "The Octopus's Sneakers," "It's Moving Backwards," and "Not Enough Time" (Lubart & Sternberg, 1995; Sternberg & Lubart, 1995). A team of six judges was trained to rate the stories. Each of six judges rated the stories for originality, complexity, emotional evocativeness, and descriptiveness on 5-point scales.

3. Oral stories. Participants were presented with five sheets of paper, each containing a set of 11 to 13 images linked by a common theme (keys, money, travel, animals playing music, and humans playing music). After choosing one of the pages, the participant was given 15 min. to formulate a short story and dictate it into a cassette recorder, which was timed by the proctor for the paper assessments and by the internal computer clock for the computer assessments. There were no restrictions on the minimum or maximum number of images that needed to be incorporated into the stories. As with the written stories, each judge rated the stories for originality, complexity, emotional evocativeness, and descriptiveness on 5-point scales.

In a sample of 793 first-year college students from around the United States, in colleges ranging from not selective at all to very selective, we found that a separate creativity factor emerged that separated the creative performance tests from the other tests. We also found that adding our creative measures to analytical as well as practical measures roughly doubled the predictive value of the SAT for our sample in predicting grades for first-year college students (Sternberg & the Rainbow Collaborators, 2006). The measures also served to *decrease* ethnic differences between groups.

Creativity is as much a decision about and an attitude toward life as it is a matter of ability. Creativity is often obvious in young children, but it may be harder to find in older children and adults because their creative potential has been suppressed by a society that encourages intellectual conformity.

Instruction

One can teach students to think more creatively (Sternberg & Williams, 1996; Williams, Markle, Brigockas, & Sternberg, 2001). However, the emphasis in our research has been on evaluating our ideas about creativity in the classroom for instruction of conventional subject matter.

In a first set of studies, we explored the question of whether conventional education in school systematically discriminates against children with creative and practical strengths (Sternberg & Clinkenbeard, 1995; Sternberg, Ferrari, Clinkenbeard, & Grigorenko, 1996; Sternberg et al., 1999). Motivating this work was the belief that the systems in most schools strongly tend to favor children with strengths in memory and analytical abilities.

To validate our ideas, we have carried out a number of instructional studies. In one study, we used the STAT (Sternberg, 1993). The test was administered to 326 children around the United States and in some other countries who were identified by their schools as gifted by any standard whatsoever. Children were selected for a Yale summer program in (college-level) psychology if they fell into one of five ability groupings: high analytical, high creative, high practical, high balanced (high in all three abilities), or low balanced (low in all three abilities). Students who came to Yale were then divided into four instructional groups. Students in all four instructional groups used the same introductory psychology textbook (a preliminary version of Sternberg, 1995) and listened to the same psychology lectures. What differed among them was the type of afternoon discussion section to which they were assigned. They were assigned to an instructional condition that emphasized either memory, analytical, creative, or practical instruction. For example, in the memory condition, they might be asked to describe the main tenets of a major theory of depression. In the analytical condition, they might be asked to compare and contrast two theories of depression. In the creative condition, they might be asked to formulate their own theory of depression. In the practical condition, they might be asked how they could use what they had learned about depression to help a friend who was depressed.

Students in all four instructional conditions were evaluated in terms of their performance on homework, a midterm exam, a final exam, and an independent project. Each type of work was evaluated for memory, analytical, creative, and practical quality. Thus, all students were evaluated in exactly the same way.

First, we observed when the students arrived at Yale, that the students in the high creative and high practical groups were much more diverse in terms of racial, ethnic, socioeconomic, and educational backgrounds than were the students in the high analytical group, suggesting that correlations of measured intelligence with status variables such as these may be reduced by using a broader conception of intelligence. Thus, the kinds of students identified as strong differed in terms of populations from which they were drawn in comparison with students identified as strong solely by analytical measures. More important, just by expanding the range of abilities measured, we discovered intellectual strengths that might not have been apparent through a conventional test.

Second, we found that all three ability tests—analytical, creative, and practical—significantly predicted course performance. When multiple regression analysis was used, at least two of these ability measures contributed significantly to the prediction of each of the measures of achievement. Perhaps as a reflection of the difficulty of deemphasizing the analytical way of teaching, one of the significant predictors was always the analytical score.

Third and most important, there was an aptitude treatment interaction whereby students who were placed in instructional conditions that better matched their pattern of abilities outperformed students who were mismatched. In other words, when students are taught in a way that fits how they think, they do better in school. Children with creative or practical abilities, who are almost never taught or assessed in a way that matches their pattern of abilities, may be at a disadvantage in course after course, year after year.

A follow-up study (Sternberg, Torff, & Grigorenko, 1998a, 1998b) examined learning of social studies and science by third graders and eighth graders. The 225 third graders were students in a very low-income neighborhood in Raleigh, North Carolina. The 142 eighth graders were students who were largely middle to upper-middle class studying in Baltimore, Maryland, and Fresno, California. In this study, students were assigned to one of three instructional conditions. In the first condition, they were taught the course that basically they would have learned had there been no intervention. The emphasis in the course was on memory. In a second condition, students were taught in a way that emphasized critical (analytical) thinking. In the third condition, they were taught in a way that emphasized analytical, creative, and practical thinking. All students' performance was assessed for memory learning (through multiple-choice assessments) as well as for analytical, creative, and practical learning (through performance assessments).

As expected, students in the analytical, creative, practical combined condition outperformed the other students in terms of the performance assessments. One could argue that this result merely reflected the way they were taught. Nevertheless, the result suggested that teaching for these kinds of thinking succeeded. More important, however, was the result that children in the successful-intelligence condition outperformed the other children, even on the multiple-choice memory tests. In other words, to the extent that one's goal is just to maximize children's memory for information, teaching for creative as well as analytical and practical thinking is still superior. It enables children to capitalize on their strengths and to correct or to compensate for their weaknesses, and it allows children to encode material in a variety of interesting ways.

We have extended these results to reading curricula at the middle and the high school levels. In a study of 871 middle school students and 432 high school students, we taught reading, either creatively, analytically, and practically or through the regular curriculum. At the middle school level, reading was taught explicitly. At the high school level, reading was infused into instruction in mathematics, physical sciences, social sciences, English, history, foreign languages, and the arts. In all settings, students who were taught using our expanded model substantially outperformed students who were taught in standard ways (Grigorenko, Jarvin, & Sternberg, 2002).

Thus, the results of three sets of studies suggest that teaching for creative thinking, as well as for analytical and practical thinking, is worthwhile. Some kinds of students do not maximally profit from conventional instruction, but they may profit from the kinds of expanded instruction we can offer. For example, when I took introductory psychology as a freshman, I was a creative learner in a memory course. My grade showed it: Despite my efforts, I got a C in the course.

Kinds of Creative Contributions

Creative contributors make different *decisions* regarding *how* to express their creativity. We proposed a propulsion theory of creative contributions (Sternberg, 1999b; Sternberg, Kaufman, & Pretz, 2001, 2002) that addresses this issue of how people decide to invest their creative resources. The basic idea is that creativity can be of different kinds, depending on how it propels existing ideas forward. When developing creativity, we can develop different kinds of creativity, ranging from minor replications to major redirections in thinking.

Creative contributions differ not only in their amounts but also in the kinds of creativity they represent. For example, both Sigmund Freud and Anna Freud were highly creative psychologists, but the nature of their contributions appears in some way or ways to have been different. Sigmund Freud proposed a radically new theory of human thought and motivation and Anna Freud largely elaborated on and modified Sigmund Freud's theory. How do creative contributions differ in quality and not just in quantity of creativity?

The type of creativity exhibited in a creator's works can have at least as much of an effect on judgments about that person and his or her work as does the amount of creativity exhibited. In many instances, it may have more of an effect on these judgments. For example, a contemporary artist might have thought processes, personality, motivation, and even background variables similar to those of Monet, but that artist, painting today in the style of Monet, probably would not be judged to be creative in the way Monet was judged. He or she was born too late. Artists, including Monet, have experimented with impressionism, and unless the contemporary artist introduced some new twist, he or she might be viewed as imitative rather than creative.

The importance of context is illustrated by the difference, in general, between creative discovery and rediscovery. For example, BACON and related programs of Langley, Simon, Bradshaw, and Zytgow (1987) rediscover important scientific theorems that were judged to be creative discoveries in their time. The processes by which these discoveries are made via computer simulation are presumably not identical to those by which the original discoverers made their discoveries. One difference derives from the fact that contemporary programmers can provide, in their programming of information into computer simulations, representations and particular organizations of data that may not have been available to the original creators. Moreover, the programs solve problems but do not define them. However, putting aside the question of whether the processes are the same, a rediscovery might be judged to be creative with respect to the rediscoverer, but it would not be judged to be creative with respect to the field at the time the rediscovery is made.

Given the importance of purpose, creative contributions must always be defined in some context. If the creativity of an individual is always judged in a context, then it will help to understand how the context interacts with how people are judged. In particular, what are the types of creative contributions a person can make within a given context? Most theories of creativity concentrate on the attributes of the individual (see Sternberg, 1999a; Ward, Smith, & Vaid, 1997). However, to the extent that creativity is in the interaction of person with context, we need to concentrate as well on the attributes of the individual and the individual's work relative to the environmental context.

A taxonomy of creative contributions needs to deal with the question not only of in what domain a contribution is creative but also of what the type of creative contribution is (Gardner, 1993). What makes one work in biology more creative or creative in a different way from another work in biology, or what makes its creative contribution different from that of a work in art? Thus, a taxonomy of domains of work is insufficient to elucidate the nature of creative contributions. A field needs a basis for scaling how creative contributions differ quantitatively and, possibly, qualitatively.

A creative contribution represents an attempt to propel a field from wherever it is to wherever the creator believes the field should go. Thus, creativity is, by its nature, *propulsion.* It moves a field from some point to another. It also always represents a decision to exercise leadership. The creator tries to bring others to a particular point in the multidimensional creative space. The attempt may or may not succeed. There are different kinds of creative leadership that the creator may attempt to exercise, depending on how he or she decides to be creative.

The propulsion model suggests eight types of contributions that can be made to a field of endeavor at a given time. Although the eight types of contributions may differ in the extent of creative contribution they make, the scale of eight types presented here is intended as closer to a nominal one than to an ordinal one. There is no fixed a priori way of evaluating *amount* of creativity on the basis of the *type* of creativity. Certain types of creative contributions probably tend, on average, to be greater in amounts of novelty than are others. However, creativity also involves quality of work, and the type of creativity does not make any predictions regarding quality of work.

The eight types of creative contributions are divided into three major categories, contributions that accept current paradigms, contributions that reject current paradigms, and paradigms that attempt to integrate multiple current paradigms. There are also subcategories within each of these categories: paradigm-preserving contributions that leave the field where it is (Types 1 and 2), paradigm-preserving contributions that move the field forward in the direction it already is going (Types 3 and 4), paradigm-rejecting contributions that move the field in a new direction from an existing or preexisting starting point (Types 5 and 6), paradigm-rejecting contributions that move the field in a new direction from a new starting point (Type 7), and paradigm-integrating contributions that combine approaches (Type 8).

Thus, Type 1, the limiting case, is not crowd defying at all (unless the results come out the wrong way!). Type 2 may or may not be crowd defying, if the redefinition goes against the field. Type 3 typically leads the crowd. Type 4 goes beyond where the crowd is ready to go and so may well be crowd defying. Types 5 through 8 typically are crowd defying to at least some degree. Obviously, there often is no "crowd" out there just waiting to attack. Rather, there is a field representing people with shared views regarding what is and is not acceptable, and if those views are shaken, the people may not react well.

Types of Creativity That Accept Current Paradigms and Attempt to Extend Them

1. Replication. The contribution is an attempt to show that the field is in the right place. The propulsion keeps the field where it is rather than moving it forward.

This type of creativity is represented by stationary motion, as of a wheel that is moving but staying in place.

2. Redefinition. The contribution is an attempt to redefine where the field is. The current status of the field thus is seen from different points of view. The propulsion leads to circular motion, such that the creative work leads back to where the field is but as viewed in a different way.

3. Forward incrementation. The contribution is an attempt to move the field forward in the direction it already is going. The propulsion leads to forward motion.

4. Advance forward incrementation. The contribution is an attempt to move the field forward in the direction it is already going but by moving beyond where others are ready for it to go. The propulsion leads to forward motion that is accelerated beyond the expected rate of forward progression.

Types of Creativity That Reject Current Paradigms and Attempt to Replace Them

5. Redirection. The contribution is an attempt to redirect the field from where it is toward a different direction. The propulsion thus leads to motion in a direction that diverges from the way the field is currently moving.

6. Reconstruction/Redirection. The contribution is an attempt to move the field back to where it once was (a reconstruction of the past) so that it may move onward from that point, but in a direction different from the one it took from that point onward. The propulsion thus leads to motion that is backward and then redirective.

7. Reinitiation. The contribution is an attempt to move the field to a different, as-yet-unreached, starting point and then to move from that point. The propulsion is thus from a new starting point in a direction that is different from that the field previously has pursued.

A Type of Creativity That Synthesizes Current Paradigms

8. Integration. The contribution is an attempt to integrate two formerly diverse ways of thinking about phenomena into a single way of thinking about a phenomenon. The propulsion thus is a combination of two different approaches that are linked together.

The eight types of creative contributions described above are largely qualitatively distinct. Within each type, however, there can be quantitative differences. For example, a forward incrementation can represent a fairly small step forward or a substantial leap. A reinitiation can restart a subfield (e.g., the work of Leon Festinger on cognitive dissonance) or an entire field (e.g., the work of Einstein on relativity theory). Thus, the theory distinguishes contributions both qualitatively and quantitatively.

Conclusions

In this chapter, I have reviewed some of the theory and research my collaborators and I have developed in our efforts to understand the nature of creativity. We have not dealt with every question that a complete theory of creativity must answer—far from it. However, we have tried to consider at least a sampling of its aspects. Our fundamental premise is that creativity is in large part a decision that anyone can make but that few people actually do make because they find the costs to be too high. Society can play a role in the development of creativity by increasing the rewards and decreasing the costs. E. Paul Torrance was one of the pioneers in recognizing that creativity can be understood by scientific means. We are proud to follow in his footsteps.

References

Amabile, T. M. (1983). *The social psychology of creativity.* New York: Springer.

Cattell, R. B., & Cattell, A. K. (1973). *Measuring intelligence with the Culture Fair Tests.* Champaign, IL: Institute for Personality and Ability Testing.

Csikszentmihalyi, M. (1988). Society, culture, and person: A systems view of creativity. In R. J. Sternberg (Ed.), *The nature of creativity* (pp. 325–339). New York: Cambridge University Press.

Dweck, C. S. (1999). *Self-theories: Their role in motivation, personality, and development.* Philadelphia: Psychology Press/Taylor & Francis.

Frensch, P. A., & Sternberg, R. J. (1989). Expertise and intelligent thinking: When is it worse to know better? In R. J. Sternberg (Ed.), *Advances in the psychology of human intelligence* (Vol. 5, pp. 157–188). Hillsdale, NJ: Erlbaum.

Garcia, J., & Koelling, R. A. (1966). The relation of cue to consequence in avoidance learning. *Psychonomic Science, 4,* 123–124.

Gardner, H. (1993). *Creating minds.* New York: Basic Books.

Grigorenko, E. L., Jarvin, L., & Sternberg, R. J. (2002). School-based tests of the triarchic theory of intelligence: Three settings, three samples, three syllabi. *Contemporary Educational Psychology, 27,* 167–208.

Guilford, J. P. (1950). Creativity. *American Psychologist, 5,* 444–454.

Grigorenko, E. L., & Sternberg, R. J. (2001). Analytical, creative, and practical intelligence as predictors of self-reported adaptive functioning: A case study in Russia. *Intelligence, 29,* 57–73.

Langley, P., Simon, H. A., Bradshaw, G. L., & Zytkow, J. M. (1987). *Scientific discovery: Computational explorations of the creative processes.* Cambridge, MA: MIT Press.

Lubart, T. I. (1994). Creativity. In R. J. Sternberg (Ed.), *Thinking and problem solving* (pp. 290–332). San Diego, CA: Academic.

Lubart, T. I., & Sternberg, R. J. (1995). An investment approach to creativity: Theory and data. In S. M. Smith, T. B. Ward, & R. A. Finke (Eds.), *The creative cognition approach* (pp. 269–302). Cambridge, MA: MIT Press.

Niu, W., & Sternberg, R. J. (2001). Cultural influences on artistic creativity and its evaluation. *International Journal of Psychology, 36,* 225–241.

O'Hara, L. A., & Sternberg, R. J. (2000–2001). It doesn't hurt to ask: Effects of instructions to be creative, practical, or analytical on essay-writing performance and their interaction with students' thinking styles. *Creativity Research Journal, 13,* 197–210.

Rubenson, D. L., & Runco, M. A. (1992). The psychoeconomic approach to creativity. *New Ideas in Psychology, 10,* 131–147.

Simonton, D. K. (1994). *Greatness.* New York: Guilford.

Sternberg, R. J. (1981). Intelligence and nonentrenchment. *Journal of Educational Psychology, 73,* 1–16.

Sternberg, R. J. (1982). Natural, unnatural, and supernatural concepts. *Cognitive Psychology, 14,* 451–488.

Sternberg, R. J. (1985). *Beyond IQ: A triarchic theory of human intelligence.* New York: Cambridge University Press.

Sternberg, R. J. (1988). Mental self-government: A theory of intellectual styles and their development. *Human Development, 31,* 197–224.

Sternberg, R. J. (1993). *Sternberg Triarchic Abilities Test.* Unpublished test.

Sternberg, R. J. (1995). *In search of the human mind.* Orlando, FL: Harcourt Brace.

Sternberg, R. J. (1997a). *Successful intelligence.* New York: Plume.

Sternberg, R. J. (1997b). *Thinking styles.* New York: Cambridge University Press.

Sternberg, R. J. (Ed.). (1999a). *Handbook of creativity.* New York: Cambridge University Press.

Sternberg, R. J. (1999b). A propulsion model of creative contributions. *Review of General Psychology*, 3, 83–100.

Sternberg, R. J. (2001). Teaching psychology students that creativity is a decision. *General Psychologist*, 36(1), 8–11.

Sternberg, R. J. (Ed.). (2003a). *Psychologists defying the crowd: Stories of those who battled the establishment and won*. Washington, DC: American Psychological Association.

Sternberg, R. J. (2003b). *Wisdom, intelligence, and creativity synthesized*. New York: Cambridge University Press.

Sternberg, R. J., Castejón, J. L., Prieto, M. D., Hautamäki, J., & Grigorenko, E. L. (2001). Confirmatory factor analysis of the Sternberg triarchic abilities test in three international samples: An empirical test of the triarchic theory of intelligence. *European Journal of Psychological Assessment, 17*(1), 1–16.

Sternberg, R. J., & Clinkenbeard, P. R. (1995). The triarchic model applied to identifying, teaching, and assessing gifted children. *Roeper Review, 17*, 255–260.

Sternberg, R. J., Ferrari, M., Clinkenbeard, P. R., & Grigorenko, E. L. (1996). Identification, instruction, and assessment of gifted children: A construct validation of a triarchic model. *Gifted Child Quarterly, 40*, 129–137.

Sternberg, R. J., & Gastel, J. (1989a). Coping with novelty in human intelligence: An empirical investigation. *Intelligence, 13*, 187–197.

Sternberg, R. J., & Gastel, J. (1989b). If dancers ate their shoes: Inductive reasoning with factual and counterfactual premises. *Memory and Cognition, 17*, 1–10.

Sternberg, R. J., & Grigorenko, E. L. (1995). Styles of thinking in school. *European Journal for High Ability, 6*, 201–219.

Sternberg, R. J., Grigorenko, E. L., Ferrari, M., & Clinkenbeard, P. (1999). A triarchic analysis of an aptitude–treatment interaction. *European Journal of Psychological Assessment, 15*(1), 1–11.

Sternberg, R. J., & Kalmar, D. A. (1997). When will the milk spoil? Everyday induction in human intelligence. *Intelligence, 25*, 185–203.

Sternberg, R. J., Kaufman, J. C., & Pretz, J. E. (2001). The propulsion model of creative contributions applied to the arts and letters. *Journal of Creative Behavior, 35*, 75–101.

Sternberg, R. J., Kaufman, J. C., & Pretz, J. E. (2002). *The creativity conundrum*. New York: Psychology Press.

Sternberg, R. J., & Lubart, T. I. (1991). An investment theory of creativity and its development. *Human Development, 34*(1), 1–31.

Sternberg, R. J., & Lubart, T. I. (1995). *Defying the crowd*. New York: Free Press.

Sternberg, R. J., & Lubart, T. I. (1996). Investing in creativity. *American Psychologist, 51*, 677–688.

Sternberg, R. J., & The Rainbow Collaborators. (2006). The Rainbow Project: Enhancing the SAT through assessments of analytical, practical and creative skills. *Intelligence, 34*, 321–350.

Sternberg, R. J., Torff, B., & Grigorenko, E. L. (1998a). Teaching for successful intelligence raises school achievement. *Phi Delta Kappan, 79*, 667–669.

Sternberg, R. J., Torff, B., & Grigorenko, E. L. (1998b). Teaching triarchically improves school achievement. *Journal of Educational Psychology, 90*, 374–384.

Sternberg, R. J., & Williams, W. M. (1996). *How to develop student creativity*. Alexandria, VA: Association for Supervision and Curriculum Development.

Tetewsky, S. J., & Sternberg, R. J. (1986). Conceptual and lexical determinants of nonentrenched thinking. *Journal of Memory and Language, 25*, 202–225.

Torrance, E. P. (1962). *Guiding creative talent*. Englewood Cliffs, NJ: Prentice Hall.

Torrance, E. P. (1974). *Torrance tests of creative thinking*. Lexington, MA: Personnel Press.

Ward, T. B., Smith, S. M., & Vaid, J. (Eds.). (1997). *Creative thought: An investigation of conceptual structures and processes*. Washington, DC: America Psychological Association.

Williams, W. M., Markle, F., Brigockas, M., & Sternberg, R. J. (2001). *Creative intelligence for school (CIFS): 21 lessons to enhance creativity in middle and high school students*. Needham Heights, MA: Allyn & Bacon.

Practical Intelligence and Tacit Knowledge: Advancements in the Measurement of Developing Expertise

5

Anna T. Cianciolo
Elena L. Grigorenko
Linda Jarvin
Guillermo Gil
Michael E. Drebot
Robert J. Sternberg

Practical intelligence and the related construct, tacit knowledge, first were advanced as individual differences constructs in the mid- to late-1980s (Sternberg, 1988; Wagner & Sternberg, 1985). Although the concepts of "naturalistic intelligence" and "knowing without telling" were not new (Neisser, 1976; Polanyi, 1958, 1966), Sternberg and his colleagues applied them in novel ways to address emerging perspectives in differential psychology and intelligence research. The advancement of practical intelligence was driven in part by an interest in accounting for the less than perfect relation between general tests of intelligence and occupational performance. More broadly, the purpose of advancing practical intelligence was to demonstrate a scientific basis for the commonly held belief that there is more to success in everyday life than can be captured by tests of intelligence that target academic knowledge or modes of thinking (McClelland, 1973; Sternberg, Conway, Ketron, & Bernstein, 1981).

The definition of the word practical—"of or concerned with the actual doing or use of something rather than with theory and ideas" (*New Oxford American Dictionary*, 2001)—makes a distinction between the realms of the concrete and of the abstract, between the immediate and the more general application of thought and action. In concert with this distinction, Sternberg (1988) defined practical intelligence as an ability—distinct from general or academic intelligence—to perform successfully in naturalistic settings in a way that is consistent with one's goals. Wagner and Sternberg (1985) have asserted also that practical intelligence enables people to determine adaptive (as opposed to "unambiguously correct"; Legree, 1995) solutions to ill-defined problems.

Wagner and Sternberg (1985) proposed using a knowledge-based approach to assessing practical intelligence, analogous to the use of knowledge tests to assess general or academic intelligence (Sternberg, 1988). Consistent with Polanyi (1966), Wagner and Sternberg (1985) defined tacit knowledge as the generally unspoken knowledge gained from experience (as opposed to explicit instruction), which distinguishes more and less expert individuals in a particular domain. Practical intelligence therefore can be viewed as developing expertise (Sternberg, 1998), and tacit knowledge its manifest indicator (Sternberg et al., 2000). That is, performance on assessments of tacit knowledge reflects the confluence of overall neurological functioning, experience dealing with practical matters, and exposure to successful adaptive behavior, much as crystallized intelligence reflects the confluence of fluid intelligence and enculturation (Horn & Cattell, 1966) and job knowledge, as traditionally assessed, reflects the confluence of general intelligence and job experience (Schmidt & Hunter, 1993).

The validity of the constructs of practical intelligence and tacit knowledge and their measurement has been investigated for nearly two decades (e.g., Colonia-Willner, 1998; Hedlund et al., 2003; Legree, Heffner, Psotka, Martin, & Medsker, 2003; Tan & Libby, 1997; Wagner & Sternberg, 1985, 1990a; Wagner, Sujan, Sujan, Rashotte, & Sternberg, 1999). This research has focused on demonstrating a distinction between practical intelligence and general (or fluid) intelligence, crystallized intelligence, and such nonability constructs as personality and motivation. In keeping with the initial interest in better accounting for individual differences in job performance, tacit-knowledge inventories such as the Tacit-Knowledge Inventory for Managers (TKIM; Wagner & Sternberg, 1990b) and the Tacit-Knowledge Inventory for Military Leaders (TKML; Hedlund et al., 2003) have been designed to capture specialized, job-related knowledge acquired from experience. For this reason, some validation research has also explored the distinction between tacit knowledge and technical job knowledge (Tan & Libby, 1997).

In general, practical intelligence has been shown to be distinct from other intelligence constructs. Scores on tacit-knowledge inventories generally show relatively weak (below .20 and sometimes negative) correlation with measures of general intelligence and crystallized intelligence [Legree et al., 2003; Sternberg et al., 2001; Tan & Libby, 1997; Wagner, 1987; Wagner & Sternberg, 1985, 1990a, 1990b; though see Colonia-Willner, 1998, for slightly higher correlations between the TKIM and scores on Raven's Progressive Matrices and the Differential Aptitude Battery, r(reflected) = .28 and .32, respectively]. Practical intelligence also appears to be distinct from aspects of personality, including sociability, self-control, and achievement via conformity (Wagner & Sternberg, 1990a; r = .14, .19, and −.05, respectively), though it may bear a relation to social presence (Wagner & Sternberg, 1990a, r = .29).

Although relatively less studied, the relation between tacit knowledge and job knowledge has been reported to be weak. Tan and Libby (1997) found a correlation of .22 between a technical knowledge composite for auditing and scores on an auditing tacit-knowledge inventory. Tan and Libby also found that although top and bottom (determined by annual evaluations and pay increments) senior-level auditors (i.e., managers) did not differ in the amount of their technical knowledge they did differ significantly in their amount of tacit knowledge. The opposite pattern was found for lower-level auditors (i.e., staff and seniors).

Tacit-knowledge inventories and similar tacit-knowledge assessment methodologies also repeatedly have shown a meaningful relation to performance (Colonia-Willner, 1998; Hedlund, Wilt, Nebel, Ashford, & Sternberg, 2006; Tan & Libby, 1997; Wagner, 1987; Wagner & Sternberg, 1985; Wagner et al., 1999). In the research of Sternberg and his colleagues, the correlation between tacit-knowledge inventories and various performance criteria generally is .35 or greater. One exception to this general pattern was found in Hedlund et al.'s (2003) study of military leaders in which scores on the TKML generally correlated less than .20 with ratings of leadership effectiveness. The leadership effectiveness ratings data presented in Hedlund et al. suggest that lack of variance in the ratings may partially account for these lower relationships. In independent research, Legree et al. (2003) found that drivers within one standard deviation below the mean on a tacit knowledge for driving test were 2.3 times more likely to be involved in a crash than those drivers scoring within one standard deviation above the mean. Drivers scoring one standard deviation below the mean were 5 times more likely.

Assessments measuring specialized, job-related knowledge may overshadow the general nature of practical intelligence, however. The relation between scores on tacit-knowledge inventories and some criterion performances may obscure the importance to successful performance of a more general ability to learn from everyday experience. Moreover, the use of specialized tacit-knowledge inventories and relatively range-restricted samples in much of the above-described research has fostered doubt among some scholars that practical intelligence—as distinct from other forms of knowledge, from general intelligence, or from personality—exists (Gottfredson, 2003; Jensen, 1993; Schmidt & Hunter, 1993).

Despite the challenges involved in assessing practical intelligence and tacit knowledge, interest in reliably and validly capturing constructs that reflect success in "naturalistic" settings is high in educational domains (Brookhart, 2004; Mitri, 2003; Sternberg & the Rainbow Project Collaborators, 2005, 2006). Assessments designed to capture tacit knowledge that can be acquired from common everyday experiences may illuminate, at least to some degree, the role in intelligent behavior of the relatively general ability to learn from everyday experience and to apply knowledge to practical problem solving. Such assessments would be more flexible across research and occupational settings than their predecessors and would extend scientific understanding of skilled performance.

The objective of this chapter is to present and discuss the measurement properties and the construct-validation data for three new tacit-knowledge inventories. Rather than assessing specialized, job-related knowledge, these inventories are designed to assess tacit knowledge acquired from situations commonly experienced in everyday American life (college undergraduate living, entry-level workplace positions, and everyday practical situations). These inventories collectively reflect individual differences in the ability to acquire and use practical knowledge—that is, practical intelligence—because they present situations likely to have been experienced by all of the examinees in less range-restricted samples.

To achieve this objective, this chapter has three goals. The first goal is to demonstrate that the new tacit-knowledge inventories are internally consistent and stable cross-sample measures of a single construct, tacit knowledge. The second goal is to demonstrate that common variance among tacit-knowledge inventories can be accounted for by a single construct, practical intelligence. The third goal is to demonstrate that practical intelligence is distinguishable from general intelligence (cf. Gottfredson, 2003; Jensen, 1993).

Overview

This chapter presents three studies in which the validity of three new tacit-knowledge inventories was evaluated. In this overview, we briefly describe the inventories and the approach we used to validate them.

Summary of the New Tacit-Knowledge Inventories

General Format

Each new tacit-knowledge inventory—the College Life Questionnaire (CLQ), the Common Sense Questionnaire (CSQ), and the Everyday Situational Judgment Inventory (ESJI)—was designed to capture knowledge to which most American college students and people entering the workforce are exposed. Because the design and development process for the inventories used in practical-intelligence research has been described in detail elsewhere (Sternberg et al., 2000), only the format of the inventories is described here.

The general format of the tacit-knowledge inventories, like that of their predecessors, can be described as a situational judgment test in that it features a set of common problem situations that are presented either via paper-and-pencil or live-action venues (see McDaniel, Morgeson, Finnegan, Campion, & Braverman, 2001, for a comprehensive review of situational judgment testing). Individuals are asked to indicate the appropriateness of multiple response strategies for each problem situation using a rating scale of 1 (extremely bad) to 7 (extremely good). Administration of the tacit-knowledge inventories is untimed.

College Life Questionnaire

The College Life Questionnaire (CLQ) contains 15 brief written vignettes that describe everyday situations encountered by college undergraduates, such as dealing with a roommate who has annoying borrowing habits or making a dreaded trip to the Bursar's Office to pay a tuition bill. The number of response strategies associated with each vignette ranges from 8 to 22.

Common Sense Questionnaire

The Common Sense Questionnaire (CSQ) contains 15 brief written vignettes that describe everyday situations encountered by individuals who are employed or seeking work in entry- to mid-level jobs. The situations are ones such as completing a tedious task or being asked to work on a day off. Each vignette is accompanied by eight possible strategies for handling the situation presented.

Everyday Situational Judgment Inventory

The Everyday Situational Judgment Inventory (ESJI) features a set of seven live-action vignettes that are shown to examinees via videocassette and television or via computer. The vignettes capture everyday problem situations encountered by average American young adults, such as going to a party where no one looks familiar or realizing after a meal out that one does not have enough cash to tip the waitress. Each vignette is accompanied by six response strategies.

Scoring the Tacit-Knowledge Inventories

Conceptually, the "score" on a tacit-knowledge inventory represents the deviation of an individual's ratings of the quality of each response strategy from the mean quality ratings of a designated comparison sample, although the exact methods for computing this score may differ (see Sternberg et al., 2000). The comparison sample may be a group of "experts" in a particular field, or the sample to which the individual belongs (Legree, 1995). Given that the vignettes used in the present research called on tacit knowledge about general societal norms, and therefore no definitive expert could be meaningfully identified, scoring was based on deviations from the sample mean. Prior research has shown that correlations between the mean ratings of expert and nonexpert samples are very high (.95, Legree, 1995; .91, Mayer, Salovey, Caruso, & Sitarenios, 2003), which provides some evidence that the ratings based on each reference group are interchangeable for research purposes.

For all three tacit-knowledge inventories, vignette-level scores assigned to each participant were derived by calculating the squared Mahalanobis distance (D^2) of the participant's vector of ratings in a given vignette from the centroid of the sample to which the participant belonged. The squared Mahalanobis distance is considered a standardized distance because it corrects differences from the mean on a particular set of solution strategies for two criteria: (1) the variance in the ratings for each solution strategy, and (2) the intercorrelation of the solution strategy ratings (see Rencher, 1995). That is, one's distance from the mean rating for a particular solution strategy receives less weight if the variance of the ratings is large and if the ratings correlate weakly with those of the other strategies in the same vignette. Overall scores for each inventory were determined by averaging the vignette scores and then taking the square root of this average to return the value to its original metric. In order to ease the interpretation of the analyses in this article, these scores were reflected such that a higher score indicated "greater" tacit knowledge.

Summary of the Three Studies

Confirmatory factor analysis was used to accomplish the three goals of this chapter (see Legree, 1995 and Wagner, 1987 for analogous approaches). First, in all three studies, single-factor models were tested for their fit to the covariance among the vignettes comprising each new tacit-knowledge inventory. The stability of these single-factor models across independently sampled groups (American and Spanish samples in Study 1, and the samples from Studies 2 and 3) also was evaluated. Second, in Study 2, a single-factor model was tested for its fit to the covariance among the three new tacit-knowledge inventories and the Practical subscale from the Sternberg

5.1 Participants to Which Each Measure in Each Study Was Administered				
Measure	N (Study 1) U.S.	N (Study 1) Spain	N (Study 2)	N (Study 3)
Cattell Culture Fair Test of g				676
Mill Hill Vocabulary Scale				678
Sternberg Triarchic Abilities Test-Practical (STAT-Practical)			527	653
Common Sense Questionnaire (CSQ)	228	227	387	374
College Life Questionnaire (CLQ)			390	413
Everyday Situational Judgment Inventory (ESJI)			679	393
Performance ratings	100	114		

Triarchic Abilities Test (Sternberg, 1991; Sternberg & the Rainbow Project Collaborators, 2005, 2006). Third and finally, two models were tested in Study 3 for their fit to the covariance among latent practical intelligence and fluid and crystallized intelligence factors. The first model allowed practical intelligence, fluid intelligence, and crystallized intelligence to correlate freely as primary factors (see Horn & Cattell, 1966). The second model featured the specification of a higher-order g factor to account for the covariance among the latent fluid and crystallized intelligence factors (see Carroll, 1993; Gustafsson, 1984) and the correlation between practical intelligence and g was freely estimated.

Table 5.1 provides a summary of the measures administered in each of the three studies, and the number of participants who took each measure. More detail on each study will be provided in the following sections.

Study 1

In Study 1, the fit of a single-factor model to the Common Sense Questionnaire (CSQ) was assessed within and across two samples of working adults, one from the United States and one from Spain. Study 1 also involved an initial examination of the relation between scores on the CSQ and perceptions of workplace performance.

Method

Participants

Participants in both the United States and Spain were recruited through advertisements in local newspapers, flyers placed in public places (e.g., universities, local grocery stores), and work supervisors. All participants were paid $20 for their participation.

U.S. Participants. There were 228 U.S. participants (149 female, 76 male, and 3 participants who did not report their gender). Ages ranged from 17 to 72 years with a median age of 34. The job classifications of the participants included custodians, dining hall food-service staff, restaurant waitstaff, salespeople, postal-service workers, taxi drivers, office personnel, and schoolteachers. The mean time that participants had spent in the workplace was 6.7 years, with a standard deviation of 7.9. The mean time spent in current position was 1.3 years with a standard deviation of 1.0.

Spanish Participants. There were 227 Spanish participants (112 female, 112 male, and 3 participants who did not report their gender). Ages ranged from 21 to 64 years with a median age of 34. The job classifications of the participants included clerks, bank office staff, photography and film developing studio personnel, biology laboratory staff, law office support personnel, librarians, educational researchers, textbook editors, university teachers, air traffic controllers, administrative personnel of diverse institutions, and psychiatrists. The mean time that participants had spent in the workplace was 7.6 years, with a standard deviation of 8.6. The mean time spent in current position was 4.0 years with a standard deviation of 3.6.

Materials

In addition to the CSQ, a two-part supervisor rating scale of occupational performance was administered (see Appendix A). The scale asked supervisors to give ratings of employee work performance according to the three dimensions of successful intelligence: analytic, creative, and practical (Sternberg, 1997). In addition, overall ratings of work performance were requested.

Design and Procedure

A trained research assistant administered the CSQ to individual participants via paper and pencil. Supervisor ratings of occupational performance were collected for a subset of the participants who were recruited by their supervisors (N = 100 and 114 in the U.S. and Spain samples, respectively).

Results

Descriptive Statistics

The descriptive statistics for the measures used in Study 1 are shown in Table 5.2. The internal-consistency reliability of the CSQ was good (Spain, α = .83; U.S., α = .92), but notably lower for the Spain sample than for the U.S. sample. However, the average ratings of the Spain and U.S. samples for each vignette response strategy correlated substantially (r = .91), indicating that relative preferences for response options were quite similar across the two nations. The correlation between U.S. scores on the CSQ using the U.S. sample as the comparison group and using the Spain sample as the comparison group was .92. The analogous correlation in the Spain sample was .94.

The mean supervisor ratings of performance in both the Spain and U. S. samples were relatively high with somewhat restricted standard deviations, suggesting that the scale developed as part of this study was susceptible to halo effects. The high

5.2 Descriptive Statistics in Each Study

Measure	Number of Items or Vignettes	Mean	SD	r_{xx}[a]
STUDY 1				
CSQ—U.S.	15 vignettes	.95	.26	.92
CSQ—Spain	15 vignettes	.97	.18	.82
Ratings—U.S.	12 items	7.01	1.57	.97
Ratings—Spain	12 items	7.43	1.02	.92
STUDY 2				
STAT-Practical	12 items	6.42	2.13	.47
CSQ	15 vignettes	.95	.24	.91
CLQ	15 vignettes	.96	.22	.89
ESJI	7 vignettes	.95	.21	.76
STUDY 3				
Cattell	50 items	31.68	3.43	.54
Mill Hill	66 items	35.55	5.23	.71
STAT-Practical	20 items	12.13	2.91	.56
CSQ	15 vignettes	.95	.23	.88
CLQ	15 vignettes	.97	.17	.82
ESJI	7 vignettes	.95	.21	.70

[a]Reliabilities for all tacit-knowledge inventories, Cattell, and for the supervisor ratings were computed using Cronbach's alpha. The reliability of the Cattell was corrected for length because subscales were used to compute alpha. Reliability for STAT-Practical was computed using the split-half method. Reliability for Mill Hill was computed by using the Spearman-Brown formula on the correlation between the two parts of the test.

internal-consistency reliability of the two sets of ratings ($\alpha = .97$ and .92 in the U.S. and Spain, respectively) further suggests that the twelve items in the scale are strongly related to one another.

Underlying Structure of the CSQ

As would be expected from the above-reported reliabilities of the CSQ and from previous research (Wagner, 1987), the fit of a single-factor model to the covariance among the CSQ vignettes in both the U. S. and Spain samples conforms to general standards of acceptable fit for confirmatory factor analysis (e.g., Byrne, 1998; Kline, 1998). That is, although the χ^2 values for these models are significant, Table 5.3 shows that (a) the comparative fit index (CFI) values for both models are above .90 (.93 for both models); (b) the root mean square error of approximation (RMSEA) values are at .08 or lower (.05 for the Spain model and .07 for the U. S. model) and have a 90% confidence interval whose upper bound is .08 or lower; and (c) the standardized root mean residual (SRMR) for both models is .05 or lower (.05 for both models).

Although the fit indices presented in Table 5.3 are comparable across the two samples, the median communality (R^2) of the 15 vignettes was somewhat different in each sample, suggesting that the vignettes were differential indicators of the latent

5.3	Fit Indices for the Single-Factor CFAs in Each Study				
Measure	$\chi^2(df)$	CFI	RMSEA (90% C.I.)	SRMR	Median R^2
STUDY 1					
CSQ—Spain	133.79 (90)**	.93	.05 (.03; .06)	.05	.29
CSQ—U.S.	172.70 (90)**	.93	.07 (.05; .08)	.05	.44
STUDY 2					
CSQ	193.69 (90)**	.95	.06 (.05; .07)	.04	.42
CLQ	248.94 (90)**	.92	.07 (.06; .08)	.05	.35
ESJI	20.53 (14)	.99	.03 (.00; .03)	.02	.31
STUDY 3					
CSQ	147.08 (90)**	.96	.05 (.02; .08)	.04	.32
CLQ	172.77 (90)**	.92	.05 (.04; .06)	.05	.24
ESJI	26.52 (14)*	.96	.04 (.03; .05)	.04	.26

*$p < .05$; **$p < .001$.

tacit-knowledge factor across samples. Two separate analyses do not test the degree to which the loadings on the tacit-knowledge factor differ across samples, however. The measurement equivalence of the CSQ across the Spanish and U.S. samples therefore was tested using nested multisample confirmatory factor analysis. The nested models in such an analysis involve placing increasingly restrictive cross-sample equality constraints on the parameter estimates and testing the resulting change in χ^2 for significance (e.g., see Byrne, 1998). A significant change in χ^2 indicates that the added equality constraint has produced a significant reduction in model fit and signals the limit of measurement equivalence.

First, a baseline single-factor model was specified simultaneously for both the U.S. and Spain samples. As shown in Table 5.4, the fit indices for this baseline model are acceptable [CFI = .93, RMSEA (90% C.I.) = .06 (.05; .07), SRMR = .05], suggesting that the covariance structure underlying the data from both samples can be accounted for by a single factor. The more restrictive model of equivalent factor loadings therefore was specified next. The change in χ^2 as a result of these restrictions was significant [$\Delta\chi^2(df) = 55.51(14)$, $p < .001$], indicating that the vignettes in the CSQ are differential indicators of the latent tacit-knowledge factor across samples.

Post hoc examination of the factor loadings for each vignette indicated that the loadings of only 3 of the 15 vignettes result in a significant increase in χ^2 when constrained to be equal. A follow-up set of nested models in which these three vignettes were removed (CSQ2) showed a nonsignificant increase in χ^2[$\Delta\chi^2$ $(df) = 17.46(11)$] when the factor loadings were constrained to be equal (the fit of the baseline model is shown in Table 5.4). Constraining the latent factor variances of CSQ2 to be equal across samples, however, resulted in a significant increase in χ^2[$\Delta\chi^2(df) = 33.46(1)$, $p < .001$].

5.4 Fit Indices for the Multisample, Single-Factor CFAs

Measure	χ^2 (df)	CFI	RMSEA (90% C.I.)	SRMR	$\Delta\chi^2$ (df)
Spain/U.S.					
CSQ—baseline model	339.04 (180)**	.93	.06 (.05; .07)	.05	
CSQ—equal factor loadings					55.51 (14)**
CSQ2	228.04 (108)**	.92	.07 (.06; .08)	.05	
CSQ2—equal factor loadings					17.46 (11)
CSQ2—equal factor variance					33.46 (1)**
Samples 2/3					
CSQ—baseline model	340.77 (180)**	.96	.05 (.04; .06)	.04	
CSQ—equal factor loadings					16.72 (14)
CSQ—equal factor variance					.15 (1)
CSQ—equal item reliability					141.95 (14)**
CLQ—baseline model	421.72 (180)**	.92	.06 (.06; .07)	.05	
CLQ—equal factor loadings					43.30 (14)**
CLQ2—baseline model	318.38 (154)**	.94	.06 (.05; .06)	.04	
CLQ2—equal factor loadings					18.26 (13)
CLQ2—equal factor variance					28.68 (1)**
ESJI—baseline model	47.05 (28)*	.98	.04 (.02; .05)	.04	
ESJI—equal factor loadings					8.92 (6)
ESJI—equal factor variance					.17 (1)
ESJI—equal item reliability					64.61 (6)**

*$p = .01$; **$p < .001$.

Criterion-Related Validity

Prior to examining the criterion-related validity of the CSQ, an exploratory factor analysis oft he supervisor performance ratings was conducted separately in the Spain and U.S. samples. Factors were extracted using the principal-axis method, and the number of factors chosen was based on a combined examination of the Kaiser criterion and scree plots.[1] The results are presented in Table 5.5, with loadings below .30 not shown.

A single-factor solution characterized the correlation data in both samples, with the factor accounting for 77% of the variance in the U.S. sample and 51% of the variance in the Spain sample. Examination of the bivariate correlations among the ratings in the Spain sample suggests that Spanish supervisors made more of a distinction between collective and individual aspects of work performance than did American supervisors (e.g., the correlation between ratings of group work and autonomous work was .38 in the Spain sample, but .79 in the U.S. sample). A single average score

---

[1]As the Kaiser criterion is known to overestimate the number of factors present, scree plots were consulted when a solution containing more than one factor was produced. If the two sources of information were in disagreement, the scree plot was used. Judgment regarding the number of factors present was also influenced by the substantial consistency among the ratings in both samples as indicated by Cronbach's alpha.

5.5 Factor Analysis of Supervisor Ratings

Item	U. S. I.	Spain I.
My relationship with this employee is good.	.83	.76
I think highly of this employee.	.93	.92
I am satisfied with this employee.	.94	.89
This employee's relationships with other coworkers are good.	.77	.55
How would you rate this employee's common-sense ability?	.88	.70
How would you rate this employee's academic ability?	.79	.58
How would you rate this employee's creative ability?	.86	.60
How would you rate this employee at working by him/herself?	.93	.68
How would you rate this employee at working with others?	.89	.68
How good is this employee at motivating him/herself?	.88	.53
How good is this employee at managing tasks?	.92	.85
How responsible is this employee?	.89	.66

for the entire set of ratings was formed based on the results of the factor analysis. The bivariate correlation among the CSQ and supervisor ratings was .39 ($p < .01$) in the U.S. sample and .11 (ns) in the Spain sample.

Discussion

The results presented in Study 1 indicate that one of the three new tacit-knowledge inventories, the Common Sense Questionnaire (CSQ), has an underlying single-factor structure. The results also suggest that a tacit-knowledge inventory sampling relatively common, everyday tacit-knowledge has some measurement equivalence across different, international samples. In both the U.S. and Spain samples, the covariance among the CSQ vignettes could be accounted for by a single factor and, with a few exceptions, the vignettes served as roughly equivalent indicators of this latent factor. In addition, the relative pattern of responding to the vignettes was consistent across the samples. The factor variance and some factor loadings were found to be nonequivalent across samples, however, suggesting that the CSQ may have measured something slightly different in each culture.

Study 1 also presents a very preliminary exploration of the criterion-related validity of the CSQ. The results from the U.S. sample tentatively indicate that the CSQ correlates with workplace ratings in a manner consistent with previous research (Colonia-Willner, 1998; Tan & Libby, 1997; Wagner, 1987; Wagner & Sternberg, 1985; Wagner et al., 1999; see also McDaniel et al., 2001). Although the data collected do not definitively address the issue, the small correlation between the CSQ and supervisory ratings in the Spain sample could be due to multiple factors. First, there may have been differences across countries regarding the level of familiarity and comfort supervisors had with providing ratings of employee performance. Such differences may reduce the validity of these ratings. Second, the tacit-knowledge captured by the CSQ may have been valued differentially by supervisors in the U.S. versus Spain.

Study 2

In Study 2, the underlying factor structure of each of the three new tacit-knowledge inventories was analyzed. The factor structure underlying the covariance among the inventories also was analyzed along with the Practical subscale from the Sternberg Triarchic Abilities Test (Sternberg & the Rainbow Project Collaborators, 2005, 2006). In particular, a single higher-order factor was specified to account for the variance among three latent tacit-knowledge factors and a latent practical knowledge-application factor.

Method

Participants

Study 2 involved 2 high schools, 8 four-year colleges, and 5 community colleges distributed nationwide: Northview High School, Mepham High School, Brigham Young University, Florida State University, James Madison University, California State University–San Bernardino, University of California–Santa Barbara, Southern Connecticut State University, Stevens Institute of Technology, Yale University, Mesa Community College, Coastline Community College, Irvine Valley Community College, Orange Coast Community College, and Saddleback Community College. From a total sample of 1007,[2] the data from college students only are reported here (N = 793; 498 female). In this subsample, participants either received course credit or payment of $20 for their participation. Ages ranged from 16 to 52 years with a median age of 19 years (four participants did not report their age).

Materials

In addition to the three new tacit-knowledge inventories [the College Life Questionnaire (CLQ), the Common Sense Questionnaire (CSQ), and the Everyday Situational Judgment Inventory (ESJI)], the Practical subscale from the Sternberg Triarchic Abilities Test (STAT) was administered. The Creative and Analytic subscales of the STAT also were administered to this sample as part of a larger study, but are analyzed elsewhere (Sternberg & the Rainbow Project Collaborators, 2005, 2006).

The STAT-Practical assesses the application of knowledge to solving common practical problems in three different content areas: quantitative, verbal, and figural. Practical–Quantitative problems require examinees to correctly solve everyday mathematical problems, such as changing the quantities of ingredients in a recipe. In Practical–Verbal problems, the examinee must read a short description of a problem typical in

---

[2]The sample presented in this article is a subset of the sample used in the larger study, which has been reported elsewhere (Sternberg & the Rainbow Project Collaborators, 2005, 2006). However, the analyses of the data presented in this chapter are original and have not been previously reported. Small differences in sample size between this chapter and publications of the larger study are due to eliminations required to conduct meaningful analyses for the larger study but not required for the present analyses.

the life of a young adult and choose the best solution to the problem. Practical–Figural problems require examinees to use a map to select from among four alternatives the optimal route to get from one place to another. STAT-Practical problems are multiple-choice. They therefore reflect practical problems for which a single correct solution can be identified but that require the application of knowledge in a way that often is not explicitly taught. The STAT-Practical is untimed and features four problems in each content area, totaling 12 problems for the overall subscale. The score for each content area is the number of problems answered correctly (range = 0–4).

Design and Procedure

The measures in this study were administered in two sessions using either a paper-and-pencil or computer-based format, depending on the school where they were administered. Table 5.1 shows the number of participants who provided complete data for each measure. In Session 1, The STAT-Practical and the ESJI were administered along with additional measures of interest to the larger study (e.g., demographic surveys). As part of an intentionally incomplete overlapping group design, which enables the resource-effective administration of numerous measures to a single sample (see McArdle, 1994), the STAT-Practical was administered to two thirds of the entire sample ($N = 527$). The ESJI was presented to all participants either on videocassette or computer, depending on the school where it was administered. The number of participants with ESJI data is lower than expected (86% instead of 100% of the total N) because several participants experienced technological difficulties with the computer-based version of the inventory.

The CLQ or CSQ was administered in Session 2 along with additional measures of interest to the larger study (e.g., measures of creative ability). As part of the intentionally incomplete overlapping group design, roughly half of the sample received the CLQ and the other half received the CSQ.

Results

Descriptive Statistics

Descriptive statistics are shown in Table 5.2. The split-half reliability of the STAT-Practical scale is low ($r_{xx'} = .47$), perhaps due to the small number of items in each half. The internal-consistency reliability of two of the new tacit-knowledge inventories is high ($\alpha = .91$ and .89 for the CSQ and CLQ, respectively). The relatively lower reliability of the ESJI is comparable to that of the longer CSQ and CLQ when the Spearman–Brown formula is used to determine the reliability of the ESJI at 15 vignettes instead of 7 ($\alpha_{corrected} = .87$).

Underlying Structure of the Tacit-Knowledge Inventories

The fit of a single-factor model to the covariance among the vignettes in each of the three tacit-knowledge inventories was tested using confirmatory factor analysis. The fit indices for these three models are shown in Table 5.3. Consistent with the internal-consistency reliability data, the fit for each of the models is acceptable (CFI = .92, RMSEA = .07, SRMR = .05), with one model (ESJI) producing a nonsignificant χ^2 value.

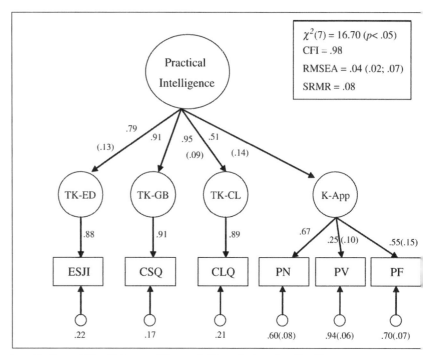

5.1

Hierarchical confirmatory factor analysis of tacit knowledge and practical intelligence. Note, standard errors of the parameter estimates for freely estimated values are indicated in parentheses. TK-ED = Tacit-Knowledge, Everyday; TK-GB = Tacit-Knowledge, General Business; TKCL = Tacit-Knowledge, College Life; K-App = (Formal) Knowledge Application.

Hierarchical Factor Analyses

Hierarchical confirmatory factor analysis was used to analyze the covariance among the new tacit-knowledge inventories and the STAT-Practical problems. Given the single-factor structure of each of the tacit-knowledge inventories, each was specified as a single indicator of its respective latent tacit-knowledge variable. Simplifying the model in this way enabled model identification. Also to enable model identification, the factor loadings and residual variances of the tacit-knowledge inventories were fixed according to Wheaton, Muthén, Alwin, and Summers (1977) and Bollen (1989), respectively, using the actual (as opposed to corrected) reliabilities of the measures. A latent variable representing practical knowledge application (K-App) was specified using the three content composites (quantitative, verbal, and figural) of the STAT-Practical as manifest indicators. Finally, a higher-order factor was specified, with the three Tacit-Knowledge factors and the Knowledge-Application factor as indicators.

Parameter estimation was accomplished using full-information maximum likelihood estimation (FIML; see Allison, 1987; Wothke, 2000). FIML is used for studies involving intentionally incomplete overlapping group designs because it enables the estimation of model parameters without the use of data-imputation techniques to replace large quantities of missing data. Rather than individual data points, FIML estimates the means, standard deviations, and covariance of the variables from the available data. Therefore, the present analysis was conducted on an estimated covariance matrix.[3] The results of this analysis are depicted in Figure 5.1.

---

[3]Estimated correlation matrices among the manifest indicators can be obtained by contacting the primary author.

As can be seen in Figure 5.1, the loadings of the manifest indicators on their respective latent factors are substantial. One exception is the Practical–Verbal subscale of the STAT, which evidently requires some enhancement as an indicator of practical knowledge application. Each of the Tacit-Knowledge factors and the Knowledge-Application factor in turn loaded substantially on the higher-order factor. Not surprisingly, the loading of the Knowledge-Application factor on this higher-order factor was lower than that of the three Tacit-Knowledge factors. The fit of this model was good [CFI = .98; RMSEA = .04 (.02; .07), SRMR = .08].

Discussion

The results from Study 2 provide more complete evidence that the new tacit-knowledge inventories, in contrast to other situational judgment tests (McDaniel et al., 2001), each have an underlying single-factor structure. In addition, content composites of problems from the Practical subscale of the STAT—each of which require knowledge application to practical problem solving—also loaded on a single factor. The hierarchical confirmatory factor analysis results demonstrate that the covariance among the latent Tacit-Knowledge factors and the latent Knowledge-Application factor can be accounted for by a single, higher-order latent factor, which we have labeled Practical Intelligence. This result provides some evidence that practical intelligence is not simply a method factor stemming from the use of situational judgment testing methodology or Mahalanobis distance scoring techniques, but does not yet elucidate the distinction between practical intelligence and other intelligence constructs.

Study 3

Study 3 replicates the analyses conducted in Study 2. In addition, the cross-sample stability of the new tacit-knowledge inventories using the samples from Study 2 and Study 3 was analyzed. Finally, two analyses were conducted in which the relation between the higher-order Practical Intelligence factor and other intelligence constructs was examined.

Method

Participants

Six hundred ninety-seven Brigham Young University (BYU) undergraduates (455 female, 239 male, and 3 participants who did not report their gender) received course credit in undergraduate psychology courses for their participation in this study. Ages ranged from 17 to 48 years with a median age of 19 (20 participants did not report their age).

Materials

In addition to measures of tacit knowledge and practical knowledge application, measures of fluid and crystallized intelligence were administered. Fluid intelligence (g–f) was measured using the Cattell Culture Fair Test of g (Cattell & Cattell, 1973),

Scale, Form B. The Cattell test consists of four timed subscales—series, classification, matrices, and conditions—totaling 50 items. The items in each subscale require examinees to determine the relation among figural representations and then to select from up to five options a related or unrelated figure. The score for this test is the number of items answered correctly.

Crystallized intelligence (g–c) was measured using the Mill Hill Vocabulary Scale (Raven, Court, & Raven, 1994) Senior Form 1, Set B. The Mill Hill is an untimed 33-item test in which examinees are presented with words of increasing difficulty and must select from among four options the closest synonym to the word presented. As with the Cattell test, the score for the Mill Hill is the number of correct answers.

The STAT-Practical administered in this study was a predecessor of the STAT-Practical used in Study 2 (see Sternberg, 2003). This older version of the STAT contained a greater number of problems, and some of the problems themselves have been changed. Otherwise, the structure, scoring, and administration of the STAT-Practical subscale used in Study 2 and Study 3 were the same. As in Study 2, the Creative and Analytic scales of the STAT were administered as part of a larger study, but are not analyzed here as the revised STAT has superceded its older version (Sternberg, 2003).

Design and Procedure

Participants took the ability measures in two sessions. In the first session, all measures except the ESJI were administered via paper and pencil. The ESJI was administered via computer in the second session. Table 5.1 shows the number of participants who took each measure. As in Study 2, an intentionally incomplete overlapping group design was used such that roughly half of the sample received the College Life Questionnaire (CLQ) and the other half received the Common Sense Questionnaire (CSQ). The entire sample received the Everyday Situational Judgment Inventory (ESJI), the STAT, and a demographic survey.

As shown in Table 5.1, the number of participants with usable ESJI data is fewer than expected (only 58% of the full sample). This difference occurred because the ESJI was not ready for administration at the same time that the paper-and-pencil testing occurred, and several participants did not return for the additional testing when the ESJI was ready. In addition, some demographic data taken during ESJI administration were lost due to a technical error, so ESJI data collected via the computer could not be linked to previously collected paper-and-pencil data. The ESJI data for the participants lacking demographic data are not presented. Participants with missing STAT-Practical data did not complete the STAT due to time constraints.

Results

Descriptive Statistics

Descriptive statistics are shown in Table 5.2. Consistent with the previous two studies, the internal-consistency reliabilities of the new tacit-knowledge inventories are acceptable (α = .88 and .82 for the CSQ and CLQ, respectively; ESJI $\alpha_{corrected}$ = .83). Consistent with Study 2, the split-half reliability of the STAT is low ($r_{xx'}$ = .56), as is the internal consistency of the Cattell subscales (α = .37) and the split-half reliability of the Mill Hill ($r_{xx'}$ = .55). When corrected for length, the reliabilities of the Cattell and Mill Hill are .54 and .71, respectively. The low intercorrelations among the components of the fluid and crystallized intelligence tests suggest that the present sample, although less range restricted than previous samples used in practical intelligence research (see Gottfredson, 2003), may have somewhat higher average intellectual ability than the samples on which these intelligence tests were normed (Legree, Pifer, & Grafton, 1996).

Underlying Structure of the Tacit-Knowledge Inventories

Replicating the findings of Studies 1 and 2, the fit indices of single-factor models fit to the covariance data of the new tacit-knowledge vignettes are good [CFI $\geq$ .92, RMSEA (90% C.I.) $\leq$ .08, SRMR $\leq$ .05—see Table 5.3].

Multisample Analyses

The stability of the factor structure of each tacit-knowledge inventory across the samples in Studies 2 and 3 was analyzed using nested multisample confirmatory factor analysis (see also Study 1). The results of these analyses are presented in Table 5.4. As shown in Table 5.4, the fit of the baseline single-factor model for each inventory—fit the two samples simultaneously—was good [CFI $\geq$ .92, RMSEA (90% C.I.) $\leq$ .07, SRMR $\leq$ .05]. Equality constraints on the factor loadings therefore were placed, resulting in a nonsignificant increase in χ^2 for the CSQ and the ESJI, but a significant change in χ^2 for the CLQ [$\Delta\chi^2(df) = 43.30(14), p < .001$]. Post hoc examination indicated that the loadings of only one of the CLQ vignettes resulted in a significant increase in χ^2 when constrained to be equal. This vignette therefore was removed in order to more fully evaluate the measurement properties of the rest of the inventory. The fit indices for the baseline model of the abridged CLQ (CLQ2) were good and constraining the factor loadings to be equal did not result in a significant increment in $\chi^2[\Delta\chi^2(df) = 18.26(13)]$.

Constraining the factor variance to be equal across samples produced similar results to constraining the factor loadings to be equal. That is, such constraints did not result in a significant increase in χ^2 for the CSQ and ESJI [$\Delta\chi^2(df) = .15(1)$ and .17(1), respectively], but did result in a significant change for the CLQ2 [$\Delta\chi^2(df) = 28.68(1), p < .001$]. Further equality constraints therefore were not placed on the CLQ2.

A final set of equality constraints were placed on the CSQ and the ESJI such that the reliability of each vignette was constrained to be equal across samples. When the residuals for the indicators of the latent CSQ and ESJI factors were constrained to be equal, a significant increase in χ^2 was observed [$\Delta\chi^2(df) = 141.95(14)$ and 64.61(6) for CSQ and ESJI, respectively].

Relation of Practical Intelligence and Tacit Knowledge to *g–f* and *g–c*

The bivariate correlation between each of the new tacit-knowledge inventories and the Cattell test were small (Cohen, 1988) but significant at the .01 level (ESJI, $r = .20$; CLQ, $r = .14$; CSQ, $r = .15$). Corrected for range restriction, these correlations increase only slightly (ESJI, $r = .23$; CLQ, $r = .16$; CSQ, $r = .17$). Similar correlation coefficients were found between the new tacit-knowledge inventories and the Mill Hill Vocabulary Scale, but only one was significant (ESJI, $r = .08$; CLQ, $r = .03$; CSQ, $r = .19, p < .01$).[4]

---

[4]Because the standard deviation of the corresponding norm sample for the Mill Hill could not be obtained from the publisher, corrections of correlation coefficients involving the Mill Hill could not be made.

Although the above results suggest that practical intelligence as reflected in the acquisition of everyday tacit knowledge is distinct from fluid and crystallized intelligence, a more nearly complete examination would be enabled by a confirmatory factor analysis in which latent variables free of measurement error represent the theoretical constructs. There are two ways in which such a model might be specified. First, practical intelligence may be allowed to correlate freely with fluid and crystallized intelligence, such that it is posited as a primary ability along with fluid and crystallized intelligence (see Horn & Cattell, 1966). In this model, practical intelligence must show a small, nonsignificant correlation with fluid and crystallized intelligence to support the claim that practical intelligence is "distinct" from these intelligence constructs. Second, and consistent with more recent research (Carroll, 1993; Gustafsson, 1984), fluid and crystallized intelligence may be specified as indicators of a higher-order general factor of intelligence (g). In this case, the correlation between practical intelligence and g must be small and nonsignificant to support the claim that practical intelligence is "distinct" from general intelligence.

Figures 5.2 and 5.3 show the results of the confirmatory factor analyses in which these two models were specified. As in Study 2, FIML was used to estimate model parameters given the intentionally incomplete overlapping group design.[5] Also consistent with Study 2, each tacit-knowledge inventory served as a single indicator of its respective latent tacit-knowledge factor with its factor loading and residual variance fixed to enable model identification. The higher-order latent Practical Intelligence factor was indicated by the latent Tacit-Knowledge factors and the latent Practical Knowledge Application (K-App) factor, indicated by the STAT-Practical content composites. The Cattell test and the Mill Hill Vocabulary Scale served as single indicators of their respective latent fluid (g–f) and crystallized (g–c) intelligence factors.[6]

As shown in Figure 5. 2, the loadings of the latent Tacit-Knowledge factors (.75–.90) on the higher-order Practical Intelligence factor were substantial. The loading of K-App on Practical Intelligence was lower (.43), but still significant. The correlations among the latent factors of Practical Intelligence and g–f and g–c (r = .34 and .20, respectively), which are free of measurement error, are significant and larger than those among their respective indicators, which have low reliabilities. The correlation between g–f and g–c (r = .44) is higher than the correlation between either of these latent factors and Practical Intelligence. The high–moderate correlation between K-App and g–f (r = .48) suggests the presence of a multiple-choice method factor. The fit of this model was quite good ($\chi^2(16)$ = 25.56, ns; CFI = .97; RMSEA = .03 (.00; .05); SRMR = .03).

Figure 5.3 differs from Figure 5. 2 in that the correlation among g–f and g–c is accounted for by a higher-order g factor. This specification was consistent with previous ability–structure research indicating that g accounts for the relation between fluid and crystallized intelligence (Carroll, 1993; Gustafsson, 1984). The correlation between practical intelligence and g was freely estimated. As shown in Figure 5.3, the correlation between Practical Intelligence and g (r = .48) is high–moderate. As with the previous model, there is a high–moderate correlation (r = .42) between K-App and g–f. The fit of this model was acceptable ($\chi^2(17)$ = 43.82, p < .001; CFI = .93; RMSEA = .05 (.03; .07); SRMR = .04).

---

[5]Estimated correlation matrices among the manifest indicators can be obtained by contacting the primary author.
[6]Although it is preferable to have multiple indicators of these latent variables, there were limitations to the amount of time available to administer measures and to the number of variables that could permit model identification due to the requirement of estimating the means and standard deviations of the sample data.

5.2

Hierarchical confirmatory factor analysis: Practical, fluid, and crystallized intelligence as primary factors. Note, standard errors of the parameter estimates for freely estimated values are indicated in parentheses. TK-ED = Tacit-Knowledge, Everyday; TK-GB = Tacit-Knowledge, General Business; TK-CL = Tacit-Knowledge, College Life; K-App = (Formal) Knowledge Application.

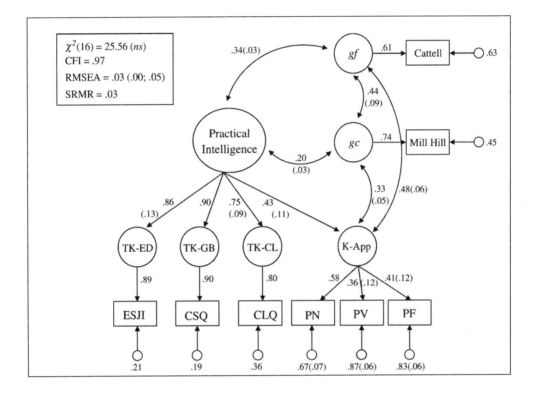

An alternative way to specify to this model without influencing fit is to change the bidirectional arrow between Practical Intelligence and g such that g has a causal influence on Practical Intelligence. This alternative specification obviously results in a loading of .48 for Practical Intelligence on a higher-order general intelligence factor. This model is statistically equivalent to the model depicted in Figure 5.3, but is less consistent with practical-intelligence theory, which places practical intelligence equivalent to g in the hierarchy of abilities (Sternberg, 1988, 1997).

Discussion

The results from Study 3 support the results from Studies 1 and 2, indicating that each of the new tacit-knowledge inventories has a single-factor structure that is stable across samples. The results of the hierarchical confirmatory factor analyses conducted in this study revealed that practical intelligence is not the same construct as fluid and

5.3

Hierarchical confirmatory factor analysis: Correlation between practical intelligence and *g*. Note, standard errors of the parameter estimates for freely estimated values are indicated in parentheses. TK-ED = Tacit-Knowledge, Everyday; TK-GB = Tacit-Knowledge, General Business; TKCL = Tacit-Knowledge, College Life; K-App = (Formal) Knowledge Application.

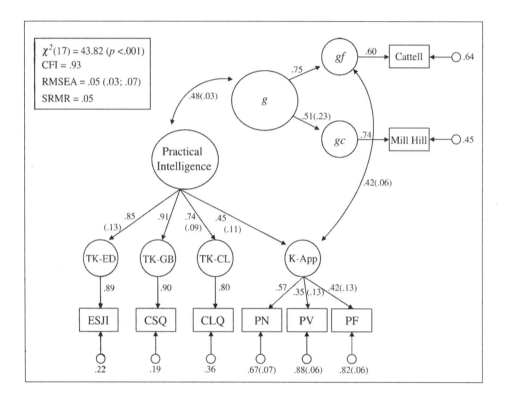

crystallized intelligence or general intelligence, but that these constructs do overlap. The high–moderate correlation between Practical Intelligence and *g* reflects common variance that may be due to shared demand for neurological functioning and/or shared performance requirements (i.e., test-taking versus other types of performances). Further empirical study that does not rely on the correlational approach is required to clarify the nature of the relation between practical intelligence and *g*.

General Discussion and Conclusions

The work described here represents an attempt to clarify the relation between practical intelligence and other intelligence constructs through the analysis of three new tacit-knowledge inventories. The new tacit-knowledge inventories were designed to capture tacit knowledge acquired from common everyday experiences such that individual differences on these measures would better reflect the general capacity to acquire tacit knowledge and apply knowledge to practical problem solving (i.e., practical intelligence). In addition, the samples used in this research were relatively less range-restricted on intellectual abilities than in previous studies (see Gottfredson, 2003; Schmidt & Hunter, 1993), further making it possible to demonstrate the equivalence of practical and general intelligence if such equivalence exists.

Measurement Properties of the New Tacit-Knowledge Inventories

Lievens (2005) has argued that situational judgment tests differ fundamentally from tests of cognitive ability or personality in that they are designed to sample specific performances rather than a generalizable construct. This difference accounts for the generally lower reliabilities and higher criterion validities of this type of assessment (Lievens, 2005; McDaniel et al., 2001). Tacit-knowledge inventories, in contrast, are designed to capture a generalizable construct—practical intelligence—using a knowledge-based method. This approach results in desirable measurement properties but also enables the assessment of abilities as developing expertise (Sternberg, 1998). Analyses from all three studies indicate that the everyday tacit-knowledge inventories have acceptable measurement properties and an underlying single-factor structure consistent with previous research (e.g., Wagner, 1987). The present findings indicate that it is feasible and productive from a psychometric standpoint to apply a theory-based approach to constructing situational judgment tests.

This chapter also presents one of the first attempts to study empirically the cross-sample stability of tacit-knowledge inventories. The multisample analyses in Study 1 and across Studies 2 and 3 indicated that each of the new tacit-knowledge inventories measured largely the same construct across samples, even when the samples came from different countries. These results suggest that performance on tacit-knowledge inventories is not strictly culture bound and support the impression that the inventories capture a general construct (see Lievens, 2005). The criterion-related validity of the Common Sense Questionnaire as explored in Study 1 was different across cultures (.11 and .34 in Spain and the U.S., respectively), however, indicating that the inventory captured less overlapping predictor and criterion spaces in the Spanish sample than in the U.S. sample (Lievens, 2005). Without further research it remains unknown whether this lack of overlap was due to the way the criterion performance was assessed (supervisor ratings) or to differential value placed on tacit-knowledge of everyday business by Spanish and American supervisors.

The criterion-related validity of the Common Sense Questionnaire in the American sample was consistent with previous research in the United States using other tacit-knowledge inventories (Colonia-Willner, 1998; Tan & Libby, 1997; Wagner, 1987; Wagner & Sternberg, 1985; Wagner et al., 1999). More important, scores on a new tacit-knowledge inventory designed to capture common, everyday knowledge have shown a comparable correlation to ratings of job performance as have measures of much more specialized job knowledge, including conventional situational judgment tests (McDaniel et al., 2001). This finding raises the question of whether the correlation found between scores on tacit-knowledge inventories and occupational performance criteria really was due to the measurement of job knowledge, as some have argued (Schmidt & Hunter, 1993), or to the measurement of practical intelligence.

Practical Intelligence and Other Intelligence Constructs

In keeping with previous research (e.g., Legree et al., 2003; Tan & Libby, 1997; Wagner, 1987; Wagner & Sternberg, 1985, 1990a, 1990b), the zero-order relation between scores on the new tacit-knowledge inventories and measures of fluid and crystallized intelligence were weak ($r \leq .23$), even when corrected for range restriction. This result cannot be due to the use of tacit-knowledge inventories requiring specialized knowledge because no such inventories were used in the present research. However, bivariate correlations alone are not enough to clarify the relation between practical intelligence and other intelligence constructs, particularly in light of the low reliabilities of the tests used to measure fluid and crystallized intelligence.

In Study 2, the covariance among the new tacit-knowledge inventories and the Practical subscale of the Sternberg Triarchic Abilities Test was accounted for by a single factor. This finding indirectly suggests that the weak relation between the tacit-knowledge scores and the tests of fluid and crystallized intelligence was not due to differences in test format (multiple-choice versus situational judgment) but to the measurement of different constructs. The first hierarchical confirmatory factor analysis conducted in Study 3 supports this conclusion. In this model, the correlation among the latent constructs of practical, fluid, and crystallized intelligence—free of measurement error—did not exceed .34. In addition, the Practical subscale of the Sternberg Triarchic Abilities Test had an independent correlation of .48 with fluid intelligence, perhaps due to shared method variance.

The second hierarchical confirmatory factor analysis conducted in Study 3, in which fluid and crystallized intelligence both loaded on a higher-order general intelligence factor, produced a correlation of .48 between practical intelligence and general intelligence. In a statistically equivalent model in which the relation between general intelligence and practical intelligence is causal, the loading of practical intelligence on g is also .48. The determination of which model is "correct" depends on one's theoretical orientation. According to the data, practical intelligence could be considered with equal validity to be a second-stratum ability below (and partially caused by) g (Carroll, 1993) or a first-stratum ability alongside (and sharing common variance with) g (Sternberg, 1988, 1997, 1998). Because of model equivalence, further correlational research will not address the relative correctness of these theoretical orientations.

In either case, the findings indicate that although practical and general intelligence are not equivalent constructs, they clearly overlap. The present data do not address the nature of this overlap but indicate that the investigation of its causes is necessary in order to advance the theory of practical intelligence. Studies that examine the neurological substrates of performance on tests of practical and general intelligence may illuminate the nature of their similarities and differences as would research that explores the development and comprehensive validation of performance-based (as opposed to test-based) measures of tacit knowledge and practical intelligence.

Limitations

There are a number of limitations to the present research, without which more comprehensive conclusions about the validity of practical intelligence and tacit knowledge could be drawn. First, although there is no clear theoretical link among personality, practical intelligence, and tacit knowledge (though see Jensen, 1993), it was not possible to test the distinction between these constructs because the new tacit-knowledge inventories were not evaluated along with measures of personality. Demonstrating such distinctiveness in light of the relation between conventional situational judgment tests and personality (McDaniel & Nguyen, 2001) would buttress the current construct validation effort.

Second, although practical intelligence was shown in Study 3 to be distinguishable from general intelligence, conclusions regarding the criterion-related validity of everyday tacit-knowledge inventories relative to tests of general intelligence cannot be drawn from the present research (though see Hedlund et al., 2006). In addition, the rating-scale criterion used in Study 1 appeared susceptible to a substantial halo effect and was not demonstrably tied to critical workplace behaviors or attitudes. Further evaluation of the criterion-related validity of everyday tacit knowledge and practical intelligence must be assessed within the context of generally accepted predictors and criteria of job success. These predictors should include multiple measures of cognitive ability and measures of personality traits such as conscientiousness and social presence.

Third, stronger multisample and cross-cultural research would involve more diverse samples than those presented here, such as those from cultures that are not steeped in Western European traditions (see Lievens, 2005). In addition, exploration of the comparison samples used for scoring tacit-knowledge inventories is necessary. Although there is initial work investigating differences between expert- and sample-based scoring methodologies (Legree, 1995; Mayer et al., 2003), there is no definitive guidance regarding the use of expert—versus sample—based scoring methodologies. Further research into implications of using different scoring methodologies (e.g., distance scores, correlations, other measures of association) for the measurement properties of tacit-knowledge inventories also is needed.

Conclusions

The present chapter has shown that practical intelligence and general intelligence do overlap when practical intelligence is measured in less range-restricted samples with inventories that capture common, everyday tacit knowledge. This finding does not obviate the theory of practical intelligence because the two constructs are not equivalent (see Sternberg et al., 2001); however, this finding does warrant investigation of the reasons for this overlap.

Appendix A: Statements Included in the Performance Evaluation Form (Study 3, U.S. Sample[7])

Part I[8]

1. My relationship with this employee is good.
2. I think highly of this employee.

---

[7]Spanish participants received the same form, translated into Castilian Spanish.
[8]The rating scale for Part I was as follows: 1 = definitely no, 5 = not sure, 9 = definitely yes.

3. I am satisfied with this employee.
4. This employee's relationships with other coworkers are good.

Part II[9]

1. How would you rate this employee's common-sense ability?
2. How would you rate this employee's academic ability?
3. How would you rate this employee's creative ability?
4. How would you rate this employee at working by him/herself?
5. How would you rate this employee at working with others?
6. How good is this employee at motivating him/herself?
7. How good is this employee at managing tasks?
8. How responsible is this employee?

References

Allison, P. D. (1987). Estimation of linear models with incomplete data. *Sociological Methodology, 17,* 71–103.

Bollen, K. A. (1989). *Structural equations with latent variables.* New York: Wiley.

Brookhart, S. M. (2004). Developing measurement theory for classroom assessment purposes and uses. *Educational Measurement, Issues and Practice, 22*(4), 5–12.

Byrne, B. M. (1998). *Structural equation modeling with LISREL, PRELIS, and SIMPLIS: Basic concepts, applications, and programming.* Mahwah, NJ: Erlbaum.

Carroll, J. B. (1993). *Human cognitive abilities: A survey of factor-analytic studies.* New York: Cambridge University Press.

Cattell, R. B., & Cattell, H. E. P. (1973). *Measuring intelligence with the Culture Fair Tests.* Champaign, IL: Institute for Personality and Ability Testing.

Cohen, J. (1988). *Statistical power analysis for the behavioral sciences* (2nd ed.). Mahwah, NJ: Erlbaum.

Colonia-Willner, R. (1998). Practical intelligence at work: Relationship between aging and cognitive efficiency among managers in a bank environment. *Psychology and Aging, 13*(1), 45–57.

Gottfredson, L. S. (2003). Dissecting practical intelligence theory: Its claims and evidence. *Intelligence, 31,* 343–397.

Gustafsson, J. (1984). A unifying model for the structure of intellectual abilities. *Intelligence, 8,* 179–203.

Hedlund, J., Forsythe, G. B., Horvath, J. A., Williams, W. M., Snook, S., & Sternberg, R. J. (2003). Identifying and assessing tacit knowledge: Understanding the practical intelligence of military leaders. *Leadership Quarterly, 14,* 117–140.

Hedlund, J., Wilt, J. M., Nebel, K. R., Ashford, S. J., & Sternberg, R. J. (2006). Assessing practical intelligence in business school admissions: A supplement to the Graduate Management Admissions Test. *Learning and Individual Differences, 16,* 101–127.

Horn, J. L., & Cattell, R. B. (1966). Refinement and test of the theory of fluid and crystallized general intelligences. *Journal of Educational Psychology, 57,* 253–270.

Jensen, A. R. (1993). Test validity: *g* versus "tacit knowledge." *Current Directions in Psychological Science, 2*(1), 9–10.

Kline, R. B. (1998). *Principles and practice of structural equation modeling.* New York: Guilford Press.

Legree, P. J. (1995). Evidence for an oblique social intelligence factor established with a Likert-based testing procedure. *Intelligence, 21,* 247–266.

Legree, P. J., Heffner, T. S., Psotka, J., Martin, D. E., & Medsker, G. J. (2003). Traffic crash involvement: Experiential driving knowledge and stressful contextual antecedents. *Journal of Applied Psychology, 88*(1), 15–26.

Legree, P. J., Pifer, M. E., & Grafton, F. C. (1996). Correlations among cognitive abilities are lower for higher ability groups. *Intelligence, 23,* 45–57.

---

[9]The rating scale for Part II was as follows: 1 = extremely bad, 5 = neither bad nor good, 9 = extremely good.

Lievens, F. (2005). International situational judgment tests. In J. A. Weekly & R. E. Ployhart (Eds.), *Situational judgment tests: Theory, measurement, and application.* Mahwah, NJ: Erlbaum.

Mayer, J. D., Salovey, P., Caruso, R., & Sitarenios, G. (2003). Measuring emotional intelligence with the MSCEIT V2.0. *Emotion, 3*(1), 97–105.

McArdle, J. J. (1994). Structural factor analysis experiments with incomplete data. *Multivariate Behavioral Research, 29*(4), 409–454.

McClelland, D. C. (1973). Testing for competence rather than for "intelligence." *American Psychologist, 28*, 1–14.

McDaniel, M. A., Morgeson, F. P., Finnegan, E. B., Campion, M. A., & Braverman, E. P. (2001). Use of situational judgment tests to predict job performance: A clarification of the literature. *Journal of Applied Psychology, 86*, 730–740.

McDaniel, M. A., & Nguyen, N. T. (2001). Situational judgment tests: A review of practice and constructs assessed. *International Journal of Selection and Assessment, 9*(1/2), 103–113.

Mitri, M. (2003). Applying tacit knowledge management techniques for performance assessment. *Computers and Education, 41*, 173–189.

Neisser, U. (1976). General, academic, and artificial intelligence. In L. B. Resnick (Ed.), *The nature of intelligence* (pp. 135–144). Hillsdale, NJ: Erlbaum.

New Oxford American Dictionary. (2001). New York: Oxford University Press.

Polanyi, M. (1958). *Personal knowledge: Towards a post-critical philosophy.* Chicago: University of Chicago Press.

Polanyi, M. (1966). *The tacit dimension.* New York: Doubleday.

Raven, J. C., Court, J. H., & Raven, J. (1994). *Mill Hill Vocabulary Scale,* 1994 edition. Oxford, UK: Oxford Psychologists Press.

Rencher, A. C. (1995). *Methods of multivariate analysis.* New York: Wiley.

Schmidt, F. L., & Hunter, J. E. (1993). Tacit knowledge, practical intelligence, general mental ability, and job knowledge. *Current Directions in Psychological Science, 2*, 8–9.

Sternberg, R. J. (1988). *Beyond IQ: A triarchic theory of human intelligence.* New York: Cambridge University Press.

Sternberg, R. J. (1991). Theory-based testing of intellectual abilities: Rationale for the Triarchic Abilities Test. In H. A. Rowe (Ed.), *Intelligence: Reconceptualization and measurement* (pp. 183–202). Hillsdale, NJ: Erlbaum.

Sternberg, R. J. (1997). *Successful intelligence.* New York: Plume Books.

Sternberg, R. J. (1998). Abilities are forms of developing expertise. *Educational Researcher, 27*(3), 11–20.

Sternberg, R. J. (2003). Issues in the theory and measurement of successful intelligence: A reply to Brody. *Intelligence, 31*, 331–337.

Sternberg, R. J., Conway, B. E., Ketron, J. L., & Bernstein, M. (1981). People's conception of intelligence. *Journal of Personality and Social Psychology, 41*, 37–55.

Sternberg, R. J., Forsythe, G. B., Hedlund, J., Horvath, J. A., Wagner, R. K., Williams, W. M., et al. (2000). *Practical intelligence in everyday life.* Cambridge, UK: Cambridge University Press.

Sternberg, R. J., Nokes, K., Geissler, P. W., Prince, R., Okatcha, F., Bundy, D. A., et al. (2001). The relationship between academic and practical intelligence: A case study in Kenya. *Intelligence, 29*, 401–418.

Sternberg, R. J., & the Rainbow Project Collaborators. (2005). Augmenting the SAT through assessments of analytical, practical, and creative skills. In W. Camara & E. Kimmel (Eds.), *Choosing students: Higher education admission tools for the 21st century* (pp. 159–176). Mahwah, NJ: Erlbaum.

Sternberg, R. J., & the Rainbow Project Collaborators. (2006). The Rainbow Project: Enhancing the SAT through assessments of analytical, practical, and creative skills. *Intelligence, 34*, 321–350.

Tan, H., & Libby, R. (1997). Tacit managerial versus technical knowledge as determinants of audit expertise in the field. *Journal of Accounting Research, 35*(1), 97–113.

Wagner, R. K. (1987). Tacit knowledge in everyday intelligent behavior. *Journal of Personality and Social Psychology, 52*(6), 1236–1247.

Wagner, R. K., & Sternberg, R. J. (1985). Practical intelligence in real-world pursuits: The role of tacit knowledge. *Journal of Personality and Social Psychology, 49*, 436–458.

Wagner, R. K., & Sternberg, R. J. (1990a). Street smarts. In K. E. Clark & M. B. Clark (Eds.), *Measures of leadership* (pp. 493–504). West Orange, NJ: Leadership Library of America.

Wagner, R. K., & Sternberg, R. J. (1990b). *Tacit-knowledge inventory for managers.* San Antonio: The Psychological Corporation.

Wagner, R. K., Sujan, H., Sujan, M., Rashotte, C. A., & Sternberg, R. J. (1999). Tacit knowledge in sales. In R. J. Sternberg & J. A. Horvath (Eds.), *Tacit knowledge in professional practice* (pp. 155–182). Mahwah, NJ: Erlbaum.

Wheaton, B., Muthén, B., Alwin, D. F., & Summers, G. F. (1977). Assessing reliability and stability in panel models. In David R. Heise (Ed.), *Sociological methodology* (pp. 85–136). San Francisco: Jossey-Bass.

Wothke, W. (2000). Longitudinal and multigroup modeling with missing data. In T. D. Little, K. U. Schnabel, & J. Baumert (Eds.), *Modeling longitudinal and multilevel data* (pp. 219–240). Mahwah, NJ: Erlbaum.

Component Processes in Analogical Reasoning

6

Robert J. Sternberg

Reasoning by analogy is pervasive in everyday experience. We reason analogically whenever we make a decision about something new in our experience by drawing a parallel to something old. When we buy a new goldfish because we liked our old one, or when we listen to a friend's advice because it was correct once before, we are reasoning analogically. In all walks of life, "analogy is inevitable in human thought" (Oppenheimer, 1956, p. 129).

Analogical reasoning has played a key role in psychological theory as well as in everyday practice. Differential psychologists have long recognized the close relation between analogical reasoning and intelligence. Spearman's three qualitative principles of cognition—apprehension of experience, eduction of relations, and eduction of correlates—correspond to three principal operations in analogical reasoning. Indeed, Spearman (1927) claimed that "it is certain that [analogy] tests—if properly made and used—have correlations with all that are known to contain g [Spearman's general factor of intelligence]" (p. 181). Raven, like Spearman, viewed analogical reasoning as central to intelligence and defined intellectual ability as the "ability to reason by analogy from awareness of relations between experienced characters" (Esher, Raven, & Earl, 1942, cited in Burke, 1958, p. 202). In Guilford's (1967) "structure of intellect" model, "one of the best types of CFR [cognition of figural relations] tests is a figure-analogies form" (p. 86). "We might expect a verbal-analogies test to be one of the best for factor CMR [cognition of semantic relations], and this seems to be the case" (p. 88).

Because of its prominent role in differential theories of intelligence, analogical reasoning ability is measured by many well-known psychometric ability tests. Raven's "progressive matrices," one of the most widely studied and highly regarded tests of general ability, was defined by Raven (1938) as "a test of a person's present capacity to form comparisons, reason by analogy, and develop a logical method of thinking regardless of previously acquired information" (p. 12). The Miller Analogies Test, widely used for graduate school admission, is composed exclusively of verbal analogies. Many other ability tests, such as the Scholastic Aptitude Test, the Graduate Record Examination, and the Concept Mastery Test, include analogies as one of several item types.

Analogical reasoning has played an important part in information-processing as well as differential theories of intelligence. Reitman's (1965) ARGUS, a computer program for solving verbal analogies, served as a first step toward a general theory of intelligence. The ANALOGY computer program of Evans (1968) solved geometric analogies taken from a standard intelligence test, and the program of Winston (Note 1) extended ANALOGY's algorithms to solving analogies with representations of three-dimensional objects. Rumelhart and Abrahamson (1973) have investigated the representation of information used in analogical reasoning and have proposed a way in which their spatial representation can be used in rank ordering the correctness of analogy options.

Despite its everyday pervasiveness and theoretical importance, analogical reasoning is still only poorly understood. Fundamental questions about analogical reasoning remain unanswered, or have been answered in conflicting ways. The present chapter addresses some of these questions.

First, the chapter describes alternative theoretical positions regarding (a) the component information processes used in analogical reasoning and (b) strategies for combining these processes. Second, the chapter presents results from three experiments on analogical reasoning. The experiments help (a) distinguish among alternative theories of the component processes used in analogical reasoning; (b) distinguish among models of strategies for combining component processes; (c) test the generality of the preferred theory and strategy model across different analogy contents, formats, and difficulties; (d) establish the durations of the various information processes used in the solution of the different kinds of analogies; (e) investigate the relations between component processes in analogical reasoning and intelligence. Third, the chapter summarizes and discusses progress made in elucidating each of these five issues.

Theoretical Viewpoints

Information Processes in Analogical Reasoning

Theoretical Issues

What are the basic information processes in analogical reasoning? Theorists seem to agree that (a) the reasoner must begin analogy solution by *encoding* analogy terms, that is, translating them into an internal representation on which further mental operations can be performed; and (b) the reasoner must complete analogy solution by indicating a *response.* Theorists disagree about the roles of three intermediate comparison operations, called *inference, mapping,* and *application* in this essay. The set of operations will be described with reference to a simple analogy example, Red:Stop: :Green:(a. Go, b. Halt).

Theoretical Positions

Theory with Inference, Mapping, and Application. According to one theory (Sternberg, 1977), inference, mapping, and application, as well as encoding and response, are all used in analogy solution. The reasoner (a) encodes the terms of the analogy, (b) infers the relation between Red and Stop (a red light means stop), (c) maps the relation between Red and Green (both are colors of traffic signals), (d) applies a relation analogous to the inferred one from Green to each answer option, choosing the closer option (a green light means go, not halt), (e) responds.

Theory with Inference and Application, but Not Mapping. According to a second theory, presented in different forms by Johnson (1962), Shalom and Schlesinger (Note 2), and Spearman (1923), only inference and application, in addition to encoding and response, are used in analogy solution. Mapping is not used. The reasoner (a) encodes the terms of the analogy, (b) infers the relation between Red and Stop, (c) applies a relation analogous to the inferred one from Green to each answer option, choosing the closer option, (d) responds. The various theorists use different labels for what are here called inference and application. Johnson refers to the inductive operation and the deductive operation, Shalom and Schlesinger to the formation of the connection formula and the application of the connection formula, and Spearman to the eduction of relations and the eduction of correlates.

Theory with Inference and Mapping, but Not Application. According to a third theory, only inference and mapping, in addition to encoding and response, are used in analogy solution. Application is not used. This theory is a distillation and simplification of the complex theories presented by Evans (1968) and Winston (Note 1) in their analogy-solving computer programs. The reasoner (a) encodes the terms of the analogy, (b) infers the relation between Red and Stop, (c) infers the relation between Green and each of the answer options, (d) maps the relation between the (Red, Stop) relation and each of the (Green, Go) and (Green, Halt) relations, choosing the closer one, (e) responds. In this theory, mapping rather than application is used as the final comparison operation that determines which answer correctly solves the analogy.

Information-Processing Strategies in Analogical Reasoning

Preview

In this section, four alternative models of analogical-reasoning strategies are proposed. First, the models are described in terms of the information-processing theory including inference, mapping, and application (Sternberg, 1977). Second, applicability of the models to different contents is discussed. Third, applicability of the models to different item formats is discussed. Fourth, a special dual-processing strategy is described for dealing with items among which are a degenerate class of analogies (A:A::A:A, A:A::B:B, A:B::A:B). Fifth, extension of the models to information-processing theories without mapping and without application is described.

Although the models specify in some detail the alternative ways in which attribute information can be combined to arrive at a solution for analogy problems, the models do not specify what the possible attributes are for different types of analogies, nor do they specify how subjects discover these attributes in the first place. A complete model of analogical reasoning would have to specify this further information; something that has not yet been done.

Four Basic Models

General Characteristics. The four basic models under the Sternberg (1977) theory share two characteristics: (a) The component processes are the same, and (b) the combination rule for component processes is the same: The processes are executed one immediately following another (serially). The models differ in the sequencing of the component processes and in the number of times each component process needs to be executed (exhaustively or with self-termination).

A schematic flow chart for the four models is presented in Figure 6.1.[1] Names of component processes are indicated inside the boxes of the flow chart, and latency parameters assigned to those processes (and discussed later) are indicated next to the boxes. Model I may be understood by following the flow chart down the left side of the figure, and then moving right at the bottom of the figure. Models II, III, and IV branch off from Model I at successively earlier points in the sequence of operations and also contain feedback loops of different sizes. Roman numerals along arrows indicate at what point each of these models branches off from Model I, and also indicate the respective scopes of the feedback loops. The models are illustrated by working through the example analogy, Washington:1::Lincoln:(a. 10, b. 5), as shown in Table 6.1.

Model 1. In Model I, the subject begins analogy solution with attribute identification: He or she encodes the first analogy term, *Washington,* and then the second term, *1.* In encoding each analogy term, the subject identifies the term, retrieves from long-term memory the attributes that may be relevant for analogy solution, retrieves from long-term memory a value corresponding to each attribute, and stores the results as an attribute-value list in working memory. Potentially relevant attributes are those that experience has indicated are useful in relating one concept to other concepts. In the example, the subject stores in working memory the facts that Washington was the first president, has his portrait on a dollar bill, and was a Revolutionary War hero. Facts that are possibly relevant for the numeral *1* are that it can represent the first counting number, the first ordinal position, or a unitary amount.

Next the subject infers the relation between all values of corresponding attributes in the first two analogy terms. The relation is stored as a list of attributes with corresponding values in working memory. Attribute comparison in inference is exhaustive with respect to the encoded attributes (although it is obviously not exhaustive with respect to all attributes stored in long-term memory that might have been

---

[1]Detailed flow charts for all models are presented in Sternberg (1977).

6.1

Flow chart for Models I, II, III, IV. Models II, III, and IV branch off from Model I at different points, and also contain feedback loops of different sizes. Branching points of each model are indicated by Roman numerals corresponding to the model number.

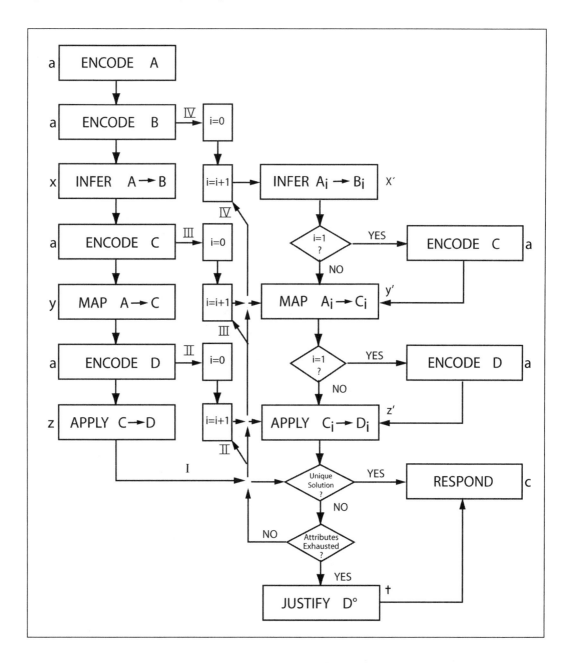

6.1 Attribute-Value List for Analogy Example—Washington:1::Lincoln:(a. 10, b. 5)

Process	Analogy Term or Relation	Relevant Attributes and Values
Encoding	*Washington*	[(president (first)), (portrait on currency (dollar)), (war hero (Revolutionary))]
	1	[(counting number (one)), (ordinal position (first)), (amount (one unit))]
	Lincoln	[(president (sixteenth)), (portrait on currency (five dollars)), (war hero (Civil))]
	10	[(counting number (ten)), (ordinal position (tenth)), (amount (ten units))]
	5	[(counting number (five)), (ordinal position (fifth)), (amount (five units))]
Inference	*Washington → 1*	[(president (ordinal position (first)), (portrait on currency (amount (dollar), (0))]
Mapping	*Washington → Lincoln*	[(presidents (first, sixteenth)), (portraits on currency (dollar, five dollars)), (war heroes (Revolutionary, Civil))]
Application	*Lincoln → 10*	[(0), (0), (0)]
	Lincoln → 5	[(0), (portrait on currency (amount (five dollars))), (0)]

placed in working memory). In the example, two of the three attributes encoded for *Washington* can be used to relate that analogy term to the second term, *1*. The inferred relation states that Washington was the first president and has his portrait on a dollar bill. No relation to *1* could be found for the third attribute-value pair identifying Washington as a Revolutionary War hero, and so this attribute-value pair is assigned a null value (0) in the inference relation.

The subject then encodes the third analogy term, *Lincoln,* enabling him or her to map the relation between the first and third analogy terms. Mapping, like inference, is exhaustive with respect to the attributes stored in working memory. Once the relation between the first and third terms has been discovered, it is stored in working memory as an attribute-value list. In the example, the subject recognizes that both Washington and Lincoln (a) were presidents, (b) have their portraits on currency, and (c) were war heroes.

The final required encodings are of the answer options, *10* and *5*. Once these terms are encoded, the subject attempts to apply from *Lincoln* to each answer option a relation analogous to the one previously inferred. Application, like inference and mapping, is exhaustive. An attempt to construct an analogous relation from *Lincoln* to *10* results in a null relation, because no analogy can be found: Lincoln was neither the 10th president nor is he the portrait on a 10-dollar bill. An analogous relation can be constructed from *Lincoln* to *5*, however, because Lincoln's portrait appears on a 5-dollar bill. Hence, a unique solution has been found. (Note that the solution is uniquely correct with respect to the available answer options, not with respect to any possible answer option that might have been employed.) Having solved the item, the subject responds with option *b,* completing the analogy problem.

In some instances, the component processes previously described are insufficient to reach a unique analogy solution. Suppose, for example, that the subject had failed to encode that Washington's portrait is on a 1-dollar bill, or that the subject had mistakenly believed that Lincoln's portrait is on a 20-dollar bill. In each case, neither of the presented answer alternatives would have met the subject's criterion for a correct answer. An additional, optional process would be required in which the subject justifies an answer option as somehow meeting this criterion, either because the subject's initial evaluation of the option was incorrect, or because the option is the best of the given alternatives. In true–false analogies, justification may be used when the presented answer option is neither clearly true nor clearly false: The presented answer does not meet the subject's criterion for correctness, but it is not clearly false either. Justification requires the subject to check previous operations to determine whether either (a) an error has been made or (b) additional information can be obtained to reach a unique solution.

Model II. The strategy on which Model II is based is identical to the Model I strategy through the encoding of D (including D_1 and D_2). At this point, an "attribute counter" is set equal to 0, and then incremented by 1.[2] Only one attribute is applied. This attribute, that Lincoln was the 16th president, fails to distinguish between answer options. So the subject returns to the attribute counter and again increments it by 1. He or she now applies the second attribute. In doing so, the subject recognizes that 5 refers to the amount of the bill on which Lincoln appears. Since the second option leads to an analogous rule, the subject responds *b.* Had neither option led to an analogous rule, even after all attributes had been examined, the subject would have attempted to justify one of the answer options as the better one.

Note that in Model II, inference and mapping are exhaustive, but application is self-terminating. Whereas in Model I all attributes were applied, in Model II only as many attributes are applied as are needed to reach a unique solution. The subject never reaches the third attribute-value pair identifying Lincoln as a Civil War hero, because the second attribute permitted a unique solution.

Model III. The strategy for Model III is identical to that for Model II through the encoding of the third analogy term. At this point, the subject enters the attribute-testing loop that in Model II includes only application. The subject maps one attribute, recognizing that Washington and Lincoln were both presidents, the 1st and 16th, respectively. Since $i = 1$ (the subject is traveling through the loop for the first time), the subject encodes D. He will not reencode D should subsequent iterations through the loop be necessary (since in subsequent iterations, $i \neq 1$). Next the subject applies the first attribute, that Lincoln was the 16th president. This application fails to yield a unique solution, so the subject returns to the beginning of the loop. As in Model II, the second trip through the loop does yield a unique answer.

Note that in Model III, inference is exhaustive, but mapping and application are self-terminating. Whereas Model II required mapping of all three attributes to solve the analogy, Model III requires mapping of only two attributes.

Model IV. The strategy for Model IV is the same as that for Model III through the encoding of the second analogy term. At this point, the subject sets $i = 0$ and then

---

[2]These bookkeeping operations are assumed in general to consume trivial amounts of time.

enters the attribute-testing loop. Once again, the loop is arranged so that analogy terms are encoded only on the first trip through the loop. The subject infers, maps, and then applies an attribute, trying to select a unique answer. If he or she cannot, it is necessary to return to the beginning of the loop. The subject infers, maps, and then applies another attribute, continuing the iterative process until the analogy is solved, or until justification is necessary.

Note that in Model IV, inference, mapping, and application are all self-terminating. Whereas Model III required inference of all three attributes to solve the analogy, Model IV requires only two inferences.

Analogy Content

The four models described above can be applied to analogies differing widely in content. As was true in the illustrative verbal analogy, information is represented in an attribute-value format. A second type of analogy used in the experiments to be described is the "people-piece" analogy. People pieces are schematic pictures of people varying on four binary attributes. A tall, blue, fat male, for example, could be represented as [(height (tall)), (color (blue)), (girth (fat)), (sex (male))]. Still another type of analogy to be considered is the geometric one. A black square inside a white circle might be represented as [((shape (square)), (position (surrounded)), (color (black))), ((shape (circle)), (position (surrounding)), (color (white)))]. The animal name analogies used by Rumelhart and Abrahamson (1973) might also be represented in an attribute-value format: [(size (x)), (ferocity (y)), (humanness (z))], where x, y, and z are amounts of each attribute. This representation for animal name analogies, and possibly representations for other types of analogies as well, appears to be formally isomorphic to Rumelhart and Abrahamson's spatial representation.

Analogy Format

True–False Analogies.   In true–false analogies, the subject proceeds through the analogy and tries to determine whether a relation can be constructed from C to D that is analogous to the relation from A to B. If such a relation can be constructed, the analogy is true; otherwise, it is false.

Forced-Choice Analogies.[3]   In forced-choice analogies, the subject proceeds through the analogy and tries to determine which option best forms a C to D relation that is analogous to the A to B relation. In applying the analogous rule from C to D, two basic strategies may be followed. The essential aspects of the two strategies are presented schematically in Figure 6.2.

In *sequential option scanning,* the subject applies attributes onto one option before applying any attributes onto another option. It is assumed that as a safeguard against premature decisions, the subject checks all options. Consider the example in Table 6.1. The subject initiates application by applying the first attribute-value pair for *Lincoln,* (president (16th)), onto *10.* This fails to yield a match, as do subsequent

---

[3]Application of the models to an option-ranking format in which one is required to rank order options from best to worst is described in Sternberg (1977).

6.2

Alternative strategies in scanning options of forced-choice analogies.

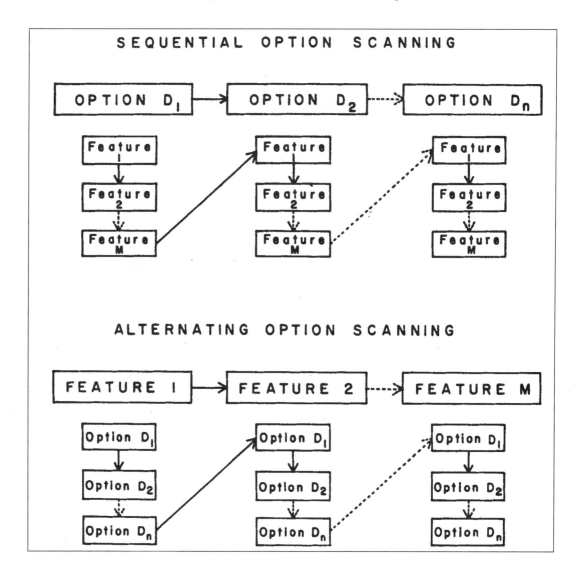

applications onto *10.* Next, the subject applies each of the attribute-value pairs onto *5,* finding a match for (portrait on currency (5 dollars)).

In *alternating option scanning,* the subject applies an attribute onto each option before applying any further attributes. Again, the subject is assumed to check all options. In the example, the subject initiates application by applying (president (16th)) first onto *10,* then onto *5.* This fails to yield a match. The subject then applies (portrait on currency (5 dollars)) onto *10*, and then *5*, obtaining a match. Note that whereas sequential option scanning required application of all attributes onto the first answer option, alternating option scanning required application of only two attributes onto this answer.

Dual Processing

Exploratory investigation revealed that for some types of analogies, the models described above need to be supplemented by an additional holistic scanning operation. This holistic scanning is tentatively suggested to occur in parallel with the processes of the models as described.[4] In holistic scanning, the subject quickly surveys the terms of the analogy for identities between two or more analogy terms. If the search is successful, the analogy may be solved by template matching: The correct option must match one (or more) of the terms of the analogy stem. The attribute comparisons of the four models, begun in parallel with holistic scanning, continue only if holistic scanning fails to solve the analogy.

Dual processing of the sort described above seems only to be used when (a) at least some of the analogies to be solved have identities in terms (as in analogies of the forms A:A::A:A, A:A::B:B, A:B::A:B), and (b) the analogy terms are highly overlearned. Dual-processing models have also been proposed by Bamber (1969) and Lockhead (1972) in the context of perceptual tasks, and by Collins and Quillian (1969) in the context of a sentence verification task. Hunt (1974) has suggested two alternative algorithms by which Raven's progressive matrix problems can be solved, and these also seem to correspond closely to the two types of processes described here.

Applicability of the Models to Alternative Process Theories

Models I to IV have been described in terms of the process theory including inference, mapping, and application, but the models are applicable as well to the other two theories described. In the theory including inference and application but not mapping, Model I consists of exhaustive inference and application; Models II and III are equivalent, consisting of exhaustive inference but self-terminating application; Model IV consists of self-terminating inference and application. In the theory including inference and mapping but not application, Model I consists of exhaustive inference and mapping; Models II and III are again equivalent, consisting of exhaustive inference but self-terminating mapping; Model IV consists of sell-terminating inference and mapping.

Experimental Data

Preview

This section is divided into eight parts. The first part describes the methods for the three experiments. The second part shows how the design of the experiments was used in the mathematical formulation of the strategy models. The third part presents

---

[4]The two types of processes are believed to occur in parallel because the use of holistic scanning does not appear to add to the time taken in standard attribute processing.

6.3

Typical people-piece analogies.

global aspects of the experimental data. The fourth part contains qualitative tests of the response-time models. The fifth part contains quantitative tests of the response-time models. The sixth part contains quantitative tests of the response-error models. The seventh part describes the distribution of processing time in analogy solution. The eighth part analyzes individual differences in analogical reasoning.

Method

Materials

People-Piece Analogy Experiment. Stimuli in the first experiment were Elementary Science Study (ESS) "people pieces," schematic drawings of people varying on four binary attributes: height (tall–short), color (blue–red), sex (male–female), and girth (fat–thin). The pictures were drawn on mimeograph stencil, reproduced, colored, and then pasted on tachistoscope cards. Items were true–false in format. Sample items of various types are shown in Figure 6.3. Color is indicated by shading: White figures were red in the experiment, and black figures were blue.

There were three general types of items: degenerate, semidegenerate, and nondegenerate. The first pictured item is a degenerate one, or one in which the number of attribute values changed both from A to B and from A to C is zero. These analogies are of the form, A:A::A:A. A correct fourth term will always match all the other terms. The pictured item is a true one.

The second pictured item is an example of a semidegenerate one, or one in which the number of values changed either from A to B, or from A to C (but not both) is zero. These analogies are of the form A:A::B:B, or A:B::A:B. The pictured item is of the latter form; it is, however, a false item, since a correct completion of a semidegenerate analogy will always match either the second or third analogy term.

The third and fourth pictured examples are nondegenerate analogies of the standard form, A:B::C:D. A correct fourth term of a nondegenerate analogy will not match any other term of the analogy. The third pictured item is true and the fourth item is false.

Verbal Analogy Experiment.   Stimuli in the second experiment were verbal analogies typed in large capital letters (International Business Machines Orator typeface) on tachistoscope cards. A representative sample of verbal analogies is shown in Table 6.2. The first digit of the number preceding each analogy indicates whether it is true (0) or false (1). The correct answer to false items is shown in the table proceeding the last analogy term, although of course these answers were not shown to subjects. Degenerate and semidegenerate analogies are shown at the bottom of the table and are numbered between 73 and 84 in their last two digits.

Geometric Analogy Experiment.   Stimuli in the third experiment were geometric analogies. Analogies were selected (with permission) from the Analogies subtests of the 1934, 1941, 1946, and 1947 editions of the American Council on Education Psychological Examination for College Freshmen (Thurstone & Thurstone, Note 3). All items selected for use in the experiment were modified in two ways: (a) the number of answer options was reduced from five to two, including the keyed option and a randomly selected option; (b) items were drawn by an artist in enlarged form on tachistoscope cards. In addition, some of the items were converted to degenerate and semidegenerate form.

The agreement permitting use of the test items prohibited their reproduction in a published piece. Figure 6.4 displays items similar to those used in the experiment.

Ability Tests.   Subjects participating in the experiments received ability tests similar to ones used by Thurstone (1938) in his investigations of the primary mental abilities. The tests measured reasoning and perceptual-speed abilities.

The reasoning tests included homemade word grouping and letter series tests, and Forms A and B of Level 3 of the Cattell Culture-Fair Test of g (Cattell & Cattell, 1963). The word grouping test required subjects to select one word (from a group of five) that did not belong with the others, for example, (1) hammer, (2) wrench, (3) screwdriver, (4) nail, (5) drill (answer—4). The letter series test required subjects to complete a series of letters, for example, c d c f g f i j (1) i, (2) j, (3) k, (4) m (answer—1).

The perceptual-speed tests included homemade same–different recognition and letter identification tests, and Tests P-1, P-2, and P-3 (Finding As, Number Comparisons, and Identical Pictures) from the French Kit of Reference Tests for Cognitive Factors (French, Ekstrom, & Price, 1963). The same–different recognition test required

	6.2 Typical Verbal Analogies	
No.	Analogy	Correct Answer to False Items
006	HAND:FOOT::FINGER:TOE	
009	MERCHANT:SELL::CUSTOMER:BUY	
010	DIME:10::NICKEL:5	
014	ATTORNEY:LAW::DOCTOR:MEDICINE	
019	PISTOL:BOW::BULLET:ARROW	
025	WORD:LETTER::PARAGRAPH:SENTENCE	
045	YOUR:MY::YOURS:MINE	
047	HEAR:SEE::DEAF:BLIND	
071	COWARDICE:ENVY::YELLOW:GREEN	
103	LEOPARD:TIGER::SPOTS:SOUP	stripes
108	AUTOMOBILE:ROAD::TRAIN:CABOOSE	track
117	LIME:LEMON::GREEN:ANIMAL	yellow
119	THUNDER:LIGHTNING::HEAR:TASTE	see
126	TRAIN:ENGINEER::PLANE:NOISE	pilot
127	SILENCE:DARKNESS::SOUND:MOON	light
130	REFRIGERATOR:FOOD::WALLET:PATIENCE	money
132	BOTH:EITHER::AND:CONJUNCTION	or
144	THEN:NOW::PAST:KIND	present
073	ARTIST:ARTIST::ARTIST:ARTIST	
078	HAMMER:HAMMER::NAIL :NAIL	
084	TREE:FOREST::TREE:FOREST	
175	MACHINE:MACHINE::MACHINE:GRASS	machine
177	CLOUD:CLOUD::RAIN:SECTION	rain
183	WINTER:SEASON::WINTER:MONTH	season

Note. The first digit of the number indicates whether the analogy is true (0) or false (1).

subjects to recognize whether pairs of numbers were the same or different, for example, 295699_____295899 (answer—"D" for *different*). The letter identification test required subjects to draw a slash through each *l* and a dot inside each *o* in a string of letters, for example, n t v l c k d f b l u o (answer—ntv/lckdfb/lue).

Subjects

People-Piece and Verbal Analogy Experiments. The identical set of 16 subjects participated in the people-piece and verbal analogy experiments. Of the subjects, 11 were men and 5 were women. Subjects were selected on the basis of composite reasoning and perceptual-speed scores on the homemade ability tests. These tests were administered to 268 Psychology 1 students at Stanford University in order to select four groups of four subjects each. Subjects were selected so as to be high in both reasoning and perceptual speed, high in reasoning but low in perceptual speed, low in reasoning

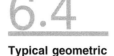

Typical geometric analogies.

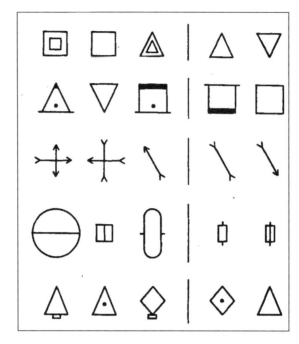

but high in perceptual speed, or low in both reasoning and perceptual speed. High scores were defined as those exceeding the 80th percentile; low scores were defined as those between the 10th and 30th percentiles. The median proportion of shared variance between reasoning and perceptual-speed tests (r^2) was .046 in the Psychology 1 subject pool, suggesting that the use of a "pseudo-orthogonal" design probably did not much affect interpretation of results (see Humphreys & Fleishman, 1974).

Geometric Analogy Experiment. Twenty-four subjects participated in the geometric analogy experiment, 12 of them men and 12 of them women. The homemade word grouping test was administered to 441 Psychology 1 students at Stanford University in order to select 12 high-reasoning and 12 low-reasoning subjects for the experiment. High scores were defined as those between the 75th and 95th percentiles; low scores were defined as those between the 5th and 25th percentiles.

Procedure

People-Piece Analogy Experiment. Subjects solved analogies presented via an Iconix three-field tachistoscope. Each test trial consisted of two parts, as in Johnson's (1960, 1962) method of serial analysis. The first part of the trial involved precueing, whereas the second part involved presentation of the full analogy.

The first part of the trial began with the appearance of a fixation point. This point was located at the spot where the first term of the analogy would appear. After 1,000 msec, the fixation point vanished and a certain number of "cues" appeared on the screen. The number of cues could be either 0, 1, 2, or 3. In the 0-cue condition, a lighted but blank field appeared. In the 1-cue condition, the first term of the analogy appeared; in the 2-cue condition, the first two terms of the analogy appeared; in the 3-cue condition, the first three terms of the analogy appeared. Subjects were given as long as they wanted to view whatever cues appeared, but they were told that they should take only as long as they really needed. After a subject was ready to continue, he indicated this by pressing a red button on the button panel. The second part of the trial then began. A fixation point appeared on the screen for 1,000 msec, followed by the full analogy. The subject then solved the analogy. Subjects were told to solve analogies as quickly as they could under the constraint that they should make almost no errors. High accuracy was rewarded with a bonus.

All testing sessions were conducted by two experimenters. One experimenter carried out the physical manipulation of the cards. The other experimenter recorded item number, cue time, solution time, and the presence of an error if one was made. Trials on which errors occurred were repeated at the end of blocks of trials.

Analogy testing was spread out over four sessions, with each session of test trials preceded by 48 practice trials. Items were blocked within cueing condition, and order of cueing conditions was counterbalanced in a Latin-square arrangement. Presentation of test items was divided into four blocks per testing session. Subjects were informed of the number of errors they had made after each block was completed.

Since subjects indicated that they did not remember analogies over sessions, all items were presented once in each cueing condition. Thus, the 288 people-piece items were presented over a total of 1,152 trials.

Verbal Analogy Experiment. The procedure in this experiment was the same as that in the preceding experiment, except that (a) error trials were not repeated, (b) each session of test trials was preceded by 12 practice trials, (c) items were presented only once to each subject. The 168 verbal items were thus presented over 168 trials. Although the items were each presented only once, they were divided into four quasiparallel forms, so that each item type was nevertheless presented in each cueing condition.

Geometric Analogy Experiment. The procedure in this experiment was the same as that in the people-piece analogy experiment, except that (a) error trials were not repeated; (b) each session of test trials was preceded by 12 practice trials; (c) subjects indicated readiness to begin the second part of the trial by pushing a foot pedal; (d) there were only two cue conditions, 0 and 2. The 90 geometric analogy items were presented twice each (once in each cueing condition) over 180 trials.

Design

Precueing conditions were crossed with attribute-value changes. Items differed in numbers of value changes from (a) the A to B analogy terms, (b) the A to C analogy terms, (c) the D analogy term(s) to D_T (the true or keyed answer). In the people-piece analogy experiment, numbers of value changes were objectively determined. In the other two experiments, ratings were used to estimate value changes. Subjects (otherwise uninvolved in any of the experiments) were asked to rate "distances" or "relatedness" (depending on the experiment) between pairs of analogy terms. Underlying this procedure were the assumptions that (a) the ratings represent an implicit linear scale of latent value transformations in the attribute-value representation for information, and that (b) these value transformations form the basis of item difficulty.

Mathematical Formulation of the Strategy Models

Process Theory with Inference, Mapping, and Application

Parameters. Latency and error parameters were assigned to each component operation in the information-processing models. The latency parameters represent the duration of each operation; the error parameters represent the difficulty of each operation. The latency parameters corresponding to the duration of each operation are shown next to the appropriate boxes in the flow chart (Figure 6.1). Durations of self-terminating operations are indicated by primed parameters (e.g., x' for self-terminating inference), whereas durations of exhaustive operations are indicated by unprimed parameters (e.g., x for exhaustive inference).

Additivity. Response time is hypothesized to equal the sum of the amounts of time spent on each component operation. Hence, a simple linear model predicts response time to be the sum across the different component operations of the number of times each component operation is performed (as an independent variable) multiplied by the duration of that component operation (as an estimated parameter).

Proportion of response errors is hypothesized to equal the (appropriately scaled) sum of the difficulties encountered in executing each component operation. A simple linear model predicts proportion of errors to be the sum across the different component operations of the number of times each component operation is performed (as an independent variable) multiplied by the difficulty of that component operation (as an estimated parameter). This additive combination rule is based on the assumption that each subject has a limit on processing capacity (or space; see Osherson, 1974). Each execution of an operation uses up capacity. Until the limit is exceeded, performance is flawless except for constant sources of error (such as motor confusion, carelessness, momentary distractions, etc.). Once the limit is exceeded, however, performance is at a chance level.

In the response-time models (with solution latency as dependent variable), all component operations must contribute significantly to solution latency, since by definition each execution of an operation consumes some amount of time. In the response-error models (error rate as dependent variable), however, all component operations need not contribute significantly to proportion of errors. The reason for this is that some operations may be so easy that no matter how many times they are executed, they contribute only trivially to prediction of errors.

Parameter Estimation. Mathematical modeling was done by multiple regression. Parameters of the models were estimated as unstandardized regression coefficients. Table 6.3 shows the basic equations for Models I, II, III, and IV, assuming that analogies are of the form A:B::C:D. In the geometric analogy experiment, there were five terms rather than four to encode, and since analogy terms varied widely in complexity, the multiplier for the encoding parameter (*a*) was determined by figure complexity ratings (obtained from subjects otherwise uninvolved in the experiments).

All parameters of each model enter into analogy processing in the 0-cue condition. The subjects must encode all four terms of the analogy, as well as perform the inference, mapping, application, and response processes. The 1-cue condition differs only slightly. The first term was presented during precueing and is assumed to have been encoded

6.3	**Basic Equations for the Models of Analogical Reasoning**	

No. Cues	Equation
	Model I
0	$ST_0 = 4a + fx + gy + fz + c$
1	$ST_1 = 3a + fx + gy + fz + c$
2	$ST_2 = 2a + \quad + gy + fz + c$
3	$ST_3 = a + \quad + \quad + fz + c$
	Model II
0	$ST_0 = 4a + fx + gy + f'z' + c$
1	$ST_1 = 3a + fx + gy + f'z' + c$
2	$ST_2 = 2a + \quad gy + f'z' + c$
3	$ST_3 = a + \quad + \quad + f'z' + c$
	Model III
0	$ST_0 = 4a + fx + g'y' + f'z' + c$
1	$ST_1 = 3a + fx + g'y' + f'z' + c$
2	$ST_2 = 2a + \quad + g'y' + f'z' + c$
3	$ST_3 = a + \quad + \quad + f'z' + c$
	Model IV
0	$ST_0 = 4a + f'x' + g'y' + f'z' + c$
1	$ST_1 = 3a + fx' + g'y' + f'z' + c$
2	$ST_2 = 2a + \quad + g'y' + f'z' + c$
3	$ST_3 = a + \quad + \quad f'z' + c$

Note. Symbol definitions: ST_i = solution time i; a = exhaustive figure scanning and encoding time; x = exhaustive inference time; y = exhaustive mapping time; z = exhaustive application time; x' = self-terminating inference time; y' = self-terminating mapping time; z' = self-terminating application time; c = constant response time. N = total number of attributes; T = truth index (0 = true; 1 = false). f = number of values changed from A to B; g = number of values changed from A to C; h = number of D values correctly matched to D'. $f' = [(N + T)/(N - h + 1)] \cdot (f)/(N)$; $g' [(N+T)/(N - h+1)] \cdot (g)/(N)$.

at that time. Hence, the 1-cue condition requires the encoding of just three analogy terms rather than all four. In the 2-cue condition, the A and B terms of the analogy were precued, and it is assumed that inference occurred during precueing. Hence, the inference parameter $(x$ or $x')$ drops out, and there is again one less term to encode. In the 3-cue condition, the A and C terms were precued, and hence it is assumed that mapping as well as inference occurred during precueing. The mapping parameter $(y$ or $y')$ therefore drops out, and there is again one less term to encode. In general, the successive cueing conditions are characterized by the successive dropout of model parameters.

Although they are not shown in the table, parameter dropouts also resulted from null transformations in which no changes occurred from A to B and/or from A to C. These dropouts occurred in the degenerate and semidegenerate analogies. (Indeed, these types of analogies were originally included to provide a zero baseline for parameter estimation.) For example, in the 0-cue condition, the inference and application parameters drop out when no changes occur from A to B, and the mapping parameter drops out when no changes occur from A to C. The same type of selective dropout occurs in all four cueing conditions.

The models make separate attribute-comparison time or error "charges" only for (objective or rated) value transformations. This type of "difference parameter" was used throughout the experiments, and has been used by others as well (e.g., Clark & Chase, 1972). Value identities are not separately charged. Subjects are assumed to be preset to recognize null transformations ("sames"), and the parameter is assumed to represent amount of time or difficulty involved in alteration of the initial state.

Where needed, the optional justification parameter was estimated as a function of the product of the distance from the keyed option to the ideal option times the number of previous attribute-comparison operations to be checked, both as determined by subjects' ratings. The further the keyed option is from the ideal one, the more likely is checking to be necessary. If the keyed and ideal options are identical, then the value of the justification parameter will be zero, and hence it will be irrelevant to analogy solution. If, however, not even the best presented option corresponds to the ideal option, then justification is required. This parameter was used only in the forced-choice geometric analogies.

In those experiments with degenerate and semidegenerate analogies and with highly overlearned analogy terms (the people-piece and verbal analogy experiments), holistic scanning was incorporated into the models by introducing two new assumptions: (a) that in holistic processing, all attribute comparison is "same–different"; (b) "different" transformations take longer than "same" (null) ones. Two major implications follow from the new assumptions. First, if no changes occur from A to B, then it does not matter how many value changes occur from A to C, if any values are changed at all. Similarly, if no changes occur from A to C, it does not matter how many values are changed from A to B, if any values are changed at all. Second, a "same" match from D to D_T (the true keyed answer) is assumed to be faster than a "different" mismatch. Thus, "true" responses are predicted to be faster than "false" responses for degenerate and semidegenerate analogies.

Mathematically, the identical equations are used for both types of processing. The only difference in independent variables is for semidegenerate analogies. In these analogies, a match is treated identically to 0 value changes, and a mismatch is treated identically to 1 value change. Thus, the number of "values changed" was always 0 or 1 in these analogies.

Process Theory with Inference and Application, but Not Mapping

The mathematical models for the process theory without mapping were identical to those for the process theory with mapping, except that the mapping parameter was omitted from all calculations. This omission meant that the number of attribute values changed from the A to C analogy terms was assumed to have no effect on analogy solution latency or error rate.

Process Theory with Inference and Mapping, but Not Application

The mathematical models for the process theory without application were identical to those for the process theory with application, except that (a) inference and application were combined into a single inference parameter and (b) mapping was assumed

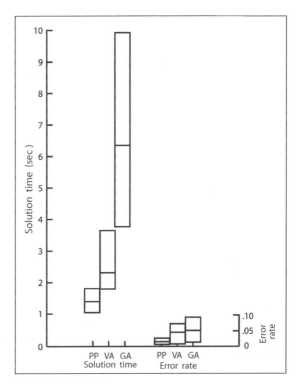

6.5

Ranges of solution times and error rates across subjects in analogy experiments. Median values are indicated by bar dividing upper and lower parts of each bar. (Abbreviations: PP = people-piece analogies; VA = verbal analogies; GA = geometric analogies.)

to be required during solution of items presented in the 3-cue condition (since in this theory, mapping is assumed to occur as the last attribute-comparison process).

Global Aspects of Information Processing

The bar graph in Figure 6.5 presents solution times and error rates for the full (0-cue) people-piece, verbal, and geometric analogies. Bars represent range of times and error rates across subjects, and the horizontal line dividing each bar into two parts represents the median solution time or error rate. As expected, solution times and error rates increased across experiments. Solution times and error rates were highly correlated across item types within each experiment.

Qualitative Tests of the Response-Time Models

Process Theory with Inference, Mapping, and Application

Convergent Predictions of Models. In order for any of the strategy models to be correct, the latency data must conform to certain qualitative predictions shared by all the models. The degree of conformity of the data to these predictions shows the extent to which the process theory with inference, mapping, and application is tenable, regardless of the particular model.

Figure 6.6 summarizes solution time data for different types of true people-piece analogies administered in each cueing condition. Observed solution times are shown by solid lines. Predicted solution times for Model III are shown by broken lines. The deviations of predicted from observed solution times are not statistically significant, $F(295, 852) .77$. Conclusions from comparable data for verbal and geometric analogies follow those described below.

1. The effects of dual processing can be seen readily in the graphs. Degenerate and semi-degenerate analogies, shown by open circles, seem to be solved using holistic, same–different comparisons. Pairs of analogy terms are treated as matching or mismatching: There is no increase in solution latency across non-zero numbers of value changes. Nondegenerate analogies, indicated by blackened circles, do, however, show increases in solution latency with increased numbers of value changes. Such increases are consistent with a serial attribute-comparison strategy.

2. Slopes across numbers of value changes from A to B and from A to C should decrease with higher numbers of cues, since fewer comparison processes per value change are involved in analogy solution as attribute-comparison operations drop out in successive cueing conditions. The one exception to this trend should be in the succession from 0 to 1 cue, since only an encoding operation (but no attribute-comparison operations) drops out between these two cueing conditions (see Table 6.3). Figure 6.6 shows that the data are consistent with this prediction.

3. Solution-time curves should be displaced downward with higher numbers of cues, since less encoding is required as analogy terms dropout in each successive cueing condition. The data are consistent with this prediction.

Divergent Predictions of the Models. Figure 6.7 shows people-piece analogy solution times averaged over all cueing conditions for true analogies and for false analogies differing in degree of falsity. Observed values are shown by solid and dotted lines. Predicted values for Model III are shown by broken lines composed of dashes. These data enable one to distinguish between the fully exhaustive Model I on the one hand, and the at least partially self-terminating Models II, III, and IV on the other hand.

1. According to the fully exhaustive Model I, true and false nondegenerate analogies should take equal amounts of time to solve, since the subject always tests all attributes. According to the self-terminating models, true nondegenerate analogies should take longer to solve than false ones, since in these models a subject responds "true" only after finding that he or she was unable to falsify the D analogy term on the basis of any of its attributes. The data are clearly consistent with the models positing self-terminating application.

2. According to Model I, false analogies of different degrees of falsity (numbers of attributes incorrectly matched between D and ideal D') should take equal amounts of time, since subjects always test all attributes. According to the models with self-terminating application, solution times should decrease with increasing degree of falsity, since the subject responds "false" to the analogy as soon as he has disconfirmed any attributes of the D term. Again, the data clearly support the models with self-terminating application. In the geometric

6.6

Solution times for true people-piece analogies in the 0 (upper left), 1 (upper right), 2 (lower left), and 3 (lower right) cue conditions. Observed values are shown by solid lines, predicted values for Model III by broken lines.

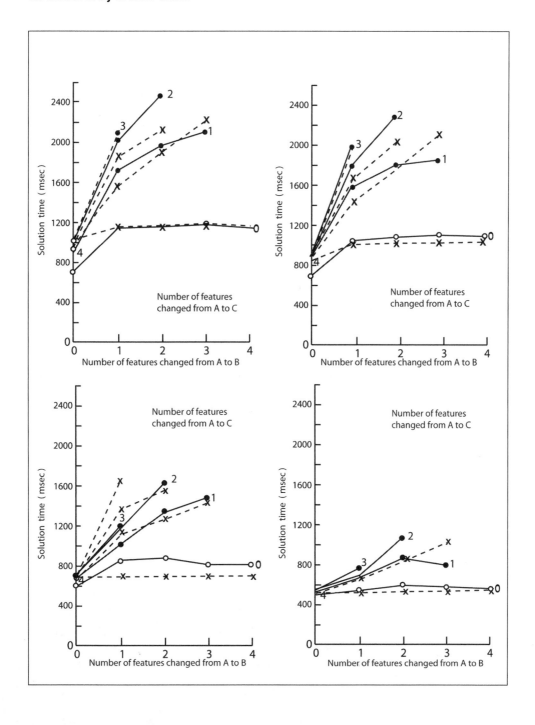

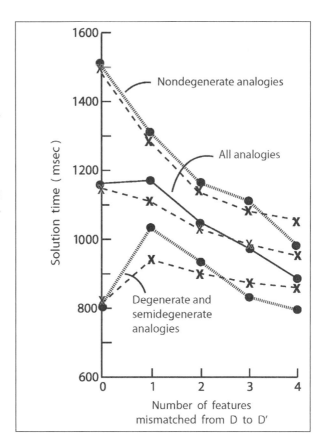

6.7

Solution times for people-piece analogies differing in degree of truth and falsity. Observed values are shown by solid and dotted lines, predicted values for Model III by broken dashed lines.

analogies, the comparable effect is that solution latency decreases as the degree of falsity of the incorrect answer option increases.

Process Theory with Inference and Application, but Not Mapping

The predictions of this theory are comparable to those of the theory with mapping, except for one major difference: According to this theory, there is no mapping operation taking the A analogy term into the C analogy term, and hence there should be no effect of A to C value changes upon solution latency. An examination of Figure 6.6 belies this prediction. The number of attribute values changed from A to C had a pronounced effect on solution latencies. Indeed, the effect is comparable to the effect of the number of attribute values changed from A to B. The qualitative pattern of the data in the people-piece analogy experiment, and in the other two experiments as well, is inconsistent with the process theory excluding mapping.

Process Theory with Inference and Mapping, but Not Application

The predictions of this theory are comparable to those of the theory with application (and mapping), except for two major differences: First, the slopes of the observed latency curves in Figure 6.6 should be the same in the 3-cue condition (bottom-right panel) as in the 2-cue condition (bottom-left panel), since the attribute-comparison operations affecting slope—mapping and inference—are both included in each condition; only the intercepts should differ, since there is one less term to be encoded in the 3-cue condition than in the 2-cue condition (see Table 6.3). Second, since mapping is assumed by the theory to occur as the final attribute-comparison operation, there should be an effect of A to C value changes on solution times in the 3-cue condition.

The qualitative data contrasting this theory to the first theory are mixed. On the one hand, there is a clear decrease in the slopes of the solution time curves from the 2-cue to the 3-cue condition. This decrease is consistent with the deletion of an attribute-comparison operation (mapping), and hence with the first theory. On the other hand, there is an effect of A to C value changes in the 3-cue condition. Although this effect is smaller than that in the 2-cue condition (contrary to the prediction of this theory), the effect is not negligible. This mixture of findings is common to the verbal analogy data as well. In the geometric analogies, there was no 3-cue condition, and predictions could not be tested.

Quantitative Tests of the Response-Time Models

Process Theory with Inference, Mapping, and Application

Comparison Between Alternating and Sequential Option Scanning. The geometric analogy experiment permitted a comparison between alternating and sequential option scanning models. The best alternating model (III) accounted for over 80% of the variance in the data, whereas the worst alternating scanning model (I) accounted for 74%. The best sequential model (I) accounted for 74% of the variance in the data, whereas the worst sequential model (IV) accounted for 64%. Thus, the best of the sequential models was comparable to the worst of the alternating models. Furthermore, Model III in its sequential form accounted for only 68% of the variance in the data, compared to 80% in its alternating form. The data therefore support the alternating option scanning models.

Comparison Among Models I, II, Ill, IV. Model fits in each of the three experiments are shown in Table 6.4 for (a) all analogies, (b) full analogies only (administered in the 0-cue condition), and (c) nondegenerate analogies only. In the people-piece analogy experiment, trials on which errors occurred were rerun at the end of blocks of trials to obtain a "correct" response time. Error times were replaced with these correct times. In the other two experiments, all data were used in model fitting. Degrees of freedom (shown in the table) are equal to 1 less than the number of data points to be predicted minus the number of regression parameters in each model. In data from the 0-cue condition only, parameter estimates for encoding and response were confounded; parameter estimates for inference and application were also confounded in Models I and IV, but not in Models II and III, resulting in 1 more degree of freedom for the former models.

In every case, the fully exhaustive Model I provides the worst fit to the data. Model II is generally the second worst. In no case are Models III and IV well distinguished, although Model III generally provides slightly better fits than Model IV. These data indicate that application is almost certainly self-terminating, mapping is

6.4 Component Model Comparison: Solution Time Percent Variance Accounted For

Model	Experiment		
	People Piece	Verbal	Geometric
	Full set of analogies		
I	76	83	74
II	85	85	80
III	92	86	80
IV	91	85	80
df	295	163	174
	0-cues only		
I	65	50	72
II	82	58	80
III	89	62	80
IV	88	59	79
df	71 or 72	38 or 39	84 or 85
	Nondegenerate analogies only		
I	71	82	62
II	85	84	69
III	93	85	70
IV	93	85	70
df	115	139	102

most probably self-terminating, and inference may be exhaustive (although here the distinction is unclear).

Model III is adopted here as the preferred model, although it cannot be well distinguished from Model IV in these data. Model III accounted for 92% of the variance in the people-piece analogy data, with a root-mean-square deviation *(RMSD)* of 130 msec. The (internal consistency) reliability of the data was .97, suggesting that of the 8% unexplained variance, 5% was systematic and 3% unsystematic. Model III accounted for 86% of the variance in the verbal analogy data, with an *RMSD* of 261 msec. Since there were no exact replications of item types, reliability of the data could not be computed. Model III accounted for 80% of the variance in the geometric analogy data, with an *RMSD* of 1,680 msec. The (intersession) reliability of the data was .89, suggesting that of the 20% unexplained variance, 9% was systematic and 11% unsystematic.

In each experiment, all parameters estimated on the full set of data for Model III differed significantly from zero at beyond the 1% level: In the people-piece experiment, each parameter was at least 10.0 times its standard error; in the verbal analogy experiment, each parameter was at least 4.5 times its standard error; in the geometric analogy experiment, each parameter was at least 3.9 times its standard error.

	Component Model Comparison for Alternative Theories: Solution Time Percent Variance Accounted For		

6.5

	Experiment		
Model	People Piece	Verbal	Geometric[a]
		Theory with inference and application, but not mapping	
I	65	80	71
II[b]	79	81	78
III[b]	79	81	78
IV	81	81	78
		Theory with inference and mapping, but not application	
I	75	82	75
II[b]	84	84	80
III[b]	84	84	80
IV	88	83	80

[a]Models assume alternating option scanning for inference between C and D.
[b]Models II and III are indistinguishable under this theory.

Process Theory with Inference and Application, but Not Mapping

Model fits across cue conditions for this theory are shown in Table 6.5 for all three experiments. The decrease in explained variance for Model III was 13% in the people-piece analogy experiment, 5% in the verbal analogy experiment, and 2% in the geometric analogy experiment. Does mapping carry its weight as a parameter in the model? This question can be answered in at least two ways:

1. In each experiment, the contribution of the mapping parameter was statistically significant: $F(1, 295) = 478$, $p < .01$ for the people-piece analogy experiment; $F(1, 163) = 50$, $p < .01$ for the verbal analogy experiment; $F(1, 174) = 22$, $p < .01$ for the geometric analogy experiment.
2. In two of the three experiments, both the raw and standardized regression coefficients were higher for mapping than either for inference or application, the other two common attribute-comparison operations. In the other experiment, the verbal analogy experiment, the coefficients for mapping were second highest (after inference).

These data, combined with the qualitative data discussed earlier, provide strong support for the existence of a mapping operation in the three experiments.

6.6	Component Model Comparison: Error Rate Percent Variance Accounted For		
	Experiment		
Model	People Piece	Verbal	Geometric
I	12	10	37
II	48	11	47
III	59	12	50
IV	60	14	50

Process Theory with Inference and Mapping, but Not Application

Model fits across cue conditions for this theory are also shown in Table 6.5 for all three experiments. The quantitative data, like the qualitative data, are equivocal. The decrease in explained variance for Model III was 8% for the people-piece analogy experiment (but only 4% relative to Model IV under this theory), 2% for the verbal analogy experiment, and .5% for the geometric analogy experiment. Since this theory is not a subset of the first theory, it cannot be compared directly to that theory. The decreases in fit, however, are small, and are perhaps a small price to pay for the deletion of a parameter. Both the qualitative and quantitative data are inadequate to distinguish between this theory and the theory including application as a separate operation from inference.

Tests of the Response-Error Models

Error rates generally followed the same qualitative patterns as solution times, which is to be expected since the two dependent variables were highly correlated. We shall focus here on quantitative tests of the response-error models. Inference, mapping, and applicaltion were all included in the analyses. Degenerate and semidegenerate analogies were excluded from consideration from people-piece analogies, since almost no errors were made on these items. Except for this exclusion, all item types were retained in the analyses to be reported. Excluding all items on which no errors were made resulted in minor decreases in fit, with no changes in the relative performances of the models.

Model fits using error rate as the dependent variable are shown in Table 6.6. Two conclusions follow from the data. First, Models III and IV provide the best fits to the data, followed by II and then I. Second, none of the models adequately accounted for errors in the verbal analogy experiment (although all fits differed significantly from 0). A possible reason for the poorer fits in this experiment is that a rather large proportion of errors appear to have been due to idiosyncratic knowledge gaps for the vocabulary and general information required to solve particular items.

A final result of interest, not shown in the table, is that not all difficulty parameters contributed to error prediction. Only self-terminating difficulty parameters made substantial contributions to the models. Thus, it appears that although self-terminating

6.8

Amounts of time spent in each component operation in people-piece (upper left), verbal (upper right), and geometric (lower center) analogy experiments. Included are component latencies of encoding (*a*), inference (*x*), mapping (*y'*), application (*z'*), response (*c*), and justification (*t*).

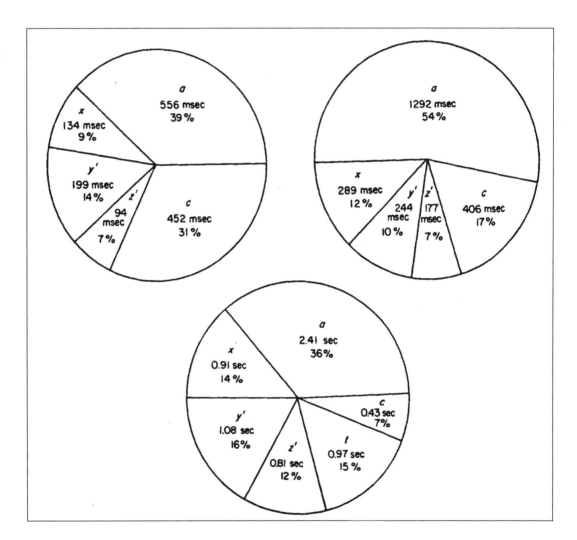

operations decrease the amount of time needed to solve analogies, they increase the probability of making an error. There is a speed–accuracy trade-off in the use of self-terminating versus exhaustive operations.

Distribution of Processing Time in Analogy Solution

How is overall processing time distributed among the various information-processing components? Figure 6.8 addresses this question, assuming Model III of the process theory including inference, mapping, and application (Sternberg, 1977). It displays the mean amount and proportion of time spent on each component operation in a typical people-piece, verbal, and geometric analogy. Times were obtained by multiplying the duration of each component (parameter estimate) by the mean number of times the component was executed. It is worth noting that neither these results nor any of the results presented subsequently would have been substantially altered had Model IV rather than Model III been adopted.

In the people-piece analogy experiment, only 30% of processing time was spent in attribute-comparison operations (inference, mapping, application). Almost 40% of a typical subject's time was spent in encoding, and just over 30% was spent in response.

The partitions for the verbal analogies show that again only 30% of the subject's time was spent in attribute-comparison operations. The relative times for the encoding and response components have changed, however. Encoding now accounts for more than half the subject's solution time. These data indicate that encoding of words is much more time-consuming than encoding of simple schematic figures, a reasonable finding. Note that the amount of time spent in response was about the same as for the people-piece analogies, as would be expected, since the magnitude of the response parameter should be constant across different types of analogies. However, the proportion of time for the response component has decreased, reflecting the greater amount of time overall that verbal analogies take.

In the geometric analogy experiment, the value of the response parameter was again about the same as in the preceding experiments; but because geometric analogies take longer to solve than either verbal or people-piece analogies, the proportion of time spent in response has decreased to a mere 7%. Attribute comparisons are much more difficult to make in this experiment than in the preceding ones, as is reflected by the fact that attribute comparisons now take about 57% of total processing time. Encoding was still the most time-consuming operation, but the proportion of time spent in encoding was closer to that in the people-piece analogies than in the verbal analogies.

These breakdowns of time spent in each component operation provide a useful way of evaluating solution processes in single experiments. The results show that the sources of solution latency are variable. In the verbal analogies, for example, encoding was particularly time-consuming, whereas in the geometric analogies, attribute comparisons were particularly time-consuming.

Individual Differences in Analogical Reasoning

Preview

This section is divided into five further parts. In the first three parts, individual differences in latencies of (a) the attribute-comparison components (inference, mapping, application, justification), (b) the attribute-identification component (encoding), and (c) the response component are related to individual differences in inductive reasoning as measured by standard ability tests. In the fourth part, individual differences in the fit of Model III to each subject's data are related to individual differences in inductive reasoning. In the fifth part, individuals' latencies for the six component operations are combined into a linear model to predict individual differences in inductive reasoning.

Model III was applied to each subject's data, and individual latency parameters were estimated. The parameters were not consistently related to each other, except for encoding and response (median $r = - .60, p < .05$) and application and justification in the geometric analogy experiment ($r = .61, p < .01$). Following the lead of Hunt, Frost, and Lunneborg (1973), a two-way analysis of variance was performed on scores for the four groups of subjects in the people-piece and verbal analogy experiments, and a one-way analysis of variance was performed upon scores for the two groups of subjects in the geometric analogy experiment. Correlational analyses yielded comparable results. Table 6.7 shows the results of these planned comparisons for the reasoning contrast, including means for each group, F values for the contrast, ω^2 for the contrast,[5] and the internal consistency reliability of each parameter on which a contrast is based. None of the Fs for the perceptual-speed contrast were statistically significant, nor were any of the interaction terms significant; hence, these values are not included in the table. In the geometric analogy experiment, only the application and justification parameters were reliable for individual subjects, and hence only results for these parameters are displayed. In this experiment, there was a strong speed–accuracy trade-off, and so error rate was used as a covariate.

Attribute-Comparison Components

Consider first the pattern of results for the people-piece analogy experiment. Durations of the three attribute-comparison components did not differ significantly across high and low reasoning subjects. Why is there no significant effect of reasoning level? One possibility is that the durations of attribute-comparison operations simply do not generate individual differences in reasoning. An alternative and more intuitively satisfying explanation is the use in all people-piece analogies of the identical attributes. Perhaps the critical element leading to individual differences in reasoning is not mere testing of attributes, which obviously was required, but rather discovery of attributes, which was required only trivially. If this explanation is correct, then significant differences between high and low reasoning subjects should be obtained in the verbal and geometric analogy experiments, where discovery of attributes was required on each trial. Indeed, all of the reliable parameters except application in the verbal analogy experiment show significant differences.

Attribute-Identification Component

An unexpected finding was the significant difference in the verbal analogy experiment between high and low reasoning subjects in encoding. Moreover, the direction of the difference was that high reasoning subjects were slower in encoding! This difference might suggest that encoding time and reasoning ability are inversely related. Such inverse relationships are rare in the human abilities literature, however, and a strategy explanation might better account for the results. Greater amounts of time spent in encoding may ultimately pay off in terms of lesser amounts of time spent in operating on these encodings. "Messy" encodings may hinder subsequent operations, and hence result in poorer performance in tasks such as reasoning, where subsequent operations (such as inference, mapping, and application) are of signal importance.

---

[5]The ω^2 statistic is a measure of the strength of association between two variables (see Hays, 1973).

6.7 Differences Between Groups in Analogical Reasoning Performance

Performance Measure	Ability Group M[a]				F	df	ω^2	Parameter Reliability
	Hi$_R$ Hi$_P$	Hi$_R$ Lo$_P$	Lo$_R$ Hi$_P$	Lo$_R$ Lo$_P$				
Attribute comparison parameters								
People-piece analogy experiment								
Inference	143	109	123	144	.04	1, 12	.00	.91
Mapping	299	246	309	309	3.92	1, 12	.14	.95
Application	126	129	154	204	1.89	1, 12	.06	.85
Verbal analogy experiment								
Inference	82	96	134	136	5.63*	1, 12	.25	.35
Mapping	156	135	345	246	4.67*	1, 12	.20	.54
Application	188	216	238	260	.38	1, 12	.00	.26
Geometric analogy experiment[b]								
Application	952		1,864		3.71	2, 21	.26	.54
Justification	4,524		6,287		3,50*	2, 21	.25	.78
Attribute identification parameter								
People-piece analogy experiment								
Encoding	133	160	123	144	.56	1, 12	.00	.84
Verbal analogy experiment								
Encoding	392	391	283	308	4.75*	1, 12	.21	.45
Response parameter								
People-piece analogy experiment								
Response	385	328	565	528	7.26*	1, 12	.30	.97
Verbal analogy experiment								
Response	151	123	695	387	20.04**	1, 12	.49	.82

[a]Hi = high; Lo = low; R = reasoning; P = perceptual speed.
[b]Error rate was used as a covariate in the geometric analogy experiment.
*$p < .05$.
**$p < .001$.

If the strategy explanation is correct, then the important variable is not absolute amount of time spent in encoding, but amount of time relative to amounts of time spent in other operations. "Relative" times may be estimated by standardizing parameters within subjects. Such standardized parameters are provided by the regression beta weights, which reflect amounts of time spent on each operation relative to amounts of time spent on other operations. According to the ability explanation, differences between groups in encoding time should become trivial, because standardized parameters represent relative amounts of time per component within subject. According to the strategy explanation, differences should actually increase, because the effect of encoding time is infra- rather than interindividual.

The magnitude of the effect greatly increased in the verbal analogy experiment. The value of $F(1, 12)$ for the standardized encoding component is 22.82, $p < .001$, and the value of ω^2 is .60. The effect also increased in the people-piece experiment to the point of statistical significance, $F(1, 12) = 6.12$, $p < .05$, $\omega^2 = .22$.

Response Component

A third interesting pattern in the data is found in the contrast between groups on the response parameter. In both the people-piece and verbal analogy experiments, this contrast was highly significant. Relations between the "constant" component and higher order abilities have been replicated in a developmental study of analogical reasoning (Sternberg & Rifkin, Note 4), in a study of linear syllogistic reasoning (Sternberg, Note 5), and in the work of other investigators (see, for example, Hunt, Lunneborg, & Lewis, 1975). This replicable pattern of results suggests that some constant factor, such as motivation, attention, or higher order planning, may be important in reasoning performance, regardless of problem difficulty.

Combining the Components

An important aspect of reasoning would seem to be a systematic way of combining information-processing components into an efficient overall strategy for solving problems. If better reasoners are more systematic in their attacks on problems, then this should be reflected in more systematic data protocols. Specifically, if Model III (or any other model) provides an adequate account of analogical reasoning processes, then one might expect better model fits for individual subjects to be associated with higher reasoning scores. Such a conjecture is obviously highly speculative, but was in fact supported by the data from the verbal analogy experiment, $F(1, 12) = 11.17$, $p < .01$, $\omega^2 = .41$.

The statistic for percent variance accounted for was unreliable in the geometric analogy experiment. The effect was not obtained in the people-piece experiment, $F(1, 12) = .22$, perhaps because of the constancy and obviousness of the relevant analogy attributes across trials. The statistic for percent variance accounted for may be related to individual differences in reasoning only when definition of the task attributes is a nontrivial task, and places a burden on subjects in addition to that of merely working within the attribute structure once it is well defined.[6] This interpretation is obviously parallel to that for the failure of inference, mapping, and application durations to differ significantly between high and low reasoning subjects for the people-piece analogies. It would also seem related to findings of Chase and Simon (1973) and of DeGroot (1965) in their studies of the locus of chess-playing skill. The difference

---

[6]For children, definition of the task attribute structure may be less trivial, and indeed, the correlation between percent variance accounted for and higher order reasoning ability is statistically significant for people-piece-type analogies when measured across ages ranging from 7 to adulthood (Sternberg & Rifkin, Note 4).

between better and worse players appeared to be in their abilities to structure meaningfully the complex pattern on the chessboard. The ability to impose a meaningful organization on an ill-defined stimulus would appear to be crucial in complex reasoning tasks.

Models of Inductive Reasoning Processes

The components of analogical reasoning would seem to be general to other kinds of inductive reasoning tasks as well. The high loadings of analogical reasoning tests on the g factor suggest the generality of the process components used in analogical reasoning, and recent theoretical work points in the same direction. Egan and Greeno (1974) and Simon and Lea (1974) have recently proposed unified views of inductive reasoning processes; my own current research program is also directed toward this end. If the components are truly general, then one might expect individual differences in component durations to account at least partially for individual differences in overall inductive reasoning performance as measured by a composite factor score for the various inductive reasoning tests used in the experiments, The multiple correlations between component latencies and reasoning scores were .74 in the people-piece experiment, .87 in the verbal analogy experiment, and .68 in the geometric analogy experiment. The multiple correlation for the geometric analogy experiment includes error rate because of the strong speed–accuracy trade-off noted earlier. These results suggest that there is considerable overlap between the components of analogical reasoning and those of other kinds of induction.

Discussion

How well do the experimental data enable us to deal with the five theoretical issues to which the experiments were addressed? This question will be answered in this final section of the essay.

Component Information Processes

Three alternative information-processing theories were described: a theory including inference, mapping, and application operations; a theory including inference and application, but not mapping; and a theory including inference and mapping, but not application. The theory without mapping was shown to be inadequate: Mapping proved to be a statistically and practically significant parameter in each of the three experiments. The data were equivocal in distinguishing between the other two theories: The qualitative pattern of the data partially supported both theories but fully supported neither; the quantitative data showed a small increase in fit for the theory including application as a separate parameter, but at the expense of an additional parameter. The theory including all three attribute-comparison operations (Sternberg, 1977) was adopted, although more conclusive tests are needed to distinguish between the two theories.

Information-Processing Strategies

Four alternative strategy models were described: In Model I, inference, mapping, and application are all exhaustive; in Model II, inference and mapping are exhaustive, but application is self-terminating; in Model III, inference is exhaustive, but mapping and application are self-terminating; in Model IV, inference, mapping, and application are all self-terminating. These models were shown to be applicable (with adjustments) to any of the three process theories considered. The models were compared using both latency and error rate as dependent variables. Regardless of the process theory adopted, Model I provided the worst account of the data. Models II and III were formally indistinguishable under two of the theories, but under the Sternberg (1977) theory, Model II provided the second-worst account of the data. Models III and IV generally provided equally good accounts. Model III was adopted because it seemed slightly superior. Mapping and application, therefore, are most probably self-terminating. It is not clear whether inference is self-terminating or exhaustive.

Two different strategies for scanning answer options during application were also described: In an alternating strategy, scanning of attributes alternates successively between options; in a sequential strategy, all attributes of one option are scanned before any attributes of another option are scanned. The data clearly supported the alternating strategy.

Generality of the Preferred Theory and Model

The data suggest that subjects are remarkably consistent in their approaches to analogy problems, even with problems differing widely in content, format, and difficulty. The process theory including inference, mapping, and application was shown to be applicable in all three experiments. The general rank-ordering of the models was also the same: Models III and IV were always closely tied for best, followed by Model II and then by Model I, which was well behind the other models.

Durations of Component Information Processes

The breakdowns of analogy solution time in Figure 6.8 enable one to pinpoint the absolute and relative amounts of time spent in each operation for each of the three types of analogies. The distribution of component latencies differs widely across item types, but makes sense in the context of each particular type of analogy. In verbal analogies, for example, encoding is particularly time-consuming, whereas in geometric analogies, attribute comparison is particularly time-consuming. The duration of the response component was always about 400 to 450 msec, although the proportion of time spent on this component decreased as the difficulty of the analogy increased.

Analogical Reasoning and Intelligence

Finally, we come to the well-established relationship between analogical reasoning and intelligence. Why is analogical reasoning such a good measure of general intellectual ability, or g? Four discoveries in the analysis of individual differences are pertinent to this question:

1. Latencies of the constant response component are highly correlated with scores on tests of general ability. Since the components are viewed here as causal and elementary, the response component is suggested to be a *source* of individual

differences in g. The relation between the response component and g might be even closer, however. Like g, the response component is in a certain sense "general." Its generality is across types of analogies (and very possibly across other item types as well), rather than across subjects. Individual differences in a general or constant component in an across-items analysis, however, could lead to the appearance of a general factor, such as g, in an across-subjects factor analysis. The constant component and the general factor, in this case, would be different manifestations of the same thing.

2. In analogies in which discovery of relevant attributes is a nontrivial task (which includes all analogies found in intelligence tests), latencies of the attribute-comparison components (inference, mapping, application, justification) were shown to be correlated with scores on tests of general ability. If, as my present research hopes to show, these same components are used in a wide variety of induction tasks, then the high intercorrelations between various tests of general ability (which are composed largely of induction items) might be understood in terms of common attribute-comparison components as well as the common response component.

3. There was some indication that relatively longer amounts of time spent in encoding of analogy terms are associated with higher scores on general ability tests. Although the modeling of error rates showed that encoding itself (an exhaustive component) contributed only trivially to error rate, more careful encoding might well lead to superior performance in operations upon the encodings, and thus to superior performance in analogical and other types of reasoning.

4. There was an indication in the verbal analogy experiment (and in a developmental study with people pieces) that the percentage of variance accounted for in a subject's data by the best model may be associated with higher ability scores. A consistent, systematic strategy for solving complex analogies appears to be one element that separates high-ability subjects from low-ability ones.

The results of the experiments suggest that analogical reasoning may be an excellent measure of general intelligence because so many aspects of it, even nonobvious ones, tap higher order general intelligence. The data presented here are a beginning toward understanding just what is meant by the term "general intelligence."

Reference Notes

Winston, P. H. (1970). *Learning structural descriptions from examples* (Report AI TR-231). Cambridge: Massachusetts Institute of Technology, Artificial Intelligence Laboratory.

Shalom, H., & Schlesinger, I. M. (1972). Analogical thinking: A conceptual analysis of analogy tests. In R. Feuerstein, I. M. Schlesinger, H. Shalom, & H. Narrol (Eds.), *Studies in cognitive modifiability* (Report 1, Vol. 2). Jerusalem: Hadassah Wizo Canada Research Institute.

Thurstone, L. L., & Thurstone, T. G. (1934, 1941, 1946, 1947). *American Council on Education Psychological Examination for College Freshmen.* Washington, DC: American Council on Education.

Sternberg, R. J., & Rifkin, B. (1979). The development of analogical reasoning processes. *Journal of Experimental Child Psychology, 27*, 195–232.

Sternberg, R. J. (1976, November). *A model of linear syllogistic reasoning.* Paper presented at the meeting of the Psychonomic Society, St. Louis.

References

Bamber, D. (1969). Reaction times and error rates for "same–different" judgments of multidimensional stimuli. *Perception & Psychophysics, 6,* 169–174.

Burke, H. R. (1958). Raven's progressive matrices: A review and critical evaluation. *Journal of Genetic Psychology, 93,* 199–228.

Cattell, R. B., & Cattell, A. K. S. (1963). *Test of g: Culture Fair, Scale 3.* Champaign, IL: Institute for Personality and Ability Testing.

Chase, W. G., & Simon, H. A. (1973). The mind's eye in chess. In W. G. Chase (Ed.), *Visual information processing.* New York: Academic Press.

Clark, H. H., & Chase, W. (1972). On the process of comparing sentences against pictures. *Cognitive Psychology, 3,* 472–517.

Collins, A. M., & Quillian, M. R. (1969). Retrieval time from semantic memory. *Journal of Verbal Learning and Verbal Behavior, 8,* 240–247.

DeGroot, A. D. (1965). *Thought and choice in chess.* The Hague: Mouton.

Egan, D., & Greeno, J. G. (1974). Theory of rule induction: Knowledge acquired in concept learning, serial pattern learning, and problem solving. In L. W. Gregg (Ed.), *Knowledge and cognition.* Potomac, MD: Erlbaum.

Esher, F. J. S., Raven, J. C., & Earl, C. J. C. (1942). Discussion on testing intellectual capacity in adults. *Proceedings of the Royal Society of Medicine, 35,* 779–785.

Evans, T. G. (1968). A program for the solution of geometric-analogy intelligence test questions. In M. Minsky (Ed.), *Semantic information processing.* Cambridge, MA: MIT Press.

French, J. W., Ekstrom, R. B., & Price, I. A. (1963). *Kit of reference tests for cognitive factors.* Princeton, NJ: Educational Testing Service.

Guilford, J. P. (1967). *The nature of human intelligence.* New York: McGraw-Hill.

Hays, W. L. (1973). *Statistics for the social sciences* (2nd ed.). New York: Holt, Rinehart & Winston.

Humphreys, L. G., & Fleishman, A. (1974). Pseudo-orthogonal and other analysis of variance designs involving individual-differences variables. *Journal of Educational Psychology, 66,* 464–472.

Hunt, E. B. (1974). Quote the raven? Nevermore! In L. W. Gregg (Ed.), *Knowledge and cognition.* Potomac, MD: Erlbaum.

Hunt, E. B., Frost, N., & Lunneborg, C. L (1973). Individual differences in cognition: A new approach to intelligence. In G. Bower (Ed.), *Advances in learning and motivation* (Vol. 7). New York: Academic Press.

Hunt, E., Lunneborg, C., & Lewis, J. (1975). What does it mean to be high verbal? *Cognitive Psychology, 7,* 194–227.

Johnson, D. M. (1960). Serial analysis of thinking. In *Annals of the New York Academy of Sciences* (Vol. 91). New York: New York Academy of Sciences.

Johnson, D. M. (1962). Serial analysis of verbal analogy problems. *Journal of Educational Psychology, 153,* 86–88.

Lockhead, G. R. (1972). Processing dimensional stimuli: A note. *Psychological Review, 79,* 410–419.

Oppenheimer, J. R. (1956). Analogy in science. *American Psychologist, 11,* 127–135.

Osherson, D. N. (1974). *Logical abilities in children. Logical inference: Underlying operations* (Vol. 2). Potomac, MD: Erlbaum.

Raven, J. C. (1938). *Progressive matrices: A perceptual test of intelligence* (1938, individual form). London: Lewis.

Reitman, W. (1965). *Cognition and thought.* New York: Wiley.

Rumelhart, D. E., & Abrahamson, A. A. (1973). A model for analogical reasoning. *Cognitive Psychology, 5,* 1–28.

Simon, H. A., & Lea, G. (1974). Problem solving and rule induction: A unified view. In L. W. Gregg (Ed.), *Knowledge and cognition.* Potomac, MD: Erlbaum.

Spearman, C. (1923). *The nature of "intelligence" and the principles of cognition.* London: Macmillan.

Spearman, C. (1927). *The abilities of man.* New York: Macmillan.

Sternberg, R. J. (1977). *Intelligence, information processing, and analogical reasoning: The componential analysis of human abilities.* Hillsdale, NJ: Erlbaum.

Thurstone, L. L. (1938). *Primary mental abilities.* Chicago: University of Chicago Press.

Section III

Successful Intelligence in the Schools

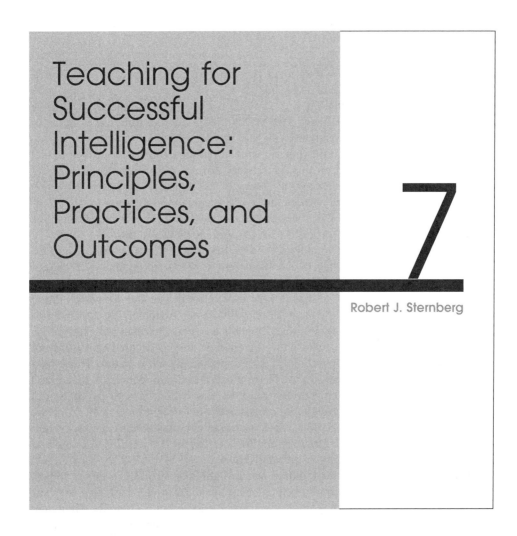

Teaching for Successful Intelligence: Principles, Practices, and Outcomes

7

Robert J. Sternberg

Our goal is to raise the achievement of all students by teaching them in a way that matches the way they learn. The question, of course, is how to do it. We think we have a way. Of course, it is not the only way. But, so far, it seems to work for a wide variety of students of varied ages and in diverse subject-matter areas.

The Problem: Schools That Work for Some Students but Not Others

The problem is that some children seem to benefit well from the schooling they get, but others do not. Teachers try very hard to reach all students, but rather frequently find that there are some students who just seem to be hard to reach. There can be many reasons why certain students are hard to reach—disabilities, disorders, motivational problems, health problems, and so forth. One reason, though, can be the mismatch between a pattern of strengths and weaknesses on the part of the student and the particular range of methods that a teacher is using in trying to reach that student. "Teaching for successful intelligence" provides a series of techniques for reaching as many students as possible (Sternberg & Grigorenko, 2000; Sternberg & Spear-Swerling, 1996; Sternberg & Williams, 2002).

Teaching for successful intelligence is based on a psychological theory, the theory of successful intelligence (Sternberg, 1997). This theory is quite different from traditional theories of intelligence, which posit that intelligence is just a single construct, sometimes called *g*, or general intelligence, and sometimes known in terms of the IQ measure. The methods based on this new theory are not the only series of teaching methods based on a new psychological theory of intelligence. Gardner (1983, 1999) has proposed a different theory with somewhat different, although sometimes overlapping, methods of instruction. But I believe that our methods are particularly effective and, moreover, have hard empirical data to support their usefulness.

The theory of successful intelligence holds that some students who do not do well in conventional courses may, in fact, have the ability to succeed, if they are taught in a way that is a better fit to their patterns of abilities. For example, when I took my introductory psychology course, I was very motivated to become a psychologist. I received a grade of "C" in the course. The grade was as extremely discouraging to me as was my instructor's comment that "There is a famous Sternberg in psychology, and judging from this grade, there won't be another one." I decided that I did not have the ability to major in psychology, so I switched to mathematics. This was a fortunate decision for me, because at midterm in advanced mathematics, I got a grade of "F." Now, the C was looking pretty good, so I switched back to psychology. I received higher grades in subsequent courses and, this year, I am President of the American Psychological Association, a national organization of about 155,000 psychologists. Incidentally, Phil Zimbardo, a former President of the Association, also received a grade of C in his introductory psychology course.

The problem is that many children who might like to study a given subject area—whether language, arts, mathematics, history, science, foreign language, or whatever—may give up because they think they cannot succeed in their study. They may either stop taking courses in the subject area, or just give up on the courses they are taking. Teaching for successful intelligence can give these students the chance to succeed that they might not otherwise have.

What Is Successful Intelligence?[1]

Successful intelligence is the ability to succeed in life, given one's own goals, within one's environmental contexts. Thus, successful intelligence is a basis for school achievement, but also life achievement. A key aspect of the theory is that success is defined in terms of a person's individual goals with the context in which that person lives, rather than in terms of more generalized goals that somehow are supposed to apply to everyone.

One is successfully intelligent to the extent that one effectively adapts to, shapes, and selects environments, as appropriate. Sometimes, one modifies oneself to fit the environment (adaptation), as when a teacher or student enters a new school, and tries

---

[1]In my earlier work (e.g., Sternberg, 1985), I proposed a "triarchic theory" of human intelligence. The present theory builds on the earlier one by defining intelligence in terms of people's ability to choose the personal and professional goals they set for their own lives.

to fit into the new environment. Other times, one modifies the environment to fit oneself, as when a teacher or student tries to improve the school environment to make it a better place in which to work. And yet other times, one selects a new environment, as when one decides that it would be better to be in another school because attempts to adapt to and/or shape the environment of the current school have not been successful.

People adapt, shape, and select by recognizing and capitalizing on strengths, and by recognizing and compensating for or correcting weaknesses. People do not achieve success in the same way. Each person has to find his or her own "recipe" for success. One of the most useful things a teacher can do is to help a student figure out how to make the most of what he or she does well, and to find ways around what he or she does not do so well.

Finally, people capitalize and compensate through a balance of analytical, creative, and practical abilities. How to teach in a way that enables students to do so is the topic of the remainder of this essay.

What Is Teaching for Successful Intelligence?

Teaching for successful intelligence involves a way of looking at the teaching–learning process that broadens the kinds of activities and assessments teachers traditionally do. Many good teachers "teach for successful intelligence" spontaneously. But, for one reason or another, most do not. Teaching for successful intelligence involves, at minimum, using a set of prompts that encourages students to engage in memory learning as well as analytical, creative, and practical learning.[2]

The key strategies are as follows.

Strategy 1: Teaching for Memory Learning

Most conventional teaching is teaching for memory learning. Teaching for successful intelligence does not ask teachers to stop what they are already doing. Rather, it asks teachers to build on it. Teaching for memory is the foundation for all other teaching because students cannot think critically (or any other way) about what they know if they do not know anything. Teaching for memory basically involves assisting or assessing students' memory of the *who* (e.g., 'Who did something?'), *what* (e.g., 'What did they do?'), *where* ('Where did they do it?'), *when* ('When did they do it?'), *why* ('Why did they do it?'), and *how* ('How did they do it?') of learning.

Here are some examples of teaching and assessing for memory learning:

- *Recall* a fact they have learned, such as the King of England during the American Revolution, or the product of 7 x 8, or the chemical formula for sodium.
- *Recognize* a fact they have learned, such as which of the following countries is in Central America: Bolivia, Ecuador, Guatemala, or Brazil; or whether the product of 7 x 8 is 54, 56, 48, or 60; or whether the chemical formula for sodium is So, Na, Sd, or Nd.

---

[2]Because this chapter is brief, it is not possible to describe each of the kinds of teaching in detail. More details are contained in Sternberg and Grigorenko (2000).

▓ *Match* one set of items of one kind with another set of items of another kind, such as list the elements hydrogen, sodium, oxygen, and potassium with the list of abbreviations H, K, Na, and O.

▓ *Verify* statements, such as whether the statement "Vladimir Putin is currently the President of Russia," or "The atomic number for uranium is 100," is true or false.

▓ *Repeat* what you have learned, such as a poem, an article of the Constitution, a scientific formula, or a mathematical formula.

Research suggests that there are certain things teachers can do to help students maximize their memory-based learning (see Sternberg & Williams, 2002). These things include (a) encouraging students to space their learning over time and study sessions rather than massing it into a small number of study sessions, (b) avoiding studying materials that are similar (e.g., French and Spanish) in close temporal proximity, to avoid confusion (or, in technical terms, proactive [forward] and retroactive [backward] interference), and studying the most important information near the beginning and the end of a session (the so-called serial-position effect, which gives a benefit to things studied near the beginning or ending of a session).

Strategy 2: Teaching for Analytical Learning

Teachers who teach for successful intelligence do not only teach for memory, because some students are not particularly adept as memory learners. I, myself, was not, as I mentioned previously, and am not until this day. Many students have the ability to learn, but fail miserably when they sit down and try to memorize a set of isolated facts, or even when they are asked merely to recall a set of isolated facts.

Here are examples of teaching and assessing for analytical learning and thinking:

▓ *Analyze* an issue, such as why genocides continue to occur even today, or why certain elements are radioactive, or why children today still find *Tom Sawyer* entertaining, or how to solve a particular algebraic factoring problem.

▓ *Evaluate* an issue, such as why unlimited political contributions can lead to corruption in a political system, how the Internet is vulnerable to catastrophic sabotage, what part of speech a certain word is, or how best to make a cake.

▓ *Explain* how the British parliamentary system works, or a wool blanket can produce static electricity, or how to solve an arithmetic word problem, or why a character in a short story acted the way she did.

▓ *Compare and contrast* two or more items, such as the systems of government in China and England, or igneous and sedimentary rocks, or two different ways of proving a geometric theorem, or two novels.

▓ *Judge* the value of characteristics of something, such as a law, or a scientific experiment, or a poem, or the metric system of measurement.

We have found it useful, in teaching for analytical thinking, to teach students how to use a problem-solving cycle in their thinking. The steps of the problem-solving cycle are what we refer to as metacomponents, or higher-order executive processes that are used to plan, monitor, and evaluate problem solving (Sternberg, 1985). First, students need to recognize the existence of a problem (e.g., the need to write a term paper). Second, they need to define exactly what the problem is (e.g., what the topic of the term paper will be). Third, they need to allocate resources for the problem (e.g., how much time to spend on the term paper). Fourth, they need to represent information about the problem (e.g., using note cards, outlines, etc.). Fifth, they need to formulate a strategy for solving the problem (e.g., getting the paper done). Sixth, they need to monitor their progress as they solve the problem (e.g., is the paper getting done or has one gotten stuck on some aspect of it?). Finally, they need to evaluate their work after it is done (e.g., proofread the paper and see how it reads).

Strategy 3: Teaching for Creative Learning

Teaching for successful intelligence also involves encouraging students to use and develop their creative-thinking skills. Such skills involve production of ideas that are novel, high in quality, and appropriate to the task at hand (Sternberg & Lubart, 1995). Teachers who teach for successful intelligence recognize that some students learn best when they are allowed to find their own ways to learn material, and when they are free to explore ideas that go beyond those likely to be in books or lectures.

Here are some examples of teaching and assessing for creative learning and thinking:

- Create a game for learning the names of the States, or a poem, or a new numerical operation, or a scientific experiment.
- *Invent* a toy, or a new way of solving a difficult mathematics problem, or a new system of government that builds on old systems of government, or a haiku.
- *Explore* new ways of solving a mathematics problem beyond those taught by the teacher, or how to achieve a certain chemical reaction, or different ways of reading so as to improve your reading comprehension, or the nature of volcanoes.
- *Imagine* what it would be like to live in another country, or what will happen if temperatures on the Earth keep rising, or what Picasso might have been thinking when he painted Guernica, or what might happen if the Government of England made it a crime to speak ill of the Government.
- *Suppose* that people were paid to inform on their neighbors to the political party in power—what would happen?, or that all lakes instantly dried up— what would happen?, or that schools stopped teaching mathematics—what would happen?, or that Germany had won World War II—what would have happened?
- *Synthesize* your knowledge of the Gulf War and the recent War in Afghanistan to propose a set of battle techniques that are likely to work in many unfamiliar kinds of terrains.

I believe that, to a large extent, creative thinking represents a decision to do thinking in certain ways and to do certain things. To teach students to think creatively, they need to learn to make these decisions (Sternberg, 2000). These decisions include, among other things, (a) redefining problems rather than merely accepting the way problems are presented, (b) being willing to take intellectual risks, (c) being willing to surmount obstacles when people criticize one's attempts at being creative, (d) being willing to work to persuade people of the value of one's creative ideas, and (e) believing that one truly has the potential to produce creative ideas in the first place.

Strategy 4: Teaching for Practical Learning

Some students are primarily practical learners. They do not catch on unless they see some kind of practical use for what they are learning. That is, they learn best if the material facilitates their adaptation to, shaping of, and selection of environments (Sternberg et al., 2000). Here are some examples of teaching and assessing for practical learning and thinking:

- *Put into practice* what you have learned about measurement in baking a cake; your foreign-language instruction in speaking with a foreigner; your knowledge of soils to determine whether a particular plant can grow adequately in a given soil.
- *Use* your knowledge of percentages or decimals in computing discounts; a lesson learned by a character in a novel in your own life; your knowledge of the effects of particulate matter in the atmosphere on vision to figure out whether a car driving behind you in the fog is substantially closer than it appears to be.
- *Utilize* a physical formula to figure out the speed at which a falling object will actually hit the ground; your understanding of cultural customs to figure out why someone from another culture behaves in a way you consider to be strange; the lesson you learned from a fable or a proverb to change your actual behavior with other people.
- *Implement* a plan for holding a classroom election; a strategy for conserving energy in your home; what you have learned in a driver-education class in your actual driving; a psychological strategy for persuading people to raise money for charity
- *Apply* your knowledge of political campaigns in history to running for class president; your knowledge of the principles of mixture problems to mixing paints to achieve a certain color; your understanding of the principles of good speaking to giving a persuasive talk.

Part of teaching for practical thinking is teaching students to adopt certain attitudes in their intellectual work (Sternberg, 1986). These attitudes include, for example, (a) combating the tendency to procrastinate, (b) organizing oneself to get one's work done, (c) figuring out how one learns best, (d) avoiding the tendency to use self-pity as an excuse for working hard, and (e) avoiding blaming others for one's own failings.

Some General Principles

In teaching for successful intelligence, one is helping all students to make the most of their skills by addressing all students at least some of the time. It is important to realize that teaching for successful intelligence does not mean teaching everything three times. Rather, one balances one's teaching strategies so that one is teaching in each of the ways part of the time. An advantage of this procedure is that one does not have to know each student's exact strengths and weaknesses. By teaching in all of the ways, one is addressing some students' strengths at the same time as one is addressing other students' weaknesses at each point. Balancing teaching strategies guarantees that one will be addressing all students' strengths at least some of the time. But one does not want only to teach to strengths, as students also need to learn how to compensate for and correct weaknesses.

It is also important to ensure that one's assessment practices match one's teaching practices. Sometimes, teachers teach in one way, but assess in another way. For example, they may encourage critical thinking in class, but then give tests that merely measure recall. Students quickly learn that the real game of getting good marks in the class is not the apparent game. The students then respond to the way they are assessed, not to the way they are taught. So it is crucial that teachers value the same things in their assessment as in their teaching.

Comparison to Other Theories

No psychological theory or set of teaching techniques is completely new. Rather, theories and the teaching techniques that derive from them build on each other. It is thus useful to point out similarities and differences between teaching for successful intelligence and other ways of teaching, based on different theories.

One well-known theory is that of Bloom (1976; Bloom, Engelhart, Frost, Hill, & Krathwohl, 1956), known as Bloom's taxonomy. Bloom proposes a six-level taxonomy: knowledge, comprehension, application, analysis, synthesis, and evaluation. Teaching for memory is related to teaching for knowledge and comprehension; teaching for analytical thinking, to teaching for analysis and evaluation; teaching for creative thinking, to teaching for synthesis; and teaching for practical thinking, to teaching for application. There are a few differences between the current theory and Bloom's. Here are four main ones.

First, the theory of successful intelligence does not view the three kinds of abilities as "hierarchically related." For example, one does not need to think for application (practically—lower in Bloom's hierarchy) in order to think for synthesis (creatively —higher in Bloom's hierarchy). On the contrary, much creative thinking is not necessarily practical at all (e.g., most academic scholarships), and much practical thinking is not necessarily creative (e.g., the thinking involved in filling out bureaucratic forms).

Second, the theory of successful intelligence parses skills differently. Analysis and evaluation are separated by synthesis, in Bloom's theory, but in the theory of successful intelligence, they are seen as more related to each other than either is to synthetic thinking.

Third, the concepts of analytical, creative, and practical thinking are each somewhat broader than the terms of Bloom's taxonomy. As shown above, each of the three kinds of teaching includes, but is not limited to, the terms in Bloom's taxonomy. For example, synthesis is part of teaching for creative thinking, but only a small part of it.

Fourth, the techniques involved in teaching for successful intelligence derive from a theory of intelligence that has been tested in many different ways. Bloom's theory is not and was not intended to be a theory of intelligence.

Another related theory is that of Gardner (1983, 1993, 1999). Gardner's theory of multiple intelligences, like the theory of successful intelligence, attempts to extend our thinking about the nature of intelligence. Again, though, there are some key differences.

First, Gardner's theory deals with domains, positing linguistic intelligence, logical/mathematical intelligence, spatial intelligence, musical intelligence, naturalistic intelligence, bodily-kinesthetic intelligence, interpersonal intelligence, intrapersonal intelligence, and possibly existential intelligence. The theory of successful intelligence specifies classes of processes. Thus, at one level, the theories are largely complementary. One can teach analytically, creatively, or practically, for example, in the linguistic domain (analytical—analyze a poem, creative—write a short story, practical—write a persuasive essay), or in any other domain.

Second, Gardner includes as intelligences sets of skills that perhaps would not be viewed as intelligences in the theory of successful intelligence. For example, in order to survive in the world, everyone has to have at least some ability to think analytically, creatively, and practically. But it is not clear that, in order to survive in the world, everyone has to think musically.

Third, the theory of successful intelligence has been extensively validated predictively, and these predictions have been largely upheld. For example, in a series of studies, we have shown that the exploratory and confirmatory factor structures of sets of tests designed to measure triarchic abilities do indeed provide distinct factors corresponding to analytical, creative, and practical abilities, and that the model proposing these three separate factors is superior to alternative factorial models (Sternberg, Grigorenko, Ferrari, & Clinkenbeard, 1999; Sternberg, Castejón, Prieto, Hautamäki, & Grigorenko, 2001). In other studies, we have shown that the theory holds up cross-culturally, for example, that the analytical and practical aspects of intelligence can be distinguished as well in countries outside of the United States as they can be in the United States (e.g., Grigorenko & Sternberg, 2001; Sternberg, Nokes, et al., 2001). I am unaware of any predictive tests of the theory of multiple intelligences. Although such tests may seem like an abstract detail to many teachers, validation of a theory helps ensure that it does, indeed, characterize how people really think, rather than merely the investigators' or others' opinions of how they really think.

Generally, then, there are similarities and differences between the theory of successful intelligence, on the one hand, and two other theories—those of Bloom and Gardner—on the other. Probably, effective teachers will not totally "buy into" any one theory. Rather, they will select those techniques from each theory that work most effectively for them in their teaching.

The truth is that most educational programs are based on *no* theory. Rather, they are simply programs that their proponents believe to be successful, often without any data to back their efficacy. Why even base an educational program on a theory in the first place? There are at least four reasons.

First, a theory potentially suggests what should be taught, how it should be taught, when it should be taught, to whom it should be taught, and why it should be taught. Atheoretical programs do not have this kind of motivation. Second, in a theory-based program, it is possible to state what are the essential aspects of the program (i.e., those based on the theory) and what are the nonessential aspects. With an atheoretical program, it is hard to distinguish what is necessary from what is not. Third, a theory-based program suggests what forms assessments should take to match instruction. Atheoretical programs do not suggest assessment options. Finally, use of a theory-based program can advance scientific knowledge by testing the theory. If the theory is good, the program should work. If the program does not work, either the theory is wrong or the operationalization of the theory is inadequate. Atheoretical programs do not advance science in this way.

Does Teaching for Successful Intelligence Work?

Teachers want—indeed, some demand—some level of assurance that, if they take the trouble to use a method of teaching, it really will work. We have completed a series of studies showing that teaching for successful intelligence really can work, at least in the instances in which we have examined it. The common element of all these studies is the possibility that when students are taught for successful intelligence, they are better able to capitalize on their strengths and to correct or compensate for their weaknesses, so that they learn at higher levels. Although the data from the studies are not conclusive, they are at least suggestive of the value of teaching for successful intelligence.

In a first study (Sternberget al., 1999), for example, we pinpointed high school children identified as gifted analytically, creatively, practically, in all three ways, or in none of these ways, for their patterns of analytical, creative, and practical abilities. We then taught these children a rigorous psychology course that either fit their pattern of abilities particularly well, or did not do so. For example, a highly creative child might receive an instructional program that emphasized creative learning and thinking (good fit), or one that emphasized memory learning (not so good fit). We found that children who were taught in a way that, at least some of the time, enabled them to capitalize on their strengths, outperformed students who were not so taught. In a second study (Sternberg, Torff & Grigorenko, 1998a, 1998b), we taught third-grade students social studies and eighth-grade science in one of three ways. Either we emphasized just memory learning, or primarily analytical (critical) thinking, or teaching for successful intelligence (memory, analytical, creative, and practical learning). All students received the same quantity of instruction and for the same time period, and all students received the same assessments for memory learning as well as for analytical, creative, and practical learning. We found that students who were taught for successful intelligence outperformed students who were taught either for memory or critical thinking, pretty much regardless of grade level, subject matter, or type of assessment. Even on memory assessments, the children taught for successful intelligence outperformed the children in the other two groups.

In a third study (Grigorenko, Jarvin & Sternberg, 2002), we helped primarily inner-city urban students at the middle and high school levels develop their reading skills. At the middle school level, reading was taught as a separate subject area, whereas at the high school level, reading was infused into other subject areas, such as English, science, foreign-language, and history instruction. Students were taught either for successful intelligence or in a standard way that emphasized memory-based instruction. The students who were taught for successful intelligence outperformed the students taught in the more conventional way on all assessments, whether for vocabulary or reading comprehension, and whether emphasizing memory-based, analytical, creative, or practical thinking.

Why Teaching for Successful Intelligence Is Successful

Why does teaching for successful intelligence work? There are at least six reasons:

■ *Helping students capitalize on strengths.* Teaching for successful intelligence helps students learn in ways that work for them, rather than forcing them to learn in ways that do not work.

■ *Helping students correct or compensate for weaknesses.* Teaching for successful intelligence helps students correct deficient skills, or at least to develop methods of compensation for these skills.

■ *Multiple encodings.* This form of teaching encourages students to encode material not just in one way, but in three or four different ways (memory, analytical, creative, practical), so the students are more likely to retrieve the material when they need it.

■ *Deeper encodings.* Teaching in this way also helps students encode material more deeply because the presentation of the material is more meaningful and closely related to what they already know.

■ *Motivation.* Teaching for successful intelligence is more interesting to most students, and hence increases motivation.

■ *Job relevance.* Much of what students learn, and the way they learn it, bears little resemblance to what these students will need later to succeed in a job. For example, a typical introductory psychology course may require memorizing a great amount of material, but psychologists do not spend much of their time memorizing books or retrieving facts from books. Teaching for successful intelligence better helps students prepare for what they later will need to do in a job.

Objections

When any new system for teaching and assessment is introduced, teachers and administrators sometimes have objections. What kinds of objections have we encountered with the system of teaching for successful intelligence, and what are our replies? Here are five typical objections.

■ *It is only for gifted students.* Some teachers believe that their students have enough problems learning the conventional way. Why introduce other ways that will just confuse them more, especially teaching for creative thinking, which these teachers may see as high-falutin'? But these teachers have things backwards. The problem is that many students simply do not learn well in conventional ways. Teaching in other ways, rather than confusing them, enlightens them. Unless they are taught in other ways, they just will not learn much. And teaching for creative thinking is not high-falutin'. In these times of rapid change, all students need to learn to think in a way that maximizes their flexibility.

■ *It is only for weak students.* Then there are teachers who say that teaching for successful intelligence is only for weak students. Their regular students learn well with the current system. But do they really learn so well? And is it ever the case that their learning cannot be improved? We believe that teaching always can be improved, and that teaching for successful intelligence is one way of doing it. Moreover, many good students are "good" in the sense of having developed adequate memory and analytical skills. But, later in life, they will need creative and practical skills too. Schools should help students develop these skills.

■ *It takes too much time to teach everything three ways.* This objection is based on a misunderstanding of what teaching for successful intelligence requires. It does not require everything to be taught three times in three ways. Rather, the idea is for teachers to alternate, so that some material is being taught one way and other material, another way.

■ *It is too hard to do.* Good teachers naturally teach for successful intelligence. They need only the bare minimum of instruction. Other teachers need more time to catch on. But once one catches on—which usually does not take an inordinate amount of time—it becomes like second nature. It is no harder, and perhaps even easier, than teaching in the regular way, because one begins to see alternative natural ways of teaching the same material.

■ *My supervisor (principal, director, etc.) will not allow it.* This might be true in some instances. But our experience has been that school administrators are open to almost any form of teaching that is ethical as long as it improves student achievement and motivation.

Conclusions

Successful intelligence involves teaching students for memory as well as analytically, creatively and practically. It does not mean teaching everything in three ways. Rather, it means alternating teaching strategies so that teaching reaches (almost) every student at least some of the time. Teaching for successful intelligence also means helping students to capitalize on their strengths and to correct or compensate for their weaknesses. We believe we have good evidence to support teaching for successful intelligence. Teaching for successful intelligence improves learning outcomes, even if the only outcome measure is straightforward memory learning. We, therefore, encourage teachers to seriously consider use of this teaching method in their classrooms—at all grade levels and for all subject areas.

New techniques and programs are being developed all the time. For example, at this time, we have active research sites testing the efficacy of our programs in many parts of the United States and abroad. We have also developed a software system, "CORE," which enables teachers to communicate with us and with each other if they encounter any problems while using our materials. In this way, they can receive immediate feedback to help them solve problems, rather than waiting until someone can help them, perhaps much later.

Teaching for successful intelligence potentially provides benefits at multiple levels. It helps students to achieve at a level that is commensurate with their skills, rather than letting valuable skills, which could be used in facilitating learning, go to waste. It helps schools reach higher levels of achievement as a whole. And in these days of school accountability, reaching higher average scores is a goal virtually every school wants to achieve. Finally, it helps society make better use of its human resources.

There is no reason for a society to waste its most precious resource—its human talent. Teaching for successful intelligence helps ensure that talent will not go to waste.

References

Bloom, B. S. (1976). *Human characteristics and school learning.* New York: McGraw-Hill.

Bloom, B. S., Engelhart, M. B., Furst, E. J., Hill, W. H., & Krathwohl, O. R. (1956). *Taxonomy of educational objectives: The classification of educational goals: Handbook 1: The cognitive domain.* New York: Longman.

Gardner, H. (1983). *Frames of mind: The theory of multiple intelligences.* New York: Basic Books.

Gardner, H. (1993). *Multiple intelligences: The theory in practice.* New York: Basic Books.

Gardner, H. (1999). *Reframing intelligence.* New York: Basic Books.

Grigorenko, E. L., Jarvin, L., & Sternberg, R. J. (2002). School-based tests of the triarchic theory of intelligence: Three settings, three samples, three syllabi. *Contemporary Educational Psychology, 27,* 167–208.

Grigorenko, E. L., & Sternberg, R. J. (2001). Analytical, creative, and practical intelligence as predictors of self-reported adaptive functioning: A case study in Russia. *Intelligence, 29,* 57–73.

Sternberg, R. J. (1985). *Beyond IQ: A triarchic theory of human intelligence.* New York: Cambridge University Press.

Sternberg, R. J. (1986). *Intelligence applied.* San Diego, CA: Harcourt.

Sternberg, R. J. (1997). *Successful intelligence.* New York: Plume.

Sternberg, R. J. (2000). Creativity is a decision. In A. L. Costa (Ed.), *Teaching for intelligence II* (pp. 85–106). Arlington Heights, IL: Skylight.

Sternberg, R. J., Castejón J. L., Prieto, M. D., Hautamäki, J., & Grigorenko, E. L. (2001). Confirmatory factor analysis of the Sternberg triarchic abilities test in three international samples: An empirical test of the triarchic theory of intelligence. *European Journal of Psychological Assessment, 17,* 1–16.

Sternberg, R. J., Forsythe, G. B., Hedlund, J., Horvath, J., Snook, S., Williams, W. M., Wagner, R. K., & Grigorenko, E. L. (2000). *Practical intelligence in everyday life.* New York: Cambridge University Press.

Sternberg, R. J., & Grigorenko, E. L. (2000). *Teaching for successful intelligence.* Arlington Heights, IL: Skylight.

Sternberg, R. J., Grigorenko, E. L., Ferrari, M., & Clinkenbeard, P. (1999). A triarchic analysis of an aptitude-treatment interaction. *European Journal of Psychological Assessment, 15*(1), 1–11.

Sternberg, R. J., & Lubart, T. I. (1995). *Defying the crowd: Cultivating creativity in a culture of conformity.* New York: Free Press.

Sternberg, R. J., Nokes, K., Geissler, P. W., Prince, R., Okatcha, F., Bundy, D. A., & Grigorenko, E. L. (2001). The relationship between academic and practical intelligence: A case study in Kenya. *Intelligence, 29,* 401–418.

Sternberg, R. J., & Spear-Swerling, L. (1996). *Teaching for thinking.* Washington, DC: American Psychological Association.

Sternberg, R. J., Torff, B., & Grigorenko, E. L. (1998a). Teaching for successful intelligence raises school achievement. *Phi Delta Kappan, 79,* 667–669.

Sternberg, R. J., Torff, B., & Grigorenko, E. L. (1998b). Teaching triarchically improves school achievement. *Journal of Educational Psychology, 90,* 374–384.

Sternberg, R. J., & Williams, W. M. (2002). *Educational psychology.* Boston: Allyn-Bacon.

Teaching Triarchically Improves School Achievement

8

Robert J. Sternberg
Bruce Torff
Elena L. Grigorenko

Ever since Binet and Simon (1916) proposed their concept of "mental orthopedics," some theorists of intelligence have sought not just to understand intelligence or to measure it but to use theory to improve learning and perhaps even the intellectual abilities underlying learning as well. Ideally, instruction and assessment based on a theory of intelligence would enhance learning and the performance outcomes associated with it.

Although many instructional programs based on cognitive theory have been suggested (e.g., Baron & Sternberg, 1987; Bransford & Stein, 1993; Costa, 1985; Feuerstein, 1980; Halpern, 1996; Nickerson, 1994; Nickerson, Perkins, & Smith, 1985; Sternberg & Bhana, 1986), relatively few have been based explicitly on theories of intelligence. Some, like the structure of intellect program of Meeker (1969), which is based on the theory of Guilford (1967), or the intelligence applied program of Sternberg (1986), which is based on Sternberg's (1985) own theory, have been separate programs designed to use aspects of a theory of intelligence to improve thinking skills. However, many educators have turned to the question of how to infuse such a theory into existing instructional programs (e.g., Swartz, 1987).

Perhaps the best known attempts are based on the theory of multiple intelligences proposed by Gardner (1983, 1993). These attempts have met with mixed success

(Callahan, Tomlinson, & Plucker, 1997), although many of the evaluations are informal or uncontrolled so that it is hard to know exactly what the outcomes have been (Gardner, 1993, 1995). As with any theory, there is a potential danger in any of these programs that the infusion will be less than true to the vision of the theorist (Gardner, 1995), so it becomes even more difficult to know whether the theory leads to success when infused into classroom instruction and assessment.

Although one might expect teachers to flock to the use of such programs, in fact, teachers are often reluctant because of the specter of the need to prepare students for the various kinds of mastery tests or other achievement tests the students will need to take. Teachers sometimes believe that teaching for thinking will undermine students' performance on these tests, which, they believe, measure primarily mastery of facts rather than higher order thinking with these facts (Sternberg, 1996; Sternberg & Spear-Swerling, 1996). Moreover, teachers may be skeptical even that the program will, in fact, produce superior knowledge or ability to use knowledge in their students, regardless of how these outcomes are measured.

The goal of the two studies reported in this chapter is to test the efficacy at the primary and secondary levels of instruction on the basis of the triarchic theory of intelligence (Sternberg, 1985) that is infused into existing curricula. According to the triarchic theory (Sternberg, 1985), human intelligence comprises three main aspects: analytical, creative, and practical. Infused into instruction and assessment, analytical tasks involve analyzing, judging, evaluating, comparing and contrasting, and critiquing; creative tasks involve creating, inventing, discovering, imagining, and supposing; and practical tasks involve implementing, using, applying, and seeking relevance (Sternberg, 1994a, 1994b). More conventional memory-based instruction involves memorizing, remembering, recalling, recognizing, and repeating.

In earlier work, we attempted to infuse a portion of this theory (the practical part) into the curriculum, combining it with Gardner's theory of multiple intelligences (Gardner, Krechevsky, Sternberg, & Okagaki, 1994; Sternberg, Okagaki, & Jackson, 1990; Williams et al., 1996), but the studies described here represent an infusion of all aspects of the theory.

In more recent work (Sternberg & Clinkenbeard, 1995; Sternberg, Ferrari, Clinkenbeard, & Grigorenko, 1996), we have infused the triarchic theory into instruction and assessment in psychology of high school students selected for a special summer program at Yale University. Students were chosen to represent particular ability patterns and then were given instruction that either more closely or more distantly matched their patterns of abilities. All students were assessed for achievement in terms of multiple-choice memory tests as well as for analytical, creative, and practical performances. We found that students who were better matched to instruction in terms of their patterns of abilities outperformed those students who were more poorly matched.

The basic design of the two studies described here involved groups receiving instruction in existing curriculum units that was either enhanced by use of the triarchic theory or that was not enhanced. Two control conditions were used for evaluation of the efficacy of the instruction. The first was a traditional-instruction group, in which students received exactly the instruction that they would receive without the experimental intervention. The second and stronger control group was one that received instruction enhanced by the infusion of critical-thinking (analytical-thinking) skills, which represent the most frequently used kind of infusion but which represent only part of what the triarchic theory would suggest needs ideally to be infused into the curriculum.

In order to ensure, to the best of our ability, an adequate test of the model, we used both memory-based multiple-choice assessments, which were already part of the existing curriculum, and our own performance-based assessments, which measured achievement in terms of the utilization of analytical, creative, and practical abilities. Thus, it would be possible to determine whether triarchic instruction improved performance on the performance assessments of achievement following from the theory, and even on memory-based assessments that did not follow directly from the theory but that were already being used as part of the assessment program for the courses being taught. At the primary level, we also used self-report assessments.

We predicted that triarchic instruction would improve achievement—both on memory-based multiple-choice items and on analytically, creatively, and practically based performance assessments. There were two reasons for this prediction, following from the triarchic theory (Sternberg, 1996; Sternberg & Spear-Swerling, 1996).

First, triarchic instruction should enable students to encode the information to be learned in three different ways (analytically, creatively, and practically), as well as for memory. The multiple encodings of information should improve learning. Using this approach, students think to learn and simultaneously learn to think.

Second, triarchic instruction should enable students to capitalize on their strengths and to compensate for or to correct their weaknesses, a key aspect of triarchic instruction, as well as of all instruction based on notions of aptitude–treatment interaction (Cronbach & Snow, 1977). In other words, there should be at least some instruction that would be compatible with almost all students' strengths, enabling the students to bring these strengths to bear on the work at hand. At the same time, at least some of the instruction would probably not correspond to students' strengths, encouraging the students to develop modes of compensation for and correction of weaknesses. Instruction that enables students to capitalize on strengths is also likely to motivate students more than instruction that does not allow such capitalization.

The basic strategy for our studies was to (a) divide students into three groups, using standardized ability measures to analyze the comparability of the groups; (b) provide different instructional treatments, corresponding to the three types of instruction discussed previously (triarchic, critical-thinking, and traditional); and (c) administer knowledge-based assessment measures, to examine differences that might obtain in outcomes generated by the three instructional treatments. Hence, each student took a standardized ability test, received training over an extended period, and then was given a battery of knowledge-based assessment instruments. This protocol was conducted with two groups of students and teachers, one in a primary-school setting and the other in a middle-school setting.

Study 1: The Primary-School Project

Method

Participants

In the primary-school project, the participants included 213 third-grade students (106 boys and 107 girls) in two elementary schools in Raleigh, North Carolina. Both schools serve a diverse population of primarily lower socioeconomic status students, including large groups of African American, Hispanic, and Asian students. Both schools are designated by the school district as gifted and talented magnet schools, but they serve both gifted and nongifted populations. A total of nine classes of 20–25 students each participated in the research. These classes were taught by nine experienced teachers who were certified to teach third grade in North Carolina.

Ability Testing

Participating students took a standardized test of cognitive abilities, the Otis-Lennon Intelligence Scales (Otis & Lennon, 1967), as part of a district-wide testing program for identification of giftedness. In the *Results and Discussion* section that follows, we use the Otis-Lennon scores as a covariate with the effects of different instructional treatments.

Instructional Treatments

Prior to the intervention, participating teachers were divided into three groups, one for each form of instructional treatment. The teachers then received extensive training programs focusing on techniques for implementation of the appropriate instructional strategies. Each of the training programs comprised a series of workshops that included (a) descriptions and models of appropriate teaching strategies and (b) opportunities for teachers to create lesson plans and classroom activities and to receive feedback on their work. Each workshop included techniques for infusing the appropriate strategy into all aspects of instruction, including lecture, discussion, collaborative-learning groups, and individual assignments.

There were three training programs in all, one for each instructional treatment. In the triarchic group, the teachers participated in workshops devoted to techniques for using and strengthening analytical, creative, and practical skills in the classroom. The critical-thinking group focused exclusively on analytical abilities. The traditional-instruction group participated in workshops focusing on an irrelevent topic— procedures for portfolio assessment. None of the teachers collected portfolios during the intervention.

Because primary-school teachers have only one class at a time, each teacher was trained for only the instructional treatment to which he or she was assigned. The five teachers at School A, where the triarchic and critical-thinking groups were located, were divided between the triarchic and critical-thinking groups. All teachers at School B, which functioned only as a control school in this study, were assigned to the traditional-instruction group. The separation of the traditional control group by school was intended to minimize the cross-contamination that can result within a school when experimental-group teachers interact with control-group teachers.

During the intervention, the students received an instructional unit on the topic of communities—a social-studies unit required for third-grade students in North Carolina. The unit centered on four curriculum objectives published in the Curriculum Guide given to teachers by the North Carolina Department of Education. Curriculum objectives for the unit included (a) citizenship; (b) similarities and differences between individuals, families, and communities; (c) concepts of authority, responsibility, and justice; and (d) relationships between people and their governments. No text was used for the unit—materials for the courses were developed individually by the teachers. The intervention took place for 10 weeks, 4 days per week, 45 min per day, for a total of 30 hr of instruction.

A total of nine sections of the unit were taught at the two schools. Of the five sections at School A, three were given triarchic instruction ($n = 74$) and two received critical-thinking instruction ($n = 45$). At School B, all four sections received traditional instruction ($n = 92$).

To illustrate the three different instructional treatments, consider three ways in which a third-grade unit on public services (e.g., fire, police) can be taught. The approach taken in traditional instruction is to have children memorize the names and functions of the various public services. In critical-thinking instruction, an additional analytical effort is undertaken, perhaps one assigning students to compare and contrast the different services and evaluate which ones to keep in case of a budget crisis. In the triarchic group, creative and practical skills are used as well as analytical ones; students might be assigned to come up with their own public service, to describe its means and ends, and to compare this new public service with conventional ones.

During the intervention, the students received instruction that reflected the differences among these three instructional treatments. A typical activity in the traditional-instruction group emphasized memory abilities:

> A police officer came to visit the class. He answered questions from the students and talked about what police officers do. He also talked about the equipment police officers use and how a person goes about becoming a police officer. After he left, each student wrote a letter thanking him and describing what [the student] learned during his visit.

In the critical-thinking group, the teachers designed and implemented activities that encouraged students to engage in analytical reasoning:

> Class discussion concerning authority figures: each student records information on a sheet with three columns. At the top of each column is a symbol for the following: USA/President, NC/Governor, and Raleigh/Mayor. The students take notes in each column as a range of issues are discussed (e.g., comparative powers, privileges, responsibilities).

Analytical activities as such were also used in the triarchic instruction group, which also focused on activities drawing on creative and practical skills:

> The students invented their own government agency. They had to decide what service to provide, give it a name, tell why it's important, and why the government should pay for it. Then [students were asked to] make an advertisement for [the invented government agency]. [The class] shared the agencies for the rest of the class time. (Creative)

> The students were given a problem situation of littering in the community. They brainstormed consequences that could be used in that situation. The teacher listed them on the board. Students then decided which consequences were appropriate (fair versus unfair). Then we tied our "make believe" littering-in-the-community problem to our real-life problem of litter on the school grounds. In groups, the students brainstormed possible solutions to the problem. They regrouped to pick the best solution and discuss consequences for future "offenders." They came up with a school-wide litter pick-up day for each grade level. (Practical)

Knowledge-Based Assessment

Following the intervention, students completed a battery of assessment instruments designed to capture how much they learned and how they were able to use that knowledge. Three types of assessments were used: (a) a total of 16 multiple-choice items; (b) essay items designed to capture analytical, creative, and practical abilities; and (c) performance assessments (assignments relying less heavily on students' writing skills, such as drawing a map) were also implemented to measure analytical, creative, and practical abilities.

The battery of assessments included three essay items—an analytical one, a creative one, and a practical one—that required students to compose paragraph-long responses to the following prompts:

Essay Item 1 (Analytical)

Select one of the positions of authority on the list below. Write a page explaining what a person in this position does. Say why the position is needed and why it is a position of authority. Describe its privileges and limitations.

1. Governor of North Carolina
2. Mayor of Raleigh
3. animal control officer (dog catcher)
4. judge
5. Internal Revenue Service worker (tax collector)

Essay Item 2 (Creative)

Imagine a place where no one tried to be a good citizen—where no one followed most of the rules at school or in the community. Write a story about a third grader's visit to this place. Discuss several different things that you might see during your visit. Why do you think these things might happen? Be creative with your answer!

Essay Item 3 (Practical)

A group of 8-year-old students from England is going to visit. You are in charge of teaching them about the different kinds of governmental services that we have in Raleigh. You want the visitors to have a general understanding of how Raleigh's system of government works. Write a paragraph describing what you will do and why. What do you want the visitors to learn, and why? What methods of teaching will work best?

In addition, the assessment battery included performance items—again, in terms of analytic, creative, and practical abilities—which are less dependent on students' writing skills:

Performance Item 1 (Analytical)

Some people believe that taxes ought to be lowered. Other people disagree; they believe that the current level of taxation is appropriate.

Task 1: Make a list of the *advantages* of lowering taxes. Make a second list of the *disadvantages* of lowering taxes.

Task 2: Write a paragraph stating your recommendation whether or not taxes should be lowered. Be sure to say *why* you believe taxes should (or should not) be lowered.

Performance Item 2 (Creative)

Design an "ideal community" with different kinds of organizations that serve the public. What organizations would your ideal community have? Why are the services provided by these organizations needed? Draw a map or a picture of your community. Be sure to describe the services you want your ideal community to have; also, say *why* you want to include them. Be creative!

Performance Item 3 (Practical)

Your school is holding an election to choose a class president, and you are the new Election Commissioner. Your job is to organize the election so that all the students have a chance to vote.

Below is a list of steps you might take to make the election a success. You don't have time to do them all, so *pick the five most important steps* to take. Place an "x" next to the steps you think are most important. You can pick only five steps. For each step you have selected, write a few words saying *why* you selected it. Don't write anything about the steps you choose NOT to take.

Why did you select this step?

——have ballots printed

——become one of the candidates

——count the votes after the polls close

——tell students whom to vote for

——create political parties among the students

——make sure that the election is fair

——have a debate between the candidates

——make sure a polling place is available

——decide whom to vote for

——discuss the important issues of the election

——publicize the date and time of the election

Self-Assessments

Students were asked to respond to three self-assessment questions: (a) How much did you like the course? (b) How much do you think you learned [in the course]? (c) How well do you think you did [in the course]? Responses were made on a 5-point Likert-type scale.

Data Analysis

Following the intervention, the performance assessments were scored by three raters—undergraduate students majoring in psychology who had no knowledge of the research design or hypothesis. The raters used a 5-point Likert-type scale to rate the overall quality of each of the responses. The raters met frequently for several weeks to tune the rating process and to increase interrater reliability. For the 15 items that required subjective ratings (1 item, Performance Item 3, could be scored directly), interrater correlations for pairs of raters ranged from .77 to .88. The overall interrater correlation of .83 was deemed sufficiently high to provide a reliable assessment of students' responses to the essay items and performance assessments.

Results and Discussion

Outcome Measures

As described in the Method section, there were 10 main outcome measures of this study: a multiple-choice test score, 6 performance measures (analytical, creative, and practical assessed by the means of a project and an essay), and 3 students' self-evaluation scores. The corresponding ability measures correlated significantly (project–essay correlations for analytical, creative, and practical abilities were .25, .56, and .21, respectively, all $p < .001$), suggesting that derivation of summary scores across the two types of evaluation would be appropriate. This conclusion was supported by the principal-component analyses, where for all three abilities (analytical, creative, and practical) there was only one component, accounting for from 60% (for practical) to 78% (for creative) of the variance in the data. The correlations between the summary ability measures and ability scores as assessed by the project and the essay ranged between .78 and .88, demonstrating that both project and essay assessments contributed highly to the summary scores. Consequently, in the following analyses, 7 outcome measures were used: (a) ability measures (analytical, creative, and practical) and the multiple-choice measure and (b) 3 self-evaluation measures.

Preliminary Analyses

Prior to conducting a series of analyses directed toward testing the hypotheses of the study, we investigated the association between the outcome performance variables (analytical, creative, practical, and multiple choice) and potential covariates, such as gender and scores on the Otis–Lennon ability test. The results revealed no significant differences between performance of boys and girls on any of the dependent measures. Moreover, there was no difference in the pattern of correlations between boys and girls.

In contrast, students' performance was significantly associated with the Otis-Lennon score. The significant correlation coefficients varied between .17 ($p < .02$), for performance-based scores obtained on the project, and .66 ($p < .0001$), for the multiple-choice test. Consequently, even though there were no differences in Otis-Lennon scores between the treatment groups, the patterns of correlation between the outcome measures and the ability measures differed across treatment groups. Thus, although all outcome measures correlated significantly with the Otis-Lennon scores in the triarchic and critical-thinking groups, only the multiple-choice performance score correlated with the Otis-Lennon score in the control group. In order to control the variance in the response to the treatment that might have had differential impact on children with different levels of abilities, the Otis-Lennon score was used as a covariate in all subsequent analyses of the four performance measures.

Students' self-assessments neither differentially correlated with the Otis-Lennon ability score nor showed mean differences between the treatment groups. Similarly, we did not find any gender-related differences. Therefore, in these analyses, the ability measure was not included as a covariate in the equation.

Treatment Effects

Multivariate analysis of variance (MANOVA), profile analysis, and pairwise least-squares means comparisons were implemented to evaluate the effect of teaching on students' performance. Two sets of analyses, one for the ability measures and the multiple-choice score and the other for self-evaluation scores, were conducted.

Performance Measures

Three different tests were performed comparing the profiles of scores in the three treatment groups. The least-squares means groups' profiles are shown in Figure 8. 1. The first test, the so-called flatness test of the group profiles, investigated whether, with groups combined, the differences between various assessments differed from zero (i.e., whether the group profiles were nonhorizontal). For this test, Wilks's lambda was equal to 0.94, $F(3, 207) = 4.35$, $p < .01$, suggesting that the obtained profiles were not horizontal. The second test, the parallelism test, asked if the difference between, for example, analytical and creative assessments was the same for students receiving instructions based on the triarchic theory, the critical-thinking approach, and traditional teaching. For this test, Wilks's lambda was equal to 0.71, $F(6, 414)$ 12.90, $p < .0001$, leading to rejection of the hypothesis of parallelism. In other words, the profiles of Figure 8.1 were not parallel. Finally, the levels test examined differences between the means of the three treatment groups combined over the four evaluations. This analysis demonstrated that, overall, there was a significant difference between treatment groups in average performance on different types of assessments, $F(2, 209) = 47.16$, $p < .0001$. The subsequent contrast analysis conducted on the transformed performance variables showed that the triarchic group performed consistently better than either the critical-thinking group (the contrast estimate was 0.75, with a standard deviation of 0.30) or the traditional group (the contrast estimate was 2.38, with a standard deviation of 0.25).

A series of subsequent univariate analyses revealed significant F values for the equations, modeling the sources of variation in the four dependent variables (see Table 8.1). Specifically, the performance on analytical tasks model was statistically significant, $F(3, 212) = 41.24$, $p < .0001$, for the total model; $F(2, 212) = 38.03$, $p < .0001$, for the effect of group; and $F(2, 212) = 34.34$, $p < .0001$, for the effect of the ability test, and accounted for 37% of the variance. Similarly, the F statistic for the performance on the practical-tasks model was significant, $F(3, 212) = 18.84$, $p < .0001$, for the total model; $F(2, 212)$ 15.42, $p < .0001$, for the effect of group; and $F(2, 212) = 22.31$, $p < .0001$, for the effect of the ability test. The R^2 for this model was equal to .21. The model for the performance on creative tasks accounted for 56% of the variance, $F(3, 212) = 88.94$, $p < .0001$, for the total model; $F(2, 212) = 98.07$, $p < .0001$, for the effect

8.1

Means in Study 1: Assessments of achievement.

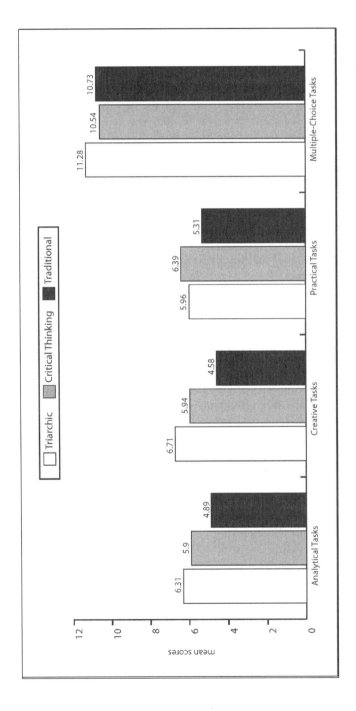

8.1 Effects of Instructional Condition in Study 1			
Assessment	$F(3,212)$	p	R^2(%)
Analytical	41.24	< .0001	37
Creative	88.94	< .0001	56
Practical	18.84	< .0001	21
Multiple-choice tasks	58.95	< .0001	46

of group; and $F(2, 212) = 44.84$, $p < .0001$, for the effect of the ability test. Finally, the multiple-choice model explained 46% of the variance in the children's performance, $F(3, 212) = 58.95$, $p < .0001$, for the total model; $F(2, 212) = 2.65$, $p < .07$, for the effect of group and $F(2, 212) = 16\ 1.16$, $p < .0001$, for the effect of the ability test.

These results were followed up by a series of pairwise comparisons of least-squares means (see Figure 8.1). For performance on analytical tasks, the triarchic group performed significantly better than did both the critical-thinking, $t(114) = 2.04$, $p < .05$, and the traditional, $t(164) = 8.45$, $p < .0001$, groups. Moreover, the critical thinking group performed better than did the traditional group, $t(135) = 5.23$, $p < .0001$. For performance on practical tasks, there was no significant difference between the triarchic and critical-thinking groups, but both groups performed better than did the traditional-teaching group, $t(164) = 3.66$, $p < .001$ and $t(135) = 5.26$, $p < .0001$, for the triarchic and critical-thinking traditional groups, respectively. On the creative tasks, students from the triarchic group performed significantly better than did students either in the critical-thinking, $t(117) = 4.14$, $p < .0001$, or the traditional-teaching groups, $t(164) = 13.76$, $p < .0001$. Students in the critical-thinking group were also better in their creative performance than were those in the traditional-teaching group, $t(135) = 7.66$, $p < .0001$. Finally, the triarchic-group students performed better on the multiple-choice test. This difference was statistically significant when compared with the performance of the students whose teaching was based on the critical-thinking approach $t(117) = 2.07$, $p < .05$, and borderline significant when compared with the performance of the traditional-teaching group, $t(164) = 1.85$, $p < .06$. The performance of students from the critical-thinking group did not differ from the performance of students from the traditional group.

Self-Assessments

The profiles of least-squares means for the three self-assessment questions are shown in Figure 8.2. As is obvious from Figure 8.2, the profiles were horizontal, so the hypothesis of flatness could not be rejected, Wilks's $\Lambda = 0.98$, $F(2, 209) = 1.66$, ns. The profiles, however, were not parallel, Wilks's $\Lambda = 0.93$, $F(4, 418) = 3.62$, $p < .01$, and the levels test was significant, $F(2, 210) = 38.24$, $p < .0001$. The contrast analyses pointed to the differences between the averaged transformed variables: The students' self-evaluations in the triarchic group were consistently higher than those of the students in both the critical-thinking (the contrast estimate was equal to 0.93 with a standard

8.2

Means in Study 2: Self-assessments.

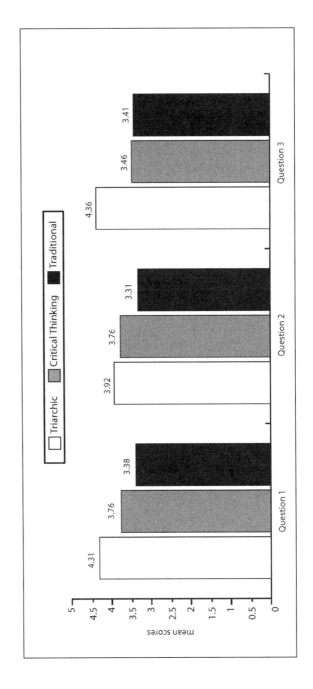

deviation of .20) and the traditional-teaching groups (the contrast estimate was 1.44 with a standard deviation of .17).

A series of subsequent univariate analyses revealed significant F values for all three dependent measures, $F(2, 212) = 25.89$, $p < .0001$, $R^2 = .20$, for Question 1; $F(2, 212) = 8.26$, $p < .001$, $R^2 = .07$, for Question 2; and $F(2, 212) = 32.31$, $p < .0001$, $R^2 = .24$, for Question 3.

A series of pairwise comparisons of least-squares means decomposed the observed multivariate effects. For the first question (how much the students liked the course), the triarchic-group students scored the highest. Their ratings were significantly higher than both the critical-thinking group students, $t(117) = 3.51$, $p < .001$, and the traditional-group students, $t(164) = 7.19$, $p < .0001$. Critical-thinking group students were more satisfied with the course than were the traditional-group students, $t(135) = 2.56$, $p < .05$. For the second question (how much the students thought they learned), there was no difference between the triarchic and critical-thinking groups, but both groups showed ratings significantly higher than those of the traditional-teaching group, $t(164) = 3.92$, $p < .0001$, and $t(135) = 2.50$, $p < .01$, for the triarchic and critical-thinking groups, respectively. Finally, for the third question (how well the students thought they did) the triarchic-group students gave higher ratings than did the students in either the critical-thinking group $t(117) = 5.95$, $p < .0001$, or the traditional group, $t(135) = 7.54$, $p < .0001$, but the two nontriarchic groups did not differ from each other.

Study 2: Middle-School Project

Method

Participants

The middle-school project was conducted in collaboration with the Center for Academic Advancement (CAA), a program in gifted education at Johns Hopkins University. In the summer of 1996, researchers at Yale University designed and implemented a summer-school course in introductory psychology for CAA students. The participants included 141 rising eighth-grade students (68 boys and 73 girls). Drawn from around the nation, the predominantly White student population hailed largely from middle-class and upper-middle-class backgrounds. The course was taught by six experienced teachers of secondary-level psychology, all of whom were active in Teaching of Psychology in Secondary Schools, a special-interest group of the American Psychological Association.

Ability Testing

A central goal of CAA is to identify gifted students and to provide them with academically challenging courses. CAA uses scores on the verbal battery of the Scholastic Assessment Test (SAT) as the basis for identification of the gifted. Students were admitted to the psychology course on the basis of an SAT-verbal score of 420 or higher. Admitted students had a mean SAT-verbal score of 471.13, with a standard deviation of 40.85.

Instructional Treatment

As in the primary-school project, participating secondary-school teachers received an extensive training program prior to the intervention. The training program focused on techniques for infusing the appropriate instructional strategy into all aspects of the course—lecture, discussion, collaborative-learning groups, and individual assignments. In the triarchic instruction group, teachers participated in workshops emphasizing the application of analytic, creative, and practical skills to the teaching of psychology. For example, having students frame their own research questions and design their own experiments were considered as tactics for bringing creative abilities to bear in the classroom. The critical-thinking training program was devoted to explication of the use of analytical reasoning in psychology; for example, tactics suggested for encouraging critical thinking in the classroom included having students analyze the flaws in a research project. The traditional-instruction group received a training program on an irrelevant topic—portfolio assessment in the middle-school classroom. None of the teachers collected portfolios during the intervention.

The 10-section course took place in two intensive 3-week sessions. Classes met 5 days per week with 7 hr of class time per day. An introductory psychology text by Myers (1996) was used in all sections. Topics included neuroscience, development, perception, consciousness, learning, memory, language, intelligence, motivation, affect, personality, psychological disorders, therapy, and social psychology.

Research activities were conducted at two sites. At Goucher College in Baltimore, Maryland, eight sections of the course were taught to 120 students. Of these eight sections, four received triarchic instruction ($n = 60$), two received critical-thinking instruction ($n = 30$), and two received traditional instruction ($n = 30$). At the State University of California at Fresno, two sections of the course were taught to 21 students. Students at Fresno received critical-thinking instruction, bringing to 51 the total number of students in the critical-thinking group. Six teachers were involved in the project, five located at Goucher and one at Fresno. Two teachers were assigned to each of the three instructional treatments.

To illustrate the three different teaching strategies as they apply to introductory psychology, it is useful to compare three ways to teach about a common psychological disorder—depression. In traditional instruction, a typical approach is to have students memorize theoretical constructs and research findings (e.g., summarize a biological perspective on depression). In critical-thinking instruction, students are typically asked to compare, contrast, and evaluate different theories of depression (e.g., compare and contrast the biological and cognitive perspectives). In triarchic instruction, students are encouraged to bring a combination of analytical, creative, and practical abilities to the fore; for example, students might be asked to generate their own theories of depression (creative), design therapeutic regimes that draw on the new theories (practical), and contrast these ideas with the work of biological and cognitive theorists (analytical).

During the intervention, students received instruction that reflected the differences among the three strategies. In the traditional-instruction group, the students participated in activities (e.g., discussions, writing tasks) that emphasized memory abilities:

Obedience to authority is a topic of interest to social psychologists. Who are some of the psychologists that conducted important research on obedience? What motivated this research? What sorts of research methods did they use? What did the researchers find?

In the critical-thinking group, the activities typically required students to use analytical-reasoning abilities:

> Sigmund Freud and Gordon Allport put forth different theories of human personality. What did each theorist seek to explain? On what assumptions does each theory rely? How are the theories similar? How are they different? Which of the two do you more agree with, and why?

In the triarchic-instruction group, creative and practical abilities were emphasized as well as analytical and memory-based abilities:

> Why do you think that people sometimes fail to transfer skills or information when they need to? Think of a time when you did transfer when you should not have. Then think of a time when you did not transfer but should have. Why did these things happen? From your own life, come up with an explanation for why transfer does and does not occur when it is appropriate. (Creative)

> Measurement error is a problem for many kinds of tests. This error is due to extraneous influences that can make people's scores unreliable. Imagine that you have a new job at the Educational Testing Service to reduce measurement error on the Scholastic Assessment Test. What kinds of measurement errors do you want to reduce, and how will you do it? Feel free to suggest strategies that ETS might not like but which you think will reduce measurement error. (Practical)

Knowledge-Based Assessment

To evaluate student achievement during the course, two types of assessment instruments were used. First, multiple-choice questions from the Myers (1996) test bank were used to capture students' understanding of course content. The midterm examination and the final examination each included 21 multiple-choice questions, yielding a total of 42 multiple-choice items. Second, performance assessments were used to capture students' abilities on analytical, creative, and practical tasks. The midterm and final exams included analytical, creative, and practical performance assessments in the form of short-answer essay items. There also were three assignments in the form of extended essays (one each was analytical, creative, and practical). The three short-answer items on the final exam gave the flavor of the performance assessments used in the study:

> June is so preoccupied with keeping her house absolutely spotless that she has no time to do anything but clean. After each meal she not only washes the dishes, but also the table, chairs, floor, and cupboards. Although these cleaning rituals irritate her family, June is unable to discontinue them without experiencing intense feelings of discomfort. Use the *psychoanalytic* and *learning* perspectives to explain June's behavior. How do these perspectives compare and contrast? What are the strengths and weaknesses of each approach? (Analytical)

> Psychologists have shown that people sometimes cling to their beliefs in the face of contrary evidence. This is called belief perseverance. Give an example of belief perseverance. Then come up with your own theory that explains why people

act this way. Be specific about how the theory explains your example of belief perseverance. (Creative)

   You are in charge of the fundraising committee for a club at school. You want to make sure that candy bar sales are strong. How would you go about training your club members to be effective salespersons? Design and describe your sales program, basing it on principles of social psychology. (Practical)

Data Analysis

As in the primary-school project, the performance assessments were scored by three raters who had no knowledge of the research design or hypothesis. The raters used a 5-point Likert-type scale to rate the overall quality of each of the responses and met frequently for several weeks to tune the rating process. Correlations among the ratings given by pairs of raters for the nine performance items ranged from .76 to .80. The overall correlation of .83 is sufficiently high for us to conclude that the ratings provide a reliable assessment of learners' responses to the performance assessments.

Results and Discussion

Outcome Measures

To reduce the number of dependent variables, we investigated whether summary measures of the students' performance on the two exams and the homework assignment would be adequate representations of the initial nine outcome measures. The principal-component analyses resulted in a one-component solution for the analytical performance measure, and in two-component solutions for both practical and creative performance measures. In both cases, the first component accounted for about 40% of shared variance in exams and assignment measures, whereas the second component (about 35% for both) was introduced by the variance in the assessment method (the examination scores and the assignment score loaded with opposite signs). On the basis of these results, in the subsequent analyses, six different outcome measures were used: analytical, creative, and practical measures for both the homework assignment and the two exams (summary measure). Thus, there were seven main outcome variables in the analyses: measures of assignment and examination performance on analytical, creative, and practical tasks, and the multiple-choice measures.

Preliminary Analyses

Two variables—gender and the SAT ability score—were considered to be of potential importance in the treatment-effect analyses. A MANOVA did not reveal the presence of gender effects on any of the outcome variables. Similarly, the SAT scores did not appear to be significantly related to the performance measures. When the correlations between the SAT scores and the initial performance measures (two examinations and the assignment) were examined, only one correlation, the correlation with the analytical subtest of the final exam, was significant $(r = .189, p < .05)$. Moreover, there were no SAT-related group differences or differentiative correlation patterns across the treatment groups. Therefore, the subsequent analyses of variance did not include any covariates.

Treatment Effects

MANOVA, profile analysis, and pair-wise least-squares means comparisons were implemented to evaluate the effect of teaching on students' performance.

Three different tests were performed comparing the profiles of scores in the three treatment groups. The least-squares means groups' profiles are shown in Figure 8.3. The flatness test of the group profiles suggested that the investigated group profiles were nonhorizontal: For this test, Wilks's lambda was .01, $F(6, 133) = 1,718.27$, $p <$ .0001. The parallelism test demonstrated that the compared profiles were different for the three groups, Wilks's $\Lambda = 0.54$, $F(12, 266) = 7.93$, $p < .0001$. Finally, the levels test examined differences among the means of the three treatment groups combined over the seven assessments. This analysis demonstrated that, overall, there was a significant difference between treatment groups in average performance on different types of assessments, $F(2, 138) = 50.04$, $p < .0001$. Specifically, the contrast analyses across averaged transformed variables resulted in the following estimates: 2.08, with a standard deviation of .30 (the triarchic group versus the critical-thinking group) and 3.35, with a standard deviation of .36 (the triarchic group vs. the traditional group). There were no differences between the critical-thinking and the traditional group. These results suggest that the triarchic group, on average, performed significantly better than either the critical-thinking group or the traditional-teaching group.

A series of subsequent univariate analyses revealed significant F values for six out of the seven investigated equations (see Table 8.2).

These results were followed up by a series of pairwise comparisons of least-squares means (see Figure 8.3). For performance on analytical tasks assessed through homework, both the triarchic group and the critical-thinking group performed better than did the traditional group, $t(88) = 3.34$, $p < .001$, and $t(58) = 2.98$, $p < .005$, respectively, but did not differ from each other. Similarly, for homework-assignment performance on creative tasks, there was no significant difference between the triarchic and critical-thinking groups, but both groups performed better than did the traditional group, $t(88) = 5.34$, $p < .0001$, and $t(58) = 3.81$, $p < .001$, for critical-thinking and traditional groups, respectively. The pattern was also replicated for the practical homework assignment. Students from both the triarchic and the critical-thinking groups performed significantly better than did students from the traditional-teaching group $t(88) = 3.08$, $p < .005$, and $t(58) = 2.12$, $p < .05$, respectively. The two groups, however, did not differ from each other.

For the examinations, the pattern of the least-squares means was very different. The three groups did not differ in their average performance on the analytical tasks of the examination. The groups differed significantly, however, on both creative and practical tasks. For the creative tasks, the triarchic group did better than did either the critical-thinking groups, $t(88) = 9.38$, $p < .0001$, or the traditional group, $t(88) = 6.07$, $p < .0001$. The difference between the critical-thinking and the traditional groups was marginally significant $(p < .07)$, with the traditional group performing slightly better than did the critical-thinking group. Similarly, on the practical tasks, the triarchic-group performance was the highest and significantly different from the performance of both the critical-thinking group, $t(88) = 5.46$, $p < .0001$, and the traditional group, $t(88) = 3.81$, $p < .001$. Students in the critical-thinking group and the traditional-teaching group did not differ.

Finally, the triarchic-group students performed better on the multiple-choice test. This difference was statistically significant both when compared with the performance

8.3

Means in Study 3: Assessments of achievement. A = homework assignments; E = examinations.

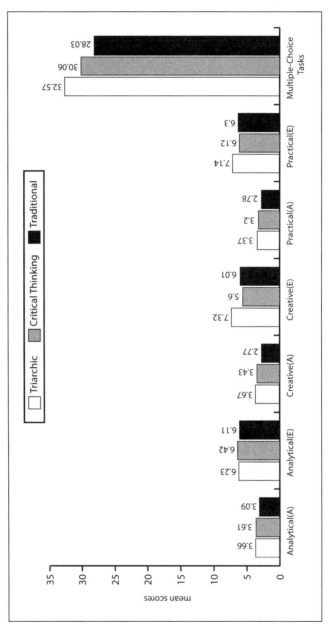

8.2 Effects of Instructional Condition in Study 2			
Assessment	$F(2, 140)$	p	R^2 (%)
Assignment			
Analytical	6.16	< .005	8
Creative	14.37	< .0001	17
Practical	4.75	< .01	6
Examination			
Analytical	0.66	ns	
Creative	47.39	< .0001	41
Practical	16.56	< .0001	19
Multiple-choice tasks	19.55	< .0001	22

of the students who received teaching based on the critical-thinking approach, $t(88)$ = 3.91, $p < .0001$, and when compared with the performance of those who received teaching based on the traditional-teaching approach, $t(88) = 6.02, p < .0001$. Moreover, the critical-thinking group did better than did the traditional-teaching group, $t(58)$ = 2.61, $p < .01$.

General Discussion

Students in two studies who received triarchic instruction generally learned more than did students who received either traditional memory-based or analytically based instruction. Greater learning was shown for a variety of kinds of assessments, including both memory-based ones that were already in use and performance-based ones that were designed especially for this project. The two experiments reported here thus suggest that students benefit from triarchic instruction, not only if it is matched to their pattern of strengths (Sternberg et al., 1996), but also if it is given in equal fashion to all students.

Of course, we make no claim that only triarchic instruction will improve achievement. Instruction based on other theories of intelligence (e.g., Gardner, 1993) might also result in enhanced achievement. Moreover, the two studies here represent tests of the theory at just two age levels, for two subject-matter areas, and in a limited number of settings. Clearly, it is premature to make any generalizations. At the very least, though, the results suggest that further testing of the triarchic theory in the classroom might be worthwhile.

Quasi-experimental studies done in actual classroom settings often have certain design limitations, and it behooves us to mention some of these possible limitations here as they apply to our own work.

First, we used intact classes in which neither assignment of pupils nor of teachers to classes was random. Ideally, of course, these assignments would be random. In order to compensate for nonrandom assignment of pupils to classes (and hence to conditions), we used mental-ability test scores as covariates. These covariates (the

Otis-Lennon Intelligence Scale in Study 1 and the SAT in Study 2) proved to be only weakly correlated with outcomes, however. It is not immediately obvious what might have served as more appropriate covariates. A measure of socioeconomic class is a possibility, but within study, there was not much variation in socioeconomic class among the participants (generally lower in Study 1 and middle to upper-middle in Study 2). Scores on a triarchic ability test might be appropriate, but we have no such test for the age levels we studied, and moreover, the test we have is not normed and standardized. A measure of achievement would be inappropriate because then we would be using achievement both as a dependent measure and as a covariate, which does not make sense. In sum, we chose plausible measures as covariates, but they proved to be only weakly related to treatment effects. In any case, the similarity of patterns of results for the two studies tends to counterindicate prior group differences as being responsible for the results.

Second, one might argue, as did a reviewer of an earlier version of our essay, that "the traditional instruction sounds deadly," and thus might have produced weaker gains because it encouraged students "to tune out." This argument is not an indictment of our study but of the existing system in which children are educated. Students in the traditional-instruction group received the regular instruction they would have received if we had not intervened. Their instruction was of the kind that millions of students in the United States and elsewhere receive every day.

Third, one could argue that the results were due to some kind of Hawthorne effect, whereby teachers or students in better performing groups were more motivated to do well or to please the researchers than were students and teachers in the weaker performing groups. This explanation is implausible, however. All teachers received an intervention that was designed to improve their teaching competencies. There is no a priori or a posteriori reason to believe that our interventions with different groups of teachers were differentially motivating.

Finally, it may be, as a reviewer suggested, that the advantage of triarchic instruction is that it is more "exciting." If that is the reason for the greater gain in the triarchic condition, we accept the reason with pleasure. We are all in favor of producing teaching that stimulates and excites students and thereby leads to improved performance. We cannot and would not rule out greater excitement as one possible source of our effects, although the generality of the gains across ages, subject matter, and dependent measures suggests that perhaps other factors were operating as well.

We believe that there is a strong need for teaching to all abilities and then assessment of achievement based on such broad teaching. Too often, teaching and assessment do not match. For example, one might teach to broad aspects of intelligence but then assess students' achievement for only memory-based outcomes. We believe that modern-day theories of intelligence and related cognitive functions have a great deal to offer to the education of children. The sooner educators incorporate in the "school-reform" efforts not just restructuring based on theories of management but also restructuring taking into account modern theories of intelligence and learning, the sooner we will see enhanced learning outcomes on the part of students.

References

Baron, J. B., & Sternberg, R. J. (Eds.). (1987). *Teaching thinking skills: Theory and practice.* New York: Freeman.

Binet, A., & Simon, T. (1916). *The development of intelligence in children.* Baltimore: Williams & Wilkins. (Original work published 1905)

Bransford, I. D., & Stein, B. S. (1993). *The ideal problem solver: A guide for improving thinking, learning, and creativity* (2nd ed.). New York: Freeman.

Callahan, C. M., Tomlinson, C. A., & Plucker, J. (1997). *Project START: Using a multiple intelligences model in identifying and promoting talent in high-risk students* (Research monograph no. 95136). Storrs, CT: University of Connecticut, National Research Center on the Gifted and Talented.

Costa, A. L. (Ed.). (1985). *Developing minds: A resource for teaching thinking.* Alexandria, VA: Association for Supervision and Curriculum Development.

Cronbach, L. J., & Snow, R. E. (1977). *Aptitudes and instructional methods.* New York: Irvington.

Feuerstein, R. (1980). *Instrumental enrichment: An intervention program for cognitive modifiability.* Baltimore, MD: University Park Press.

Gardner, H. (1983). *Frames of mind: The theory of multiple intelligences.* New York: Basic Books.

Gardner, H. (1993). *Multiple intelligences: The theory in practice.* New York: Basic Books.

Gardner, H. (1995). Reflections on multiple intelligences: Myths and messages. *Phi Delta Kappan, 77,* 200–203, 206–209.

Gardner, H., Krechevsky, M., Sternberg, R. J., & Okagaki, L. (1994). Intelligence in context: Enhancing students' practical intelligence for school. In K. McGilly (Ed.), *Classroom lessons: Integrating cognitive theory and classroom practice* (pp. 105–127). Cambridge, MA: Bradford Books.

Guilford, J. P. (1967). *The nature of human intelligence.* New York: McGraw-Hill.

Halpern, D. F. (1996). *Thought and knowledge: An introduction to critical thinking* (2nd ed.). Mahwah, NJ: Erlbaum.

Meeker, M. (1969). *The structure of intellect: Its interpretations and uses.* Columbus, OH: Charles E. Merrill.

Myers, D. (1996). *Exploring psychology* (3rd ed.). New York: Worth.

Nickerson, R. S. (1994). The teaching of thinking and problem solving. In R. J. Steinberg (Ed.), *Thinking and problem solving* (pp. 409–449). San Diego, CA: Academic Press.

Nickerson, R. S., Perkins, D. N., & Smith, E. E. (1985). *The teaching of thinking.* Hillsdale, NJ: Erlbaum.

Otis, A. S., & Lennon, R. T. (1967). *Otis-Lennon Mental Ability Test.* New York: Harcourt, Brace & World.

Sternberg, R. J. (1985). *Beyond IQ: A triarchic theory of human intelligence.* New York: Cambridge University Press.

Sternberg, R. J. (1986). *Intelligence applied: Understanding and increasing your intellectual skills.* San Diego, CA: Harcourt Brace Jovanovich.

Sternberg, R. J. (1994a). Allowing for thinking styles. *Educational Leadership, 52,* 36–40.

Sternberg, R. J. (1994b). Diversifying instruction and assessment. *Educational Forum, 59,* 47–53.

Stemberg, R. J. (1996). *Successful intelligence.* New York: Simon & Schuster.

Sternberg, R., & Bhana, K. (1986). Synthesis of research on the effectiveness of intellectual skills programs: Snake-oil remedies or miracle cures? *Educational Leadership, 44(2),* 60–67.

Sternberg, R., & Clinkenbeard, P. (1995). A triarchic view of identifying, teaching, and assessing gifted children. *Roeper Review, 17,* 255–260.

Sternberg, R. J., Ferrari, M., Clinkenbeard, P., & Grigorenko, E. L. (1996). Identification, instruction, and assessment of gifted children: A construct validation of a triarchic model. *Gifted Child Quarterly, 40,* 129–137.

Sternberg, R. J., Okagaki, L., & Jackson, A. (1990). Practical intelligence for success in school. *Educational Leadership, 48,* 35–39.

Sternberg, R. J., & Spear-Swerling, L. (1996). *Teaching for thinking.* Washington, DC: American Psychological Association.

Swartz, R. J. (1987). Teaching for thinking: A developmental model for the infusion of thinking skills into mainstream instruction. In J. B. Baron & R. J. Sternberg (Eds.), *Teaching thinking skills: Theory and practice* (pp. 182–218). New York: Freeman.

Williams, W. M., Blythe, T., White, N., Li, J., Sternberg, R. J., & Gardner, H. I. (1996). *Practical intelligence for school: A handbook for teachers of grades 5-8.* New York: HarperCollins.

A Triarchic Analysis of an Aptitude–Treatment Interaction

9

Robert J. Sternberg
Elena L. Grigorenko
Michel Ferrari
Pamela Clinkenbeard

Is it possible to instruct students and assess their achievement in ways that capitalize on the students' patterns of intellectual abilities? If so, such instruction and assessment might lead us to find aptitude–treatment interactions in the schools as a result of the extent of match of students' patterns of intellectual abilities to the ways in which they are instructed and assessed for their achievement. The work reported in this chapter addresses the existence and nature of one such interaction.

This essay is divided into three main parts. First, we briefly discuss ways of conceptualizing and measuring human intelligence and their implications for instruction and assessment of achievement, as well as for understanding aptitude–treatment interactions (ATI). Next, we present an experiment on the use of the triarchic theory of human intelligence (Sternberg, 1985, 1988) as a basis for eliciting ATIs. Finally, we discuss some general implications of our findings.

Historically, measurement of intelligence in academic settings dates back to Binet and Simon, who developed a scale to distinguish normal children from children deficient in mental ability (Binet & Simon, 1905, 1908). The Binet-Simon scale consisted of a series of 30 tasks of increasing difficulty. Although varied, most of the tasks relied on understanding language and on ability to reason using verbal or nonverbal (spatial and mathematical) materials. This test was later adapted by Terman to create the American *Stanford-Binet Intelligence Scale* (Terman, 1916; Thorndike, Hagen, & Sattler, 1986), and to create similar tests such as the *Wechsler Intelligence Scale for Children-III* (Wechsler, 1991).

Although Binet and Simon (1905) proposed a theory of intelligence, whereby more intelligent individuals are ones who show higher levels of adaptation, direction, and self-criticism, the theoretical bases by which intelligence test scores are understood are more likely to derive from the work of psychometric theorists such as Spearman (1904), Thurstone (1938), Cattell (1971), Vernon (1971), and, more recently, Carroll (1993). With the exception of Thurstone, these theorists have tended to view intelligence hierarchically, with a general ability *(g)* at the top of the hierarchy, major and minor group factors below general ability, and specific factors at the bottom of the hierarchy.

Conventional tests of intelligence have yielded what might be seen as somewhat disappointing results when used in studies of ATI. In particular, to the extent that such ATIs have been found, they have tended to be primarily with respect to the general factor *(g)* of intelligence (Cronbach & Snow, 1977). Results of early studies were so weak and fleeting that the study of ATI all but disappeared from the educational-psychology literature (see Snow, 1994; Woolfolk, 1995). One interpretation of this development would be that such interactions are limited, few, and far between. Another interpretation, which we begin to examine here, is that the paucity of robust ATIs may reflect narrowness in the conventional conceptualizations of intelligence as operationalized by traditional psychometric tests of abilities as well as failure to apply a unified model of intelligence to assessment of intellectual abilities, instruction, and assessment of achievement.

Conventional theories and tests of intelligence tend to encompass what Sternberg (1985, 1996; Sternberg & Spear-Swerling, 1996) refers to as memory and analytical abilities. Even theories positing multiple abilities and tests still deal largely with this class of abilities. The paucity of sustainable ATIs in the literature may reflect the possibility that the range of abilities conceptualized and then tested is too narrow to permit such ATIs to show themselves. Moreover, in this literature, it is rare that a single theory of intelligence is explicitly used as the unified basis for not just the conceptualization of abilities, but also for measurement of abilities, instruction, and assessment of achievement. The use of "off-the-shelf" measures of abilities and achievement combined with instruction that is typically based on no particular theory of intelligence may weaken whatever effects might otherwise have been attained.

We propose here to conduct an ATI investigation in which a single, relatively broad theory of intelligence is used as the basis for conceptualization of abilities, and then as well for measurement of abilities, instruction, and assessment of achievement.

The proposed theory, the triarchic theory of human intelligence (Sternberg, 1985, 1988), posits three basic kinds of abilities: analytical, creative, and practical abilities. All three of these kinds of abilities draw on a common set of information-processing components. They differ in the range of experience and the contexts to which the components apply. Thus, analytical abilities are applied to more familiar kinds of material; creative abilities are applied to relatively novel kinds of material or to familiar material conceptualized in a novel way; and practical abilities are applied to familiar or novel material for the purposes of adaptation to, shaping of, and selection of environmental contexts.

In the present study, we examined whether the triarchic theory would give rise to an ATI in the context of a college-level psychology course taught to high school students who were selected for triarchic ability pattern, taught in a way that either better or more poorly matched their triarchic pattern of abilities, and whose achievement was assessed triarchically as well.

Method

Participants

The participants in the present study were high school students, ranging in age from 14 to 18, who attended the 1993 Yale Summer Psychology Program (YSPP). The program was advertised through brochures and newsletters distributed to schools in the United States and abroad. Schools were asked to submit nominations of gifted and talented students, by whatever criteria they used, to the Program Committee of the YSPP. A selection procedure was based on the students' performance on the *Sternberg Triarchic Abilities Test* (STAT), Level H, designed for advanced high school and college students (Sternberg, 1993). The STAT was sent to schools that placed nominations, where the test was administered to the nominated students.

A total of 199 students (146 females and 53 males), from among 326 who were tested, were selected for participation in the summer program of 1993, on the basis of their patterns of ability-test scores (as described below). Of these students, 3 (1.5%) were entering grade 9, 25 (12.6%) were entering grade 10, 77 (38.7%) were entering grade 11, and 94 (47.2%) were entering grade 12. The program participants were fairly widely distributed ethnically (based on students' own reports): 60% European American, 11% African American, 6% Hispanic American, and 17% American from another ethnic minority. Furthermore, 4% of the students were from South Africa, and 2% "other."

The STAT subtest scores for the students were standardized, so they could be compared across different subtests. Based on their STAT performance, all students enrolled in the program were classified into five different groups. Students were identified as "high" in an aspect of ability based on their strongest test score and their score in respect to group average. For students to be classified as "high" in analytical, creative, or practical ability, their total score for a given ability was required to be at least a half–standard deviation above the group average and at least a half–standard deviation above their own scores for the other two abilities measured by the STAT (e.g., analytical higher than creative and practical). Thus, the first three groups included: (1) a group in which students were high in analytical ability ($N = 39$, 19.6%); (2) a group in which students were high in creative ability ($N = 38$, 19.1%); and (3) a group in which students were high in practical ability ($N = 35$, 17.6%). In addition, a "high balanced" group was also defined ($N = 40$, 20.1%). For students to be classified as high balanced, they had to score above the group average for all three abilities. Finally, the fifth group comprised students who scored at or below the group average for all three abilities ($N = 47$, 23.6%). This was a "low balanced" group.

Materials

Ability Test

Description of Test

Participants for this study were selected on the basis of scores on the Sternberg Triarchic Abilities Test (STAT) (Sternberg, 1991a, 1991b, 1991c, 1993), a research instrument constituting one theory-based alternative to traditional intelligence tests. The test is based on the triarchic theory of intelligence (Sternberg, 1985), which views intelligence as comprising three aspects: an analytical aspect, a creative aspect, and a practical aspect.

In a nutshell, the analytical aspect of intelligence involves analyzing, evaluating, and critiquing given knowledge; the creative aspect involves discovering, creating, and inventing new knowledge; and the practical aspect involves using, implementing, and applying knowledge in everyday contexts.

The test has nine four-option multiple-choice subtests, each comprising four items. The test takes roughly 11 hours to administer, which was the maximum time that participating schools wished to allow for testing. In addition, the test includes three performance or essay subtests—one emphasizing analytical, the second creative, and the third practical thinking.

The nine multiple-choice subtests represent a crossing of three kinds of process domains specified by the triarchic theory—analytic, creative, and practical—with three major content domains—verbal, quantitative, and figural. The idea behind this design is to measure the three aspects of processing in content domains that involve different basic abilities. Because the test is unpublished and is not widely known, it is briefly described here.

The nine multiple-choice subtests plus the three performance tests are:

1. *Analytical-Verbal* (neologisms [artificial words]). Students see a novel word embedded in a paragraph, and have to infer its meaning from the context.
2. *Analytical-Quantitative* (number series). Students have to say what number should come next in a series of numbers.
3. *Analytical-Figural* (matrices). Students see a figural matrix with the lower right entry missing, and have to say which of the options fits into the missing space.
4. *Practical-Verbal* (everyday reasoning). Students have to solve a set of everyday problems in the life of an adolescent (e.g., what to do about a friend who seems to have a substance-abuse problem).
5. *Practical-Quantitative* (everyday math). Students have to solve math problems based on scenarios requiring the use of math in everyday life (e.g., buying tickets for a ballgame or making chocolate chip cookies).
6. *Practical-Figural* (route planning). Students are presented with a map of an area (e.g., an entertainment park), and have to answer questions about navigating effectively through the area depicted by the map.
7. *Creative-Verbal* (novel analogies). Students are presented with verbal analogies preceded by counterfactual premises (e.g., money falls off trees), and must solve the analogies as though the counterfactual premises were true.
8. *Creative-Quantitative* (novel number operations). Students are presented with rules for novel number operations (e.g., *flix*, for which numerical manipulations differ

depending on whether the first of two operands is greater than, equal to, or less than the second). Students have to use the novel number operations to solve presented math problems.

9. *Creative-Figural* (novel series completion). Students are first presented with a figural series that involves one or more transformations; they then must apply the rule of the original series to a new figure with a different appearance, to complete a new series.

There are also three essay items, one each stressing analytical, creative, and practical thinking. In the current version, the analytical problem requires students to analyze the advantages and disadvantages of having police or security guards in a school building. The creative problem requires students to describe how they would reform their school system to produce an ideal one. The practical problem requires students to specify a problem in their lives, and to state three practical solutions for solving it. Essays are scored for analytical, creative, and practical qualities, respectively, by trained raters.

Psychometric Properties of the Test

Because the test we used is unfamiliar, we briefly describe here its main psychometric properties as elicited from our sample.

Basic statistics for the STAT took into account both multiple-choice and essay items. Scores for essays represent an average of two independent raters. Maximum score for each essay (analytical, creative, and practical) was 4. Mean scores ($N = 267$) were 2.78 ($SD = 0.73$) for analytical; 2.54 ($SD = 0.71$) for creative; and 2.85 ($SD = 0.81$) for practical essays. Maximum score for each of the analytical, creative, and practical multiple-choice sections was 12. Multiple-choice subtest means for all students initially screened ($N = 326$) were 7.90 ($SD = 2.52$) for the analytical section, 8.75 ($SD = 2.09$) for the creative section, and 8.09 ($SD = 2.11$) for the practical section. These statistics show what appear to be acceptable levels of mean performance and dispersions around these means.

Total ability (analytical, creative, and practical) scores are all calculated as sums of standardized scores on the multiple-choice and essay sections of the test. Overall correlations across subtests, all statistically significant at the $p < .01$ level, were .47 between analytical and creative, .41 between analytical and practical, and .37 between creative and practical. In general, multiple-choice items tended to intercorrelate with each other moderately (median $r = .52$) and the essay items to intercorrelate weakly (median $r = .21$), although all intercorrelations were statistically significant. The median intercorrelation of multiple-choice with essay items was also weak (median $r = .14$) but statistically significant.

Because we used two different forms of test items (multiple-choice and essay) and hypothesized three latent abilities (analytical, creative, and practical), the multitrait-multimethod approach via structural-equation modeling (Bollen, 1989) was utilized in order to assess what the correlations across the abilities would be if method variance were accounted for. In this model, we allowed the abilities (analytical, creative, and practical) to correlate, but the abilities and methods were uncorrelated. The errors were fixed rather than estimated. The overall fit of the model was satisfactory ($\chi^2_{(5)} = 9.8$, $p = .08$; GFI = .99; RMSEA = .06). The analysis enabled us to take out elements of the intersubtest correlations that are due solely to shared forms of testing (which

9.1 Estimates of Influence of Three Abilities (Analytical, Creative, and Practical) and Two Methods (Multiple-Choice and Essay) on Observed Ability Indicators

Observed Variables	Abilities			Methods		Error Variance
	Analytical	Creative	Practical	Multiple Choice	Essay	
Multiple choice						
Analytical	.57			.77		.10
Creative		.05		.73		.44
Practical			.07	.70		.44
Essay						
Analytical	.13				.94	.10
Creative		.89			.33	.10
Practical			.92		.22	.10

are especially relevant to the multiple-choice subtests). Using such analysis, we found the correlations between latent abilities (as measured by multiple-choice subtests and essays) to be −.07 for analytical and creative, .00 for analytical and practical, and .06 for creative and practical. The correlation between the methods was 0.25. Other details of this analysis are presented in Table 9.1.

The KR-20 internal-consistency reliabilities of the multiple-choice items, averaging across contents, were .63 for the analytical items, .62 for the creative items, and .48 for the practical items. These reliabilities are relatively weak, but perhaps reflect the facts that item content was diverse (verbal, quantitative, figural) and the number of items was small (12 for each of the analytical, creative, and practical sections). Interrater reliabilities (Spearman-Brown corrected correlation coefficients) of the essays were .69 for the analytical, .58 for the creative, and .68 for the practical essays.

In a pilot use of the STAT with a similar population (Sternberg & Clinkenbeard, 1995), a variety of tests of abilities was administered to 64 participants. The other tests used were the Terman Concept Mastery Test (primarily a test of crystallized abilities), the Watson-Glaser Critical Thinking Appraisal (a verbal test of critical think-ing), the Cattell Culture Fair Test of *g* (primarily a test of fluid abilities), and a homemade test of insight problems (adapted from Sternberg, 1986). Respective correla-tions of the STAT with these tests were, for the analytical, .49, .50, .50, and .47 (all significant); for the creative, .43, .53, .55, and .59 (all significant); and for the practical, .21, .32, .36, and .21 (the second and third significant).

Instructional Material

The text for the course was a prepublication version of *In Search of the Human Mind* (Sternberg, 1995), an introductory-psychology text comprising 20 chapters. The text covers at a college level the topics typical of introductory-psychology courses. It includes analytical, creative, and practical questions embedded within each chapter and at the end of each chapter. Thus, all students, regardless of instructional placement, received at least some triarchic instruction through their reading.

Assessment of Achievement

Students in the program were evaluated in three ways: They were given two assignments, a final project, and two examinations (midterm and final). Each of the assessments involved analytical, creative, and practical thinking, as well as use of memory.

With regard to homework, one assignment required students to (a) compare and contrast two theories of depression (analytical); (b) propose their own, improved theory, which could be based in part on past theories (creative); and (c) show how they could apply their theory of depression to help a depressed friend (practical). The other homework required similar thought processes applied to the Festinger-Carlsmith (1959) forced-compliance paradigm.

With regard to the examinations, the midterm consisted of a multiple-choice portion measuring primarily recall but also simple inference, and three essays: one analytical, one creative, and one practical. The final exam again consisted of multiple-choice and essay sections, differing from the midterm only in the length of the multiple-choice section (it was longer) and the number of essays (three per type rather than one).

The independent project required students to come up with their own investigation and to pursue it analytically, creatively, and practically.

Four raters scored all performance assessments (i.e., assignments, exam essays, final project). Each (analytical, creative, practical) part of each assessment was rated for analytical, creative, and practical quality. To reduce redundancy, and to arrive at a purer assessment of each of these abilities, analyses are reported in this chapter only for ratings matched to assessments (e.g., analytical ratings for the analytical performances, creativity ratings for the creative performances, and practical ratings for the practical performances). Results were similar when all three ratings were used for all three types of performance.

All ratings were on a scale of 1 (low) to 9 (high). Raters met frequently in order to ensure common standards and use of the rating scales. Averaged Pearson interrater reliabilities for quality ratings by the four judges of the achievement measures were .59 for the assignments, .45 for the final project, and .71 for the examinations, and were comparable for analytical, creative, and practical ratings. If one applied the Spearman-Brown formula to take into account the use of the four judges whose ratings were ultimately averaged, the reliabilities rose to .85, .78, and .90, respectively. The ratings were subjected to principal-component analyses. First principal component standardized scores were utilized in the subsequent analyses as the measures of course performance.

Design

Students were selected on the basis of their ability-test score profiles to be either (a) high-analytical, (b) high-creative, (c) high-practical, (d) high-balanced, or (e) low-balanced. They were then placed at random in sections of the introductory-psychology course that emphasized (a) analytical instruction, (b) creative instruction, (c) practical instruction, or (d) memory instruction (control). Thus, some students were better matched, and others more poorly matched, with respect to ability patterns and instructional treatment. All students were assessed for (a) analytical, (b) creative, (c) practical, and (d) memory achievement. Thus, participant ability and method of instruction were between-subjects variables, and method of assessment was a within-subjects variable.

Procedure

Ability tests were sent out to schools from which students were nominated. The tests were administered in the schools, and then returned to us for scoring and data analysis. Students were then selected for participation in the study on the basis of their ability pattern. They came to the 4-week summer program at Yale, where instruction lasted all day. The students were housed in a common dormitory. Students used a common text and attended common lectures in the morning, given by a psychology professor who had won a university teaching award.

In the afternoons, students were assigned to sections, which constituted the experimental treatment. There were eight sections in all, two for each of the four instructional conditions. Half the sections were taught by high school advanced-placement psychology teachers, the other half by trained graduate assistants. The two types of teachers were equally distributed across instructional conditions. Although students and their parents signed informed consent forms and thus knew they were part of a study, they did not know exactly what the study was about, nor that it involved ability patterns. Of course, they did not know their test scores, nor how the sections were intended to differ. All examinations were administered in class. At the end of the course, participants were debriefed.

Results

Predictive Validity of STAT for Course Performance

Before testing for ATI, we wanted to ascertain whether the STAT even had empirical validity for predicting course performance.

Simple correlations between the STAT and various aspects of course performance are shown in Table 9.2.

Subtests for all three processing domains measured by the STAT reliably predicted each of the analytical, creative, and practical aspects of course performance. Of course, because the subtests are themselves correlated, there may be redundancy in these predictions. Hence, we need to use multiple regression in order to assess levels of prediction for all three ability subtests.

The results of multiple regressions, addressing the question of relative levels of prediction of course performance, are shown in Table 9.3. In every case, at least two variables, and in one case, all three variables, significantly contributed to prediction: the analytical and either or both of the creative and practical scores.

Analysis of Variance

To investigate the effects of the demographic factors, three sets of multivariate analyses of variance were conducted. These analyses separately employed multiple measures

9.2 Correlations of Combined STAT Multiple-Choice and Essay Scores with Course Assessments

| STAT Scores | Assignments | | | |
	Analytical	Creative	Practical	Overall Average
Analytical	.35**	.32**	.27**	.34**
Creative	.27**	.29**	.28**	.30**
Practical	.24**	.19**	.14**	.20**
STAT Scores	Final Project			
	Analytical	Creative	Practical	Overall Average
Analytical	.29**	.21**	.34**	.36**
Creative	.34**	.28**	.32**	.33**
Practical	.26**	.24**	.29**	.24**
STAT Score	Exams			
	Analytical	Creative	Practical	Overall Average
Analytical	.30**	.36**	.34**	.33**
Creative	.30**	.30**	.33**	.37**
Practical	.25**	.20**	.21**	.31**
STAT Score	Total Overall Assessments (Assignments, Final Project, Exams)			
	Analytical	Creative	Practical	Overall Average
Analytical	.43**	.43**	.45**	.46**
Creative	.38**	.38**	.41**	.41**
Practical	.31**	.28**	.26**	.30**

$^*p < .05$, $^{**}p < .01$

of performance on analytical, creative, and practical tasks as dependent measures and gender, ethnicity, and grade as independent measures. With the exception of one test (the main effect of ethnicity for performance on practical tasks), none of the multivariate tests of the main effects or interactions was significant. For the statistically significant test, Pillai's Trace value was 0.158 ($F_{15,516} = 1.92$, $p < .05$). The follow-up univariate analyses revealed that there were significant differences for three out of the five measures of performance on practical tasks: the second homework assignment ($F_{3,174} = 3.63$, $p < .05$), the final exam ($F_{3,174} = 3.47$, $p < .05$), and the independent project ($F_{3,174} = 3.19$, $p < .05$). Closer analyses of the means showed that these differences were consistently due to the lower performance of Black students on these tasks. However, when conservative Bonferroni procedures correcting for the level of significance were applied, these findings were no longer significant.

The overall conclusion from the analyses of possible differences in task performance due to demographic factors showed that the students' performance did not vary significantly depending on such characteristics as their gender, ethnicity, and grade. Consequently, in the further investigation, these demographic factors were excluded from the tested models.

To investigate the effect of the interaction between the students' abilities and the method of teaching, a set of repeated-measures analyses of variance was conducted.

9.3	Multiple Regression of Course Performance on STAT Multiple-Choice Items and Essays				
				STAT Beta Score	
Dependent Measure	F Value	R^2	Analytical	Creative	Practical
Assignments					
Overall	10.0***	.12	.25**	.16**	.01
Analytical	10.0***	.13	.27**	.09	.06
Creative	8.7***	.11	.22**	.16*	.01
Practical	7.2***	.10	.19*	.19*	−.05
Independent Project					
Overall	13.4***	.17	.14*	.22**	.14*
Analytical	10.3***	.12	.13	.22**	.09
Creative	6.6***	.09	.04	.19*	.13
Practical	11.8***	.15	.19*	.16*	.13
Exams					
Overall	12.0***	.14	.24**	.19**	.04
Analytical	9.0***	.11	.16*	.16*	.10
Creative	10.9***	.13	.27**	.15	.00
Practical	11.1***	.15	.22**	.21*	.01

$* p < .05, ** p < .01, *** p < .001$

Mean and standard deviations for the five assessments (two homework assignments, two exams, and an independent project) of the three abilities (analytical, creative, and practical) across two groups of students (matched and mismatched) are presented in Table 9.4. In these analyses, students were considered as matched if they scored high on the ability test (analytical, creative, practical) corresponding to the instructional condition (analytical, creative, practical), and mismatched otherwise. Thus, high balanced were always matched, low balanced always mismatched.

The repeated-measures analyses of variance employed five different assessment procedures as different assessment points spaced in time. The within-subjecteffect was specified as the assessment factor and the match/mismatch was specified as the between-subjects effect.

For the measures of performance on the analytical tasks, there were no significant assessment or assessment-by-match effects. However, the between-subject effect of match was significant ($F_{1,197} = 20.00$, $p < .000$). The estimated marginal means are graphed in Figure 9.1. The follow-up profile analysis, which allowed a comparison between performance of matched and mismatched groups across all five measures, showed the significant differences in level of performance of matched and mismatched students. The tests of parallelism and flatness were nonsignificant: The profiles appear to be parallel and the various forms of assessment elicited the same average responses from both matched and mismatched students.

For creative tasks, there were no significant assessment or assessment-by-match effects. However, the between-subject effect of match was significant ($F_{1,197} = 3.86$, $p < .05$). The estimated marginal means are graphed in Figure 9.2. The follow-up profile

| | Analytical | | Creative | | Practical | |
Groups	Mean	SD	Mean	SD	Mean	SD
Better Matched						
Assignment 1	.26	0.97	.09	1.06	.11	1.06
Assignment 2	.23	1.13	.08	1.05	.07	1.13
Midterm Examination	.31	1.02	.23	0.97	.17	1.01
Final Examination	.22	1.06	.03	1.05	.10	1.03
Independent Project	.29	1.00	0.8	1.00	.26	1.00
More Poorly Matched						
Assignment 1	−.15	0.99	−.06	0.97	−.09	0.96
Assignment 2	−.16	0.95	−.10	1.00	−.08	0.95
Midterm Examination	−.23	0.94	−.13	0.96	−.19	0.94
Final Examination	−.13	0.93	−.07	0.97	−.08	0.96
Independent Project	−.22	0.93	−.11	0.99	−.13	0.98

9.4 Aptitude–Treatment Interaction Analysis for Total Sample[1]

[1] The table presents the means and standard deviations of the first principal component standardized scores obtained from the four judges' ratings. The scores range from −1 to 1.

9.1

Analytical task performance.

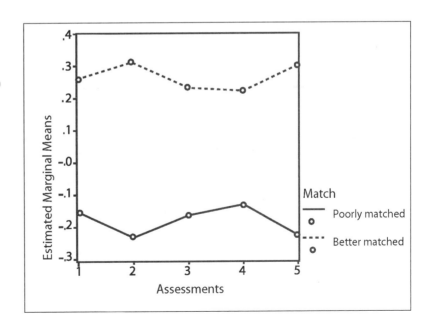

9.2

Creative task performance.

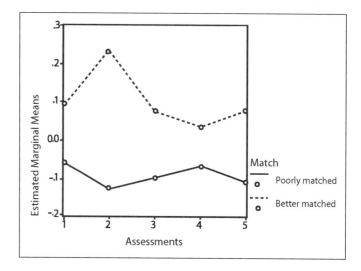

analysis, which allowed a comparison between performance of matched and mis-matched groups across all five measures, showed significant differences in levels of performance of matched and mismatched students. The tests of parallelism and flatness were nonsignificant: The profiles appear to be parallel and the various forms of assessment elicited the same average responses from both matched and mis-matched students.

Finally, for practical tasks, there also were no significant assessment or assessment-by-match effects. However, the between-subject effect of match was significant ($F_{1,197}$ = 6.56, $p < .01$). The estimated marginal means are graphed in Figure 9.3. The follow-up profile analysis, which allowed a comparison between performance of matched and mismatched groups across all five measures, showed significant differences in levels of performance of matched and mismatched students. The tests of parallelism and flatness were nonsignificant: The profiles appeared to be parallel and the various forms of assessment elicited the same average responses from both matched and mismatched students.

The total sample of 326 children was recruited through the children's schools, which nominated them for participation in the program as gifted and talented. Thus, even the total sample comprised fairly selected children. The selection of 199 children for participation in the ATI analyses gave us groups with balanced as well as unbal-anced patterns of triarchic abilities. Yet, one could argue that the observed difference between the matched and mismatched groups might have resulted from the fact that the "high" ability group was included in the matched group and the "low" balanced group were included in the mismatched group, thus confounding the ATI-based effect with the effect of the g-factor (i.e., general intelligence). To test this hypothesis, we repeated the analyses described above on a subsample of children that included only those high on specific abilities (analytical, creative, or practical). The balanced groups were not included in this analysis.

9.3

Practical task performance.

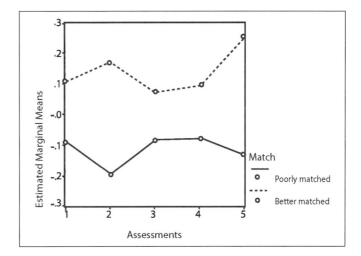

This procedure, however, significantly decreased the size of the sample, especially the size of the matched group ($N = 71$ to $N = 31$). In such a small sample, random fluctuations of scores (which might have been due to the impact of nonacademic factors of the YSPP, such as staying up late in the dormitory, etc.) are especially noticeable. In order to control for the impact of random variance, the data were screened for deviant scores, and those extreme scores were deleted from the analyses.

In the framework of repeated-measures analyses of variance, the between-subject effect of match was significant for the measures of performance on the analytical ($F_{1,71} = 12.3$, $p < .001$) and creative ($F_{1,71} = 4.2$, $p < .05$) tasks. There was no overall effect of match on the performance of the five practical tasks, but the effect held for three of the five individual tasks (first homework assignment, final exam, and independent project, $F_{1,71} = 3.8$, $p < .05$). For these analyses, the observed means are shown in Table 9.5 and the estimated marginal means are graphed in Figure 9.4.

Discussion

Our results suggest that students performed better when they were better rather than more poorly matched in instruction vis-à-vis their triarchic pattern of abilities. In particular, analytically, creatively, and practically oriented students all performed at higher levels when the afternoon discussion sections matched their patterns of abilities. The pattern of external validation is thus consistent both with our theory and with its implications for instruction.

In some ways, our treatment manipulation was relatively mild, consisting only of differences in the afternoon discussion sections, although these differences did last the length of a full, all-day, 4-week course. All students received at least some triarchic instruction through the text (Sternberg, 1995), and all students received a common lecture. That we were able to obtain interaction effects that went beyond a mere

	Analytical		Creative		Practical	
Groups	Mean	*SD*	Mean	*SD*	Mean	*SD*
Better Matched						
Assignment 1	.37	.64	.28	.82	.21	.66
Assignment 2	.54	.72	.26	.82	.18	.90
Midterm Exam	.50	.79	.18	.78	.06	.75
Final Exam	.24	.76	−.04	.77	.05	.74
Independent Project	.15	.91	.12	.82	.30	.79
More Poorly Matched						
Assignment 1	.00	.81	.09	.76	.01	.87
Assignment 2	−.09	.91	.00	.98	−.08	.93
Midterm Exam	−.15	.97	−.07	.83	−.12	.73
Final Exam	−.12	.86	.01	.93	.06	.93
Independent						
Project	−.14	.78	−.06	.79	.02	.72

9.5 Aptitude–Treatment Interaction Analysis (Reduced Sample)

general-ability based effect (see Cronbach & Snow, 1977) suggests that, in ATI studies, there may be an advantage to using a broad-based theory of intelligence that serves as a common conceptualization for the measurement of intellectual abilities, instruction, and the assessment of achievement. Of course, we evaluated only high school students studying psychology, and broader evaluations are needed.

Our results might be interpreted to suggest that, ideally, schools would expand their instruction and assessment to take into account creative and practical, and not just memory and analytical abilities. Because it is important for all students to compensate for and remediate weaknesses as well as to capitalize on strengths (Cronbach & Snow, 1977; Sternberg, 1994a, 1994b), all students ideally would receive at least some of the three kinds of instruction and assessment, as in our study, and not just the kind that matches their ability pattern.

In sum, the purpose of this investigation was to examine the interaction between ability patterns and school achievement as a function of type of instruction. The results of the investigation show, we believe, at least some promise both for the triarchic theory of intelligence and for further development of ability testing, instruction, and assessment of achievement based on the theory.

9.4

Top: Analytical task performance. Middle: Creative task performance. Bottom: Practical task performance.

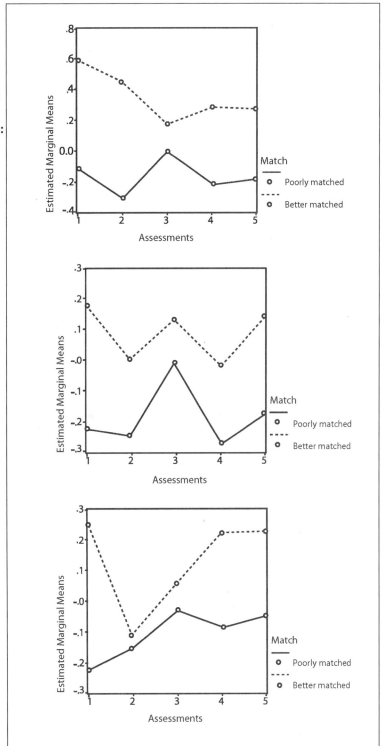

References

Binet, A., & Simon, T. (1905). Méthodes nouvelles pour le diagnostique du niveau intellectuel des anormaux (New methods for diagnosing the intellectual level of subnormals). *L'année psychologique, 11,* 191–336.

Binet, A., & Simon, T. (1908). Le developpement de l'intelligence chez les enfants (The development of intelligence in children). *L'année psychologique, 14,* 1–94.

Bollen, K. A. (1989). *Structural equations with latent variables.* New York: Wiley.

Carroll, J. B. (1993). *Human cognitive abilities: A survey of factor-analytic studies.* Cambridge: Cambridge University Press.

Cattell, R. B. (1971). *Abilities: Their structure, growth, and action.* Boston: Houghton Mifflin.

Cronbach, L. J., & Snow, R. E. (1977). *Aptitudes and instructional methods.* New York: Irvington.

Festinger, L., & Carlsmith, J. M. (1959). Cognitive consequences of forced compliance. *Journal of Abnormal and Social Psychology, 58,* 203–210.

Gardner, H. (1983). *Frames of mind: The theory of multiple intelligences.* New York: Basic Books.

Snow, R. E. (1994). Aptitude-treatment interaction. In R. J. Sternberg (Ed.), *Encyclopedia of human intelligence* (Vol. 1, pp. 117–121). New York: Macmillan.

Spearman, C. E. (1904). "General intelligence" objectively determined and measured. *American Journal of Psychology, 15,* 201–293.

Spearman, C. E. (1927). *The abilities of man.* London: Macmillan. (Reprinted: New York: AMS Publishers, 1981)

Sternberg, R. J. (1984). What should intelligence tests test? Implications of a triarchic theory of intelligence for intelligence testing. *Educational Researcher, 13,* 5–15.

Sternberg, R. J. (1985). *Beyond IQ: A triarchic theory of human intelligence.* New York: Cambridge University Press.

Sternberg, R. J. (1986). *Intelligence applied.* Orlando, FL: Harcourt Brace Jovanovich.

Sternberg, R. J. (1988). *The triarchic mind: A new theory of human intelligence.* New York: Viking.

Sternberg, R. J. (1990). *Metaphors of mind.* New York: Cambridge University Press.

Sternberg, R. J. (1991a). Giftedness according to the triarchic theory of human intelligence. In N. Colangelo & G. A. Davis (Eds.), *Handbook of gifted education* (2nd ed., pp. 45–54). Needham Heights, MA: Allyn & Bacon.

Sternberg, R. J. (1991b). Theory-based testing of intellectual abilities: Rationale for the Triarchic Abilities Test. In H. Rowe (Ed.), *Intelligence: Reconceptualization and measurement* (pp. 183–202). Hillsdale, NJ: Erlbaum.

Sternberg, R. J. (1991c). Triarchic abilities test. In D. Dickinson (Ed.), *Creating the future: Perspectives on educational change* (pp. 76–81). Aston Clinton, Bucks, UK: Accelerated Learning Systems.

Sternberg, R. J. (1992). Toward better intelligence tests. In M. C. Wittrock (Ed.), *Testing and cognition.* Englewood Cliffs, NJ: Prentice-Hall.

Sternberg, R. J. (1993). *Sternberg Triarchic Abilities Test,* High School Level. Unpublished test.

Sternberg, R. J. (1994a). Diversifying instruction and assessment. *Educational Forum, 59(1),* 47–53.

Sternberg, R. J. (1994b). A triarchic model for teaching and assessing students in general psychology. *General Psychologist, 30,* 42–48.

Sternberg, R. J. (1995). *In search of the human mind.* Orlando: Harcourt Brace College Publishers.

Sternberg, R. J. (1996). Matching abilities, instruction, and assessment: Reawakening the sleeping giant of ATI. In I. Dennis & P. Tapsfield (Eds.), *Human abilities: Their nature and measurement* (pp. 167–181). Mahwah, NJ: Erlbaum.

Sternberg, R. J., & Clinkenbeard, P. R. (1995). A triarchic model of identifying, teaching, and assessing gifted children. *Roeper Review, 17,* 255–260.

Sternberg, R. J., & Davidson, J. E. (Eds.). (1986). *Conceptions of giftedness.* New York: Cambridge University Press.

Sternberg, R. J., & Spear-Swerling, L. (1996). *Teaching for thinking.* Washington, DC: American Psychological Association.

Terman, L. M. (1916). *The measurement of intelligence: An explanation of and a complete guide for the use of the Stanford revision and extension of the Binet-Simon intelligence scale.* Boston: Houghton Mifflin.

Thorndike, R. L., Hagen, E. P., & Sattler, J. M. (1986). *Technical manual for the Stanford-Binet Intelligence Scale: Fourth edition.* Chicago: Riverside.

Thurstone, L. L. (1938). Primary mental abilities. *Psychometric Monographs,* 1.

Vernon, P. E. (1971). *The structure of human abilities.* London: Methuen.

Wechsler, D. (1991). *The Wechsler Intelligence Scales for Children–third edition* (WISC-111). San Antonio, TX: Psychological Corporation.

Woolfolk, A. (1995). *Educational psychology.* Boston: Allyn-Bacon.

Using the Theory of Successful Intelligence as a Basis for Augmenting AP Exams in Psychology and Statistics

10

Steven E. Stemler
Elena L. Grigorenko
Linda Jarvin
Robert J. Sternberg

Each year, millions of students across the country take high-stakes achievement tests that will have an important infuence on their academic and professional future (Heubert & Hauser, 1999); yet, many of these tests are not aligned with modern theories of student learning and cognitive processing. As a result, students with strengths in cognitive skills not assessed by these tests may have their future opportunities curtailed (Sternberg, 1997). For example, many students with strong creative or practical skills but weaker memory and analytical skills never have the opportunity to reach the highest levels of education, where they might thrive, because the tests that are used as gatekeepers tend to emphasize a more limited range of skills (e.g., memory and analytical skills) than might be optimal. Yet, a narrow range of skills, such as memory and analytical skills, taken alone is not sufficient to succeed in the professional world. Instead, a balance of a wider range of cognitive skills is important, regardless of one's professional domain.

Broadening the range of cognitive skills assessed is important not only at the individual level. It has potentially important implications at the group level as well. Sternberg and colleagues (Sternberg & The Rainbow Project Collaborators, 2006;

235

Sternberg, Torff, & Grigorenko, 1998a, 1998b; Sternberg et al., 2004) have shown that when assessments are designed to measure a broad range of cognitive skills, the achievement gap typically observed between White students and underrepresented minority students (Chubb & Loveless, 2002; Jencks & Phillips, 1998) appears to be reduced substantially.

In recent years, designers of large-scale testing programs, recognizing the important social, economic, and ethical consequences associated with standardized testing, have become increasingly interested in linking educational assessment to modern theories of cognitive processing skills (Embretson & Reise, 2000; Irvine & Kyllonen, 2002). To the extent that high-stakes exams draw on sound traditions of research in psychological theory and educational assessment, the results will be more construct valid and defensible.

Therefore, in the spirit of infusing cognitive theory into educational assessment, the aim of the current study was to create a series of augmented exams for the College Board's Advanced Placement (AP) program that would be explicitly based on one validated theory of cognitive processing (Sternberg, 1985, 1997, 1999), the theory of successful intelligence. We were particularly interested in examining individual and ethnic group differences in cognitive processing skills within the context of AP Psychology and Statistics.

Of course, this is not the only theory that could serve as a basis for such an assessment. There are many others (Alexander, Jetton, & Kulikowich, 1995; Carroll, 1993; Cattell, 1971; Ceci, 1996; Gardner, 1983; Luria, 1973) that might also serve as a basis for augmentation of existing tests. Perhaps future studies will compare alternative theories as a basis for such augmentation. We chose the theory of successful intelligence, in particular, because (a) it has been validated through converging operations in a number of different studies, (b) it has rather clear implications for operationalization in the context of item construction for AP exams, (c) past studies had shown incremental validity for theory in the context of assessment, and (d) we are familiar with the theory and its implications.

Background

To set the context for the study, we begin with a brief description of the AP program. We then present our theoretical framework for the study and briefly review the literature related to individual differences in cognitive skills and ethnic differences in achievement. This section concludes with a statement of the specific research questions under investigation.

The Advanced Placement Program

The College Board's Advanced Placement program, started in 1955, was originally designed as a mechanism for granting exceptional high school students the opportunity for advanced study that would be equivalent to college-level programming. Since then, the program has expanded both in terms of the kinds of students eligible to take the courses and in the number of different subject areas covered by the program. Over time, the program has become widely disseminated. In 2002, a total of 937,951 students (about 10% of all high school students) took an exam in one of the 34 courses across 19 subject areas offered by the AP program.[1]

Each spring, students enrolled in AP courses are given the opportunity to take a high-stakes exam to demonstrate their mastery of the subject area. The exams are graded on a scale from 1 to 5, "with five indicating a student who is extremely well-qualified to receive college credit and/or advanced placement based on an AP exam grade" (College Board, 2004). Typically, students scoring 3 or higher on the exam are eligible in many colleges to receive college credit for their course. Thus, the results of the test have potentially important financial implications, as placing out of the college courses potentially can save a student thousands of dollars in tuition in subsequent years. The limited number of chances to take the test, coupled with the potentially significant financial savings associated with the outcome, qualifies the AP exam as a high-stakes test.

Traditionally, the chief concern of the AP exam developers has been with the assessment of particular subdomains of academic content and skills rather than with the explicit assessment of students' cognitive skills. Given the high consequences attached to the test results of AP exams, the designers of the AP program are now seeking to ensure that its tests are aligned with the latest thinking about how students learn.

Theoretical Framework

According to Sternberg's theory of successful intelligence (1984, 1985, 1997, 1999), a common set of processes underlies all aspects of problem solving. These processes, although not their behavioral manifestations, are hypothesized to be universal (Sternberg, 2003). For example, although the solutions to problems that are considered intelligent in one culture may be different from the solutions considered to be intelligent in another culture, the need to define problems and translate strategies to solve these problems exists in any culture. *Metacomponents,* or executive processes, plan what to do, monitor things as they are being done, and evaluate things after they are done. *Performance components* execute the instructions of the metacomponents. *Knowledge-acquisition components* are used to learn how to solve problems or simply to acquire declarative knowledge in the first place.

Although the same components are used for all three aspects of intelligence universally, these processes are applied to different kinds of tasks and situations, depending on whether a given problem requires analytical thinking, creative thinking, practical thinking, or a combination of these kinds of thinking. In particular, *analytical* thinking is invoked when components are applied to fairly familiar kinds of problems abstracted from everyday life. *Creative* thinking is invoked when the components are applied to relatively novel kinds of tasks or situations. *Practical* thinking is invoked when the components are applied to experience to adapt to, shape, and select environments. Thus, the same components, applied in different contexts, yield different kinds

---

[1] The 34 courses offered by the AP program include: Art History, Biology, Calculus AB, Calculus BC, Chemistry, Computer Science A, Computer Science AB, Economics: Macro, Economics: Micro, English Language and Composition, English Literature and Composition, Environmental Science, European History, French Language, French Literature, German Language, Government and Politics: Comparative, Government and Politics: United States, Human Geography, International English Language/APIEL, Latin Literature, Latin: Vergil, Music Theory, Physics B, Physics C: Electricity and Magnetism, Physics C: Mechanics, Psychology, Spanish Language, Spanish Literature, Statistics, Studio Art: 2-D Design, Studio Art: 3-D Design, Studio Art: Drawing, U.S. History, World History.

of thinking—analytical, creative, and practical. Ultimately, one needs creative thinking to generate new ideas, analytical thinking to determine if they are good ideas, and practical thinking to implement the ideas and to persuade others of their value.

The theory of successful intelligence is not wholly incompatible with aspects of other theories, such as Bloom's (1956) taxonomy of cognitive skills and Gardner's (1983) theory of multiple intelligences. Ultimately, however, the usefulness of any one theory for augmentation of a test such as the AP exam is shown by empirical data examining what happens when the test is augmented by the particular theory.

A key advantage to using an expanded theory of cognitive-processing skills in test construction is that it can provide useful information about and for individual students. Within the theoretical framework of the theory of successful intelligence, students could receive a score report showing their specific profile of strengths and weaknesses across a variety of cognitive skills, which they then could use in future learning opportunities to capitalize on their strengths and compensate or correct for their weaknesses. Furthermore, by measuring a broader range of cognitive skills, individuals who might have been labeled as low achievers when assessed on a limited set of cognitive skills may have better opportunities to demonstrate their content area mastery.

Differences in Student Achievement

One of the biggest challenges facing the AP program is in the recruitment of minority students to participate in the program. In 2002, approximately 14% of all students who took one or more exams were African American or Latino, a figure substantially lower than their relative representation in the high school population of 30%.[2] The demographic breakdown of participants varies some by subject area. For example, in 2002, 70% of test-takers in AP Psychology were White students, 5% were African American, and 7% were Latino. In AP Statistics, 68% of the test-takers were White, 4% were African American, and 6% were Latino.

In addition to the problem of low minority student enrollment in advanced courses, one of the most persistent problems in instruction and assessment over the years has been the existence of systematic differences in student achievement by ethnicity. Many authors have noted the persistent presence of a Black–White test score gap (first documented in 1966), with White students tending to outperform minority students on most conventional tests of achievement by nearly a full standard deviation (Chubb & Loveless, 2002; Jencks & Phillips, 1998). Researchers have proposed several possible reasons for these results, including genetic differences (Herrnstein & Murray, 1994), cultural differences (Fordham & Ogbu, 1986; Williams, 2004), and social psychological differences (Steele, 1997). We believe that one reason for this persistent difference is that traditional achievement tests tend to assess a fairly limited range of cognitive skills, ignoring other important skills.

Sternberg and colleagues (Sternberg & The Rainbow Project Collaborators, 2006; Sternberg et al., 1998a, 1998b) have shown in a series of studies that when assessments are designed to expand the range of cognitive skills assessed, the achievement gap between White students and minority students can be reduced. For example, in a

---

[2]African American and Latino students represented 30% of the secondary school population in 1996, the last year this information was collected by NCES's Youth survey, and their numbers have continued to grow.

recent study designed to create assessments that would augment the predictive power of the SAT, Sternberg and the Rainbow Project collaborators found that adding assessments of creative and practical skills roughly doubled the power to predict first-year-college GPA compared with the use of the SAT alone. Furthermore, differences in achievement between White students and Black students were drastically reduced (typically by about 0.5 *SD)* on measures of creative skills as compared with assessments emphasizing analytical skills (Sternberg & The Rainbow Project Collaborators, 2005, 2006). Similarly, differences between White students and Latino students were reduced on assessments emphasizing practical skills and creative skills as compared with analytical skills (typically about 0.8 *SD* on both creative and practical assessments). Thus, it appears that not only do individual differences in profiles of strengths and weaknesses exist across cognitive skills, but there are also systematic group differences as well.

Research Questions and Hypotheses

The purpose of this study was to examine individual and group differences in achievement with respect to cognitive-processing skills within the contexts of AP Psychology and Statistics. In particular, we were interested in examining the following research questions:

1. Is it possible to develop psychometrically sound assessments based on the theory of successful intelligence in the context of AP Psychology and Statistics?
2. Do students, in general, show uneven profiles of strengths and weaknesses across different cognitive skills or do students generally exhibit a relatively even profile of strengths and weaknesses across cognitive skills?
3. Are there systematic ethnic-group differences in achievement across different cognitive-skill areas, regardless of the content domain assessed?

In our study, we hypothesized that the analytical and memory subscale scores from the augmented exams would exhibit the strongest relationship with the scores from the actual AP exam. This hypothesis was based on the view that traditional tests are strongest at measuring memory and analytical rather than creative and practical skills.

Methods

In this section, we describe the process by which the AP exams in Psychology and Statistics used in this study were developed. We then describe how each exam used in this study compared with the actual AP exam in that same subject area. This section then concludes with a description of the sample of students and teachers used in this study.

Instruments

To investigate our research questions, it was necessary to develop alternative versions of the AP exams in Psychology and Statistics. These "augmented" exams were designed to mimic the actual AP exams as much as possible; however, the augmented exams were also developed with an eye toward explicitly balancing items for the cognitive skills they assessed.

The newly developed items for both exams were systematically designed to follow a particular structure. Memory-based items tended to ask the respondent to recall or recognize simple factual information. The stem often provided direct cues or asked for definitions. Items designed to tap analytical skills tended to ask respondents to compare and contrast, critique, evaluate, or judge something. (Memory is not a separate part of the theory of successful intelligence, but rather, is important in all of its other parts. Analytical, creative, and practical processing all operate on information stored in long-term memory and working memory. Moreover, traditional tests emphasize memory for information, and hence it was important that our augmented exams, like traditional exams, include items assessing primarily memory-based performance.) Analytical items typically dealt with abstract and academic, rather than concrete or practical, concepts. They required participants to analyze, evaluate, critique, or compare and contrast. Creative items required the respondent to imagine, suppose, discover, or invent. Creative items often involved a novel analogy, a low-probability situation, or a suspension of conventional beliefs. Practical items required the respondent to apply, use, or implement a concept within a social context. The stem of a practical item typically presented the respondent with a goal or a context for solving the problem. The response options for multiple-choice items often included the application of a concept rather than a naming of the concept. In the next session, we present some example items that were designed to tap each of the aforementioned processing skills.

Assessing Memory, Analytical, Creative, and Practical Abilities: Example Items

Memory items require students to recall and/or recognize who did certain things (e.g., proposed a theory), what things they did (e.g., the nature of the theory), how certain things are done (e.g., computing a standard deviation), when certain things are done (e.g., when squaring of terms is done in a formula), etc.

For example, consider the following multiple-choice question:

According to the psychologist Carl Rogers, which are the three conditions for promoting human growth and fulfillment?

(a) gentleness, kindness, and empathy
(b) genuineness, acceptance, and empathy
(c) agreeableness, acceptance, and extroversion
(d) genuineness, generosity, and extroversion
(e) creativity, generosity, and empathy

The correct answer to this question (underlined) requires knowledge of the theory of Carl Rogers. The student needs to rely in part on his or her long-term memory, answering this question. However, the question can also be answered through a combination of memory and analytical abilities: If the participant understands the theory of Rogers, he or she can infer what the three conditions are most likely to be. Indeed, many memory items require, or can be solved through, the use of at least some inference. Items were classified as "memory" if they were adjudged to require primarily memory for correct solution.

Analytical items require students to analyze (e.g., Freud's theory of depression), critique (e.g., the design of an experiment), evaluate (e.g., whether a certain formula is appropriate for solving a statistical problem), compare and contrast (e.g., two statistical tests of significance), and so on.

For example, consider the following multiple-choice question:

Suppose you earned 75 points on the most recent exam in statistics. The teacher announced that the mean score for the class was 87 points with a variance of 27.04. What can you conclude about your grade in relation to that of your peers?

(a) Your performance was slightly lower than that of the rest of the class.
(b) Your grade is substantially lower than that of the rest of the class.
(c) Your grade is higher than the majority of your classmates.
(d) Statistically speaking, your grade is about the same as the rest of the class.
(e) There is not enough information given to allow making any conclusions regarding your grade in relation to the rest of the class.

In finding the correct answer (underlined), the student is expected to rely on his or her understanding of the normal curve to analyze the proposed choices. Unlike the memory item above, this item *cannot* be solved purely by memory.

Creative items require students to create (e.g., the design of an experiment), imagine (e.g., how a theory of intelligence would apply cross-culturally), invent (e.g., a theory), or suppose (e.g., what would happen if an achievement test designed for American children was translated and then administered to children in rural Kenya?).

For example, consider the following multiple-choice question:

Imagine that you had to produce a TV sitcom to illustrate Freud's personality theory. Which of the following characters would best represent the superego?

(a) A firefighter
(b) An action-movie hero
(c) A nurse
(d) An artist
(e) A Supreme Court judge

Answering this question, the student is expected to imagine the described theory and map it onto the offered selection of answer options.

Practical items require students to apply (e.g., the formula for conducting an independent-samples *t* test to an everyday problem involving comparing prices of two brands of gasoline measured across various service stations), use (e.g., a theory of dreaming to understand why someone had a certain dream), apply what has been learned (e.g., the difference among the mean, median, and mode to deciding which statistic should be used in computing average incomes in a highly right-skewed sample of incomes).

For example, consider the following item:

By mowing your neighbor's lawn for pay, you started earning your own money in 1994. Since then, your personal income has grown every year. Your best summer was the summer of 1997—you had a great job and made some money. You decided to analyze the dynamics of your income over the 7 years (1994–2000) and fitted a least-squares regression line to these data. Then you decided to recode the data so that the year 1997 was labeled as 0. Now the years are coded by {−3, −2, −1, 0, 1, 2, 3}. Using these coded data, you fitted another least squares regression line. Compare the slope and intercept of the newly fitted regression line to those of the original regression line. Which of the following is true?

(a) Slope stayed the same, intercept decreased.
(b) Slope stayed the same, intercept increased.
(c) Slope increased, intercept increased.
(d) Slope decreased, intercept increased.
(e) No change of slope or intercept.

In answering this item, the students are expected to activate their knowledge of Exploratory Data Analysis and apply their knowledge in the context specified by the stem above.

In addition to assessing these cognitive skills using multiple-choice types of items, we assessed the skills with a series of open-response items. A single item could have up to four subcomponents, each relating to a different processing skill, as in the following examples:

A variety of explanations have been proposed to account for why people sleep.

(a) Describe the Restorative Theory of sleep.
(b) An alternative theory is an evolutionary theory of sleep, sometimes referred to as the "Preservation and Protection" theory. Describe this theory and compare and contrast it with the Restorative Theory. State what you see as the two strong points and two weak points of this theory compared to the Restorative Theory.
(c) How might you design an experiment to test the Restorative Theory of sleep? Briefly describe the experiment, including the participants, materials, procedures, and design.
(d) A friend informs you that she is having trouble sleeping. Based on your knowledge of sleep, what kinds of helpful (and health-promoting) suggestions might you giver her to help her fall asleep at night?

Part (a) would be an example of an item primarily requiring memory abilities. Parts (b)–(d) would be examples of items primarily requiring analytical, creative, and practical abilities, respectively. Another example open-ended item is presented below, this time from the domain of statistics:

A manufacturer claims that under typical road-travel conditions, the wear of tire tread after 50,000 miles for the manufacturer's tire is approximately normally distributed with a mean of 2 mm and *SD* of 0.2 mm. A tire is determined to be unsafe if the wear is more than 2.1 mm. You are called in to help with a research study designed to assess the wear of a set of 1000 of the manufacturer's tires that have just reached the 50,000-mile mark. Use the random-number table to answer the following questions.

94163	81961	18731	89627	42895
00981	83906	68499	16409	92391
77880	41991	73241	65897	40517
27740	35486	56466	93298	71440

(a) Describe how you would use the random-number table to sample 100 of the 1000 available tires for wear.

(b) Assume you have a similar random-digit table consisting of different sets of numbers. If you selected another random sample of 100 tires and compared it to the first random sample of 100, what could you conclude with regard to which sample is best to use in the experiment? Explain.

(c) The company vice-president asks you why you have to use the random-number table. He wonders why you cannot simply take the first 100 tires that became available. What should you tell him?

(d) Generate your own method of sampling tires to determine wear and state why it would be an effective design.

Part (a) would be an example of an item primarily requiring memory abilities. Parts (b) (d) would be examples of items primarily requiring analytical, creative, and practical abilities, respectively.

Item Development

From the summer of 2000 until the spring of 2002, item development proceeded in eight stages: (1) item development; (2) internal review; (3) review by the first expert panel of school teachers and college faculty; (4) review by consultants at the Educational Testing Service (ETS); (5) piloting of selected items by consulting teachers on the project; (6) review by the second expert panel of college faculty; (7) final review and item selection, and preparation of final assessment forms; and (8) post hoc evaluation. In March 2002, all items that had successfully passed through peer review were assembled into the assessments. Next, we describe the contents and structure of each of the augmented exams.

Psychology. For the actual AP Psychology test in 2002, students were given 70 min to complete the multiple-choice section (100 items) and 50 min to complete the open-response section (2 items) of the exam. The items were designed to cover 14 content subdomains. Table 10.1 gives a breakdown of each subdomain covered by the AP Psychology exam, along with the percentage of items on the test devoted to each topic. It is important to note that many more items were developed than successfully passed through the item review process. Thus, the items that did pass through the item review process were not necessarily perfectly reflective of a balanced distribution across content areas, but were the best items developed at the time of administration.[3]

---

[3]In an ideal world, we would have revised items or developed new items until a perfect balance was achieved. In reality, however, the amount of time required for the item review process is substantial, and at the end of the day, there are deadlines and issues of timing with regard to when the tests must be administered. Thus, the items chosen for the exam were the best of all items at the time. We could have deleted items in categories that were overrepresented to achieve a balance at the level of the lowest common denominator, but that would have resulted in a loss of information about otherwise strong items that successfully passed through the rigorous item review process.

10.1	Content Areas Covered by the Actual AP Psychology Exam and the Augmented AP Psychology Exam and the Percentage of Items Devoted to Each	
Content	MC Actual AP Exam[a] (%)	Total Augmented AP Exam (%)
Abnormal	7–9	7
Biological basis of behavior	8–10	2
Cognition	8–10	13
Developmental	7–9	1
History	2–4	4
Learning	7–9	8
Methods	6–8	14
Motivation and emotion	7–9	7
Personality	6–8	7
Sensation and perception	7–9	5
Social	7–9	9
States of consciousness	2–4	4
Testing and individual differences	5–7	8
Treatment	5–7	11

[a] *Note.* Data downloaded on 4/20/03 from http://www.collegeboard.com/ap/students/psych/cours_2002.html.

The exams were scored on a scale from 1 (lowest) to 5 (highest). Consistent with the scoring of the actual AP exam, the multiple-choice section of the augmented exam was worth 50% of the total exam grade, and the open-response section was worth 50% of the total exam grade.

The augmented AP Psychology exam was designed to mimic, in many ways, the actual AP Psychology exam. A total of 85 new items were developed and piloted for the augmented AP Psychology exam, many of which were designed as open-response items. To maximize the number of items we could pilot test and to maintain some basis for equating the scores, the open-response items were distributed across two different forms, whereas the same 50 multiple-choice items appeared on both versions of the augmented AP Psychology exam. For the open-response section of the augmented exam, each version had 20 open-response items. For equating purposes, a subset of items appeared on both forms of the exam. Items 15–20 on Form A corresponded to Items 1–5 on Form B (see Appendix A for a breakdown). In the augmented exam, students were given 40 min to complete the multiple-choice section (50 items) and 110 min to complete the open-response section of the exam (20 items). Thus, the augmented exam required slightly more time than the regular exam. The difference in amount of time derived from the estimated time required to respond to our items, based on the piloting of these items with a group of students. In order for the exam to be practical, we did not want to go much over the normally allocated time, and did not.

Consistent with the actual AP Psychology exam, the new items were distributed across 14 content subdomains. At the low end of the spectrum, items assessing the Biological Basis of Behavior constituted 2% of the test items. At the high end, items from the domain of Research Methods constituted 14% of the items (see Table 10.1). The distribution of the items corresponded closely to those on the actual AP Psychology exam. The 85 newly developed items were distributed in the following way across the four areas of primary cognitive demand: 28% memory, 31% analytical, 19% creative, and 22% practical. (For further information, see Stemler, Grigorenko, Jarvin, Macomber, & Sternberg, 2003a).[4]

Statistics. For the actual AP Statistics exam in 2002, students were given 90 min to complete the multiple-choice section (40 items) and 90 min to complete the open-response section of the exam (6 items). The items were designed to cover the following five content areas: (i) Experimental Design; (ii) Exploratory Data Analysis; (iii) Randomness and Sampling; (iv) Regression; and (v) Significance Testing. The augmented AP Statistics exam was designed to mimic the existing AP Statistics exam. Students were given 75 min to complete the multiple-choice section (50 items) and 75 min to complete the open-response section of the exam (6 items). Thus, the augmented exam required slightly less time than the regular exam. The difference in amount of time derived from the estimated time required to respond to our items, based on the piloting of these items with a group of students.

A total of 80 new items were developed and piloted on the augmented AP Statistics exam. Because an important condition of the study was that the teachers could use the augmented exam as a practice test for the existing exam, it was important that the amount of time required for testing be as close as possible to the existing exam. At the same time, an important goal of the project was to evaluate the psychometric properties of the newly developed items. For the augmented AP Statistics exam, many of these items were open-ended response items. Thus, to pilot-test all of the newly developed items, keeping time constant, items were distributed across three test forms. The same 50 multiple-choice items appeared on all versions of the augmented AP Statistics exam to provide an easy basis for linking the scores from the various forms, and because more of the items that required pilot testing were of the open-response variety. Appendix B provides a breakdown of the number of items on each form as well as the overlap and the number of people taking each form.

Consistent with the actual AP Statistics exam, the items developed for the augmented AP Statistics exam were distributed across five content subdomains.[5] Items from the subdomain of Regression constituted a low of 8% of the items. Items from the subdomain of Exploratory Data Analysis, as well as items from the subdomain of Randomness and Sampling, constituted a high of 26% of the items each. The 80

---

[4]Many more items were developed that did not successfully pass through the item-review process. Thus, the items that did pass through the item review process were not necessarily perfectly reflective of a balanced distribution, but were the best items developed at the time of administration. The matter here is a practical one. In an ideal world, we would have revised items or developed new items until a perfect balance was achieved. In reality, however, the amount of time required for the item-review process is substantial, and at the end of the day, there are deadlines and issues of timing with regard to when the tests must be administered. Thus, the items chosen for the exam were the best of all items at the time. We could have deleted items in categories that were overrepresented to achieve a balance at the level of the lowest common denominator, but that would have resulted in a loss of information about otherwise strong items that successfully passed through the rigorous item review process. We believe that our procedure maximized the amount of information obtained.

[5]The College Board did not report the percentage of items measuring each subdomain on the 2002 AP Statistics examination.

newly developed items were distributed in the following way across the four areas of cognitive demand: 11% memory, 35% analytical, 20% creative, and 34% practical. (For further information, see Stemler, Grigorenko, Jarvin, Macomber, & Sternberg, 2003b).

Sample

In the fall of 2000, a first wave of recruitment letters was sent out. They went to AP Psychology and Statistics teachers who had been recommended by the AP Psychology and Statistics Development Committees. This strategy failed to yield a sufficient numbers of replies. Therefore, a second wave of letters was sent out to all practicing AP teachers whose e-mail and regular mail addresses were available on different functional lists through the College Board. This mailing, carried out in the early months of 2001, included a cover letter from the College Board inviting teachers to participate in the project. The information was distributed to a large group of teachers $(N = 224)$, which resulted in much greater success for our recruitment efforts.

The recruitment package comprised a cover letter from the College Board Executive Director of Advanced Placement Program and a brief outline of the program. Potential participants were informed that the purpose of the project was to promote effective teaching techniques and to help classroom teachers create formative assessments that tap higher order thinking skills. They were also told that participation in the project would require them to arrange for the administration of the newly developed practice exam (the enhanced AP exam) sometime in the spring of the following academic year (spring 2002), prior to the actual AP exam. All teachers were compensated monetarily for their participation at the rates specified by ETS and the College Board in their collaboration with AP teachers.

In response to our recruitment efforts, a total of 33 AP Psychology and 23 AP Statistics teachers volunteered to participate in this study. Participating teachers were drawn from across the U.S.A. and represented a total of 19 different states, with each participating teacher representing a different school. The number of years of prior teaching experience for AP Psychology teachers ranged from 1 to 10 (mean = 7.08, mode = 10), with 20 teachers having experience as readers for the AP national test. Participating AP Statistics teachers ranged in years of teaching experience from 0 to 6 years (mean = 3.5, mode = 5), with nine having experience as readers for the AP national test.

Table 10.2 presents the demographic breakdown of the students taking the augmented exams in AP Statistics and AP Psychology. Note that, in this project, no students took both the Statistics and Psychology exams. We were able to obtain information on the ethnicity of 452 of the 1262 students (36%) taking the augmented AP Psychology exam. The ethnic breakdown of these 452 students was 75% White, 3% Black, 5% Latino, 13% Asian, and 4% Other. These numbers are roughly comparable to the proportion of students from each ethnic group who took the actual AP Psychology exam in 2002 (cf. 70% White, 5% Black, 7% Latino, 12% Asian, and 4% Other). Despite the low response rate, an analysis of the test score data revealed no statistically significant differences in their overall score on the augmented AP Psychology exam between those reporting ethnic information and those not reporting ethnic information.

Of the 633 students who took the augmented AP Statistics exam, we were able to obtain ethnic background information for 306 students (48%). The ethnic breakdown

10.2 Demographic Breakdown for Participating Students	Statistics	Psychology
Gender		
Male	232	349
Female	284	635
Missing	117	278
Ethnicity		
White	210	338
Black	13	14
Hispanic	11	23
Asian	54	60
Other	18	17
Missing	327	810
Total N	633	1262

of these 306 students was 68% White, 4% Black, 4% Latino, 18% Asian, and 6% Other. These numbers are also nearly identical to the proportion of students from each ethnic group who took the actual AP Statistics exam in 2002 (cf. 68% White, 4% Black, 6% Latino, 17% Asian, and 4% Other). An analysis of the data revealed that those for whom we did not have ethnic information showed significantly lower levels of achievement overall on the augmented AP Statistics exam than either White students or Asian students, but did not show statistically significant differences in achievement from Black or Latino students.

Results

Main Findings for Research Question 1: Psychometric Properties of the Instruments

The data were analyzed using both classical test theory (Crocker & Algina, 1986) and Rasch measurement (Bond & Fox, 2001; Rasch, 1960/1980; Wright & Stone, 1979). In this essay, we report the results from the Rasch analysis as they provide the most precise estimates of student ability (Bond & Fox, 2001; R. Smith, 1996; E. Smith, 2001; Wright & Stone, 1979). Evidence in the psychometric literature suggests that Rasch estimates are more precise estimates of latent abilities than classical estimates (R. Smith, 1996; E. Smith, 2001). Classical analyses assume that the true scores of all test takers are measured equally well (i.e., they are assigned a uniform standard error of estimate). With Rasch analyses, each participant may be assigned a distinct standard error of estimate depending on which items the participant got correct or incorrect. This feature greatly increases the precision of estimates of latent abilities (or true scores) as compared with classical test theory methods. (For further details see E. Smith, 2001; R. Smith, 1996.)

The data for each of the exams were analyzed using the many-facets Rasch model (Linacre, 1988, 1994; Linacre, Wright, & Lunz, 1990). This approach has several advantages over classical test theory. First, it puts each of the items onto a linear scale. Second, it effectively deals with incorporating information from multiple raters, correcting for rater severity in the ability estimate. Third, it is an effective technique for combining the results of multiple-choice and open-response items into a single ability estimate.

A series of five separate Rasch analyses were run for each domain (i.e., Psychology and Statistics). The first analysis included all items for an overall ability estimate. The next four analyses were designed to generate ability estimates for each subscale using only items that were explicitly designed for to measure the said process (e.g., scale 1 = memory items, scale 2 = analytical items).

There is always a fundamental tension in test construction between the desire for the measurement of a unidimensional construct (e.g., Statistics ability), and the recognition that the construct itself may be divided into various subdomains on the basis of content areas (e.g., probability, sampling) or kinds of processes (e.g., creative, analytical). Thus, few would ever argue that we can attain a purely unidimensional construct. Nevertheless, Rasch analysis does not require this strict interpretation to be useful. In fact, the underlying dimension driving the ability estimate is Statistics ability. This overarching construct comprises subcomponents—domain-specific knowledge as well as specific cognitive skills. They are useful both for the purposes of test construction, as well as for diagnostic purposes (such as the identification of areas in which participants exhibit strengths and weaknesses).

Consistent with the way the actual AP exam is scored, the multiple-choice and open-response sections of the augmented exams received equal weighting. Each student received an ability estimate for the overall exam, as well as an ability estimate for each of the subscales assessing memory, analytical, creative, and practical skills. To aid interpretation of the scale and avoid the use of the negative logit values associated with the Rasch approach, each of the Rasch ability estimates was rescaled to have a mean of 250 and a SD of 50. In addition, five proficiency levels were developed for each scale, corresponding to students at quintile intervals (e.g., students scoring 2 on the scale represent students scoring from the 21st to the 40th percentile).

Content-Related Validity Evidence

Content-related validity evidence for the augmented exams was gathered following the eight-step process described above and detailed elsewhere (Stemler et al., 2003a, 2003b). To summarize briefly, items were systematically developed based on Sternberg's theory of successful intelligence. They were then sent out to expert teachers and test developers for review. The evaluation criteria were (a) the extent to which each item accurately tapped into memory, analytical, creative, or practical abilities and (b) its central position in the content domain. Moreover, the content of the items was thoroughly evaluated.

Once a set of multiple-choice and open-ended items had been reviewed and revised internally, two separate test forms were created and sent out for evaluation and review to a panel of six active AP teachers and six college faculty in statistics (N = 12) and to eight active AP teachers and eight college faculty in psychology (N = 16). The results of the evaluation indicated that the majority of the items fitted the

10.3	Bivariate Correlations Between the Actual AP Score and the Overall and Subscale Scores of the Augmented AP Psychology Exam				
Scale	1	3	4	5	6
1. Actual AP exam	1.00				
2. Augmented AP exam	0.61**				
3. Memory subscale	0.52**	1.00			
4. Analytic subscale	0.54**	0.47**	1.00		
5. Creative subscale	0.41**	0.40**	0.53**	1.00	
6. Practical subscale	0.33**	0.42**	0.43**	0.41**	1.00

N for actual AP exam with other scales = 633; *N* for other scales = 1262. **Correlation is significant at the 0.01 level (two tailed).

described item specifications. All relevant comments from the reviewers were incorporated in the new revision of the items.

After the completion of the first external review, the items were revised once again and sent out for another round of reviews, this time to an AP psychology coordinator and an AP statistics coordinator at Educational Testing Service (ETS). The reviewers were asked to evaluate the items and provide detailed comments, which were incorporated in yet another revision of the items.

Next, a number of AP teachers consulting on the project ($N = 16$) were asked to pilot the items with their students and to provide their feedback and the students' comments on the items. All relevant suggestions were incorporated.

Finally, four independent consultants, individuals who worked at universities and who had expertise in the relevant content area as well as expertise in item development, were hired to review the items for content, clarity, and potential bias. The reviewers' comments were then used to modify items before creating the final exam booklets.

Criterion-Related Validity Evidence

Criterion-related validity evidence was gathered by correlating scores from the augmented exam with scores from the actual AP exam for a subset of individuals. The results, reported in Table 10.3, were generally in line with our research hypothesis. The analytical subscale was correlated most highly with the actual AP exam score ($r = .54$, $p < .01$), whereas the practical subscale was least correlated with the actual AP exam score ($r = .33$, $p < .01$). A test for the difference between two dependent correlation coefficients from the same sample (Blalock, 1972, p. 407) was conducted for each pair of correlation coefficients (e.g., memory vs. practical). A total of six paired comparisons were conducted. The results showed that the difference between the correlation of the memory subscale with the actual exam score and the correlation of the analytical

10.4	Bivariate Correlations Between the Actual AP Score and the Overall and Subscale Scores of the Augmented AP Statistics Exam					
Scale	1	3	4	5	6
1. Actual AP exam	1.00				
2. Augmented AP exam	0.49**				
3. Memory subscale	0.45**	1.00			
4. Analytic subscale	0.39**	0.35**	1.00		
5. Creative subscale	0.36**	0.43**	0.43**	1.00	
6. Practical subscale	0.43**	0.44**	0.46**	0.55**	1.00

N for actual AP exam with other scales = 393; *N* for subscales = 633.
**Correlation is significant at the 0.01 level (two tailed).

subscale and the actual exam score was nonsignificant. The differences between all other pairs of correlations were statistically significant at the .05 α level. A Bonferroni adjustment for 6 multiple-comparisons yielded a critical t value of 2.64 for a two-tailed test at the .05 a level. The differences in correlations provide some evidence that the subscales are measuring constructs that differ significantly from each other (memory–analytical, N.S.; memory–creative $t = 4.04$, $p < .01$; memory–practical $t = 6.83$, $p < .01$; analytical–creative $t = 5.77$, $p < .01$; analytical–practical $t = 7.85$, $p < .01$; creative–practical $t = 2.53$, $p < .05$).

In addition, the results in Table 10.4 reveal that the total score from the augmented version of the AP Statistics exam and the existing AP Statistics exam were moderately correlated ($r = .49$, $p < .001$). We also hypothesized that the correlations involving the memory subscale, the analytical subscale, and the actual AP Statistics exam would be greater than the correlations involving the creative subscale, the practical subscale, and the actual AP exam, as the existing exam consists mostly of items tapping memory and analytical skills. The results presented in Table 10. 4 were generally in line with our predictions. The memory subscale was correlated most highly with the actual AP exam score ($r = .45$, $p < .01$), whereas the creative subscale was least correlated with the actual AP exam score ($r = .36$, $p < .01$). However, after correcting for multiple comparisons, no significant differences between coefficients were found.

Because multiple comparisons were made for each test, the Bonferroni correction procedure was used. Although the Bonferroni correction diminishes the probability of Type I error, it will inflate the probability of Type II error. Given that this is the first study of its kind, the decision to use this correction may have been overly conservative.

Construct-Related Validity Evidence

Evidence of the construct validity of the exams was provided through various statistics from the many-facets Rasch model. The Rasch person-reliability and item-reliability estimates for the augmented AP Psychology exam are presented in Table 10.5. The Rasch reliability estimates are interpreted in the same way as Cronbach's α, but provide estimates that are more precise (see Fisher, 1992; E. Smith, 2001). Table 10.6 presents the same information for the augmented AP Statistics exam.

In general, separation values greater than 2.0 indicate that the scale is working as desired (Bond & Fox, 2001). Larger item-separation values indicate that the items are targeted at varying levels of difficulty rather than all being targeted at approximately the same level of difficulty. Within the context of Rasch measurement, high item-reliability values suggest that if the same test were given to a different sample of participants with similar abilities, the relative positioning of item difficulties would be expected to remain constant.

Table 10.5 reveals that the item-separation index for the overall scale of the augmented AP Psychology exam was 18.96, indicating that there was a substantial spread of items along the logit scale. In other words, the items were not all targeted around a limited set of ability levels, or at the same level of difficulty. The item reliability for the overall scale was 1.0. The average person ability was 0.06 logits, meaning that the ability level of this sample of test-takers was almost perfectly matched to the difficulty level of the items on the test.

Figure 10.1 presents an item map for the overall augmented AP Psychology exam and Figure 10.2 presents an item map for the overall augmented AP Statistics exam. It is easy to see from the item map that there is a spread of items associated with each of the process areas. The items on the item map are labeled with a prefix indicating their specific process area (e.g., M14 means that item 14 assesses a memory process).

The 12 raters who scored the open-response items on the augmented AP Psychology exam differed somewhat in terms of their severity and the range in severity differed across subscales. Within the domain of psychology, the range in rater severity was approximately 1.75 logits for the memory subscale, 1.25 logits for the analytical subscale, and 2.3 logits for the creative and practical subscales.

In addition, the rater fit statistics show that raters were fairly consistent in their application of the scoring rubric, with only 2 raters exhibiting greater than expected variation in their ratings on each of the memory, analytical, and creative subscales. Interestingly, although the rater severity spans the greatest range for the practical items, the rater fit statistics reveal that all of the raters remained faithful to their interpretation of the scoring rubric (i.e., there were no misfitting raters).

For statistics, the six raters who scored the various open-response items on the augmented AP Statistics exam differed somewhat in terms of their severity and the range in severity differed across subscales. Within the domain of statistics, the range in rater severity was approximately 0.37 logits for the memory subscale, 1.64 logits for the analytical subscale, 0.86 logits for the creative subscale, and 1.63 logits for the practical subscale.

In addition, the rater fit statistics show that raters were fairly consistent in their application of the scoring rubric, with only 2 raters exhibiting greater than expected variation in their ratings on the analytical scale, and no raters exhibiting misfit on each of the memory, creative, or practical subscales.

Summary

Overall, the various sources of evidence support the validity of using the theory of successful intelligence as a basis for creating augmented exams in AP Psychology

		Person and Item Estimates: Augmented AP Psychology Exam			
10.5					
	Overall	Memory	Analytical	Creative	Practical
Psychology—item summary					
Summary of item estimates					
Mean	0.00	0.00	0.00	0.00	0.00
SD	1.23	1.47	1.02	1.14	1.09
Reliability of estimate	1.00	1.00	1.00	1.00	1.00
Separation	18.96	18.42	17.04	18.74	18.19
N of items	85	24	26	16	19
Summary of fit statistics					
Infit mean square					
Mean	1.20	1.10	1.10	1.10	1.00
SD	0.40	0.30	0.20	0.30	0.10
Outfit mean square					
Mean	1.20	1.20	1.10	1.20	1.10
SD	0.60	0.30	0.30	0.40	0.20
Infit z					
Mean	2.10	2.60	1.50	1.30	1.40
SD	3.40	3.60	3.70	4.70	4.20
Outfit z					
Mean	2.20	2.70	1.60	1.90	1.50
SD	3.50	3.30	3.70	4.90	4.10
Psychology—person summary					
Summary of person estimates					
Mean	0.06	−0.22	0.07	0.31	0.11
SD	0.66	0.99	0.85	1.07	0.94
Reliability of estimate	0.92	0.79	0.82	0.75	0.76
Separation	3.28	1.94	2.17	1.75	1.79
N of test-takers	1262	1262	1262	1262	1262
Summary of fit statistics					
Infit mean square					
Mean	1.30	1.30	1.10	1.00	1.00
SD	0.50	0.80	0.60	0.70	0.60
Outfit mean square					
Mean	1.20	1.20	1.10	1.10	1.10
SD	0.40	0.80	0.50	1.00	0.80
Infit z					
Mean	1.40	0.40	0.00	−0.30	−0.20
SD	2.00	1.60	1.60	1.50	1.50
Outfit z					
Mean	0.80	0.10	0.00	−0.10	−0.10
SD	1.60	1.10	1.30	1.30	1.30

10.6	Person and Item Estimates: Augmented AP Psychology Exam				
	Overall	Memory	Analytical	Creative	Practical
Statistics—item summary					
Summary of item estimates					
Mean	0.00	0.00	0.00	0.00	0.00
SD	1.05	1.33	1.17	1.02	0.95
Reliability of estimate	0.99	0.99	1.00	0.99	0.99
Separation	12.87	12.79	14.22	11.70	11.27
N of items	80	9	27	15	26
Summary of fit statistics					
Infit mean square					
Mean	1.10	1.00	1.20	1.10	1.00
SD	0.50	0.30	0.20	0.20	0.10
Outfit mean square					
Mean	1.20	0.30	1.30	1.10	1.10
SD	0.60	4.70	0.30	0.30	0.20
Infit z					
Mean	1.20	1.20	3.60	1.20	0.80
SD	3.00	0.50	2.90	4.10	3.50
Outfit z					
Mean	1.40	0.80	3.80	1.10	1.30
SD	3.10	5.00	3.00	4.40	3.80
Statistics—person summary					
Summary of person estimates					
Mean	−0.23	0.54	−0.36	0.08	0.02
SD	0.67	1.31	0.79	1.14	0.98
Reliability of estimate	0.94	0.57	0.91	0.82	0.85
Separation	3.90	1.15	3.18	2.11	2.38
N of test-takers	633	633	633	633	633
Summary of fit statistics					
Infit mean square					
Mean	1.70	0.90	1.50	0.90	1.00
SD	0.90	0.50	0.80	0.60	0.40
Outfit mean square					
Mean	1.40	1.20	1.30	1.10	1.00
SD	0.60	1.30	0.70	0.70	0.50
Infit z					
Mean	2.50	−0.40	1.30	−0.50	−0.30
SD	3.10	1.00	2.30	1.50	1.60
Outfit z					
Mean	1.80	−0.10	0.80	−0.20	−0.10
SD	2.60	1.00	1.70	1.30	1.40

10.1

Item map for the augmented AP Psychology exam.

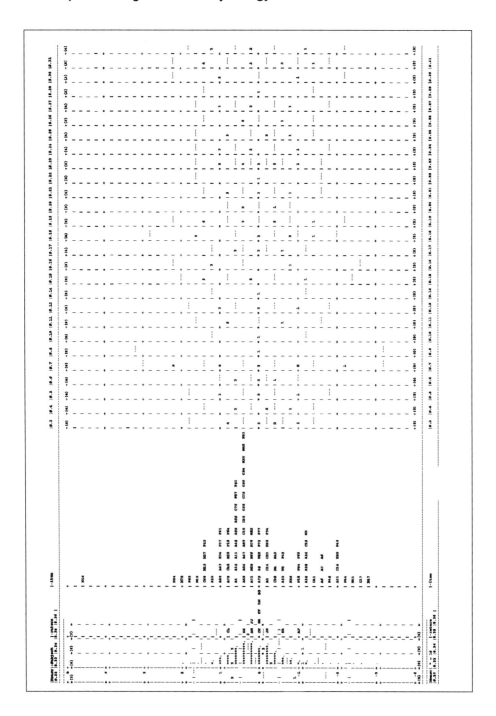

10.2

Item map for the augmented AP Statistics exam.

and Statistics. Items tapping memory, analytical, creative, and practical skills are distinguishable on the basis of their content. In addition, the subscales containing items tapping each different cognitive process showed the expected pattern of correlations with the actual AP exam results. Finally, the various subscales exhibited acceptable levels of internal consistency and other item statistics, with the single exception of the memory subscale of the Statistics exam, whose internal consistency (for persons, not items) was substandard.

Main Findings for Research Question 2: Individual Differences in Cognitive Processes

To examine the extent to which individuals exhibited different profiles of strengths and weaknesses across the four cognitive-skill areas under investigation, we conducted a cluster analysis using the Q-factor analysis approach (Hair, Anderson, Tatham, & Black, 1998). Under this approach, students with similar patterns of relative strengths and weaknesses, regardless of differences in absolute levels of achievement, are identified as belonging to the same cluster. The results will now be discussed for each content area.

Psychology

Using principal components extraction with a promax rotation, we obtained three factors with eigenvalues greater than 1.0 that accounted for 100% of the variance in the dataset. The three factors correspond to three distinct profiles of achievement primarily found in the dataset. Each participant thus had a factor loading corresponding to each of the three extracted factors. Table 10.7 presents an abridged structure matrix of factor loadings for each participant in the augmented AP Psychology exam.

Table 10.7 illustrates that some students had a clear, high positive loading on a single factor, whereas other students had factor loadings that were high, but in the negative direction.

To gain a deeper appreciation for the meaning behind each of these factors, Figure 10.3 presents the profiles of achievement for 12 participants. The four participants in the first row had high positive loadings on the first factor; the four participants shown in the second row had high positive loadings on the second factor; and the four participants shown in the third row had high positive loadings on the third factor.

An examination of Figure 10.3 reveals that those participants with high loading on the first factor tend to exhibit profiles of achievement with relatively low scores on the memory subscale compared with their achievement on the analytical, creative, and practical subscales. At the same time, their scores on the analytical, creative, and practical subscales were roughly equivalent.

Students with high loadings on the second factor (second row of Figure 10.3) tended to have weaker levels of achievement on items tapping practical thinking skills; however, their achievement on the memory, analytical, and creative scales was roughly equivalent to one another.

Finally, students with high loadings on the third factor (third row of Figure 10.3) showed a pattern of relative strength on creative items, relative weakness on the analytical items, and moderate achievement on the memory and practical items.

Although three principal components were extracted from the Q-factor analysis, it is important to note that some participants had high positive loadings on a factor,

10.7	Abridged Output of Factor Loadings for Each Participant: Augmented AP Psychology Exam		
	Component		
SID	1	2	3
K_01060061	**0.998**		
K_00020051	**0.997**		
K_00080081	**0.996**		
K_02080015	**0.996**		
K_02020017	0.996		
K_00120027	0.995		
K_02030014		−0.982	
K_02100027		−0.982	
K_02080064		**0.977**	
K_00120034		**0.976**	
K_00080003		**0.976**	
K_00080102		**0.976**	
K_00140006		−0.975	
K_02080019			−0.996
K_00140017			**0.995**
K_00010021			**0.995**
K_02090013			**0.995**
K_00020083			**0.993**
K_00070008			0.992
K_02100017			0.991

SIDs listed in bold correspond to person profiles shown in Figure 10.3.

and other participants had high negative loadings on the same factor. Participants with high negative loadings on the first factor show a pattern of achievement that is the mirror image of those students with positive loadings on that factor. Specifically, participants with high negative loadings on the first factor exhibit relatively strong achievement on memory items, and lower but relatively equal achievement on analytical, creative, and practical items. Thus, although three factors were extracted, these factors yielded six distinct profiles of achievement.

Table 10.8 presents a summary of the number of participants whose profile is associated with each of the six empirically distinguishable profiles of achievement. For example, 30% of the 1262 participants exhibited a profile of achievement associated with a high positive loading on Factor 1 (relative weakness on memory skills), whereas 19% of participants exhibited a profile of achievement associated with high positive loadings on Factor 3 (i.e., relative strength in creative skills and relative weakness in analytical skills). These findings suggest that tests developed with items measuring primarily memory and analytical skills would fail to detect the relative strengths of many participants.

10.3

Augmented AP Psychology exam—exemplary empirical profiles of achievement.
1 = Memory subscale score (logits), 2 = analytical subscale score, 3 = creative subscale score,
4 = practical subscale score.

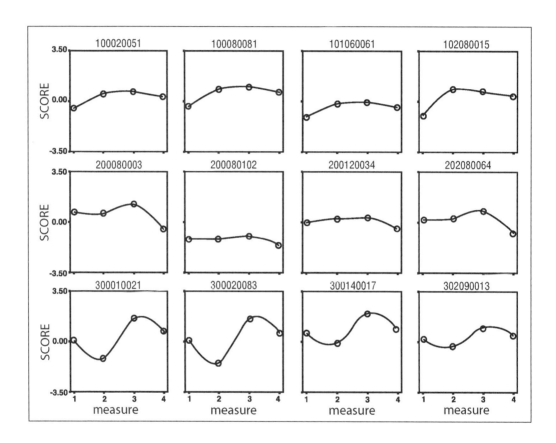

Statistics

Using principal components extraction with a promax rotation, we obtained three factors with eigenvalues greater than 1.0 that accounted for 100% of the variance in the dataset. The three factors correspond to three distinct profiles of achievement primarily found in the dataset. Each participant thus had a factor loading corresponding to each of the three extracted factors. Table 10.9 presents an abridged structure matrix of factor loadings for each participant in the augmented AP Statistics exam.

Table 10.9 illustrates that some students had a clear high positive loading on a single factor, whereas other students had factor loadings that were high, but in the negative direction. The findings from the Q-factor analysis show that there are three empirically distinguishable profiles of achievement that come out in the data.

10.8	Summary of Participants Associated with Each Cluster Analysis Profile: Augmented AP Psychology Exam				

	Psychology				
	Positive Loading		Negative Loading		
	N	%	N	%	
Cluster 1	377	30	122	10	
Cluster 2	211	17	201	16	
Cluster 3	243	19	108	9	

10.9	Abridged Output of Factor Loadings for Each Participant: Augmented AP Statistics Exam

SID	Component 1	2	3
K_05020027	**0.998**		
K_03040019	**0.998**		
K_03090002	**0.997**		
K_05030039	**0.997**		
K_03040037	−0.995		
K_03010012	0.995		
K_04070009		**0.999**	
K_03010017		**0.997**	
K_05090001		**0.995**	
K_04060021		**0.995**	
K_03070012		−0.991	
K_03050010		0.990	
K_05060016			**0.999**
K_04080004			**0.996**
K_05090016		0.318	**0.993**
K_05020042	0.333	0.314	**0.990**
K_03070004		0.361	0.989
K_03090004			0.989
K_05020005			0.984
K_03040063			0.982

SIDs listed in bold correspond to person profiles shown in Figure 10.4.

10.4

Augmented AP Statistics exam—exemplary empirical profiles of achievement.
1 = Memory subscale score (logits), 2 = analytical subscale score, 3 = creative subscale score,
4 = practical subscale score.

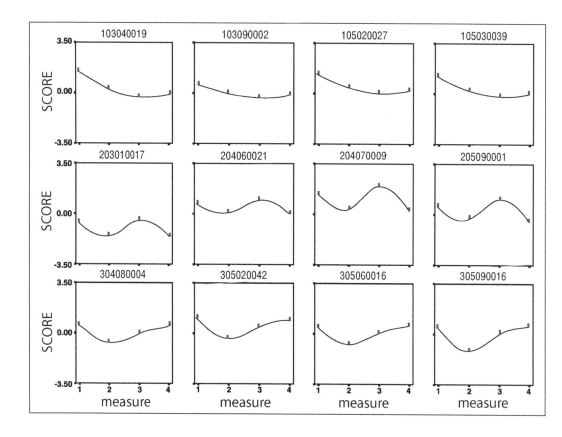

For illustration purposes, Figure 10.4 presents the profiles of achievement for 12 participants. The four participants in the first row had high positive loadings on the first factor. The four participants shown in the second row had high positive loadings on the second factor, and the four participants shown in the third row had high positive loadings on the third factor.

An examination of Figure 10.4 reveals that those participants with high loading on the first factor tend to exhibit relatively high scores on the memory subscale compared with the analytical, creative, and practical subscales. At the same time, the relative achievement on the analytical, creative, and practical subscales was roughly equivalent.

	Statistics			
	Positive		Negative	
	N	%	*N*	%
Cluster 1	184	29	76	12
Cluster 2	142	22	43	7
Cluster 3	155	24	33	5

10.10 Summary of Participants Associated with Each Cluster Analysis Profile: Augmented AP Statistics Exam

Students with high loadings on the second factor (second row of Figure 10.4) tend to have weaker levels of achievement on items tapping analytical thinking skills and relatively strong achievement on items assessing creative skills.

Finally, students with high loadings on the third factor (third row of Figure 10.4) show a pattern of relative weakness on items assessing analytical thinking skills. Yet, their average achievement on items tapping memory, creative, and practical skills is roughly equivalent.

Although three principal components were extracted from the Q-factor analysis, it is important to note that some participants had high positive loadings on a factor, and other participants had high negative loadings on the same factor. Participants with high negative loadings on the first factor show a pattern of achievement that is the mirror image of those students with positive loadings on that factor. Specifically, participants with high negative loadings on the first factor exhibit relatively weak achievement on memory items, and lower but relatively equal achievement on analytical, creative, and practical items. Thus, although three factors were extracted, these factors yielded six distinct profiles of achievement.

Table 10.10 presents a summary of the number of participants whose profile is associated with each of the six empirically distinguishable profiles of achievement. For example, 24% of the 633 participants taking the augmented AP Statistics exam exhibited a profile of achievement associated with a high positive loading on Factor 3 (relative weakness on analytical skills), whereas 22% of participants exhibited a profile of achievement associated with high positive loadings on Factor 2 (i.e., relative strength in creative skills). These findings suggest that tests developed with items measuring primarily memory and analytical skills would fail to detect the relative strengths of many participants.

Summary

Overall, the findings from the cluster analyses presented here provide empirical support for the assertion that individuals exhibit different profiles of strengths and weaknesses across memory, analytic, creative, and practical skills. These findings suggest that tests that measure a limited range of processes may fail to detect the strengths of a substantial proportion of test-takers.

Main Findings for Research Question 3: Ethnic Differences in Achievement

Table 10.11 presents the mean scale scores and standard deviation by student ethnicity on the actual AP exam, as well as for the overall augmented AP Psychology exam and each of the cognitive processing subscales. Recall that the actual AP exam is scored on a scale of 1 (lowest) to 5 (highest); the mean for all test-takers on the augmented exam and each of the subscales is 250, with a *SD* of 50 points.

A psychometric analysis of item difficulty found that items across all subscales of the augmented AP exams represented a broad range of difficulty levels. Consequently, higher ability estimates on creative and practical subscales are independent of the difficulty level of the items. In other words, the results demonstrated that creative and practical items are just as difficult (from a psychometric perspective) as items tapping analytical and memory items across the entire sample of test takers. This finding held for items on both the augmented AP Psychology exam and the augmented AP Statistics exam.

Psychology

The results from Table 10.11 indicate that, on the actual AP Psychology exam administered in 2002, the standardized difference in achievement between Black students and White students was fairly large, with Black students scoring nearly three-quarters of

10.11	Augmented AP Psychology Exam Subscale Scores by Ethnicity					
	White		Black		Latino	
Scale	Mean	*SD*	Mean	*SD*	Mean	*SD*
Actual AP exam (2002)	3.43	(1.23)	2.52	(1.29)	2.70	(1.31)
N	35,386		2724		3324	
Augmented exam	250	(49)	238	(56)	233	(44)
Memory subscale	252	(46)	254	(50)	230	(48)
Analytic subscale	247	(47)	234	(56)	238	(47)
Creative subscale	253	(47)	252	(57)	237	(54)
Practical subscale	253	(51)	231	(45)	247	(40)
N	338		14		23	

Note. The actual AP exam is scored on a 1–5 performance scale. We did not have access to students' raw scores, but rather only to the overall performance level scores. By contrast, the data from the Augmented exam are based on raw scores that were scaled using Rasch measurement. Each of the scales of the Augmented exam has a mean of 250 and a *SD* of 50 when the data for all participants are analyzed together.

10.12	Augmented AP Statistics Exam Subscale Scores by Ethnicity					
	White		Black		Latino	
Scale	Mean	SD	Mean	SD	Mean	SD
Actual AP exam (2002)	2.84	(1.29)	1.90	(1.14)	2.05	(1.20)
N	33,368		1950		2879	
Augmented AP exam	262	(38)	207	(60)	232	(61)
Memory subscale	257	(47)	220	(47)	244	(47)
Analytic subscale	258	(37)	200	(72)	210	(67)
Creative subscale	263	(42)	248	(57)	243	(43)
Practical subscale	263	(43)	227	(48)	240	(47)
N	210		13		11	

Note. The actual AP exam is scored on a 1–5 performance scale. We did not have access to students' raw scores, but rather only to the overall performance level scores. By contrast, the data from the Augmented exam are based on raw scores that were scaled using Rasch measurement. Each of the scales of the Augmented exam has a mean of 250 and a SD of 50 when the data for all participants are analyzed together.

a standard deviation below White students (Cohen's $d = -0.72$). By way of comparison, White students also tended to have the highest scores overall on the augmented AP Psychology exam. Black students in our sample scored approximately one-quarter of a standard deviation (Cohen's $d = -0.23$) lower than the mean of White students on the overall exam, and on the analytical subscale ($d = -.025$). A key finding, however, is that the effect size difference between Black students and White students was virtually nonexistent for both the creative subscale ($d = -0.02$) and the memory subscale ($d = 0.04$). To our surprise, the biggest gap in achievement between this sample of Black students and White students was observed on the practical subscale ($d = -0.45$).

In addition, a comparison of the standardized difference in achievement between Latino students and White students on the actual AP exam reveals that Latino students scored a little more than half a standard deviation below White students ($d = -0.58$). By way of comparison, Latino students scored about one-third of a standard deviation below White students on the overall augmented AP Psychology scale ($d = -0.37$). The largest difference between Latino students and White students was observed on the memory subscale of the augmented AP Psychology exam, wherein Latino students scored approximately one-half a standard deviation below the White students ($d = -0.47$). Yet, the effect size difference between Latino students and White students was somewhat lower on the creative subscale ($d = -0.32$), and substantially lower on the practical subscale ($d = -0.13$).

In general, then, our exam reduced differences between ethnic groups relative to the actual AP exam. Thus, it appears simultaneously to measure a broader range of skills and to reduce differences between groups.

Statistics

Table 10.12 presents the mean scale scores and standard deviation by ethnicity for the actual AP Statistics exam from 2002, as well as the augmented AP Statistics exam and each of the cognitive processing subscales. The results indicate that Black students scored approximately three-quarters of a standard deviation below White students ($d = -0.77$) on the actual AP exam. By way of comparison, the results from Table 10.12 show that White students and Asian students tended to have the highest scores overall on the augmented exam for Statistics. Black students in the sample scored one full standard deviation below the mean of the White students on the overall subscale ($d = -1.10$). In addition, we observed a similar gap in achievement on the analytical (d $= -1.01$) subscale. The effect size difference between Black students and White students was somewhat lower on both the memory ($d = -0.79$) and practical subscales ($d = -0.77$), and was drastically reduced on the creative subscale ($d = -0.30$). To put these findings into context, the effect size difference between White students and Black students on the actual exam ($d = -0.77$) means that a White student scoring at the 50th percentile of the White student distribution would outscore 78% of the Black students taking the same exam. By contrast, a White student scoring at the 50th percentile on the creative subscale would outscore 63% of Black students on the creative subscale.

Interestingly, whereas Black students tended to exhibit smaller differences in achievement on the creative subscale, Latino students exhibited smaller differences in achievement on the practical subscales. Latino students scored approximately one standard deviation below the White students on the analytical subscale of the augmented exam ($d = -0.89$). Yet, the effect size difference between Latino students and White students was somewhat lower on the creative ($d = -0.47$) and practical subscales ($d = -0.50$), and much lower on the memory subscale ($d = -0.28$). These results can be compared with the results of the actual AP Statistics exam in 2002 shown in Table 10.12 in which Latino students scored approximately two-thirds of a standard deviation below White students ($d = -0.63$).

Summary

In summary, the augmented exam thus generally reduced differences between groups on the Statistics exam, as on the Psychology exam.

Discussion

This study has provided some suggestive answers to our three research questions. First, the results indicate that it is possible to create psychometrically sound instruments based on the theory of successful intelligence that measure students' cognitive skills in the context of AP Psychology and AP Statistics.

Second, students do exhibit somewhat different profiles of strengths and weaknesses across different cognitive skills, regardless of content domain. Indeed, the results shown here demonstrate that a subset of students even exhibit extreme differences in their achievement, scoring at the lowest levels on one skill and the highest levels of other skills. Thus, tests that measure only one cognitive skill may tend to miss important information about individuals with strengths in other cognitive skill areas. Tests that measure only a narrow range of cognitive skills may therefore lead to less valid inferences of student ability.

Third, the results of an analysis of ethnic differences in achievement show that ethnic minority students appear to benefit from assessments that measure a broader range of cognitive skills. Some evidence for this assertion comes from the fact that the pervasive achievement gap between Black students and White students that has been consistently observed across many achievement tests was also observed on the analytical subscales for both of the augmented exams created for this study. Yet, the Black–White test score differences were eliminated or greatly reduced on the creative subtests for both AP Psychology and Statistics. In addition, the differences in achievement between White students and Latino students were greatly reduced on the practical subtest of the augmented exams. Although the sample size on which these findings are based is rather small and the sample is not necessarily representative, the findings suggest that tests that measure only a limited range of cognitive skills, or that make no effort to explicitly balance the range of cognitive skills assessed, may inadvertently not reveal the full range of important skills of at least some members of particular ethnic groups. To ensure equity for individuals and ethnic groups, it is important to develop tests that assess a wide range of cognitive skills.

Limitations

One important limitation of the study relates to the sample sizes of the ethnic minority students in the study. Although the results of our analyses are suggestive, they must be interpreted with caution, given the small n's of the ethnic minority students on which the results are based. Nevertheless, the results of this study provide first estimates of the effect sizes. Thus, future researchers may use these data to calculate sampling strategies for future studies that are powerful enough to detect the desired effects.

The small number of ethnic minority students taking our exam is somewhat reflective of a larger problem with the AP program itself. Indeed, proportionately, the percentage of students from various ethnic groups taking our exams was nearly identical to the percentage of students from each ethnic group taking the actual AP exam. A great challenge facing the AP program is in recruiting minority students to participate. We also cannot and do not claim that our data are fully representative of the various groups that we tested.

Directions for Future Research

The results of this study suggest that the theory of successful intelligence provides a useful basis for test construction. Future studies that replicate this approach in different content domains are warranted to further test the generalizability of this approach. In addition, the findings from the examination of ethnic group differences must be replicated with a larger sample of students before any firm conclusions can be drawn. Future studies should be conducted that explicitly oversample students from the underrepresented minority groups of interest to more fully examine the extent to which the preliminary findings presented here hold.

Conclusions

Overall, the results reported here are promising. Explicitly balancing tests for both content and cognitive processing skill appears to be potentially beneficial at both the individual and group levels. At the individual level, a profile-oriented approach to scoring may lead to the identification of students with strengths in areas not traditionally measured by tests of achievement. At the group level, broadening the range of cognitive skills assessed on tests of achievement may lead to greater equity and increased validity in using the results to make inferences about students' level of content mastery. Broadening the range of cognitive skills assessed may allow us to create a more comprehensive assessment system, whereby diverse cognitive-processing skills are valued and rewarded. Educational institutions may be better able to select students who exhibit a range of cognitive processing skills, thereby enriching the academic experience of all students and creating greater equity within the context of a high-stakes testing program.

Appendix A

Breakdown of Open-Response Items on the Augmented AP Psychology Exam and Their Relative Scale Scores

Item Number	Total Points	Weighting Value	Form A	Form B
51	1	2.50	2.5	
52	5	0.50	2.5	
53	4	0.63	2.5	
54	4	0.63	2.5	
55	4	0.83	3.3	
56	6	0.55	3.3	
57	2	1.65	3.3	
58	1	2.50	2.5	
59	2	1.25	2.5	
60	3	0.83	2.5	
61	4	0.63	2.5	
62	1	2.50	2.5	
63	2	1.25	2.5	
64	4	0.63	2.5	
65	3	0.83	2.5	
66	4	0.63	2.5	2.5
67	5	0.50	2.5	2.5
68	5	0.50	2.5	2.5
69	3	0.83	2.5	2.5
70	4	0.63		2.5
71	2	1.25		2.5
72	6	0.42		2.5
73	4	0.63		2.5
74	4	0.63		2.5
75	3	0.83		2.5
76	4	0.63		2.5
77	2	1.25		2.5
78	1	2.50		2.5
79	3	0.83		2.5
80	5	0.50		2.5
81	4	0.63		2.5
82	3	0.83		2.5
83	4	0.63		2.5
84	4	0.63		2.5
85	3	0.83		2.5
			49.9	50

Appendix B

Breakdown of Open-Response Items on the Augmented AP Statistics Exam and Their Relative Scale Scores

Item Number	Total Possible Raw Score Points	Weight Value	Form A— Maximum Score After Rescaling	Form B— Maximum Score After Rescaling	Form C— Maximum Score After Rescaling
51	8	0.416	3.33	3.33	3.33
52	8	0.416	3.33	3.33	3.33
53	8	0.416	3.33	3.33	3.33
54	5	0.336	1.68		
55	2	0.840	1.68		
56	3	0.560	1.68		
57	3	0.560	1.68		
58	5	0.666	3.33	3.33	
59	2	1.665	3.33	3.33	
60	1	3.330	3.33	3.33	
61	2	1.665	3.33	3.33	
62	2	1.665	3.33	3.33	
63	4	0.833	3.33		3.33
64	2	1.665	3.33		3.33
65	1	3.330	3.33		3.33
66	3	1.110	3.33		3.33
67	4	0.833	3.33		3.33
68	2	1.390		2.78	
69	1	2.780		2.78	
70	3	0.927		2.78	
71	2	1.390		2.78	
72	2	1.390		2.78	
73	3	0.927		2.78	
74	4	0.833		3.33	3.33
75	4	0.833		3.33	3.33
76	3	1.110			3.33
77	4	0.833			3.33
78	2	1.665			3.33
79	2	1.665			3.33
80	3	1.110		3.33	
			50.01	49.98	49.95

References

Alexander, P. A., Jetton, T. L., & Kulikowich, J. M. (1995). Interrelationship of knowledge, interest, and recall: Assessing a model of domain learning. *Journal of Educational Psychology, 87,* 559–575.

Blalock, H. M. (1972). *Social statistics* (second ed.). New York: McGraw-Hill.

Bloom, B. S. (Ed.). (1956). *Taxonomy of educational objectives, handbook i: Cognitive domain.* New York: Longmans Green.

Bond, T., & Fox, C. (2001). *Applying the Rasch model.* Mahwah, NJ: Erlbaum.

Carroll, J. B. (1993). *Human cognitive abilities: A survey of factor-analytic studies.* New York: Cambridge University Press.

Cattell, R. B. (1971). *Abilities: Their structure, growth, and action.* Boston: Houghton-Mifflin.

Ceci, S. J. (1996). *On intelligence* (expanded ed.). Cambridge, MA: Harvard University Press.

Chubb, J. E., & Loveless, T. (Eds.). (2002). *Bridging the achievement gap.* Washington, DC: Brookings Institute.

College Board. (2004). *Exam scoring.* Available from: http://apcentral.collegeboard.com/article/0,3045,152-167-0-1994,00.html

Crocker, L., & Algina, J. (1986). *Introduction to classical and modern test theory.* Orlando, FL: Harcourt Brace Jovanovich.

Embretson, S. E., & Reise, S. P. (2000). *Item response theory for psychologists.* Mahwah, NJ: Erlbaum.

Fisher, W. P. (1992). Reliability statistics. *Rasch Measurement Transactions, 6*(3), 238.

Fordham, S., & Ogbu, J. U. (1986). Black students' school success: Coping with the "burden of 'acting white.' " *Urban Review, 18,* 176–206.

Gardner, H. (1983). *Frames of mind: The theory of multiple intelligences.* New York: Basic Books.

Hair, J. F., Anderson, R. E., Tatham, R. L., & Black, W. C. (1998). *Multivariate data analysis* (5th ed.). Upper Saddle River, NJ: Prentice Hall.

Herrnstein, R. J., & Murray, C. (1994). *The bell curve.* New York: Free Press.

Heubert, J. P., & Hauser, R. M. (Eds.). (1999). *High stakes: Testing for tracking, promotion, and graduation.* Washington, DC: National Research Council.

Irvine, S. H., & Kyllonen, P. C. (Eds.). (2002). *Item generation for test development.* Mahwah, NJ: Erlbaum.

Jencks, C., & Phillips, M. (Eds.). (1998). *The black–white test score gap.* Washington, DC: Brookings Institution Press.

Linacre, J. M. (1988). *Facets: A computer program for many-facet Rasch measurement* (Version 3.3.0). Chicago: MESA Press.

Linacre, J. M. (1994). *Many-facet Rasch measurement.* Chicago: MESA Press.

Linacre, J. M., Wright, B. D., & Lunz, M. E. (1990). *A facets model for judgmental scoring* (MESA Memo No. 61). Chicago: MESA.

Luria, A. R. (1973). *The working brain.* London: Penguin.

Rasch, G. (1960/1980). *Probabilistic models for some intelligence and attainment tests* (Expanded ed.). Chicago: University of Chicago Press.

Smith, E. V. (2001). Evidence for the reliability of measures and validity of measure interpretation: A Rasch measurement perspective. *Journal of Applied Measurement, 2,* 281–311.

Smith, R. M. (1996). A comparison of methods for determining dimensionality in Rasch measurement. *Structural Equation Modeling, 3*(1), 25–40.

Steele, C. M. (1997). A threat in the air: How stereotypes shape intellectual identity and performance. *American Psychologist, 52*(6), 613–629.

Stemler, S. E., Grigorenko, E. L., Jarvin, L., Macomber, D., & Sternberg, R. J. (2003a). *Examining the utility of the theory of successful intelligence for enhancing the construct validity of the advanced placement psychology exam*: Research Report submitted to the College Board.

Stemler, S. E., Grigorenko, E. L., Jarvin, L., Macomber, D., & Sternberg, R. J. (2003b). *Examining the utility of the theory of successful intelligence for enhancing the construct validity of the advanced placement statistics exam.* Research Report submitted to the College Board.

Sternberg, R. J. (1984). Toward a triarchic theory of human intelligence. *Behavioral and Brain Sciences, 7,* 269–287.

Sternberg, R. J. (1985). *Beyond IQ: A triarchic theory of human intelligence.* New York: Cambridge University Press.

Sternberg, R. J. (1997). *Successful intelligence: How practical and creative intelligence determine success in life.* New York: Plume.

Sternberg, R. J. (1999). The theory of successful intelligence. *Review of General Psychology, 3,* 292–316.

Sternberg, R. J. (2003). Culture and intelligence. *American Psychologist, 59,* 325–338.

Sternberg, R. J., & The Rainbow Project Collaborators. (2005). Augmenting the SAT through assessments of analytical, practical, and creative skills. In W. Camara & E. Kimmel (Eds.), *Choosing students. Higher education admission tools for the 21st century* (pp. 159–176). Mahwah, NJ: Erlbaum.

Sternberg, R. J., & The Rainbow Project Collaborators. (2006). The Rainbow Project: Enhancing the SAT through assessments of analytical, practical, and creative skills. *Intelligence, 34,* 321–350.

Sternberg, R. J., The Rainbow Project Collaborators, & University of Michigan Business School Project Collaborators. (2004). Theory based university admissions testing for a new millennium. *Educational Psychologist, 39,* 185–198.

Sternberg, R. J., Torff, B., & Grigorenko, E. L. (1998a). Teaching for successful intelligence raises school achievement. *Phi Delta Kappan, 79,* 667–669.

Sternberg, R. J., Torff, B., & Grigorenko, E. L. (1998b). Teaching triarchically improves school achievement. *Journal of Educational Psychology, 90,* 374–384.

Williams, B. (Ed.). (2004). *Closing the achievement gap: A vision for changing beliefs and practices.* Alexandria, VA: Association for Supervision and Curriculum Development.

Wright, B. D., & Stone, M. H. (1979). *Best test design.* Chicago: MESA.

Section IV

Successful Intelligence and School Admissions

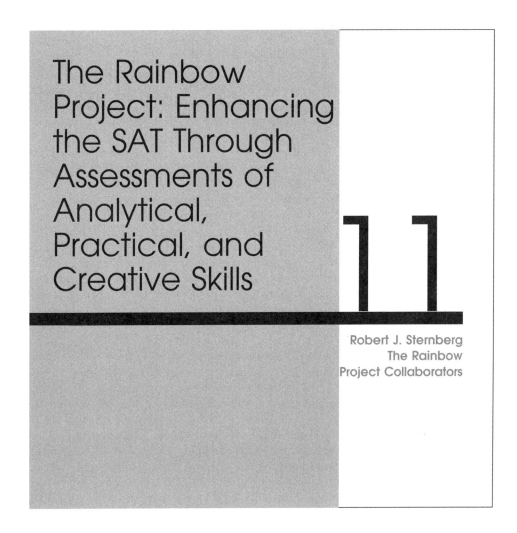

The Rainbow Project: Enhancing the SAT Through Assessments of Analytical, Practical, and Creative Skills

11

Robert J. Sternberg
The Rainbow
Project Collaborators

Standardized tests are frequently used in the United States and abroad as a basis for making high-stakes decisions about educational opportunities, placements, and diagnoses. One of the most widely used tests for these purposes is the SAT. Many colleges and universities in the U.S. use the SAT, usually taken during the high school years, as a predictor of success in college.

The SAT I is a 3-hr examination that measures verbal comprehension and mathematical thinking skills (also referred to as reasoning abilities); new in recent years is an added writing component. A wide variety of studies have shown the usefulness of the SAT as a predictor of college success (Bridgeman, McCamley-Jenkins, & Ervin, 2000; Ramist, Lewis, & McCamley-Jenkins, 1994; Willingham, Lewis, Morgan, & Ramist, 1990). Each SAT II is a 1-hr subject-specific test that measures achievement in designated areas such as mathematics, foreign languages, various sciences, and so forth.

A recent meta-analysis of the predictive validity of the SAT, encompassing roughly 3000 studies and more than one million students, suggested that the SAT is a valid predictor of early-college academic performance (as measured by first-year grade

273

point average [GPA]), with validity coefficients generally in the range of .44 to .62 (Hezlett et al., 2001). The validity coefficients for later-college performance were somewhat lower but still substantial—generally ranging from the mid .30s to the mid .40s. Ramist et al. (1994) found that the validity of the SAT I at 38 colleges was better than high school GPA for predicting one specified course grade, but that high school GPA was a better predictor of overall first-year GPA. The correlations (corrected for restriction of range and criterion unreliability) with freshman GPA were .60 for SAT-Verbal (SAT-V), .62 for SAT-Math (SAT-M), .65 for SAT-Combined (SAT-C), and .69 for high school GPA. The corrected multiple correlation of high school GPA and SAT-C with freshman grades was .75. SAT-V and SAT-M predicted differentially for different courses. The difference favoring the SAT-V scores was greatest (~30%) for various types of English courses and history. The differences favoring the SAT-M scores were greatest (~35%) for mathematics and physical sciences/engineering courses. Correlations for females were generally higher than for males. Correlations also differed somewhat for different ethnic groups: the predictive effectiveness of the SAT-C varied from the highest (.64) for White students to the lowest (.50) for Native American students, with Asian American (.63), Black (.62), and Hispanic (.53) students taking intermediate positions in the order specified here.

Kobrin, Camara, and Milewski (2002) examined the validity of the SAT for college admission decisions in California and elsewhere in the United States. They found that, in California, SAT I and SAT II both showed moderate correlations with family income (in the range of .25 to .55 for SAT I and in the range of .21 to .35 for SAT II) and parental education (in the range of .28 to .58 for SAT I and in the range of .27 to .40 for SAT II). These findings indicate that SAT scores may be a function, in part, of social class. Predictive effectiveness of the SAT was similar for different ethnic groups; however, there were important mean differences and differences in changes in score across time (see also Bridgeman, Burton, & Cline, 2001). The group differences are reflected by the number of standard deviations (SD) away from the White students' mean each group scored. When all SAT scores were aggregated (i.e., when both SAT-I and SAT-II scores were considered), in comparison with White students on average, African American students scored about one full SD lower, Latino students scored 0.9 SD lower, and Native Americans scored about half a SD lower. Asian students demonstrated slightly lower scores (by .2 of SD) than did White students for the aggregated score. In particular, they scored higher than White students by about .03 (SAT I) to .07 (SAT II) SDs on the math tests, but about a third (SAT I) to half a (SAT II) SD lower on the verbal/writing tests.

All together, these results suggest good predictive validity for the SAT for freshman college performance. But as is always the case for any single test or type of test, there is room for improvement. The prediction of tests of "general" ability typically can be improved upon, and there is evidence indicating that the SAT is mainly a test of g (Frey & Detterman, 2004), although the interpretation of these findings has generated some controversy (Bridgeman, 2004; Frey & Detterman, 2005).

The theory of successful intelligence (Sternberg, 1997, 1999a) provides one basis for improving prediction and possibly for establishing greater group equity. It suggests that broadening the range of skills tested to go beyond the analytical and memory skills typically tapped by the SAT, to include practical and creative skills as well, might significantly enhance the prediction of college performance beyond current levels.

Thus, the theory does not suggest replacing, but rather, augmenting the SAT in the college admissions process. A collaborative team of investigators sought to study how successful such an augmentation could be.

The Triarchic Theory of Successful Intelligence

This study was motivated by the triarchic theory of successful intelligence (Sternberg, 1997, 1999a). Our goal was to construct-validate the theory and also to show its usefulness in a practical prediction situation. At the same time, we recognize that there are other useful theories of intelligence (see discussions in Carroll, 1993; Ceci, 1996; Cianciolo & Sternberg, 2004; Deary, 2000; Gardner, 1983; Jensen, 1998; Mackintosh, 1998; Sternberg, 1990, 2000). We are not claiming that our theory is somehow the "correct" one: no contemporary theory is likely to be final! Rather, we merely wish to show that this theory, as operationalized, is construct valid and that it is useful in increasing predictive validity, and, at the same time, in reducing ethnic group differences in scores.

The approach we take was in many respects pioneered by Hunt (Hunt, 1980; Hunt, Frost, & Lunneborg, 1973; Hunt, Lunneborg, & Lewis, 1975), as well as by Carroll (1976), Detterman (1986), Sternberg (1977), and others (see Sternberg & Pretz, 2005, for a review of cognitive approaches to intelligence). The fundamental idea is to use modern cognitive theory to understand and measure intelligence as it pertains to school as well as other forms of success. We recognize that other approaches, such as those based on working memory (e.g., Engle, Tuholski, Laughlin, & Conway, 1999), processing speed (Neubauer & Fink, 2005), inspection time (Deary, 2000), or the combination of abilities and personality (Ackerman, Kanfer, & Goff, 1995), may ultimately prove as successful or more successful than our approach.

The Definition of Successful Intelligence

The construct that forms the basis for our work is successful intelligence.

1. Successful intelligence is defined in terms of the ability to achieve success in life in terms of one's personal standards, within one's sociocultural context. The field of intelligence has at times tended to put the cart before the horse, defining the construct conceptually on the basis of how it is operationalized rather than vice versa. This practice has resulted in tests that stress the academic aspect of intelligence, or intelligence relevant only to the classroom, which is not surprising given the origins of modern intelligence testing in the work of Binet and Simon (1916) in designing an instrument that would distinguish children who would succeed from those who would fail in school. But the construct of intelligence needs to serve a broader purpose, accounting for the bases of success in all areas of one's life.

We refer to the construct as successful intelligence to avoid getting into disagreements over the "true" definition of intelligence, as there is, arguably, no one true definition. Indeed, Sternberg and Detterman (1986) asked two dozen experts in the field to define intelligence, and each one gave a different definition. Our concern is with intelligence as it relates to the achievement of goals one sets for oneself within one's sociocultural context—because intelligence is a social construction. Some languages do not even have a single word for it. Our goal in this chapter is to propose a definition of successful intelligence, and then to operationalize that definition and test this operationalization.

Binet and Simon (1916) originally operationalized intelligence in terms of the skills one needs for success in school. We believe this operationalization was too narrow, as indeed, did Binet, whose conceptualization was much broader than his operationalization through his test (Binet & Simon, 1916). For one thing, it would mean that intelligence is undefined for children who never go to school, and that it becomes undefined for children or adults when they leave school. For another thing, it suggests that the most important adaptation people do is to school rather than to the large majority of the years they will spend outside of it in the workforce. It is precisely against this kind of narrow and academic operationalization of intelligence that we argue. Indeed, it is this glorification of the academic experience that, in our opinion, often leads academic viewpoints to be viewed with suspicion by those outside the academy. The abilities needed to succeed in school are certainly an important part of intelligence, and they are important in the workforce (Hunt, 1995). But the abilities measured by conventional tests are not all there is, as Binet and later Wechsler (1939) both recognized in their conceptualizations of intelligence. Indeed, even intelligence, broadly defined, is only part of what is needed for success in school and in life (Sternberg, 2003). If intelligence is to be defined as what the tests test (Boring, 1923), then perhaps we at least need broader tests.

The use of societal criteria of success (e.g., school grades, personal income) can obscure the fact that conventional operationalizations often do not capture people's personal notions of success. Some people choose to concentrate on extracurricular activities such as athletics or music and pay less attention to grades in school; others may choose occupations that are personally meaningful to them but that never will yield the income they could gain doing work that is less personally valuable. Although scientific analysis of some kinds requires nomothetic operationalizations, the definition of success for an individual is idiographic. In the theory of successful intelligence, however, the conceptualization of intelligence is always within a sociocultural context. Although the processes of intelligence may be common across such contexts, what constitutes success is not. Being a successful member of the clergy of a particular religion may be highly rewarded in one society and viewed as a worthless pursuit in another culture.

2. One's ability to succeed requires capitalizing on one's strengths and correcting or compensating for one's weaknesses. Theories of intelligence typically specify some relatively fixed set of skills, whether one general factor and a number of specific factors (Spearman, 1904), seven multiple factors (Thurstone, 1938), eight multiple intelligences (Gardner, 1983, 1999), or 150 separate intellectual abilities (Guilford, 1982). Such nomothetic specification is useful in establishing a common set of skills to be tested. But people achieve success, even within a given occupation, in many different ways. For example, successful teachers and researchers achieve success through many different blends of skills rather than through any single formula that works for all of them. One reviewer of this manuscript suggested that our definition of successful intelligence in terms of capitalization on strengths and correcting or compensating for weaknesses is trivial—what else is there, he asked? This view, we believe, is incorrect. Positive psychology (e.g., Peterson & Seligman, 2004) emphasizes almost exclusively capitalization on strengths. Peterson and Seligman have argued that it is strengths that are important for understanding human capabilities, not weaknesses. Moreover, the traditional view in schools emphasizes correcting weaknesses—learning how to accomplish the tasks one has not mastered—rather than compensation for weaknesses—having someone else do these tasks. Indeed, compensation by seeking outside help on a test is often viewed as cheating. One is supposed to do all the work oneself. As Greenfield (1997) pointed out, only a collectivist society,

such as the Maya she has studied, would view collaboration on a test as proper test-taking behavior and therefore acceptable. Indeed, intelligence is viewed differently, and manifests itself differently, in diverse cultures and other groupings (Sternberg, 2004; Sternberg, Grigorenko, & Kidd, 2005).

3. A balance of skills is needed to adapt to, shape, and select environments. Definitions of intelligence have traditionally emphasized the role of adaptation to the environment ("Intelligence and Its Measurement," 1921; Sternberg & Detterman, 1986). But intelligence involves not only modifying oneself to suit the environment (adaptation), but also modifying the environment to suit oneself (shaping), and sometimes, finding a new environment that is a better match to one's skills, values, or desires (selection).

Not all people have equal opportunities to adapt to, shape, and select environments. In general, people of higher socioeconomic standing tend to have more opportunities than do people of lower socioeconomic status. The economy or political situation of the society also can be factors. Other variables that may affect such opportunities are education and especially literacy, political party, race, religion, and so forth. For example, someone with a college education typically has many more possible career options than does someone who has dropped out of high school to support a family. Thus, how and how well an individual adapts to, shapes, and selects environments must always be viewed in terms of the opportunities the individual has.

4. Success is attained through a balance of three aspects of intelligence: analytical, practical, and creative skills. Analytical skills are the skills primarily measured by traditional tests. But success in life requires one not only to analyze one's own ideas as well as the ideas of others, but also to generate ideas and persuade other people of their value. This necessity occurs in the world of work, as when a subordinate tries to convince a superior of the value of his or her plan; in the world of personal relationships, as when a child attempts to convince a parent to do what he or she wants or when one spouse tries to convince the other to do things his or her preferred way; and in the world of school, as when a student writes an essay arguing for a point of view.

Defining the Three Aspects of Successful Intelligence

According to the proposed theory of human intelligence and its development (Sternberg, 1980, 1984, 1985, 1997, 1999a), a common set of processes underlies all aspects of intelligence. These processes are hypothesized to be universal. For example, although the solutions to problems that are considered intelligent in one culture may be different from the solutions considered to be intelligent in another culture, the need to define problems and translate strategies to solve these problems exists in any culture. However, although the same processes are used for all three aspects of intelligence universally, these processes are applied to different kinds of tasks and situations depending on whether a given problem requires analytical thinking, practical thinking, creative thinking, or a combination of these kinds of thinking.

Analytical Intelligence

Analytical intelligence involves skills used to analyze, evaluate, judge, or compare and contrast. It is typically used when processing components are applied to relatively familiar kinds of problems that require abstract judgments.

Practical Intelligence

Practical intelligence involves skills used to implement, apply, or put into practice ideas in real-world contexts. It involves individuals applying their abilities to the kinds of daily problems they confront on the job or at home. Practical intelligence is the application of the components of intelligence to experience to (a) adapt to, (b) shape, and (c) select environments.

Much of the work done by Sternberg et al. on practical intelligence has involved the concept of tacit knowledge. They have defined this construct as the knowledge that one is not explicitly taught and that often is not even verbalized but that one needs to work effectively in an environment (Sternberg et al., 2000; Sternberg & Hedlund, 2002; Sternberg & Wagner, 1993; Sternberg, Wagner, & Okagaki, 1993; Sternberg, Wagner, Williams, & Horvath, 1995; Wagner, 1987; Wagner & Sternberg, 1986). Sternberg et al. represent tacit knowledge in the form of production systems, or sequences of "if–then" statements that describe procedures one follows in various kinds of everyday situations (Sternberg et al., 2000). For example, if one needs to write a paper for a class (or a journal, for that matter), one can make one's way through a production system with "if . . . then" statements such as "If there are insufficient references on a topic, then change topics," "If the topic is too broad, then narrow it," "If the paper is too one-sided, include information on other points of view," and so on. According to this view, one essentially constructs one's actions by going through the production system.

Creative Intelligence

Creative intelligence involves skills used to create, invent, discover, imagine, suppose, or hypothesize. Tests of creative intelligence go beyond tests of analytical intelligence in measuring performance on tasks that require individuals to deal with relatively novel situations. Sternberg has shown that assessing a range of abilities beyond that assessed by conventional tests of intelligence allows one to tap sources of individual differences measured little or not at all by these tests (Sternberg, 1985). Thus, it is important to include problems that are relatively novel in nature. These problems can call for either convergent or divergent thinking.

More details on the theory of successful intelligence and its validation can be found in Sternberg (1985, 1997, 1999a); see also Sternberg, Lautrey, and Lubart (2003).

The current study applied the theory of successful intelligence to the creation of assessments that capture analytical, practical, and creative skills. This battery was administered to more than a thousand students at a variety of institutions across the country, and was used to predict success in school as measured by GPA. The hypotheses were twofold: first, we expected that the battery of assessments based on the theory of successful intelligence would predict a substantial proportion of variance in GPA above and beyond that captured by the SAT. Second, we expected that this battery would reduce the socially defined racial and ethnic differences typically found in scores on current standardized college entrance exams such as the SAT.

Method

Here we outline the basic methodology used in Phase 1 of the Rainbow Project to test the hypotheses outlined previously. First, we describe the participants and institutions that participated in data collection. We then describe in detail the measures used in the study, including baseline measures and the measures we are introducing as candidates for supplementing the SAT. These measures include three multiple-choice measures from the Sternberg Triarchic Abilities Test (STAT), three practical performance tasks, and three creativity performance tasks. Finally, we conclude the Methods section with a discussion of the study design and procedure.

Participating Institutions

Data were collected at 15 schools across the United States, including 8 four-year colleges, 5 community colleges, and 2 high schools.[1] Here, however, we present only the data from the colleges ($n = 13$). Most of the data were collected from mid-April 2001 through June 2001, although some institutions extended their data collection somewhat further into the summer. All institutions were supportive of our efforts to collect the data; when technical problems did occur, they tended to be with the online administration of the measures. Such technical difficulties are perhaps expected, given the fact that online data collection using these new tests of analytical, practical, and creative skills has not been done before.

The following institutions participated in the project: Brigham Young University; Florida State University; James Madison University; California State University, San Bernardino; University of California, Santa Barbara; Southern Connecticut State University; Stevens Institute of Technology; Yale University; Mesa Community College; Coastline Community College; Irvine Valley Community College; Orange Coast Community College; Saddleback Community College; Mepham High School; and Northview High School. Students from University of California, Irvine, and from William & Mary also participated; however, the n was less than 5 at each of these schools, so the participants were removed from subsequent analyses. In addition, 14 students failed to report institutional information, and were therefore removed from subsequent analyses for this chapter.

Participants

Participants were recruited on a volunteer basis through fliers distributed on each campus and through psychology courses at the university and college level, and through psychology classes at the high school level. Participants either received course credit or were paid $20 for their participation.

The participants were 1013 students predominantly in their first year of college or their final year of high school. Six participants were removed from the analyses because of procedural errors, 14 students did not report institutional information, and another 3 students from 2 participating institutions were removed because the institutions did not meet the criteria for inclusion in this report (i.e., they did not have

---

[1]The following institutions participated in the project: Brigham Young University; Florida State University; James Madison University; California State University, San Bernardino; University of California, Santa Barbara; Southern Connecticut State University; Stevens Institute of Technology; Yale University; Mesa Community College; Coastline Community College; Irvine Valley Community College; Orange Coast Community College; Saddleback Community College; Mepham High School; and Northview High School. Students from University of California, Irvine, and from William & Mary also participated; however, the n was less than 5 at each of these schools, so the participants were removed from subsequent analyses. In addition, 14 students failed to report institutional information, and were therefore removed from subsequent analyses for this chapter.

$n > 5$ students). Therefore, the total number of participants whose data were available for analyses was 990.

In this chapter, we include analyses[2] only for college students, except where otherwise noted.[3] Although the data from the high school students have their own utility, we analyze in detail only data from the college students because we were interested in the extent to which our new measures predict success in college, not success in high school. Thus, the final number of participants for the prediction studies presented in detail here was 777. The number of participants from each institution, their demographic characteristics, and a listing of the number of participants who completed each assessment are summarized in Tables 11.1 and 11.2. WebTable 1 is a complete by-institution-type table of means and standard deviations for all measures. See http://pace.tufts for this and other WebTables.

Materials

Baseline Assessments

Baseline measures of standardized test scores and high school GPA were collected to evaluate the predictive validity of current tools used for college admission criteria, and to provide a contrast for our current measures. Students' scores on standardized college entrance exams were obtained from the College Board. For most students, we accessed performance on the SAT (math and verbal sections separately, SAT-M and SAT-V), and when these scores were not available, PSAT or ACT scores were obtained. In a small number of instances where students had ACT but not SAT data, the ACT scores were transformed to match the scaling of SAT scores via the algorithm described in Dorans (1999). For the college students, high school GPA was collected from the SAT files provided by the College Board.

There is a potential concern about restriction of range in scores using the SAT when considering students from a select sample of universities. However, our sample was taken from institutions with a wide range of selectivity, from community colleges to highly selective four-year institutions. Additionally, the SD of the SAT scores (for the college sample, $SD_{\text{SAT-V}} = 118.2$, and $SD_{\text{SAT-M}} = 117.5$) was comparable with the SD of the SAT tests in the norm-group ($SD = 100$) selected to represent the broader population. If anything, a chi-squared test for differences between sample variance and population variance (Glass & Hopkins, 1996) suggests that the variance for the sample for these items is statistically larger than for the norm-group of SAT examinees (SAT-V $\chi^2(456) = 637.08$, $p < .001$; SAT-M $\chi^2(456) = 629.57$, $p < .001$). For these reasons, the concern of restriction of range of SAT scores across the whole sample is alleviated.

The Rainbow Measures: An Overview

The Rainbow measures are designed to assess analytical, creative, and practical abilities along the lines specified by the theory of successful intelligence. The instruments consisted of both multiple-choice tests (the Sternberg Triarchic Abilities Test, STAT) and performance measures of creative and practical skills. They were thus designed to sample across ability domains as well as methods of assessment.

---

[2]Also note that psychometric scaling was done on the college sample only, unless otherwise specified.
[3]The means, medians, and standard deviations for all items for the high school students are available from the authors.

11.1 Demographic Breakdown by Institution

School	Gender			Ethnicity								
	Female	Male	Total	Missing	Asian	White	Latino	Native American	Pacific Islander	Black	Other	Total
Brigham Young University	74	65	139	52	4	75	6	1	1	0	0	139
Coastline Community College	14	4	18	2	5	4	6	0	0	0	1	18
Florida State University	3	4	7	0	0	1	3	0	0	1	2	7
Irvine Valley Community College	11	7	18	2	5	8	1	0	0	0	2	18
James Madison University	31	26	57	17	0	37	1	0	0	2	0	57
Mesa Community College	77	42	119	7	3	71	14	7	1	5	11	119
Orange Coast Community College	16	6	22	2	8	2	4	1	1	0	4	22
Saddleback Community College	8	4	12	1	2	4	3	0	0	0	2	12
California State University, San Bernadino	84	27	111	19	9	37	30	0	2	9	5	111
University of California, Santa Barbara	42	17	59	9	4	37	7	0	1	1	0	59
Southern Connecticut State University	23	27	50	19	1	15	0	2	1	12	0	50
Stevens Institute of Technology	30	68	98	15	25	32	9	0	4	7	6	98
Yale University	46	21	67	12	11	25	5	0	0	10	4	67
Total	459	318	777	157	77	348	89	11	11	47	37	777

11.2	Demographic Data and Number of College Students Completing Each of the Rainbow Measures	
	College Students	
	N	Percentage
Gender		
Men	318	40.9
Women	459	59.1
Ethnicity		
White	348	44.8
Black	47	6.0
Latino	89	11.5
Asian	77	9.9
Pacific Islander	11	1.4
Native American	11	1.4
Other	37	4.8
Not reported	157	20.2
Completed assessments		
STAT		
Analytical	500	64.3
Practical	502	64.6
Creative	490	63.1
Creativity		
Written	441	56.8
Oral	197	25.4
Cartoons	757	97.4
Practical		
Common sense	379	48.8
College life	383	49.3
Movies	671	86.4
Year in school		
College		
First	706	90.9
Second	63	8.1
Third	6	.8
Fourth	2	.3

The Sternberg Triarchic Abilities Test

The STAT was developed as a means of capturing analytical, practical, and creative skills using multiple-choice questions (Sternberg & Clinkenbeard, 1995; Sternberg, Ferrari, Clinkenbeard, & Grigorenko, 1996). Level H of the test (Sternberg, 1993) was designed to measure cognitive skills among secondary school and college students, and was used in this study. The STAT briefly measures each of the triarchic skills with three types of item content: verbal, quantitative, and figural. As a result, the STAT scale is composed of nine subscales: analytical–verbal, analytical–quantitative, analytical–figural, practical–verbal, practical–quantitative, practical–figural, creative–verbal, creative–quantitative, and creative–figural. Essay items from the STAT were not used. Each subscale included 5 items for a total of 45 items. Nine of these items (one for each of the ability × modality combinations) were new to the STAT. The particular contents of the items that compose these scales have been described elsewhere (e.g., Sternberg et al., 1996). Each multiple-choice item in the STAT had four different response options, from which the correct response could be selected. A scoring key was used for computing the STAT scores for participants who completed the tests in paper-and-pencil format. In this format, participants circled their response. The responses on the computer-administered tests were keyed into a computer file. Ability scores were then computed by combining the responses to the subscales, using item response theory (IRT) to create three final scales representing analytical, practical, and creative skills (STAT$_{Analytical}$, STAT$_{Practical}$, and STAT$_{Creative}$).[4] The psychometric properties of these scales are presented in the Results section.

Creative Skills—Performance Tasks

In addition to the creative skill measured by the STAT, creativity was measured using open-ended measures. These performance tasks were expected to tap an important aspect of creativity that might not be measured using multiple-choice items alone, because open-ended measures require more spontaneous and free-form responses.

For each of the tasks, participants were given a choice of topic or stimuli on which to base their creative stories or cartoon captions. Although these different topics or stimuli varied in terms of their difficulty for inventing creative stories and captions, these differences are accounted for in the derivation of IRT ability estimates.

Each of the creativity performance tasks were rated on criteria that were determined a priori as indicators of creativity.[5]

Cartoons. Participants were given five cartoons, minus their captions, purchased from the archives of the *New Yorker*.[6] The participants' task was to choose three cartoons, and to provide a caption for each cartoon. Two trained judges rated all the cartoons for cleverness, humor, originality, and task appropriateness on 5-point scales. A combined creativity score was formed by summing the individual ratings on each dimension except task appropriateness, which, theoretically, is not a pure measure of creativity per se. Task appropriateness did not, and would not be expected to, correlate with the other ratings of creativity; however, it is a necessary prerequisite for a product to be creative with respect to a given task. In other words, a creative product is expected to be task appropriate.

Written Stories. Participants were asked to write two stories, spending about 15 min on each, choosing from the following titles: "A Fifth Chance," "2983," "Beyond the Edge," "The Octopus's Sneakers," "It's Moving Backwards," and "Not Enough Time" (Lubart & Sternberg, 1995; Sternberg & Lubart, 1995). A team of six judges was trained to rate the stories. Each judge rated the stories for originality, complexity, emotional evocativeness, and descriptiveness on 5-point scales. Because the reliability based on

---

[4]Further details on the IRT analyses are available from the authors.
[5]Further detail about the rating systems and the training of judges who rated the students' responses are available from the authors.
[6]A sample of the cartoons used in the study is available from the authors.

the total score for each story was satisfactory (see Results section), for efficiency purposes 64.7% of the stories were rated by one of the six judges.

Oral Stories. Participants were presented with five sheets of paper, each containing a set of 11 to 13 images linked by a common theme (keys, money, travel, animals playing music, and humans playing music).[7] There were no restrictions on the minimum or maximum number of images that needed to be incorporated into the stories. After choosing one of the pages, the participant was given 15 min to formulate a short story and dictate it into a cassette recorder. The process was timed by the proctor for the paper assessments and by the internal computer clock for the computer assessments. For dictation of the stories in the paper-and-pencil administration of the test, participants simply pressed the "record" button on a cassette recorder to begin dictation, and pressed "stop" when they were finished. For the computer administration, participants dictated their story into a computer microphone that translated the stories into a *.wav* file that was automatically saved onto the computer. In both cases, the actual dictation period for each story was not to be more than 5 min long. The process was then repeated with another sheet of images so that each participant dictated a total of two oral stories. Six judges were trained to rate the stories. As with the written stories, each judge rated the stories for originality, complexity, emotional evocativeness, and descriptiveness on 5-point scales. Because inter-rater reliability based on the total score for each story was satisfactory (see Results section), for efficiency purposes 48.4% of the stories were rated by only one of the six judges.

In the process of preparing this manuscript for publication, one reviewer suggested that Oral Stories may be a measure of verbal fluency rather than creativity. However, we view verbal fluency as part of creativity, and hence have no argument with this viewpoint. We agree that, at this early stage, we cannot be sure that our tests are pure measures of the constructs we seek to assess. We are hoping that the refined tests and larger sample we will use in the anticipated next phase of the Rainbow Project will help resolve such issues. Like Thurstone (1938), we think it important to separate the fluency aspect of verbal ability from its comprehension aspect (see also Carroll, 1993).

Practical Skills—Performance Tasks

As outlined in Sternberg (1997), practical skills include the ability to acquire useful knowledge from experience, including "tacit knowledge" that is not explicitly taught and is often difficult to articulate, and to apply this knowledge to solving complex everyday problems. Complex everyday problems are distinguished from academic problems in that they are practical, must be solved with incomplete information, and often do not have a single correct answer. In addition to the practical skills measured by the STAT, practical skill was assessed using three situational judgment inventories: the Everyday Situational Judgment Inventory (Movies), the Common Sense Questionnaire, and the College Life Questionnaire, each of which taps different types of tacit knowledge. The general format of tacit knowledge inventories has been described in detail elsewhere (Sternberg et al., 2000), so only the content of the inventories used in this study will be described here.[8]

---

[7]A sample of the exact images used is available from the authors.
[8]To avoid compromising the validity of the items in the measure, we do not present actual items used in the College Life and Common Sense measures, but instead present representative item types used in these tests. These items are available from the authors.

Unlike the creativity performance tasks, in these practical performance tasks the participants were not given a choice of situations to rate. For each task, participants were told that there was no "right" answer, and that the options described in each situation represented variations on how different people approach different situations. That no single correct answer could be determined in our assessment situations is consistent with the kind of everyday problems that individuals with practical skills handle successfully. Even "experts" show a great deal of variability in their problem-solving strategies. The uncertainty surrounding solutions to ill-defined problem situations and the link between a particular response and resulting outcomes represents a qualitative difference between traditional cognitive testing and testing for practical skill (see Legree, 1995; Legree, Psotka, Tremble, & Bourne, 2005).

Everyday Situational Judgment Inventory (ESJI or Movies). This video-based inventory included seven brief vignettes that capture problems encountered in everyday life, such as determining what to do when one is asked to write a letter of recommendation for someone one does not know particularly well. Each situation was accompanied by six written options for how one might handle the situation. For each option, participants were asked to rate how appropriate each option was for resolving the problem on a scale from 1 (a very bad course of action) to 7 (an extremely good course of action). The ESJI took approximately 30 min to administer.

Common Sense Questionnaire (CSQ). This written inventory included 15 vignettes that capture problems encountered in general business-related situations, such as managing tedious tasks or handling a competitive work situation. Each situation was accompanied by eight written options for how one might handle the situation. Like the movie task described above, each option was rated on its quality for resolving the problem on a scale from 1 (extremely bad) to 7 (extremely good). The CSQ took approximately 30 min to administer.

College Life Questionnaire (CLQ). This written inventory included 15 vignettes that capture problems encountered in general college-related situations, such as handling trips to the bursar's office or dealing with a difficult roommate. Each situation was accompanied by several written options (with the number of options varying depending on the situation). The mean number of options for how one might handle the situation was 8. The participant indicated how characteristic and how good the option was as a means of handling the situation on a scale from 1 (e.g., not at all characteristic, not a very good choice) to 7 (e.g., extremely characteristic, a very good choice). The CLQ took approximately 30 min to administer.

School Performance

School performance was measured using cumulative GPA as obtained from college transcripts, that is, this measure was GPA assessed at the end of the year. Clearly, GPA provides only a limited assessment of the totality of school performance. Our goal in Phase 1 of the Rainbow Project, represented here, was to see whether our measures met the minimum necessity of improving prediction of GPA.

Additional Measures

All students at all institutions completed self-report measures of school involvement, satisfaction with school, time spent on leisure activities, competencies with computers, beliefs about the stability of cognitive skills and character, and perceptions of interpersonal competencies. These data are not presented here because preliminary analyses suggested that they did not contribute to our understanding of success in college.[9]

Design and Procedure

College students filled out the assessment battery either in paper-and-pencil format (41%) or on the computer via the World Wide Web (59%).[10] Participants were either tested individually or in small groups. During the oral stories section, participants who were tested in the group situation either wore headphones or were directed into a separate room so as not to disturb the other participants during the story dictation.

There was at least one proctor, and often two, present during the administration of the tests. Proctors read instructions to the participants for both types of administrations, and were available for questions at all times. There were two discrete sessions, conducted one after the other, for each participant. The first session included the informed-consent procedure, demographics information, the movies, the STAT items, and the cartoons, followed by a short debriefing period. The second session included obtaining consent again, followed by the rest of the demographics and "additional measures" described earlier, the Common Sense or College Life Questionnaire (depending on the condition), the Written or Oral Stories (depending on the condition), and ending with the final debriefing. The order was the same for all participants. No strict time limits were set for completing the tests, although the instructors were given rough guidelines of about 70 min per session. The time taken to complete the battery of tests ranged from 2 to 4 hr.

As a result of the lengthy nature of the complete battery of assessments, participants were administered parts of the battery using an intentional incomplete overlapping design, as described in McArdle and Hamagami (1992; also McArdle, 1994). The participants were randomly assigned to the test sections they were to complete. Table 11.2 depicts the layout of the overlapping groups, which shows that each student completed two of the three sections of the STAT, two of the three creativity performance tasks, and two of the three practical performance tasks. The baseline (e.g., SAT-V and SAT-M) and school performance measures (e.g., GPA) were intended to be collected for all participants.

Although half the participants were to receive the oral stories, we were unable to assign the oral stories to many participants because of technical problems involving the recording equipment across different institutions. Those participants who were unable to receive the oral-stories manipulation because of these technical problems were assigned the written stories instead.

Data were also missing not only by design, but also for other reasons, mainly because of technical problems administering the tests by computer. The data that were missing for reasons other than design are listed in Table 11.3.

---

[9]An example item is available from the authors.

[10]The type of administration, whether paper-based or computer-based, typically depended on the institution. Because of this confound, it is difficult to determine whether there are important differences between the pencil-based versus computer-based methodologies.

11.3	Missing Data That Occurred Not Because of the Intentional Missing Data Scheme That Was Part of the Study Design	
	College Students	
	N	Percentage
STAT		
Missing all assessments	9	1.2
Missing 1 of 2 assigned assessments	44	5.7
Practical		
Missing Movies	106	13.6
Missing both CS and CL	15	1.9
Creativity		
Missing Cartoons	20	2.6
Missing both Written and Oral	139	17.9

All missing data in the sample were managed using the full-information maximum likelihood (FIML) technique. McArdle (1994) presented the practical advantages of using FIML to estimate the parameters in structural equation model methods for handling missing data, namely, that other methods such as listwise or pairwise deletion or mean imputation result in the loss of information and potentially inaccurate computations of means and covariance data (Wothke, 2000). The particular advantage of interest here is that careful consideration of FIML during the study-design phase results in the ability to administer more assessments to a given sample where data are incomplete. Keeping the number of groups relatively constrained, unmeasured variables in a particular group (i.e., assessments not administered) can be treated as latent variables in a multigroup analysis of the entire sample including all of the measured variables (Allison, 1987; Dempster, Laird, & Rubin, 1977; McArdle, 1994; Wothke, 2000). In large-scale studies such as the one presented here, this advantage allows for the consideration of a larger number of individual differences variables.

Careful consideration should be given to the relative size of the sample groups when using FIML estimation, as large amounts of incomplete data will inflate the standard error of the estimates and reduce the power of a model (McArdle & Hamagami, 1992). That said, examples of structural equation models using FIML estimation presented in the literature feature samples with up to 80% incomplete data with generally good results for model fit and parameter estimation (e.g., McArdle & Hamagami, 1992; Wothke, 2000). The present research reflects both intentionally incomplete (i.e., by design) and unintentionally incomplete data (i.e., nonsystematic missing data), resulting in larger differences in sample groups than intended. Estimates should thus be considered somewhat tentative. Future attempts to design our studies with intentionally incomplete data should reflect a smaller difference in sample size across groups to reach more stable estimates.

Results

We begin the Results section with a discussion of the descriptive statistics for the baseline assessments, namely, college GPA, and the SAT-V, SAT-M, and SAT C. We continue with analyses of the reliability and internal factor structure of the STAT multiple-choice tests. This discussion is followed by tests of the structure of the items measuring creative abilities and the items measuring practical abilities. Following this are hierarchical multiple regressions showing the unique variance in college GPA that is accounted for by all the tests used in this study, and another multiple regression that considers a reduced number of predictors. Finally, we present an analysis of the group differences that exist for each of the measures in this study.

There is no one perfect way of analyzing these data. A major point of discussion throughout the review process of the manuscript has been with regard to the outcome variable, college GPA. As noted above, we used an incomplete design, which does not permit an execution of comparable analyses within institutions. Originally, we simply used GPAs of college students, uncorrected for the school they attended. A set of external referees used by the College Board took exception to this approach, so we corrected for level of school, using *US News and World Report* ratings of colleges as a basis for correction. But a second set of external referees used by the College Board disputed the use of this procedure. So we went back to uncorrected GPAs. Clearly, there is no perfect procedure. To satisfy the referees, we completed the analyses with both GPA and SAT standardized across the full sample of college students and GPA and SAT standardized within each college. Note that the correlation coefficient, r, for GPA_{Across} and GPA_{Within} is .91 ($p < .001$), for $SAT-V_{Across}$ and $SAT-V_{Within}$ is .69 ($p < .001$), and for $SAT-M_{Across}$ and $SAT-M_{Within}$ is .71 ($p < .001$). There were also additional points of contention, such as (a) whether SAT-V and SAT-M should be analyzed as two separate variables or as a single combined variable (SAT-C, a simple sum of SAT-V and SAT-M) and (b) whether high school student data should or should not be a part of these analyses. All of these suggestions have been carefully considered and proper data analyses were carried out. In sum, we have analyzed the results multiple ways, and they are largely the same, regardless of method of analysis. Indeed, the general conclusions of this research hold for any of the many ways we analyzed the data over the course of our own exploratory data analyses and the various reviewers' comments. That is, no conclusions in this chapter change as a result of which way the data are analyzed. However, because the book has limited space, only one set of analyses is presented here. All other analyses are available at our Website (http://pace.tufts.edu) and/or from the authors (robert.sternberg@tufts.edu).

In brief, in this essay, we standardize across institutions following the recommendation of the College Board (Sternberg and the Project Rainbow Collaborators, 2003); the analyses with standardization within institutions are available on the Web through WebTables. We present analyses for SAT-V and SAT-M because the test is designed, scaled, and promoted to measure different constructs (http://www.collegeboard.-com/highered/ra/sat/sat.html). Although colleges often use combined SAT scores in their decision making, some liberal arts colleges put more weight on SAT-V and many schools of engineering emphasize SAT-M. Because the College Board recommends the use of separate scores rather than combined scores (Wayne Camara, personal communication, 8/6/05), we do so in our work. Yet, to satisfy the reviewers and interested readers, we share a set of analyses with SAT-C on the Web (see corresponding WebTables).

Baseline Assessments

As Table 11.4 shows, when examining college students alone, one can see that this sample shows a slightly higher mean level of SAT than that found in colleges across the country. Using a one-sample z-test to compare the sample means with a population mean of 500 for the verbal and mathematics SAT we find statistically significant differences (for SAT-V, $z = 10.19$, $p < .001$; for SAT-M, $z = 14.4$, $p < .001$). The higher means in our sample may reflect that many students at these universities were recruited through their psychology courses and participated for course credit, and might capture a type of motivation that could be associated with slightly higher SAT scores overall. A more likely explanation, however, is that a relatively large proportion of the sample was enrolled in highly selective 4-year colleges. Finally, among the college students, GPA and SAT scores indicate other substantive differences, such that White and Asian students have higher GPAs and test scores than do underrepresented minority students. Group differences on these and the other measures have been found in other research (e.g., Kobrin et al., 2002) and will be discussed in detail in a later section.

Another point that should be made explicit here is that estimates of the correlations between college and high school GPA and SAT-M and SAT-V (see also WebTables for SAT-C) obtained in our study are comparable, although closer to the lower boundary, with those in the literature (Hezlett et al., 2001; Ramist, Lewis, & McCamley-Jenkins, 1994). Our correlations tend to be somewhat lower than others because we do not correct for (a) attenuation, (b) restriction of range, (c) differences in grading practices and standards across very diverse colleges and universities, or (d) reliability of the indicators in the analyses.

Sternberg Triarchic Abilities Test

The 45 items from the STAT were analyzed together as a single test and as separate 15-item analytical, practical, and creative subtests. [11] A three-factor between-item Rasch analysis was performed on the 45-item set, representing analytical, practical, and creative constructs. In addition, to explore the verbal, numerical, and figural content of each of the 15-item subtests, the multidimensional random-coefficients multinomial logit model (MRCMLM; Adams, Wilson, & Wang, 1997) was applied using the Con-Quest program (Wu, Adams, & Wilson, 1998).

Briefly, the Schmidt et al. analyses indicate that the IRT item reliability estimate for the 45-item STAT was good (.79). The STAT best fits a 3-factor between-item model (analytical, practical, creative) over a 1-factor model, and, when analyzed by 15-item subtest, a 3-factor model (verbal, numerical, figural) appears necessary only for the analytical subtest. Both the practical and creative subtests of the STAT appear to need only one factor to describe the dimensionality. The Cronbach alpha estimates of reliability are satisfactory but not high (.67, .56, and .72 for the analytical, practical, and creative subtests, respectively), in part because the subtests are short. The corresponding Rasch person reliability estimates for the same sample on the analytical,

---

[11]The ability estimates derived from the Rasch analyses were based on the combined high school and college student sample. This approach served to increase the precision of the estimates, but did not alter in a substantive way the difference between scores of participants as the IRT estimates are sample-free (Bond & Fox, 2001; Wright & Stone, 1979). The details of these analyses, based on the combined high school and college sample ($N = 1013$), are provided in the technical report prepared independently by the Jefferson Psychometric Lab (Schmidt, Bowles, Kline, & Deboeck, 2002).

11.4 College Sample Descriptive Statistics for GPA, SAT-V, SAT-M, and SAT-C

	GPA			SAT-V			SAT-M			SAT-C		
	Mean	SD	N	Mean	SD	N	Mean	SD	N	Mean	SD	N
Institution type												
Total college sample	3.03	(0.68)	756	547.7	(118.2)	457	567.6	(117.5)	457	1115.9	(220.5)	458
2-year college only	3.05	(0.73)	183	489.6	(116.0)	48	507.9	(100.3)	48	996.2	(195.3)	47
4-year college only	3.02	(0.66)	573	554.5	(116.7)	409	574.6	(117.5)	409	1129.6	(219.3)	411
College students by gender												
Men	2.92	(0.73)	312	559.1	(113.6)	193	592.5	(110.4)	193	1151.6	(208.3)	192
Women	3.10	(0.63)	444	539.3	(121.0)	264	549.4	(119.4)	264	1090.1	(225.9)	266
College students by ethnicity												
White	3.08	(0.69)	341	576.5	(105.1)	206	589.0	(100.1)	206	1165.68	(189.6)	206
Black	2.57	(0.77)	43	498.1	(126.5)	31	506.1	(126.1)	31	1007.4	(240.0)	31
Asian	3.13	(0.64)	76	557.3	(123.7)	41	635.1	(110.0)	41	1190.8	(211.6)	40
Latino	2.97	(0.53)	86	464.5	(98.3)	53	487.2	(106.7)	53	951.7	(196.4)	53
Native American	2.40	(0.71)	10	502.5	(129.2)	4	510.0	(49.7)	4	1037.5	(146.8)	4
Pacific Islander	3.15	(0.49)	11	510.0	(62.7)	7	570.0	(89.1)	7	1080	(136.9)	7
Other	2.99	(0.60)	36	579.5	(117.4)	21	568.6	(123.0)	21	1153.81	(227.9)	21
Not specified	3.06	(0.68)	153	541.2	(127.7)	94	559.0	(129.8)	94	1101.2	(241.7)	96

practical, and creative subtests were slightly lower (.59, .53, .60, respectively), which is most likely due to the presence of a ceiling effect for some particularly easy items in this test.[12] Together, these analyses support the use of separate subtest scores. In subsequent analyses, the IRT ability estimates for the analytical, practical, and creative subtests based on both high school and college students are used in preference to the raw scores.

Creative Abilities—Performance Tests

Cartoons[13]

As described previously, the cartoon task was scored along multiple dimensions, including cleverness, humor, and originality, leaving out task appropriateness because the responses were all largely appropriate to the task. Using facets analysis (an extension of the Rasch model), we derived a single ability estimate related to the cartoons for each participant (Linacre, 1989). The four measurement facets used were the same as for the Written and Oral Stories: person ability, item dimension differences (i.e., for cartoons the dimensions of this facet used were: cleverness, humor, and originality), rater severity, and story difficulty. Using the many-facets Rasch model for analysis has two distinct advantages in this context. First, the ratings from multiple judges may be accurately combined into a single score. Second, each of the facets under examination may have its elements compared on a common scale (i.e., the logit scale). Thus, we can get an empirical estimate of which items were most difficult, which raters were most severe, which item dimensions were most difficult, and which students had the highest ability. Because the estimates for each facet are on a common scale, person ability estimates can then be accurately adjusted for differences in the severity of the judges scoring each person's items, the difficulty level of the items that were selected, and the difficulty level for each of the creativity dimensions. This yields a single overall ability estimate for each student that has been adjusted for each of the facets in the model.

Table 11.5 reports the zero-order correlations between these ability-based scores (not adjusted for selectivity) and shows evidence that our judges were able to differentiate task appropriateness from other measures thought to capture creativity. The IRT reliability for the composite person ability-based estimates was very good (CHO = .86). The results also indicate slight differences in the level of severity between the raters; however, all raters fit the model very well, such that any differences between raters could be reliably modeled (reliability = .99). Finally, the results indicate that the range in difficulty from one cartoon to the next was small (−.16 to .18). Therefore, fit statistics indicate that each of the items fit the model well, and that the variance in difficulty could be reliably modeled (reliability = .96; see Schmidt et al., 2002, for an independent report on item analyses).

---

[12]Within the many-facets Rasch model, responses are modeled at the item level. Thus, each item and person has a corresponding standard error, which allows for a more accurate computation of reliability than a simple Cronbach's alpha, which is determined based on the error of a hypothetical "average" test-taker. Ceiling effects are likely to cause item response patterns that are too consistent, resulting in low infit scores and low person separation. Cronbach's alpha is less sensitive to these effects. These data, available from the authors, show the distribution of scores for each of the STAT subscales, as well as their correlations with college GPA.
[13]The ability estimates derived from the Rasch analyses were based on the combined high school and college student sample. This approach served to increase the precision of the estimates, but did not alter in a substantive way the difference between scores of participants as the IRT estimates are sample-free (Bond & Fox, 2001; Wright & Stone, 1979).

11.5	Intercorrelations Between Creativity Components (Rasch Estimates) of the Cartoons Task				
	C	H	O	TA	CHO
Cleverness (C)	1.00				
Humor (H)	0.82	1.00			
Originality (O)	0.76	0.72	0.100		
Task appropriateness (TA)	0.39	0.41	0.23	1.00	
Composite (CHO)	0.93	0.92	0.90	0.37	1.00

$N = 757.$

Written and Oral Stories

The raw scores assigned by the raters were analyzed by the many-facets Rasch model (FACETS; Linacre, 1989, 1994) using the FACETS computer program (Linacre, 1998).[14] Four measurement facets were used: person ability, item dimension differences, rater severity, and story difficulty. Student ability estimates were derived for the complexity, emotionality, descriptiveness, and originality dimensions on which the responses were rated. Table 11.6 reports the zero-order correlations between these components for each task. The Rasch reliability indices for the composite person ability estimates for the Written and Oral Stories were very good (.79 and .80, respectively). The judges for both the Written and Oral Stories varied greatly in terms of their severity of ratings for the stories. For the Written Stories, the judges also ranged in their fit to the model, although the reliability was still sound (rater reliability = .94).

For the Oral Stories, all the judges fit the model very well, so their differences could be reliably modeled (rater reliability = .97). Finally, the results indicate that differences between the choice of story titles for the Written Stories and images sheets for the Oral Stories were modest (–.15 to .14 for the Written Stories, and –.15 to .10 for the Oral Stories), such that differences could be reliably modeled (reliability for Written Story titles = .91, for Oral Story images = .81). Further, independent item analyses are reported in detail by Schmidt et al. (2002). One conclusion reached from the item analyses is that the originality component needs some refinement, at least in terms of scoring; however, removing the originality scores did not substantially change the reliability of the measures. Therefore, the ability estimates for the Written and Oral Stories were based on the four rated dimensions, each of which was used in subsequent analyses.

Latent Factor Structure of Performance Measures of Creativity

The experimental design does not allow direct comparison of the relationship between the creativity measures because participants received either the Oral Stories or the

---

[14]The ability estimates derived from the Rasch analyses were based on the combined high school and college student sample. This approach served to increase the precision of the estimates, but did not alter in a substantive way the difference between scores of participants as the IRT estimates are sample-free (Bond & Fox, 2001; Wright & Stone, 1979).

11.6	Intercorrelations Between Components of Written (A) and Oral (B) Stories (Rasch Estimates)				
A. Written Stories	CO	EM	DE	OR	WS
Complexity (CO)	1.00				
Emotionality (EM)	0.77	1.00			
Descriptiveness (DE)	0.63	0.56	1.00		
Originality (OR)	0.35	0.33	0.29	1.00	
Composite Written Stories (WS)	0.82	0.78	0.76	0.58	1.00
N = 441					
B. Oral Stories	CO	EM	DE	OR	OS
Complexity (CO)	1.00				
Emotionality (EM)	0.68	1.00			
Descriptiveness (DE)	0.61	0.48	1.00		
Originality (OR)	0.46	0.37	0.29	1.00	
Composite Oral Stories (OS)	0.82	0.74	0.75	0.65	1.00
N = 197					

Written Stories, but not both; however, all participants received the Cartoons task (see Method section). Therefore, the covariance matrix for these measures was estimated using the full-information maximum likelihood (FIML; Allison, 1987; Dempster et al., 1977; McArdle, 1994) method as implemented in Mplus version 3.13 (Muthen & Muthen, 2002). The estimation algorithm is assisted by additional variables that have overlapping samples of respondents, and so the standardized college GPA, high school GPA, the SAT-V and SAT-M, as well as the $STAT_{Creative}$ measures were included in the analyses. The estimated correlation matrix for these variables is provided in Table 11.7. Note that Oral Stories and $STAT_{Creative}$ correlate almost as highly or higher with college GPA as the SAT-V and SAT-M (Table 11.7) or SAT-C (WebTable 7) do with high school GPA.

The Rasch analyses suggest that the separate performance measures of creativity have appropriate internal psychometric properties. However, the inter-correlations between pairs of the creativity tasks are themselves quite small, suggesting that the possibility of identifying a single common latent factor uniting these variables (i.e., variables 2, 3, 4, and 5 in Table 11.7 for SAT-V and SAT-M and WebTable 7 for SAT-C) is low. As has been stated elsewhere, creativity is, at least in part, domain specific (Sternberg, Grigorenko, & Singer, 2004; Sternberg & Lubart, 1995). It becomes domain general only when measured solely in the most trivial ways (such as through very simple fluency measures).

The model summarized in Figure 11.1 explores the incremental prediction of such a latent creativity factor and reports the fit statistics, standardized path coefficients and their standard errors, and the squared multiple correlation between college GPA and all variables in the model. The overall fit is good ($\chi^2(9)) = 16.74$, $p = .053$, CFI =

11.7 Estimated Correlations Between Creative Abilities, SAT, and High School and College GPA							
	1	2	3	4	5	6	7
1. College GPA[a]	1.00						
2. Oral Stories	.28	1.00					
3. Written Stories	.13	.07	1.00				
4. Cartoon	.08	.16	.23	1.00			
5. STAT$_{Creative}$	.34	.08	.30	.28	1.00		
6. SAT-V[a]	.27	.22	.37	.38	.54	1.00	
7. SAT-M[a]	.29	.19	.29	.27	.59	.75	1.00
8. High school GPA[a]	.37	.05	.20	.20	.46	.50	.57

Nominal $N = 777$; the nominal n of 777 represents the n of all students taking any portion of any test. There are no students who took every portion of every test. When the FIML procedure is used, the correlation matrix is estimated based on all of the information available from all tests for all participants. Rather than using pairwise or listwise deletion techniques to compute correlations, the FIML technique computes pairwise correlation values, and then adjusts the value of the correlation based on the information from other variables in the model. Further information on the FIML procedure may be found in McArdle (1994) and McArdle and Hamagami (1992).
[a] z-score transformation applied.

11.1

Prediction of College GPA (GPA) by Creative Abilities, SAT-V and SAT-M, and High School GPA (HSGPA).

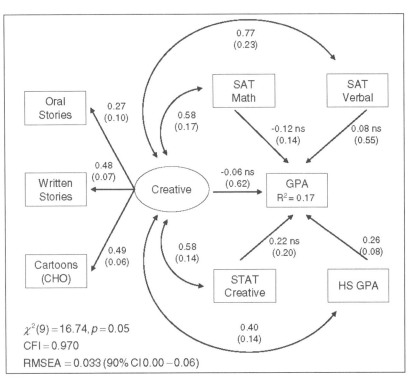

$\chi^2(9) = 16.74, p = 0.05$
$CFI = 0.970$
$RMSEA = 0.033 \, (90\% \, CI \, 0.00 - 0.06)$

0.970, RMSEA = .033, 90% CI = .000–.058), based on standard criteria of CFI indices larger than .95 and RMSEA indices equal to or lower than .05. The creative component of the STAT contributed significantly to the incremental prediction of college GPA; however, the composite performance measure of creativity did not. There are substantial correlations between the SAT-V and the latent creativity factor, which suggests that, for this sample, the performance measures of creative ability and the verbal test of the SAT are tapping common content to an important extent. The zero-order correlations between the SAT-V and the Oral, Written, and Cartoon measures are .22, .37, and .38, respectively, whereas the correlation between SAT-V and STAT$_{Creative}$ is .54 (see Table 11.7). WebFig. 1 Presents This Model With SAT-C.

Practical Abilities—Performance Tests[15]

For all three tacit knowledge measures, the scores assigned to each participant were derived by calculating the Mahalanobis distance (D^2) of the participant's ratings for each possible solution strategy from the mean ratings of the sample to which the participant belonged. A brief description of the calculation of D^2 follows, using the Everyday Situational Judgment (Movies) Inventory as an example to illustrate how the calculation was done (see also Rencher, 1995). The same procedure was used on the Common Sense Questionnaire and the College Life Questionnaire, and the following example could be applied to those tests as well.

For each of the six possible solution strategies accompanying each of the seven vignettes in the Everyday Situational Judgment Inventory (Movies), the sample's mean rating (excluding the rating of the participant of interest) was subtracted from the participant's rating. These computations resulted in a vector of six simple difference scores for each participant, for each of the seven vignettes, and thus $7 \times N$ vectors in all. Then, the vectors of difference scores were each multiplied by the inverse of the variance–covariance matrix of the six possible response strategies from which the difference scores were created. The resulting 6×1 vector was then multiplied by the transpose of the original difference-score vector, resulting in a scalar, called the Mahalanobis distance, or D^2. These computations, then, resulted in seven D^2 values per individual, one per vignette, and thus $7 \times N$ in all. The D^2 values were then averaged, and their square root was taken to return the value to its original metric. The individual's total score for the Everyday Situational Judgment Inventory (Movies) was determined by averaging the resulting vignette-level values.[16]

Situational judgment inventories, used in personnel research for decades, traditionally feature a set of response options from which the examinee is asked to select either the best response or the best and worst response (Legree, 1995; Legree et al., 2005; Motowidlo, Hanson, & Crafts, 1997). The use of a Likert-type scale for rating the quality of response options and a distance-score methodology for determining relative performance levels has been shown to improve the reliability and construct validity of situational judgment inventories for assessing interpersonal skills (Legree, 1995; Legree et al., 2005). Although the use of Mahalanobis distance scores to indicate

---

[15]The scaling for all of the practical tests was done using the college student sample only. The reason for this approach is because the practical measures were scored using a group-based scoring approach rather than an item response theory approach (as was used in scoring the creative tasks).

[16]Although there is a conceptual difference between using the Euclidian distance measure (d^2) and the Mahalanobis distance measure (D^2), the results were run using both approaches. The correlation between the two sets of distance measures was greater than 0.97 for the entire sample.

practical abilities is a novel application of this statistic, it represents an extension of earlier work and is logically consistent with the use of D^2 to detect outliers in multivariate distributions. Yet, to ensure the consistency of our results, we also computed distances at the option level. For example, the movies had 7 scenarios with 6 options each, resulting in 42 responses at the option level. Correspondingly, whereas the Mahalanobis distance scores use only summative information from the 7 scenarios, absolute deviation values obtained at the option level use all available information from all responses. Unsurprisingly, the reliability estimates at the option level tend to be higher than at the scenarios/vignettes level. Below we present reliability estimates for both types of scoring and the correlations between the scoring approaches. Because the correlations are very substantial, we resort to the use of the more conceptually appropriate, from our point of view, method of scoring with the Mahalanobis distances.

As noted earlier, scores on the practical ability performance measures were determined in reference to the average, or consensual, responses of the sample. Important concerns arise when consensual scoring techniques become imbalanced with regard to race, ethnicity, or sex, as such imbalances might be biased against minority group members; other problems arise with regard to defending the basis of any particular individual's score against the average responses of the sample. However, using an "expert group" as a reference instead of the average responses of the sample might lead to similar problems, for example, with determining the demographic characteristics of those individuals comprising such an "expert group." Legree (1995) demonstrated that the ratings of experts and nonexperts on a situational judgment inventory were highly correlated ($r = .72$ and $.95$), indicating that a fairly knowledgeable nonexpert consensus was as sensitive to relative differences in solution quality as were the experts. Mayer, Salovey, Caruso, and Sitarenios (2003) have shown that an expert panel shows more within-group consistency than a general sample in selecting the "correct" answer on emotional intelligence items; however, there appears to be a great deal of between-group agreement in terms of these items, suggesting that both expert panels and general samples tend to agree on the overall correct answers to emotional intelligence items.

Everyday Situational Judgment Inventory (Movies)

Of the 777 college students included in the analysis for this study, 670 produced complete data, and 2 students produced usable but incomplete data. Missing data were a result of technological difficulties in either showing the films or collecting data via computer. Two exceptions were participants who were removed from analyses for apparent malfeasance (e.g., rating all 42 response options with a "1"). All of the items on the test require procedural rather than factual/declarative knowledge to be answered correctly. That is, there are no problems that can be answered on the basis of declarative knowledge alone because all require problem solving, even if declarative knowledge is used in such problem solving.

Measurement Properties. The internal-consistency reliability of a scale composed of the seven distance scores was determined using Cronbach's alpha. This reliability was .76 for the Mahalanobis distance (D^2) and .80 for absolute deviation values (for the two scoring approaches, $r = .95$, $p < .001$), which is comparable with that of many conventional ability tests containing more items.

Underlying Structure. Consistent with Wagner (1987), the fit of a single-factor model to the data was tested via confirmatory factor analysis (CFA). The fit of this model was very good ($\chi^2(14) = 21.65$, $p = .09$; CFI = .99; RMSEA = .03, 90% CI = .00–.05), with loadings of the vignettes on the latent factor ranging between .50 and .60. The variance accounted for in the vignettes by the latent factor (R^2) ranged between .25 and .36, however, indicating that the vignettes could be improved in their measurement of practical abilities as represented in the acquisition and use of general, everyday tacit knowledge. Although the shared variance among the vignettes could be accounted for by a single factor, much unique variance remained. To some degree, unique variance should be expected, as each vignette features a different problem situation. Furthermore, the commonalities (amount of common variance) for these vignettes are comparable with, if not higher than, those reported for measures of cognitive abilities as traditionally defined (e.g., Cattell's Culture Fair Test of *g*, Engle et al., 1999; Arithmetic Reasoning, Kyllonen & Christal, 1990; Raven's Progressive Matrices, Rogers, Hertzog, & Fisk, 2000) or for working memory (Alphabet Recoding, Kyllonen & Christal, 1990; Operation Span, Reading Span, and Computation Span, Engle et al., 1999) in CFAs where they were specified to load on a single, construct-relevant higher-order factor (e.g., *gf* or general working memory). The results of this analysis justified the formation of a single composite for further analyses, representing practical abilities as reflected in the acquisition of general, everyday tacit knowledge. This composite was formed by taking the unit-weighted average of the Mahalanobis distances across all 7 vignettes.

Common Sense Questionnaire

Roughly half of the 777 college students included in these analyses ($n = 377$) produced complete data for the College Student Questionnaire as a result of the intentional incomplete overlapping-group design described earlier (McArdle, 1994). Three participants were removed from analyses for apparent malfeasance.

Measurement Properties. The internal-consistency reliability of a scale composed of the 15 vignettes was determined using Cronbach's alpha. This reliability was .91 for D^2 and .95 for the absolute deviation values ($r = .93$, $p < .001$), which is comparable with that of many conventional ability tests.

Underlying Structure. As with the data from the video-based vignettes, a CFA was used to test the fit of a single-factor model to the data. The fit of this model was good ($\chi^2(90) = 217.91$, $p = .00$; CFI = .94; RMSEA = .06, 90% CI = .05–.07), with loadings of the vignettes on the latent factor ranging between .58 and .70. The commonalities for the vignettes ranged between .34 and .49, indicating that the vignettes are reasonable measures of practical abilities as reflected in the acquisition of general, business-related tacit knowledge. Once again, the vignettes appear to be comparable in structure with conventional measures of cognitive abilities or working memory. The results of this analysis justified the formation of a single composite for further analyses. This composite was formed by taking the unit-weighted average of the Mahalanobis distances across all 15 vignettes.

College Life Questionnaire

Roughly half of the 777 college students included in these analyses ($n = 385$) were administered the College Life Questionnaire as a result of the intentional incomplete overlapping-group design. Ten participants were removed from analyses for apparent malfeasance or failure to follow directions.

Measurement Properties. The internal-consistency reliability of a scale composed of the 15 vignettes was determined using Cronbach's alpha. This reliability was .89 at the vignette level and .95 at the option level ($r = .93$, $p < .001$), again comparable with that of many conventional ability tests.

Underlying Structure. As with the data from the video-based vignettes and the Common Sense Questionnaire, a CFA was used to test the fit of a single-factor model to the data. The fit of this model was marginal ($\chi^2 > (90) = 244.42$, $p = .00$; CFI = .92; RMSEA = .07, 90% CI = .06–.08). The loadings of the vignettes on the latent factor ranged between .53 and .70, with the exception of one vignette that had a loading of .38. The majority of the commonalities for the vignettes ranged between .28 and .49, indicating that the vignettes are reasonable measures of the underlying construct of practical abilities as reflected in the acquisition and use of general, college-related tacit knowledge. The vignette with the relatively low loading, whose commonality was .14, appears to be an exception.

Examination of the content of this vignette reveals that participants were asked to indicate their preference for particular school-related activities, rather than rate the quality of the activities as a strategy for achieving a particular goal. As tacit knowledge is applied toward achieving a particular goal (adapting to, shaping, or selecting the environment), this vignette did not capture a key aspect of using practical abilities. The relatively poor measurement of the construct by this vignette suggested that it should be removed from further analyses. The same CFA when fit to the data with this variable excluded had acceptable fit ($\chi^2(77) = 205.814$ $p = .00$; CFI = .92; RMSEA = .07, 90% CI = .06–.08). The results of this analysis justified the formation of a single composite composed of 14 items for further analyses, representing practical abilities as reflected in the acquisition of general, college-related tacit knowledge captured across vignettes. This composite was formed by taking the unit-weighted average of the Mahalanobis distances across all 14 vignettes.

In summary, all three indicators of practical ability have adequate internal consistencies and concur with the anticipated theoretical structure. In fact, the reported reliabilities compare favorably with those for many situational judgment tasks (SJTs). For example, in a meta-analysis of SJTs, McDaniel et al. (McDaniel, Morgeson, Finnegan, Campion, & Braveman, 2001) reported a median reliability of .795, with a range of values from .43 to .94, with half the values below .80 and one-third below .70. As per Nunnally's (1978) recommendation of viewing a reliability value of .80 as a minimum level for applied projects, and .70 for basic research, our indicators of practical ability meet the required standards.

Practical Abilities, SAT, and GPA

The intercorrelations between the vignette-based practical ability measures, the STAT$_{Practical}$ composite, SAT-V, SAT-M, and GPA are shown in Table 11.8 (see WebTable 8 for SAT-C). These intercorrelations were estimated for nearly the entire sample of college students ($N = 777$) in Mplus using FIML estimation.

These intercorrelations indicate that practical abilities, as reflected in the acquisition of tacit knowledge of differing content, show some relation to GPA. This finding

	1	2	3	4	5	6	7
11.8 Estimated Correlations Between Practical Abilities, SAT-V, SAT-M, and High School and College GPA							
1. College GPA[a]	1.00						
2. Everyday Situational Judgment	.14	1.00					
3. College Life Questionnaire	.15	.59	1.00				
4. Common Sense Questionnaire	.27	.54	.31	1.00			
5. STAT$_{Practical}$	.25	.28	.28	.36	1.00		
6. SAT-V[a]	.28	.28	.24	.27	.54	1.00	
7. SAT-M[a]	.29	.26	.26	.30	.57	.75	1.00
8. High school GPA[a]	.37	.17	.23	.26	.45	.50	.57

Nominal $N = 777$; FIML used to estimate statistics.
[a]z-score transformation applied.

is particularly true for the Common Sense Questionnaire, which assesses general business tacit knowledge. Surprisingly, the College Life Questionnaire and the Everyday Situational Judgment Inventories (Movies), which depicted problem situations typically experienced during undergraduate education, showed relatively smaller relations to college GPA.

Next, a full structural equation model was fit to the data to examine the simultaneous relations between these measures and college GPA. As with the intercorrelations presented previously, the estimates presented in this model were derived using data from nearly the entire sample ($N = 777$) and FIML estimation. Figure 11.2 shows the model and the corresponding fit indices, standardized path coefficients, and correlations. The fit of this model is good, as indicated by a nonsignificant χ^2, a CFI of .99, and an RMSEA of .02, whose 90% confidence interval contains .00. As shown in Figure 11.2, the three tacit knowledge measures each load highly on a single general practical abilities factor, as expected. Because of a compromise to model fit that occurs when the STAT$_{Practical}$ items are included with the performance items, it was not specified to load on the practical latent variable. These problems may occur because the STAT scale uses a different methodology compared with the other practical performance measures. Nevertheless, there is a significant correlation between the STAT$_{Practical}$ and the latent variable comprising the practical performance items, suggesting that each is tapping a similar construct.

Importantly, the general practical abilities factor shows a significant path coefficient to college GPA, the only significant path coefficient to college GPA other than high school GPA. SAT-M and SAT-V, when analyzed simultaneously with general practical abilities, do not significantly account for variance in GPA. Both SAT-M and SAT-V show a significant relation to the practical latent variable. In the case of SAT-V, this relation may occur because general practical abilities in our tests are indicated

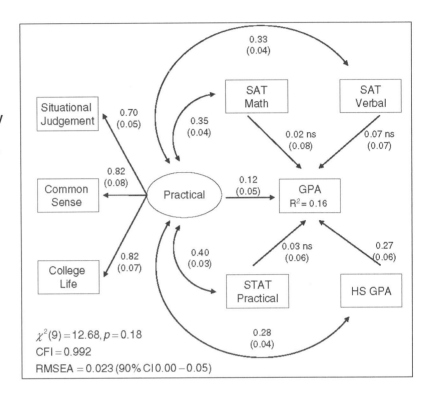

11.2

Prediction of College GPA (GPA) by Practical Abilities, SAT-V and SAT-M, and High School GPA (HS GPA).

by measures that require verbal processing to complete. The relation between SAT-M and the general practical ability factor was not expected, but could perhaps be explained by a reasoning or problem-solving component that may be common to both types of measures. Nevertheless, overall, the fit of this model and the significant path from general practical ability to college GPA show some promise in using vignette-based practical ability measures to supplement SAT scores when considering candidates for college admission. WebFig. 2 presents this model with SAT-C.

Factor Structure of the Triarchic Measures

An exploratory factor analysis was conducted to investigate the factor structure underlying the triarchic measures. The results of these analyses are reported in Table 11.9. Specifically, because the three factors are not theorized to be completely orthogonal, a promax rotation was performed. Three factors were extracted with eigenvalues greater than 1 and these accounted for 62.8% of the variation among the measures. Table 11.9 presents the pattern matrix, as well as the intercorrelations among the three factors.

The results suggest that, consistent with the analyses reported above, evidence for a unidimensional latent creativity factor is unclear, although the four creativity indicators load on this factor with coefficients ranging from .20 to .79. The practical ability measures clearly define a latent factor, again consistent with the analyses reported above. That the STAT variables define a latent factor is expected to the extent

11.9 Exploratory Factor Analysis of Triarchic Measures

	Estimated Correlations[a]								F1	F2	F3
	1	2	3	4	5	6	7	8			
1. Oral Stories	1.00								**.57**	−.06	−.06
2. Written Stories	.07	1.00							**.79**	.01	−.02
3. Cartoons	.14	.24	1.00						**.20**	**.28**	−.08
4. STAT_Creative	.11	.27	.29	1.00					.00	**.73**	.09
5. STAT_Analytical	.14	.24	.21	.58	1.00				**.80**	−.04	−.06
6. STAT_Practical	.14	.31	.29	.61	.63	1.00			**.81**	−.02	.03
7. Movies	.02	.22	.14	.29	.17	.26	1.00		.12	.05	**.52**
8. College Life	.01	.13	.12	.38	.24	.30	.59	1.00	−.13	.01	**1.00**
9. Common sense	.03	.30	.05	.38	.38	.33	.55	.33	.12	−.01	**.92**

Factor intercorrelations

	F1	F2	F3
F1	1.00		
F2	.45	1.00	
F3	.30	.40	1.00

62.8% of variation explained; Nominal $N = 776$. Bolded numbers indicate salient loadings on factor.
[a] Correlations estimated using FIML.

that methodology (multiple choice) and to some extent content (numerical, figural, verbal) is common across the analytical, practical, and creative items. It would seem that, in this sample, the common methodological factor might overwhelm the unique creative, practical, and analytical contribution offered by the different STAT subtests.

Model Comparisons

When using structural equation models to evaluate predictive validity, it is important to compare competing explanatory models. Thus, Table 11.10 shows a comparison of five potential explanatory models.

Model 1 is the standard g-based model, which specifies that each of the manifest variables in the model loads on a common general ability factor. This g-factor is then used to predict freshman GPA. According to the results listed in Table 11.10, the g-based model was not a good fit to the data, as indicated by a statistically significant χ^2, a CFI of .83, and an RMSEA of .080, whose 90% confidence interval does not contain .05, suggesting the data do not support this model.

Model 2 is indicated as a strict triarchic model, in which all manifest variables were forced to load on one of three latent variables (i.e., analytical, creative, or practical). Although this model was a slight improvement over the g-based model, the strict triarchic model was not a good fit to the data as indicated by a statistically significant χ^2, a CFI of .86, and an RMSEA of .076, whose 90% confidence interval does not contain .05.

Model 3 specifies a "method model" in which the latent variables simply represent method variance. Thus, those variables that were measured using some form of multiple-choice assessment were specified to load on the multiple-choice latent variable, and those manifest indicators that were measured in a performance-oriented way were specified to load on a performance latent. High school GPA did not fit well into either of the latent method indicators, and therefore was also included in the model as a manifest variable independently of the two latents. The fit for this model was better than the first two models, but was again not very good by traditional SEM criteria. The χ^2 test is statistically significant, the CFI is .89, and the RMSEA is .065, with a 90% confidence interval that does not contain .05.

Model 4 specifies three latent variables. The first is composed of the performance measures of creative ability. The second is composed of the performance measures of practical abilities, and the third latent variable is the STAT, viewed in this model as largely a g-based (i.e., analytical) test. This model showed a substantial improvement in fit over all previous models, and indeed showed good fit by standard SEM criteria. Model 4 had a nonsignificant chi-squared statistic, a RMSEA of .030, and a CFI of 0.98.

Finally, Model 5 shows a modified version of Model 4. The key difference between these two models is that in Model 5, each of the three components of the STAT are kept as manifest indicators that do not load on any latent factors. In this way, the model reflects that the STAT does not measure *only g*. Model 5 also showed very good fit to the data, although it did not show substantial improvement over and above Model 4.

In summary, Models 4 and 5 showed much better fit to the data than did any of the first three models. Therefore, in the next section, the regression equations are presented for the subcomponents presented in Model 5.

11.10 Structural Equation Model Comparisons

Model		Chi-Squared	df	RMSEA	90% CI	CFI	R^2
Model 1	*g* model	377.60	63	.080	.072–.088	.827	.136
Model 2	Strict triarchic[a]	319.31	58	.076	.068–.084	.856	.172
Model 3	Method[b]+hsgpa model	251.60	59	.065	.057–.073	.894	.164
Model 4	Perf_C <[c]+Perf_P[d]+STAT+zhsgpa+zsat_m+zsat_v	78.34	46	.030	.018–.041	.975	.177
Model 5	Perf_C <[a]+Perf_P[a]+STATcre+STATanl+STATpra+zhsgpa +zsat_m+zsat_v	53.94	34	.027	.012–.041	.970	.178

[a] Creative = oral, written, cartoon, $STAT_{Creative}$; Practical = movies, college, common, $STAT_{Creative}$; Analytic = sat_m, sat_v, hsgpa, $STAT_{Analytic}$.
[b] Multiple-choice = $STAT_{analytic}$, $STAT_{Creative}$, $STAT_{Practical}$; SAT-V, SAT-M; Performance = oral, written, cartoons, movies, college, common.
[c] Perf_C = cartoons, oral, written.
[d] Perf_P = movies, college, common.

Complete Hierarchical Regressions

Regressions are described below. None are corrected for restriction of range, attenuation, or shrinkage; hence these figures are not directly comparable with those of other investigators who have done such corrections.

Many investigators correct correlation coefficients for restriction of range. We do not, for several reasons: (a) we think the assumptions underlying corrections are somewhat dubious, and (b) we do not know what the mean and standard deviation for creative and practical tests for this population would be, as no norming studies exist for these measures.

Many investigators also correct correlation coefficients for attenuation. We do not, although not because we have any great objection in principle to doing so. But we believe that such corrections once again entail dubious assumptions, at times even leading to correlations greater than 1. Moreover, the lower the reliability of the test and the greater the correction, the less likely it seems to be to represent reality. There is, of course, value in corrections, and some investigators prefer corrected correlations. But we believe the greatest value is in reporting what the data were, not what they might have been had certain (sometimes dubious) assumptions been met.

Predicting College GPA[17]

To test the incremental validity provided by triarchic measures above and beyond the SAT in predicting GPA, a series of hierarchical regressions was conducted that included the items analyzed above in the creative and practical abilities. To complete the third dimension of the triarchic model, we also included the $STAT_{Analytic}$ measure. The estimated correlation matrix on which these analyses are based is provided in Table 11.11A[18] (see WebTable 11 for correlation coefficients computed using the SAT-C indicator). Table 11.11B provides the calculated correlation matrix. The hierarchical regressions that include all three dimensions of the triarchic model are shown in Tables

---

[17]One problem when using college GPA from students across different colleges is that a high GPA from a less selective institution is equated to a high GPA from a highly selective institution. One could make the argument that the skills needed to achieve a high GPA at a selective college are greater than the skills needed to achieve a high GPA at a less selective college. There are a number of ways one could account for this problem of equated GPAs. (1) One could assign a weight to GPA based on the selectivity of the students' institution, such that more selective institutions are given a weight that increases the GPA relative to less selective institutions. However, this procedure assumes that the variables used to predict GPA are measured independently of the weight, namely, selectivity of the school. Because SAT is used to determine the selectivity of the school to which a student matriculates, and therefore results in a violation of independence of independent and dependent variables, we could not run this procedure because it would artificially inflate the relationship between SAT and weighted GPA. Adjusting for the SAT/Selectivity relationship by partialling out selectivity from the SAT would artificially deflate the relationship between SAT and weighted GPA. (2) A second procedure would be to standardize all scores, including the dependent variable and all independent variables, within levels of selectivity of the institution, or even within each school, and then run these scores together in all analyses. This standardization procedure effectively equates students at highly selective institutions with students from less selective institutions, and produces results that would be essentially a rough summary of the analyses done within each level of selectivity or within each school. One problem with this procedure is that it loses the elegance of involving schools in a large range of selectivity (e.g., University of California at Santa Barbara versus Mesa Community College) if all students become equated by standardization. Nevertheless, when this procedure is run, the pattern of results is essentially the same as an analysis that does not use a standardization adjustment to the data; in fact, the only substantive change is that, across the board, all coefficients become attenuated (including correlations, beta coefficients, R^2, et cetera). Consequently, we have chosen to report the results based on scores that are unadjusted for institutional selectivity.

[18]The estimation of correlations in FIML is partially dependent on the variables included in the model. This results in minor differences in the estimated values as will be noted for instance in the comparison of Table 11.9 with Table 11.10. For comparison with the raw correlations of the measures without FIML computation (i.e., with incomplete samples), contact the authors.

11.11A Intercorrelations Between Rainbow Measures, GPA, and SAT

	Mean	1	2	3	4	5	6	7	8	9	10	11	12	
1. College GPA[a]	.00	1.00												
2. High school GPA[a]	−.04	.36	1.00											
3. SAT-M[a]	−.12	.28	.57	1.00										
4. SAT-V[a]	−.11	.26	.50	.75	1.00									
5. Oral Stories	−.23	.29	.06	.19	.22	1.00								
6. Written Stories	−.42	.12	.19	.28	.37	.11	1.00							
7. Cartoon	.03	.08	.20	.27	.38	.15	.24	1.00						
8. $STAT_{Creative}$	1.04	.35	.47	.60	.55	.07	.27	.28	1.00					
9. $STAT_{Practical}$	.46	.25	.43	.57	.53	.14	.32	.29	.61	1.00				
10. $STAT_{Analytical}$	1.50	.24	.43	.62	.53	.12	.22	.22	.57	.62	1.00			
11. Everyday Situational Judgment	−.94	.14	.17	.26	.28		.12	.23	.14	.28	.26	1.00		
12. College Life Questionnaire	−.96	.16	.23	.27	.24	.02	.15	.12	.39	.30	.23	.17	1.00	
13. Common Sense Questionnaire	−.95	.27	.24	.28	.26	.20	.31	.04	.38	.32	.26	.55	.59	.33

Nominal $N = 777$; FIML used to estimate statistics.
The estimation of correlations in FIML is partially dependent on the variables included in the model. The correlations reported in Table 11.11A are used for the hierarchical regressions reported in Tables 11.12 and 11.13.
[a] z-score transformation applied

11.11B Actual Correlation Coefficients Computed in SPSS Using Only Complete Data with Pairwise Deletion of Missing Data

	Mean	SD	1	2	3	4	5	6	7	8	9	10	11	12
1. College GPA[a]	.00	1.00	756	654	372	370	450	450	186	433	736	477	491	487
2. Everyday Situational Judgment	-.95	.21	.14	671	346	315	425	425	169	368	655	429	439	431
3. College Life Questionnaire	-.96	.22	.10	.60	383	0	226	226	94	222	374	239	245	246
4. Common Sense Questionnaire	-.95	.24	.31	.54	(a)	379	227	227	99	210	369	242	249	245
5. SAT-M[a]	-.04	1.02	.29	.27	.29	.29	457	457	96	256	444	273	310	303
6. SAT-V[a]	-.05	1.03	.27	.29	.25	.26	.75	457	96	256	444	273	310	303
7. Oral Stories	-.18	.97	.25	.07	.08	.08	.19	.21	197	0	188	129	124	127
8. Written Stories	-.41	.97	.12	.24	.10	.32	.30	.40	(a)	441	435	274	284	287
9. Cartoon	.03	.86	.08	.14	.10	.06	.25	.36	.17	.23	757	476	495	485
10. STAT Creative	1.03	1.18	.35	.30	.38	.38	.59	.54	.16	.30	.30	490	236	235
11. STAT Practical	.43	.97	.24	.30	.32	.37	.56	.53	.15	.30	.33	.65	502	253
12. STAT Analytical	1.55	1.31	.25	.13	.18	.25	.61	.52	.03	.24	.17	.53	.62	500
13. High school GPA[a]	.00	1.00	.36	.20	.30	.24	.56	.48	-.01	.27	.20	.45	.46	.47

Correlation coefficients are listed in the bottom triangle. Sample sizes for each correlation coefficient are listed on the top triangle.
[a]Cannot be computed because at least one of the variables is constant.

11.12 and 11.13. Note that the creativity measures in these hierarchical regressions are separated from their latent variable because, as noted earlier, these items did not include enough common variance.

As shown in Table 11.12 (1 and 2), SAT-V, SAT-M, and high school GPA were included in the first step of the regression because these are the standard measures used today to predict college performance. Here SAT and GPA indicators were standardized across institutions. (See WebTables 12 A–N for parallel analyses with indicators standardized within and across institutions in difference combinations and with SAT-C.)

Only high school GPA contributed uniquely to R^2. In Step 2 we added the analytical subtest of the STAT, because this test is closest conceptually to the SAT tests. The inclusion of the analytical subtest of the STAT did not contribute to the explained variance, and in fact, suggests the presence of a trivial suppressor effect, indicating that it had nothing substantive to contribute and may have been capitalizing on chance or minor variations in the data. In Step 3, the measures of practical ability were added, resulting in a small increase in R^2. Notably, the latent variable representing the common variance among the practical performance measures and high school GPA were the only variables to significantly account for variance in college GPA in Step 3. The inclusion of the creative measures in the final step of this regression indicates that by supplementing the SAT and high school GPA with measures of analytical, practical, and creative abilities a total of 24.8% of the variance in GPA can be accounted for. Inclusion of the triarchic measures in Steps 2, 3, and 4 represents an increase of about 90% (from .159 to .248) in the variance accounted for over and above the typical predictors of college GPA. Table 11.12 (1 and 2) presents the analyses with and without high school GPA (see WebTables 12 A–N for various parallel analyses). The pattern of results was similar even when the SAT and high school GPA variables were entered into the regression equation after the creative, analytic, and practical indicators (Table 11.13).[19] In sum, across multiple models tested, the triarchic measure added to the prediction by anywhere from 5% to 10.2% (7.4% on average), accounting for up to 50% of the total explained variance in the criterion.

Group Differences

Although one important goal of the present study was to predict success in college, another important goal involved developing measures that reduce socially defined racial and ethnic group differences in mean levels. There are a number of ways one can test for group differences in these measures, each of which involves a test of the size of the effect of race. We chose two: omega square (ω^2), and Cohen's d.

We first considered the omega-square coefficients. This procedure involves conducting a series of one-way analyses of variance (ANOVA) considering differences in mean performance levels among the six ethnic and socially defined racial groups reported, including White, Asian, Pacific Islander, Latino, Black, and Native American, for the following measures: the baseline measures (SAT-V and SAT-M), the STAT ability scales, the creativity performance tasks, and the practical ability performance tasks. The omega-squared coefficient indicates the proportion of variance in the variables that is accounted for by the self-reported ethnicity of the participant. The F-statistic

---

[19]A complete set of corresponding tables paralleling WebTables 12 A–N is available on request.

11.12 Incremental Prediction of College GPA Using the Triarchic Abilities (1) Above and Beyond the SAT and High School GPA and (2) Above and Beyond SAT

1.	Step 1	Step 2	Step 3	Step 4
SAT/HSGPA				
Verbal[a]	.098	.084	.066	.005
Math[a]	.070	.011	−.008	−.069
High school GPA[a]	.285*	.276*	.267*	.270*
Analytical				
Analytical STAT		.096	.054	.012
Practical				
Performance latent[b]			.119*	.049
Practical STAT			.025	−.033
Creative				
Written				.003
Oral				.273*
Cartoons				−.072
Creative STAT				.258*
R^2	.156	.152	.159	.248
2.				
SAT				
Verbal[a]	.145*	.125	.098	.039
Math[a]	.188*	.114	.082	.021
Analytical				
Analytical STAT		.122*	.068	.021
Practical				
Performance latent[b]			.133*	.058
Practical STAT			.055	−.015
Creative				
Written				−.003
Oral				.252*
Cartoons				−.068
Creative STAT				.290*
R^2	.098	.099	.110	.199

Entries are standardized beta coefficients. *$p < .05$; $N = 777$.
[a]z-score transformation applied; [b]see Figure 11.2.

for each ANOVA, its significance, the n on which each analysis was based, and the omega squared for each analysis are presented in Table 11.14.

The test of effect sizes using the Cohen's d statistic allows one to consider more specifically a standardized representation of specific group differences. The Cohen's d statistic is represented in Table 11.15. For the test of ethnic group differences, each entry represents how far away from the mean for Whites each group performs in

11.13	Predicting College GPA Above and Beyond the Triarchic Abilities Using SAT and High School GPA				
	Step 1	Step 2	Step 3	Step 4	Step 5
Practical					
Performance latent[b]	.163*	.378	.058	.058	.049
Practical STAT	.165*	−.032	−.025	−.015	−.033
Creative					
Written		.018	.020	−.003	.003
Oral		.258*	.258*	.252*	.273*
Cartoons		−.065	−.069	−.068	−.072
Creative STAT		.356*	.330*	.290*	.257*
Analytical					
Analytical STAT			.026	.021	.012
SAT					
Verbal[a]			.039	.005	
Math[a]				.021	−.069
HSGPA					
High school GPA[a]					.270*
R^2	.075	.208	.201	.199	.248

Entries are standardized beta coefficients.
*$p < .05$; $N = 777$.
[a]z-score transformation applied; [b]see Figure 11.2

terms of standard deviations. For the test of gender differences, the entries represent how far away women perform from men in terms of standard deviations.

These results indicate two general findings. First, in terms of overall differences represented by omega squared, the triarchic tests appear to reduce race and ethnicity differences relative to traditional assessments of abilities such as the SAT. Second, in terms of specific differences represented by Cohen's *d*, it appears that Latino students benefit the most from the reduction of group differences. Black students, too, seem to show a reduction in difference from the White mean for most of the triarchic tests, although a substantial difference appears to be maintained with the practical performance measures. Important reductions in differences can also be seen for Native Americans relative to Whites; however, the very small sample size suggests that any conclusions about Native American performance should be made tentatively. In addition, mean differences between groups are a function of score reliabilities (Table 11.15). Although the reliabilities for the Rainbow tests are adequate (see discussion above), the brevity of the tests decreases their values somewhat. Correspondingly, the levels of reliabilities of the Rainbow scores should be kept in mind and these group results should be interpreted with caution.

11.14 Amount of Variance in Each Assessment Accounted for by Ethnicity, Using the Omega-Square Effect Size Statistic

Measure	F	p	N	Omega Squared (ω^2)
SAT				
Verbal	35.8	< .001	341	.09
Math	15.2	< .001	341	.04
Total (combined)	28.2	< .001	340	.07
STAT				
Analytical	0.5	ns	370	.00
Practical	12.8	< .001	374	.03
Creative	6.7	< .01	369	.02
Practical performance				
EDSJ (Movies)	5.9	< .05	493	.01
Common Sense	2.6	ns	273	.01
College Life	8.4	< .01	298	.02
Creative performance				
Cartoon captions	14.0	< .001	569	.02
Oral Stories	6.0	< .05	152	.03
Written Stories	3.1	ns	329	.01

Although the group differences are not perfectly reduced, these findings suggest that measures can be designed that reduce ethnic and socially defined racial group differences on standardized tests, particularly for historically disadvantaged groups such as Blacks and Latinos. These findings have important implications for reducing adverse impact in college admissions.

Discussion

Summary of Findings

The SAT is based on a conventional psychometric notion of cognitive skills. Based on this notion, it has had substantial success in predicting college performance. But perhaps the time has come to move beyond conventional theories of cognitive skills. Based on multiple regression analyses, for our sample, the triarchic measures alone approximately double the predicted amount of variance in college GPA when compared with the SAT alone (comparative R^2 values of .199 to .098, respectively). Moreover, the triarchic measures predict an additional 8.9% of college GPA beyond the initial 15.6% contributed by the SAT and high school GPA. These findings, combined with the substantial reduction of between-ethnicity differences, make a compelling case for furthering the study of the measurement of analytical, creative, and practical skills for predicting success in college.

11.15 Group Differences as Represented by the Cohen's d Statistic

Test	Reliability	Black d	(N)	Latino d	(N)	Asian d	(N)	Native Am. d	(N)	Women d	(N)
SAT measures											
Math		-.74	31	-.98	53	.35	48	-1.00	4	-.37	264
Verbal		-.67	31	-1.10	53	-.23	48	-.62	4	-.17	264
Total (combined)		-.73	31	-1.10	53	.04	47	-.76	4	-.28	266
STAT											
Analytical	0.59	-.19	31	-.36	55	.34	51	-.33	8	-.30	290
Practical	0.53	-.47	31	-.53	53	.09	55	-.66	7	-.18	297
Creative	0.60	-.67	31	-.46	61	-.03	55	-1.15	7	-.18	288
Practical performance											
ESDJ (Movies)	0.76	-.51	46	-.35	77	.05	82	-.77	4	.19	384
Common sense	0.91	-.89	15	-.22	44	.21	37	-.40	8	.52	222
College life	0.89	-.68	32	-.22	41	-.22	50	.20	3	-.05	229
Creative performance											
Cartoon captions	0.86	-.24	45	-.51	86	-.16	85	-.39	10	-.13	443
Oral Stories	0.79	-.14	16	-.46	27	-.50	25	.50	2	.04	111
Written Stories	0.80	-.26	21	-.11	51	-.25	45	.01	7	.00	269

For ethnicity, Whites are the reference group. For gender, men are the reference group.

Analytical Skills: SAT, HSGPA, STAT_{Analytical}

It is not surprising to find that analytical skills as tapped by the SAT, high school GPA, and the STAT$_{Analytical}$, are important to successful performance in college. And it is not altogether surprising that high school GPA turns out to be the best predictor, subsuming the unique contribution of other largely analytical measures and including other variance as well.

High school GPA is such a good predictor because the best predictor of future behavior of a certain kind is past behavior of the same kind. The best predictor of grades should be—and generally is— grades. GPA is psychologically complex. It thus is not of much use as a psychological predictor because it contains so many things confounded within it, including conscientiousness.

We concur that analytical abilities are necessary for success in many academic disciplines. However, we have also suggested that these abilities may not be sufficient for college success—particularly for disadvantaged students. Although the zero-order correlation between the STAT$_{Analytical}$ test and GPA was approximately the same magnitude as the correlation between the SAT and GPA, the analytical section of our test added little in terms of predictive power over and above the SAT. Because the SAT is already a well-developed, reliable, and valid measure of analytical skills, we plan to dispense with the analytical section in future versions of the Rainbow Project and simply use the SAT as our analytical measure.

Given that traditional pedagogy emphasizes memory and analytical skills, it may not be particularly clear what other student characteristics might determine success. The theory of successful intelligence proposes that creative and practical abilities are also important for success in many areas of life, including college; for example, creative abilities are important in creating course projects, written essays, and papers, and practical skills are important in understanding how to study for exams, manage time, and infer professors' expectations for coursework.

Creative Skills: Cartoons, Oral Stories, Written Stories, STAT_{Creative}

The creative performance measures provide modest reliability and zero-order prediction of college GPA. Research in creativity has repeatedly demonstrated the multidimensional characteristic of this construct (see, for example, Sternberg, 1999b), and our analyses suggest that our measures of creativity show similar multidimensionality. Our measures do show some common variation with verbal skills; however, there is evidence to suggest that reliable variation in the Oral Stories is being determined by skills distinct from the traditional academic abilities assessed by the SAT-V. When incremental prediction is considered, both the Oral Stories task and the STAT$_{Creative}$ remain significant predictors of academic performance (college GPA) beyond SAT.

Practical Skills: Movies, Common Sense, College Life, STAT_{Practical}

The failure of the STAT$_{Practical}$ to load on the practical measure suggests that there are very strong method factors. Practical skills cannot be fully measured by the kinds of multiple-choice measures that appear on the original STAT. For this reason, in the new Rainbow measures, creative and practical items will be mostly performance-based.

The practical performance measures have good reliability and appear to be effective measures of tacit knowledge and practical skill. Together, the three practical performance tests load on a higher-order practical-skill factor, although they did not significantly predict college GPA at the .05 alpha level after the creative measures were entered into the regression equation.

There are a number of issues yet to be resolved, including deciding on an appropriate criterion against which to assess responses to the practical measures, and whether it should be sample-based or expert-based. Another issue with practical intelligence is that cumulative high school GPA is likely to reflect some and perhaps many of the practical skills necessary for academic success, particularly because it reflects academic success over an extended period of time and not simply in a single testing situation.

Incremental Predictive Power

Overall, in the full regression, the only analytical indicator that provided statistically significant prediction of college GPA was high school GPA. The practical performance measures did load on a common factor, and the practical variables were statistically significant predictors of college GPA when they were the only variables in the model. However, when the full range of analytical, practical, and creative measures were added to the regression prediction equation, the latent practical factor was not a statistically significant predictor of college GPA. With regard to the creative measures, two of the four indicators (i.e., the $STAT_{Creative}$, the Oral Stories, and the Cartoons) were statistically significant predictors in the final regression equation, even after including SAT and high school GPA variables, as well as practical indicators. Yet, we need to issue a note of caution here, hoping that others in the field or our future studies will explore certain unexpected results. For example, the Cartoons variable demonstrated a negative regression weight, indicating, in combination with a relatively low correlation with GPA, the likely presence of negative net suppression in the regression (Krus & Wilkinson, 1986). In an attempt to explain this connection, we suggest that the Cartoons indicator might also capture and reflect the trait of humor. Humor, in its different aspects, might positively relate to creativity, but might also negatively relate to academic success. In theoretical models of humor, there is typically a facet of challenge to authority and disobedience (Barron, 1999). Clearly, these aspects of humor, when demonstrated in the classroom, might not positively influence college, especially freshman, GPA. Because we do not have data to explain this effect completely, we acknowledge this as a limitation of our study. Yet, suppression effects are rather common in complex models and are not viewed as a flaw of a measure, design, or model (Cohen, Cohen, West, & Aiken, 2003). In our case, further research is needed to explain this finding completely.

Group Differences

One important goal for the current study, and future studies, is the creation of standardized test measures that reduce the different outcomes between different groups as much as possible in a way that still maintains test validity. Our measures suggest positive results toward this end. Although the group differences in the tests were not reduced to zero, the tests did substantially attenuate group differences relative to other measures such as the SAT. This finding could be an important step toward ultimately ensuring fair and equal treatment for members of diverse groups in the academic domain.

There has been a lot of buzz in the psychological literature about relations of ability-test scores to socially defined ethnic group membership. People have widely differing views on score differences and what they mean (e.g., Rushton & Jensen, 2005, versus Sternberg, 2005; see also Hunt & Sternberg, 2006). We do not wish to contribute to the noise level of this debate. Our results suggest, however, that there may be variation relevant to college performance that is not tapped by conventional tests.

Methodological Issues

Although this first study presents a promising start for the investigation of an equitable yet powerful predictor of success in college, the study is not without its share of methodological problems. Future development of these tests will help sort out some of the problems borne out of the present findings.

Problems with the Sample

At this stage of the project, our goal was to recruit a broad range of higher education institutions to participate in the investigation. Participating institutions included community colleges, 4-year colleges, and universities. It is important to note, however, that the participants in this project reflect a purposive sample rather than a truly random sample of higher education institutions.

Problems with the Creativity Tests

One important problem raised by the creativity tests is that they risk tapping into verbal skills too much. The structural equation model suggests a very strong path between the creativity latent variable and SAT-V (0.78); however, the correlations between the SAT-V test and the individual creativity performance measures (Cartoons, Oral and Written Stories) were consistently less than .40. This finding, along with the fact that creativity measures do predict college GPA above and beyond the SAT, suggests that there is more to the creativity tests than mere verbal-expression skills. Moreover, the best predictor was Oral, not Written Stories, and Oral Stories require less sophisticated verbal and especially lexical skills than do written ones.

But other research has shown that verbal skills may play an important role in creativity anyhow. Measures of "verbal fluency" have had a long history in the conceptualization of measures of creativity, from Guilford (1967) to Mednick and Mednick (1967) to Torrance (1974). Recent empirical evidence shows that raters on written story products often have difficulty removing quality of written expression from their judgments of creativity (Sternberg et al., 1996). Although verbal fluency can be distinguished from strict verbal comprehension (Carroll, 1993; Sincoff & Sternberg, 1987; Thurstone, 1938), one should not expect the relationship between creativity and verbal skills to be completely orthogonal.

Why might SAT-V correlate with our verbal creativity measures? For one thing, there may be content effects due to shared verbal representations. Both sets of tests presumably access the same lexical mental representations. Better scores would be associated with richer and more interconnected representations. In addition, retrieval processes may be shared. In both cases, the participant needs to access the representations, and the retrieval processes may be related or identical for the two tasks. But the two tasks are not the same, in that one requires primarily verbal comprehension, and the other, verbal production (cf., e.g., Thurstone's [1938] distinction between verbal comprehension and verbal fluency).

Nevertheless, future studies could encourage raters to discriminate more between verbal ability and creative skills in their judgments of creativity of stories and captions. For example, we could simplify the ratings by using only two or three dimensions for judgment per task, and having one of those dimensions directly involve a judgment of verbal expression. This system might help future judges distinguish between verbal ability and creativity, much the same way our judges were able to distinguish between task appropriateness and indicators of creativity on the Cartoon task. Including this rating could allow judges to more easily recognize a well-written but not particularly creative story, or a poorly written but highly creative story, sharpening our measurement of creativity.

Future studies should also allow for more than one judge for all written and oral stories. We were able to demonstrate unique predictive power for our creative measures that involved one rater for many stories; however, no single rater can be a perfect judge of creativity. In conjunction with more refined rubrics, having multiple raters could allow for a more accurate, and more powerful, measure of the creativity construct.

Problems with the Practical Tests

Although the tests of practical skills did show zero-order relationships to college GPA, these relationships were reduced to marginal significance in the context of a multiple regression that included all variables. One interpretation of this finding is that our operationalization of practical skills may not fully capture the kinds of practical skills necessary for success in college. For example, the different types of scenarios or response options might possibly better capture the kinds of practical skills necessary for success in college.

A second possibility is that the effects of practical skills could be reduced because of the use of the sample-based profile against which our participants' scores were determined. Using an expert panel (e.g., scores of already successful undergraduates) might provide a more refined profile for determining participants' scores, and could reduce the possibility that our measures are merely capturing conformity to peers. However, there are problems that arise from using expert panels, as discussed earlier. Expert panels show a great deal of variation in terms of appropriate responses on measures of practical skills; they might introduce cultural or group biases depending on the composition of the panel, and they might not contribute a more powerful profile of practical intelligence than would a sample-based profile.

One might argue that the failure of the STAT multiple-choice tests to provide independent prediction is an embarrassment to the theory of successful intelligence. We disagree. Galton's (1883) initial measurements of simple constructs were not very successful. For many years, people concluded, wrongly, that all such measures were invalid. Eventually, in the 1970s, investigators such as Hunt et al. (1973) showed that this thinking was wrong. The early measures were just too crude. In the same way, our initial multiple-choice measures of practical skills did not prove to be psychometrically distinct from g. Had we never found any measures that were psychometrically distinct from g, that would have been a problem. But we have (see also Sternberg et al., 2000).

So our data suggest that the problem was with the initial measures, not the theory. Over time, still better measures perhaps will be created.

Problems with Test Length

The test as constructed was too long to administer in its entirety to our participants. Hence, we used the incomplete design and short versions of the assessments. This was an exploratory study to suggest ways of cutting down the length of the test to the 2-h maximum that will be imposed in any future version. Inevitably, this situation impacted the reliabilities of our measures and our ability to manipulate complete data.

Conclusions

The theory of successful intelligence appears to provide a strong theoretical basis for augmented assessment of the skills needed for college success. There is evidence to indicate that it has good incremental predictive power, and serves to increase equity. As teaching improves and college teachers emphasize further the creative and practical skills needed for success in school and life, the predictive power of the test may increase. Cosmetic changes in testing over the last century have not made great differences to the construct validity of assessment procedures. The theory of successful intelligence could provide a new opportunity to increase construct validity. We are not suggesting that this theory is unique in providing such opportunities. But we do believe that, given the data, its value in creating a new generation of assessments for future use in college admissions is at least worthy of exploration.

References

Ackerman, P. L., Kanfer, R., & Goff, M. (1995). Cognitive and noncognitive determinant and consequences of complex skill acquisition. *Journal of Experimental Psychology. Applied, 6*, 259–290.

Adams, R. J., Wilson, M., & Wang, W. (1997). The multidimensional random coefficients multinomial logit model. *Applied Psychological Measurement, 21*, 1–23.

Allison, P. D. (1987). Estimation of linear models with incomplete data. *Sociological Methodology, 17*, 71–103.

Barron, J. W. (Ed.). (1999). *Humor and psyche: Psychoanalytic perspectives.* Hillsdale, NJ: Analytic Press.

Binet, A., & Simon, T. (1916). *The development of intelligence in children.* Baltimore: Williams and Wilkins. (Originally published in 1905)

Bond, T. G., & Fox, C. M. (2001). *Applying the Rasch model: Fundamental measurement in the human sciences.* Mahwah, NJ: Erlbaum.

Boring, E. G. (1923, June 6). Intelligence as the tests test it. *New Republic,* 35–37.

Bridgeman, B. (2004). Unbelievable results when predicting IQ from SAT scores. *Psychological Science, 16*, 745–746.

Bridgeman, B., Burton, N., & Cline, F. (2001). *Substituting SAT II: Subject tests for SAT I: Reasoning test: Impact on admitted class composition and quality.* New York: College Entrance Examination Board College Board Report No. 2001–3.

Bridgeman, B., McCamley-Jenkins, L., & Ervin, N. (2000). *Predictions of freshman grade-point average from the revised and recentered SAT I: Reasoning test.* New York: College Entrance Examination Board College Board Report No. 2000–1.

Carroll, J. B. (1976). Psychometric tests as cognitive tasks: A new structure of intellect. In L. B. Resnick (Ed.), *The nature of intelligence* (pp. 27–56). Hillsdale, NJ: Erlbaum.

Carroll, J. B. (1993). *Human cognitive abilities: A survey of factor analytical studies.* Cambridge, England: Cambridge University Press.

Ceci, S. J. (1996). *On intelligence* (expanded ed.). Cambridge, MA: Harvard University Press.

Cianciolo, A. T., & Sternberg, R. J. (2004). *A brief history of intelligence.* Malden, MA: Blackwell.

Cohen, J., Cohen, P., West, S. G., & Aiken, L. S. (2003). *Applied multiple regression/correlation analysis for the behavioral sciences.* Mahwah, NJ: Erlbaum.

Deary, I. J. (2000). *Looking down on human intelligence.* Oxford, UK: Oxford University Press.

Dempster, A. P., Laird, N. M., & Rubin, D. B. (1977). Maximum likelihood from incomplete data via the EM algorithm. *Journal of the Royal Statistical Society, 39,* 1–38.

Detterman, D. K. (1986). Human intelligence is a complex system of separate processes. In R. J. Sternberg & D. K. Detterman (Eds.), *What is intelligence?* (pp. 57–61). Norwood, NJ: Ablex.

Dorans, N. J. (1999). *Correspondences between ACT and SAT I scores.* College Board Rep. No. 99-1; ETS Rep. RR. No. 99–2.

Engle, R. W., Tuholski, S. W., Laughlin, J. E., & Conway, A. R. A. (1999). Working memory, short-term memory and general fluid intelligence: A latent variable approach. *Journal of Experimental Psychology. General, 128,* 309–331.

Frey, M. C., & Detterman, D. K. (2004). Scholastic assessment or *g*? *Psychological Science, 15,* 373–378.

Frey, M. C., & Detterman, D. K. (2005). Regression basics. *Psychological Science, 16,* 747.

Galton, F. (1883). *Inquiry into human faculty and its development.* London: Macmillan.

Gardner, H. (1983). *Frames of mind: The theory of multiple intelligences.* New York: Basic.

Gardner, H. (1999). *Intelligence reframed: Multiple intelligences for the 21st century.* New York: Basic Books.

Glass, G. V., & Hopkins, K. H. (1996). *Statistical methods in education and psychology.* Boston: Allyn and Bacon.

Greenfield, P. M. (1997). You can't take it with you: Why abilities assessments don't cross cultures. *American Psychologist, 52,* 1115–1124.

Guilford, J. P. (1967). *The nature of human intelligence.* New York: McGraw-Hill.

Guilford, J. P. (1982). Cognitive psychology's ambiguities: Some suggested remedies. *Psychological Review, 89,* 48–59.

Hezlett, S., Kuncel, N., Vey, A., Ones, D., Campbell, J., & Camara, W. J. (2001). *The effectiveness of the SAT in predicting success early and late in college: A comprehensive meta-analysis.* Paper presented at the annual meeting of the National Council of Measurement in Education, Seattle, WA.

Hunt, E. B. (1980). Intelligence as an information-processing concept. *British Journal of Psychology, 71,* 449–474.

Hunt, E. B. (1995). *Will we be smart enough? A cognitive analysis of the coming workforce.* New York: Russell Sage Foundation.

Hunt, E., Frost, N., & Lunneborg, C. (1973). Individual differences in cognition: A new approach to intelligence. In G. Bower (Ed.), *The psychology of learning and motivation* (Vol. 7, pp. 87–122). New York: Academic Press.

Hunt, E. B., Lunneborg, C., & Lewis, J. (1975). What does it mean to be high verbal? *Cognitive Psychology, 7,* 194–227.

Hunt, E., & Sternberg, R. J. (2006). Sorry, wrong numbers: An analysis of a study of a correlation between skin color and IQ. *Intelligence, 34,* 131–137.

Intelligence and its measurement: A symposium. (1921). *Journal of Educational Psychology, 12,* 123–147, 195–216, 271–275.

Jensen, A. R. (1998). *The g factor.* Westport, CT: Praeger-Greenwood.

Kobrin, J. L., Camara, W. J., & Milewski, G. B. (2002). *The utility of the SATI and SATII for admissions decisions in California and the Nation.* New York: College Entrance Examination Board College Board Report No. 2002–6.

Krus, D. J., & Wilkinson, S. M. (1986). Demonstration of properties of a suppressor variable. *Behavior Research Methods, Instruments, and Computers, 18,* 21–24.

Kyllonen, P. C., & Christal, R. E. (1990). Reasoning ability is (little more than) working-memory capacity? *Intelligence, 14,* 389–433.

Legree, P. J. (1995). Evidence for an oblique social intelligence factor established with a Likert-based testing procedure. *Intelligence, 21,* 247–266.

Legree, P. J., Psotka, J., Tremble, T., & Bourne, D. (2005). Using consensus based measurement to assess emotional intelligence. In R. Schulze & R. D. Roberts (Eds.), *International handbook of emotional intelligence.* Berlin, Germany: Hogrefe and Huber.

Linacre, J. M. (1989). *FACETS user's guide.* Chicago: MESA Press.

Linacre, J. M. (1994). *Many-facet Rasch measurement.* Chicago: MESA Press.

Linacre, J. M. (1998). *Many-facet Rasch measurement* [on-line]. Available: http://www.winsteps.com/facetman/index.htm

Lubart, T. I., & Sternberg, R. J. (1995). An investment approach to creativity: Theory and data. In S. M. Smith, T. B. Ward, & R. A. Finke (Eds.), *The creative cognition approach* (pp. 269–302). Cambridge, MA: MIT Press.

Mackintosh, N. J. (1998). *IQ and human intelligence.* Oxford: Oxford University Press.

Mayer, J. D., Salovey, P., Caruso, D. R., & Sitarenios, G. (2003). Measuring emotional intelligence with the MSCEIT v2.0. *Emotion, 3*(1), 97–105.

McArdle, J. J. (1994). Structural factor analysis experiments with incomplete data. *Multivariate Behavioral Research, 29,* 409–454.

McArdle, J. J., & Hamagami, F. (1992). Modeling incomplete longitudinal and cross-sectional data using latent growth structural models. *Experimental Aging Research, 18,* 145–166.

McDaniel, M. A., Morgeson, F. P., Finnegan, E. B., Campion, M. A., & Braveman, E. P. (2001). Use of situational judgment tests to predict job performance: A clarification of the literature. *Journal of Applied Psychology, 86,* 730–740.

Mednick, S. A., & Mednick, M. T. (1967). *Remote associates test examiner's manual.* Boston: Houghton-Mifflin.

Motowidlo, S. J., Hanson, M. A., & Crafts, J. L. (1997). Low-fidelity simulations. In D. L. Whetzel & G. R. Wheaton (Eds.), *Applied measurement methods in industrial psychology.* Palo Alto, CA: Davies-Black Publishing.

Muthen, L. K., & Muthen, B. O. (2002). *Mplus user's guide* (2nd ed.). Los Angeles, CA.

Neubauer, A. C., & Fink, A. (2005). Basic information processing and the psychophysiology of intelligence. In R. J. Sternberg & J. E. Pretz (Eds.), *Cognition and intelligence* (pp. 68–87). New York: Cambridge University Press.

Nunnally, J. C. (1978). *Psychometric theory.* New York: McGraw-Hill.

Peterson, C., & Seligman, M. E. (2004). *Character strengths and virtues.* New York: Oxford University Press.

Ramist, L., Lewis, C., & McCamley-Jenkins, L. (1994). *Student group differences in predicting college grades: Sex, language and ethnic groups.* New York: College Entrance Examination Board College Board Report No. 93-1, ETS RR No. 94-27.

Rencher, A. C. (1995). *Methods of multivariate analysis.* New York: Wiley.

Rogers, W. A., Hertzog, C., & Fisk, A. D. (2000). An individual differences analysis of ability and strategy influences: Age-related differences in associative learning. *Journal of Experimental Psychology. Learning, Memory, and Cognition, 26*(2), 359–394.

Rushton, J. P., & Jensen, A. R. (2005). Thirty years of research on race differences in cognitive ability. *Psychology, Public Policy, and Law, 11,* 235–294.

Schmidt, K. M., Bowles, R. P., Kline, T. L., & Deboeck, P. (2002, (March). *Psychometric Scaling Progress Report: The Rainbow Project Data—revised.* Technical report presented to the College Board.

Sincoff, J., & Sternberg, R. J. (1987). Two faces of verbal ability. *Intelligence, 11,* 263–276.

Spearman, C. (1904). 'General intelligence,' objectively determined and measured. *American Journal of Psychology, 15*(2), 201–293.

Sternberg, R. J. (1977). *Intelligence, information processing, and analogical reasoning: The componential analysis of human abilities.* Hillsdale, NJ: Erlbaum.

Sternberg, R. J. (1980). Sketch of a componential subtheory of human intelligence. *Behavioral and Brain Sciences, 3,* 573–584.

Sternberg, R. J. (1984). Toward a triarchic theory of human intelligence. *Behavioral and Brain Sciences, 7,* 269–287.

Sternberg, R. J. (1985). *Beyond IQ: A triarchic theory of human intelligence.* New York: Cambridge University Press.

Sternberg, R. J. (1990). *Metaphors of mind.* New York: Cambridge University Press.

Sternberg, R. J. (1993). *Sternberg Triarchic Abilities Test.* Unpublished test.

Sternberg, R. J. (1997). *Successful intelligence.* New York: Plume.

Sternberg, R. J. (1999a). The theory of successful intelligence. *Review of General Psychology, 3,* 292–316.

Sternberg, R. J. (Ed.) (1999b). *Handbook of creativity.* New York: Cambridge University Press.

Sternberg, R. J. (Ed.) (2000). *Handbook of intelligence.* New York: Cambridge University Press.

Sternberg, R. J. (2003). *Wisdom, intelligence, and creativity, synthesized.* New York: Cambridge University Press.

Sternberg, R. J. (2004). Culture and intelligence. *American Psychologist, 59*(5), 325–338.

Sternberg, R. J. (2005). There are no public-policy implications: A reply to Rushton and Jensen. *Psychology, Public Policy, and Law, 11,* 295–301.

Sternberg, R. J., & Clinkenbeard, P. R. (1995). A triarchic model applied to identifying, teaching, and assessing gifted children. *Roeper Review, 17*(4), 255–260.

Sternberg, R. J., & Detterman, D. K. (1986). *What is intelligence?* Norwood, NJ: Ablex Publishing Corporation.

Sternberg, R. J., Ferrari, M., Clinkenbeard, P. R., & Grigorenko, E. L. (1996). Identification, instruction, and assessment of gifted children: A construct validation of a triarchic model. *Gifted Child Quarterly, 40*, 129–137.

Sternberg, R. J., Forsythe, G. B., Hedlund, J., Horvath, J., Snook, S., Williams, W. M., et al. (2000). *Practical intelligence in everyday life.* New York: Cambridge University Press.

Sternberg, R. J., Grigorenko, E. L., & Kidd, K. K. (2005). Intelligence, race, and genetics. *American Psychologist, 60*, 46–59.

Sternberg, R. J., Grigorenko, E. L., & Singer, J. L. (Ed.) (2004). *Creativity: The psychology of creative potential and realization.* Washington, DC: American Psychological Association.

Sternberg, R. J., & Hedlund, J. (2002). Practical intelligence, *g*, and work psychology. *Human Performance, 15*(1/2), 143–160.

Sternberg, R. J., Lautrey, J., & Lubart, T. I. (Ed.). (2003). *Models of intelligence for the new millennium.* Washington, DC: American Psychological Association.

Sternberg, R. J., & Lubart, T. I. (1995). *Defying the crowd: Cultivating creativity in a culture of conformity.* New York: Free Press.

Sternberg, R. J., & Pretz, J. E. (Ed.). (2005). *Cognition and intelligence.* New York: Cambridge University Press.

Sternberg & Project Rainbow Collaborators. (2003 revision). *The Rainbow Project: Enhancing the SAT through assessments of analytical, practical, and creative skills.* Technical report submitted to the College Board.

Sternberg, R. J., & Wagner, R. K. (1993). The *g* ocentric view of intelligence and job performance is wrong. *Current Directions in Psychological Science, 2*(1), 1–4.

Sternberg, R. J., Wagner, R. K., & Okagaki, L. (1993). Practical intelligence: The nature and role of tacit knowledge in work and at school. In H. Reese & J. Puckett (Eds.), *Advances in lifespan development* (pp. 205–227). Hillsdale, NJ: Erlbaum.

Sternberg, R. J., Wagner, R. K., Williams, W. M., & Horvath, J. A. (1995). Testing common sense. *American Psychologist, 50*(11), 912–927.

Thurstone, L. L. (1938). *Primary mental abilities.* Chicago: University of Chicago Press.

Torrance, E. P. (1974). *Torrance tests of creative thinking: Norms—technical manual.* Lexington, MA: Ginn.

Wagner, R. K. (1987). Tacit knowledge in everyday intelligent behavior. *Journal of Personality and Social Psychology, 52*, 1236–1247.

Wagner, R. K., & Sternberg, R. J. (1986). Tacit knowledge and intelligence in the everyday world. In R. J. Sternberg & R. K. Wagner (Eds.), *Practical intelligence: Nature and origins of competence in the everyday world* (pp. 51–83). New York: Cambridge University Press.

Wechsler, D. (1939). *The measurement of adult intelligence.* Baltimore: Williams and Wilkins.

Willingham, W. W., Lewis, C., Morgan, R., & Ramist, L. (Eds.). (1990). *Predicting college grades: An analysis of institutional trends over two decades.* Princeton, NJ: Educational Testing Service.

Wothke, W. (2000). Longitudinal and multigroup modeling with missing data. In T. Little, K. Schnabel, & J. Baumert (Eds.), *Modeling longitudinal and multilevel data.* Mahwah, NJ: Erlbaum.

Wright, B. D., & Stone, M. H. (1979). *Best test design.* Chicago: MESA.

Wu, M., Adams, R. J., & Wilson, M. R. (1998). *ConQuest: User's manual.* Australia: ACER.

Assessing Practical Intelligence in Business School Admissions: A Supplement to the Graduate Management Admissions Test

12

Jennifer Hedlund
Jeanne M. Wilt
Kristina L. Nebel
Susan J. Ashford
Robert J. Sternberg

The admission process in Masters of Business Administration (MBA) programs involves assessing each candidate's demonstrated and potential abilities to be a successful student and business leader. The Graduate Management Admissions Test (GMAT) is perhaps the most widely used uniform criterion in business school admissions (Dobson, Krapljan-Barr, & Vielba, 1999; Hancock, 1999; Wright & Palmer, 1994). Like many standardized admission tests, the GMAT consistently explains about 20% of the variance in graduate GPA (Ahmadi, Raiszadeh, & Helms, 1997; Graham, 1991; Hancock, 1999; Nilsson, 1995; Paolillo, 1982; Wright & Palmer, 1994; Youngblood & Martin, 1982). Although 20% is impressive in regard to psychological measurement, 80% of the variance in school performance remains unexplained. Furthermore, there is evidence to suggest that the GMAT's predictive validity may be limited largely to performance in graduate school (Bretz, 1989).

Another potential limitation with the use of standardized admissions tests is their potential for adverse impact (Bracey, 2001; Darling-Hammond, 1991). Researchers have consistently found mean differences on tests of general cognitive ability and related abilities for different racial/ethnic groups; most notably, blacks tend to score one standard deviation lower than whites on these tests (Hartigan & Wigdor, 1989; Jensen, 1998; Schmidt, 1988; Williams, 2000). The GMAT, in particular, has been found to exhibit disparities in test scores across both gender and racial/ethnic subgroups (Dobson et al., 1999; Hancock, 1999). These differences tend to favor males over females and whites over blacks. Most notably, blacks tend to score more than one standard deviation lower than whites on the GMAT. Identifying a supplement to the GMAT that could potentially reduce, or compensate for, these differences while at the same time increasing prediction, could be of great benefit to business school admissions.

The purpose of our research was to explore alternative ways to assess a business school candidate's potential for success that address, although certainly do not fully circumvent, some of the limitations identified above. The goal is not to replace the GMAT or comparable assessments, but rather to supplement them and thus to improve the process of business school admissions. Our efforts focused on the incorporation of measures of practical abilities as complements to the analytically oriented GMAT, with the aim of improving the prediction of business-school performance and, ultimately, business success. This chapter presents the development and preliminary validation of measures of practical intelligence for use in MBA admissions.

Exploring Alternatives to Conventional Standardized Admissions Tests

Before pursuing a supplement to the GMAT, it was important to consider what constructs the test purports to measure, and thus, what constructs it does not intend to assess. The GMAT is comparable to other standardized admissions test (e.g., SAT, LSAT) in that it consists of multiple-choice questions that measure verbal and quantitative skills. The GMAT further includes an essay component aimed at measuring analytical skills. According to Jaffe and Hilbert (1994), "The purpose of the GMAT is to measure your ability to think systematically and to employ the verbal and mathematical skills that you have acquired throughout your years of schooling" (p. 3). Thus, like the SAT (Frey & Detterman, 2004), the GMAT can be characterized as a traditional measure of intelligence, or a test of general cognitive ability (g).

Given the above-mentioned limitations associated with standardized admissions tests, researchers have suggested broadening the attributes considered in selection and admissions decisions (Sacket, Schmitt, Ellington, & Kabin, 2001). These attributes might include personality, motivation, interpersonal skills, and prior experience, to name a few. Some researchers argue that measures of these attributes, such as biographical data, structured interviews, personality tests, and situational-judgment tests, are potentially useful additions to selection and admission decisions because they tap "noncognitive" factors relevant to performance (Oswald, Schmitt, Kim, Ramsay, & Gillespie, 2004; Sacket et al., 2001). Furthermore, there is evidence to suggest that such measures reduce subgroup differences and increase predictive validity (Hough, Oswald, & Ployhart, 2001; Pulakos & Schmitt, 1996).

These so-called noncognitive predictors have traditionally been used in business school admissions, along with GMAT scores. Applicants often are asked to provide résumés, letters of recommendation, and essays, which are used to evaluate work experience as well as academic and leadership potential. Some programs further recommend or require an interview, which can be used to evaluate interpersonal skills, in addition to the previously mentioned characteristics. Unfortunately, most of these items are difficult to quantify and receive limited weight in admissions decisions. In reality, they typically are used only for a small number of candidates who have GMAT scores that fall near or below an established cutoff score. If these attributes are important for success as a business school student and as a business leader, ideally, they should be considered along with GMAT scores for all candidates.

Oswald et al. (2004) explored the potential value of adding quantifiable measures of noncognitive attributes to college admissions. Specifically, they developed a biographical measure and a situational-judgment inventory (SJI) for college undergraduate students. Biographical (biodata) measures consisted of standardized questions regarding an individual's prior experiences. Situational-judgment inventories consisted of hypothetical problems relevant to those encountered in the performance domain. These measures were developed to assess 12 dimensions of college performance, such as learning, leadership, citizenship, adaptability, perseverance, and ethics.

Oswald et al. (2004) examined the validity of these measures relative to the SAT/ACT in predicting school performance. They found that scores on 12 biodata scales and an overall score on the SJI accounted for significant variance in GPA, absenteeism, and self- and peer-ratings of college performance beyond SAT/ACT scores and the Big Five personality traits. These increments ranged from $\Delta R^2 = .06$ with GPA to $\Delta R^2 = .22$ with self-ratings of performance. In regard to group differences, they found that females scored lower than males on the SAT/ACT, but tended to score higher than males on the biodata items and the SJI. They also found that subgroup differences on the biodata items tended to be relatively small compared to those observed for the SAT/ACT. Additionally, there were no significant differences across subgroups on the SJI. These findings suggest that inclusion of noncognitive measures may help reduce the potential for adverse impact, while also increasing prediction in comparison with relying solely on traditional admissions tests.

An alternative but related strategy for dealing with the limitations of standardized admissions tests is based on a different conceptualization of cognitive abilities. In particular, some researchers propose that definitions of intelligence should include aspects such as interpersonal intelligence (Gardner, 1993, 1999), emotional intelligence (Goleman, 1998; Mayer, Salovey, & Caruso, 2000), and creative and practical intelligence (Sternberg, 1985, 1997, 1999; Sternberg et al., 2000). Rather than view all alternatives to general cognitive ability tests as noncognitive, these perspectives view cognitive ability tests as measuring one aspect of intelligence. These broader conceptualizations of intelligence recognize that individuals have different strengths, and that these strengths may not be identified through traditional approaches to measuring intelligence.

Practical intelligence is a component of a broader definition of intelligence, which also includes creative and analytical intelligence (Sternberg, 1997, 1999). Practical intelligence is defined as the ability that individuals use to find a more optimal fit between themselves and the demands of the environment through adapting to the environment, shaping (or changing) the environment, or selecting a new environment in the pursuit of personally valued goals (Sternberg, 1985, 1997). It can be characterized as "street smarts" or "common sense," and can be contrasted with analytical intelligence or "book smarts." In order to succeed in life, individuals need "common sense" as well as "book smarts." The concept of practical intelligence encompasses many of the attributes that others have labeled as noncognitive, such as interpersonal skills, perseverance, and good judgment. These attributes are important to performance, whether it be in school or on-the-job, but are not necessarily captured by standardized admissions or selection tests. We argue that measures of practical intelligence offer one means of addressing the limitations associated with more analytically oriented admissions tests, in particular, the GMAT.

Practical Intelligence and MBA Admissions

Measures of so-called practical abilities have been used in the area of job selection for nearly 50 years. For example, in-basket tests were designed to assess an individual's ability to deal with job-related tasks under some of the same constraints (e.g., deadlines) found on the actual job (Frederiksen, 1966; Frederiksen, Saunders, & Wand, 1957). Assessment centers also are used to observe an individual's performance in situations that have been created to represent aspects of the actual job situation. Assessment centers typically present small groups of individuals with a variety of tasks, including in-basket tests, simulated interviews, and simulated group discussions (Bray, 1982; Thornton & Byham, 1982). Responses to these simulations are considered to represent the actual, or close approximations of, responses that individuals would exhibit in real situations. Situational-judgment inventories represent yet another approach to measuring practical abilities, and have even been viewed as low-fidelity simulations of actual work situations (Motowidlo, Dunnette, & Carter, 1990). There is also evidence to suggest that some of these measures (e.g., work sample tests) can exhibit higher validity than general cognitive ability tests (Schmidt & Hunter, 1998). In other words, there is evidence to suggest that measures intended to reflect more closely actual job performance may be equally, if not more, valid than measures of general cognitive ability.

We chose to explore the use of measures of practical abilities as supplements to the GMAT in MBA admissions. In particular, we pursued two alternative methods of measuring practical intelligence, one knowledge-based and the other skill-based. These measures draw on prior efforts to assess practical abilities in the area of job performance.

Tacit Knowledge

Practical intelligence often has been equated with the notion of "common sense." It involves knowing how to navigate effectively through the problems of everyday life. Individuals who are successful at solving these everyday problems also are said to rely, to some extent, on their "intuition."

In other words, they develop effective solutions to problems without necessarily being able to explain or justify their decisions. This "intuition" or "common sense" has been attributed in the practical-intelligence literature to tacit knowledge (see Polanyi, 1976; Sternberg, Wagner, Williams, & Horvath, 1995). The concept of tacit knowledge reflects the idea that much of the knowledge relevant to performance is acquired through everyday experiences without conscious intent and guides our actions without being easily articulated.

Sternberg and his colleagues (Sternberg & Horvath, 1999; Sternberg et al., 2000) have focused on tacit knowledge as a means of providing insight into practical intelligence. They have studied tacit knowledge in domains as diverse as bank management, sales, academic psychology, primary education, clerical work, and military leadership

(Hedlund et al., 2003; Sternberg & Wagner, 1993; Sternberg et al., 2000; Wagner, 1987; Wagner & Sternberg, 1985; Wagner et al., 1999).

Tacit knowledge (TK) typically is measured via situational-judgment inventories. Individuals are presented with written descriptions of situations that represent actual situations or approximations of actual situations in the domain of interest (e.g., a salesperson making a phone solicitation). They are asked to rate the quality or appropriateness of potential solutions. Then their responses are scored relative to a standard based on expert or consensus judgment. This score is considered to be a measure of an individual's tacit knowledge and is viewed as an indicator of his or her practical intelligence.

Previous research has examined the relationship of TK scores to domain-specific experience, general cognitive ability, and various indicators of performance. Generally, individuals with greater experience in a domain (e.g., business managers vs. business students) receive better TK scores (Hedlund, Sternberg, & Psotka, 2001; Sternberg, Wagner, & Okagaki, 1993; Wagner, 1987). Tacit knowledge scores also correlate fairly consistently with performance across a variety of domains. Individuals with higher TK scores have been found to have higher salaries, better performance ratings, more productivity, and to work in more prestigious institutions (Hedlund et al., 2003; Sternberg et al., 1993, 1995; Wagner, 1987; Wagner & Sternberg, 1985).

Finally, TK tests appear to tap abilities that are distinct from those measured by traditional intelligence or ability tests. The correlations between scores on TK tests and scores on traditional intelligence tests have ranged from negative to moderately positive (Sternberg et al., 1993, 2000, 2001; Wagner & Sternberg, 1985). More important, TK scores have been found to explain performance above and beyond that accounted for by tests of general cognitive ability (Hedlund et al., 2003; Wagner & Sternberg, 1990). Colonia-Willner (1998) also found that TK significantly predicted an index of managerial skill, whereas psychometric and verbal reasoning did not.

Other researchers have demonstrated the potential value of using SJIs to measure practical abilities (e.g., Chan & Schmitt, 1998; Fox & Spector, 2000; Pulakos, Schmitt, & Chan, 1996). Fox and Spector administered a SJI to undergraduate students participating in a simulated interview. The students were asked to select the response they would most likely or least likely take to several work-related situations. They found that practical intelligence significantly predicted evaluations of the interviewee's qualifications. They also found that scores on the practical-intelligence test exhibited a moderate, significant correlation (.25) with a measure of general intelligence. Pulakos et al. (1996), using a SJI specifically designed for entry-level professionals in a federal investigative agency, found that practical intelligence predicted both peer and supervisory ratings of performance, and that the effects of practical intelligence were not accounted for by a test of general cognitive ability. Finally, Chan and Schmitt (1998) reported that SJIs tend to correlate with performance ratings for various jobs in the range of .13 to .37. Thus, TK tests, and SJIs in general, offer a promising approach for assessing an individual's practical abilities.

Practical Problem-Solving Skills

Another approach to assessing practical intelligence focuses on the skills involved in solving practical problems. The types of problems individuals encounter in their everyday lives differ from those found on traditional admissions tests, in that they tend to be poorly defined, to lack complete information, to have multiple possible solutions, and to be embedded in a context (Neisser, 1976; Sternberg, 1997; Wagner & Sternberg, 1986). According to Sternberg (1985, 1997), individuals who effectively solve practical problems are able to recognize that a problem exists, to define the problem clearly, to allocate appropriate resources to the problem, to formulate strategies for solving the problem, to monitor their solutions, and to evaluate the outcomes of those solutions. Furthermore, in order to understand the problem in the first place, individuals need to be able to filter relevant information from irrelevant information, relate new information to existing knowledge, and compile information into a meaningful picture. The effective use of these skills to solve practical, everyday problems can be viewed as an indicator of one's practical intelligence. Thus, measures of practical problem-solving skills can serve as an alternative to knowledge-based measures of practical intelligence.

Study Overview

The purpose of our research was twofold: (1) to develop and compare two alternative measures of practical intelligence, and (2) to validate those measures as potential supplements to the GMAT. In regard to the first goal, we chose to explore a knowledge-based and a skill-based approach to measuring practical intelligence. Although TK tests have exhibited concurrent validity with performance in academic and work settings, it is not known how well they will predict future performance. In other words, it is not clear if they are suitable for applicants who are not required to possess domain-specific knowledge (e.g., business school applicants). Therefore, we also considered using a measure of an applicant's ability (or potential) to solve problems like those that might someday be encountered in the business world. In regard to the second goal, we evaluated the new measures on four factors: (a) predictive validity relative to indicators of academic and employment success; (b) incremental validity relative to GMAT scores and undergraduate GPA; (c) potential for adverse impact via disparities in test scores; and (d) applicants' reactions to the measures (e.g., face validity, endorsement). We first describe the development of the practical intelligence (PI) measures. Then we present two studies aimed at assessing their validity.

Instrument Development

The development of both PI measures began with the identification of the types of problems MBA graduates might experience as business leaders. To identify such problems, we considered existing taxonomies of managerial/leadership skills (see Mintzberg, 1980; Yukl, 1998), along with the types of business functions (marketing, accounting, information systems, general management) and business settings (finance, manufacturing, technology, nonprofit) in which MBA graduates typically work. We generated 12 problem ideas that incorporated at least one leadership skill (e.g., managing conflict), one business function (e.g., general management), and one business setting (e.g., technology). In consultation with business-school faculty and admissions personnel, we selected six of the most promising ideas for further measurement development.

Measures of Problem-Solving Skills

For the skill-based measure of practical intelligence, we sought to create items with enough detail to allow an individual to demonstrate various problem-solving skills, such as problem recognition, solution generation, and outcome monitoring. We drew on several techniques that have been used to measure practical abilities in the area of personnel selection (e.g., in-basket tests, work samples, case-based interviews). Because the format of our measures was unique to our purpose, we labeled them case scenario problems (CSPs). The CSPs presented a fictitious business case, which consisted of a brief overview of the problem, the respondent's role, and a history of the organization. In addition, respondents were provided various documents such as organizational charts, departmental memos, email correspondence, financial tables, and/or product descriptions. In developing the materials, we sought to include enough information to assess problem-solving skills while at the same time avoiding details that would favor individuals with prior business experience. The 6 scenarios we developed are briefly summarized in Table 12.1.

Respondents were instructed to read through all the materials and to answer a set of questions aimed at assessing the following problem-solving skills:

- *Problem identification and rationale.* What do you see as the main problem in this situation? Why do you consider it to be the main problem? What additional problems need to be addressed?
- *Solution generation and rationale.* What would you do to address the main problem you have identified? What alternative courses of action did you consider? Why did you choose your particular course of action?
- *Information processing.* What information did you focus on in developing a response to the situation? How did you use the information to arrive at a response to the situation? Did you draw on any personal experiences in developing a response to the situation? If so, please explain. What additional information/resources would you need to address this problem?
- *Outcome monitoring and obstacle recognition.* What outcome do you hope will result from the course of action you have chosen? What obstacles, if any, do you anticipate to obtaining this outcome?

Next, 27 business-school alumni and students provided answers to the scenarios and rated them in regard to: (a) time requirements, (b) realism, (c) accuracy and sufficiency of information, (d) prerequisite knowledge or experience, and (e) types of skills/abilities addressed. It took the reviewers, on average, 20–40 min to complete each scenario. Overall, the reviewers believed that the scenarios were realistic, presented clear problems, and provided enough information to generate an appropriate response. Mean ratings were all above 3.5 on a scale of 1 (strongly disagree) to 5 (strongly agree). Next, although reviewers considered the scenarios to be challenging, the majority thought that prior knowledge or experience in a specific management function (e.g., marketing, accounting) was not necessary to respond effectively to the problems. Lastly, reviewers were asked to indicate which of nine leadership skills were addressed by each scenario (see Table 12.2). As expected, the nine leadership skills were well represented, suggesting that the case-scenario problems (CSPs) provide good coverage of skills that are relevant to effective leadership. When asked to express in their own words what skills and/or abilities were measured by the CSPs, the reviewers

12.1 Scenario Titles and Descriptions

Scenario Title	Description
S1: personnel shortage	You are the human resource manager of a manufacturing plant facing a personnel shortage. Your employees are working excessive amounts of overtime and morale is low. Materials provided: Current employment figures and job-satisfaction survey results.
S2: strategic decision making	You are a management consultant working for a newspaper that is struggling to gain new subscribers and is entering the world of electronic media. Materials provided: Memos pertaining to a potential union strike, summary of an evaluation of the web-based paper, and the newspaper's third quarter financial report.
S3: problem subordinate	You are the director of research and development for a communications technology company. You have a subordinate manager who is technically sound but lacks managerial skills. Materials provided: Organizational chart, résumé and evaluations of the problem subordinate, and memos and email exchanges among project managers and the director.
S4: consulting challenge	You are a financial consultant to a medium-sized beverage company. The company's president has sought your services and you discover that he is part of the problem. Materials provided: Press releases, industry performance and market share data, net income chart, and transcripts of interviews with top management.
S5: interdepartmental negotiations	You are a director of a nonprofit agency and in charge of developing the floor plan for a new building. One of your colleagues is creating conflict by refusing to compromise. Materials provided: Résumé of the design consultant, memos regarding floor planning process, email and voice-mail communications among planning team members.
S6: project management	You are a project manager in a technology-consulting firm. You recently were given additional responsibilities in preparation for a promotion. In addition, your teams are behind on several projects, with critical deadlines approaching. Materials provided: Organization charts, project calendar, communications among project staff and clients.

mentioned creative thinking, adaptability, common sense, and analytical thinking, among others, thus providing support for the face validity of the items.

The final step of instrument development was to generate rating scales for the open-ended questions of the CSPs. To do so, we compiled all the responses provided by the initial sample of 27 alumni and student reviewers into a survey. A set of expert reviewers, hand-picked for each scenario based on their background and functional area, were asked to evaluate the quality of these responses relative to the problem-solving dimension they represented (i.e., problem identification, solution generation, information processing, and outcome monitoring). Ratings were obtained from 8 to 10 experts per scenario (total $n = 55$). These ratings were used to identify benchmarks of more and less effective answers to include, along with anchors, for 5-point rating scales developed for each problem-solving dimension (e.g., problem identification, solution generation, information use, outcome identification) as well as overall quality.

12.2	Managerial Skills Addressed by Each Scenario ·					
Skill / Ability	S1%	S2%	S3%	S4%	S5%	S6%
Planning, organizing, and coordinating	25	18.8	43.8	36.4	90.9	90
Decision making	100	100	68.8	90.9	81.8	90
Managing projects/subordinates	25	6.3	100	9.1	63.6	100
Adapting to changing work demands	62.5	31.3	37.5	9.1	18.2	90
Collecting and interpreting data	75	100	25	90.9	27.3	0
Handling stress	25	12.5	43.8	0	45.5	100
Developing subordinates	6.3	6.3	100	9.1	18.2	40
Communicating and informing others	37.5	37.5	50	54.5	100	70
Interacting effectively with others	62.5	31.3	93.8	27.3	100	70

Cell values represent the percentage of reviewers who indicated that the scenario addressed the ability.

Measures of Tacit Knowledge

Past efforts to develop measures of TK have involved soliciting critical incidents from individuals with domain-relevant experience, and developing written descriptions that summarize the main problem in those incidents (Hedlund et al., 2003; Wagner, 1987; Wagner & Sternberg, 1985). Because our goal was to measure more general knowledge (or common sense) and to be able to compare the knowledge-based approach to a skill-based approach to measuring practical intelligence, we employed a different method of item development.

First, we identified a set of subproblems in each of the 6 case scenarios described above. For example, in Scenario 1, we isolated problems pertaining to understaffing, employee turnover, and job satisfaction. Although in the overall scenario these problems were all symptoms of a larger problem (e.g., a mismatch between employee values and management policies), they all can be viewed as significant problems themselves. For each subproblem, we developed a brief description that attempted to capture, in a paragraph, the key issues pertaining to that problem. We then generated a set of possible solutions for each problem, using the reviewers' responses to the question "What would you do to address the main problem you have identified?" For example, suggestions for dealing with the problem of understaffing included hiring temporary employees, offering overtime to current employees, asking individual departments to evaluate their personnel needs, and hiring full-time employees with the understanding that they may be laid off if demand decreases. Because this process differed from previous efforts to develop TK tests as well as other situational-judgment inventories, we differentiate our measures by labeling them situational-judgment problems (SJPs). The process of developing these items resulted in a total of 18 SJPs (three problems representing each of the six scenarios). An example of a SJP is shown in Figure 12.1.

To develop a scoring key for the SJPs, we compiled all 18 problems into one instrument and asked a sample of 30 experts to rate the options on a scale from 1 (extremely bad) to 7 (extremely good). Again, the experts were selected to represent

12.1

Sample situational-judgment problem (SJP).

Scenario 1: Personnel Shortage

1a. You are a senior level manager in the human resources department of a medium-sized manufacturing plant (2,500 employees). Your primary responsibility is to oversee employee selection and staffing. The plant has found itself in a unique situation in which product demand has been high but unemployment levels are low. This situation has resulted in a personnel shortage in key areas of the plant (20 % in production, 15% in maintenance, and 25% in engineering). To avoid layoffs and reduce overhead costs, the company has previously used temporary laborers to compensate for fluctuations in product demand. For the past six months, product demand has been very high and future projections continue to be positive for the next three to six months. In the short term (three months or less), temporary workers are more cost effective, however, their commitment to the job and work quality is less than full-time employees. In the long-term (six months or more), hiring full-time employees is more cost effective. However, if production demands drop, as they often do, the plant would have to lay off employees, which it has never done in its entire 25-year history.

Given this situation, rate the effectiveness of the options below using the following scale:

1	2	3	4	5	6	7
Extremely Bad	Bad	Somewhat Bad	Neither Good Nor Bad	Somewhat Good	Good	Extremely Good

___ Hire temporary employees to compensate for the immediate shortage and reassess the situation in three months.

___ Hire full-time employees but let them know that if production demands decrease, you will have to let them go.

___ Hire a few full-time employees to fill some of the positions and fill the rest with temporary employees to minimize layoffs should production demand diminish.

___ Ask each department to evaluate their own personnel needs and recommend the best approach for their own department.

___ Research the situation in more detail to get a better indication of future product demand and of the relative costs and benefits of various staffing options before making any final decisions.

___ Present the available information to top management and have them make a final decision on how to best handle the personnel shortage.

___ Offer overtime hours for existing employees to see if they would like the opportunity to make more money before hiring temporary laborers or full-time employees.

a variety of backgrounds and leadership positions. The mean ratings of all the experts on each response option served as the scoring key for the SJPs.

Study 1

Methodology

Sample

The initial validation of the PI measures took place with a sample of 422 incoming MBA students at the University of Michigan Business School during orientation in the Fall of 1999. The sample consisted of 313 (74%) males and 109 (26%) females. The racial/ethnic composition was 28 (7%) African American, 124 (29%) Asian, 213 (50%) Caucasian, 22 (5%) Hispanic, and 26 (6%) classified as "Other." Nine (2%) did not provide information regarding race/ethnicity. The majority (81%) of the students were between the ages of 26 and 35 and none were over age 45.

Measures

Two methods of measuring PI were administered to the students, the CSPs and the SJPs. Due to the time constraints, the number of CSPs administered to each student was limited to two. Each student also was administered six SJPs representing two alternate scenarios. This resulted in three different pairings of CSPs and SJPs (1 and 6; 2 and 5; 3 and 4). We paired scenarios based on their time requirements, level of difficulty, functional areas addressed, and leadership skills measured. We also alternated the order of the CSPs and SJPs so as to control for potential effects of fatigue and time constraints on performance. Each student received one score for the SJPs and another for the CSPs. Scores on the SJPs represented the similarity of the student's ratings to those of the experts across all response options. For our purposes, we chose a similarity index (Pearson correlation), which looks at how closely the profile of ratings provided by the student relates to the profile provided by the experts. The Pearson r was preferred as it allowed for more straightforward interpretation of the results and enabled comparisons to be made across SJPs.[1] Scores on the CSPs reflect the overall quality rating of an individual's answers to a series of open-ended questions. Ratings were based on a scoring key derived from expert judgments and ranged from 1 (poor answer) to 5 (excellent answer).[2]

In addition to the PI measures, we administered measures of student demographics (age, gender, race/ ethnicity, citizenship), prior work experience, and prior academic performance (undergraduate GPA, GMAT score). Where available, we used GMAT scores and undergraduate GPA from business-school records to avoid potential unreliability in the self-report data. Finally, a reaction questionnaire was administered after each test format, which asked students to evaluate the measures on five dimensions: overall quality, self-assessed performance, job-relatedness, face validity, and potential use.

---

[1]The SJP scores were transformed for the purpose of analysis into Fisher z values in order to correct for non-normality in the distribution of correlation scores.
[2]Because ratings on all the CSP dimensions were highly intercorrelated, we chose to use the overall quality ratings in our analyses for parsimony.

12.3 Descriptive Statistics for Predictor and Outcome Variables (Study 1)					
Variable	N	Min	Max	Mean	SD
Prior work experience	409	12	216	63	27
GMAT score	406	530	790	677	44
Undergraduate GPA	373	2.00	4.00	3.34	.43
SJP score	387	−.17	.92	.66	.21
CSP score	421	1.00	5.00	3.05	.71
1st year GPA	361	1.40	3.93	2.93	.49
Consulting project grade	283	1.00	4.00	3.10	.62
Final GPA	358	2.07	3.96	3.05	.38
Club participation	365	0	6	2.02	1.33
Volunteer participation	365	0	5	.46	.75
Leadership positions	365	0	5	.99	.96
Internship interviews	295	0	47	9.55	6.59
Internship offers	295	0	10	2.70	1.62
Job interviews	354	0	64	7.66	8.00
Job offers	354	0	13	1.74	1.82
Base salary	309	28,000	180,000	93,216	17,166

Several criteria were used to assess student success. Performance in the MBA program was measured using GPA at the end of the 1st year and the end of the program, as well as a score on an applied team-consulting project completed during the student's first year. The consulting project was evaluated on a scale of 1 = Low Pass, 2 = Pass, 3 = Good, or 4 = Excellent. Success outside the classroom was assessed using indicators of participation in extracurricular activities, including participation in student clubs, involvement in volunteer organizations, and leadership positions held while in the MBA program. Finally, we obtained initial indicators of employment success, including the number of interviews and offers received for internships and jobs, as well as starting salary.

Procedure

The PI measures were administered on the first day of orientation week for incoming MBA students. The researchers provided a brief overview of the study's purpose and then assigned students to one of six classrooms. Second-year MBA students served as proctors and administered the measures to the students. Before completing the assessment, students read and signed a consent form to allow members of the research team to access prior and future records of performance (e.g., GMAT scores, job placement, MBA grades).

Results

Table 12.3 presents the descriptive statistics for all study variables. The average score on the SJPs was .66, indicating that students' ratings, on average, correlated fairly well with the experts' ratings. Because scores on the SJPs represented Pearson rs, we assessed reliability using Spearman–Brown split-half coefficients on the scores students received on the two sets of SJPs they completed. Reliabilities ranged from .61 to .73 across the three versions that were administered. These values are consistent with the reliabilities typically observed for situational-judgment tests, in general, and have been viewed as indicators of the multidimensional nature of such measures (Chan & Schmitt, 1998; Oswald et al., 2004). Scores on the CSPs represent the average quality rating an individual received on the two scenarios she or he completed, and ranged from 1 (poor) to 5 (excellent). The mean score on the CSPs was 3.05, indicating that students, on average, received a satisfactory rating. Intraclass correlation coefficients were used to assess the reliability across raters. The inter-rater reliabilities ranged from .62 to .79, with an average of .70 across CSPs. The average grade on the consulting project was 3.10 on a 4-point scale, with 65% of the students receiving a rating of 3 or "good," suggesting a possible leniency effect in these ratings. Finally, it is important to note that because many of the extracurricular and placement variables were skewed (e.g., the majority of students had 0 as an answer), these measures were log transformed prior to the analyses.

Predictive Validity

We first performed correlational analyses to determine the predictive validity of SJP and CSP scores relative to other predictors and the various performance criteria (see Table 12.4). Scores on both PI measures were predictive of academic success.[3] Students with higher scores on the SJPs had significantly higher 1st year and final GPAs ($r =$ .18 and .21, respectively), and also received higher grades on the team-consulting project ($r = .17$). Similarly, students with higher scores on the CSPs had significantly higher 1st year and final GPAs ($r = .21$ and .30, respectively) and higher consulting project grades ($r = .17$).

Both GMAT scores and undergraduate GPA also were significant predictors of 1st year GPA ($r = .44$ and .30, respectively) and final GPA ($r = .40$ and .32, respectively). However, GMAT scores did not correlate significantly with the consulting project grade ($r = .06$, ns). Prior work experience did not correlate with MBA grades, and actually exhibited modest negative correlations with PI measures ($r = -.12$) and undergraduate GPA ($r = -.22$).

SJP and CSP scores exhibited modest, but significant correlations with involvement in extracurricular activity. Students who scored higher on the SJPs participated in more student clubs ($r = .15$) and held more leadership positions ($r = .11$). Students with higher CSP scores held more leadership positions ($r = .18$).

Finally, there were few significant predictors of internship or job placement success as measured by the number of interviews, number of offers, and base salary. Students with higher CSP scores received more full-time job offers ($r = .11$) and students with higher GMAT scores received higher base salaries ($r = .13$). The latter finding may be attributable to the fact that many employees look at the GMAT scores of job applicants, which ultimately may influence the salary they offer.

---

[3]All correlations reported in the text are significant at $p < .05$ unless otherwise indicated.

12.4 Correlations Among Predictor and Outcome Variables (Study 1)

	1	2	3	4	5	6	7	8	9	10	11	12	13	14	15	16
1. Prior work experience	1.00															
2. GMAT score	.06	1.00														
3. Undergraduate GPA	-.22**	.18**	1.00													
4. SJP score	-.12*	.08	.03	1.00												
5. CSP score	-.12*	.04	.12*	.29**	1.00											
6. 1st year GPA	-.00	.44**	.30**	.18**	.21**	1.00										
7. Consulting project grade	-.05	.06	.15*	.17**	.17*	.12*	1.00									
8. Final GPA	.00	.40**	.32**	.21**	.30**	.85**	.36**	1.00								
9. Club participation	-.10	-.13*	-.06	.15**	.05	-.08	.02	-.06	1.00							
10. Volunteer participation	-.01	-.12	.02	.07	.03	-.11*	.00	-.08	.12*	1.00						
11. Leadership positions	-.13*	-.05	.01	.11*	.18**	-.01	.09	.05	.19**	.07	1.00					
12. Internship interviews	-.05	.08	.01	-.03	-.09	-.04	-.10	-.05	.00	-.06	.05	1.00				
13. Internship offers	-.06	-.03	.02	.01	-.01	.03	-.05	.07	.02	.03	.11	.54**	1.00			
14. Job interviews	.06	-.01	.01	-.04	-.05	-.08	-.14*	-.16	.07	-.11*	.03	.23**	.04	1.00		
15. Job offers	-.05	.01*	.04	.02	.11*	-.03	-.08	-.06	.06	.01	.16**	.11	.22**	.54**	1.00	
16. Base salary	.08	.13*	.07	-.02	.09	.03	-.11	-.01	-.06	.04	.03	.14*	.19**	.03	.06	1.00

Square-root transformations were performed on club participation, volunteer participation, and leadership positions in order to normalize the data prior to analysis.
$*p < .05$; $**p < .01$.

12.5	Hierarchical Regression Analyses of MBA Grades on Predictor Variables (Study 1)					
Step	**1st Year GPA**			**Final GPA**		
	R	ΔR^2	Beta	R	ΔR^2	Beta
1. GMAT score	.52	.27**	.41**	.50	.25**	.38**
Undergraduate GPA			.23**			.24**
2. SJP score	.55	.03**	.18**	.54	.04**	.19**
1. GMAT score	.51	.26**	.41**	.50	.25**	.37**
Undergraduate GPA			.21**			.22**
2. CSP score	.54	.03**	.18**	.55	.06**	.24**
1. GMAT score	.52	.27**	.40**	.50	.25**	.36**
Undergraduate GPA			.21**			.22**
2. CSP score	.57	.06**	.16**	.57	.08**	.21**
SJP score			.14**			.14**

*$p < .05$; **$p < .01$.

Incremental Validity

Next, we sought to determine the validity of the SJPs and CSPs relative to the two most commonly used criteria in MBA admissions, undergraduate GPA and GMAT scores. First we observed that neither SJP nor CSP scores correlated significantly with GMAT scores ($r = .08$ and $.04$, respectively, ns), suggesting that the PI measures tap distinct abilities from the GMAT. Similarly, SJP scores did not correlate with undergraduate GPA ($r = .03$, ns), but CSP scores exhibited a modest correlation with undergraduate GPA ($r = .12$).

We conducted a series of hierarchical regression analyses in order to determine the extent to which SJP and CSP scores explained individual differences in MBA performance beyond undergraduate GPA and GMAT scores. In the following hierarchical regressions, we entered GMAT scores and undergraduate GPA in the first step, followed in the second step by either SJP scores, CSP scores, or both PI measures (see Table 12.5). Based on the zero-order correlations, we chose to focus only on 1st year and final GPA in the hierarchical regression analyses.

Both SJP and CSP scores accounted for significant variance in MBA grades beyond GMAT scores and undergraduate GPA. In predicting 1st year GPA, SJP and CSP scores each accounted for an additional 3% of variance beyond GMAT and undergraduate GPA. In predicting final GPA, SJP and CSP scores accounted for 4% and 6% incremental validity, respectively.[4]

We also compared CSP and SJP scores directly and found that CSP scores were better predictors of final GPA than were SJP scores ($\beta = .21$ and $.14$, respectively). In addition, CSP scores accounted for an additional 4% variance in final GPA after accounting for SJP scores. In comparison, SJP scores only accounted for 2% variance beyond CSP scores. There were virtually no differences between SJP and CSP scores

---

[4]The calculation of final GPA includes grade received for the team-consulting project.

12.6	Differences in Test Scores as a Function of Self-Reported Race/Ethnicity (Study 1)					
		N	Mean	SD	F	p	d
GMAT	AfrAm	25	625	48	11.58	.00	-1.24
	Asian	119	684	41			.07
	Caucasian	206	681	43			–
	Hispanic	21	665	46			−.36
	Other	26	667	36			−.31
SJP	AfrAm	24	.65	.22	3.42	.01	−.14
	Asian	117	.62	.23			−.38
	Caucasian	198	.67	.19			–
	Hispanic	19	.68	.13			.09
	Other	22	.68	.20			.05
CSP	AfrAm	28	2.94	.77	9.20	.00	−.42
	Asian	123	2.79	.73			−.63
	Caucasian	213	3.24	.66			–
	Hispanic	22	2.83	.67			−.57
	Other	26	3.13	.69			−.15

in regard to predicting 1st year GPA. Finally, as shown in Table 12.5, when both scores were considered together, they explained as much as 8% additional variance in MBA grades beyond GMAT scores and undergraduate GPA.

Group Differences

Because there is evidence that females and African Americans score significantly lower on the GMAT than do other gender and racial/ethnic groups (Dobson et al., 1999; Hancock, 1999), we assessed the extent to which group differences emerged in scores on the SJPs and CSPs, and compared them to differences in GMAT scores. First, we found significant gender differences for GMAT scores, SJP scores, and CSP scores. Males scored .34 of a standard deviation higher than did females on the GMAT ($Ms = 681$ and 666, respectively, $t = -3.05$, $p < .0$ 1). Females, however, scored .24 of a standard deviation higher than did males on the SJPs ($Ms = .68$ and .65, respectively, $t = 2.29$, $p < .05$) and .39 of a standard deviation higher on the CSPs ($Ms = 3.26$ and 2.98, respectively, $t = 3.53$, $p < .01$). Using our new measures in addition to the GMAT thus helps "cancel out" the gender differences obtained when only the GMAT is used in assessment.

Second, in regard to race/ethnicity, individuals were classified based on self-report data as African American, Asian, Caucasian, Hispanic, or Other. The results of analyses of variance (ANOVAs) to test for group differences are presented in Table 12.6. We computed d values for all groups relative to Caucasians. African Americans scored 1.24 standard deviations lower than did Caucasians on the GMAT. In contrast, African Americans scored only .14 of a standard deviation lower on the SJPs and .42 of a standard deviation lower on the CSPs than did Caucasians.

Other patterns of disparities emerged on the PI measures that were not found on the GMAT. Overall, the racial/ethnic-group differences on the SJPs were modest, with the most notable disparity between Caucasians and Asians ($d = -.38$), favoring Caucasians. Differences on the CSPs were more pronounced, with the largest disparities between Caucasians and Asians ($d = -.63$), favoring Caucasians, followed by Caucasians and Hispanics ($d = -.57$), also favoring Caucasians.

One possible explanation for the pattern of disparities on the SJPs and CSPs is that not all students were native English speakers. In fact, 34% of the students in the sample classified themselves as non-U.S. citizens. These students may have had more difficulty successfully completing the measures, given the extensive reading and writing requirements. After controlling for citizenship status, differences in scores among racial/ethnic groups on the SJPs were reduced to nonsignificance. Differences in CSP scores remained, but were somewhat mitigated. Most notably, the disparity in scores between Asians and Caucasians was reduced from $-.63$ to $-.24$. Interestingly, differences in scores among racial/ethnic groups on the GMAT were only exacerbated after controlling for citizenship status. The disparity between African Americans and Caucasians increased to 1.43 standard deviations, which represents a disparity 3 times greater than that for the CSPs. Overall, these findings indicate that the SJPs and CSPs mitigate some of the disparities inherent in the GMAT, although it is clear that the CSPs present some of their own disparities that need to be addressed in further test development.

Student Reactions

The final criterion we examined was how the students perceived the PI measures. Students rated the CSPs and SJPs in terms of overall quality (16 items), self-assessed performance (3 items), job-relatedness (5 items), face validity (4 items), and potential use (4 items). Items were rated on a 5-point scale (1 = Strongly Disagree to 5 = Strongly Agree). The results of these ratings are summarized in Table 12.7.

The ratings of the SJPs and CSPs were somewhat mixed. The mean ratings for overall quality were 3.65 for the SJPs and 3.50 for the CSPs. In general, students enjoyed completing the problems, found them to be interesting and challenging, and preferred them to other assessments they have completed. Students also generally felt that they answered the questions effectively and performed as well as or better than did others in their cohort ($M = 3.35$ and 3.23 for SJPs and CSPs, respectively). Ratings regarding job-relevance and potential use, however, were more nearly neutral, indicating that there was neither agreement nor disagreement about the relevance of the new measures to MBA admissions or job performance. The lowest ratings were for face validity ($M = 2.71$ and 2.73 for SJPs and CSPs, respectively), indicating that students did not necessarily believe that the measures were fully valid indicators of their own abilities. This finding may reflect the novelty of the measures. That is, students may be reluctant to rate an assessment as a valid measure of their ability without knowing how well they actually scored on that assessment.

We also compared the students' reactions across the two measures. Significant differences were observed for all dimensions except for face validity. In general, students believed that the quality of the items and their own performance was higher on the SJPs. The CSPs, however, were seen as having greater job-relevance and potential use in admissions and selection decisions.

12.7 Student Reactions to PI Measures (Study 1)

Format / Dimension	N	M	SD	Alpha
Situational-judgment problems				
Overall quality*	346	3.65	0.46	.81
Self-assessed performance*	343	3.35	0.53	.55
Job relatedness*	343	2.92	0.71	.80
Face validity	340	2.71	0.71	.81
Potential use*	340	2.86	0.75	.80
Case scenario problems				
Overall quality	378	3.50	0.48	.80
Self-assessed performance	369	3.23	0.60	.65
Job relatedness	369	3.06	0.71	.82
Face validity	360	2.73	0.76	.83
Potential use	355	2.95	0.75	.80

*Indicates significant mean difference as a function of measurement type.

Study 2

Study 2 served as a replication of Study 1 with a new sample of MBA students.

Method

Study 2 followed the methodology of Study 1 only with slight variations as specified below.

Measures

We administered the PI measures in the same format and collected the same performance criteria as in Study 1 with the exception of placement data. Due to poor economic conditions at the time of data collection (Summer of 2002), many job offers were postponed or withdrawn. Thus, we were unable to include this information in our study.

Sample

The sample for Study 2 consisted of 370 students who entered the MBA program at University of Michigan Business School in Fall of 2000. The sample consisted of 262 (71%) males and 106 (29%) females. The racial/ethnic composition was 31 (9%) African American, 98 (27%) Asian, 191 (52%) Caucasian, 24 (7%) Hispanic, and 18 (5%) classified as "Other." Eight (2%) did not provide information regarding race/ethnicity. The majority of the sample (81%) was between the ages of 26 to 35, and no students were over the age of 45.

	12.8	Descriptive Statistics for Predictor and Outcome Variables (Study 2)				
Variable		N	Min	Max	Mean	SD
Prior work experience		346	12	204	64	27
GMAT score		356	530	770	672	47
Undergraduate GPA		328	2.12	4.30	3.32	.39
SJP score		307	.07	.87	.66	.21
CSP score		355	1.00	5.00	2.86	.76
1st year GPA		327	1.33	3.91	2.85	.51
Consulting project grade		241	1.00	4.00	2.97	.76
Final GPA		289	2.03	3.83	2.99	.42
Club participation		321	0	6	2.36	1.08
Volunteer participation		321	0	3	.60	.78
Leader positions		321	0	4	.63	.80
Internship interviews		314	0	27	8.97	5.34
Internship offers		314	0	11	1.93	1.53

Procedures

The PI measures were administered following the same procedures used in Study 1. However, there were some differences in regard to the conditions of administration. In Study 1 the PI measures were administered as part of the first day of student orientation. In Study 2 they were administered as part of a workshop held by the Office of Career Development in the evening following the first full day of classes. As a result, the sample size was smaller (377 vs. 422) and the testing conditions were less favorable (evening vs. day) in Study 2 than in Study 1.

Results

Table 12.8 presents the descriptive statistics for the Study 2 variables. Study 2 students performed comparably to Study 1 students on most of the predictor and outcome variables. The average split-half reliability on the SJPs was .65 and the average inter-rater reliability on the CSPs was .72. The only noteworthy difference is that Study 2 students scored slightly lower on the CSPs, on average, than did Study 1 students ($M = 2.86$ vs. 3.05).

Predictive Validity

The patterns of correlations observed in Study 2 were generally comparable to those found in Study 1, with a few exceptions (see Table 12.9). SJP scores correlated significantly with consulting project grade ($r = .14$) and final GPA ($r = .16$) but did not correlate with 1st year GPA ($r = .08$, ns). CSP scores correlated significantly with 1st year GPA ($r = .14$) and final GPA ($r = .18$) but only exhibited a marginally significant correlation with the consulting project grade ($r = .12$, $p < .10$).

Similar to Study 1, GMAT scores and undergraduate GPA correlated significantly with 1st year GPA ($r = .44$ and .23, respectively) and final GPA ($r = .36$ and .22,

Correlations Among Predictor and Outcome Variables (Study 2)

	1	2	3	4	5	6	7	8	9	10	11	12	13
1. Prior work experience	1.00												
2. GMAT score	-.00	1.00											
3. Undergraduate GPA	-.16**	.01	1.00										
4. SJP score	.04	-.06	-.05	1.00									
5. CSP score	-.02	.03	.05	.20**	1.00								
6. 1st year GPA	-.06	.44**	.23**	.08	.14*	1.00							
7. Consulting project grade	-.06	.00	.06	.14*	.12*	.19**	1.00						
8. Final GPA	-.02	.36**	.22**	.16*	.18**	.89**	.48**	1.00					
9. Club participation	.01	.03	.07	-.05	.14*	-.02	.06	-.01	1.00				
10. Volunteer participation	-.09	.10	.03	.07	.08	-.01	.00	.02	.13*	1.00			
11. Leadership positions	-.07	-.03	.02	.14*	.12*	-.03	.03	.02	.12*	.10	1.00		
12. Internship interviews	.05	-.01	.04	-.06	-.02	-.01	-.14*	-.12	.17*	.04	-.01	1.00	
13. Internship offers	-.01	-.07	.03	.01	.18**	.13*	.04	.10	.08	.07	.14*	.42**	1.00

Square-root transformations were performed on club participation, volunteer participation, and leadership positions in order to normalize the data prior to analysis.
$^*p < .05$; $^{**}p < .01$.

	Hierarchical Regression Analyses of MBA Grades on Predictor Variables (Study 2)					
12.10						

	1st Year GPA			Final GPA		
Step	R	ΔR^2	Beta	R	ΔR^2	Beta
1. GMAT score	.46	.21**	.41**	.37**	.14**	.33**
Undergraduate GPA			.21**			.19**
2. SJP score	.48	.01	.11	.41**	.03**	.18**
1. GMAT score	.50	.25**	.43**	.43**	.19**	.36**
Undergraduate GPA			.24**			.22**
2. CSP score	.51	.01*	.11*	.46**	.02**	.15**
1. GMAT score	.46	.21**	.40**	.38	.14**	.33**
Undergraduate GPA			.22**			.19**
2. CSP score	.48	.01	.07	.43	.04*	.11
SJP score			.09			.15*

*$p < .05$; **$p < .01$.

respectively). Once again, neither variable correlated significantly with consulting project grade ($r = .00$ and $.06$, respectively, ns).

Also consistent with Study 1, students with higher SJP and CSP scores held more leadership positions ($r = .14$ and $.12$, respectively). In addition, students with higher CSP scores participated in more clubs ($r = .14$). In contrast to Study 1, GMAT scores did not correlate with any of the extracurricular activity variables. As indicated previously, we were unable to fully examine job-placement success. However, we did collect data on the number of internship interviews and offers received. We found that CSP scores correlated significantly with the number of internship offers received ($r = .18$), whereas in Study 1 we observed a relationship between CSP scores and job offers.

Incremental Validity

Similar to Study 1, scores on the SJPs and CSPs exhibited no significant relationship with scores on the GMAT ($r = -.06$ and $.03$, respectively, ns) or undergraduate GPA ($r = -.05$ and $.05$, respectively, ns). SJP and CSP scores also explained variance in MBA performance beyond GMAT scores and undergraduate GPA, but to a lesser degree than in Study 1 (see Table 12.10). The most variance explained was for final GPA, with SJP scores accounting for 3% variance and CSP scores explaining 2% variance beyond GMAT scores and undergraduate GPA. When both PI measures were considered in combination, the incremental validity in regard to final GPA increased to 4%.

In Study 1, CSP scores appeared to be slightly better predictors of academic success than were SJP scores. In Study 2, SJP scores accounted for 2% of the variance beyond CSP scores while CSP scores accounted for only 1% of the variance beyond SJP scores, but the differences were not statistically significant.

12.11	Differences in Test Scores as a Function of Self-Reported Race/Ethnicity (Study 2)					
		N	Mean	SD	F	p	d
GMAT	AfrAm	31	627	57	13.81	.00	−1.00
	Asian	93	686	40			.26
	Caucasian	185	674	44			−
	Hispanic	23	641	42			−.70
	Other	17	682	41			.17
SJP	AfrAm	23	.66	.22	4.89	.00	−.29
	Asian	88	.62	.25			−.57
	Caucasian	156	.69	.17			−
	Hispanic	19	.68	.23			−.05
	Other	15	.63	.13			−.48
CSP	AfrAm	29	2.63	.65	4.69	.00	−.50
	Asian	94	2.66	.78			−.46
	Caucasian	188	3.01	.75			−
	Hispanic	23	2.89	.71			−.16
	Other	15	2.63	.65			−.50

Group Differences

Consistent with Study 1, we found significant gender differences for GMAT scores and CSP scores. Males scored .53 standard deviation higher than did females on the GMAT (Ms = 679 and 654, respectively, t = -4.61, $p < .01$). Females scored .29 standard deviation higher than did males on the CSPs (Ms = 3.01 and 2.79, respectively, t = 2.48, $p < .05$). In contrast to Study 1, there were no significant gender differences on the SJPs (Ms = .67 and .66 for females and males, respectively).

Similar patterns of racial/ethnic group differences emerged in Study 2 as were found in Study 1 (see Table 12.11). African Americans scored 1.00 standard deviation lower than Caucasians on the GMAT. In comparison, African Americans scored only .29 of a standard deviation lower than did Caucasians on the SJPs and .50 of a standard deviation lower on the CSPs. Once again, differences on the SJPs and CSPs appear to be attributable to discrepancies between Caucasians and all other groups. However, only one of these differences was larger than half a standard deviation. Asians scored .57 of a standard deviation lower than Caucasians on the SJPs.

As with Study 1, we conducted follow-up analyses to test for the influence of citizenship status on racial/ethnic group differences. Once again, differences in SJP scores were reduced to nonsignificance (F = .99, p = .41), with the most notable reduction in the disparity in scores between Asians and Caucasians (d = −.57 before and .00 after controlling for citizenship). A similar change was observed on the CSPs, with the difference between Asians and Caucasians reducing from d = −.46 before to d = −.08 after controlling for citizenship. Controlling for citizenship, however, had little effect on other group differences.

Format / Dimension	N	M	SD	Alpha
12.12 Student Reactions to PI Measures (Study 2)				
Situational-judgment problems				
Overall quality*	281	3.50	.46	.79
Self-assessed performance*	278	3.35	.52	.60
Job relatedness	279	2.77	.74	.83
Face validity*	272	2.50	.78	.87
Potential use	272	2.70	.78	.82
Case scenario problems				
Overall quality	281	3.29	.55	.79
Self-assessed performance	259	3.13	.66	.75
Job relatedness	257	2.87	.78	.87
Face validity	242	2.37	.80	.88
Potential use	242	2.67	.81	.84

*Indicates significant mean difference as a function of measurement type.

Student Reactions

The pattern of ratings across the five dimensions (overall quality, self-assessed performance, job relevance, face validity, and potential use) was consistent with Study 1, but, overall, the mean ratings tended to be slightly lower in Study 2 (see Table 12.12). Students tended to rate the measures favorably in regard to quality ($M = 3.50$ for SJPs and 3.29 for CSPs), and they were more likely to agree than disagree that they answered the questions effectively ($M = 3.35$ for SJPs and 3.13 for CSPs). In Study 2, the students were less likely to agree that the problems were job relevant, face valid, or potentially useful for selection or admissions purposes. Again, the lowest ratings were for face validity ($M = 2.50$ for SJPs and 2.37 for CSPs).

In comparing students' ratings across measures, we again found that the SJPs were rated higher on overall quality and self-assessed performance than were the CSPs. However, in contrast to Study 1, there were no significant differences between the SJPs and CSPs in regard to job-relatedness or potential use.

General Discussion

Our research was prompted by concerns regarding the potential over-reliance on conventional standardized testing in graduate admissions, with specific focus on the GMAT in graduate business school admissions. The concerns with standardized tests like the GMAT are that (a) they measure a limited set of skills relevant to success, accounting for only 20% to 25% of the variance in criterion performance, and (b) they produce disparities in scores among gender and racial/ethnic groups. Our goal was not to replace, but rather to supplement, the GMAT by measuring abilities it does not intend to assess. Specifically, we sought to develop measures of practical intelligence (PI) to complement the analytical emphasis of the GMAT. We administered two types of PI measures (knowledge-based situational-judgment problems and skill-based case scenario problems) to two samples of incoming MBA students and evaluated their predictive validity and potential for adverse impact relative to the GMAT. We summarize and discuss the key findings below.

Adding Value Beyond GMAT Scores

First and foremost, we examined the extent to which the PI measures predicted success in the MBA program. In general, scores on the PI measures correlated significantly with performance in the program as indicated by graduate GPA and faculty evaluations on a team-consulting project. In addition, CSP and SJP scores correlated moderately with indicators of success outside the classroom, such as the number of leadership positions held and the number of internship and job offers received. As expected, GMAT scores and undergraduate GPA correlated significantly with graduate GPA, but GMAT scores failed to correlate significantly with the consulting project grade. The latter results suggest that some aspects of graduate school performance are not accounted for by GMAT scores and also are consistent with the finding of Peiperl and Trevelyan (1997) that GMAT scores were not predictive of how students performed on group assignments. It is important to note that GMAT scores did correlate significantly with base salary in Study 1, which does support the findings of Kuncel, Hezlett, and Ones (2004) that analytically oriented tests like the GMAT have predictive validity in regard to work-related criteria.

We next addressed the incremental validity of the PI measures relative to GMAT scores and undergraduate GPA. First, we found no significant correlations between GMAT scores and PI scores, suggesting that the SJPs and CSPs are measuring abilities that are distinct from those measured by the GMAT. Second, both the SJPs and CSPs explained significant variance in grades, particularly final GPA, beyond GMAT scores and undergraduate GPA. Although these increments may be considered modest (ranging from 2% to 6%), Oswald et al. (2004) argued that even an increment of 6% has the potential of adding practical value in college admissions. Further, when both PI measures are considered together, they account for as much as 8% of the variance beyond GMAT scores and undergraduate GPA. Thus a combination of the two measures might provide even greater value to MBA admissions.

In general, the findings of Study 2 are comparable to the findings of Study 1. In both studies, the SJPs and CSPs were predictive of academic performance and accounted for significant variance beyond GMAT scores and undergraduate GPA. However, the effect sizes were slightly smaller in Study 2 compared with Study 1. One possible explanation for the smaller effect sizes in Study 2 was differences in the conditions under which the measures were administered. In Study 2 the PI measures were administered during an optional evening workshop following the first full day of classes, whereas in Study 1 they were administered during the daytime as part of new student orientation. Additionally, in Study 1 the researchers provided a brief overview of the study's purpose, whereas no such overview was provided in Study 2. As a result, the students in Study 2 may have been less motivated and may have been fatigued, which could have negatively affected their performance. Some direct comparisons of the data from Studies 1 and 2 support this explanation. On the CSPs, which require more effort than the SJPs, students in Study 2 scored significantly lower than students in Study 1 ($M = 2.86$ and 3.05, respectively, $t = 3.71$, $p < .01$). In addition, students in Study 2 rated both PI measures significantly lower in terms of overall quality, job relevance, face validity, and potential use than students in Study 1, which may indicate a generally less positive attitude toward the test.

Reducing the Potential for Adverse Impact

The second main limitation of the GMAT that we attempted to address is the existence of disparities in scores across gender and racial/ethnic groups. Our findings were consistent with previous research in that females scored lower than males and African American students scored lower than other groups that were tested (Dobson et al., 1999; Hancock, 1999). The largest disparity was between African American and Caucasian students, with differences equal to or greater than one standard deviation found in both studies.

We also found significant group differences on the new measures, but the differences tended to be smaller in magnitude and dissimilar in pattern to those observed on the GMAT. Gender differences on the PI measures were comparable in magnitude to the GMAT, but in contrast to the GMAT, females scored higher than males on both the CSPs and SJPs. In regard to self-reported racial/ethnic group, Asian students, rather than African American students, had the lowest scores of all groups on the PI measures. These differences were found to be attributable, in part, to citizenship status. After controlling for citizenship status, differences between Asian and Caucasian students were substantially reduced, if not altogether eliminated. Differences remained between African American and Caucasian students, but these disparities were less than half the magnitude of those found for the GMAT. Therefore, PI measures have the potential to correct or to at least partially compensate for some of the disparities in GMAT scores, and thus to reduce the possibility of adverse impact in admissions.

Knowledge vs. Skill-Based Measures of Practical Intelligence

We chose to explore two ways of measuring practical intelligence. The SJPs were patterned after a knowledge-based approach used in previous research (Hedlund et al., 2003; Wagner, 1987; Wagner et al., 1999). This approach assesses an individual's ability to identify more and less appropriate responses to brief problem descriptions, in other words, the individual's tacit knowledge. The concern with using this type of measure was that it could give those applicants with prior managerial experience an unfair advantage in the admission process. The CSPs represented an alternative approach that involves assessing a specific set of skills associated with solving practical problems. These skills include problem identification, information processing, solution generation, and outcome monitoring. The concern with using this type of assessment is that it can be lengthy to administer and difficult to score.

It is clear from our findings that there are some inherent differences between the two PI measures. The CSPs exhibited slightly better predictive and incremental validities than the SJPs in regard to academic performance. The SJPs, on the other hand, produced less disparity in scores than the CSPs. There also were some notable differences in the ratings of the SJPs and CSPs. The students preferred the format of the SJPs and evaluated their own performance to be higher on the SJPs, but they tended to view the CSPs as more relevant to job performance and more potentially useful in an admission process. Finally, prior work experience was unrelated to scores on both measures, thus eliminating the main concern with using the SJPs with this population. This finding also suggests that the SJPs may be measuring general knowledge (e.g., common sense or good judgment) rather than job-specific knowledge, as has been proposed by past research on tacit knowledge.

Unfortunately, the results do not unilaterally favor one PI measure over the other. Instead, they suggest that both PI measures, through further development, may add value to the MBA admissions process. We also found that using both measures, along with GMAT scores and undergraduate GPA, further improves the prediction of graduate school performance beyond using either measure alone. This result indicates that the CSPs and SJPs are tapping into somewhat different aspects of practical intelligence, as intended, and that both aspects are relevant to performance.

Limitations and Directions for Future Research

There are several limitations of our work that need to be addressed through future research. First, our studies were conducted with just one institution and may not be representative of the results that would be obtained with other MBA programs. Depending on the emphasis placed on the development of practical skills, the SJPs and CSPs may be more or less predictive in other MBA programs. However, the predictive validity of the GMAT in our studies were consistent with those found with samples from other institutions, which suggests that our results may generalize to other schools. Nevertheless, further studies need to be conducted to replicate our findings with other MBA programs.

Second, the validation samples involved students who have already been selected on several criteria, including GMAT scores. Thus, our results indicate predictive validity only within a restricted range of scores. However, because we do not have population estimates for the PI measures, we did not and could not correct for range restriction in our analyses.[5] It is likely that our findings represent conservative estimates of the actual validity of the measures. Ideally, the measures should be validated with a sample from an extensive and broad MBA applicant pool.

Third, group differences emerged on our measures that were unexpected. In particular, we found differences that appeared to be attributable, in part, to the influence of citizenship status (and the background variables for which it is presumably a proxy variable). That is, non-U.S. citizens received lower scores on the measures than did U.S. citizens. These findings may reflect cultural differences in managerial or leadership styles or first-language differences. The sample used to develop the scoring key for the SJPs and the raters who scored the CSPs were predominantly U.S. citizens. If there are cultural variations in the proper way to solve business problems, than it is possible that the responses of non-U.S. citizens would be inconsistent with those viewed as appropriate according to our expert standard, thus resulting in lower scores. In an increasingly global economy, the existence of such differences merits further attention, particularly as they relate to graduate admissions.

---

[5]Corrections for range restriction were computed on zero-order correlations involving GMAT scores. These corrections did not result in any substantial increases or decreases in effect sizes.

Fourth, there is a need to conduct more extensive longitudinal research in order fully to assess the predictive validity of the measures relative to work-related criteria. Our studies tracked students only through the first summer after completing the program. In Study 2, our data collection was negatively affected by poor economic conditions that reduced the number of opportunities for MBA graduates. There were preliminary indicators that CSP and SJP scores may predict success after graduation in terms of job search outcomes, but it will be important to determine the extent to which they predict long-term career success.

Finally, it is important to note that this study represents the initial development and administration of PI measures for MBA admissions. In addition, this study involves the first specific attempt to develop a skill-based measure of practical intelligence. In contrast, the GMAT has been in use since 1954. Clearly, further instrument development is needed to improve the quality of the measures. Post hoc analyses indicated that some versions of the PI measures, which included different sets of CSPs and SJPs, were more predictive than others. With further item development, it is plausible, although not certain, that the predictive and incremental validity of the SJPs and CSPs would improve. It also is worth exploring the possibility of combining the CSP and SJP in some way that maximizes the predictive and incremental validity offered by adding PI to the admission process.

Conclusions

We sought to broaden the range of abilities considered in MBA admission beyond those tapped by the GMAT and undergraduate GPA. Our results indicate that measures of PI predict performance inside and outside the classroom, explain individual differences in MBA grades modestly to moderately beyond GMAT scores, predict performance on a team consulting project better than the GMAT, and generally exhibit less disparity across groups than the GMAT. In the increasingly competitive business environment, it is important to understand what it takes to succeed and to know how to identify and develop the talent that leads to success. The traditional admissions process, which relies primarily on GMAT scores and undergraduate grades, does not take into account the full range of abilities that are important for success. Our research showed that PI measures have the potential to improve the prediction of success in business school and beyond. Furthermore, PI measures may ultimately prove beneficial to graduate and undergraduate admissions in general.

References

Ahmadi, M., Raiszadeh, F., & Helms, M. (1997). An examination of the admission criteria for the MBA programs: A case study. *Education, 117,* 540–546.

Bracey, G. W. (2001). Test scores in the long run. *Phi Delta Kappan,* 637–638.

Bray, D. W. (1982). The assessment center and the study of lives. *American Psychologist, 37,* 180–189.

Bretz, R. D. (1989). College grade point average as a predictor of adult success: A meta-analytic review and some additional evidence. *Public Personnel Management, 18,* 11–22.

Chan, D., & Schmitt, N. (1998). Video-based versus paper-and-pencil method of assessment in situational judgment tests: Subgroup differences in test performance and face validity perceptions. *Journal of Applied Psychology, 82,* 143–159.

Colonia-Willner, R. (1998). Practical intelligence at work: Relationship between aging and cognitive efficiency among managers in a bank environment. *Psychology and Aging, 13,* 45–57.

Darling-Hammond, L. (1991). The implications of testing policy for quality and equality. *Phi Delta Kappan, 73*, 220–225.

Dobson, P., Krapljan-Barr, P., & Vielba, C. (1999). An evaluation of the validity and fairness of the Graduate Management Admissions Tests (GMAT) used for MBA selection in a UK business school. *International Journal of Selection and Assessment, 7*, 196–202.

Fox, S., & Spector, P. E. (2000). Relations of emotional intelligence, practical intelligence, general intelligence, and trait affectivity with interview outcomes: It's not all just 'G.' *Journal of Organizational Behavior, 21*, 203–220.

Frederiksen, N. (1966). Validation of a simulation technique. *Organizational Behavior and Human Performance, 1*, 87–109.

Frederiksen, N., Saunders, D. R., & Wand, B. (1957). The in-basket test. *Psychological Monographs, 71.*

Frey, M. C., & Detterman, D. K. (2004). Scholastic assessment or g? The relationship between the scholastic assessment test and general cognitive ability. *Psychological Science, 15*, 373–378.

Gardner, H. (1993). *Multiple intelligences: The theory in practice.* New York: Basic Books.

Gardner, H. (1999). *Reframing intelligence.* New York: Basic Books.

Goleman, D. (1998). *Working with emotional intelligence.* New York: Bantam Books.

Graham, L. D. (1991). Predicting academic success of students in a Masters of Business Administration Program. *Educational and Psychological Measurement, 51*, 721–727.

Hancock, T. (1999). The gender difference: Validity of standardized American tests in predicting MBA performance. *Journal of Education for Business, 75*, 91–94.

Hartigan, J. A., & Wigdor, A. K. (Eds.). (1989). *Fairness in employment testing: Validity generalization, minority issues, and the general aptitude test battery.* Washington, DC: National Academy Press.

Hedlund, J., Forsythe, G. B., Horvath, J., Williams, W. M., Snook, S., & Sternberg, R. J. (2003). Identifying and assessing tacit knowledge: Understanding the practical intelligence of military leaders. *Leadership Quarterly, 14*, 117–140.

Hedlund, J., Sternberg, R. J., & Psotka, J. (2001). *Tacit knowledge for military leadership: Seeking insight into the acquisition and use of practical knowledge* (Tech. Rep. No. 1105). Alexandria, VA: U.S. Army Research Institute for the Behavioral and Social Sciences.

Hough, L. M., Oswald, F. L., & Ployhart, R. E. (2001). Determinants, detection and amelioration of adverse impact in personnel selection procedures: Issues, evidence and lessons learned. *International Journal of Selection and Assessment, 9*, 152–194.

Jaffe, E. D., & Hilbert, S. (1994). *How to prepare for the graduate management admission test* (10th ed.). Hauppauge, NY: Barron's Educational Series.

Jensen, A. R. (1998). *The g factor.* Westport, CT: Greenwood-Praeger.

Kuncel, N. R., Hezlett, S. A., & Ones, D. S. (2004). Academic performance, career potential, creativity, and job performance: Can one construct predict them all? *Journal of Personality and Social Psychology, 86*, 148–161.

Mayer, J. D., Salovey, P., & Caruso, D. (2000). Competing models of emotional intelligence. In R. J. Sternberg (Ed.), *Handbook of intelligence* (pp. 396–420). New York: Cambridge University Press.

Mintzberg, H. (1980). *The nature of managerial work.* Englewood Cliffs, NJ: Prentice-Hall.

Motowidlo, S. J., Dunnette, M. D., & Carter, G. W. (1990). An alternative selection procedure: The low-fidelity simulation. *Journal of Applied Psychology, 75*, 640–647.

Neisser, U. (1976). *Cognition and reality.* San Francisco: Freeman.

Nilsson, J. E. (1995). The GRE and the GMAT: A comparison of their correlations to GGPA. *Educational and Psychological Measurement, 55*, 637–641.

Oswald, F. L., Schmitt, N., Kim, B. H., Ramsay, L. J., & Gillespie, M. A. (2004). Developing a biodata measure and situational judgment inventory as predictors of college student performance. *Journal of Applied Psychology, 89*, 187–207.

Paolillo, J. (1982). The predictive validity of selected admissions variables relative to grade point average earned in a Masters of Business Administration program. *Educational and Psychological Measurement, 42*, 1163–1167.

Peiperl, M. A., & Trevelyan, R. (1997). Predictors of performance at business school and beyond: Demographic factors and the contrast between individual and group outcomes. *Journal of Management, 16*, 354–363.

Polanyi, M. (1976). Tacit knowledge. In M. Marx & F. Goodson (Eds.), *Theories in contemporary psychology* (pp. 330–344). New York: Macmillan.

Pulakos, E. D., & Schmitt, N. (1996). An evaluation of two strategies for reducing adverse impact and their effects on criterion-related validity. *Human Performance, 9*, 241–258.

Pulakos, E. D., Schmitt, N., & Chan, D. (1996). Models of job performance ratings: An examination of ratee race, ratee gender, and rater level effects. *Human Performance, 9*, 103–119.

Sacket, P. R., Schmitt, N., Ellington, J. E., & Kabin, M. B. (2001). High-stakes testing in employment, credentialing, and higher education: Prospects in a post-affirmative-action world. *American Psychologist, 56*, 302–318.

Schmidt, F. L. (1988). The problem of group differences in ability test scores in employment selection. *Journal of Vocational Behavior, 33*, 272–292.

Schmidt, F. L., & Hunter, J. E. (1998). The validity and utility of selection methods in personnel psychology: Practical and theoretical implications of 85 years of research findings. *Psychological Bulletin, 124*, 262–274.

Sternberg, R. J. (1985). *Beyond IQ: A triarchic theory of human intelligence*. New York: Cambridge University Press.

Sternberg, R. J. (1997). *Successful intelligence*. New York: Plume Books.

Sternberg, R. J. (1999). Intelligence as developing expertise. *Contemporary Educational Psychology, 24*, 259–375.

Sternberg, R. J., Forsythe, G. B., Hedlund, J., Horvath, J. A., Wagner, R. K., Williams, W. M., et al. (2000). *Practical intelligence in everyday life*. New York: Cambridge University Press.

Sternberg, R. J., & Horvath, J. A. (Eds.). (1999). *Tacit knowledge in professional practice*. Mahwah, NJ: Erlbaum.

Sternberg, R. J., Nokes, K., Geissler, P. W., Prince, R., Okatcha, F., Bundy, D. A., & Grigorenko, E. L. (2001). The relationship between academic and practical intelligence: A case study in Kenya. *Intelligence, 29*, 401–418.

Sternberg, R. J., & Wagner, R. K. (1993). The geocentric view of intelligence and job performance is wrong. *Current Directions in Psychological Science, 2*, 1–5.

Sternberg, R. J., Wagner, R. K., & Okagaki, L. (1993). Practical intelligence: The nature and role of tacit knowledge in work and at school. In H. Reese & J. Puckett (Eds.), *Advances in lifespan development* (pp. 205–227). Hillsdale, NJ: Erlbaum.

Sternberg, R. J., Wagner, R. K., Williams, W. M., & Horvath, J. A. (1995). Testing common sense. *American Psychologist, 32*, 912–927.

Thornton, G. C., & Byham, W. C. (1982). Developing managerial talent through simulation. *American Psychologist, 45*, 190–199.

Wagner, R. K. (1987). Tacit knowledge in everyday intelligent behavior. *Journal of Personality and Social Psychology, 52*, 1236–1247.

Wagner, R. K., & Sternberg, R. J. (1985). Practical intelligence in real-world pursuits: The role of tacit knowledge. *Journal of Personality and Social Psychology, 49*, 436–458.

Wagner, R. K., & Sternberg, R. J. (1986). Tacit knowledge and intelligence in the everyday world. In R. J. Sternberg & R. K. Wagner (Eds.), *Practical intelligence: Nature and origins of competence in the everyday world* (pp. 51–83). New York: Cambridge University Press.

Wagner, R. K., & Sternberg, R. J. (1990). Street smarts. In K. E. Clark & M. B. Clark (Eds.), *Measures of leadership* (pp. 493–504). West Orange, NJ: Leadership Library of America.

Wagner, R. K., Sujan, H., Sujan, M., Rashotte, C. A., & Sternberg, R. J. (1999). Tacit knowledge in sales. In R. J. Sternberg & J. A. Horvath (Eds.), *Tacit knowledge in professional practice* (pp. 155–182). Mahwah, NJ: Erlbaum.

Williams, W. M. (2000). Perspectives on intelligence testing, affirmative action, and educational policy. *Psychology, Public Policy, and Law, 6*, 5–19.

Wright, R. E., & Palmer, J. C. (1994). GMAT scores and undergraduate GPAs as predictors of performance in graduate business programs. *Journal of Education for Business, 69*, 344–349.

Youngblood, S. A., & Martin, B. J. (1982). Ability testing and graduate admissions: Decision process modeling and validation. *Educational and Psychological Measurement, 42*, 1153–1161.

Yukl, G. (1998). *Leadership in organizations* (4th ed.). Upper Saddle River, NJ: Prentice-Hall.

Section V

Successful Intelligence, Leadership, and Wisdom

A Balance Theory of Wisdom

13

Robert J. Sternberg

Wisdom can be defined as the "power of judging rightly and following the soundest course of action, based on knowledge, experience, understanding, etc." *(Webster's New World College Dictionary,* 1997, p. 1533). Such a power would seem to be of vast importance in a world that at times appears bent on destroying itself. My goal in this essay is to provide the beginnings of a psychological theory of wisdom and to relate it to other psychological constructs. I will first review some major attempts to understand wisdom, then describe the proposed approach to wisdom, and finally suggest how wisdom might be measured and developed. Other more comprehensive reviews can be found elsewhere (Baltes, 2004; Sternberg, 1990b).

Major Approaches to Understanding Wisdom

A number of scholars have attempted to understand wisdom in different ways. The approaches underlying some of these attempts are summarized in Sternberg (1990a). The approaches might be classified as *philosophical, implicit theoretical,* and *explicit theoretical* approaches.

Philosophical Approaches

Philosophical approaches have been reviewed by Robinson (1990; see also Robinson, 1989, with regard to the Aristotelian approach in particular, and Labouvie-Vief, 1990, for further review). Robinson noted that the study of wisdom has a history that long antedates psychological study, with the Platonic dialogues offering the first intensive Western analysis of the concept of wisdom. Robinson pointed out that, in these dialogues, there are three different senses of wisdom: wisdom as (a) *sophia,* which is found in those who seek a contemplative life in search of truth; (b) *phronesis,* which is the kind of practical wisdom shown by statesmen and legislators; and (c) *episteme,* which is found in those who understand things from a scientific point of view.

Aristotle distinguished between *phronesis,* the kind of practical wisdom mentioned above, and *theoretikes,* or theoretical knowledge devoted to truth. Robinson noted that, according to Aristotle, a wise individual knows more than the material, efficient, or formal causes behind events. This individual also knows the final cause, or that for the sake of which the other kinds of causes apply.

Other philosophical conceptions of wisdom have followed up on the early Greek ones. Of course, it is not possible to review all of these conceptions here. But as an example, an early Christian view emphasized the importance of a life lived in pursuit of divine and absolute truth. To this day, most religions aim for wisdom through an understanding not just of the material world, but also of the spiritual world and its relationship to the material world.

Implicit Theoretical Approaches

Implicit theoretical approaches to wisdom have in common the search for an understanding of people's folk conceptions of what wisdom is. Thus, the goal is not to provide a "psychologically true" account of wisdom, but rather an account that is true with respect to people's beliefs, whether these beliefs are right or wrong.

Some of the earliest work of this kind was done by Clayton (1975, 1976, 1982; Clayton & Birren, 1980), who multidimensionally scaled ratings of pairs of words potentially related to wisdom for three samples of adults differing in age (younger, middle aged, older). In her earliest study (Clayton, 1975), the terms scaled were ones such as *experienced, pragmatic, understanding,* and *knowledgeable.* In each study, participants were asked to rate similarities between all possible pairs of words. Two consistent dimensions of wisdom, which Clayton referred to as an *affective dimension* and a *reflective dimension,* emerged from the results of the scalings among age cohorts. There was also a suggestion of a dimension relating to age. The greatest difference among the age cohorts was that mental representations of wisdom seemed to become more differentiated (i.e., to increase in dimensionality) with increases in the ages of the participants.

Holiday and Chandler (1986) also used an implicit-theories approach to understanding wisdom. Approximately 500 participants were studied across a series of experiments. The investigators were interested in determining whether the concept of wisdom could be understood as a *prototype* (Rosch, 1975), or central concept. Principal-components analysis of one of their studies revealed five underlying factors: Exceptional Understanding, Judgment and Communication Skills, General Competence, Interpersonal Skills, and Social Unobtrusiveness.

Sternberg (1985b) has reported a series of studies investigating implicit theories of wisdom. In one study (Sternberg, 1985b), 200 professors each of art, business, philosophy, and physics were asked to rate the characteristics of each of the behaviors obtained in a prestudy from the corresponding population with respect to the professors' ideal conception of each of an ideally wise, intelligent, or creative individual in their occupation. Laypersons were also asked to provide these ratings but for a hypothetical ideal individual without regard to occupation. Correlations were computed across the three ratings. In each group except philosophy, the highest correlation was between wisdom and intelligence; in philosophy, the highest correlation was between intelligence and creativity. The correlations between wisdom and intelligence ratings ranged from .42 to .78, with a median of .68. For all groups, the lowest correlation was between wisdom and creativity. Correlations between wisdom and creativity ratings ranged from−.24 to .48, with a median of .27. The only negative correlation (−.24) was for ratings of professors of business.

In a second study (Sternberg, 1985b), 40 college students were asked to sort three sets of 40 behaviors each into as many or as few piles on the basis of similarity as they wished. The 40 behaviors in each set were the top-rated wisdom, intelligence, and creativity behaviors from the previous study. The sortings were then each subjected to nonmetric multidimensional scaling. For wisdom, six components emerged: *Reasoning Ability, Sagacity, Learning From Ideas and Environment, Judgment, Expeditious Use of Information,* and *Perspicacity.*

Examples of behaviors showing high loadings under reasoning ability were, "has the unique ability to look at a problem or situation and solve it," "has good problem-solving ability," and "has a logical mind." Participants characterized sagacity by identifying behaviors such as "displays concern for others," "considers advice," and "understands people through dealing with a variety of people." They characterized learning from ideas and environment with such qualities as "attaches importance to ideas," "is perceptive," and "learns from other people's mistakes." "Acts within own physical and intellectual limitations," "is sensible," and "has good judgment at all times" showed high loadings for judgment. The qualities "is experienced," "seeks out information, especially details," and "has age, maturity, or long experience" were key for expeditious use of information. "Has intuition," "can offer solutions that are on the side of right and truth," and "is able to see through things—read between the lines" showed high loadings for perspicacity.

In this same study, components for intelligence were *Practical Problem-Solving Ability, Verbal Ability, Intellectual Balance and Integration, Goal Orientation and Attainment, Contextual Intelligence,* and *Fluid Thought.* Components for creativity were *Nonentrenchment, Integration and Intellectuality, Aesthetic Taste and Imagination, Decisional Skill and Flexibility, Perspicacity, Drive for Accomplishment and Recognition, Inquisitiveness,* and *Intuition.*

In a third study (Sternberg, 1985b), 50 adults were asked to rate descriptions of hypothetical individuals for intelligence, creativity, and wisdom. Correlations were computed between pairs of ratings of the hypothetical individuals' levels of the three traits. Correlations between the ratings were .94 for wisdom and intelligence, .62 for wisdom and creativity, and .69 for intelligence and creativity, again suggesting that wisdom and intelligence are highly correlated in people's implicit theories.

Explicit Theoretical Approaches

Explicit theories are constructions of (supposedly) expert theorists and researchers rather than of laypeople. In the study of wisdom, most explicit-theoretical approaches are based on constructs from the psychology of human development.

The most extensive program of research in this area has been that conducted by Baltes and his colleagues. For example, Baltes and Smith (1987, 1990) gave adult participants life-management problems, such as, "A 14-year-old girl is pregnant. What should she, what should one, consider and do?" and "A 15-year-old girl wants to marry soon. What should she, what should one, consider and do?" Baltes and Smith tested a five-component model on participants' protocols in answering these and other questions, based on a notion of wisdom as expert knowledge about fundamental life matters (Smith & Baltes, 1990) or of wisdom as good judgment and advice in important but uncertain matters of life (Baltes & Staudinger, 1993).

A model of wisdom emerged from the work of Baltes and his colleagues (Baltes, 2004): Three kinds of factors—general person factors, expertise-specific factors, and facilitative experiential contexts—facilitate wise judgments. These factors are used in life planning, management, and review. Wisdom is in turn then reflected in five components: (a) rich factual knowledge (general and specific knowledge about the conditions of life and its variations); (b) rich procedural knowledge (general and specific knowledge about strategies of judgment and advice concerning matters of life); (c) life-span contextualism (knowledge about the contexts of life and their temporal [developmental] relationships); (d) relativism (knowledge about differences in values, goals, and priorities); and (e) uncertainty (knowledge about the relative indeterminacy and unpredictability of life and ways to manage). An expert answer should reflect more of these components, whereas a novice answer should reflect fewer of them. The data that Baltes has collected to date generally have been supportive of the model.

Over time, Baltes and his colleagues (e.g., Baltes, Smith, & Staudinger, 1992; Baltes & Staudinger, 1993) have collected a wide range of data showing the empirical usefulness of the proposed theoretical and measurement approaches to wisdom. For example, Staudinger, Lopez, and Baltes (1997) found that measures of intelligence and personality as well as their interface overlap with but are not identical to measures of wisdom in terms of constructs measured. Also, Staudinger, Smith, and Baltes (1992) showed that human-services professionals outperformed a control group on wisdom-related tasks. They also showed that older adults performed as well on such tasks as did younger adults and that older adults did better on such tasks if there was a match between their age and the age of the fictitious characters about whom they made judgments. Baltes, Staudinger, Maercker, and Smith (1995) found that older individuals nominated for their wisdom performed as well as did clinical psychologists on wisdom-related tasks. They also showed that up to the age of 80, older adults performed as well on such tasks as younger adults. In another set of studies, Staudinger and Baltes (1996) found that performance settings that were ecologically relevant to the lives of their participants and that provided for actual or "virtual" interaction of minds substantially increased wisdom-related performance.

Sternberg (1990b) also proposed an explicit theory, suggesting that the development of wisdom can be traced to six antecedent components: (a) knowledge, including an understanding of its presuppositions and meaning as well as its limitations; (b) processes, including an understanding of what problems should be solved automatically and what problems should not be so solved; (c) a judicial thinking style, characterized by the desire to judge and evaluate things in an in-depth way; (d) personality, including tolerance of ambiguity and of the role of obstacles in life; (e) motivation, especially the motivation to understand what is known and what it means; and (f) environmental context, involving an appreciation of the contextual factors in the environment that lead to various kinds of thoughts and actions. Whereas my (Sternberg, 1990b) theory specified a set of antecedents of wisdom, the balance theory I propose here specifies the processes (balancing of interests and of responses to environmental contexts) in relation to the goal of wisdom (achievement of a common good). My earlier theory is incorporated into the balance theory as specifying antecedent sources of developmental and individual differences, as discussed later.

Some theorists have viewed wisdom in terms of post–formal-operational thinking, thereby viewing wisdom as extending beyond the Piagetian stages of intelligence (Piaget, 1972). Wisdom thus might be a stage of thought beyond Piagetian formal operations. For example, some authors have argued that wise individuals are those who can think reflectively or dialectically, in the latter case with the individuals' realizing that truth is not always absolute but rather evolves in a historical context of theses, antitheses, and syntheses (e.g., Basseches, 1984; Kitchener, 1983, 1986; Kitchener & Brenner, 1990; Kitchener & Kitchener, 1981; Labouvie-Vief, 1980, 1982, 1990; Pascual-Leone, 1990; Riegel, 1973). Consider a very brief review of some specific dialectical approaches.

Kitchener and Brenner (1990) suggested that wisdom requires a synthesis of knowledge from opposing points of view. Similarly, Labouvie-Vief (1990) emphasized the importance of a smooth and balanced dialogue between logical forms of processing and more subjective forms of processing. Pascual-Leone (1990) argued for the importance of the dialectical integration of all aspects of a person's affect, cognition, conation (motivation), and life experience. Similarly, Orwoll and Perlmutter (1990) emphasized the importance of an integration of cognition with affect to wisdom. Kramer (1990) suggested the importance of the integration of relativistic and dialectical modes of thinking, affect, and reflection. And Birren and Fisher (1990), putting together a number of views of wisdom, also suggested the importance of the integration of cognitive, conative, and affective aspects of human abilities.

Other theorists have suggested the importance of knowing the limits of one's own extant knowledge and of then trying to go beyond it. For example, Meacham (1990) suggested that an important aspect of wisdom is an awareness of one's own fallibility and a knowledge of what one does and does not know. Kitchener and Brenner (1990) also emphasized the importance of knowing the limitations of one's own knowledge. Arlin (1990) linked wisdom to problem finding, the first step of which is the recognition that how one currently defines a problem may be inadequate. Arlin views problem finding as a possible stage of post–formal operational thinking. Such a view is not necessarily inconsistent with the view of dialectical thinking as such a post–formal-operational stage. Dialectical thinking and problem finding could represent distinct post–formal-operational stages or two manifestations of the same post–formal-operational stage.

Although most developmental approaches to wisdom are ontogenetic, Csikszentmihalyi and Rathunde (1990) have taken a philogenetic or evolutionary approach, arguing that constructs such as wisdom must have been selected for over time, at least in a cultural sense (see also Csikszentmihalyi, 1988). In other words, wise ideas should survive better over time than unwise ideas in a culture. The theorists define *wisdom* as having three basic dimensions of meaning: (a) that of a *cognitive process*, or a particular way of obtaining and processing information; (b) that of a *virtue*, or socially valued pattern of behavior; and (c) that of a good, or personally desirable state or condition.

Tacit Knowledge as the Core of Wisdom

The Nature of Tacit Knowledge

The view of wisdom proposed here has at its core the notion of tacit knowledge (Polanyi, 1976) about oneself, others, and situational contexts. *Tacit* knowledge is action oriented, typically acquired without direct help from others, and allows individuals to achieve goals they personally value (Sternberg, Wagner, Williams, & Horvath, 1995). Tacit knowledge thus has three main features: (a) it is procedural, (b) it is relevant to the attainment of goals people value, and (c) it typically is acquired with little help from others. Tacit knowledge is an important part of practical intelligence, and indeed, the particular notion of tacit knowledge used here derives from my triarchic theory of intelligence (Sternberg, 1985a, 1997a). An advantage of the proposed theory is that it draws on a theory of intelligence (the triarchic one) at the same time that it makes explicit how wisdom is different from the various aspects of intelligence as they are typically encountered.

When people refer to tacit knowledge as being procedural and as intimately related to action, they are viewing it as a form of "knowing how" rather than of "knowing that" (Ryle, 1949). In our work (Sternberg et al., 1995), we view condition–action sequences (production systems) as a useful formalism for understanding the mental representation of tacit knowledge (see also Horvath et al., 1996). For example, if one needs to deliver bad news to one's boss, and it is Monday morning, and the boss's golf game was rained out the day before, and the boss's staff seems to be "walking on eggshells," then it is better to wait until later to deliver the news. Note that tacit knowledge is always wedded to particular uses in particular situations or classes of situations.

Tacit knowledge also is practically useful. It is instrumental to the attainment of goals that people value. Thus people use this knowledge in order to achieve success in life, however they may define success. Abstract academic knowledge about procedures for solving problems with no relevance to life would not be viewed, in this perspective, as constituting tacit knowledge. Finally, tacit knowledge typically is acquired without direct help from others. At best, others can guide one to acquire this knowledge. Often, environmental support for the acquisition of this knowledge is minimal, and sometimes organizations actually suppress the acquisition of tacit knowledge. For example, an organization might not want its employees to know how personnel decisions are really made, as opposed to how they are supposed to be made. From a developmental standpoint, this view suggests that wisdom is not taught so much as indirectly acquired. One can provide the circumstances for the development of wisdom and case studies to help students develop wisdom, but one cannot teach particular courses of action that would be considered wise, regardless of circumstances. Indeed, tacit knowledge is wedded to contexts, so that the tacit knowledge that would apply in one context would not necessarily apply in another context. To help someone develop tacit knowledge, one would provide mediated learning experiences rather than direct instruction as to what to do, when.

Measurement of Tacit Knowledge

In a series of studies (summarized in Sternberg, Wagner, & Okagaki, 1993; Sternberg et al., 1995), my colleagues and I have sought to develop assessments of tacit knowledge in real-world pursuits. The methodology for constructing assessments is rather complex (Horvath et al., 1996), but it involves interviewing individuals for how they have handled critical situations on their jobs. We then extract the tacit knowledge implicit in these interviews. Assessments then are constructed that ask people to solve the kinds of problems they find in managing themselves, others, and tasks on the job. Examples of two tacit-knowledge problems, one for an academic psychologist and one for a business manager, are shown in the Appendix of Sternberg et al. (1995). Each of these problems typically presents a scenario about a job-related problem along with possible options for dealing with that problem. For example, an academic psychologist might be asked to solve a problem in which a psychology professor has too much to do in the time available to do it. The participant (an academic psychologist) would be given statements suggesting how the hypothetical professor might allocate his or her time, and would be asked to rate the goodness of each of the options on a 1- to 9-point Likert scale. The response profile for all items then is typically scored against the averaged profile of a nominated expert group.

Tacit Knowledge as an Aspect of Practical Intelligence

My colleagues and I argued that tacit knowledge is a key aspect of *practical intelligence* (Steinberg, 1985b, 1997b; Sternberg & Wagner, 1993; Sternberg et al., 1993; Sternberg et al., 1995), or the ability to apply various kinds of information-processing components of intelligence to experience for the purposes of adaptation to, shaping of, and selection of environments. Practical intelligence requires adaptation, shaping, and selection, in that different kinds of environments and environmental situations require different kinds of responses. It has been distinguished conceptually and statistically in research from analytical and creative aspects of intelligence (Sternberg, 1985a; Sternberg, Ferrari, Clinkenbeard, & Grigorenko, 1996; Sternberg, Grigorenko, Ferrari, & Clinkenbeard, 1999).

In a series of studies (see review in Sternberg et al., 1995), my colleagues and I showed that tacit knowledge tends to increase with experience on a job, but it is what one learns from the experience rather than the experience itself that seems to matter. Measures of tacit knowledge tend to be correlated with each other, both within and across measures for different occupations. For example, Wagner (1987) found a correlation at the .6 level between scores on tacit-knowledge measures for academic psychology and management with undergraduates as participants. Our measures of tacit knowledge also predict actual performance in jobs such as sales, management, and college teaching. Not only is this prediction statistically significant and fairly substantial in magnitude (with correlations typically at about the .3 level), but this prediction is largely independent of the prediction provided by conventional tests of academic intelligence. In a study at the Center for Creative Leadership (described in Sternberg et al., 1993), my colleagues and I found that tacit knowledge for management was the best single predictor of performance on two managerial simulations and that even after entering (conventional) cognitive abilities, personality-scale measures, styles, and interpersonal orientation into a hierarchical regression equation predicting performance on the simulations, tacit knowledge still contributed significantly and substantially to prediction of performance on the simulations. This is true within a fairly broad range of academic abilities (Eddy, 1988). But the prediction is not always independent. In one study among Kenyan school children, we actually found a significant negative correlation between tacit knowledge relevant to environmental adaptation (knowledge of natural herbal medicines believed to fight infections) and performance on measures of crystallized abilities (see Sternberg & Grigorenko, 1997a).

Why should tacit knowledge be relatively independent of academic abilities or even, in some cases, inversely related to them? Along with Neisser (1979), we believe it is in part because the characteristics of academic and practical problems differ. In particular, academic problems tend to be (a) formulated by others; (b) intrinsically uninteresting for the most part; (c) self-contained, in that all needed information is available from the beginning; (d) disembedded from an individual's ordinary experience; (e) well defined; (f) characterized by a "correct" answer; and (g) characterized by a single method of obtaining the correct answer. In contrast, practical problems tend to be (a) unformulated or in need of reformulation; (b) personally interesting; (c) lacking information necessary for solution; (d) related to everyday experience; (e) poorly defined; (f) characterized by multiple correct or at least "acceptable" solutions, each with liabilities as well as assets; and (g) characterized by multiple methods for picking a problem solution (Sternberg et al., 1995).

Practical intelligence and the role of tacit knowledge in it provide an entree for understanding wisdom, but they do not provide a complete basis for its understanding. Consider the balance theory of wisdom in more detail.

Sketch of a Balance Theory of Wisdom

Balance is a crucial construct in the theory proposed here. Several of the theories described above also emphasize the importance of various kinds of integrations or balances in wisdom. At least three major kinds of balances have been proposed: balance among various kinds of thinking (e.g., Labouvie-Vief, 1990); among various self-systems, such as the cognitive, conative, and affective (e.g., Kramer, 1990); and among various points of view (e.g., Kitchener & Brenner, 1990). The view presented here expands on but also differs from these kinds of notions in providing for particular kinds of balance in wisdom.

The balance theory views wisdom as inherent in the interaction between an individual and a situational context, much as intelligence (Sternberg, 1997a; Valsiner & Leung, 1994) involves a person–context interaction, as does creativity (Csikszentmihalyi, 1996; Sternberg & Lubart, 1995). For this reason, the balances proposed by the theory are in the interaction between a person and his or her context, rather than, say, in internal systems of functioning (such as cognitive, conative, and affective). On the current view, someone could be balanced in terms of the internal systems by which he or she processes information but not in the products that result from these processes. Because wisdom is in the interaction of person and situation, information processing in and of itself is not wise or unwise. Its degree of wisdom depends on the fit of a wise solution to its context.

On this view, the same balance of cognitive, conative, and affective processes that in one situational context might result in a wise solution in another context might not. This result might derive, for example, from a lack of tacit knowledge or incorrect tacit knowledge about one situation but not another. Judgments in any domain require a substantial tacit-knowledge base in order to be wise consistently.

Wisdom as Tacit Knowledge Used for Balancing Interests

The definition of wisdom proposed here (see Figure 13.1) draws both on the notion of tacit knowledge, as described previously, and on the notion of balance. In particular, wisdom is defined as the application of tacit knowledge as mediated by values toward the goal of achieving a common good (a) through a balance among multiple intrapersonal, interpersonal, and extrapersonal interests and (b) in order to achieve a balance among responses to environmental contexts: adaptation to existing environmental contexts, shaping of existing environmental contexts, and selection of new environmental contexts.

In its application to wisdom, the features of tacit knowledge take on a special cast. Wisdom is procedural knowledge; it is about what to do in usually difficult and complex circumstances. Wisdom is also relevant to the attainment of particular goals people value, although not just any goals, but rather, a balance of responses to the environment—adaptation, shaping, and selection—so as to achieve a common good for all relevant stakeholders. Finally, wisdom is typically acquired with little direct help from others. One typically learns it from experience, not from formal instruction. Formal instruction might give one contexts in which to develop wisdom, but one cannot impart wisdom the way, say, multiplication facts can be imparted.

Wisdom is probably best developed through role modeling and through the incorporation of dialectical thinking into one's processing of problems (Basseches, 1984; Labouvie-Vief, 1990; Pascual-Leone, 1990; Riegel, 1973; Sternberg, 1998, 1999). Thinking can be dialectical either with respect to time or with respect to place. When it is with respect to time, it involves the recognition that ideas evolve over time through an ongoing, unending process of thesis, followed by antithesis, followed by synthesis, with the synthesis in turn becoming the next thesis (Hegel, 1807/1931). When dialectical thinking occurs with respect to place (or space), it involves the recognition that at a given point in time, people may have diverging viewpoints on problems that seem uniquely valid or at least reasonable to them.

Thus, wisdom is related to practical intelligence in that it draws on tacit knowledge about oneself, others, and situational contexts, but it is only a refined subset of the tacit knowledge involved in practical intelligence. Practical intelligence has been defined in terms of maximizing practical outcomes. The practical outcomes may be for any one or more particular individuals, but usually these outcomes are the outcomes of an individual and most typically of oneself. For example, when one manages oneself, others, or tasks (Wagner, 1987; Wagner & Sternberg, 1985), one's ultimate goal often is to maximize one's self-interest. Wisdom is involved when practical intelligence is applied to maximizing not just one's own or someone else's self-interest, but rather a balance of various self-interests (intrapersonal) with the interests of others (interpersonal) and of other aspects of the context in which one lives (extrapersonal), such as one's city or country or environment or even God.

Thus, whereas practical intelligence can be applied toward the maximization of any set of interests—whether of an individual or a collective—wisdom is practical

13.1

A balance theory of wisdom. Tacit knowledge underlying practical intelligence is applied to balance intrapersonal, interpersonal, and extrapersonal interests to achieve a balance of the responses to the environmental context of adaptation to, shaping of, and selection of environments in order to achieve a common good. Values mediate how people use their tacit knowledge in balancing interests and responses.

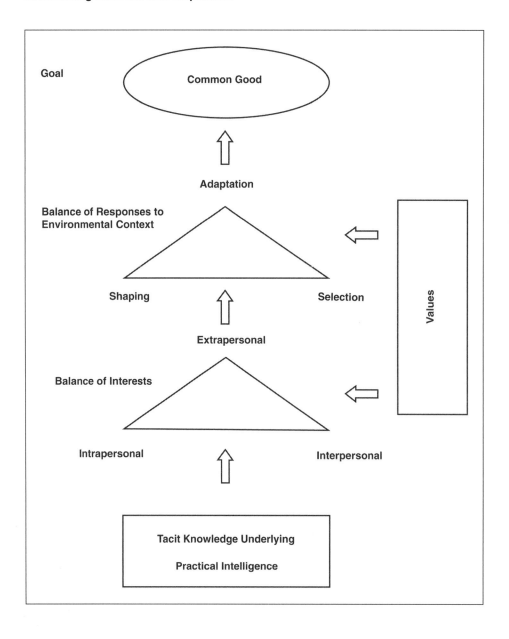

intelligence applied in particular to a balance of intrapersonal, interpersonal, and extrapersonal interests. It is a very special case of practical intelligence, one that requires balancing of multiple and often competing interests. Practical intelligence may or may not involve a balancing of interests, but wisdom must. Its output is typically in the form of advice, usually to another person, but sometimes for oneself.

An implication of this view is that when one applies practical intelligence, one deliberately may seek outcomes that are good for oneself or one's family and friends but bad for the common good. For example, despots typically are practically intelligent, managing to control an entire country largely for their own benefit. Despots such as Hitler or Stalin even may have balanced factors in their judgments, but not for the common good. Or one may apply practical intelligence to maximize someone else's benefit, as does a lawyer. In the subset of practical intelligence that is wisdom, one certainly may seek good ends for oneself (intrapersonal interests), but one also seeks to balance them with good outcomes for others (interpersonal interests) and with the contextual factors (extrapersonal interests) involved. The balance is then used to adapt to, shape, and select environments. For example, after hearing about as many relevant factors as possible, one might advise a college student to stay with his or her major but to work harder (adapt), to stay with the major but try to obtain waiver of a certain requirement or set of requirements (shape), or to find another major (select).

If one's motivations are to maximize certain people's interests and minimize other people's, wisdom is not involved. In wisdom, one seeks a common good, realizing that this common good may be better for some than for others. A person who uses his mental powers to become an evil genius may be academically or practically intelligent, but the person cannot be wise. I do not attempt here a disquisition on what constitutes "good" and "evil," believing such questions to be better dealt with by moral philosophy and religion.

I refer here to *interests,* which, together with the perceived facts of a situation, are the content to which wisdom is applied. Interests are related to the multiple points of view that are a common feature of many theories of wisdom (as reviewed in Sternberg, 1990a). Diverse interests encompass multiple points of view and thus the use of the term *interests* is intended to include points of view. Interests go beyond points of view, however, in that they include not only cognitive aspects of divergences but affective and motivational divergences also. Sometimes differences in points of view derive not so much from differences in cognitions as from differences in motivations. For example, executives in the tobacco industry for many years have defended their products. Their point of view may be divergent from those of many others, but the motivation of maintaining a multimillion dollar business may have more to do with the divergences in points of view than do any kinds of cognitive analysis. Economic interests no doubt motivate these executives to adopt a point of view favorable to the continued use in society of tobacco products. In order to be wise, therefore, one must understand not only people's cognitions, but also their motivations and even their affects. Such understanding may involve applying one's own cognitions, motivations, and affects to the understanding of other people's. Wisdom involves, then, understanding people's cognitions, motivations, and affects.

Problems requiring wisdom always involve at least some element of each of intrapersonal, interpersonal, and extrapersonal interests, although the weights may be different in different instances, just as they may be different for adaptation, shaping, and selection. For example, one might decide that it is wise to go to college, a problem that seemingly involves only one person. But many people are typically affected by an individual's decision to go to college—parents, friends, significant others, children, and the like. And the decision always has to be made in the context of the whole range of available options. In making the decision, one selects a future environment and, in doing so, adapts to and shapes one's current environment, as well as the environments of others. Similarly, a decision about whether to have an abortion requires wisdom because it involves not only oneself, but the baby who would be born; others to whom one is close, such as the father; and the rules and customs of the society. One also simultaneously is profoundly adapting to, shaping, and selecting the environment, both for oneself and for a potential infant.

The Role of Values

It is impossible to speak of wisdom outside the context of a set of values, which in combination may lead one to a moral stance or, in Kohlberg's (1969, 1983) view, a stage. Values mediate how one balances interests and responses and collectively contribute even to how one defines a common good. I do not believe it is the mission of psychology, as a discipline, to specify what the common good is or what values should be brought to bear in what proportion toward its attainment. Such specifications are perhaps more the job of religion or moral philosophy. I, at least, would be skeptical of any psychologist who claims to specify what people should think rather than how or why they think or should think. But I believe the intersection of wisdom with the moral domain can be seen by there being some overlap in the notion of wisdom presented here and the notion of moral reasoning as it applies in the two highest stages (4 and 5) of Kohlberg's (1969) theory. At the same time, wisdom is broader than moral reasoning. It applies to any human problem involving a balance of intrapersonal, interpersonal, and extrapersonal interests, regardless of whether moral issues are at stake.

Mental Processes Underlying Wisdom

As is true with all aspects of practical intelligence (Sternberg, 1985a, 1997a), wisdom involves a balancing not only of the three kinds of interests, but also of three possible courses of action in response to the balancing of interests: adaptation of oneself or others to existing environments, shaping of environments in order to render them more compatible with oneself or others, and selection of new environments. In adaptation, the individual tries to find ways to conform to the existing environment that forms his or her context. Sometimes adaptation is the best course of action under a given set of circumstances. But typically one seeks a balance between adaptation and shaping, realizing that fit to an environment requires not only changing oneself, but changing the environment also. When an individual finds it impossible or at least implausible to attain such a fit, he or she may decide to select a new environment altogether, leaving, for example, a job, a community, a marriage, or whatever.

Underlying wisdom in action is a series of processes executed in a manner that is typically cyclical and variable with respect to order of process execution. Among these processes are what I have referred to as *metacomponents* of thought (Sternberg, 1985a), which include (a) recognizing the existence of a problem, (b) defining the nature of the problem, (c) representing information about the problem, (d) formulating a strategy for solving the problem, (e) allocating resources to the solution of a problem,

(f) monitoring one's solution of the problem, and (g) evaluating feedback regarding that solution. In deciding about college, for example, one first has to see both going to college and not going as viable options (problem recognition); then figure out exactly what going or not going to college would mean for oneself (defining the problem); then consider the costs and benefits to oneself and others of going or not going to college (representing information about the problem); and so forth. In wisdom, these processes are applied to balancing off the various interests of parties about which one needs to make a judgment or series of judgments.

The balance theory suggests that wisdom is at least partially domain specific, in that tacit knowledge is acquired within a given context or set of contexts. It typically is acquired by selectively encoding new information that is relevant for one's purposes in learning about that context, selectively comparing this information to old information in order to see how the new fits with the old, and selectively combining pieces of information in order to make them fit together into an orderly whole (Sternberg et al., 1993). These processes are referred to as *knowledge-acquisition components* in the triarchic theory of intelligence (Sternberg, 1985a).

The use of metacomponents and knowledge acquisition in wisdom or any other kind of practical intelligence points out a key relationship between wisdom and intelligence (as conceptualized by the triarchic theory). All aspects of intelligence—analytical, creative, and practical—involve use of metacomponents for executive processing and of knowledge-acquisition components for learning. What differs is the kind of context in which they are applied. Analytic intelligence is called on for relatively familiar, decontextualized, abstract, and often academic kinds of situations. Creative intelligence is called on for relatively unfamiliar, novel kinds of situations. Practical intelligence is called on for highly contextualized situations encountered in the normal course of one's daily life.

People who acquire wisdom in one context may be those who would be well able to develop it in another context, but the tacit knowledge needed to be wise in different contexts may itself differ. For example, the wise individual in one society may be able to give useful advice in the context of that society. But the same advice might be suicidal in another society (e.g., to criticize a governmental policy as it applies to a particular individual). Thus the ability to be wise may transfer, but the actual content of wise advice may vary. A wise person will therefore know not only when to give advice, but when not to (see Meacham, 1990) because the individual will know the limitations of his or her own tacit knowledge.

As noted above, however, research has found significant correlations on scores of tacit knowedge across domains. For example, my colleagues and I found that scores on tests of tacit knowledge for academic psychology and management correlate significantly (Wagner & Sternberg, 1985), as do scores on tests of tacit knowledge for management and military leadership (Forsythe et al., 1998). Thus, although one's development of wisdom might be domain specific, the tacit knowledge one learns in one domain can extend to other domains.

Although tacit knowledge is acquired within a domain, it more typically applies to a field, following a distinction made by Csikszentmihalyi (1988, 1996). Csikszentmihalyi refers to the domain as the *formal knowledge of a socially defined field*. So, for example, knowing how to construct, conduct, or analyze the results of experiments would be knowledge important to the domain of experimental psychology. But knowing how to speak about the results persuasively, how to get the results published, or knowing how to turn the results into the next grant proposal would constitute knowledge of the field. Thus, academic intelligence seems to apply primarily in the domain, whereas practical intelligence in general, and wisdom in particular, seem to apply primarily in the field. Because the field represents the social organization of the domain, it is primarily in the field that intrapersonal, interpersonal, and extrapersonal interactions take place.

The much greater importance for wisdom of the field than of the domain helps to clarify why, in the balance theory, tacit, informal knowledge rather than explicit formal knowledge is the basis of wisdom. Formal knowledge about the subject matter of a discipline is certainly essential to expertise in that discipline (Chi, Glaser, & Farr, 1988; Hoffman, 1992), but domain-based expertise is neither necessary nor sufficient for wisdom. Most people know domain-based experts who seem pretty near the bottom of any scale when it comes to wisdom. At least some people also know very wise individuals who have little formal education. Their education is in the "school of life," which is in the acquisition of tacit (informal) knowledge.

Sources of Developmental and Individual Differences in Wisdom

The balance theory suggests a number of sources of developmental and individual differences in wisdom. In particular, there are two kinds of sources, those directly affecting the balance processes and those that are antecedent.

Individual and Developmental Differences Directly Affecting the Balance Processes

There are five such sources:

1. Goals: People may differ in terms of the extent to which they seek a common good and thus in the extent to which they aim for the essential goal of wisdom.
2. Balancing of responses to environmental contexts: People may differ in their balance of responses to environmental contexts. Responses always reflect an interaction of the individual making the judgment and the environmental context, and people can interact with contexts in myriad ways.
3. Balancing of interests: People may balance interests in different ways.
4. Practical intelligence manifested as tacit knowledge: People bring different kinds and levels of tacit knowledge to judgmental situations, which are likely to affect their responses.
5. Values: People have different values mediating their utilization of tacit knowledge in the balancing of interests and responses.

These sources of differences produce variation in how wise people are and in how well they can apply their wisdom in different kinds of situations. The way in which wisdom typically is associated with greater intellectual and even physical maturity presumably is based on the development of tacit knowledge and of values. Wisdom is something that unfolds over the course of the life span and not just during childhood or even in early years of adulthood.

The above sources of individual differences pertain to the balancing processes. Other sources are antecedent to these processes.

Developmental and Individual Differences in Antecedent Variables

Antecedent variables leading to developmental and individual differences are those specified by my earlier theory (Sternberg, 1990b). They include (a) knowledge, (b) analytical and creative as well as practical thinking (Sternberg, 1997a), (c) a judicial thinking style (Sternberg, 1997b), (d) personality variables, (e) motivation to think wisely, and (f) environmental variables.

Relation of the Proposed Balance Theory to Other Balance Theories in Psychology

The idea of balance in psychological theories is certainly not new. For example, Heider (1958) proposed a balance theory of interpersonal attraction, although the balance to which he referred was between polarities (positive or negative) in the interpersonal relationships among all three pairings of the triad among three persons (i.e., the A to B, A to C, and B to C relationships linking A, B, and C). The triad was said to be balanced when there was an even number of negatives (e.g., A and B both feel negatively toward C and vice versa, but A and B both feel positively toward each other). An odd number of negatives resulted in an unbalanced, unstable triad (e.g., A and B feel positively toward C, and vice versa, but negatively toward each other). These balances are not relevant to the present theory of wisdom, however.

In the cognitive and developmental literatures, balance has been suggested as important in some theories of intelligence. For example, Piaget (1972) proposed that the development of intelligence involves an equilibration, or balance, between assimilation (modification of the way one understands an object or concept in order to fit it into existing cognitive schemas) and accommodation (modification of one's existing cognitive schemas in order to fit the way one understands a concept or object). As another example, Sternberg and Frensch (1989) proposed a balance-level theory of intelligent thinking involving a balance between coping with novelty and procedure. These kinds of balance, too, are not directly relevant to the theory proposed in this chapter.

The notion of balance also has played an important role in theories of wisdom. Philosophical conceptions of wisdom (reviewed in Baltes, 2004; see especially Hartshorne, 1987) and especially Chinese conceptions (reviewed in Yang, 2001) note the importance of balance, as do psychological theories such as the ontogenetic theory of wisdom proposed by Baltes and his colleagues (see Baltes, 1993; Staudinger & Baltes, 1994; Staudinger et al., 1997).

Staudinger and Baltes (1996) specified a family of five criteria, mentioned previously, that characterize wisdom and wisdom-related performance. In contrast, the theory proposed here views wisdom as inherent in the extent to which a task requires a person to balance the interests of him or herself, others, and the context for a common good, such that the decision making leads to adaptation to, shaping of, and selection of environments. Although the basic claim is simple, the actual balancing is extremely complex, and it is unlikely that any theory of wisdom can provide a normative "formula" to be used to achieve this balance.

What is new in the balance theory is not the concept of balance, per se, but the proposed specification of the particular conjunction of elements that are balanced (intrapersonal, interpersonal, and extrapersonal interests balanced to achieve a common good through a balance among adaptation to, shaping of, and selection of environments). Also new is the proposed specification of the relation between wisdom and practical intelligence, in particular, and intelligence, more generally.

The balance theory is further related to other theories of wisdom in a variety of ways. Consider some of the main theories and the relation to the balance theory proposed here.

Wisdom requires an individual to see the other's point of view, a skill emphasized in Kitchener's (1986) model of reflective judgment. But wisdom requires not only the ability to see each point of view, but further requires the ability to formulate a solution that takes into account these points of view and that also will be acceptable to all parties to a negotiation. Thus, one needs not only understand each party's perspective, but also to understand how to craft a solution, given these points of view. It further requires one to recognize the interests underlying the points of view, as mentioned earlier. Wisdom in the balance theory is also directed toward a good, as in Csikszentmihalyi and Rathunde's (1990) theory.

The nature of balance in the theory proposed here is somewhat different from the nature of balance in some of the other models (e.g., Kramer, 1990), which are intrapersonal balances of cognitive, conative, and affective systems. In the present model, the individual can use whatever internal systems he or she wants in making judgments. But the individual must understand how these systems work in him or herself and in others. Intrapersonal balance refers not to a balance of such systems, but of the various kinds of interests one has oneself. For example, wisdom from an intrapersonal standpoint might balance one's own short- and long-term interests, or one's desire to engage in an activity that one enjoys with the recognition that the activity one enjoys poses substantial risks.

Relation of Wisdom to Other Constructs

According to the balance view, wisdom is related to practical intelligence, a point also made in the extensive work of Baltes and his colleagues (e.g., Baltes & Smith, 1990), but the two constructs are not the same. In practical intelligence in general, tacit knowledge typically is used in a way that does not balance interests to achieve a common good. The subset of practical intelligence that is wisdom applies when the tacit knowledge is used maximally to advance the balanced joint interests of oneself, others, and the context for a common good to adapt to, shape, and select environments. One may actually take a loss for oneself in advancing the joint benefit. On this view, wisdom and egocentricity are incompatible. People who are practically intelligent but not wise, however, can be quite egocentric, Some of the most successful individuals, at least by the conventional standards of society, seem to be people who have gotten where they are by not taking other people's interests into account or even by actively thwarting the interests of others. They might be viewed as practically intelligent, but on the view proposed here, they would not be viewed as wise.

Consider a concrete example in which practical intelligence and wisdom are not the same. In a negotiation between management and a union, negotiators are often chosen for their practical intelligence—their ability maximally to advance the interests of their respective parties. But negotiations in which the two sides seek only to advance their own interests typically go nowhere. If the two parties do not have the wisdom to reach an agreement, sometimes a third party is brought in who, it is hoped, will have the wisdom to help the negotiating parties reach a settlement. Such an individual must take into account his or her own (intrapersonal) role, as well as the interpersonal and extrapersonal factors involved in the negotiation. Similarly, in international relations, if the parties to a dispute cannot reach an agreement, a mediating party (such as the United Nations) is hoped to have the wisdom to help the disputants reach some kind of settlement.

Wisdom seems to bear at least some relation to constructs such as social intelligence (Cantor & Kihlstrom, 1987; Sternberg & Smith, 1985), emotional intelligence (Goleman, 1995; Mayer & Salovey, 1993; Salovey & Mayer, 1990), and interpersonal and intrapersonal intelligences (Gardner, 1983). There are also differences, however. Social intelligence can be applied to understanding and getting along with others, to any ends, for any purposes. Wisdom seeks out a good through a balancing of interests. Thus, a salesperson who figures out how to sell a worthless product to a customer might do so through using social intelligence to understand the customer's wants, but has not applied wisdom in the process. Emotional intelligence involves understanding, judging, and regulating emotions. These skills are an important part of wisdom. But making wise judgments requires going beyond the understanding, regulation, or judgment of emotions. It requires processing the information to achieve a balance of interests and formulating a judgment that makes effective use of the information to achieve a common good. Moreover, wisdom may require a balance of interpersonal and intrapersonal intelligences, but it also requires an understanding of extrapersonal factors and a balance of these three factors to attain a common good. Thus wisdom seems to go somewhat beyond these two theoretically distinct kinds of intelligences also. Perhaps the most salient difference among constructs is that wisdom is applied toward the achievement of ends that are perceived as yielding a common good, whereas the various kinds of intelligences may be applied deliberately toward achieving either good ends or bad ones, at least for some of the parties involved. Interestingly, the conception of wisdom proposed here is substantially closer to Chinese conceptions of intelligence than to many European and American conceptions of intelligence (Yang & Sternberg, 1997a, 1997b). Indeed, one of the words used in Chinese to characterize intelligence is the same as the word used to characterize wisdom.

Problems Measuring (and Not Measuring) Wisdom

If one looks at the kinds of problems that have been used to measure wisdom in empirical work, notably of Baltes and his colleagues, one can evaluate the degree to which they measure wisdom, at least according to this balance theory. A life-planning task (Baltes et al., 1995) would be an excellent task for measuring wisdom because it involves one's own interests, but may and usually will take into account the interests of others about whom one cares deeply as well as the context in which one lives and may live in the future. A task in which one must decide what to do when a good friend calls and says he or she wants to commit suicide (Staudinger & Baltes, 1996) would also involve the interests of the other, one's own interest in getting involved and possibly failing to convince the person not to commit suicide, and also the difficulty of acting in the context of an unexpected telephone call. Similarly, counseling a 14-year-old girl who is pregnant or a 16-year-old boy who wants to marry soon (Baltes &

Smith, 1990) both involve balancing of the interests of the individuals to be counseled, the other people in their lives, and the costs of giving the wrong advice.

Perhaps the ideal problems for measuring wisdom, in light of the balance theory proposed here, are complex conflict-resolution problems involving the formation of judgments, given multiple competing interests and no clear resolution of how these interests can be reconciled (see, e.g., Stemberg & Dobson, 1987; Sternberg & Soriano, 1984). For example, one might be asked to resolve a conflict between a couple over whether the husband's mother should be allowed to come to live with the couple. Given the relevance of such problems, it makes sense that Baltes and his colleagues (Smith, Staudinger, & Baltes, 1994) would have found that clinical psychologists would do particularly well on wisdom-related tasks. Another group who might be expected to do well would be experienced foreign-service officers and other negotiators who have helped nations in conflict reach resolutions of their disagreements.

Part of wisdom is deciding not only what course of action best balances off various interests, but whose interests are at stake and what the contextual factors are under which one is operating. A high-level display of wisdom requires identification of all relevant stakeholders. Thus some wisdom might be involved in resolving a conflict between management and a trade union in a way that provides equitable benefits to both. But a higher level of wisdom might be needed to take into account as well that other stakeholders' interests are involved, including shareholders, customers, people who live near to the organization, and perhaps others also.

The tacit-knowledge approach to measurement described above might present a useful way of measuring wisdom. The exact problems would differ, however, from those we have used to measure practical intelligence. In particular, the problems would involve solutions that maximize not just one's own self-interest, but a variety of intrapersonal, interpersonal, and extrapersonal interests. The stakes, therefore, would be higher and more complex, because so many different interests would be involved. In our current work, my colleagues and I are using tacit-knowledge problems of these kinds to assess wisdom and its relation to other constructs.

In contrast to problems such as the ones suggested above or the ones Baltes (2004) and his colleagues have used, typical problems found on conventional tests of intelligence, such as the Stanford-Binet (Thorndike, Hagen, & Sattler, 1986) or the Wechsler (Wechsler, 1991), measure wisdom minimally or not at all, according to the balance theory. There is no obvious similarity between these problems and the kinds of problems described above that would measure wisdom. Even when they measure thinking in a variety of domains, they typically do not involve balancing judgments about intrapersonal, interpersonal, and extrapersonal interests for purposes of adapting to, shaping, and selecting environments. Similarly, there is little apparent similarity between problems measuring wisdom and those measuring creativity, whether from a psychometric point of view (e.g., Torrance, 1974) or from a systems point of view (e.g., Sternberg & Lubart, 1995). For example, wisdom-related problems seem remote either from finding unusual uses for a paper clip or from writing creative short stories, drawing creative pictures, or devising creative scientific experiments or explanations.

Although wisdom problems seem remote from problems found on conventional intelligence tests, people's implicit theories of wisdom are rather close to their implicit theories of intelligence and people expect, to a large degree, that people high in wisdom will be high in intelligence. The same relation holds true, but to a lesser extent, for creativity (see Sternberg, 1985b). Scores on wisdom-related tasks also overlap with scores on tasks measuring intelligence and other abilities as well as tasks measuring personality and thinking styles (Staudinger et al., 1997). For example, the groups of participants that Baltes and his colleagues have tested and identified as high in wisdom, such as expert clinical psychologists, could be expected to be high in IQ. But the evidence is not clear that other groups as high or higher in IQ (e.g., expert physicists or mathematicians) necessarily would be as wise (and of course they might be wiser—no one knows at this point). The evidence that old adults perform about as well as young adults on wisdom-related tasks (e.g., Staudinger, Smith, & Baltes, 1992) suggests that, to the extent that wisdom covaries with intelligence, it covaries more with crystallized than with fluid abilities (Cattell, 1971).

Much is still to be learned about how wisdom functions as an individual-differences variable. It is plausible to speculate that the potential for wisdom may be in part genetic, given that other kinds of potentials seem to be at least in part genetic (see Sternberg & Grigorenko, 1997b). But the tacit knowledge necessary for wisdom must be environmentally acquired, so that genetic factors could only be necessary but never sufficient for the development of wisdom. (Indeed, the same argument could be made for any ability, as abilities always manifest themselves in an environmental context.) Far more important, it seems, would be the kinds of experiences one has and what one learns from them. The development and display of wisdom also would seem to be partly attitudinal, involving a decision that one wishes to use one's tacit knowledge for the balanced benefit of others and the environment, not just for the benefit of oneself.

There is one source of evidence that suggests that, as individual-difference variables, wisdom and intelligence might be rather different "kettles of fish." Researchers have shown that IQs have been rising substantially over the past several generations (Flynn, 1987; Neisser, 1998). The gains have been experienced both for fluid and for crystallized abilities, although the gains are substantially greater for fluid than for crystallized abilities. Yet it is difficult for some to discern any increase in the wisdom of the peoples of the world. Of course tests administered over time might have revealed otherwise. But the levels of conflict in the world show no sign of deescalating, and conflicts recently have intensified in many parts of the world where formerly they lay dormant (as in the former Yugoslavia). So maybe it is time that psychologists, as a profession, take much more seriously the measurement of wisdom and the formulation of theories and theory-based measures of wisdom. Although there has been work in the area, the amount of work is dwarfed by work on intelligence. And perhaps psychologists even need to be concerned about how they might create experiences that would guide people to develop wisdom as much as psychologists have been concerned in some quarters about guiding people to develop their intelligence (see, e.g., Perkins & Grotzer, 1997).

From a theoretical standpoint, wisdom is quite distinct both from intelligence as traditionally defined and from creativity. In terms of the triarchic theory (Sternberg, 1985a), wisdom derives primarily from practical intelligence, traditional intelligence primarily from analytical intelligence, and creativity primarily from creative intelligence. The three aspects of intelligence are statistically quite distinct (Sternberg, 1997a). In terms of the theory of mental self-government (Sternberg, 1997b), wisdom draws primarily on a judicial (judgmental, evaluative) style, traditional intelligence primarily on an executive (implementing, executing) style, and creativity primarily on a legislative (inventive, rebellious) style. The wise person uses knowledge primarily to make balanced judgments about problems in the context of a field, whereas the creative person typically uses knowledge primarily in extending a domain, often in a decidedly unbalanced and extreme way. The traditionally intelligent person is someone who has shown an ability to use knowledge that is as abstracted as possible from traditional context-rich domains (as can be seen by the inclusion of abstract-reasoning items on conventional intelligence tests). In terms of personality, the wise individual seeks to resolve ambiguities, whereas the traditionally intelligent person excels in problems that have few or no ambiguities (and thus can be "objectively" scored as right or wrong). The creative person often creates ambiguity or at least must be tolerant of it (according to the investment theory of creativity; Sternberg & Lubart, 1995).

To the extent psychologists want people to be simultaneously intelligent, creative, and wise, they need to develop different skills and dispositions in people. Psychologists also have to realize that in the future as in the past, the people who are notable for being traditionally intelligent, creative, or wise often may not be the same people. None of these attributions is any guarantee of any of the others. Schools cannot assume that developing or measuring one will spill over into developing or measuring another.

Schools place a great deal of emphasis on developing academic skills. But in a society that seems largely ruled by self-interests, students often start to develop practical skills in order to use schooling primarily to maximize their self-interests. Perhaps if schools put into the development of wisdom even a small fraction of the effort they put into the development of an often inert knowledge base, some of the conflicts that have arisen so quickly in the world would also disappear, if not quickly, at least in due course. One cannot know for sure, but is it not worth the effort to find out?

References

Arlin, P. K. (1990). Wisdom: The art of problem finding. In R. J. Sternberg (Ed.), *Wisdom: Its nature, origins, and development* (pp. 230–243). New York: Cambridge University Press.

Baltes, P. B. (1993). The aging mind: Potential and limits. *The Gerontologist, 33,* 580–594.

Baltes, P. B. (2004). *Wisdom: The orchestration of mind and virtue.* Berlin: Max Planck Institute for Human Development.

Baltes, P. B., & Smith, J. (1987, August). *Toward a psychology of wisdom and its ontogenesis.* Paper presented at the Annual Convention of the American Psychological Association, New York.

Baltes, P. B., & Smith, J. (1990). Toward a psychology of wisdom and its ontogenesis. In R. J. Sternberg (Ed.), *Wisdom: Its nature, origins, and development* (pp. 87–120). New York: Cambridge University Press.

Baltes, P. B., Smith, J., & Staudinger, U. M. (1992). Wisdom and successful aging. In T. Sonderegger (Ed.), *Nebraska Symposium on Motivation* (Vol. 39, pp. 123–167). Lincoln: NE University of Nebraska Press.

Baltes, P. B., & Staudinger, U. M. (1993). The search for a psychology of wisdom. *Current Directions in Psychological Science, 2,* 75–80.

Baltes, P. B., Staudinger, U. M., Maercker, A., & Smith, J. (1995). People nominated as wise: A comparative study of wisdom-related knowledge. *Psychology and Aging, 10,* 155–166.

Basseches, J. (1984). *Dialectical thinking and adult development.* Norwood, NJ: Ablex.

Birren, J. E., & Fisher, L. M. (1990). The elements of wisdom: Overview and integration. In R. J. Sternberg (Ed.), *Wisdom: Its nature, origins, and development* (pp. 317–332). New York: Cambridge University Press.

Cantor, N., & Kihlstrom, J. F. (1987). *Personality and social intelligence.* Englewood Cliffs, NJ: Prentice-Hall.

Cattell, R. B. (1971). *Abilities: Their structure, growth, and action.* Boston: Houghton-Mifflin.

Chi, M. T. H., Glaser, R., & Farr, M. J. (Eds.). (1988). *The nature of expertise.* Hillsdale, NJ: Erlbaum.

Clayton, V. (1975). Erickson's theory of human development as it applies to the aged: Wisdom as contradictory cognition. *Human Development, 18,* 119–128.

Clayton, V. (1976). *A multidimensional scaling analysis of the concept of wisdom.* Unpublished doctoral dissertation, University of Southern California, Los Angeles.

Clayton, V. (1982). Wisdom and intelligence: The nature and function of knowledge in the later years. *International Journal of Aging and Development, 15,* 315–321.

Clayton, V., & Birren, J. E. (1980). The development of wisdom across the life-span: A reexamination of an ancient topic. In P. B. Baltes & O. G. Brim (Eds.), *Life-span development and behavior* (Vol. 3, pp. 103–135). New York: Academic Press.

Csikszentmihalyi, M. (1988). Society, culture, and person: A systems view of creativity. In R. J. Sternberg (Ed.), The *nature of creativity* (pp. 325–339). New York: Cambridge University Press.

Csikszentmihalyi, M. (1996). *Creativity.* New York: HarperCollins.

Csikszentmihalyi, M., & Rathunde, K. (1990). The psychology of wisdom: An evolutionary interpretation. In R. J. Sternberg (Ed.), *Wisdom: Its nature, origins, and development* (pp. 25–51). New York: Cambridge University Press.

Eddy, A. S. (1988). *The relationship between the Tacit Knowledge Inventory for Managers and the Armed Services Vocational Aptitude Battery.* Unpublished master's thesis, St. Mary's University, San Antonio, TX.

Forsythe, G. B., Hedlund, K., Snook, S., Horvath, J. A., Williams, W. M., Bullis, R. C., Dennis, M., & Sternberg, R. J. (1998, April). *Construct validation of tacit knowledge for military leadership.* Paper presented at the Annual Meeting of the American Educational Research Association, San Diego, CA.

Flynn, J. R. (1987). Massive IQ gains in 14 nations. *Psychological Bulletin, 101,* 171–191.

Gardner, H. (1983). *Frames of mind: The theory of multiple intelligences.* New York: Basic Books.

Goleman, D. (1995). *Emotional intelligence.* New York: Bantam Books.

Hartshorne, C. (1987). *Wisdom as moderation: A philosophy of the middle way.* Albany: State University of New York Press.

Hegel, G. W. F. (1931). *The phenomenology of the mind* (2nd ed., J. D. Baillie, Trans.). London: Allen & Unwin. (Original work published 1807)

Heider, F. (1958). *The psychology of interpersonal relations.* New York: Wiley.

Hoffman, R. R. (Ed.). (1992). *The psychology of expertise: Cognitive research and empirical AI.* New York: Springer-Verlag.

Holliday, S. G., & Chandler, M. J. (1986). *Wisdom: Explorations in adult competence.* Basel, Switzerland: Karger.

Horvath, J. A., Steinberg, R. J., Forsythe, G. B., Sweeney, P. J., Bullis, R. C., Williams, W. M., & Dennis, M. (1996). *Tacit knowledge in military leadership: Supporting instrument development* (Technical Report No. 1042). Alexandria, VA: U.S. Army Research Institute for the Behavioral and Social Sciences.

Kitchener, K. S. (1983). Cognition, metacognition, and epistemic cognition: A three-level model of cognitive processing. *Human Development, 4,* 222–232.

Kitchener, K. S. (1986). Formal reasoning in adults: A review and critique. In R. A. Mines & K. S. Kitchener (Eds.), *Adult cognitive development.* New York: Praeger.

Kitchener, K. S., & Brenner, H. G. (1990). Wisdom and reflective judgment: Knowing in the face of uncertainty. In R. J. Sternberg (Ed.), *Wisdom: Its nature, origins, and development* (pp. 212–229). New York: Cambridge University Press.

Kitchener, K. S., & Kitchener, R. F. (1981). The development of natural rationality: Can formal operations account for it? In J. Meacham & N. R. Santini (Eds.), *Social development in youth: Structure and content.* Basel, Switzerland: Karger.

Kohlberg, L. (1969). Stage and sequence: The cognitive-developmental approach to socialization. In G. A. Goslin (Ed.), *Handbook of socialization theory and research* (pp. 347–380). Chicago: Rand McNally.

Kohlberg, L. (1983). *The psychology of moral development.* New York: Harper & Row.

Kramer, D. A. (1990). Conceptualizing wisdom: The primacy of affect-cognition relations. In R. J. Sternberg (Ed.), *Wisdom: Its nature, origins, and development* (pp. 279–313). New York: Cambridge University Press.

Labouvie-Vief, G. (1980). Beyond formal operations: Uses and limits of pure logic in life span development. *Human Development, 23,* 141–161.

Labouvie-Vief, G. (1982). Dynamic development and mature autonomy. *Human Development, 25,* 161–191.

Labouvie-Vief, G. (1990). Wisdom as integrated thought: Historical and developmental perspectives. In R. J. Sternberg (Ed.), *Wisdom: Its nature, origins, and development* (pp. 52–83). New York: Cambridge University Press.

Mayer, J. D., & Salovey, P. (1993). The intelligence of emotional intelligence. *Intelligence, 17,* 433–442.

Meacham, J. (1990). The loss of wisdom. In R. J. Sternberg (Ed.), *Wisdom: Its nature, origins, and development* (pp. 181–211). New York: Cambridge University Press.

Neisser, U. (1979). The concept of intelligence. In R. J. Sternberg & D. K. Detterman (Eds.), *Human intelligence: Perspectives on its theory and measurement* (pp. 179–189). Norwood, NJ: Ablex.

Neisser, U. (Ed.). (1998). *The rising curve.* Washington, DC: American Psychological Association.

Onvoll, L., & Perlmutter, M. (1990). The study of wise persons: Integrating a personality perspective. In R. J. Sternberg (Ed.), *Wisdom: Its nature, origins, and development* (pp. 160–177). New York: Cambridge University Press.

Pascual-Leone, J. (1990). An essay on wisdom: Toward organismic processes that make it possible. In R. J. Sternberg (Ed.), *Wisdom: Its nature, origins, and development* (pp. 244–278). New York: Cambridge University Press.

Perkins, D. N., & Grotzer, T. A. (1997). Teaching intelligence. *American Psychologist, 52,* 1125–1133.

Piaget, J. (1972). *The psychology of intelligence.* Totowa, NJ: Littlefield-Adams.

Polanyi, M. (1976). Tacit knowledge. In M. Marx & F. Goodson (Eds.), *Theories in contemporary psychology* (pp. 330–344). New York: Macmillan.

Riegel, K. F. (1973). Dialectical operations: The final period of cognitive development. *Human Development, 16,* 346–370.

Robinson, D. N. (1989). *Aristotle's psychology.* New York: Columbia University Press.

Robinson, D. N. (1990). Wisdom through the ages. In R. J. Sternberg (Ed.), *Wisdom: Its nature, origins, and development* (pp. 13–24). New York: Cambridge University Press.

Rosch, E. (1975). Cognitive representations of semantic categories. *Journal of Experimental Psychology: General, 104,* 192–233.

Ryle, G. (1949). *The concept of mind.* London: Hutchinson.

Salovey, P., & Mayer, J. D. (1990). Emotional intelligence. *Imagination, Cognition, and Personality, 9,* 185–211.

Smith, J., & Baltes, P. B. (1990). Wisdom-related knowledge: Age/cohort differences in response to life-planning problems. *Developmental Psychology, 26,* 494–505.

Smith, J., Staudinger, U. M., & Baltes, P. B. (1994). Occupational settings facilitating wisdom-related knowledge: The sample case of clinical psychologists. *Journal of Consulting and Clinical Psychology, 66,* 989–999.

Staudinger, U. M., & Baltes, P. B. (1994). Psychology of wisdom. In R. J. Sternberg (Ed.), *Encyclopedia of human intelligence* (Vol. 2, pp. 1143–1152). New York: Macmillan.

Staudinger, U. M., & Baltes, P. B. (1996). Interactive minds: A facilitative setting for wisdom-related performance? *Journal of Personality and Social Psychology, 71,* 746–762.

Staudinger, U. M., Lopez, D. E., & Baltes, P. B. (1997). The psychometric location of wisdom-related performance: Intelligence, personality, and more? *Personality & Social Psychology Bulletin, 23,* 1200–1214.

Staudinger, U. M., Smith, J., & Baltes, P. B. (1992). Wisdom-related knowledge in life review task: Age differences and the role of professional specialization. *Psychology and Aging, 7,* 271–281.

Sternberg. R. J. (1985a). *Beyond IQ: A triarchic theory of human intelligence.* New York: Cambridge University Press.

Sternberg, R. J. (1985b). Implicit theories of intelligence, creativity, and wisdom. *Journal of Personality and Social Psychology, 49,* 607–627.

Sternberg, R. J. (Ed.). (1990a). *Wisdom: Its nature, origins, and development.* New York: Cambridge University Press.

Sternberg, R. J. (1990b). Wisdom and its relations to intelligence and creativity. In R. J. Sternberg (Ed.), *Wisdom: Its nature, origins, and development* (pp. 142–159). New York: Cambridge University Press.

Sternberg, R. J. (1997a). *Successful intelligence.* New York: Plume.

Sternberg, R. J. (1997b). *Thinking styles.* New York: Cambridge University Press.

Sternberg, R. J. (1998). The dialectic as a tool for teaching psychology. *Teaching of Psychology, 25,* 177–180.

Sternberg, R. J. (1999). A dialectical basis for understanding the study of cognition. In R. J. Sternberg (Ed.), *The nature of cognition* (pp. 51–78). Cambridge, MA: MIT Press.

Sternberg, R. J., & Dobson, D. M. (1987). Resolving interpersonal conflicts: An analysis of stylistic consistency. *Journal of Personality and Social Psychology, 52,* 794–812.

Sternberg, R. J., Ferrari, M., Clinkenbeard, P. R., & Grigorenko, E. L. (1996). Identification, instruction, and assessment of gifted children: A construct validation of a triarchic model. *Gifted Child Quarterly, 40,* 129–137.

Sternberg, R. J., & Frensch, P. A. (1989). A balance-level theory of intelligent thinking. *Zeitschrift ftir Pädagogische Psychologie [German Journal of Educational Psychology], 3,* 79–96.

Sternberg, R. J., & Grigorenko, E. L. (1997a). The cognitive costs of physical and mental ill-health: Applying the psychology of the developed world to the problems of the developing world. *Eye on Psi Chi, 2,* 20–27.

Sternberg, R. J., & Grigorenko, E. L. (Eds.). (1997b). *Intelligence, heredity, and environment.* New York: Cambridge University Press.

Sternberg, R. J., Grigorenko, E. L., Ferrari, M., & Clinkenbeard, P. R. (1999). A triarchic analysis of an aptitude-treatment interaction. *European Journal of Psychological Assessment, 15,* 1–11.

Sternberg, R. J., & Lubart, T. I. (1995). *Defying the crowd: Cultivating creativity in a culture of conformity.* New York: Free Press.

Sternberg, R. J., & Smith, C. (1985). Social intelligence and decoding skills in nonverbal communication. *Social Cognition, 2,* 168–192.

Sternberg, R. J., & Soriano, L. J. (1984). Styles of conflict resolution. *Journal of Personality and Social Psychology, 47,* 115–126.

Sternberg, R. J., & Wagner, R. K. (1993). The g-ocentric view of intelligence and job performance is wrong. *Current Directions in Psychological Science, 2,* 1–5.

Sternberg, R. J., Wagner, R. K., & Okagaki, L. (1993). Practical intelligence: The nature and role of tacit knowledge in work and at school. In H. Reese & J. Puckett (Eds.), *Advances in lifespan development* (pp. 205–227). Hillsdale, NJ: Erlbaum.

Sternberg, R. J., Wagner, R. K., Williams, W. M., & Horvath, J. A. (1995). Testing common sense. *American Psychologist, 50,* 912–927.

Thorndike, R. L., Hagen, E. P., & Sattler, J. M. (1986). *Stanford-Binet Intelligence Scale* (4th ed.). Itasca, IL: Riverside.

Torrance, E. P. (1974). *Torrance tests of creative thinking: Technical-norms manual.* Bensenville, IL: Scholastic Testing Services.

Valsiner, J., & Leung, M.-C. (1994). From intelligence to knowledge construction: A sociogenetic process approach. In R. J. Sternberg & R. K. Wagner (Eds.), *Mind in context* (pp. 202–217). New York: Cambridge University Press.

Wagner, R. K. (1987). Tacit knowledge in everyday intelligent behavior. *Journal of Personality and Social Psychology, 52,* 1236–1247.

Wagner, R. K., & Sternberg, R. J. (1985). Practical intelligence in real-world pursuits: The role of tacit knowledge. *Journal of Personality and Social Psychology, 49,* 436–458.

Webster's New World College Dictionary. (3rd ed.). (1997). New York: Simon & Schuster.

Wechsler, D. (1991). *Wechsler Intelligence Scale for Children* (3rd ed.). San Antonio, TX: The Psychological Corporation.

Yang, S. (2001). Conceptions of wisdom among Taiwanese Chinese. *Journal of Cross-Cultural Psychology, 32,* 662–680.

Yang, S., & Sternberg, R. J. (1997a). Conceptions of intelligence in ancient Chinese philosophy. *Journal of Theoretical and Philosophical Psychology, 17,* 101–119.

Yang, S., & Sternberg, R. J. (1997b). Taiwanese Chinese people's conceptions of intelligence. *Intelligence, 25,* 21–36.

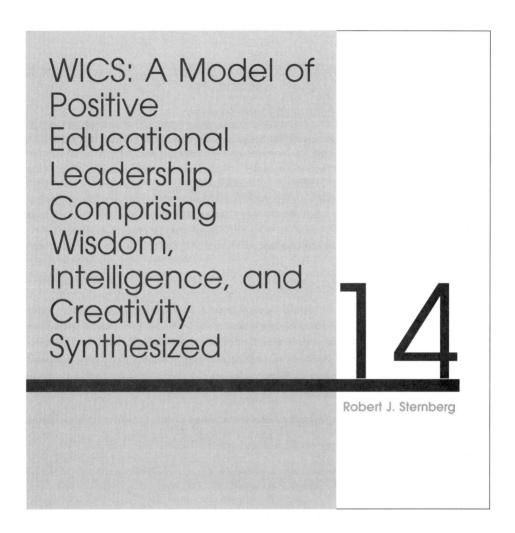

WICS: A Model of Positive Educational Leadership Comprising Wisdom, Intelligence, and Creativity Synthesized

14

Robert J. Sternberg

In this essay I propose a model, WICS, standing for *w*isdom, *i*ntelligence, and *c*reativity, synthesized. I argue that educational leaders exhibit a synthesis of the three attributes of wisdom, intelligence, and creativity. To a large extent, I argue, the development and display of these attributes is a decision over which one has substantial control, not merely some kind of innate set of predispositions. I also present a sampling of the evidence my colleagues and I have collected to date in support of the model and its various aspects. I also compare WICS with other models of leadership.

The WICS model can be applied to various kinds of leadership. But my concern here is primarily with educational leadership and how WICS can be applied to enhance it. Hence, the examples are, for the most part, educational ones.

There are many models of leadership, of course (see reviews in Antonakis et al., 2004a, 2004b). Some are examined below.

Previous Models of Leadership That Can Be Applied to Educational Settings

Antonakis and colleagues (2004a) have identified several different schools of leadership, providing a taxonomy similar to taxonomies provided by others (see Antonakis et al., 2004b; Goethals et al., 2004). Here, I discuss different leadership approaches and some of the problems associated with each. This analysis recognizes that *all* leadership approaches have associated problems. There is no one perfect approach to leadership that is devoid of problematic aspects. Leadership is a complex interlocking of many antecedent skills, attitudes, and situational variables (Hunt, 2004).

The Trait-Based Approach

A traditional approach is the trait-based approach (Zaccaro et al., 2004). The trait approach was particularly popular in the middle of the twentieth century when scholars attempted to identify traits associated with effective leadership (e.g., Bird, 1940; Stogdill, 1948). Stogdill (1948) suggested a number of traits associated with leadership, including intelligence, scholarship, dependability in exercising responsibility, activity and social participation, and higher socioeconomic status. The effective school principal, for example, would be someone who is smart, dependable, and gets along with other people. Mann (1959) also proposed a list of traits, including intelligence, good adjustment, extroversion, dominance, masculinity, and interpersonal sensitivity. He found conservatism to be negatively related to successful leadership. Many educational leaders are selected because they can be counted on *not* to rock the boat. According to Mann, they would not be among the more effective educational leaders.

There seems to be a moderate correlation between intelligence and leadership effectiveness (Stogdill, 1948; see also Morrow & Stern, 1990; Spreitzer et al., 1997; essays in Riggio et al., 2002). This positive correlation appears both in laboratory and field studies, and appears to be robust (Zaccaro et al., 2004). Certain aspects and kinds of intelligence also show positive correlations with leadership effectiveness. For example, divergent thinking is positively correlated with leadership success (Baehr, 1992; Mumford & Connelly, 1991; Mumford et al., 2002). Emotional intelligence is also a positive predictor of leadership (Caruso et al., 2002; Goleman et al., 2002; Sosik and Megerian, 1999; see also Zaccaro et al., 2004). Practical intelligence also predicts leadership success (Hedlund et al., 2003). An effective superintendent, say, would be able to come up with new ideas for the school system, be able to understand how people would respond to these ideas, and have practical ideas about how to implement the ideas.

More generally, Zaccaro et al. (2004) have proposed a model of attributes of leaders. The model comprises three distal attributes: personality, cognitive abilities, and motives and values, all three of which are viewed as overlapping with each other. The model also involves three proximal attributes: social-appraisal skills, problem-solving skills, and expertise/tacit knowledge. The last attribute points out, as we have (Sternberg et al., 2000), that an important part of leadership is understanding the system one is to lead. Superintendents frequently move from one job to the next at a fairly rapid clip. One thing they must keep in mind, if they wish to succeed, is the necessity of understanding the culture of the new system in which they are working before trying to implement serious changes. Otherwise, they risk failing for lack of understanding of the cultural environment in which they are working. What is "smart" in leadership, as in other things, depends on one's cultural context (Sternberg, 2004a).

There are at least three general problems with the trait-based approach. First, correlations of traits with leadership tend to be modest to moderate and hence can account for only a part, and generally, a fairly small part of what makes a leader successful. Second, the trait approach undervalues the importance of modifiability. Leaders are at least as much made as they are born. Leadership skills are teachable, and hence people can develop their leadership effectiveness in ways that trait theory cannot fully account for. Third, the trait approach is static, whereas leadership is dynamic. So this approach can account for part of what makes for a good leader, but certainly not all of it.

The Behavioral Approach

The behavioral approach fits into the tradition of B. F. Skinner and his behaviorist progenitors. Skinner, a radical behaviorist, believed that virtually all forms of human behavior, not just learning, could be explained by behavior emitted in reaction to the environment. Skinner rejected mental mechanisms. He believed instead that *operant conditioning*—involving the strengthening or weakening of behavior, contingent on the presence or absence of reinforcement (rewards) or punishments—could explain all forms of human behavior. Skinner applied his experimental analysis of behavior to many psychological phenomena, such as learning, language acquisition, and problem solving. Largely because of Skinner's towering presence, behaviorism dominated the discipline of psychology for several decades.

Behavioral theories are associated with mid-twentieth-century approaches at the University of Michigan and Ohio State University. Most behaviorally oriented theorists of leadership were not as extreme as Skinner. Nevertheless, they believed that the main shortcoming of trait theories was that they dealt with alleged antecedents to leadership behavior rather than with the behavior itself Bales (1951).

A typical view was that leadership involved two kinds of behaviors: those that were mission oriented and that led to productivity and those that were person oriented and that were sensitive to people's feelings. Leaders could be either high or low in initiating structure and in showing consideration (see, e.g., Blake & Mouton, 1964; Hersey & Blanchard, 1969; Stogdill & Coons, 1957). A related view was proposed by McGregor (1960). He suggested two "theories" of leadership, which he referred to as X and Y. Theory X assumes that people inherently dislike work and that nothing will much change that fact. Hence, leaders must act task and production oriented because otherwise employees will take advantage of them and work as little as possible. Theory Y assumes that people can enjoy work and feel affirmed by work if they are treated well. Hence, this theory emphasizes good treatment of employees by showing trust and respect for them and their work. According to this theory, for example, principals might treat their teachers as people committed to the caring of children. Or they might treat the teachers as people there just to collect a salary, as more loyal to their union than to their school, and as looking to goof off at the first available moment. The problem with the second (Theory X) view is that treating people that way may lead them to act that way, creating a self-fulfilling prophecy.

For example, Lewin et al. (1939) and Lewin and Lippitt (1938), studying Boy Scout and other groups, distinguished three kinds of leadership styles: authoritarian, democratic, and laissez-faire. Authoritarian leaders were directive and their subordinates were productive, but generally, only so long as the leaders were in the room or otherwise keeping close watch. Democratic leaders were the most successful leaders overall. They empowered their followers. Laissez-faire leaders were as nondirective as possible, much of the time leaving it to the followers to figure out what to do. When the followers could not figure out what to do, the groups became ineffectual.

Whereas the trait approach to leadership is still somewhat active, the behavioral approach has lost much of its appeal. Indeed, a recent encyclopedia of leadership (Goethals et al., 2004) devotes less space to this approach than to any of the major "competitors." There are several reasons why the behavioral approach has lost some of its popularity. First, whereas the trait approach assumes that leadership capabilities inhere largely in predispositions to behavior, the behavioral approach assumes that they inhere largely in the behavior itself. Each approach is incomplete without the other. Second, the behavioral approach is really a hybrid rather than a true behavioral approach. Skinner would not have likely identified the so-called behavioral approach as truly "behavioral" because it talks about internal dispositions. Third, and perhaps most important, the behavioral approach is simplistic, assuming that good leadership is a function of behavior rather than behavior in context. For example, there may be some situations in which behavior based on Theory X applies better, such as those in which the work to be done is aversive and personally unfulfilling, whereas there may be other situations in which behavior based on Theory Y applies better, such as those in which the work is personally fulfilling. Should a leader raise salaries, increase work-production quotas, or redesign jobs? Probably it depends on the situation. There is no one behavior or set of behaviors that is optimal for every situation.

Situational Approaches to Leadership

Social psychology tends to emphasize the importance of situational variables in behavior. For example, two of the most famous studies of all time (Milgram, 1974; Zimbardo, 1972) are famous precisely because they show the power of situations, in the case of Milgram, in inciting obedience, and in the case of Zimbardo, in inciting guard-like or prisoner-like behavior in a prison simulation. Situational approaches to leadership similarly emphasize the importance of situations in leadership (Ayman, 2004).

The situational view is reflected in the philosophy of Leo Tolstoy (1994), who said in *War and Peace:* "In historical events great men—so-called—are but labels serving to give a name to the event, and like labels they have the least possible connection with the event itself. Every action of theirs, that seems to them an act of their own free will, is in an historical sense not free at all, but in bondage to the whole course of previous history, and predestined from all eternity." On this theory, good principals, for example, are good largely because they had the good fortune to be given the job and were in the right place at the right time.

Research has given some support to the situational view. For example, Leavitt (1951) examined the relative effectiveness of four kinds of communication patterns in a group situation: a chain, a wheel, a Y, and a circle. He found that the person in the central junction of the Y was most likely to be identified as a leader because that person largely controlled communication in the group, merely by virtue of his position. In contrast, in a circle arrangement, each member of the group had a more nearly equal chance of being designated as a leader because no one controlled communication. Thus, the situation, rather than any particular trait or behavior, seemed to control who was viewed as a leader. In other studies, people seated at the head of a table were more likely to end up in a position of leadership (Howells & Becker, 1962). In a related study, Shartle (1951) reported that the best predictor of a manager's behavior was not his or her characteristics, but those of his or her boss. Thus, the leader merely mirrored the norms that the situation demanded.

The situational view is generally viewed today as oversimplified. First, whereas it rightfully acknowledges the importance of situations, it fails to acknowledge the importance of individual differences. Some leaders, in a given situation, fail, and hence are replaced, often by people who succeed better. For example, Steve Jobs took over the ailing Apple Computer Corporation from Gil Amelio, as Lou Gerstner took over the diminishing IBM corporation from John Akers. The successors saved their companies from further decline, showing that individuals matter, not just situations. Second, the situational approach fails to recognize the interaction between persons and situations. A given situation may work for one person and not for another. For example, Amelio or Akers might well have been more successful in another time. But the times did not fit their skills. "Comebacks" of formerly successful chief executive officers (CEOs) may or may not work, depending on whether the circumstances of the organization still call for the talents the CEO has to bring to the situation. Superintendents often are fired, and their successors find the success that they lacked. These successors are usually able to find the right blend of adaptation and shaping of the environment that enables them to bring in some kind of a vision, but that does not offend those who may not share this vision. Finally, the evidence in favor of the situational approach is rather minimal. There is no question that situations matter. But no data show situational variables to be exclusively important or even, perhaps, of primary importance.

Contingency Approaches to Leadership

Contingency models of leadership assume that there is an interaction between a leader's traits and the situation in which he or she finds him or herself. For example, Fiedler's (1978) cognitive-resource theory assumes such a contingency. Fiedler predicts that leaders who are more relationship oriented will be more effective than leaders who are task focused when there is moderate situational control; in contrast, leaders who are more task focused will be more effective in situations in which there is either high or low situational control. Fiedler also has looked at effects of intelligence. According to Fiedler, the correlation of intelligence with leadership success is moderated by a number of factors. One such factor is the stress experienced by the leader (Fiedler, 2002; Fiedler & Link, 1994), which apparently even can change the direction of the correlation. Intelligence positively predicts leadership success under conditions of low stress, but not high stress, where it may actually impede effectiveness. There is also some evidence that when a leader's cognitive skills are substantially higher than those of his or her followers, higher levels of cognitive skills may actually work against the leader's effectiveness (Simonton, 1994; Williams & Sternberg, 1988). For example, a highly intelligent superintendent might find her intelligence working against her if her preference is to apply careful and complete analysis to situations that provide neither the time nor the resources to allow such a preference to take root.

Another theory that emphasizes the interaction between a leader and the situation is that of Vroom (Vroom & Jago, 1978; Vroom & Yetton, 1973). This theory specifies what a leader's behavior should be as a function of the kind of situation he or she is in, for example, with regard to his or her own knowledge and that of the people he or she leads. Vroom's theory is based on five general strategies, two of which are autocratic, two of which are consultative, and one of which involves full participation of the group. The leader chooses a form of leadership based on four criteria, namely: improving the quality of decision making, increasing involvement of subordinates, reducing time spent in decision making, and developing subordinates. How consultative a principal should be, for example, would depend on the skill of the teachers he or she works with, how much pressure there is to reach a decision quickly, how much consultation the principal is comfortable in making, and so forth.

Path–goal theory, proposed by House (1971, 1996), identifies four types of leadership styles: directive, achievement oriented, supportive, and participative. The first two styles are more task oriented, the second two more relationship oriented. Which style works best depends on characteristics of the environment and of the followers one is to lead.

Yukl (1994) has suggested a number of variables that can enhance or diminish the effects of intervening variables in leadership. They include things such as recruitment and selection systems, geographical dispersion of the work unit, the nature of the flow of work, the size of the team, and team member characteristics.

Contingency theories represent the need for leaders to interact with the situation they are in. They remain one of the most popular kinds of theorizing today. The most difficult challenge they face is that of whether *everything* is an interaction. Probably that is not the case. For example, some reasonably high level of intelligence and openness to experience is probably associated with good leadership under most circumstances. To the extent that a theory turns everything into a contingency, it may become difficult to do what science needs to do—which is to provide a model that, in some way, reduces a phenomenon. At the extreme, if everything were a contingency, there would be nothing general to teach leaders. Nevertheless, this approach seems to be superior in recognizing that many attributes of leaders do indeed interact with situations.

Transformational Leadership Approaches

Transformational approaches to leadership originate in the work of Burns (1978). Burns suggested that there are essentially two ways of performing leadership functions. One is where there is an implicit or explicit contractual relationship between the leader and his or her followers. This type of leadership, which has come to be called *transactional leadership*, is characterized by followers agreeing to do certain stipulated things in exchange for the leader (usually a boss) doing other things. A second and more powerful kind of *transformational leadership* tries to gain converts to ideas.

Thus, transactional leaders emphasize the contractual relationship between leader and follower. For example, an employee might agree to engage in certain activities in exchange for certain rewards from the leadership of the organization by which he is employed (Sashkin, 2004). A transactional principal makes clear what he or she expects of his or her teachers. In exchange, those teachers who do what is expected of them will be adequately compensated and potentially be given benefits, such as better classes to teach, or a less demanding schedule. Transformational leaders emphasize higher needs, such as for self-actualization, and a leader–follower relationship in which followers may become leaders, and leaders, moral agents (Burns, 1978; Sashkin, 2004). In the terms of Bass and Avolio (Bass, 1985, 1998, 2002; Bass & Avolio, 1994; Bass et al., 1996), transactional leaders are more likely to pursue options that preserve current paradigms. Transformational leaders, on the other hand, are more likely to pursue any options that reject current paradigms. They are crowd-defiers. In terms of Kuhn's (1970) theory of scientific revolutions, which applies to ideas outside the sciences as well, transformational leaders revolutionize ways of thinking. They change the systems in which they work, whether they are classrooms, schools, or entire school systems.

Bass (1985) suggested that transactional and transformational leadership are not two opposite ends of a single continuum, but rather, two independent aspects of leadership. Bass developed a widely used measure, the Multifactor Leadership Questionnaire (MLQ), which assesses transactional and transformational aspects of leadership. In its latest form (Bass & Avolio, 1995), it yields five factors: idealized influence–attributions, idealized influence–behaviors, individualized consideration, intellectual stimulation, and inspirational motivation.

The transformational approach is currently popular and shows that good leadership is much more than good management. At the same time, it addresses only limited aspects of leadership. Not all organizations need to be transformed at a given time, and not all leaders who succeed are transformational. Indeed, there may be times when transformation is counter indicated, as when an organization is having great success in what it is doing or when times are such that resources are not available for substantial change. A successful school may not want to change because it has found a recipe for success. Thus, this theory addresses important aspects of leadership rather than leadership as a whole.

The Leading-Minds Approach to Leadership

Howard Gardner (1993a, 1993b, 1995) has proposed a theory of leadership based on multiple intelligences that takes a distinctly cognitive approach to understanding leadership.

Multiple Intelligences

In his earlier work, Gardner (1993b) sought to apply his theory of multiple intelligences to understanding leadership, and especially creative leadership. The theory proposes that intelligence can be understood as comprising eight or possibly nine distinct intelligences, each of which constitutes a separate symbol system. Linguistic intelligence is used in verbal communication, such as to understand newspaper articles, to write poetry, or speak articulately. Gardner used T. S. Eliot as an example of a creative leader in the linguistic domain. Logical/mathematical intelligence is used in posing and solving mathematical and logical problems. According to Gardner, Einstein was a creative leader in this domain. Bodily-kinesthetic intelligence is used in skilled physical activity, such as basketball, dance, and acrobatics. Gardner used Martha Graham as an example of a creative leader in this intelligence. Spatial intelligence is used in understanding space and form. Gardner held up Pablo Picasso as a master of this intelligence. Musical intelligence is used to read music, play an instrument, or sing a song. Gardner used Igor Stravinsky as an example of a creative leader in this intelligence. Interpersonal intelligence is used to understand other people and interact with them. Gardner used Mahatma Gandhi as an example of interpersonal intelligence. Intrapersonal intelligence is key to self-understanding. Gardner used Sigmund Freud as an example. After writing his 1993 book, Gardner (1999) added two more intelligences. Naturalist intelligence is used to understand patterns in nature, and, according to Gardner, is well exemplified by Charles Darwin. Existential intelligence, a so-called "candidate intelligence," is used to understand deeper issues of meaning in life, and might be particularly well exemplified by individuals such as Gautama Buddha.

Six Constants of Leadership

Gardner (1995) suggests that there are six constants of leadership. Different leaders excel in them to different degrees.

The first constant is a *story*. The leader must have a story to tell or some kind of message to convey. The story is more effective to the extent that it appeals to what Gardner (1991) refers to as the "unschooled mind," that is, a mind that, in terms of modern cognitive theory, is more experiential than rational in its thinking (Sloman, 1996). Stories need to address both individuals' own identities and those of the group or groups to which they belong. A story is more likely to succeed if it is central to what the leader actually does in his or her action, if the story can be unfolded over a long period of time, and if it can be stated in a time of relative calm. In times of crisis, according to Gardner, stories need to be simplified.

Stories may be inclusionary or exclusionary. Inclusionary leaders try to ensure that all of the followers for whom they are responsible somehow are made to feel inside the fold. Exclusionary leaders do not include everyone and in extreme cases, such as Hitler or Stalin, turn on segments of the population whom they are entrusted to lead.

The second constant is the *audience*. Gardner (1995) points out that no matter what the story, if there is no audience for it, it is dead. So a leader needs a story to which his or her audience will respond. The leader needs to take into account the experiential mode of thinking of the audience, and the kinds of changes in points of view to which the audience is likely to be responsive.

The third constant is the *organization*. Sooner or later, a leader needs some kind of organization or other institutional support. Sometimes, the leader starts with such backing. Other times, the leader must acquire the backing. Gardner points out that dictatorial leaders, such as Stalin, would have gotten nowhere without an organization to enforce their will. Nontotalitarian leaders, such as Churchill, discover that if they lose organizational support, they risk losing their hold on leadership.

The fourth constant is what Gardner refers to as the *embodiment*. The leader must in some way embody the story he or she tells. If the leader fails to do so, then that leader's leadership may be seen as bankrupt. For example, cover ups by Richard Nixon and Bill Clinton seriously undermined their leadership because they came to be seen as leaders who held others to one standard, and themselves to another. Many people recently have lost faith in certain church leaders who held their flocks to a standard of morality that they themselves flagrantly violated by abusing children or covering up such abuse. One cannot lead effectively if one asks people to do as one says, not as one does.

The fifth constant is *direct* and *indirect* leadership. In direct leadership, one has power of some kind over those whom one leads, as is the case for individuals in government positions. In indirect leadership, one's power stems from the symbolic products one creates. For example, the literary leadership of T. S. Eliot or the musical leadership of Igor Stravinsky was indirect. Most leaders are indirect. Their power is not necessarily lesser as a result. For example, Jesus was an indirect leader, yet one of the most powerful leaders in all of history.

The sixth constant is *expertise* (Sternberg, 1998d). A leader needs knowledge of a domain in order to lead effectively. As Gardner points out, direct leaders often have indirect knowledge; they tend to rely on the expertise of staff and other subordinates. Indirect leaders more often have direct knowledge; they themselves are experts.

Guidelines for Effective Leadership

Gardner (1995) proposes three general guidelines for effective leadership.

The first is to *appreciate the enduring features of leadership.* This means recognizing and appreciating the importance of the six constants mentioned earlier. If one loses sight of these features, one may also lose one's effectiveness as a leader.

The second is to *anticipate and deal with new trends.* Many leaders are effective at one point in time, only to lose their effectiveness and later find that they no longer have their audience. Often they have failed to cope with the changes that can happen so rapidly in the world. Thus, they cannot take their mantle of leadership for granted. They must continually reinvent it.

The third is to *encourage recognition of the problems, paradoxes, and possibilities of leadership.* A leader needs to educate his or her audience. At the same time, he or she must recognize what a difficult task this is, given the unschooled minds of most followers. There are many paradoxes in leadership, according to Gardner. One is the tension between technical expertise, on the one hand, and the need to reach the unschooled mind, on the other. Another is the need for stories that speak to many yet diverse individuals. A third is the problem that stories can build a community, or fragment it. Sometimes, there are factions that would prefer that the audience be fractionated. So a leader must live in a dialectical world in which unruly complications are the exception rather than the rule.

A Typical Exemplary Leader

Gardner (1995) has characterized what he refers to as an exemplary leader (EL). This leader is a persuasive speaker and is interested in understanding other people and how they think. The individual is energetic and resourceful and as a youngster, seems to be someone on the road to success, although it is not yet clear what form this success will take. Typically, the leader is well rounded rather than particularly strong in one particular area, although there are exceptions. The EL is willing when necessary to confront people in authority and may even do so in an abrasive way. Often, the EL feels superior in some sense toward others. ELs often lost their fathers at an early age and this loss may be part of what they feel empowers them to exercise the authority that the father is no longer there to exercise. ELs are open to experience and typically have many and diverse experiences before they actually enter into positions of leadership. He or she is attuned to the audience and sees how to capitalize on his or her experiences in creating a story that will resonate with the audience. The EL recognizes that one does not simply plop down into a position where he or she commands respect. Rather, it must be earned and then re-earned. The EL, thus, is aware of changes in the environment and capitalizes on these changes to renew his or her leadership.

Leaders Changing Minds

In his most recent work, Gardner (2004) has enumerated the steps leaders must take in order to change the minds of their followers. The first step is *research.* People can be persuaded by data. The second step is *overcoming resistances.* Leaders must expect groups of followers to resist some of the leaders' ideas. It is the leaders' responsibility to devise ways to overcome these resistances. The third step is becoming aware of *resources* and *rewards.* What does the leader have at his or her disposal to sweeten the pie—to encourage people to follow his or her leadership?

The fourth step is *representational redescription.* Ideas can be expressed in many ways. The more varied the ways in which a leader's ideas can be expressed, and the more compelling these ways are, the more likely the leader is to persuade followers to come along. The fifth step is *reason.* The leader needs to be prepared to reason with followers in order to persuade them to follow. The sixth step is *resonance.* At a given time and in a given place, certain ideas will resonate with followers, others will not. Establishing resonance can go a long way toward persuading people to listen. And the final step is incorporating *real-world events.* Followers need to see how the leader's ideas relate to the lives the followers live from day to day.

Having considered some of the main approaches to leadership, next consider the WICS theory, first through cognitive processing and then through stories of leadership on which the processes act.

The WICS Model

The WICS model is a possible common basis for identifying positive educational leaders, both developed and in development. This model is an expansion of a model of abilities for leadership proposed elsewhere (Sternberg, 2003c, 2003d, 2003e, 2003f, 2004b; Sternberg & Vroom, 2002). WICS, as noted earlier, is an acronym standing for *w*isdom, *i*ntelligence, and *c*reativity, *s*ynthesized. It builds on many of the models described earlier, but is different in systematically trying to combine wisdom, intelligence, and creativity, which are, separately, implicit in many previous models. According to the WICS model, wisdom, intelligence, and creativity synthesized provide a sine qua non for the positive educational leaders of the past, present, and future. Without a synthesis of these three attributes, someone can be a decent educational leader, and perhaps even a good one, but never a great one. A great educational leader uses creativity to generate possible depictions and solutions of problems, analytical intelligence to evaluate the quality of these depictions and solutions, practical intelligence to implement decisions and persuade others of their value, and wisdom to ensure the decisions help achieve a common good.

The history of the theory presented here has been documented, to some extent, in two earlier theoretical articles (Sternberg, 1980b, 1984). In the first article (Sternberg, 1980b), a theory of components of intelligence was presented, arguing that intelligence could be understood in terms of a set of elementary information-processing components that contributed to people's intelligence and individual differences in it. In the second article (Sternberg, 1984), the theory was expanded to include not just the analytical aspect of intelligence, which had been the emphasis of the earlier article, but the creative and practical aspects of intelligence as well. But I came to realize that intelligence, and even what I came to call *successful intelligence,* are not enough for positive educational leadership. Consider the role of a politician in educating his or her citizenry. Stalin was successfully intelligent in his own societal context, but he was not an educational leader, and certainly not a positive one. The current essay extends the theory to encompass creativity and wisdom in synthesis with each other and with intelligence.

In the remainder of this chapter, each of these attributes is discussed, although for didactic purposes, they are not discussed in the order in which they are stated earlier. The discussion starts with intelligence, which is a basis for creativity and for wisdom and so should be discussed first. Next creativity is discussed, which is essential as well for wisdom. Then, wisdom is discussed, which builds on but goes beyond intelligence and creativity. Finally, some general conclusions are drawn.

Intelligence

The Nature of Intelligence

There are many definitions of intelligence, although intelligence is typically defined in terms of a person's ability to adapt to the environment and to learn from experience (Sternberg & Detterman, 1986). The definition of intelligence here is somewhat more elaborate and is based on my (Sternberg, 1997, 1998a, 1999c) theory of successful intelligence. According to this definition, (successful) intelligence is (1) the ability to achieve one's goals in life, given one's sociocultural context; (2) by capitalizing on strengths and correcting or compensating for weaknesses; (3) in order to adapt to, shape, and select environments; (4) through a combination of analytical, creative, and practical abilities.

Consider first Item 1. Intelligence involves formulating a meaningful and coherent set of goals, and having the skills and dispositions to reach those goals. One individual may wish to be a statesperson, another, a scientist, and still another, an artist. Others may decide on careers in athletics, plumbing, politics, acting, or whatever. The question typically is not so much what goals individuals have chosen, but rather, what the individuals have done so that they can realize those goals in a meaningful way. Thus, this item actually includes three subitems: (a) identifying meaningful goals, (b) coordinating those goals in a meaningful way so that they form a coherent story of what one is seeking in life, and (c) moving a substantial distance along the path toward reaching those goals.

This first item recognizes that "intelligence" means a somewhat different thing to each individual. The individual who wishes to become a Supreme Court judge will be taking a different path from the individual who wishes to become an educational leader—but both will have formulated a set of coherent goals toward which to work. An evaluation of intelligence should focus not on what goal is chosen but on whether the individual has chosen a worthwhile set of goals and shown the skills and dispositions needed to achieve them.

Item 2 recognizes that although psychologists sometimes talk of a "general" factor of intelligence (Jensen, 1998; Spearman, 1927; see essays in Sternberg, 2000; Sternberg & Grigorenko, 2002b), really, virtually no one is good at everything or bad at everything. People who are the positive educational leaders of society have identified their strengths and weaknesses, and have found ways to work effectively within that pattern of abilities.

There is no single way to succeed in a job that works for everyone. For example, some principals are successful by virtue of their strong analytical skills. They can figure out the problems their schools are confronting, and what aspects of the school are working better and worse. Other leaders may be successful by their creative intellectual skills. They may not be the best at figuring out what is right and wrong in the present system. But they may be strong in figuring out a vision for what needs to be done. And still other principals are strong in practical skills. They get along well with people and/or know how to implement the programs their school has adopted.

This same general principle applies in any profession. Consider, for example, teaching. Educators often try to distinguish characteristics of expert teachers (see Sternberg & Williams, 2001), and indeed, they have distinguished some such characteristics. But the truth is that teachers can excel in many different ways. Some teachers are better in giving large lectures, others in small seminars, others in one-on-one mentoring. There is no one formula that works for every teacher. Good teachers figure out their strengths and try to arrange their teaching so that they can capitalize on their strengths and at the same time either compensate for or correct their weaknesses. Team teaching is one way of doing so, in that one teacher can compensate for what the other does not do well.

Candidates for positions of positive educational leadership might have different patterns of abilities. Sometimes selection committees will have feelings of discomfort, recognizing that they are obliged to choose between "apples and oranges"—that is, to evaluate people whose strengths are drastically different on a single scale that does not seem to apply across all applicants. For example, one candidate may excel in creativity, another in interpersonal skills. The two dimensions do no collapse well into one scale. When the committee looks at their task from the standpoint of the theory of successful intelligence, their job becomes easier. The question is not how well people do on some common scale, but rather, how well they do on whatever scales are relevant to their making the most of their own aspirations—in other words, how well they capitalize on their strengths without letting their weaknesses get in their way. Of course, they further need to reflect on other attributes that may be required over and above intelligence.

Item 3 recognizes that intelligence broadly defined refers to more than just "adapting to the environment," which is the mainstay of conventional definitions of intelligence. The theory of successful intelligence distinguishes among adapting, shaping, and selecting.

In adaptation to the environment, one modifies oneself to fit an environment. The ability to adapt to the environment is important in life, and is especially important to individuals entering a new program. Most of them will be entering a new environment that is quite different from the one in which they previously have spent time. If they are not adaptable, they may not be able to transfer the skills they showed in the previous environment to the new one. Over the course of a lifetime, environmental conditions change greatly. A kind of work that at one point in time may be greatly valued (e.g., forming a start-up company) may, at another point in time, be valued little if at all. In research, the problems change, and sometimes, people who were effective in solving the problems of one decade are relatively ineffective in solving the problems of another decade. In governmental leadership, some elected leaders prove to be dinosaurs—people who were able to lead the country effectively under one set of conditions but not under another set of conditions (such as when the national or world economy tanks). Clearly, adaptability is a key skill in any definition of intelligence. An educational leader ought to be able to show the ability to adapt to a variety of environments.

In life, adaptation is not enough, however. Adaptation needs to be balanced with shaping. In shaping, one modifies the environment to fit what one seeks of it, rather than modifying oneself to fit the environment. Truly great educational leaders are not just adaptors; they are also shapers. They recognize that they cannot change everything, but that if they want to have an impact on the world, they have to change some things. Part of successful intelligence is deciding what to change, and then how to change it.

When an individual enters an institution, one hopes that the individual will not only adapt to the environment, but shape it in a way that makes it a better place than it was before. Selection committees look for evidence not just of a candidate's engagement in a variety of activities but also of the individual's having made a difference in those activities. Through shaping, one has this kind of impact (see Sternberg, 2003a).

Sometimes, one attempts unsuccessfully to adapt to an environment and then also fails in shaping that environment. No matter what one does to try to make the environment work out, nothing in fact seems to work. In such cases, the appropriate action may be to select another environment.

Many of the greatest people in any one field are people who started off in another field and found that the first field was not really the one in which they had the most to contribute. Nobel Prize winner Herbert Simon is a good example. He started off working in mathematics and economics, and then later worked in political science, and then in computer science and psychology. Rather than spend their lives doing something that turned out not to match their pattern of strengths and weaknesses, they had the sense to find something else to do where they really had a contribution to make.

Item 4 points out that successful intelligence involves a broader range of abilities than is typically measured by tests of intellectual and academic skills. Most of these tests measure primarily or exclusively memory and analytical abilities. With regard to memory, they assess the abilities to recall and recognize information. With regard to analytical abilities, they measure the skills involved when one analyzes, compares and contrasts, evaluates, critiques, and judges. These are important skills during the school years and in later life. But they are not the only skills that matter for success in school and life. People need not only to remember and analyze concepts, they need to be able to generate and apply them. Memory pervades analytic, creative, and practical thinking, and is necessary for their execution; but it is far from sufficient.

According to the proposed theory of human intelligence and its development (Sternberg, 1980b, 1984, 1985a, 1990, 1997, 1999a, 2003e, 2004a), a common set of processes underlies all aspects of intelligence. These processes are hypothesized to be universal. For example, although the solutions to problems that are considered intelligent in one culture may be different from the solutions considered to be intelligent in another culture, the need to define problems and translate strategies to solve these problems exists in any culture.

Metacomponents, or executive processes, plan what to do, monitor things as they are being done, and evaluate things after they are done. Examples of metacomponents are recognizing the existence of a problem, defining the nature of the problem, deciding on a strategy for solving the problem, monitoring the solution of the problem, and evaluating the solution after the problem is solved.

Performance components execute the instructions of the metacomponents. For example, inference is used to decide how two stimuli are related, and application is used to apply what one has inferred (Sternberg, 1977).

Other examples of performance components are comparison of stimuli, justification of a given response as adequate although not ideal, and actually making the response.

Knowledge-acquisition components are used to learn how to solve problems or simply to acquire declarative knowledge in the first place (Sternberg, 1985a). Selective encoding is used to decide what information is relevant in the context of one's learning. Selective comparison is used to bring old information to bear on new problems. And selective combination is used to put together the selectively encoded and compared information into a single and sometimes insightful solution to a problem.

Although the same processes are used for all three aspects of intelligence universally, these processes are applied to different kinds of tasks and situations depending on whether a given problem requires analytical thinking, creative thinking, practical thinking, or a combination of these kinds of thinking. In particular, analytical thinking is invoked when components are applied to fairly familiar kinds of problems abstracted from everyday life. Creative thinking is invoked when the components are applied to relatively novel kinds of tasks or situations. Practical thinking is invoked when the components are applied to experience to adapt to, shape, and select environments. One needs creative skills and dispositions to generate ideas, analytical skills and dispositions to decide if they are good ideas, and practical skills and dispositions to implement one's ideas and to convince others of their worth.

More details regarding the theory can be found in Sternberg (1984, 1985a, 1997). Because the theory of successful intelligence comprises three subtheories—a componential subtheory dealing with the components of intelligence; an experiential subtheory dealing with the importance of coping with relative novelty and of automatization of information processing; and a contextual subtheory dealing with processes of adaptation, shaping, and selection—the theory has been referred to from time to time as *triarchic*.

Intelligence is not, as Edwin Boring (1923) once suggested, merely what intelligence tests test. Intelligence tests and other tests of cognitive and academic skills measure part of the range of intellectual skills. They do not measure the whole range. One should not conclude that a person who does not test well is not smart. Rather, one should merely look at test scores as one indicator among many of a person's intellectual skills.

The Assessment of Intelligence

Our assessments of intelligence have been organized around the analytical, creative, and practical aspects of it. I discuss those assessments here.

Analytical Intelligence

Analytical intelligence is involved when the information-processing components of intelligence are applied to analyze, evaluate, judge, or compare and contrast. It typically is involved when components are applied to relatively familiar kinds of problems in which the judgments to be made are of a fairly abstract nature.

In some early work, it was shown how analytical kinds of problems, such as analogies or syllogisms, can be analyzed componentially (Guyote & Sternberg, 1981; Sternberg, 1977, 1980b, 1983; Sternberg & Gardner, 1983; Sternberg & Turner, 1981), with response times or error rates decomposed to yield their underlying information-processing components. The goal of this research was to understand the information-processing origins of individual differences in (the analytical aspect of) human intelligence. With componential analysis, one could specify sources of individual differences underlying a factor score such as that for "inductive reasoning." For example, response times on analogies (Sternberg, 1977) and linear syllogisms (Sternberg, 1980a) were decomposed into their elementary performance components. The general strategy of such research is to (a) specify an information-processing model of task performance; (b) propose a parameterization of this model, so that each information-processing component is assigned a mathematical parameter corresponding to its latency (and another corresponding to its error rate); and (c) construct cognitive tasks administered in such a way that it is possible through mathematical modeling to isolate the parameters of the mathematical model. In this way, it is possible to specify, in the solving of various kinds of problems, several sources of important individual or developmental differences: (1) What performance components are used? (2) How long does it take to execute each component? (3) How susceptible is each component to error? (4) How are the components combined into strategies? (5) What are the mental representations on which the components act?

As an example, through componential analysis, it was possible to decompose inductive-reasoning performance into a set of underlying information-processing components. The analogy $A : B :: C : D$, $D1$, $D2$, $D3$, $D4$ is used as an example to illustrate the components. These components are (1) *encoding*, the amount of time needed to register each stimulus $(A, B, C, D1, D2, D3, D4)$; (2) *inference*, the amount of time needed to discern the basic relation between given stimuli $(A$ to $B)$; (3) *mapping*, the amount of time needed to transfer the relation from one set of stimuli to another (needed in analogical reasoning) $(A$ to $C)$; (4) *application*, the amount of time needed to apply the relation as inferred (and sometimes as mapped) to a new set of stimuli $(A$ to B as C to $?)$; (5) *comparison*, the amount of time needed to compare the validity of the response options $(D1, D2, D3, D4)$; (6) *justification*, the amount of time needed to justify one answer as the best of the bunch (e.g., $D1$); and (7) *preparation–response*, the amount of time needed to prepare for the problem's solution and to respond.

Studies of reasoning need not use artificial formats. In a more recent study, a colleague and I looked at predictions for everyday kinds of situations, such as when milk will spoil (Sternberg & Kalmar, 1997). In this study, the investigators looked at both predictions and postdictions (hypotheses about the past in which information about the past is unknown) and found that postdictions took longer to make than did predictions.

Research on the components of human intelligence yielded some interesting results. Consider some examples. First, execution of early components (e.g., inference and mapping) tends exhaustively to consider the attributes of the stimuli, whereas execution of later components (e.g., application) tends to consider the attributes of the stimuli in self-terminating fashion, with only those attributes processed that are essential for reaching a solution (Sternberg, 1977). Second, in a study of the development of figural analogical reasoning, it was found that although children generally became quicker in information processing with age, not all components were executed more rapidly with age (Sternberg & Rifkin, 1979). The encoding component first showed a decrease in component time with age and then an increase. Apparently, older children realized that their best strategy was to spend more time in encoding the terms of a problem so that they later would be able to spend less time in operating on these encodings. A related, third finding was that better reasoners tend to spend relatively more time than do poorer reasoners in global, up-front metacomponential planning when they solve difficult reasoning problems. Poorer reasoners, on the other hand, tend to spend relatively more time in local planning (Sternberg, 1981). Presumably, the better reasoners recognize that it is better to invest more time up front so as to be able to process a problem more efficiently later on. Fourth, it also was found in a study of the development of verbal analogical reasoning that as children grew older, their strategies shifted so that they relied on word association less and abstract relations more (Sternberg & Nigro, 1980).

Some of the componential studies concentrated on knowledge-acquisition components rather than performance components or metacomponents. For example, in one set of studies, the investigators were interested in sources of individual differences in vocabulary (Sternberg & Powell, 1983; Sternberg et al., 1983; see also Sternberg, 1987a, 1987b). We were not content just to view these as individual differences in declarative knowledge because we wanted to understand why it was that some people acquired this declarative knowledge and others did not. What we found was that there are multiple sources of individual and developmental differences. The three main sources were in knowledge-acquisition components, use of context clues, and use of mediating variables. For example, in the sentence, "The blen rises in the east and sets in the west," the knowledge-acquisition component of selective comparison is used to relate prior knowledge about a known concept, the sun, to the unknown word (neologism) in the sentence, "blen." Several context cues appear in the sentence, such as the fact that a blen rises, the fact that it sets, and the information about where it rises and sets. A mediating variable is that the information can occur after the presentation of the unknown word.

We did research such as that described earlier because we believed that conventional psychometric research sometimes incorrectly attributed individual and developmental differences. For example, a verbal analogies test that might appear on its surface to measure verbal reasoning might in fact measure primarily vocabulary and general information (Sternberg, 1977). In fact, in some populations, reasoning might hardly be a source of individual or developmental differences at all. And if researchers then look at the sources of the individual differences in vocabulary, they would need to understand that the differences in knowledge did not come from nowhere: Some children had much more frequent and better opportunities to learn word meanings than did others.

In the componential-analysis work described earlier, correlations were computed between component scores of individuals and scores on tests of different kinds of psychometric abilities. First, in the studies of inductive reasoning (Sternberg, 1977; Sternberg & Gardner, 1982, 1983), it was found that although inference, mapping, application, comparison, and justification tended to correlate with such tests, the highest correlation typically was with the preparation–response component. This result was puzzling at first because this component was estimated as the regression constant in the predictive regression equation. This result ended up giving birth to the concept of the metacomponents: higher-order processes used to plan, monitor, and evaluate task performance. It was also found, second, that the correlations obtained for all the components showed convergent–discriminant validation: They tended to be reliably related with psychometric tests of reasoning but not with psychometric tests of perceptual speed (Sternberg, 1977; Sternberg & Gardner, 1983). Moreover, third, significant correlations with vocabulary tended to be obtained only for encoding of verbal stimuli (Sternberg, 1977; Sternberg & Gardner, 1983). Fourth, it was found in studies of linear-syllogistic reasoning (e.g., *John is taller than Mary; Mary is taller than Susan; who is tallest?*) that components of the proposed (mixed linguistic–spatial) model that were supposed to correlate with verbal ability did so but did not correlate with spatial ability; components that were supposed to correlate with spatial ability did so but did not correlate with verbal ability. In other words, it was possible successfully to validate the proposed model of linear-syllogistic reasoning not only in terms of the fit of response-time or error data to the predictions of the alternative models but also in terms of the correlations of component scores with psychometric tests of verbal and spatial abilities (Sternberg, 1980a). Fifth and finally, it was found that there were individual differences in strategies in solving linear syllogisms, whereby some people used a largely linguistic model, others a largely spatial model, and most the proposed linguistic–spatial mixed model. Thus, sometimes, less than perfect fit of a proposed model to group data may reflect individual differences in strategies among participants.

Creative Intelligence

Intelligence tests contain a range of problems, some of them more novel than others. In some of the componential work we have shown that when one goes beyond the range of unconventionality of the conventional tests of intelligence, one starts to tap sources of individual differences measured little or not at all by the tests. According to the theory of successful intelligence, (creative) intelligence is particularly well measured by problems assessing how well an individual can cope with relative novelty. Thus, it is important to include problems that are relatively novel in nature in a battery of tests.

We (Sternberg, 1982) presented 80 individuals with novel kinds of reasoning problems that had a single best answer. For example, they might be told that some objects are green and others blue; but still other objects might be grue, meaning green until the year 2000 and blue thereafter, or bleen, meaning blue until the year 2000 and green thereafter. Or they might be told of four kinds of people on the planet Kyron, blens, who are born young and die young; kwefs, who are born old and die old; balts, who are born young and die old; and prosses, who are born old and die young. Their task was to predict future states from past states, given incomplete information (see also Tetewsky & Sternberg, 1986). In another set of studies, 60 people were given more conventional kinds of inductive reasoning problems, such as analogies, series completions, and classifications, but were told to solve them. The problems, though, had premises preceding them that were either conventional (dancers wear shoes) or novel (dancers eat shoes). The participants had to solve the problems as though the counterfactuals were true (Sternberg & Gastel, 1989a, 1989b).

In these studies, we found that correlations with conventional kinds of tests depended on how novel or nonentrenched the conventional tests were. The more novel are the items, the higher are the correlations of our tests with scores on successively more novel conventional tests. Thus, the components isolated for relatively novel items would tend to correlate more highly with more unusual tests of fluid abilities (e.g., that of Cattell & Cattell, 1973) than with tests of crystallized abilities.

We also found that when response times on the relatively novel problems were componentially analyzed, some components better measured the creative aspect of intelligence than did others. For example, in the "grue–bleen" task mentioned earlier, the information-processing component requiring people to switch from conventional green–blue thinking to grue–bleen thinking and then back to green–blue thinking again was a particularly good measure of the ability to cope with novelty.

Practical Intelligence

Practical intelligence involves individuals applying their abilities to the kinds of problems that confront them in daily life, such as on the job or in the home. Practical intelligence involves applying the components of intelligence to experience so as to (a) adapt to, (b) shape, and (c) select environments. Adaptation is involved when one changes oneself to suit the environment. Shaping is involved when one changes the environment to suit oneself. And selection is involved when one decides to seek out another environment that is a better match to one's needs, abilities, and desires. People differ in their balance of adaptation, shaping, and selection, and in the competence with which they balance among the three possible courses of action.

   Much of our work on practical intelligence has centered on the concept of tacit knowledge (Sternberg et al., 2000). We have defined this construct as what one needs to know in order to work effectively in an environment that one is not explicitly taught in school or at work and that often is not even verbalized explicitly (Sternberg et al., 1993, 1995, 2000; Sternberg & Wagner, 1993; Wagner, 1987; Wagner & Sternberg, 1986). An example of tacit knowledge would be knowing that if teachers are asked to do too many new things to improve their teaching, they may become confused and teach less rather than more effectively.

   We typically have measured tacit knowledge using work-related problems that present problems one might encounter on the job. We have measured tacit knowledge for both children and adults, and among adults, for people in over two dozen occupations, such as management, sales, academia, teaching, school administration, secretarial work, and the military. In a typical tacit-knowledge problem, people are asked to read a story about a problem someone faces and to rate, for each statement in a set of statements, how adequate a solution the statement represents. For example, in a paper-and-pencil measure of tacit knowledge for sales, one of the problems deals with sales of photocopy machines. A relatively inexpensive machine is not moving out of the show room and has become overstocked. The examinee is asked to rate the quality of various solutions for moving the particular model out of the show room. In a performance-based measure for sales people, the test-taker makes a phone call to a supposed customer, who is actually the examiner. The test-taker tries to sell advertising space over the telephone. The examiner raises various objections to buying the advertising space. The test-taker is evaluated for the quality, rapidity, and fluency of his or her responses on the telephone.

   In the tacit-knowledge studies (reviewed in Sternberg et al., 2000), we found, first, that practical intelligence as embodied in tacit knowledge increases with experience, but it is profiting from experience rather than experience per se that results in increased scores. Some people can have been in a job for years and still have acquired relatively little tacit knowledge. Second, we also found that subscores on tests of tacit knowledge—such as for managing oneself, managing others, and managing tasks—correlate significantly with each other. Third, scores on various tests of tacit knowledge, such as for academics and managers, are also correlated fairly substantially (at about the 0.5 level) with each other. Thus, fourth, tests of tacit knowledge may yield a general factor across these tests. However, fifth, scores on tacit-knowledge tests do not correlate with scores on conventional tests of intelligence, whether the measures used are single-score measures or multiple-ability batteries. Thus, any general factor from the tacit-knowledge tests is not the same as any general factor from tests of academic abilities (suggesting that neither kind of g factor is truly general, but rather, general only across a limited range of measuring instruments). Sixth, despite the lack of correlation of practical-intellectual with conventional measures, the scores on tacit-knowledge tests predict performance on the job as well as or better than do conventional psychometric intelligence tests. We further found, seventh, that scores on our tests of tacit knowledge for management were the best single predictor of performance on a managerial simulation. In a hierarchical regression, scores on conventional tests of intelligence, personality, styles, and interpersonal orientation were entered first and scores on the test of tacit knowledge were entered last. Scores on the test of tacit knowledge were the single best predictor of managerial simulation score. Moreover, these scores also contributed to the prediction even after everything else was entered first into the equation. In recent work on military leadership (Hedlund et al., 2003; Sternberg & Hedlund, 2002; Sternberg et al., 2000), it was found, eighth, that scores of 562 participants on tests of tacit knowledge for military leadership predicted ratings of leadership effectiveness, whereas scores on a conventional test of intelligence and on a tacit-knowledge test for managers did not significantly predict the ratings of effectiveness.

We also have done studies of social intelligence, which is viewed in the theory of successful intelligence as a part of practical intelligence (Barnes & Sternberg, 1989; Sternberg & Smith, 1985). In these studies, 40 individuals were presented with photos and were asked to make judgments about the photos. For one kind of photo, they were asked to evaluate whether a male–female couple was a genuine couple (i.e., really involved in a romantic relationship) or a phony couple posed by the experimenters. For another kind of photo, they were asked to indicate which of two individuals was the other's supervisor. Females were superior to males on these tasks. Scores on the two tasks did not correlate with scores on conventional ability tests, nor did they correlate with each other, suggesting a substantial degree of domain specificity in the task.

Even stronger results were obtained overseas. In a study in Usenge, Kenya, near the town of Kisumu, we examined school-age children's ability to adapt to their indigenous environment. We devised a test of practical intelligence for adaptation to the environment (see Sternberg & Grigorenko, 1997; Sternberg, Nokes, et al., 2001). The test of practical intelligence measured children's informal tacit knowledge for natural herbal medicines that the villagers believe can be used to fight various types of infections. At least some of these medicines appear to be effective (Dr. Frederick Okatcha, personal communication), and most villagers certainly believe in their efficacy, as shown by the fact that children in the villages use their knowledge of these medicines an average of once a week in medicating themselves and others. Thus, tests of how to use these medicines constitute effective measures of one aspect of practical intelligence as defined by the villagers as well as their life circumstances in their environmental contexts. Middle-class Westerners might find it quite a challenge to thrive or even survive in these contexts, or, for that matter, in the contexts of urban ghettos often not distant from their comfortable homes.

We measured the Kenyan children's ability to identify the medicines, where they come from, what they are used for, and how they are dosed. Based on work we had done elsewhere, we expected that scores on this test would not correlate with scores on conventional tests of intelligence (Sternberg et al., 2000). In order to test this hypothesis, we also administered to 85 children the Raven Coloured Progressive Matrices Test, which is a measure of fluid or abstract–reasoning-based abilities, as well as the Mill Hill Vocabulary Scale, which is a measure of crystallized or formal–knowledge-based abilities. In addition, we gave the children a comparable test of vocabulary in their own Dholuo language. The Dholuo language is spoken in the home; English is spoken in the schools.

We did indeed find no correlation between the test of indigenous tacit knowledge and scores on the fluid-ability tests. But to our surprise, we found negative correlations between the tacit-knowledge tests and scores on the tests of crystallized abilities. In other words, on average the higher the children scored on the test of tacit knowledge, the lower they scored on the tests of crystallized abilities. This surprising result can be interpreted in various ways, but based on the ethnographic observations of the anthropologists on the team, we concluded that a plausible scenario takes into account the expectations of families for their children.

Many children drop out of school before graduation, for financial or other reasons, and many families in the village do not particularly value formal Western schooling. There is no reason they should, as the children of many families will for the most part spend their lives farming or engaged in other occupations that make little or no use of Western schooling. These families emphasize teaching their children the indigenous informal knowledge that will lead to successful adaptation in the environments in which they will really live. Children who spend their time learning the indigenous practical knowledge of the community generally do not invest themselves heavily in doing well in school, whereas children who do well in school generally do not invest themselves as heavily in learning the indigenous knowledge—hence the negative correlations.

The Kenya (Sternberg, Castejón, et al., 2001; Sternberg, Nokes, et al., 2001) study suggests that the identification of a general factor of human intelligence may tell us more about how abilities interact with patterns of schooling and especially Western patterns of schooling than it does about the structure of human abilities. In Western schooling, children typically study a variety of subject matters from an early age and thus develop skills in a variety of skill areas. This kind of schooling prepares the children to take a test of intelligence, which typically measures skills in a variety of areas. Often, intelligence tests measure skills that children were expected to acquire a few years before taking the intelligence test. But as Rogoff (1990) and others have noted, this pattern of schooling is not universal and has not even been common for much of the history of humankind. Throughout history and in many places still, schooling, especially for boys, takes the form of apprenticeships in which children learn a craft from an early age. They learn what they will need to know in order to succeed in a trade, but not a lot more. They are not simultaneously engaged in tasks that require the development of the particular blend of skills measured by conventional intelligence tests. Hence, it is less likely that one would observe a general factor in their scores, much as the investigators discovered in Kenya. Some years back, Vernon (1971) pointed out that the axes of a factor analysis do not necessarily reveal a latent structure of the mind but rather represent a convenient way of characterizing the organization of mental abilities. Vernon believed that there was no one "right" orientation of axes, and indeed, mathematically, an infinite number of orientations of axes can be fit to any solution in an exploratory factor analysis. Vernon's point seems perhaps to have been forgotten or at least ignored by later theorists.

I have considered so far each of the aspects of intelligence separately. Next, I examine how they fare when assessed together.

All Three Aspects of Intelligence Together

Factor-Analytic Studies. Several separate factor-analytic studies support the internal validity of the theory of successful intelligence. In one study (Sternberg et al., 1999), we used the so-called Sternberg Triarchic Abilities Test (STAT—Sternberg, 1993) to investigate the internal validity of the theory. Three hundred twenty-six high school students, primarily from diverse parts of the United States, took the test, which comprised 12 subtests in all. There were four subtests each measuring analytical, creative, and practical abilities. For each type of ability, there were three multiple-choice tests and one essay test. The multiple-choice tests, in turn, involved, respectively, verbal, quantitative, and figural content. Consider the content of each test:

1. Analytical-Verbal: Figuring out meanings of neologisms (artificial words) from natural contexts. Students see a novel word embedded in a paragraph and have to infer its meaning from the context.
2. Analytical-Quantitative: Number series. Students have to say what number should come next in a series of numbers.
3. Analytical-Figural: Matrices. Students see a figural matrix with the lower-right entry missing. They have to say which of the options fits into the missing space.
4. Practical-Verbal: Everyday reasoning. Students are presented with a set of everyday problems in the life of an adolescent and have to select the option that best solves each problem.
5. Practical-Quantitative: Everyday math. Students are presented with scenarios requiring the use of math in everyday life (e.g., buying tickets for a ballgame) and have to solve math problems based on the scenarios.
6. Practical-Figural: Route planning. Students are presented with a map of an area (e.g., an entertainment park) and have to answer questions about navigating effectively through the mapped area.
7. Creative-Verbal: Novel analogies. Students are presented with verbal analogies preceded by counterfactual premises (e.g., money falls off trees). They have to solve the analogies as though the counterfactual premises were true.
8. Creative-Quantitative: Novel number operations. Students are presented with rules for novel number operations, for example, "flix," which involves numerical manipulations that differ as a function of whether the first of two operands is greater than, equal to, or less than the second. Students have to use the novel number operations to solve presented math problems.
9. Creative-Figural: In each item, students are first presented with a figural series that involves one or more transformations; they then have to apply the rule of the series to a new figure with a different appearance, and complete the new series.
10. Analytical-Essay: This essay requires students to analyze the use of security guards in high schools: What are the advantages and disadvantages and how can these be weighed to make a recommendation?

11. Practical-Essay: Give three practical solutions to a problem you are currently having in your life.
12. Creative-Essay: Describe the ideal school.

Confirmatory factor analysis on the data was supportive of the triarchic theory of human intelligence, yielding separate and uncorrelated analytical, creative, and practical factors. The lack of correlation was due to the inclusion of essay as well as multiple-choice subtests. Although multiple-choice tests tended to correlate substantially with multiple-choice tests, their correlations with essay tests were much weaker. The multiple-choice analytical subtest loaded most highly on the analytical factor, but the essay, creative, and practical subtests loaded most highly on their respective factors. Thus, measurement of creative and practical abilities should, ideally, be accomplished with other kinds of testing instruments that complement multiple-choice instruments.

In another study, conducted with 3252 students in the United States, Finland, and Spain, we used the multiple-choice section of that STAT to compare five alternative models of intelligence, again via confirmatory factor analysis (Sternberg, Castejón, et al., 2001). A model featuring a general factor of intelligence fit the data relatively poorly. The triarchic model, allowing for intercorrelation among the analytic, creative, and practical factors, provided the best fit to the data.

In a further study, we (Grigorenko & Sternberg, 2001) tested 511 Russian school children (ranging in age from 8 to 17 years) as well as 490 mothers and 328 fathers of these children. They used entirely distinct measures of analytical, creative, and practical intelligence. Consider, for example, the ability tests used for adults (similar tests were used for children) described next.

Fluid analytical intelligence was measured by two subtests of a test of nonverbal intelligence. The *Test of g: Culture Fair, Level II* (Cattell & Cattell, 1973) is a test of fluid intelligence designed to reduce, as much as possible, the influence of verbal comprehension, culture, and educational level, although no test eliminates such influences. In the first subtest, *Series*, individuals were presented with an incomplete, progressive series of figures. The participants' task was to select, from among the choices provided, the answer that best continued the series. In the *Matrices* subtest, the task was to complete the matrix presented at the left of each row.

The test of crystallized intelligence was adapted from existing traditional tests of analogies and synonyms/antonyms used in Russia. We used adaptations of Russian rather than American tests because the vocabulary used in Russia differs from that used in the United States. The first part of the test included 20 verbal analogies (KR20 = 0.83). An example is *circle–ball = square–?* *(a) quadrangular, (b) figure, (c) rectangular, (d) solid, (e) cube.* The second part included 30 pairs of words, and the participants' task was to specify whether the words in the pair were synonyms or antonyms (KR20 = 0.74). Examples are *latent–hidden,* and *systematic–chaotic.*

The measure of creative intelligence also comprised two parts. The first part asked the participants to describe the world through the eyes of insects. The second part asked participants to describe who might live and what might happen on a planet called "Priumliava." No additional information on the nature of the planet was specified. Each part of the test was scored in three different ways to yield three different scores. The first score was for originality (novelty), the second was for the amount of development in the plot (quality), and the third was for creative use of prior knowledge in these relatively novel kinds of tasks (sophistication). The measure of practical intelligence was self-report and also comprised two parts. The first part was designed as a 20-item, self-report instrument, assessing practical skills in the social domain (e.g., effective and successful communication with other people), in the family domain (e.g., how to fix household items, how to run the family budget), and in the domain of effective resolution of sudden problems (e.g., organizing something that has become chaotic). The second part had four vignettes, based on themes that appeared in popular Russian magazines in the context of discussion of adaptive skills in the current society. The four themes were, respectively, how to maintain the value of one's savings, what to do when one makes a purchase and discovers that the item one has purchased is broken, how to locate medical assistance in a time of need, and how to manage a salary bonus one has received for outstanding work. Each vignette was accompanied by five choices and participants had to select the best one. Obviously, there is no one "right" answer in this type of situation. Hence Grigorenko and Sternberg used the most frequently chosen response as the keyed answer. To the extent that this response was suboptimal, this suboptimality would work against the researchers in subsequent analyses relating scores on this test to other predictor and criterion measures.

In this study, exploratory principal-component analysis for both children and adults yielded similar factor structures. Both varimax and oblimin rotations yielded clear-cut analytical, creative, and practical factors for the tests. Thus, with a sample of a different nationality (Russian), a different set of tests, and a different method of analysis (exploratory rather than confirmatory analysis), there was again support for the theory of successful intelligence.

The analytical, creative, and practical tests the investigators employed were used to predict mental and physical health among the Russian adults. Mental health was measured by widely used paper-and-pencil tests of depression and anxiety, and physical health was measured by self-report. The best predictor of mental and physical health was the practical-intelligence measure. Analytical intelligence came second and creative intelligence came third. All three contributed to prediction, however. Thus, the researchers again concluded that a theory of intelligence encompassing all three elements provides better prediction of success in life than does a theory comprising just the analytical element.

In a recent study supported by the College Board (Sternberg & the Rainbow Project Team, 2002; Sternberg, the Rainbow Project Collaborators, & University of Michigan Business School Project Collaborators, 2004), we used an expanded set of tests on 1015 students at 15 different institutions (13 colleges and 2 high schools). Our goal was not to replace the SAT, but to devise tests that would supplement the SAT, measuring skills that this test does not measure. In addition to the multiple-choice STAT tests described earlier, we used three additional measures of creative skills and three of practical skills.

The three additional tests of creative skills were as follows:

1. *Cartoons.* Participants were given five cartoons purchased from the archives of the *New Yorker*, but with the captions removed. The participant's task was to choose three cartoons and to provide a caption for each cartoon. Two trained judges rated all the cartoons for cleverness, humor, and originality. A combined creativity score was formed by summing the individual ratings on each dimension.

2. *Written Stories.* Participants were asked to write two stories, spending about 15 min on each, choosing from the following titles: "A Fifth Chance," "2983," "Beyond the Edge," "The Octopus's Sneakers," "It's Moving Backwards," and

"Not Enough Time." A team of four judges was trained to rate the stories for originality, complexity, emotional evocativeness, and descriptiveness. These stories were based on work originally done to measure creativity (Sternberg & Lubart, 1995), which is described further later.

3. *Oral Stories.* Participants were presented with five sheets of paper, each containing a set of pictures linked by a common theme. For example, participants might receive a sheet of paper with images of a musical theme, a money theme, or a travel theme. The participant then chose one of the pages and was given 15 min to formulate a short story and dictate it into a cassette recorder. The dictation period was not to be more than 5 min long. The process was then repeated with another sheet of images so that each participant dictated a total of two oral stories. Six judges were trained to rate the stories for originality, complexity, emotional evocativeness, and descriptiveness.

The three additional tests of practical skills were as follows:

1. *Everyday Situational Judgment Inventory (Movies).* This video-based inventory presents participants with seven brief vignettes that capture problems encountered in general, everyday life, such as determining what to do when asked to write a letter of recommendation for someone you do not know particularly well.
2. *Common Sense Questionnaire.* This written inventory presents participants with 15 vignettes that capture problems encountered in general business-related situations, such as managing tedious tasks or handling a competitive work situation.
3. *College Life Questionnaire.* This written inventory presents participants with 15 vignettes that capture problems encountered in general college-related situations, such as handling trips to the bursar's office or dealing with a difficult roommate.

We found that our tests significantly and substantially improved on the validity of the SAT for predicting first-year college grades (Sternberg & the Rainbow Project Collaborators, 2005). The test also improved equity: Using the expanded test to admit a class would result in greater ethnic diversity than would using just the SAT or just the SAT and grade-point average. This expanded test is now going into Phase-2 piloting, where it will be tried out on a larger sample of individuals.

Instructional Studies. Instructional studies are a further means of testing the theory. We have used instruction both in cognitive skills, in general (Sternberg, 1987a; Sternberg & Williams, 1996; Williams et al., 2002), and in academic skills, in particular (Sternberg et al., 1998a, 1998b).

1. *Cognitive skills.* The kinds of analytical, creative, and practical abilities discussed in this chapter are not fixed but, rather, modifiable.

Analytical skills can be taught. For example, in one study, I (Sternberg, 1987a) tested whether it is possible to teach people better to decontextualize meanings of unknown words presented in context. In one study, I gave 81 participants a pretest on their ability to decontextualize word meanings. Then the participants were divided into five conditions, two of which were control conditions that lacked formal instruction. In one condition, participants were not given any instructional treatment. They were merely asked later to take a posttest. In a second condition, they were given practice as an instructional condition, but there was no formal instruction, per se. In a third condition, they were taught knowledge-acquisition component processes that could be used to decontextualize word meanings. In a fourth condition, they were taught to use context cues. In a fifth condition, they were taught to use mediating variables. Participants in all three of the theory-based formal-instructional conditions outperformed participants in the two control conditions, whose performance did not differ. In other words, theory-based instruction was better than no instruction at all or just practice without formal instruction.

Creative-thinking skills also can be taught and a program has been devised for teaching them (Sternberg & Williams, 1996; see also Sternberg & Grigorenko, 2000). In some relevant work, the investigators divided 86 gifted and nongifted fourth-grade children into experimental and control groups. All children took pretests on insightful thinking. Then some of the children received their regular school instruction, whereas others received instruction on insight skills. After instruction, all children took a posttest on insight skills. Results indicated that children taught how to solve the insight problems using knowledge-acquisition components gained more from pretest to posttest than did students who were not so taught (Davidson & Sternberg, 1984).

Practical-intelligence skills also can be taught. We developed a program for teaching practical intellectual skills, aimed at middle school students, that explicitly teaches students "practical intelligence for school" in the contexts of doing homework, taking tests, reading, and writing (Gardner et al., 1994; Williams et al., 1996, 2002). We evaluated the program in a variety of settings (Gardner et al., 1994; Sternberg et al., 1990) and found that students taught via the program outperformed students in control groups that did not receive the instruction.

Individuals' use of practical intelligence can be to their own gain in addition to or instead of the gain of others. People can be practically intelligent for themselves at the expense of others. It is for this reason that wisdom needs to be studied in its own right in addition to practical or even successful intelligence (Baltes & Staudinger, 2000; Sternberg, 1998b).

In sum, practical intelligence, like analytical intelligence, is an important antecedent of life success. Because measures of practical intelligence predict everyday behavior at about the same level as measures of analytical intelligence (and sometimes even better), the sophisticated use of such tests could double the explained variance in various kinds of criteria of success. Using measures of creative intelligence as well might increase prediction still more. Thus, tests based on the construct of successful intelligence might lead to new and higher levels of prediction. At the same time, expansions of conventional tests that stay within the conventional framework of analytical tests based on standard psychometric models do not seem likely to expand greatly our predictive capabilities (Schmidt & Hunter, 1998).

I view intelligence as a form of developing expertise (Sternberg, 1998a, 1998d, 1999a, 2003a). Indeed, some of the tests we use may seem more like tests of achievement or of developing expertise (see Ericsson, 1996; Howe et al., 1998) than of intelligence. But it can be argued that intelligence is itself a form of developing expertise—that there is no clear-cut distinction between the two constructs (Sternberg, 1998a, 1999a). Indeed, all measures of intelligence, one might argue, measure a form of developing expertise.

An example of how tests of intelligence measure developing expertise emanates from work we have done in Tanzania. A study done in Tanzania (see Sternberg &

Grigorenko, 1997; Sternberg, Grigorenko, et al., 2002) points out the risks of giving tests, scoring them, and interpreting the results as measures of some latent intellectual ability or abilities. We administered tests to 358 school children between the ages of 11 and 13 years near Bagamoyo, Tanzania, tests including a form-board classification test; a linear syllogisms test; and a Twenty Questions Test, which measure the kinds of skills required on conventional tests of intelligence. Of course, we obtained scores that they could analyze and evaluate, ranking the children in terms of their supposed general or other abilities. However, we administered the tests dynamically rather than statically (Brown & Ferrara, 1985; Budoff, 1968; Day et al., 1997; Feuerstein, 1979; Grigorenko & Sternberg, 1998; Guthke, 1993; Haywood & Tzuriel, 1992; Lidz, 1987, 1991; Sternberg & Grigorenko, 2002a; Tzuriel, 1995; Vygotsky, 1978). Dynamic testing is like conventional static testing in that individuals are tested and inferences about their abilities made. But dynamic tests differ in that children are given some kind of feedback in order to help them improve their scores. Vygotsky (1978) suggested that the children's ability to profit from the guided instruction received during the testing session could serve as a measure of children's zone of proximal development (ZPD), or the difference between their developed abilities and their latent capacities. In other words, testing and instruction are treated as being of one piece rather than as being distinct processes.

This integration makes sense in terms of traditional definitions of intelligence as the ability to learn ("Intelligence and Its Measurement," 1921; Sternberg & Detterman, 1986). What a dynamic test does is directly measure processes of learning in the context of testing rather than measuring these processes indirectly as the product of past learning. Such measurement is especially important when not all children have had equal opportunities to learn in the past.

In our assessments, children were first given the ability tests. In an experimental group, they then were given a brief period of instruction in which they were able to learn skills that would potentially enable them to improve their scores. In a control group, they were not given this intervention. Then all students were tested again. Because the instruction for each test lasted only about 5–10 min, dramatic gains were not expected. Yet, on average, the gains were statistically significant in the experimental group, and statistically greater than in the control group. In the control group, pretest and posttest scores correlated at the 0.8 level. In the experimental group, however, scores on the pretest showed only weak although significant correlations with scores on the posttest. These correlations, at about the 0.3 level, suggested that when tests are administered statically to children in developing countries, they may be rather unstable and easily subject to influences of training. The reason could be that the children are not accustomed to taking Western-style tests, and so profit quickly even from small amounts of instruction as to what is expected from them. Of course, the more important question is not whether the scores changed or even correlated with each other, but rather how they correlated with other cognitive measures. In other words, which test was a better predictor of transfer to other cognitive performance, the pretest score or the posttest score? The posttest score was the better predictor.

2. *Academic skills.* In a first set of studies, researchers explored the question of whether conventional education in school systematically discriminates against children with creative and practical strengths (Sternberg & Clinkenbeard, 1995; Sternberg et al., 1996, 1999). Motivating this work was the belief that the systems in most schools strongly tend to favor children with strengths in memory and analytical abilities. However, schools can be unbalanced in other directions as well. One school Elena

Grigorenko and I visited in Russia in 2000 placed a heavy emphasis on the development of creative abilities—much more so than on the development of analytical and practical abilities. While on this trip, we were told of yet another school—catering to the children of Russian businessmen—that strongly emphasized practical abilities, and in which children who were not practically oriented were told that, eventually, they would be working for their classmates who were practically oriented.

The investigators used the Sternberg Triarchic Abilities Test, as described earlier, in some of their instructional work. The test was administered to 326 children around the United States and in some other countries who were identified by their schools as gifted by any standard whatsoever. Children were selected for a summer program in (college-level) psychology if they fell into one of five ability groupings: high analytical, high creative, high practical, high balanced (high in all three abilities), or low balanced (low in all three abilities). Selected students who came to Yale University were then divided into four instructional groups. Students in all four instructional groups used the same introductory-psychology textbook (a preliminary version of Sternberg [1995]) and listened to the same psychology lectures. What differed among them was the type of afternoon discussion section to which they were assigned. They were assigned to an instructional condition that emphasized either memory, analytical, creative, or practical instruction. For example, in the memory condition, they might be asked to describe the main tenets of a major theory of depression. In the analytical condition, they might be asked to compare and contrast two theories of depression. In the creative condition, they might be asked to formulate their own theory of depression. In the practical condition, they might be asked how they could use what they had learned about depression to help a friend who was depressed.

Students in all four instructional conditions were evaluated in terms of their performance on homework, a midterm exam, a final exam, and an independent project. Each type of work was evaluated for memory, analytical, creative, and practical quality. Thus, all students were evaluated in exactly the same way. Results suggested the utility of the theory of successful intelligence. This utility showed itself in several ways.

First, we observed that when the students arrived at Yale University the students in the high creative and high practical groups were much more diverse in terms of racial, ethnic, socioeconomic, and educational backgrounds than were the students in the high analytical group, suggesting that correlations of measured intelligence with status variables such as these may be reduced by using a broader conception of intelligence. Thus, the kinds of students identified as strong differed in terms of populations from which they were drawn in comparison with students identified as strong solely by analytical measures. More important, just by expanding the range of abilities measured, the investigators discovered intellectual strengths that might not have been apparent through a conventional test.

Second, we found that all three ability tests—analytical, creative, and practical—predicted course performance. When multiple-regression analysis was used, at least two of these ability measures contributed significantly to the prediction of each of the measures of achievement. Perhaps as a reflection of the difficulty of deemphasizing the analytical way of teaching, one of the significant predictors was always the analytical score. (However, in a replication of our study with low-income African American students from New York, Deborah Coates of the City University of New York found a different pattern of results. Her data indicated that the practical tests were better predictors of course performance than were the analytical measures, suggesting that what ability test predicts what criterion depends on population as well as mode of teaching.)

Third, and most important, there was an aptitude–treatment interaction whereby students who were placed in instructional conditions that better matched their pattern of abilities outperformed students who were mismatched. In other words, when students are taught in a way that fits how they think, they do better in school. Children with creative and practical abilities, who are almost never taught or assessed in a way that matches their pattern of abilities, may be at a disadvantage in course after course, year after year.

A follow-up study (Sternberg et al., 1998a, 1998b) examined learning of social studies and science by third-graders and eighth-graders. The 225 third-graders were students in a low-income neighborhood in Raleigh, North Carolina. The 142 eighth-graders were students who were largely from middle- to upper-middle class homes studying in Baltimore, Maryland, and Fresno, California. In this study, students were assigned to one of three instructional conditions. In the first condition, they were taught the course that basically they would have learned had there been no intervention. The emphasis in the course was on memory. In a second condition, students were taught in a way that emphasized critical (analytical) thinking. In the third condition, they were taught in a way that emphasized analytical, creative, and practical thinking. All students' performance was assessed for memory learning (through multiple-choice assessments) as well as for analytical, creative, and practical learning (through performance assessments).

As expected, students in the successful-intelligence (analytical, creative, practical) condition outperformed the other students in terms of the performance assessments. One could argue that this result merely reflected the way they were taught. Nevertheless, the result suggested that teaching for these kinds of thinking succeeded. More important, however, was the result that children in the successful-intelligence condition outperformed the other children even on the multiple-choice memory tests. In other words, to the extent that one's goal is just to maximize children's memory for information, teaching for successful intelligence is still superior. It enables children to capitalize on their strengths and to correct or to compensate for their weaknesses, and it allows children to encode material in a variety of interesting ways.

We have now extended these results to reading curricula at the middle school and the high school level (Grigorenko et al., 2002). In a study of 871 middle school students and 432 high school students, we taught reading either triarchically or through the regular curriculum. At the middle school level, reading was taught explicitly. At the high school level, reading was infused into instruction in mathematics, physical sciences, social sciences, English, history, foreign languages, and the arts. In all settings, students who were taught triarchically substantially outperformed students who were taught in standard ways.

Thus, the results of three sets of studies suggest that the theory of successful intelligence is valid as a whole. Moreover, the results suggest that the theory can make a difference not only in laboratory tests but in school classrooms and even the everyday life of adults as well.

Creativity

The Nature of Creativity

Creativity is not an attribute limited to the historic "greats"—the Darwins, the Picassos, the Hemingways. Rather, it is something anyone can use. To a large extent, creativity is a decision.

According to the investment theory of creativity, creative leaders are like good investors: They buy low and sell high (Sternberg, 2003b; Sternberg & Lubart, 1995, 1996). Whereas investors do so in the world of finance, creative leaders do so in the world of ideas. Creative leaders generate ideas that are like undervalued stocks (stocks with a low price-to-earnings ratio), and both the stocks and the ideas are generally rejected by the public. When creative ideas are proposed, they often are viewed as bizarre, useless, and even foolish, and are summarily rejected. The person proposing them often is regarded with suspicion and perhaps even with disdain and derision. This is one of many reasons that it is so hard to change schools and school systems: People are often suspicious, rather than welcoming, of change.

Creative ideas are both novel and valuable. They potentially have impact (Sternberg, 2003a). But, they are often rejected because the creative leader stands up to vested interests and defies the crowd. The crowd does not maliciously or willfully reject creative notions. Rather, it does not realize, and often does not want to realize, that the proposed idea represents a valid and advanced way of thinking. Society generally perceives opposition to the status quo as annoying, offensive, and reason enough to ignore innovative ideas.

Evidence abounds that creative ideas are often rejected (Gardner, 1993a; Sternberg, 2003b; Sternberg & Lubart, 1995). Initial reviews of major works of literature and art are often negative. Toni Morrison's *Tar Baby* received negative reviews when it was first published, as did Sylvia Plath's *The Bell Jar*. The first exhibition in Munich of the work of Norwegian painter Edvard Munch opened and closed the same day because of the strong negative response from the critics. Some of the greatest scientific papers have been rejected not just by one journal, but even by several journals before being published. For example, John Garcia, a distinguished biopsychologist, was immediately denounced when he first proposed that a form of learning called classical conditioning could be produced in a single trial of learning (Garcia & Koelling, 1966).

From the investment view, then, the creative leader buys low by presenting a unique idea and then attempting to convince other people of its value. After convincing others that the idea is valuable, which increases the perceived value of the investment, the creative person sells high by leaving the idea to others and moving on to another idea. Leaders typically want others to embrace their ideas, but immediate universal applause for an idea usually indicates that it is not particularly creative. Many educators spend their lives feeling frustrated, waiting for the acceptance of their ideas that never is forthcoming.

Creativity is as much a decision about and an attitude toward life as it is a matter of ability. Creativity is often obvious in young children, but it is harder to find in older children and adults because their creative potential has been suppressed by a society that encourages intellectual conformity.

Creative work requires applying and balancing the three intellectual abilities— creative, analytic, and practical—all of which can be developed (Sternberg, 1985a; Sternberg & Lubart, 1995; Sternberg & O'Hara, 1999; Sternberg & Williams, 1996). Creative ability is used to generate ideas. Everyone, even the most creative person, has better and worse ideas. Without well-developed analytic ability, the creative thinker is as likely to pursue bad ideas as to pursue good ones. The creative individual uses analytic ability to work out the implications of a creative idea and to test it. Practical ability is the ability to translate theory into practice and abstract ideas into practical accomplishments. An implication of the investment theory of creativity is that good ideas do not sell themselves. The creative person uses practical ability to convince other people that an idea is valuable. For example, every organization has a set of ideas that dictate how things, or at least some things, should be done. When an individual proposes a new procedure, she or he must sell it by convincing others that it is better than the old one. Practical ability is also used to recognize ideas that have a potential audience.

Creativity requires analytic and practical as well as creative skills. Leaders may fail to be creative because they lack any of the skills. The leader who is only synthetic may come up with innovative ideas, but cannot recognize or sell them. The leader who is only analytic may be an excellent critic of other people's ideas, but is not likely to generate creative ideas. The leader who is only practical may be an excellent salesperson, but is as likely to promote ideas or products of little or no value as to promote genuinely creative ideas.

Attributes Leading to Creativity

What kinds of attributes should one look for in leaders in order to assess their creativity?

1. *Redefining problems.* Redefining a problem means taking a problem and turning it on its head. Many times in life, individuals have a problem and they just do not see how to solve it. They are stuck in a box. Redefining a problem essentially means extricating oneself from the box. This process is the synthetic part of creative thinking.

The educational leader encounters many kinds of novel situations that resist easy definition in terms of past experience. The more flexible the individual is in redefining these situations so that they make sense to him or her, the more likely the individual is to succeed. Flexible definition and redefinition of problems, thus, are essential to creativity (Davidson & Sternberg, 1984; Getzels & Csikszentmihalyi, 1976; Sternberg, 1985a). Getzels & Csikszentmihalyi's (1976) seminal research on problem finding showed that art students who produced highly original still-life drawings spent longer periods of time formulating their compositions than less creative peers.

2. *Questioning and analyzing assumptions.* Often one does not realize the nature of the assumptions one has because these assumptions are widely shared. Creative people question assumptions and eventually lead others to do the same. Questioning assumptions is part of the analytical thinking involved in creativity. When Copernicus suggested that Earth revolves around the sun, the suggestion was viewed as preposterous because everyone could see that the sun revolves around Earth. Galileo's ideas, including the relative rates of falling objects, caused him to be banned as a heretic.

Sometimes it is not until many years later that society realizes the limitations or errors of their assumptions and the value of the creative person's thoughts. The impetus of those who question assumptions allows for cultural, technological, and other forms of advancement.

Schools in particular, and society in general, tend to make a pedagogical mistake by emphasizing the answering and not the asking of questions (Sternberg, 1994). The good student is perceived as the one who rapidly furnishes the right answers. The expert in a field thus becomes the extension of the expert student—the one who knows and can recite a lot of information. As John Dewey (1933) recognized, how one thinks is often more important than what one thinks. Schools need to teach students how to ask the right questions (questions that are good, thought-provoking, and interesting) and lessen the emphasis on rote learning. Institutions perhaps do not wish to identify as educational leaders those who merely are experts in spitting back what others have previously said.

3. *Realizing that creative ideas do not sell themselves.* Everyone would like to assume that his or her wonderful, creative ideas will sell themselves. But as Galileo, Edvard Munch, Toni Morrison, Sylvia Plath, and many others have discovered, they do not. On the contrary, creative ideas are usually viewed with suspicion and distrust (see essays in Sternberg, 1998c, 2003b). Moreover, those who propose such ideas may be viewed with suspicion and distrust as well. Because people are comfortable with the ways they already think, and because they probably have a vested interest in their existing way of thinking, it is difficult to dislodge them from their current way of thinking. Superintendents often must spend more time selling their ideas than coming up with them.

4. *Recognizing that knowledge is a double-edged sword.* On the one hand, one cannot be creative without knowledge. Quite simply, one cannot go beyond the existing state of knowledge if one does not know what that state is. Many students have ideas that are creative with respect to themselves, but not with respect to the field because others have had the same ideas before. Those with a greater knowledge base can be creative in ways that those who are still learning about the basics of the field cannot be.

At the same time, those who have an expert level of knowledge can experience tunnel vision, narrow thinking, and entrenchment. Experts can become so stuck in a way of thinking that they become unable to extricate themselves from it (Adelson, 1984; Frensch & Sternberg, 1989; Sternberg & Lubart,1995). For example, Frensch and Sternberg (1989) found experts more susceptible than novices to set effects in bridge when the basic rules of the game were played. Learning must be a lifelong process, not one that terminates when a person achieves some measure of recognition. When a person believes that he or she knows everything there is to know, he or she is unlikely to ever show truly meaningful creativity again.

The upshot of this is that the teaching–learning process is a two-way process. We, as teachers, have as much to learn from our students as they have to learn from us. We have knowledge they do not have, but they have flexibility we do not have—precisely because they do not know as much as we do. By learning from, as well as teaching to, one's students, one opens up channels for creativity that otherwise would remain closed. The educational leader needs to use knowledge to move beyond where things are, rather than to replicate what others have already done or to get stuck in old ways of thinking that no longer serve a constructive purpose.

5. *Willingness to surmount obstacles.* Buying low and selling high means defying the crowd. And people who defy the crowd—people who think creatively—almost inevitably encounter resistance. The question is not whether one will encounter obstacles; that obstacles will be encountered is a fact. The question is whether the creative leader has the fortitude to persevere (Golann, 1962; Roe, 1952). I have often wondered why so many people start off their careers doing creative work and then vanish from the radar screen. Here is at least one reason why: Sooner or later, they decide that being creative is not worth the resistance and punishment. The truly creative leaders pay the short-term price because they recognize that they can make a difference in the long term. But often it is a long while before the value of creative ideas is recognized and appreciated.

Creative individuals encounter many obstacles in their lives. Some of them have led "charmed" lives. But sooner or later, the obstacles start to present themselves. The ones who go on to greatness are those who are prepared to surmount rather than succumb to these obstacles.

6. *Willingness to take sensible risks.* When creative leaders defy the crowd by buying low and selling high, they take risks in much the same way as do people who invest. Some such investments simply may not pan out. Moreover, defying the crowd means risking the crowd's wrath. But there are levels of sensibility to keep in mind when defying the crowd. Creative leaders take sensible risks and produce ideas that others ultimately admire and respect as trendsetting (Glover, 1977; McClelland et al., 1953). In taking these risks, creative people sometimes make mistakes, fail, and fall flat on their faces.

Nearly every major discovery or invention entailed some risk. When a movie theater was the only place to see a movie, someone created the idea of the home video machine. Skeptics questioned if anyone would want to see videos on a small screen. Another initially risky idea was the home computer. Many wondered if anyone would have enough use for a home computer to justify the cost. These ideas were once risks that are now ingrained in our society.

Willingness to take risks is especially important for creative leaders. Many of them got to where they are by *not* taking risks. They played the academic game with consummate gamesmanship, doing what needed to be done and playing it safe so that they would not get "burned." But there is a transition in the life of every great leader. He or she needs to start taking risks. It is important, therefore, to select people who are willing to risk.

7. *Tolerance of ambiguity.* People often like things to be in black and white. They like to think that a country is good or bad (ally or enemy) or that a given idea in education works or does not work. The problem is that there are a lot of grays in creative work. Artists working on new paintings and writers working on new books often report feeling scattered and unsure in their thoughts. They often need to figure out whether they are even on the right track. Scientists often are not sure whether the theory they have developed is exactly correct. These creative thinkers need to tolerate the ambiguity and uncertainty until they get the idea just right (Barron & Harrington, 1981; Golann, 1962).

A creative idea tends to come in bits and pieces and develops over time. However, the period in which the idea is developing tends to be uncomfortable, as Darwin found in formulating his theory of evolution over a long period of time. Without time or the ability to tolerate ambiguity, many may jump to a less than optimal solution. Creative leaders often undertake major projects in their early years. They should be individuals who are willing to tolerate ambiguity long enough to make these projects not just good, but great.

8. *Willingness to grow.* Many people have one or two creative ideas early on, but then become afraid to have any more. They may be afraid that their next idea will not be as good as their last one, or that they will embarrass themselves if the new idea does not pan out. Or they may have acquired an investment in an idea and not want to give it up. Leaders who are creative throughout their lives continue to grow and recognize that learning is lifelong (Sternberg & Lubart, 1995).

9. *Self-efficacy.* People often reach a point at which they feel as if no one believes in them or values or even appreciates what they are doing. Because creative work often does not get a warm reception, it is important that the creative leaders believe in the value of what they are doing. This is not to say that individuals should believe that every idea they have is a good idea. Rather, individuals need to believe that, ultimately, they have the ability to make a difference. In the course of their studies,

creative individuals will sometimes doubt themselves. To succeed in life, one has to believe not in each and every thing one does, but in one's ability to get done what needs to get done, and to recover from the inevitable setbacks that life throws one's way (Bandura, 1997).

10. *Finding what one loves to do.* Teachers must help students find what excites them to unleash their students' best creative performances. Teachers need to remember that this may not be what really excites them. Leaders who truly excel creatively in a pursuit, whether vocational or avocational, almost always genuinely love what they do. Certainly, the most creative leaders are intrinsically motivated in their work (Amabile, 1983, 1996; Crutchfield, 1962; Golann, 1962; Rogers, 1954). Less creative people often pick a career for the money or prestige and are bored with or loathe their career. Most often, these people do not do work that makes a difference in their field.

One often meets students who are pursuing a certain field not because it is what they want to do, but because it is what their parents or other authority figures expect them to do. One may feel sorry for such students, knowing that although they may do good work in that field, they almost certainly will not do great work. It is hard for people to do great work in a field that simply does not interest them.

Identification committees should select those students who genuinely love what they do and wish to keep doing it, not because it brings them extrinsic rewards, but because they feel a calling to do it. The people who feel such a calling are the ones who later can make a true difference.

11. *Willingness to delay gratification.* Part of being creative means being able to work on a project or task for a long time without immediate or interim rewards. Students must learn that rewards are not always immediate and that there are benefits to delaying gratification (Mischel et al., 1989). The fact of the matter is that, in the short term, people are often ignored when they do creative work or even punished for doing it.

Hard work often does not bring immediate rewards. Students do not immediately become expert baseball players, dancers, musicians, or sculptors. And the reward of becoming an expert can seem far away. Students often succumb to the temptations of the moment, such as watching television or playing video games. The people who make the most of their abilities are those who wait for a reward and recognize that few serious challenges can be met in a moment.

The short-term focus of most school assignments does little to teach children the value of delaying gratification. Long-term projects are clearly superior in meeting this goal, but it is difficult for teachers to assign home projects if they are not confident of parental involvement and support. By working on a task for many weeks or months, students learn the value of making incremental efforts for long-term gains.

Because much of schooling is about short-term rewards, many of the candidates for selective programs will not truly have learned the importance of delaying gratification. Yet it is a lesson they need to learn because the great contributions to the world are rarely made quickly.

12. *Courage.* Above all, defying the crowd takes, courage. Those who do not have courage of their convictions may be many things—they will not be creative. A creative leader can be many things. If he or she is not courageous, the other things may not matter (Amabile, 1983; Barron & Harrington, 1981; Dellas & Gaier, 1970; Golann, 1962; MacKinnon, 1962, 1965).

Kinds of Creative Leadership

Theorists of creativity and related topics have recognized that there are different types of creative leadership (see reviews in Ochse, 1990; Sternberg, 1988; Weisberg, 1993). For example, Kuhn (1970) distinguished between normal and revolutionary science. Normal science expands on an already existing paradigm of scientific research, whereas revolutionary science proposes a new paradigm. Revolutionary leading thinkers have included Newton and Einstein in the field of physics, Darwin and Wallace in the field of biology, Braque and Picasso in the field of art, and Freud and Wundt in the field of psychology. Darwin's contribution is particularly well analyzed by Gruber (1981).

Gardner (1993b, 1994) also described different types of creative contributions individuals can make. They include (a) the solution of a well-defined problem, (b) the development of an encompassing theory, (c) the creation of a "frozen work," (d) the performance of a ritualized work, and (e) a "high-stakes" performance. Other bases for distinguishing among types of creative contributions also exist. For example, psychoeconomic models such as those of Rubenson and Runco (1992) and Sternberg and Lubart (1991, 1995, 1996) can distinguish different types of contributions in terms of the parameters of the models. In the Sternberg–Lubart model, contributions might differ in the extent to which they "defy the crowd" or in the extent to which they redefine how a field perceives a set of problems. Simonton's (1997) model of creativity also proposes parameters of creativity, and contributions might be seen as differing in terms of the extent to which they vary from other contributions and the extent to which they are selected for recognition by a field of endeavor (see also Campbell, 1960; Perkins, 1995; Simonton, 1997). But in no case were these models intended explicitly to distinguish among types of creative contributions. Rather, the models can be extrapolated to suggest how different creators might differ in their contributions in terms of the parameters that are proposed to make the contributors creative.

A view that is more likely to distinguish among types of creative leadership was proposed by Gough and Woodworth (1960), who discussed stylistic variations among professional research scientists. The styles include zealots, initiators, diagnosticians, scholars, artificers, estheticians, and methodologists. For example, a zealot proposes a cause and then becomes strongly identified with that cause, sometimes with only minimal empirical support for the arguments behind the cause. A methodologist concentrates on and takes great care with the methodology of his or her contributions and perhaps with the innovation inhering in the methodology, possibly at the expense of paying attention to the substantive contribution.

Maslow (1967) distinguished more generally between two types of creativity, which he referred to as primary and secondary. Primary creativity is the kind of creativity a person uses to become self-actualized—to find fulfillment in one's life. Secondary creativity is the kind of creativity with which scholars in the field are more familiar—the kind that leads to creative achievements of the kind typically recognized by a field.

Disagreements among scholars in the field of creativity also may reflect different kinds of creative leadership. Ward et al. (1999) noted three such apparent disagreements and how the disagreements may reflect differences in kinds of creativity rather than in what "truly" underlies creativity. One apparent disagreement is regarding goal-oriented versus exploratory creativity. Ward and his colleagues noted that there is evidence to favor the roles of focusing (Bowers et al., 1990; Kaplan & Simon, 1990) and of exploratory thinking (Bransford & Stein, 1984; Getzels & Csikszentmihalyi, 1976) on creative thinking. It may be, however, that both kinds of thinking can lead to creative work of different kinds. A second distinction made by Ward and his colleagues is between domain-specific (Clement, 1989; Langley et al., 1987; Perkins, 1981; Weisberg, 1986) and universal (Finke, 1990, 1995; Guilford, 1968; Koestler, 1964) creativity skills, although both kinds of skills may be relevant to creativity. They suggested, for example, that efficient exploration of a preinventive structure depends on knowledge and experience, but that general methods may be relevant in designing a new form of transportation. Finally, Ward and his colleagues distinguished between unstructured (Bateson, 1979; Findlay & Lumsden, 1988; Johnson-Laird, 1988) and structured or systematic (Perkins, 1981; Ward, 1994; Weisberg, 1986) creativity. Unstructured creativity suggests that randomness, or perhaps blind variation in the generation of ideas, plays a major role in creativity (see, e.g., Cziko, 1998; Simonton, 1998), whereas structured creativity suggests that some kind of system is highly involved in the generation of ideas (see, e.g., Sternberg, 1999b). Again, Ward and his colleagues saw structure and lack of structure as complementary rather than contradictory. Indeed, different biological mechanisms—such as in levels or types of cortical activation—may underlie different types of creativity (Martindale, 1999).

Here, I propose that there are three basic types of creative educational leadership (Sternberg, 1999b; Sternberg, Kaufman, & Pretz, 2002, 2003). One type accepts current paradigms. This type includes replication, redefinition, forward incrementation, and advance forward incrementation. A second type rejects current paradigms. It includes redirection, reconstruction/redirection, and reinitiation. And a third type synthesizes current paradigms. It includes simply synthesis. Consider each kind.

Types of Creative Leadership That Accept Current Paradigms

Replication. This type of creative leadership is a limiting (minimally creative) case. It is an attempt to show that a field or organization is in the right place at the right time. The leader therefore attempts to maintain it in that place. The propulsion keeps the organization where it is rather than moving it. The view of the leader is that the organization is where it needs to be. The leader's role is to keep it there. This type of creativity is represented by stationary motion, as of a wheel that is moving but staying in place. The replicative leader metaphorically pedals in place, as with a stationary bicycle.

Organizations tend to choose replicative leaders when the organization is succeeding and the goal of those seeking the new leader is to maintain the perceived status, and perhaps, preeminence, of the organization. The greatest threat to the organization is likely to be perceived to be loss of current status, not failure to gain new status. The organization is seen as one that does not need to change or appear to change (cf., Sternberg, 2002). Organizations with highly successful product or service lines may seek replicative leaders who will maintain the standing of these lines. Organizations that have had a highly successful and possibly charismatic leader for some time may be happy to seek a leader who can, to the extent possible, replicate the success of the previous leader. Schools that have been successful in the past by following a certain formula may seek leaders who are like the leaders of the past.

Replicative leadership is likely to be most successful during time periods of relative stability, both in terms of consumer demands and in terms of competitive threats. In times of flux, the kind of leader who worked before may not work again, and the organization may lose preeminence by selecting a leader like the last one.

Redefinition. This type of creative leadership is an attempt to show that a field or organization is in the right place, but not for the reason(s) that others, including previous leaders, think it is. The current status of the organization thus is seen from a different point of view. The propulsion leads to circular motion, such that the creative leadership directs back to where the organization is, but as viewed in a different way. Metaphorically, this type of leadership is like riding a bicycle in a circle, so that one returns to where one is but sees it from a different vantage point. Redefiners are chosen by organizations because they can maintain a status quo but appear to justify that status quo in terms most palatable to followers. A school district might choose a redefiner as a superintendent if it wants someone who appears to change things, but who does not really change anything other than the image.

Forward Incrementation. This type of creative leadership is an attempt to lead a field or an organization forward in the direction it already is going. The propulsion leads to forward motion.

Most educational leadership is probably forward incrementation. In such leadership, one takes the helm with the idea of advancing the leadership program of whomever one has succeeded. The promise is of progress through continuity. Creativity through forward incrementation is probably the kind that is most easily recognized and appreciated as creative. Because it extends existing notions, it is seen as creative. Because it does not threaten the assumptions of such notions, it is not rejected as useless or even harmful. Forward incrementation is like riding a bike forward in the direction it has been going at a comfortable rate of speed.

Forward incrementations tend to be successful when times are changing in relatively predictable and incremental ways. The times thus match the leadership strategy, whether in terms of leadership of people or leadership of products. When times change unpredictably, leaders may find that their strategy no longer works. For example, many Internet start-ups in the late 1990s were simple forward incrementations of other such businesses. Small variants in products or even image seemed to be enough to generate investment capital, if not to start a successful business. But when the dotcom market crashed, many of the start-ups went with it. There was no longer any investment capital to be had for just another variant of what already existed, and there was insufficient customer base to support the businesses. Many school leaders are forward incrementers. They make changes but ones that are small, carefully planned, and consistent with the direction things already are going in the school.

Advance Forward Incrementation. This type of creative leadership is an attempt to move an organization forward in the direction it is already going, but by moving beyond where others are ready for it to go. The propulsion leads to forward motion that is accelerated beyond the expected rate of forward progression.

Advance forward incrementations usually are not successful at the time they are attempted because followers in fields and organizations are not ready to go where the leader wants to lead. Or significant portions of followers may not wish to go to that point, in which case they form an organized and sometimes successful source of resistance. Advance forward incrementers are often not appreciated because they want to move things ahead too fast. As a principal, the school leader may find him or herself wanting to lead teachers to places they are not ready to go. Advance forward incrementation is like riding a bike forward at a rapid rate so that people may become afraid that the bike will run them over or otherwise crash.

Types of Creative Leadership That Reject Current Paradigms

Redirection. This type of creative leadership is an attempt to redirect an organization, field, or product line from where it is headed toward a different direction. The propulsion thus leads to motion in a direction that diverges from the way the organization is currently moving.

Redirections can change a field in unpredictable ways. For example, computers were originally viewed as rapid serial information processors. Artificial-intelligence research tried to create expert programs by creating ever more rapid and powerful rapid serial processors. But then it was realized that computer learning might better occur through massive parallel distributed processing. Today many computer programs use such a model and are able to achieve higher levels of expertise than was possible through the serial information-processing model. School reformers who are redirectors generally try to change the direction in which a school is moving. Whether they succeed depends as much on the structure of the bureaucracy in which they are working as it does on their own leadership qualities. In redirection, one metaphorically continues to ride one's bike, but in a totally new direction that is different from the previous one.

Reconstruction/Redirection. This type of creative leadership is an attempt to move a field or an organization or a product line back to where it once was (a reconstruction of the past) so that it may move onward from that point, but in a new direction. The propulsion thus leads to motion that is backward and then redirective from an earlier point in time. Current attempts to move schools back to the "three R's" are, to some extent, reconstructive redirections. In reconstruction/redirection, one metaphorically rides one's bicycle backward to a point one previously reached, and sets off in a new direction from there.

Reinitiation. This type of creative leadership is an attempt to move a field, organization, or product line to a different, not yet reached starting point and then to move from that point. The propulsion is thus from a new starting point in a direction that is different from that the field, organization, or product line has previously pursued. Reinitiators are leaders who try to move an educational system in a totally different direction and from a starting point other than the one at which the school currently is. In reinitiation, one metaphorically picks up one's bike, takes it to a new location, and sets off in a new direction from one's new starting point.

A Type of Creative Leadership That Integrates Current Paradigms

Synthesis. In this type of creative leadership, the creator integrates two ideas that previously were seen as unrelated or even as opposed. What formerly were viewed as distinct ideas now are viewed as related and capable of being unified. Integration is a key means by which progress is attained in the sciences. It represents neither an acceptance nor a rejection of existing paradigms, but rather, a merger of them. Many educational leaders are synthesizers, trying to combine the best of the ideas currently available. Synthesis involves watching the routes taken by other bicyclists, and then forging a new route that takes the others into account but is different from their paths.

Assessment of Creativity

In my original work with divergent reasoning problems having no one best answer, my colleagues and I asked 63 people to create various kinds of products (Lubart & Sternberg, 1995; Sternberg & Lubart, 1991, 1995, 1996) for which an infinite variety of responses were possible. Individuals were asked to create products in the realms of writing, art, advertising, and science. In writing, they were asked to write brief stories for which we would give them a choice of titles, such as "Beyond the Edge" or "The Octopus's Sneakers" (cf. description of Rainbow tests mentioned earlier). In art, the participants were asked to produce art compositions with titles such as "The Beginning of Time" or "Earth from an Insect's Point of View." In advertising, they were asked to produce advertisements for products such as a brand of bow tie or a brand of doorknob. In science, they were asked to solve problems such as one asking them how people might detect extraterrestrial aliens among us who are seeking to escape detection. Participants created two products in each domain.

Results showed, first, that creativity comprises the components proposed by their investment model of creativity: intelligence, knowledge, thinking styles, personality, and motivation. Second, results showed that creativity is relatively, although not wholly, domain specific. Correlations of ratings of the creative quality of the products across domains were lower than correlations of ratings and generally were at about the 0.4 level. Thus, there was some degree of relationship across domains, at the same time that there was plenty of room for someone to be strong in one or more domains but not in others. Third, measures of creative performance were correlated with conventional tests of abilities. As was the case for the correlations obtained with convergent problems, correlations were higher to the extent that problems on the conventional tests were nonentrenched. For example, correlations were higher with fluid than with crystallized ability tests, and correlations were higher, the more novel the fluid test was. These results confirm that tests of creative intelligence have some overlap with conventional tests (e.g., in requiring verbal skills or the ability to analyze one's own ideas—Sternberg & Lubart, 1995) but also tap skills beyond those measured even by relatively novel kinds of items on the conventional tests of intelligence.

Wisdom

The Nature of Wisdom

Wisdom may be the most important attribute to seek in educational leaders. People can be intelligent or creative but not wise. People who use their cognitive skills for evil or even selfish purposes, or who ignore the well-being of others, may be smart—but foolish.

According to my balance theory of wisdom (Sternberg, 1998b, 2001, 2003e), wisdom is defined as the application of intelligence, creativity, and knowledge as mediated by values toward the achievement of a common good through a balance among (a) intrapersonal, (b) interpersonal, and (c) extrapersonal interests, over the (a) short- and (b) long-terms, in order to achieve a balance among (a) adaptation to existing environments, (b) shaping of existing environments, and (c) selection of new environments.

Wisdom is not just about maximizing one's own or someone else's self-interest, but also about balancing various self-interests (intrapersonal) with the interests of others (interpersonal) and about other aspects of the context in which one lives (extrapersonal), such as one's city or country or the world. The common good needs also to take into account distributive justice: the rights of individuals and subgroups within any collectivity, and what is as nearly fair as possible to all.

A person could be practically intelligent, but use his or her practical intelligence toward bad or selfish ends. In wisdom, one certainly may seek good ends for oneself, but one also seeks common-good outcomes for others. If one's motivations are to maximize certain people's interests and minimize other people's, wisdom is not involved. In wisdom, one seeks a common good, realizing that this common good may be better for some than for others.

Problems requiring wisdom always involve at least some element of each of intrapersonal, interpersonal, and extrapersonal interests. For example, one might decide that it is wise to take advantage of a particular study opportunity abroad, a decision that seemingly involves only one person. But many people are typically affected by an individual's decision to go away to study—significant others, perhaps children, perhaps parents and friends. And the decision always has to be made in the context of what the whole range of available options is.

What kinds of considerations might be included under each of the three kinds of interests? Intrapersonal interests might include the desire to enhance one's popularity or prestige, to make more money, to learn more, to increase one's spiritual well-being, to increase one's power, and so forth. Interpersonal interests might be quite similar, except as they apply to other people rather than oneself. Extrapersonal interests might include contributing to the welfare of one's school, helping one's community, contributing to the well-being of one's country, or serving God, and so forth. Different people balance these interests in different ways. At one extreme, a malevolent dictator might emphasize his or her own personal power and wealth; at the other extreme, a saint might emphasize only serving others and God.

Wisdom involves a balancing not only of the three kinds of interests but also of three possible courses of action in response to this balancing: adaptation of oneself or others to existing environments, shaping of environments in order to render them more compatible with oneself or others, and selection of new environments.

There are five primary sources of differences directly affecting the balance processes. Consider, as an example, a teacher who has been instructed by a chairperson to spend almost all of his time teaching in a way so as to maximize students' scores on standardized tests, but who believes that the chairperson is essentially forcing him to abandon truly educating his students.

1. *Goals.* People may differ in terms of the extent to which they seek a common good, and thus in the extent to which they aim for the essential goal of wisdom. They also may differ in terms of what they view as the common good. The teacher may believe that it is not in the children's best interest to engage in what he views as mindless drills for a test. The chairperson, however, may

416

have a different view. The teacher is thus left with the responsibility of deciding what is in the best interests of all concerned.

2. *Balancing of responses to environmental contexts.* People may differ in their balance of responses to environmental contexts. Responses always reflect in the interaction of the individual making the judgment and the environment, and people can interact with contexts in myriad ways. The teacher may adapt to the environment and do exactly what the chairperson has told him to do; or shape the environment and do exactly what he believes he should do; or try to find some balance between adaptation and shaping that largely meets the chairperson's goals but also largely meets his own. Or the teacher may decide that the environment of the school is sufficiently aversive to his or her philosophy of teaching that he would prefer to teach at another school.

3. *Balancing of interests.* People may balance interests in different ways. The teacher must decide how to balance his own interests in good teaching and also in staying on good terms with the chairperson, the children must balance interests in learning but also doing well on the standardized tests, the parents' balance interests in having well-educated children, and so on.

4. *Balancing of short- and long-terms.* People may differ in their emphases. The teacher may believe that, in the long run, a proper education involves much more than preparing for statewide tests, but at the same time realizes that, in the short run, the children's scores on the tests will affect their future as well as his future and possibly that of his chairperson and school.

5. *Values.* People have different values mediating their use of tacit knowledge in the balancing of interests and responses. Values may vary somewhat across space and time, as well as among individuals within a given cultural context. The teacher's values may require him to diverge at least somewhat from the instructions of the chairperson. Another teacher's values might lead him to do what the school principal says, regardless of how he personally feels.

Some leaders are intelligent and creative, but foolish. They lack wisdom. What are the characteristics of leaders who are smart, but foolish? Consider five characteristics, according to Sternberg (2002).

The first is *unrealistic optimism* with respect to the long-term consequences of what they do. They may believe themselves to be so smart that they believe that, whatever they do, it will work out all right. They may overly trust their own intuitions, believing that their brilliance means that they can do no wrong.

The second is *egocentrism.* Many smart leaders have been so highly rewarded in their lives that they lose sight of the interests of others. They start to act as though the whole world revolves around them. In doing so, they often set themselves up for downfalls, as happened to both Presidents Nixon and Clinton, the former in the case of Watergate, the latter in the case of "Monicagate."

The third characteristic is a sense of *omniscience.* Smart leaders typically know a lot. They get in trouble, however, when they start to think they "know it all." They may have expertise in one area, but then, start to fancy themselves experts in practically everything. At that point, they become susceptible to remarkable downfalls because they act as experts in areas in which they are not, and can make disastrous mistakes in doing so.

The fourth characteristic is a sense of *omnipotence.* Many smart leaders find themselves in positions of substantial power. Sometimes they lose sight of the limitations of their power and start to act as though they are omnipotent. Several U.S. presidents as well as presidents of other countries have had this problem, leading their countries to disasters on the basis of personal whims. Adolf Hitler, Josef Stalin, Mobutu Sese Seko, and Idi Amin come to mind as examples. Many corporate chieftains have also started to think of themselves as omnipotent, unfortunately, cooking the books of their corporations at will.

The fifth characteristic is a sense of *invulnerability.* Not only do the individuals think they can do anything; they also believe they can get away with it. They believe that either they are too smart to be found out or, even if found out, they will escape any punishment for misdeeds. The result is the kind of disasters the United States has seen in the recent Enron, Worldcom, and Arthur Andersen debacles.

Assessment of Wisdom

My work on wisdom is relatively recent (Sternberg, 1998b, 2002) and is still "work-in-progress"; my colleagues and I are developing and validating various assessments of wisdom. Because both wisdom and practical intelligence are measured through scenario-based measures, it might be useful to review results obtained for practical intelligence (Sternberg et al., 2000). Keep in mind that practical intelligence is related to wisdom but is not the same as wisdom. A person could be practically intelligent and look out only for his or her own interests. A wise person never could look out only for him or herself.

Wisdom scenarios differ from practical-intelligence scenarios in that they more involve balancing of interests toward a common good. Here is an example of a scenario used in our current research:

> Felicia and Alexander have been in an intimate relationship for their entire four years of college. Felicia has now been accepted for graduate school in French by a prestigious graduate program in northern California. Alexander was not admitted to the law school in this university, nor to any other law school in the northern California area. Alexander was admitted to a good although not outstanding law school in southern California, but he was also admitted to an outstanding law school in Massachusetts. Felicia has no viable opportunities for graduate study on the East Coast, at least at this time. Alexander is trying to decide whether to attend the less prestigious law school in southern California or the more prestigious one in Massachusetts. He would like to continue the relationship, as would Felicia, and both ultimately hope to get married to each other. A complicating factor is that the law school in Massachusetts has offered Alexander a half-scholarship, whereas the law school in southern California has not offered financial aid for the first year, although it has indicated that there is a possibility of financial aid in subsequent years. Alexander's parents have indicated that while they would be willing to pay his half-tuition for the more prestigious law school, they do not believe it is fair to ask them to pay full tuition for the less prestigious one. They also believe his going to the less prestigious law school will only hurt Alexander's career advancement. Felicia is torn and is leaving it to Alexander to decide what to do. What should Alexander do and why?

We do not yet have data on how students respond to these problems. We do have data on people's implicit theories of wisdom, which are consistent with, although they do not provide a direct test of, the balance theory (Sternberg, 1985b). In one study, 200 professors each of art, business, philosophy, and physics were asked to rate the characteristics of each of the behaviors obtained in a prestudy from the corresponding population with respect to the professors' ideal conception of each of an ideally wise, intelligent, or creative individual in their occupation. Laypersons were also asked to provide these ratings but for a hypothetical ideal individual without regard to occupation. Correlations were computed across the three ratings. In each group except philosophy, the highest correlation was between wisdom and intelligence; in philosophy, the highest correlation was between intelligence and creativity. The correlations between wisdom and intelligence ratings ranged from 0.42 to 0.78 with a median of 0.68. For all groups, the lowest correlation was between wisdom and creativity (which ranged from –0.24 to 0.48 with a median of 0.27).

In a second study from Sternberg (1985b), 40 college students were asked to sort three sets of 40 behaviors each into as many or as few piles as they wished. The 40 behaviors in each set were the top-rated wisdom, intelligence, and creativity behaviors from the previous study (Sternberg, 1985b). The sortings then each were subjected to nonmetric multidimensional scaling. For wisdom, six components emerged: *reasoning ability, sagacity, learning from ideas and environment, judgment, expeditious use of information,* and *perspicacity.* These components can be compared with those that emerged from a similar scaling of people's implicit theories of intelligence, which were *practical problem-solving ability, verbal ability, intellectual balance and integration, goal orientation and attainment, contextual intelligence,* and *fluid thought.* In both cases, cognitive abilities and their use are important. In wisdom, however, some kind of balance of interests appears to emerge as important that does not emerge as important in intelligence, in general.

In a third study (Sternberg, 1985b), 50 adults were asked to rate descriptions of hypothetical individuals for wisdom, intelligence, and creativity. Correlations were computed between pairs of ratings of the hypothetical individuals' levels of the three traits. Correlations between the ratings were 0.94 for wisdom and intelligence, 0.62 for wisdom and creativity, and 0.69 for intelligence and creativity, again suggesting that wisdom and intelligence are highly correlated in people's implicit theories.

The most ambitious program of research on wisdom has been that of Paul Baltes. Over time, Baltes and his colleagues (e.g., Baltes et al., 1992; Baltes & Staudinger, 1993) have collected a wide range of data showing that wisdom can be studied from an explicit-theoretical base. For example, Staudinger et al. (1997) found that measures of intelligence (as well as personality) overlap with but are nonidentical to measures of wisdom in terms of constructs measured. And, Staudinger and colleagues (1992) showed that human-services professionals outperformed a control group on wisdom-related tasks. They also showed that older adults performed as well on such tasks as did younger adults, and that older adults did better on such tasks if there was a match between their age and the age of the fictitious characters about whom they made judgments. Baltes et al. (1995) found that older individuals nominated for their wisdom performed as well as did clinical psychologists on wisdom-related tasks. They also showed that up to the age of 80, older adults performed as well on wisdom tasks as did younger adults. In a further set of studies, Staudinger and Baltes (1996) found that performance settings that were relevant to the lives of their participants and that provided for actual or "virtual" interaction of minds through collaborative discourse and endeavors increased wisdom-related performance substantially.

Synthesis

What conclusions can be drawn from the WICS framework?

The Basic Relationships

The WICS theory views intelligence, creativity, and wisdom as different, but as involving fundamental similarities. The basis for "intelligence" narrowly defined, as it is measured by successful intelligence, is the analytical aspect of successful intelligence. The basis for creativity is the creative aspect of successful intelligence. And the basis for wisdom is the practical aspect of successful intelligence, and, in particular, tacit knowledge. Thus, successful intelligence lies at the basis of conventional intelligence, creativity, and wisdom.

Successful intelligence is a basis for conventional intelligence, creativity, and wisdom, but there is more to each of these constructs than just successful intelligence. Several components are also involved.

The Role of Components

Metacomponents. Metacomponents play a key role in intelligence, creativity, and wisdom. They form the central executive functions without which none of these three attributes could operate. To think intelligently, creatively, or wisely, one needs to be able to recognize the existence of problems, define the problems, formulate strategies to solve the problems, and so forth. The difference is in the kinds of problems to which they are applied.

In intelligence, they are applied to several kinds of problems. First, when they are applied to relatively familiar kinds of problems that are somewhat abstracted from the world of everyday experience, they are applied to problems requiring analytical intelligence. Second, when they are applied to relatively novel kinds of problems that are relatively nonentrenched in nature, they are applied to problems requiring creative intelligence. Third, when they are applied to relatively practical problems that are highly contextualized in nature, they are applied to problems requiring practical intelligence.

All problems requiring creativity require creative intelligence, but not all problems requiring creative intelligence require creativity. The reason is that creativity—at least according to the investment theory—requires more than just creative intelligence. It also requires knowledge, certain thinking styles, certain personality attributes, and certain motivational attributes. Thus, people can be creatively intelligent but not creative. They may think in novel ways but perhaps lack the persistence, or the propensity toward risk-taking, or the willingness to grow that one needs in order to be fully creative. Problems requiring full creativity thus tend to be more complex than problems requiring just creative intelligence. For example, a conceptual-projection problem (about grue and bleen), as described earlier, requires creative intelligence. But it does not require creativity in the same sense that writing an important novel does. The novel involves far more components of creativity than does the conceptual-projection problem. Thus, coping with novelty is only one aspect of creativity.

Metacomponents are especially important for defining and redefining creative problems. As Getzels and Csikszentmihalyi (1976) pointed out, finding and then clearly defining good problems is an essential element of creativity. Metacomponents are also important for monitoring and evaluating one's products. No one, no matter how creative, hits the creative heights every time. A creative individual needs to devise a system to separate his or her own wheat from the chaff.

Metacomponents also apply in the solution of problems requiring wisdom. Indeed, much of the difficulty of a wisdom-related problem is in figuring out exactly what the problem is, whose interests are involved, and what their interests are. One then needs to formulate a strategy to deal with the problem and a way of monitoring whether the strategy is working.

Performance Components.   Performance components also are involved in solving each of the three kinds of problems. For example, one almost inevitably needs to make inferences in solving each kind of problem, whether it is in inferring relations in test-like analogy problems, inferring analogical relations in order to propose a new model of a phenomenon based on a model of a phenomenon (such as Freud's applying the hydraulic model to the psyche), or inferring what a participant in a negotiation really is looking for so that one can offer a wise solution that balances interests.

Knowledge-Acquisition Components.   Finally, knowledge-acquisition components are involved in all three kinds of problems as well.

In learning the meanings of new words embedded in context, the reader has to separate helpful and relevant information in context from extraneous material that is irrelevant to or may actually get in the way of learning the words' meanings. Moreover, the reader must combine the selected information into a meaningful whole, using past information about the nature of words as a guide. Deciding what things would be useful for defining a new word and deciding what to do with these useful things once they are isolated are processes that are guided by the use of old information. The reader constantly seeks to connect the context of the unknown word to something with which he or she is familiar. Thus, processing the available information requires three distinct operations: (a) locating relevant information in context, (b) combining this information into a meaningful whole, and (c) interrelating this information to what the reader already knows. These processes are referred to from now on as selective encoding, selective combination, and selective comparison, respectively.

Coping with Novelty Skills

Coping with novelty is relevant in each of conventional intelligence, creativity, and wisdom. In conventional intelligence, coping with novelty is involved in fluid abilities (see Carroll, 1993; Cattell, 1971). It is the essential ingredient of creative thinking. And most wisdom problems are at least somewhat novel; in other words, they present new aspects that old problems have not presented. When problems are more routine, they may be referred to as requiring common sense, but they are not likely to be referred to as requiring wisdom.

Practical Skills

Practical skills are involved in all three sets of skills as well. They are probably least involved in conventional intelligence. Most would apply to knowing what kinds of strategies and solutions are expected in taking tests and in school (Williams et al., 1996, 2002). Practical skills are required in creativity to render ideas so that they can be implemented and so that one can convince others of the worth of these ideas. And they are required in wisdom to solve problems. Indeed, tacit knowledge is a basis for wise thinking.

WICS and Leadership

WICS integrates many of the aspects of previous theories of leadership. It involves aspects of trait theory because it specifies the characteristics of a person needed for successful leadership. It involves aspects of behavioral theory because it also suggests the behaviors that must emanate from these characteristics, such as acting in ways that take into account the interests of all stakeholders. It involves aspects of situational theories because the situation is so important in the contextual aspect of the theory of practical intelligence: What is practical depends on the context in which it is done. And it involves aspects of transformational leadership in that the paradigm-rejecting forms of creative leadership involve transforming an organization.

Educational leadership involves three basic elements. Creativity is used to generate ideas for leadership. Academic, or analytical, intelligence is used to analyze the value of these ideas; practical intelligence is used to implement the ideas and to persuade other people of their value. Wisdom is used to ensure the ideas represent a common good for all. The critical aspect of the theory is that all of creativity, intelligence, and wisdom are largely decisions: One has to *decide* to approach a problem creatively, analytically, practically, and wisely.

In terms of selection of leaders, WICS implies that one should pay some but not too much attention to the educational credentials that usually form a major part of an individual's record. Schools traditionally have emphasized memory and analytical skills substantially more than they have emphasized creative and practical skills. WICS implies that more attention should be paid to creative and practical intelligence and, more generally, to creativity as a whole and to wisdom.

In terms of development of leaders, WICS implies that leadership skills and attitude can be developed in anyone—that leadership is in large part a decision that anyone can make. Developing leaders involves developing their decision-making skills so that they decide in ways that are creative, intelligent, and wise. For example, they would be encouraged to take risks (creative thinking), to ask whether the solution to a problem they pose is the best one they can formulate (intelligent thinking), and whether their solution represents a common good (wise thinking).

In terms of assessment of leaders, the WICS model suggests that leaders be evaluated for the creativity, intelligence, and wisdom of their decision making and their interactions with followers and superiors. Often, supervisors do not know exactly what qualities to look for in evaluating leadership in subordinates. WICS specifies such qualities in some detail.

In this chapter, I have discussed evidence that leaders of various kinds are intelligent, creative, and wise. Do leaders need all three aspects? I have argued here that each of the three lines of research described in this chapter—on intelligence, creativity, and wisdom—represents part of a puzzle. The effective educational leader uses creativity to generate novel ideas, intelligence to ensure they are of high quality, and wisdom to ensure they will be for the common good of all followers.

Consider some examples of applications of WICS. These examples are aimed at three levels of leadership: teacher, principal, and superintendent.

Consider a first example. A teacher has to decide whether to organize a dramatic production for her fourth-grade classroom. She believes in the value of dramatic productions, and the one she has in mind is of a well-known children's play. But she is under a lot of pressure from the principal and the school district to concentrate on basic skills, and she is concerned that producing a play may not be viewed in a favorable light. So she would like to do a dramatic production and at the same time be able to convince the administration that the play is a worthwhile activity for the children in terms of addressing the issue of basic skills. She has to be creative in figuring out a way to do this, such as by having children read and analyze the play first. She has to be analytic in deciding whether her plans indeed address students' basic skills. She has to be practical in convincing administrators of the value of her plan. And she has to be wise in all this by doing what is best for the children, their parents, and for the school.

Consider as a second example a decision of a school principal regarding how to deal with low reading scores among the students in her school. Creativity would be involved in planning an intervention that would raise reading levels and hence scores among the pupils. Analytical intelligence is involved in determining whether the proposed plan is indeed one that can be shown to make analytical sense in terms of what is known about reading. Practical intelligence is involved in deciding whether the plan is workable in the school, and to persuade various stakeholders to buy into the plan. Wisdom is involved in making sure the plan represented a common good for all—that it helps students, but also helps the reputation of the school, is fair to teachers in terms of what it requires of them in extra time and effort, does not put an undue burden on parents, and so on.

As a third example, consider a decision of a school superintendent as to whether to renew a contract with a commercial food-service company that provides food to the district. The price for the district is extremely competitive, but that is in part because the menus have a disproportionate amount of food that students like but that could be described as "fast food." It is relatively high in sugar and fat content and low in nutritional value. The superintendent is creative in deciding whether the terms can be renegotiated to provide more nutritive but nevertheless palatable food at a competitive price, or whether another vendor can be found who will do this. He is analytically intelligent in determining whether any new proposed plan meets budgetary, nutritional, and palatability requirements. He is practically intelligent in negotiating the best deal. And he is wise in ensuring that the deal is the best for all stakeholders in the school district. For example, he may come to believe that no matter how cost-efficient the current contract is, it cannot be justified because of the poor nutritional value for the students.

Summary

In sum, the components of intelligence are at the base of successful intelligence, creativity, and wisdom. They are applied in intelligence, broadly defined, to experience in order to adapt to, shape, and select environments. When the components are involved in fairly abstract but familiar kinds of tasks, they are used analytically. When they are involved in relatively novel tasks and situations, they are used creatively.

When they are involved in adaptation to, shaping of, and selection of environments, they are used practically.

Creative intelligence is a part of but not the entirety of human creativity. Creativity also involves aspects of knowledge, styles of thinking, personality, and motivation, as well as these psychological components in interaction with the environment. An individual with the intellectual skills for creativity but without the other personal attributes is unlikely to do creative work.

Wisdom results from the application of successful intelligence and creativity toward the common good through a balancing of intrapersonal, interpersonal, and extrapersonal interests over the short- and long terms. Wisdom is not just a way of thinking about things; it is a way of doing things. If people wish to be wise, they must act wisely, not just think wisely. We all can.

Conclusions

This chapter has presented a theory of educational leadership—WICS. The theory may have some appeal because it attempts to view educational leadership broadly. Leaders who are smart but not creative or wise, who are creative but not wise, are less likely to be the leaders who have enduring impact. Of course, some psychologists believe the theory departs too much from the conventional theory of general intelligence (Spearman, 1904): Some disagree with parts of the theory (e.g., Brody, 2003a, 2003b) and some disagree with the whole thing, vehemently (Gottfredson, 2003a, 2003b). Others believe the theory does not depart from conventional g theory enough (Gardner, 1983). Still others have theories that are more compatible, in spirit, with that proposed here, at least for intelligence (Ceci, 1996). The theory is rather newer than that of, say, Spearman (1904) and has much less work to support it, as well as a lesser range of empirical support. I doubt the theory is wholly correct—scientific theories so far have not been—but I hope at the same time it serves as a broader basis for future theories than, say, Spearman's theory of general intelligence. No doubt, there will be those who wish to preserve this and related older theories, and those who continue to do research that replicates many times that so-called general intelligence does indeed matter for success in many aspects of life. I agree. At the same time, I suspect endless replication is not sufficient, and that those who keep replicating the findings of the past are unlikely to serve as the positive educational leaders of the future. But only time will tell. As noted earlier, there is typically some value to replication in science, although after the point at which a point is established, the replication seems more to continue to produce papers than to produce new scientific breakthroughs.

In selecting the educational leaders of tomorrow, three important factors to consider are intelligence, creativity, and wisdom—synthesized so that they work together effectively. These are not the only attributes that matter. For example, motivation and energy are important as well. However, motivation is partly (although not exclusively) situational. With the proper environment, anyone can be motivated to achieve.

This essay has concentrated on "tests" as measures of intelligence and creativity, but they represent only one of many ways of assessing these attributes. Interviews, questionnaires, letters of recommendation, and project work all can help in assessing these attributes.

The educational system in the United States, as in many other countries, places great emphasis on instruction and assessments that tap two important skills: memory and analysis. Students who are adept at these two skills tend to profit from the educational system because the ability tests, instruction, and achievement tests used all largely measure products and processes emanating from these two kinds of skills. There is a problem, however—namely, that children whose strengths are in other kinds of skills may be shortchanged by this system. These children might learn and test well, if only they were given an opportunity to play to their strengths, such as of analytical, creative, or practical abilities rather than their weaknesses in these and related skills.

As a society, we can create a closed system that advantages only certain types of children and that disadvantages other types. Children who excel in memory and analytical abilities may end up doing well on ability tests and achievement tests, and hence find the doors of opportunity open to them. Children who excel in other abilities may end up doing poorly on the tests, and find the doors shut. By treating children with alternative patterns of abilities as losers, society may end up creating harmful self-fulfilling prophecies.

Institutions should consider pooling their resources and developing a common model and common methods of assessment. By working separately, they fail to leverage their strengths and to share information regarding the best ways to make decisions. In essence, each institution "reinvents the wheel." A consortium would be far more powerful than each institution working on its own. WICS is one model such a consortium might use. Doubtless there are many others. The important thing is to work together toward a common good—toward devising the best ways to select students so as to maximize their positive future impact. We all wish our educational leaders to show wisdom. We ourselves need to do the same.

References

Adelson, B. (1984). When novices surpass experts: The difficulty of a task may increase with expertise. *Journal of Experimental Psychology: Learning, Memory, and Cognition, 10*, 483–495.

Amabile, T. M. (1983). *The social psychology of creativity.* New York: Springer.

Amabile, T. M. (1996). *Creativity in context.* Boulder, CO: Westview.

Antonakis, J., Cianciolo, A. T., & Sternberg, R. J. (2004a). Leadership: Past, present, and future. In J. Antonakis, A.T. Cianciolo, & R. J. Sternberg (Eds.), *The nature of leadership* (pp. 3–15). Thousand Oaks, CA: Sage.

Antonakis, J., Cianciolo, A. T., & Sternberg, R. J. (Eds.). (2004b). *The nature of leadership.* Thousand Oaks, CA.: Sage

Ayman, R. (2004). Situational and contingency approaches to leadership. In J. Antonakis, A. T. Cianciolo, & R. J. Sternberg (Eds.), *The nature of leadership* (pp. 148–170). Thousand Oaks, CA: Sage.

Baehr, M. E. (1992). *Predicting success in higher level positions: A guide to the system for testing and evaluation of potential.* New York: Quorum.

Bales, R. F. (1951). *Interaction process analysis: A method for the study of small groups.* Reading, MA: Addison-Wesley.

Baltes, P. B., Smith, J., & Staudinger, U. M. (1992). Wisdom and successful aging. In T. B. Sonderegger (Ed.), *Psychology and aging* (pp. 123–167). Lincoln, NE: University of Nebraska Press.

Baltes, P. B., & Staudinger, U. M. (1993). The search for a psychology of wisdom. *Current Directions in Psychological Science, 2*, 75–80.

Baltes, P. B., & Staudinger, U. M. (2000). Wisdom: A metaheuristic (pragmatic) to orchestrate mind and virtue toward excellence. *American Psychologist, 55*, 122–135.

Baltes, P. B., Staudinger, U. M., Maercker, A., & Smith, J. (1995). People nominated as wise: A comparative study of wisdom-related knowledge. *Psychology and Aging, 10*, 155–166.

Bandura, A. (1997). *Self-efficacy: The exercise of control.* New York: Freeman.

Barnes, M. L., & Sternberg, R. J. (1989). Social intelligence and decoding of nonverbal cues. *Intelligence, 13,* 263–287.

Barron, F., & Harrington, D. M. (1981). Creativity, intelligence, and personality. *Annual Review of Psychology, 32,* 439–476.

Bass, B. M. (1985). *Leadership and performance beyond expectations.* New York: Free Press.

Bass, B. M. (1998). *Transformational leadership: Industrial, military, and educational impact.* Mahwah, NJ: Erlbaum.

Bass, B. M. (2002). Cognitive, social, and emotional intelligence of transformational leaders. In R. E. Riggio, S. E. Murphy, & F. J. Pirozzolo (Eds.), *Multiple intelligences and leadership* (pp. 105–118). Mahwah, NJ: Erlbaum.

Bass, B. M., & Avolio, B. J. (Eds.). (1994). *Improving organizational effectiveness through transformational leadership.* Thousand Oaks, CA: Sage.

Bass, B. M., & Avolio, B. J. (1995). *MLQ Multifactor Leadership Questionnaire for Research: Premission Set.* Redwood City, CA: Mindgarden.

Bass, B. M., Avolio, B. J., & Atwater, L. (1996). The transformational and transactional leadership of men and women. *International Review of Applied Psychology, 45,* 5–34.

Bateson, G. (1979). *Mind and nature.* London: Wildwood House.

Bird, C. (1940). *Social psychology* New York: Appleton-Century.

Blake, R. R., & Mouton, J. S. (1964). *The managerial grid.* Houston, TX: Gulf Publishing Group.

Boring, E. G. (1923, June 6). Intelligence as the tests test it. *New Republic,* 35–37.

Bowers, K. S., Regehr, G., Balthazard, C., & Parker, K. (1990). Intuition in the context of discovery. *Cognitive Psychology, 22,* 72–109.

Bransford, J. D., & Stein, B. (1984). *The IDEAL problem solver.* New York: Freeman.

Brody, N. (2003a). Construct validation of the Sternberg Triarchic abilities test: Comment and reanalysis. *Intelligence, 31,* 319–329.

Brody, N. (2003b). What Sternberg should have concluded. *Intelligence, 31,* 339–342.

Brown, A. L., & Ferrara, R. A. (1985). Diagnosing zones of proximal development. In J. V. Wertsch (Ed.), *Culture, communication, and cognition: Vygotskian perspectives* (pp. 273–305). New York: Cambridge University Press.

Budoff, M. (1968). Learning potential as a supplementary assessment procedure. In J. Hellmuth (Ed.), *Learning disorders,* Vol. 3 (pp. 295–343). Seattle, WA: Special Child.

Burns, J. M. (1978). *Leadership.* New York: Harper & Row.

Campbell, D. T. (1960). Blind variation and selective retention in creative thought and other knowledge processes. *Psychological Review, 67,* 380–400.

Carroll, J. B. (1993). *Human cognitive abilities: A survey of factor-analytic studies.* New York: Cambridge University Press.

Caruso, D. R., Mayer, J. D., & Salovey, P. (2002). Emotional intelligence and emotional leadership. In R. E. Riggio, S. E. Murphy, & F. J. Pirozzolo (Eds.), *Multiple intelligences and leadership* (pp. 55–74). Mahwah, NJ: Erlbaum.

Cattell, R. B. (1971). *Abilities: Their structure, growth and action.* Boston: Houghton Mifflin.

Cattell, R. B., & Cattell, H. E. P. (1973). *Measuring intelligence with the Culture Fair Tests.* Champaign, IL: Institute for Personality and Ability Testing.

Ceci, S. J. (1996). *On intelligence* (revised and expanded ed.). Cambridge, MA: Harvard University Press.

Clement, J. (1989). Learning via model construction and criticism: Protocol evidence on sources of creativity in science. In G. Glover, R. Ronning, & C. Reynolds (Eds.), *Handbook of creativity* (pp. 341–381). New York: Plenum.

Crutchfield, R. (1962). Conformity and creative thinking. In H. Gruber, G. Terrell, & M. Wertheimer (Eds.), *Contemporary approaches to creative thinking* (pp. 120–140). New York: Atherton Press.

Cziko, G. A. (1998). From blind to creative: In defense of Donald Campbell's selectionist theory of human creativity. *Journal of Creative Behavior, 32,* 192–208.

Davidson, J. E., & Sternberg, R. J. (1984). The role of insight in intellectual giftedness. *Gifted Child Quarterly, 28,* 58–64.

Day, J. D., Engelhardt, J. L., Maxwell, S. E., & Bolig, E. E. (1997). Comparison of static and dynamic assessment procedures and their relation to independent performance. *Journal of Educational Psychology, 89,* 358–368.

Dellas, M., & Gaier, E. L. (1970). Identification of creativity: The individual. *Psychological Bulletin, 73,* 55–73.

Dewey, J. (1933). *How we think.* Boston: Heath.

Ericsson, K. A. (Ed.). (1996). *The road to excellence.* Mahwah, NJ: Erlbaum.

Feuerstein, R. (1979). *The dynamic assessment of retarded performers: The Learning Potential Assessment Device theory, instruments, and techniques.* Baltimore, MD: University Park Press.

Fiedler, F. E. (1978). The contingency model and the dynamics of the leadership process. In L. Bekowitz (Ed.), *Advances in experimental social psychology* (Vol. 11, pp. 59–112). New York: Academic Press.

Fiedler, F. E. (2002). The curious role of cognitive resources in leadership. In R. E. Riggio, S. E. Murphy, & F. J. Pirozzolo (Eds.), *Multiple intelligences and leadership* (pp. 91–104). Mahwah, NJ: Erlbaum.

Fiedler, F. E., & Link, T. G. (1994). Leader intelligence, interpersonal stress, and task performance. In R. J. Sternberg & R. K. Wagner (Eds.), *Mind in context: Interactionist perspectives on human intelligence* (pp. 152–167). New York: Cambridge University Press.

Findlay, C. S., & Lumsden, C. J. (1988). The creative mind: Toward an evolutionary theory of discovery and invention. *Journal of Social Biology and Structures, 11,* 3–55.

Finke, R. (1990). *Creative imagery: Discoveries and inventions in visualization.* Hillsdale, NJ: Erlbaum.

Finke, R. (1995). A creative insight and preinventive forms. In R. J. Sternberg & J. E Davidson (Eds.), *The nature of insight* (pp. 255–280). Cambridge, MA: MIT Press.

Frensch, P. A., & Sternberg, R. J. (1989). Expertise and intelligent thinking: When is it worse to know better? In R. J. Sternberg (Ed.), *Advances in the psychology of human intelligence* (Vol. 5, pp. 157–188). Hillsdale, NJ: Erlbaum.

Garcia, J., & Koelling, R. A. (1966). The relation of cue to consequence in avoidance learning. *Psychonomic Science, 4,* 123–124.

Gardner, H. (1983). *Frames of mind: The theory of multiple intelligence.* New York: Basic Books.

Gardner, H. (1991). *The unschooled mind.* New York: Basic Books.

Gardner, H. (1993a). *Creating mind.* New York: Basic Books.

Gardner, H. (1993b). *Multiple intelligences: The theory in practice.* New York: Basic Books.

Gardner, H. (1994). The creator's patterns. In D. H. Feldman, M. Csikszentmihalyi, & H. Gardner (Eds.), *Changing the world: A framework for the study of creativity* (pp. 69–84). Westport, CT: Praeger.

Gardner, H. (1995). *Leading minds.* New York: Basic Books.

Gardner, H. (1999). *Intelligence reframed: Multiple intelligences for the 21st century.* New York: Basic Books.

Gardner, H. (2004). *Changing minds: The art and science of changing our own and other people's minds.* Boston: Harvard Business School Press.

Gardner, H., Krechevsky, M., Sternberg, R. J., & Okagaki, L. (1994). Intelligence in context: Enhancing students' practical intelligence for school. In K. McGilly (Ed.), *Classroom lessons: Integrating cognitive theory and classroom practice* (pp. 105–127). Cambridge, MA: MIT Press.

Getzels, J. W., & Csikszentmihalyi, M. (1976). *The creative vision: Problem finding in art.* Chicago: Van Nostrand.

Glover, J. A. (1977). Risky shift and creativity. *Social Behavior and Personality, 5,* 317–320.

Goethals, G. R., Sorenson, G. J., & Burns, J. M. (Eds.). (2004). *Encyclopedia of leadership.* Thousand Oaks, CA: Sage.

Golann, S. E. (1962). The creativity motive. *Journal of Personality, 30,* 588–600.

Goleman, D., Boyatzis, R., & McKee, A. (2002). *Primal leadership: Realizing the power of emotional intelligence.* Boston: Harvard Business School Press.

Gottfredson, L. S. (2003a). Discussion: On Sternberg's 'Reply to Gottfredson.' *Intelligence, 31,* 415–424.

Gottfredson, L. S. (2003b). Dissecting practical intelligence theory: Its claims and evidence. *Intelligence, 31,* 343–397.

Gough, H. G., & Woodworth, D. G. (1960). Stylistic variations among professional research scientists. *Journal of Psychology, 49,* 87–98.

Grigorenko, E. L., Jarvin, L., & Sternberg, R. J. (2002). School-based tests of the triarchic theory of intelligence: Three settings, three samples, three syllabi. *Contemporary Education and Psychology, 27,* 167–208.

Grigorenko, E. L., & Sternberg, R. J. (1998). Dynamic testing. *Psychological Bulletin, 124,* 75–111.

Grigorenko, E. L., & Sternberg, R. J. (2001). Analytical, creative, and practical intelligence as predictors of self-reported adaptive functioning: A case study in Russia. *Intelligence, 29,* 57–73.

Gruber, H. E. (1981). *Darwin on man: A psychological study of scientific creativity* (2nd ed.). Chicago: University of Chicago Press. (Original work published 1974)

Guilford, J. P. (1968). Intelligence has three facets. *Science, 160,* 615–620.

Guthke, J. (1993). Current trends in theories and assessment of intelligence. In J. H. M. Hamers, K. Sijtsma, & A. J. J. M. Ruijssenaars (Eds.), *Learning potential assessment* (pp. 13–20). Amsterdam: Swets & Zeitlinger.

Guyote, M. J., & Sternberg, R. J. (1981). A transitive-chain theory of syllogistic reasoning. *Cognitive Psychology, 13,* 461–525.

Haywood, H. C., & Tzuriel, D. (1992). Epilogue: The status and future of interactive assessment. In H. C. Haywood & D. Tzuriel (Eds.), *Interactive assessment* (pp. 38–63). New York: Springer-Verlag.

Hedlund, J., Forsythe, G. B., Horvath, J. A., Williams, W. M., Snook, S., & Sternberg, R. J. (2003). Identifying and assessing tacit knowledge: Understanding the practical intelligence of military leaders. *Leadership Quarterly, 14,* 117–140.

Hersey, P., & Blanchard, K. H. (1969). *Management of organizational behavior.* Englewood Cliffs, NJ: Prentice-Hall.

House, R. J. (1971). A path–goal theory of leader effectiveness. *Administrative Science Quarterly, 16,* 321–339.

House, R. J. (1996). Path–goal theory of leadership: Lessons, legacy, and a reformed theory. *Leadership Quarterly, 7,* 323–352.

Howe, M. J., Davidson, J. W., & Sloboda, J. A. (1998). Innate talents: Reality or myth? *Behavioral Brain Science, 21,* 399–442.

Howells, L. T., & Becker, S. W. (1962). Seating arrangement and leadership emergence. *Journal of Abnormal Social Psychology, 64,* 148–150.

Hunt, J. G. (2004). What is leadership? In J. Antonakis, A. T. Cianciolo, & R. J. Sternberg (Eds.), *The nature of leadership* (pp. 19–47). Thousand Oaks, CA: Sage.

"Intelligence and its measurement": A symposium. (1921). *Journal of Educational Psychology, 12,* 123–147, 195–216, 271–275.

Jensen, A. R. (1998). *The g factor: The science of mental ability.* Westport, CT: Praeger/Greenwood.

Johnson-Laird, P. N. (1988). Freedom and constraint in creativity. In R. J. Sternberg (Ed.), *The nature of creativity* (pp. 202–219). New York: Cambridge University Press.

Kaplan, C. A., & Simon, H. A. (1990). In search of insight. *Cognitive Psychology, 22,* 374–419.

Koestler, A. (1964). *The act of creation.* New York: Dell.

Kuhn, T. S. (1970). *The structure of scientific revolutions* (2nd ed.). Chicago: University of Chicago Press.

Langley, P., Simon, H. A., Bradshaw, G. L., & Zytkow, J. M. (1987). *Scientific discovery: Computational explorations of the creative processes.* Cambridge, MA: MIT Press.

Leavitt, H. J. (1951). Some effects of certain communication patterns on group performance. *Journal of Abnormal Psychology, 46,* 38–50.

Lewin, K., & Lippitt, R. (1938). An experimental approach to the study of autocracy and democracy: A preliminary note. *Sociometry, 1,* 292–300.

Lewin, K., Lippitt, R., & White, R. K. (1939). Patterns of aggressive behavior in experimentally created social climates. *Journal of Social Psychology, 10,* 271–301.

Lidz, C. S. (Ed.). (1987). *Dynamic assessment.* New York: Guilford Press.

Lidz, C. S. (1991). *Practitioner's guide to dynamic assessment.* New York: Guilford Press.

Lubart, T. I., & Sternberg, R. J. (1995). An investment approach to creativity: Theory and data. In S. M. Smith, T. B. Ward, & R. A. Finke (Eds.), *The creative cognition approach.* Cambridge, MA: MIT Press.

MacKinnon, D. W. (1962). The nature and nurture of creative talent. *American Psychologist, 17,* 484–495.

MacKinnon, D. W. (1965). Personality and the realization of creative potential. *American Psychologist, 20,* 273–281.

Mann, R. D. (1959). A review of the relationship between personality and performance in small groups. *Psychological Bulletin, 56,* 241–270.

Martindale, C. (1999). Biological bases of creativity. In R. J. Sternberg (Ed.), *Handbook of creativity* (pp. 137–152). New York: Cambridge University Press.

Maslow, A. (1967). The creative attitude. In R. L Mooney & T. A. Rasik (Eds.), *Explorations in creativity* (pp. 43–57). New York: Harper & Row.

McClelland, D. C., Atkinson, J. W., Clark, R. A., & Lowell, E. L. (1953). *The achievement motive.* New York: Appleton-Century-Crofts.

McGregor, D. M. (1960). *The human side of enterprise.* New York: McGraw-Hill.

Milgram, S. (1974). *Obedience to authority.* New York: Harper & Row.

Mischel, W., Shoda, Y., & Rodriguez, M. L. (1989). Delay of gratification in children. *Science, 244,* 933–938.

Morrow, I. J., & Stern, M. (1990). Stars, adversaries, producers, and phantoms at work: A new leadership typology. In K. E. Clark & M. B. Clark (Eds.), *Measures of leadership* (pp. 419–440). Greensboro, NC: Center for Creative Leadership.

Mumford, M. D., & Connelly, M. S. (1991). Leaders as creators: Leader performance and problem solving in ill-defined domains. *Leadership Quarterly, 2,* 289–316.

Mumford, M. D., Scott, G. M., Gaddis, B., & Strange, J. M. (2002). Leading creative people: Orchestrating expertise and relationships. *Leadership Quarterly, 13*, 705–750.

Ochse, R. (1990). *Before the gates of excellence.* New York: Cambridge University Press.

Perkins, D. N. (1981). *The mind's best work.* Cambridge, MA: Harvard University Press.

Perkins, D. N. (1995). Insight in minds and genes. In R. J. Sternberg & J. E. Davidson (Eds.), *The nature of insight* (pp. 495–534). Cambridge, MA: MIT Press.

Riggio, R. E., Murphy, S. E., & Pirozzolo, F. J. (2002), *Multiple intelligences and leadership.* Mahwah, NJ: Erlbaum.

Roe, A. (1952). *The making of a scientist.* New York: Dodd, Mead.

Rogers, C. R. (1954). Toward a theory of creativity. *ETC: A Review of General Semantics, 11*, 249–260.

Rogoff, B. (1990). *Apprenticeship in thinking. Cognitive development in social context.* New York: Oxford University Press.

Rubenson, D. L., & Runco, M. A. (1992). The psychoeconomic approach to creativity. *New Ideas in Psychology, 10*, 131–147.

Sashkin, M. (2004). Transformational leadership approaches: A review and synthesis. In J. Antonakis, A. T. Cianciolo, & R. J. Sternberg (Eds.), *The nature of leadership* (pp. 171–196). Thousand Oaks, CA: Sage.

Schmidt, F. L., & Hunter, J. E. (1998). The validity and utility of selection methods in personnel psychology: Practical and theoretical implications of 85 years of research findings. *Psychological Bulletin, 124*, 262–274.

Shartle, C. L. (1951). Studies of naval leadership. Part I. In H. Guetzkow (Ed.), *Group, leadership and men* (pp. 119–133). Pittsburgh, PA: Carnegie Press.

Simonton, D. K. (1994). *Greatness: Who makes history and why?* New York: Guilford Press.

Simonton, D. K. (1997). Creative productivity: A predictive and explanatory model of career trajectories and landmarks. *Psychological Review, 104*, 66–89.

Simonton, D. K. (1998). Donald Campbell's model of the creative process: Creativity as blind variation and selective retention. *Journal of Creative Behavior, 32*, 153–158.

Sloman, S. A. (1996). The empirical case for two systems of reasoning. *Psychological Bulletin, 119*, 3–22.

Sosik, J. J., & Megerian, L. E. (1999). Understanding leader emotional intelligence and performance: The role of self–other agreement on transformational leadership perceptions. *Group Organization and Management, 24*, 367–390.

Spearman, C. (1904). 'General intelligence,' objectively determined and measured. *American Journal of Psychology, 15*, 201–293.

Spearman, C. (1927). *The abilities of man.* London: Macmillan.

Spreitzer, G. M., McCall, M. W., Jr., & Mahoney, J. D. (1997). Early identification of international executive potential. *Journal of Applied Psychology, 82*, 6–29.

Staudinger, U. M., & Baltes, P. M. (1996). Interactive minds: A facilitative setting for wisdom-related performance? *Journal of Personality and Social Psychology, 71*, 746–762.

Staudinger, U. M., Lopez, D. F., & Baltes, P. B. (1997). The psychometric location of wisdom-related performance: Intelligence, personality, and more? *Personality and Social Psychology Bulletin, 23*, 1200–1214.

Staudinger, U. M., Smith, J., & Baltes, P. B. (1992). Wisdom-related knowledge in life review task: Age differences and the role of professional specialization. *Psychology of Aging, 7*, 271–281.

Sternberg, R. J. (1977). *Intelligence, information processing, and analogical reasoning: The componential analysis of human abilities.* Hillsdale, NJ: Erlbaum.

Sternberg, R. J. (1980a). Representation and process in linear syllogistic reasoning. *Journal of Experimental Psychology: General, 109*, 119–159.

Sternberg, R. J. (1980b). Sketch of a componential subtheory of human intelligence. *Behavioral Brain Science, 3*, 573–584.

Sternberg, R. J. (1981). Intelligence and nonentrenchment. *Journal of Educational Psychology, 73*, 1–16.

Sternberg, R. J. (1982). Natural, unnatural, and supernatural concepts. *Cognitive Psychology, 14*, 451–488.

Sternberg, R. J. (1983). Components of human intelligence. *Cognition, 15*, 1–48.

Sternberg, R. J. (1984). Toward a triarchic theory of human intelligence. *Behavioral Brain Science, 7*, 269–287.

Sternberg, R. J. (1985a). *Beyond IQ: A triarchic theory of human intelligence.* New York: Cambridge University Press.

Sternberg, R. J. (1985b). Implicit theories of intelligence, creativity, and wisdom. *Journal of Personality and Social Psychology, 49*, 607–627.

Sternberg, R. J. (1987a). Most vocabulary is learned from context. In M. G. McKeown & M. E. Curtis (Eds.), *The nature of vocabulary acquisition* (pp. 89–105). Hillsdale, NJ: Erlbaum.

Sternberg, R. J. (1987b). The psychology of verbal comprehension. In R. Glaser (Ed.), *Advances in instructional psychology* (Vol. 3, pp. 97–151). Hillsdale, NJ: Erlbaum.

Sternberg, R. J. (Ed.). (1988). *The nature of creativity: Contemporary psychological perspectives.* New York: Cambridge University Press.

Sternberg, R. J. (1990). *Metaphors of mind.* New York: Cambridge University Press.

Sternberg, R. J. (1993). *Sternberg triarchic abilities test.* Unpublished test.

Sternberg, R. J. (1994). Answering questions and questioning answers. *Phi Delta Kappan, 76,* 136–138.

Sternberg, R. J. (1995). *In search of the human mind.* Orlando, FL: Harcourt Brace.

Sternberg, R. J. (1997). *Successful intelligence.* New York: Plume.

Sternberg, R. J. (1998a). Abilities are forms of developing expertise. *Educational Research, 27,* 11–20.

Sternberg, R. J. (1998b). A balance theory of wisdom. *Reviews in General Psychology, 2,* 347–365.

Sternberg, R. J. (Ed.). (1998c). *Handbook of creativity.* New York: Cambridge University Press.

Sternberg, R. J. (1998d). Metacognition, abilities, and developing expertise: What makes an expert student? *Instructional Science, 26,* 127–140.

Sternberg, R. J. (1999a). Intelligence as developing expertise. *Contemporary Educational Psychology, 24,* 359–375.

Sternberg, R. J. (1999b). A propulsion model of types of creative contributions. *Reviews in General Psychology, 3,* 83–100.

Sternberg, R. J. (1999c). The theory of successful intelligence. *Reviews in General Psychology, 3,* 292–316.

Sternberg, R. J. (Ed.). (2000). *Handbook of intelligence.,* New York: Cambridge University Press.

Sternberg, R. J. (2001). Why schools should teach for wisdom: The balance theory of wisdom in educational settings. *Educational Psychology, 36,* 227–245.

Sternberg, R. J. (2002). Smart people are not stupid, but they sure can be foolish: The imbalance theory of foolishness. In R. J. Sternberg (Ed.), *Why smart people can be so stupid* (pp. 232–242). New Haven, CT: Yale University Press.

Sternberg, R. J. (Ed.). (2003a). *The anatomy of impact: What has made the great works of psychology great* (pp. 223–228). Washington, DC: American Psychological Association.

Sternberg, R. J. (Ed.). (2003b). *Psychologists defying the crowd: Stories of those who battled the establishment and won.* Washington, DC: American Psychological Association,.

Sternberg, R. J. (2003c). What is an expert student? *Educational Research, 32*(8), 5–9.

Sternberg, R. J. (2003d). WICS: A model for leadership in organizations. *Academy of Management Learning and Education, 2,* 386–401.

Sternberg, R. J. (2003e). *WICS: A theory of wisdom, intelligence, and creativity, synthesized.* New York: Cambridge University Press.

Sternberg, R. J. (2003f). WICS as a model of giftedness. *High Ability Student, 14,* 109–137.

Sternberg, R. J. (2004a). Culture and intelligence. *American Psychologist, 59,* 325–338.

Sternberg, R. J. (2004b). WICS: A model of educational leadership. *Educational Forum, 68*(2), 108–114.

Sternberg, R. J., Castejón, J. L., Prieto, M. D., Hautamaki, J., & Grigorenko, E. L. (2001). Confirmatory factor analysis of the Sternberg triarchic abilities test in three international samples: An empirical test of the triarchic theory of intelligence. *European Journal of Psychological Assessment, 17,* 1–16.

Sternberg, R. J., & Clinkenbeard, P. R. (1995). The triarchic model applied to identifying, teaching, and assessing gifted children. *Roeper Review, 17,* 255–260.

Sternberg, R. J., & Detterman, D. K. (Eds.). (1986). *What is intelligence?* Norwood, NJ: Ablex.

Sternberg, R. J., Ferrari, M., Clinkenbeard, P. R., & Grigorenko, E. L. (1996). Identification, instruction, and assessment of gifted children: A construct validation of a triarchic model. *Gifted Child Quarterly, 40,* 129–137.

Sternberg, R. J., Forsythe, G. B., Hedlund, J., Horvath, J., Snook, S., Williams, W. M., Wagner, R. K., & Grigorenko, E. L. (2000). *Practical intelligence in everyday life.* New York: Cambridge University Press.

Sternberg, R. J., & Gardner, M. K. (1982). A componential interpretation of the general factor in human intelligence. In H. J. Eysenck (Ed.), *A model for intelligence* (pp. 231–254). Berlin: Springer-Verlag.

Sternberg, R. J., & Gardner, M. K. (1983). Unities in inductive reasoning. *Journal of Experimental Psychology: General, 112,* 80–116.

Sternberg, R. J., & Gastel, J. (1989a). Coping with novelty in human intelligence: An empirical investigation. *Intelligence, 13,* 187–197.

Sternberg, R. J., & Gastel, J. (1989b). If dancers ate their shoes: Inductive reasoning with factual and counterfactual premises. *Memory and Cognition, 17,* 1–10.

Sternberg, R. J., & Grigorenko, E. L. (1997, Fall). The cognitive costs of physical and mental ill health: Applying the psychology of the developed world to the problems of the developing world. *Eye on Psi Chi, 2*(1), 20–27.

Sternberg, R. J., & Grigorenko, E. L. (2000). *Teaching for successful intelligence.* Arlington Heights, IL: Skylight Training and Publishing.

Sternberg, R. J., & Grigorenko, E. L. (2002a). *Dynamic testing.* New York: Cambridge University Press.

Sternberg, R. J., & Grigorenko, E. L. (Eds.). (2002b). *The general factor of intelligence: How general is it?* Mahwah, NJ: Erlbaum.

Sternberg, R. J., Grigorenko, E. L., Ferrari, M., & Clinkenbeard, P. (1999). A triarchic analysis of an aptitude–treatment interaction. *European Journal of Psychological Assessment, 15*(1), 1–11.

Sternberg, R. J., Grigorenko, E. L., Ngrosho, D., Tantufuye, E., Mbise, A., Nokes, C., Jukes, M., & Bundy, D. A. (2002). Assessing intellectual potential in rural Tanzanian school children. *Intelligence, 30*, 141–162.

Sternberg, R. J., & Hedlund, J. (2002). Practical intelligence, g, and work psychology. *Human Performance, 15*(1/2), 143–160.

Sternberg, R. J., & Kalmar, D. A. (1997). When will the milk spoil? Everyday induction in human intelligence. *Intelligence, 25*, 185–203.

Sternberg, R. J., Kaufman, J. C., & Pretz, J. E. (2002). *The creativity conundrum: A propulsion model of kinds of creative contributions.* New York: Psychology Press.

Sternberg, R. J., Kaufman, J. C., & Pretz, J. E. (2003). A propulsion model of creative leadership. *Leadership Quarterly, 14*, 455–473.

Sternberg, R. J., & Lubart, T. I. (1991). An investment theory of creativity and its development. *Human Development, 34*(1), 1–31.

Sternberg, R. J., & Lubart, T. I. (1995). *Defying the crowd: Cultivating creativity in a culture of conformity.* New York: Free Press.

Sternberg, R. J., & Lubart, T. I. (1996). Investing in creativity. *American Psychologist, 51*, 677–688.

Sternberg, R. J., & Nigro, G. (1980). Developmental patterns in the solution of verbal analogies. *Child Development, 51*, 27–38.

Sternberg, R. J., Nokes, K., Geissler, P. W., Prince, R., Okatcha, F., Bundy, D. A., & Grigorenko, E. L. (2001). The relationship between academic and practical intelligence: A case study in Kenya. *Intelligence, 29*, 401–418.

Sternberg, R. J., & O'Hara, L. (1999). Creativity and intelligence. In R. J. Sternberg (Ed.), *Handbook of creativity* (pp. 251–272). New York: Cambridge University Press.

Sternberg, R. J., Okagaki, L., & Jackson, A. (1990). Practical intelligence for success in school. *Educational Leadership, 48*, 35–39.

Sternberg, R. J., & Powell, J. S. (1983). Comprehending verbal comprehension. *American Psychologist, 38*, 878–893.

Sternberg, R. J., Powell, J. S., & Kaye, D. B. (1983). Teaching vocabulary-building skills: A contextual approach. In A. C. Wilkinson (Ed.), *Classroom computers and cognitive science* (pp. 121–143). New York: Academic Press.

Sternberg, R. J., & the Rainbow Project Collaborators. (2005). Augmenting the SAT through assessments of analytical, practical, and creative skills. In W. Camara & E. Kimmel (Eds.), *New tools for admission to higher education.* Mahwah, NJ: Erlbaum.

Sternberg, R. J., & the Rainbow Project Team. (2002, February 16). *The Rainbow Project: Augmenting the validity of the SAT.* Paper presented to American Academy of Arts and Sciences, Boston, MA.

Sternberg, R. J., the Rainbow Project Collaborators, & University of Michigan Business School Project Collaborators. (2004). Theory based university admissions testing for a new millennium. *Educational Psychology, 39*, 185–198.

Sternberg, R. J., & Rifkin, B. (1979). The development of analogical reasoning processes. *Journal of Experimental Child Psychology, 27*, 195–232.

Sternberg, R. J., & Smith, C. (1985). Social intelligence and decoding skills in nonverbal communication. *Social Cognition, 2*, 168–192.

Sternberg, R. J., Torff, B., & Grigorenko, E. L. (1998a). Teaching for successful intelligence raises school achievement. *Phi Delta Kappan, 79*, 667–669.

Sternberg, R. J., Torff, B., & Grigorenko, E. L. (1998b). Teaching triarchically improves school achievement. *Journal of Educational Psychology, 90*, 374–384.

Sternberg, R. J., & Turner, M. E. (1981). Components of syllogistic reasoning. *Acta Psychologica, 47*, 245–265.

Sternberg, R. J., & Vroom, V. H. (2002). The person versus the situation in leadership. *Leadership Quarterly, 13,* 301–323.

Sternberg, R. J., & Wagner, R. K. (1993). The geocentric view of intelligence and job performance is wrong. *Current Directions in Psychological Science, 2*(1), 1–4.

Sternberg, R. J., Wagner, R. K., & Okagaki, L. (1993). Practical intelligence: The nature and role of tacit knowledge in work and at school. In H. Reese & J. Puckett (Eds.), *Advances in lifespan development* (pp. 205–227). Hillsdale, NJ: Erlbaum.

Sternberg, R. J., Wagner, R. K., Williams, W. M., & Horvath, J. A. (1995). Testing common sense. *American Psychologist, 50,* 912–927.

Sternberg, R. J., & Williams, W. M. (1996). *How to develop student creativity.* Alexandria, VA: Association for Supervision and Curriculum Development.

Sternberg, R. J., & Williams, W. M. (2001). *Educational psychology,* Boston: Allyn & Bacon.

Stogdill, R. M. (1948). Personal factors associated with leadership: A survey of the literature. *Journal of Psychology, 25,* 35–71.

Stogdill, R. M., & Coons, A. E. (1957). *Leader behavior: Its description and measurement.* Columbus, OH: Bureau of Business Research, Ohio State University.

Tetewsky, S. J., & Sternberg, R. J. (1986). Conceptual and lexical determinants of nonentrenched thinking. *Journal of Memory and Language, 25,* 202–225.

Tolstoy, L. (1994). *War and peace* (Translated by C. Garnett). New York: Modern Library.

Tzuriel, D. (1995). *Dynamic interactive assessment: The legacy of L. S. Vygotsky and current developments.* Unpublished manuscript.

Vernon, P. E. (1971). *The structure of human abilities.* London: Methuen.

Vygotsky, L. S. (1978). *Mind in society: The development of higher psychological processes.* Cambridge, MA: Harvard University Press.

Vroom, V. H., & Jago, A. G. (1978). On the validity of the Vroom–Yetton model. *Journal of Applied Psychology, 63,* 151–162.

Vroom, V. H., & Yetton, P. W. (1973). *Leadership and decision making.* Pittsburgh, PA: University of Pittsburgh Press.

Wagner, R. K. (1987). Tacit knowledge in everyday intelligent behavior. *Journal of Personality and Social Psychology, 52,* 1236–1247.

Wagner, R. K., & Sternberg, R. J. (1986). Tacit knowledge and intelligence in the everyday world. In R. J. Sternberg & R. K. Wagner (Eds.), *Practical intelligence: Nature and origins of competence in the everyday world* (pp. 51–83). New York: Cambridge University Press.

Ward, T. B. (1994). Structured imagination: The role of conceptual structure in exemplar generation. *Cognitive Psychology, 27,* 1–40.

Ward, T. B., Smith, S. M., & Finke, R. A. (1999). Creative cognition. In R. J. Sternberg (Ed.), *Handbook of creativity* (pp. 189–212). New York: Cambridge University Press.

Weisberg, R. W. (1986). *Creativity, genius and other myths.* New York: Freeman.

Weisberg, R. W. (1993). *Creativity: Beyond the myth of genius.* New York: Freeman.

Williams, W. M., Blythe, T., White, N., Li, J., Sternberg, R. J., & Gardner, H. I. (1996). *Practical intelligence for school: A handbook for teachers of grades 5–8.* New York: HarperCollins.

Williams, W. M., Blythe, T., White, N., Li, J. Gardner, H., & Sternberg, R. J. (2002). Practical intelligence for school: Developing metacognitive sources of achievement in adolescence. *Developmental Review, 22,* 162–210.

Williams, W. M., & Sternberg, R. J. (1988). Group intelligence: Why some groups are better than others. *Intelligence, 12,* 351–377.

Yukl, G. (1994). *Leadership in organizations* (3rd ed.). Englewood Cliffs, NJ: Prentice-Hall.

Zaccaro, S. J., Kemp, C., & Bader, P. (2004). Leader traits and attributes. In J. Antonakis, A. T. Cianciolo, & R. J. Sternberg (Eds.), *The nature of leadership* (pp. 101–124). Thousand Oaks, CA: Sage.

Zimbardo, P. (1972). Pathology of imprisonment. *Society, 9*(6), 4–8.

Section VI

Robert J. Sternberg on Psychology: Brief Insights

It All Started with Those Darn IQ Tests: Half a Career Spent Defying the Crowd

15

Robert J. Sternberg

The Prehistory

If it weren't for the darn IQ tests, my whole life might have been different. As a child, I was very test anxious (and probably everything else anxious, too). The school psychologist would enter the elementary school classroom, and I immediately knew why she was there—to give us a group IQ test. Immediately, I would tighten up like a drum. She would hand out the test booklets, but all I could focus on was my test anxiety. She would say "Begin," and I would watch other students answer the problems. I would look at the problems, but I hardly could read them, so tense was I in their presence! Then the other children would start turning pages, and I was still on the first or second problem. It was over—another failure.

I eventually cured myself of the test anxiety when, as a sixth grader, I was sent back to a fifth-grade classroom to retake the fifth-grade intelligence test. The school officials apparently did not think me bright enough to be able to cope with the sixth-grade test. At that point, I was in the final grade of elementary school, and like all other sixth graders, I viewed myself as eminently superior to the younger kids, who I perceived as little more than infants. Certainly I could compete with fifth graders! So I took the test without anxiety, and the test anxiety disappeared and never returned.

What did not disappear, however, was a lifelong interest in the nature, measurement, and development of intelligence. This interest was rather strange for a young child, and it was not a whole lot less strange among the cognitive psychologists with whom I was trained in graduate school and with whom I would later associate as a professor. The interest started early: Even in elementary school, every year I would write a workbook with exercises that I thought would help children in the grade I was in to develop their intelligence. But I was interested not only in developing intelligence—I wanted to test it.

In seventh grade, at age 13, I wanted to understand intelligence, and implicitly, why I had done so poorly on the tests. Test anxiety was a concept with which I was not yet familiar; but stupidity was something I was quite familiar with, and I wondered whether I was afflicted with it. So when we were asked to come up with ideas for science projects, I generated an idea that almost certainly had not been tried by others in Mr. Adams's seventh-grade science class. I proposed to do a project on the development of mental testing. As part of the project, I invented my own test, the Sternberg Test of Mental Abilities, which, like my workbooks (and my childhood comic books), is long since lost. In visiting, for the first time, the adult section of the Maplewood, New Jersey, town library, I discovered the book *Measuring Intelligence* (Terman & Merrill, 1937), which contained the verbal materials for the Stanford-Binet Intelligence Scales (2nd ed.). I thought it would be a good idea to get some practice in administering the tests to some classmates.

The first classmate to whom I gave the test was a girl in whom I was romantically interested. I was rather shy and thought that perhaps giving her the IQ test would help break the ice. I was wrong. She did very well on the test, but the romantic relationship never got started. The second classmate to whom I gave the test was one I had known from the Cub Scouts. Another disaster. He told his mother, who told the junior high school guidance counselor, who told a school psychologist. I was called away from a social studies class one day, bawled out for 40 minutes, and informed by the psychologist that if I ever brought the book into school again, he personally would burn it. He suggested that if I had to study intelligence, I study it instead in rats. I don't think he was offering himself as a subject.

At this point, I learned a lesson about defying the crowd, a lesson I relearn on a regular basis: Defying the crowd has costs, sometimes steep ones. It almost always is easier to follow the crowd and join in the fads (Sternberg, 1997a). Fortunately, my science teacher stood up for me, and the consequences were not as serious as they might have been: No suspensions, no expulsions. I decided at that point that I had to do what I had to do. For me, it was a calling. Today, I view it as a mission. I continued to study intelligence, but went underground. I did not come out from the underground until several years later.

In tenth grade, I was suspicious that the Biological Science Curriculum Study (BSCS) biology program we were using was not really teaching us much biology. So, with the support of my biology teacher, Mrs. Stewart, I designed an experiment to test how scores of the students in BSCS biology would compare with those of comparable students in the standard biology course, both for the BSCS exams and the standard exams. True to my prediction, the two groups did equally well on the BSCS test, but the students in the standard course outperformed the BSCS students on the standard exam.

The summer after tenth grade, I went to a summer program in marine biology, and the program directors were not thrilled when I proposed to study human intelligence, but they caved in. So I studied the effects of distractions on mental test performance and discovered that neither a car headlight shining in one's eyes nor a metronome disrupted mental test performance, but a Beatles record playing "She's Got the Devil in Her Heart" improved mental test performance.

A year later, my physics teacher, Mr. Genzer, was wonderfully supportive when I did a strange physics project, the development of a physics aptitude test. I was trying, in part, to figure out why I was doing so poorly in physics. The test correlated about .65 with physics grades and was actually used by the high school for several years as a screening device for admission to the advanced physics class.

So if I ask myself why I can defy the crowd and live with it, I attribute much of it to the wonderful support I had both from my parents and from early teachers, like Mr. Adams, Mrs. Stewart, and Mr. Genzer. They provided an atmosphere in which one could go one's own way and be rewarded for it. Yet I knew from my seventh-grade experience that there were costs, and this is a lesson I keep relearning.

Ancient History

I went to college and discovered that not much was going on in intelligence research at Yale University. The one professor interested in the field was perturbed. He had spent his time using calculators to predict students' Yale grade point averages (GPAs) from variables in their admissions folders, such as scholastic aptitude test (SAT) scores and high school GPAs. But Yale had introduced computerization, and so the calculations he had lovingly done over months now took a matter of seconds. He took to checking the computer calculations by hand, but fortunately for all, retired soon thereafter.

I pursued my interests by doing research on undergraduate admissions—resulting in two published articles—and by studying thinking with Professor Alexander Wearing. The admissions office had mixed feelings about my research. They had these long admissions meetings during which they spent several weeks, meeting for many hours per day, deciding who should be admitted. I showed that, for about three-quarters of the cases, an algorithm could predict what they were doing with roughly 98% accuracy (Sternberg, 1972). In another study, I showed that the admissions office interview was a poor predictor of admissions outcomes (Sternberg, 1973). But I recommended that the office keep the interview, because students liked it and thought they did much better than they did with respect to the evaluation they received.

After my junior year, Professor Wearing took a position in Australia, and I became a student of Endel Tulving. Tulving was a wonderful mentor whose trademark, at that point, was defying the crowd. If people believed one thing, he would show them that the opposite was true. So if they believed, for example, that repetition always improved recall, he would show them that it could actually result in worse recall (Tulving, 1966). If they believed that recognition memory was always better than recall memory, he would show that recall memory could be better than recognition memory (Tulving & Thomson, 1973). Tulving was a wonderful role model: a scientist who had defied the crowd and won!

A year later, I went to Stanford University to study under Gordon Bower. For my first-year project, I continued with work I had started on negative transfer in part–whole and whole–part free recall, and I did a series of studies providing an explanation of the phenomenon that was different from Tulving's (Sternberg & Bower, 1974). One might have expected Tulving to protest. Quite the contrary. He was totally supportive, teaching me another lesson. The true scientist is out to discover the truth, wherever it may be found. And sometimes, one discovers that the truth is not where one has been looking.

Tulving and I continued to collaborate during my relatively brief time at Stanford. The collaboration was facilitated by his spending a year at the Center for Advanced Study in the Behavioral Sciences, which was nearby. We wrote an article on the measurement of subjective organization, which advocated a type of measure that was rather unpopular at that time. We submitted the article to the *Psychological Bulletin*, and it was rejected. I needed to cite the article in another article I was writing, and I asked Tulving how I should cite it. He stared me straight in the eye and replied something like, "Well, cite it as 'Rejected by *Psychological Bulletin*, of course.' " At the time, I thought this a most bizarre answer. We were going to brag about getting our article rejected? I later realized the message he was sending me (or, at least, I thought he was sending me): If you defy the crowd, you will get rejections. They are not a badge of shame, but rather, a badge of honor. If you never get anything rejected, the one thing you know about yourself is that you never took the risk of defying the crowd. Eventually, *Psychological Bulletin* accepted the article (Sternberg & Tulving, 1977). When, years later, I became editor of this same journal, I wrote an editorial encouraging people to be unconventional in their submissions. And by encouraging such submissions, and providing for others the same kind of encouragement that I myself had gotten from my mentors, the journal did indeed receive and publish articles that defied the crowd.

My heart was in intelligence research, not in memory research, however, and so I was casting about for ideas about how to study intelligence. I got some ideas the summer after my first year of graduate study, and so was born the componential analysis (Sternberg, 1977a, 1977b, 1983) of human intelligence. To his great credit, my advisor, Bower, was wholly supportive of my working in a field totally outside his area and outside the area of anyone else in the department. He even supported my research from his grant. But I also discovered that the general climate of the psychology department was not highly favorable for the kind of research I was doing. It just didn't fit. I decided to take some courses in education, an idea that also did not receive much support from the psychology department. But I went my own way and thereby met Lee Cronbach, another great influence on my life. Later, as editor of *Psychological Bulletin*, I was to discover that of the 10 most frequently cited articles in the history of the journal, Cronbach had authored or coauthored 4 of them (Sternberg, 1992). Here was a man who went his own way! He helped invent the field we now know as psychometrics.

Early History

Stanford was a wonderful place, but in some respects, I felt that the atmosphere was not right for me. I had the impression, at least at the time, that Stanford was into trends, whereas I tended to buck, or at least ignore, trends. Because I was finishing up, I applied during my third year there for some jobs, and Yale University hired me. Yale was full of idiosyncratic people who seemed to go their own offbeat ways. It was full of trend busters! It seemed right for me. And so I packed up and went back to Yale, pained, however, that my mentor Tulving had left.

Yale proved to be the right place for me. Offbeat people such as myself were valued. But as soon as I left the campus, I found that the sledding got tougher, and sometimes the sled seemed to overturn.

In my first year, I received a colloquium invitation from a major testing organization. I was thrilled. This was going to be my chance to really change things. After all, who more needed to hear what I had to say about intelligence than the old fuddy-duddies at testing organizations, who had been producing essentially the same tests for close to a century? I went to the colloquium full of enthusiasm.

The talk bombed. I was stunned. How could my wonderfully fresh and creative ideas about intelligence go over so poorly? Maybe they weren't so fresh or even so wonderful! Over time, I came to realize the nature of at least part of the problem. The testing organization had a very substantial vested interest in its existing products. What I was proposing was essentially that those products were nowhere near as good as they thought they were. This was not the message that such an organization wanted to hear. What did I expect—that people 20 or 30 years my senior would come up to this 25-year-old and thank him for saving them from wasting the rest of their careers as they had wasted them up to that point? Those who defy the crowd should not expect accolades from the crowd.

There is an even more difficult problem: The fact that one defies the crowd does not mean that one's ideas are good. There are plenty of crowd-defying ideas that are crowd-defiant simply because so few people would be foolish enough to believe them. For example, few people today believe that little green people live on Mars. Believing in such creatures would be crowd defying, but, in all likelihood, foolish as well. Wendell Garner once told me of a comment made to him by Michael Posner. The comment was that the easiest papers to get accepted by journals, and the easiest proposals to get funded by granting agencies, were those that were middling in quality. They made a contribution but offended no one. The hardest pieces to get accepted were those that were awful, because they were awful, and those that were wonderful, because they often went against the way things were being done at the time.

I have learned this lesson from both directions. Some of what I considered my best articles had to be revised many times before being accepted. But perhaps more revealing was an incident with another article. I wrote an article on the development of linear syllogistic reasoning (Sternberg, 1980a), which is the kind of reasoning used in problems such as "John is taller than Mary; Mary is taller than Susan; who is tallest?" After submitting the article, I came to realize it was really quite trivial. The article basically took a theory of linear-syllogistic reasoning I had proposed (Sternberg, 1980b) and applied it developmentally. There was nothing new in the article. I thought about withdrawing it and then decided I would just let it get rejected and die a quiet death. To my astonishment, I got back three glowing reviews. It was at that point I learned that, in the short run, the research that is most valued is often that which threatens no one. It makes a small contribution and claims to be nothing more than a small contribution.

I've found Posner's wisdom to be very useful to me over the years. The problem, of course, is that one can never be sure if one's rejected article or grant proposal is an unappreciated gem or a rightly rejected dud. I often use a "three-time" heuristic.

I submit an article or proposal to up to three places. Each time it is turned down, I try to improve it. If, after three tries, it is still rejected, I put it in a file drawer (or, today, on the hard drive of my computer) and let it incubate. I cannot be sure if the idea is a good one or a bad one; what I can be sure of is that I have not persuaded others of the value of my idea. And part of the creative process is persuading others that one's ideas have value (Sternberg & Lubart, 1995, 1996).

I have not always succeeded in persuading other people of the value of my ideas, and sometimes, for good reason. During my first year at Yale, I became convinced that Garner's (1974) viewpoint regarding structure inhering in the stimulus rather than in the interaction between person and stimulus was wrong. So I did some research to knock down his theory. I felt truly defiant: I was defying the views of a senior member of my department! I submitted the article to a journal, and it was rejected. I presented the research as a talk, and it was destroyed.

One day, Garner called me into his office. Of course, he had been one of the reviewers of the article, and a fair one. He told me that there was a lesson to be learned from this experience. The lesson was that one is judged by posterity for the positive contributions one makes, not for the negative contributions. I have tried to learn that lesson and to make contributions that seek to build rather than destroy. It is easy to be defiant and knock down someone else's work. What is hard is to come up with a better idea.

In my third year, John Anderson left to go to Carnegie–Mellon, and a senior slot opened. I applied for it but didn't get it. The department offered the position to Bill Estes. I consoled myself by telling myself he was more than twice my age. But he turned down Yale to go to Harvard, so the slot remained open, and I was again considered for the tenured position.

I started hearing rumblings that Yale was getting letters back from referees stating, implicitly or explicitly, that it was not at all clear that they should hire me for the slot. Intelligence, these referees thought, was a rather junky field, and with a limited number of senior slots, Yale might do better to select someone in a better field. This information depressed me, and I began to question whether defying the crowd and working in the field of intelligence—which indeed did not have a very good reputation—was such a great idea, after all. I talked to Garner, my informal senior faculty mentor, and told him that perhaps I had made a mistake. I said that, when all was said and done, I could have done exactly the same work I had been doing, but labeled it as work in thinking or problem solving. Both of these fields had higher prestige, and perhaps if I had labeled my work thus, my employment prospects would not now be in jeopardy. Garner gave me what I consider to be some of the best advice I have received in my entire career. It went something like this:

> You're afraid that your intelligence research may cost you your job, and you're asking me what to do about it? You're right. Your intelligence research may cost you your job. You want my advice, so I'll give you my advice. You should go on doing exactly what you have been doing. When you came here, your mission was to make a difference to the field of intelligence. And that's what you have to do, even if it does cost you your job.

Tulving and Bower gave me similar advice. I took it, and I'm still at Yale. I should say, though, that studying intelligence and related phenomena has not been cost-free.

One day, Yale was hosting a very-well-known cognitive psychologist from an esteemed institution. He came to chat with me in my office, and I mentioned some cognitive research I was doing. He commented to me something like, "You know, Bob, you're not really a cognitive psychologist anymore." At the time, I was stunned. I took pride in being a cognitive psychologist, and here I was being told by an eminence that I was anything but. I have come to realize that he was not alone: Despite Cronbach's (1957) plea for a unification of the two disciplines of scientific psychology and despite my own efforts at unification (e.g., Sternberg, 1978), the two disciplines have never become truly unified. Their practitioners often have eyed one another with suspicion. And those who choose a path that bridges them may end up being viewed with suspicion by practitioners in both camps!

Modern History

As the years went by, the character of my research began to change. Less and less of it was in the laboratory, more and more of it out in the everyday world. I was looking less and less like the standard cognitive psychologist, or psychologist of any particular kind at all. I was not entirely alone, however.

Dick Neisser wrote what I consider to be two classic books in his career. The first, *Cognitive Psychology* (Neisser, 1967), largely established Neisser's career and also was instrumental in establishing the field of cognitive psychology. It provided a theoretical framework for much laboratory-based cognitive psychology. It was well received and has been widely cited. The second book, *Cognition and Reality* (Neisser, 1976), argued for the importance of studying cognition in context. It has never had anywhere near the influence of the earlier book, and research resulting from it has even generated some broadside attacks (e.g., Banaji & Crowder, 1989).

I liked the first book and loved the second. People who study intelligence in its everyday manifestations find that it seems to behave according to different rules in everyday life than those that obtain when people solve rather structured and formal problems of the kinds found on intelligence tests (Sternberg et al., 2000). My ventures into psychology in the everyday world have met with the approbation of some and the disapproval of others. Those in the traditional intelligence fraternity have reacted in various ways to the work I have done throughout my career, some ignoring it and others attacking it in various ways. I can happily say that only one of the many attacks I have seen has been vicious and personal, and that attack is not yet published and may not be, at least in the form it was originally written.

In my intelligence and other research, I have tried to take a balanced approach (Sternberg, 1985, 1990, 1997b). I tend to believe that truth often lies in the middle ground. My style tends to be integrative—seeking, for example, a rapprochement among psychometric, cognitive, and contextualist approaches to intelligence. But sometimes one finds oneself under pressure to choose sides. The message one receives is that either you are for the "Blue Team," or you are against it. Of course, you get the same message from the "Red Team." It often takes some strength to seek and stay on a middle course.

In the early years, the work we did in my research group, balanced though it may have been, was largely ignored by testing organizations. For a while, I worked with one such organization, but when the leadership changed, I was quickly dismissed. The head of one such organization used to walk out when I gave talks. More recently, leadership changes have resulted in our working with some of the same organizations that used to shun us. It is a challenge to work with such organizations, because our views on what needs to be measured do not always correspond to theirs. But we have found that, with open-minded leadership, one can go rather far. For example, right now we are involved in a 16-site project to develop instruments that might eventually be used to supplement the SAT for use in college admission. Our idea is to create research projects that have the maximum possible impact—scientifically, educationally, and societally.

Our expanded work in the everyday world is in large part a matter of mission—we, in my group, are trying to change the world, and we think the way to change the world is by working in and being a part of it. But there is another factor that has led us in this direction, one whose influence I underestimated when I was younger. As time went on, I have written many grant proposals. Some have been accepted, others rejected. But the accepted ones tended to be ones that were school or community based, and the rejected ones tended to be ones that were laboratory based. So I found, as have so many others, that my work was shaped not only by what I wanted to do, but also by what I was able to do with the funds at hand.

Not all our work has been funded, of course. In the early 1980s, my personal life was not going well. And just as my failures on intelligence tests had led me to the study of intelligence, my personal failures led me to the study of love. Love research was, at least at the time, one of the few areas in psychology that enjoyed even less prestige than did intelligence research, a distinction not easily attained. But I had some ideas first about how the structures (not the content) of psychometric theories of intelligence could be applied to the study of love (Sternberg & Grajek, 1984). So I started studying love.

I naively thought that people would commend me for broadening out in my theory and research. Not so fast. I found the reaction to be often more negative than positive. Some said that I had gone soft in the head; others that I had run out of ideas about intelligence; others that I wanted to be another Dr. Ruth. Instead of accolades, I was getting flack. I was therefore particularly pleased when a theory article (Sternberg, 1986) was published in the *Psychological Review,* perhaps the first theory of love published in that journal. But acceptances were mixed with rejections, and I continued to muddle through, much the way I had in the work I had done on intelligence. My articles on love as a story encountered rougher sailing, although eventually I found homes for them (Sternberg, 1995, 1996; Sternberg, Hojjat, & Barnes, 2001) and eventually simply decided to write a book on the subject (Sternberg, 1998b)—a book, incidentally, which, wonderful though it was, did not sell very well.

Oddly enough, it was not just the cognitive people who questioned my entrance into the love field. Some of the people in that field viewed me as some kind of interloper. I was an intelligence researcher. Who did I think I was studying love, a topic foreign to the bulk of my research? To this day, I have never been invited to speak at any conference on love, despite having published a fair amount of work in the field. Of course, there are multiple interpretations of my failure to have been invited to speak!

In recent years, the interests of my research group have diverged even more than in the past. We still study intelligence, creativity, love, and related topics, but I think I am most excited by three aspects of our research.

The first aspect is research in other cultures (e.g., Sternberg & Grigorenko, 1997, 1999). We have come to believe that psychologists cannot understand phenomena in their own culture unless they understand how, and whether, these phenomena apply in other cultures. Many of the things we take for granted, we stop taking for granted when we look at people in diverse foreign lands.

The second aspect is research in the schools (e.g., Grigorenko, Jarvin, & Sternberg, in press; Sternberg, Torff, & Grigorenko, 1998). What we find is that by using teaching methods based on my theory of intelligence (Sternberg, 1997b), we can make a difference in students' school performance: Students can achieve at higher levels when they are taught in a way that enables them to capitalize on strengths and to compensate for or correct weaknesses.

The third aspect is our research on wisdom (e.g., Sternberg, 1998a, 2001). There are many people who are intelligent, but they are not wise. According to the balance theory, people are wise when they apply their (successful) intelligence to a common good, seeking to balance their interests with the interests of other people and institutions.

One of the wonderful things about research in psychology is that one can apply what one studies to one's own life, or at least, try to learn from it. Studying wisdom has been a special opportunity to try to become more balanced in my thought and affect. I suppose that I have achieved greater balance even in my personal life. In recent years, I have taken up the cello after a hiatus of 30 years during which I stupidly defined myself as an "ex-cellist," have continued to exercise every day, and have started the study of a third foreign language. I am amazed by the opportunities that are out there, if only one finds (or, even better, creates) them.

Although one can try to be wise in one's life, the wise course of action often is not altogether clear. For example, recently, a new problem cropped up in my life. Although early in my career I found the psychology department at Yale to be a hospitable environment, I began to question that a couple of years ago. I increasingly felt isolated. This was not the "fault" of my colleagues. Rather, it seemed more and more that my own thinking and values were departing from others'. The composition of the department had changed, and I worried whether its ways of thinking and mine were parting company. I thought about leaving but ultimately found another solution.

In 2000, we opened the Yale Center for the Psychology of Abilities, Competencies, and Expertise. The center is housed in its own building —an old house in which two U.S. Presidents, Theodore Roosevelt and William Howard Taft, slept. Since we moved there, it has been close to paradise for us. We have established our own team-oriented culture and our own set of values regarding the importance of scientific, educational, and societal impact. We believe that teams, when well managed, produce work that is more than the sum of the parts (Sternberg & Grigorenko, 2000). At the same time, we remain part of the Department of Psychology. Our building is at the northern edge of campus, and when I selected the site, I found our moving to the edge of campus to be symbolic of the way we think. We hope we always stay at this edge.

My undergraduate advisor, Tulving, once said to me that I would be surprised at the amount of time it takes to have an impact—to make a difference. He was right. I'm 51, and I often feel frustrated with the lack of impact I've had. I'm hoping my career is only half done. Maybe in the second half I'll accomplish some of what I have failed to accomplish in the first.

If I do, it will be not because I follow the crowd, but rather, because I head where I need to go, regardless of where others go. I do not believe that all creative work is crowd defying (Sternberg, 1999a, 1999b). And certainly not all my work has been crowd defying. Early in my career, I did some work on metaphor (e.g., Sternberg &

Nigro, 1983; Tourangeau & Sternberg, 1981), which at the time was a hot area. I enjoyed the work but did not enjoy the crowding. The field had too many people competing too furiously. I have always been susceptible to claustrophobia, and I felt claustrophobic. So for me, I do my best when the tune I play is the one I write. Each of us must create his or her path, and I am constantly trying to create my own.

References

Banaji, M. R., & Crowder, R. C. (1989). The bankruptcy of everyday memory. *American Psychologist, 44*, 1185–1193.

Cronbach, L. J. (1957). The two disciplines of scientific psychology. *American Psychologist, 12*, 671–684.

Garner, W. R. (1974). *The processing of information and structure.* Potomac, MD: Erlbaum.

Grigorenko, E. L., Jarvin, L., & Sternberg, R. J. (2002). School-based tests of the triarchic theory of intelligence: Three settings, three samples, three syllabi. *Contemporary Educational Psychology, 27*, 167–208.

Neisser, U. (1967). *Cognitive psychology.* New York: Appleton-Century-Crofts.

Neisser, U. (1976). *Cognition and reality.* San Francisco: W. H. Freeman.

Sternberg, R. J. (1972). A decision rule to facilitate the undergraduate admissions process. *College and University, 48*, 48–53.

Sternberg, R. J. (1973). Cost-benefit analysis of the Yale admissions office interview. *College and University, 48*, 154–164.

Sternberg, R. J. (1977a). Component processes in analogical reasoning. *Psychological Review, 84*, 353–378.

Sternberg, R. J. (1977b). *Intelligence, information processing, and analogical reasoning: The componential analysis of human abilities.* Hillsdale, NJ: Erlbaum.

Sternberg, R. J. (1978). Intelligence research at the interface between differential and cognitive psychology. *Intelligence, 2*, 195–222.

Sternberg, R. J. (1980a). The development of linear syllogistic reasoning. *Journal of Experimental Child Psychology, 29*, 340–356.

Sternberg, R. J. (1980b). Representation and process in linear syllogistic reasoning. *Journal of Experimental Psychology: General, 109*, 119–159.

Sternberg, R. J. (1983). Components of human intelligence. *Cognition, 15*, 1–48.

Sternberg, R. J. (1985). Human intelligence: The model is the message. *Science, 230*, 1111–1118.

Sternberg, R. J. (1986). A triangular theory of love. *Psychological Review, 93*, 119–135.

Sternberg, R. J. (1990). *Metaphors of mind.* New York: Cambridge University Press.

Sternberg, R. J. (1992). *Psychological Bulletin's* top 10 "Hit Parade." *Psychological Bulletin, 112*, 387–388.

Sternberg, R. J. (1995). Love as a story. *Journal of Social and Personal Relationships, 12*, 541–546.

Sternberg, R. J. (1996). Love stories. *Personal Relationships, 3*, 1359–1379.

Sternberg, R. J. (1997a). Fads in psychology: What we can do. *APA Monitor, 28(7)*, 19.

Sternberg, R. J. (1997b). *Successful intelligence.* New York: Plume.

Sternberg, R. J. (1998a). A balance theory of wisdom. *Review of General Psychology, 2*, 347–365.

Sternberg, R. J. (1998b). *Love is a story.* New York: Oxford University Press.

Sternberg, R. J. (1999a). The creativity paradox: Why everyone and no one seems to appreciate creative work. *APA Monitor, 30(10)*, 17.

Sternberg, R. J. (1999b). A propulsion theory of types of creative contributions. *Review of General Psychology, 3*, 83–100.

Sternberg, R. J. (2001). Why schools should teach for wisdom: The balance theory of wisdom in educational settings. *Educational Psychologist, 36*, 227–245.

Sternberg, R. J., & Bower, G. H. (1974). Transfer in part-whole and whole-part free recall: A comparative evaluation of theories. *Journal of Verbal Learning and Verbal Behavior, 13*, 1–26.

Sternberg, R. J., Forsythe, G. B., Hedlund, J., Horvath, J., Snook, S., Williams, W. M., et al. (2000). *Practical intelligence in everyday life.* New York: Cambridge University Press.

Sternberg, R. J., & Grajek, S. (1984). The nature of love. *Journal of Personality and Social Psychology, 47*, 312–329.

Sternberg, R. J., & Grigorenko, E. L. (1997). The cognitive costs of physical and mental ill health: Applying the psychology of the developed world to the problems of the developing world. *Eye on Psi Chi, 2(1)*, 20–27.

Sternberg, R. J., & Grigorenko, E. L. (1999). A smelly 113 degrees in the shade, or why we do field research. *APS Observer, 12*(1), 10–11, 20–21.

Sternberg, R. J., & Grigorenko, E. L. (2000). The myth of the lone ranger in psychological research. *APS Observer, 13,* 11, 27.

Sternberg, R. J., Hojjat, M., & Barnes, M. L. (2001). Empirical tests of aspects of a theory of love as a story. *European Journal of Personality, 15,* 1–20.

Sternberg, R. J., & Lubart, T. I. (1995). *Defying the crowd: Cultivating creativity in a culture of conformity.* New York: Free Press.

Sternberg, R. J., & Lubart, T. I. (1996). Investing in creativity. *American Psychologist, 51,* 677–688.

Sternberg, R. J., & Nigro, G. (1983). Interaction and analogy in the comprehension and appreciation of metaphors. *Quarterly Journal of Experimental Psychology, 35A,* 17–38.

Sternberg, R. J., Torff, B., & Grigorenko, E. L. (1998). Teaching triarchically improves school performance. *Journal of Educational Psychology, 90,* 374–385.

Sternberg, R. J., & Tulving, E. (1977). The measurement of subjective organization in free recall. *Psychological Bulletin, 84,* 539–556.

Terman, L. M., & Merrill, M. (1937). *Measuring intelligence.* Boston: Houghton-Mifflin.

Tourangeau, R., & Sternberg, R. J. (1981). Aptness in metaphor. *Cognitive Psychology, 13,* 27–55.

Tulving, E. (1966). Subjective organization and effects of repetition in multi-trial free-recall learning. *Journal of Verbal Learning and Verbal Behavior, 5,* 193–197.

Tulving, E., & Thomson, D. M. (1973). Encoding specificity and retrieval processes in episodic memory. *Psychological Review, 80,* 352–373.

Unified Psychology

16

Robert J. Sternberg
Elena L. Grigorenko

Unified psychology is the multiparadigmatic, multidisciplinary, and integrated study of psychological phenomena through converging operations. In this chapter, we propose that unified psychology can and should supplement traditional approaches to psychology. Some readers might even find it a suitable replacement for several traditional approaches. To unpack our definition, we need to look at each of its aspects. But before we do, we must summarize a major contention of our essay.

Unified psychology, as we conceive of it, involves giving up or, at least, putting aside what we believe to be three bad habits that are commonplace among some psychologists. The bad habits are (a) exclusive or almost exclusive reliance on a single methodology (e.g., response-time measurements or fMRI measurements) rather than multiple converging methodologies for studying psychological phenomena, (b) identification of scholars in psychology in terms of psychological subdisciplines (e.g., social psychology or clinical psychology) rather than in terms of the psychological phenomena they study, and (c) adherence to single underlying paradigms for the investigation of psychological phenomena (e.g., behaviorism, cognitivism, psychoanalysis).

Before we elaborate on our view of the good habits that can replace these bad ones, we discuss some previous proposals regarding the notion of a unified psychology. We also consider objections that have been raised to such proposals.

Previous Proposals Regarding the Unification of Psychology

Perhaps the whole issue of unity versus disunity—in psychology or any other science—was best framed by Berlin (1953), who argued that there are different sorts of people: *hedgehogs,* who try to relate everything to a single system or vision, and *foxes,* who pursue many different paths without trying to fit them together. (A third class of person is a fox who sees him- or herself as a hedgehog.) The distinction is based on the words of the Greek poet Archilochus, who said, "The fox knows many things, but the hedgehog knows one big thing." Therefore, those who seek unification are the hedgehogs.

Although the distinction may be too sharp, it seems roughly to apply to the literature that has grown up around the issue of unification in psychology. Consider the views of both hedgehogs and foxes.

Attempts by hedgehogs to unify psychology go back a long way, in part because psychology has a long history as a "house divided" (Kimble, 1989, p. 491). For example, Baldwin (1902) went about integrating the study of development with that of evolution; Baldwin (1897/1906) also combined social-psychological and developmental techniques in studying mental development. But many attempts at unification are much more recent.

One of the most ambitious and more recent efforts at unifying psychology was undertaken by Staats (1991), who proposed what he referred to as a "unified positivism and unification psychology" (p. 899; see also Staats, 1983, 1993). Staats suggested that psychology has suffered from a crisis of disunity and that the crisis has needed, for some time, to be resolved. He further suggested that unification could be achieved not by the old "grand theories" of psychology but through interlevel and interfield theories. An interlevel theory would seek to bridge different levels of analysis of a phenomenon, such as the application of basic learning principles to language learning. The idea here is to form connections between one level of analysis that calls on more elementary principles—in this case, presumably, learning theory—and a second level of analysis that presumably is more molar—in this case, presumably, language learning. An interfield theory would seek to bridge different fields of analysis of the same phenomenon, such as biological and psychological approaches to a problem. The idea here is to form connections between fields that may have members studying the same problem with different methods and different perspectives.

Staats (1999) further suggested that part of the reason that psychology may have failed to become unified is because it lacks an infrastructure for unification. For example, in unified sciences, there are single terms corresponding to particular theoretical constructs, such as the quark in physics. In psychology, particular theoretical constructs are often associated with multiple terms, with the distinctions among them unclear. Staats gave "self-concept," "self-image," "self-perception," "self-esteem," "self-confidence," "self," and "self-efficacy" as examples of concepts whose differences are, in his opinion, at best, ill-defined. Further problems discouraging unification are that (a) there are many theories in psychology but few attempts to interrelate them and (b) each theory must be discussed using a different language, so conversations in which theories are being compared or contrasted sometimes are virtually unintelligible.

A somewhat different approach has been taken by systems theorists (e.g., Kuo, 1967, 1976; Magnusson, 2000; Sameroff, 1983; Schneirla, 1957; Thelen, 1992; Thelen &

Smith, 1994, 1998). For example, Magnusson (2000) has proposed that a holistic approach to psychological inquiry and to the individual can provide a basis for integrating and unifying many diverse outlooks on human development. Sameroff and Bartko (1998) have applied a political-systems metaphor to child development, Lerner (1998) has also taken a systems approach, arguing that the multiple levels of organization that constitute human life—from the biological to the individual to the social and beyond—all need to be understood within a common framework. Cairns (1998) has made a similar suggestion. Bronfenbrenner (1979; Bronfenbrenner & Morris, 1998) has actually proposed such a framework, with interlocking systems of development, such as the microsystem, which encompasses the individual; the mesosystem, which encompasses the family, school, peers, religious institutions, and so forth; the exosystem, which includes the extended family, neighbors, mass media, social welfare and legal services, and so forth; and the macrosystem, which includes the attitudes and ideologies of the culture.

Other investigators, although not necessarily proposing such comprehensive frameworks, have also argued in favor of the unification of psychology and have made related suggestions regarding the need for some kind of effort at unification. For example, Royce (1970) suggested that psychology was fragmenting and needed more organization and more unity. Bevan (1991, 1994) argued that specialization can give rise to "regressive fragmentation" (Bevan, 1994, p. 505) and "self-limiting specialization" (Bevan, 1982, p. 1311), which alienate psychology from larger human concerns. Maher (1985) also spoke of the fragmentation and chaotic diversity in psychology. MacIntyre (1985) suggested that such chaos gives rise to the view that psychology is prescientific rather than scientific. Rychlak (1988) saw the problem of fragmentation as having three aspects: theoretical, methodological, and scholarly. He believed that a first step toward unification would be the development of a greater tolerance by psychologists of differences among psychologists. DeGroot (1989) suggested that for psychologists to achieve unification, they would need to reach some kind of greater consensus both as to the mission of psychology and as to what constituted its methods. Kimble (1994) suggested that unification was desirable and could be achieved by a set of principles, which he proposed in his article. Fowler (1990) also called for unification, in his case, of science and practice. Wapner and Demick (1989) argued that the unification of psychology was overdue, whereas Anastasi (1990) suggested that psychology already was making large steps toward unification.

Not everyone has believed the unification of psychology to be a good idea. Some of the foxes' critiques of unification have been in direct response to Staats's (1991) call for unification. McNally (1992) suggested, on the basis of his analysis of Kuhn (1991), that the diversity and disunity present in psychology might be a sign of health rather than of illness, Kukla (1992) proposed that the whole goal of unification is questionable: Psychologists should concentrate on producing the best theories possible and then let the chips fall where they may. And Green (1992), although not taking issue with the notion of unity, suggested that Staats's positivistic program is not the optimal way to achieve unity.

Other researchers also have questioned the prospects for unification. For example, Koch (1981) suggested that psychology, by its nature, may not be unifiable. (See Leary, 2001, for a detailed analysis of Koch's point of view.) Krech (1970) also believed that psychology, by its nature, could not be unified. Wertheimer (1988) suggested that, at best, unification would face many obstacles. Kendler (1987) suggested that a natural division exists between psychology as a natural science and as a social science and that this division would continue to express itself in psychological theory and research. In a separate article, Kendler (1970) suggested that unifying psychology requires reducing any two of the three subject matters of behavior, neurophysiological events, and phenomenal experience to the third. Messer (1988) argued that even clinical psychology, a part of the social science side of psychology, would be difficult to unify. Viney (1989) noted that unity has both pros and cons and that both must be considered before psychology moves toward unification. And Scott (1991) observed that as psychology branches out and becomes more specialized, divisions are to be expected as a natural outcome.

Clearly, then, there have been diverse points of view regarding whether unification is possible and, if so, what form it should take. In this chapter, we propose one such form that the unification of psychology might take, which we refer to here as *unified psychology.*

Converging Operations

Converging operations refers to the use of multiple methodologies for studying a single psychological phenomenon or problem. The term was first introduced by Garner, Hake, and Erikson (1956) in a groundbreaking article on psychological methodology. The basic idea is that any one operation is, in all likelihood, inadequate for the comprehensive study of any psychological phenomenon. The reason is that any methodology introduces biases of one kind or another, often of multiple kinds. By using multiple converging methodologies (i.e., converging operations) for the study of a single psychological phenomenon or problem, one averages over sources of bias.

There are many examples of how converging operations can illuminate phenomena in a way that no one operation can. (See the original Garner et al., 1956, article for examples.) Often new constructs are especially well served by such operations.

Consider, for a first example, the construct of prejudice. Prejudice traditionally has been measured in one of two ways: either by a questionnaire asking participants to characterize their feelings toward groups of people (Allport, 1929; Dovidio & Gaertner, 2000) or by observations of behavior (Sherif, Harvey, White, Hood, & Sherif, 1961/1988). Many studies have shown that attitudes are often not particularly good predictors of behavior (e.g., Dovidio, Kawakami, Johnson, Johnson, & Howard, 1997). If one wished to understand prejudices, one would have to study both participants' verbally expressed attitudes and participants' actual behavior.

Of course, one could say that the crucial measure is behavior and that the attitudes are only interesting to the extent that they predict behavior. We disagree. Behavior is as interesting a predictor of attitudes, as are attitudes of behavior. There is no ultimate dependent variable. Consider an example of this notion as it applies to attitudes and prejudices.

Recently, Greenwald, Banaji, and their colleagues (Greenwald & Banaji, 1995; Greenwald et al., 2000) have developed measures of implicit attitudes that examine a wholly different aspect of how people feel about certain groups of individuals. These measures each are referred to as an Implicit Association Test or IAT (Greenwald, McGhee, & Schwartz, 1998). The IAT is a computer-based reaction-time measure that estimates the degree of association between target concepts, such as attitudes toward African Americans and attitudes toward White Americans, and an evaluative dimension, such as pleasant–unpleasant.

For example, African American faces are paired with the words *good* or *bad,* as are White American faces. On half the trials, one pushes the same response key for White and *good,* and on the other half, one presses the same key for White and *bad.* The same holds for Black and *good* and Black and *bad.* One can then compare the time it takes to associate *good* or *bad* with White or Black. The test provides a relative measure. In other words, a target concept (attitudes toward African Americans) must have a contrasting domain (attitudes toward White Americans). A participant's responses will indicate an implicit attitude toward African Americans relative to his or her implicit attitude toward White Americans.

Using such measures, these investigators have found consistently prejudiced implicit attitudes of White Americans toward African Americans and even often of African Americans toward African Americans. They have uncovered other negative implicit attitudes as well. Their measures of implicit attitudes correlate only poorly with the traditional measures of explicit attitudes, in which one simply asks individuals to state or rate their attitudes toward members of various groups. Thus, what result one gets depends on the dependent variable one uses.

The data suggest converging operations are needed if one wishes to fully understand people's attitudes toward various groups. One may wish to look at, for example, indicators of implicit attitudes, which usually involve timed decision tasks; measures of explicit attitudes, which typically take the form of questionnaires; or assessments of behavior. Ideally, one looks at all three.

Of course, there are many other examples of attitudes failing to predict behavior. Most people would agree that drunken driving is irresponsible, but a number of these people do it anyway. Many people who know that condom use may literally save their lives by preventing transmission of the HIV virus nevertheless fail to use condoms when they know they should. People who know that smoking is killing them continue to smoke. The examples are endless.

Another example of the need for converging operations can be seen in the study and measurement of intelligence and related intellectual abilities. Sternberg, Grigorenko, Ferrari, and Clinkenbeard (1999) used both multiple-choice and essay items to assess analytical, creative, and practical intellectual abilities. One of their analyses involved the use of confirmatory factor analysis by which they investigated, among other things, how effective the two item types (multiple choice and essay) were in assessing the three different kinds of abilities. They found that the multiple-choice items were the more effective in assessing analytical abilities—the types of abilities assessed by traditional tests of intellectual skills—whereas the essay items were more effective in assessing creative and practical abilities. Using just one type of item (e.g., all multiple choice or all essay) would have resulted in inferior measurements.

The principle of converging operations applies beyond the particular kinds of test items to the kinds of investigative operations used as well. The study of intelligence traditionally has drawn heavily on factor analysis. For example, Carroll (1993) followed in a long line of investigators who have developed and tested theories of intelligence largely or exclusively on the basis of factor analysis (e.g., Guilford, 1967; Spearman, 1927; Thurstone, 1938; see reviews in Brody, 2000; Carroll, 1982; Mackintosh, 1998; Sternberg, 1990). Nothing is wrong with factor analysis per se, but any single method has advantages and drawbacks. For example, factor analysis as typically used in the study of intelligence relies solely on the use of individual differences as sources of data. But many other useful sources of information can be drawn on to study intelligence, such as cultural analysis (Laboratory of Comparative Human Cognition, 1983;

Serpell, 2000), cognitive analysis (Cooper & Regan, 1982; Deary, 2000; Estes, 1982; Lohman, 2000; Sternberg, 1982), and biological analysis (e.g., Larson, Haier, LaCasse, & Hazen, 1995; MacLullich, Seckl, Starr, & Deary, 1998; Vernon, 1997; Vernon, Wickett, Bazana, & Stelmack, 2000). These other methods of investigation can yield findings simply not susceptible to discovery by factor analysis and, in some cases, may call into question some of the results of factor analysis (e.g., Gardner, 1983, 1999; Sternberg, 1985, 1997). Our goal here is not to take a position on whether the results of factor analysis or any other single method in particular are right or wrong. It is simply to point out that converging operations can yield insights about psychological phenomena that are opaque to any single methodology.

If, as Garner, Hake, and Erikson (1956) claimed, converging operations are so superior to single operations, why do some and perhaps many psychologists rely largely or even exclusively on a single method of analysis (or, for that matter, only two methods of analysis)? We believe there are three main reasons, none of them really acceptable from a research standpoint.

Training

Psychologists may have been trained largely in the use of a single methodology. They may have subsequently invested heavily in that methodology in their work. Learning how to do structural equation modeling, neural imaging, or qualitative analysis, for example, can require a large amount of work, especially if one wishes to perfect each of the set of techniques. Researchers may seek to maximize the return on their time investment and to use what they have learned as much as possible. Even if they come to see the flaws of their preferred methodology, they may come to view the time invested as a sunken cost and seek to justify or even redeem the investment anyway. They thereby can become fixed in their use of a single method of analysis.

Panaceas

Researchers can come to view a single methodology as representing a kind of panacea for the study of a certain problem or set of problems. At one time, exploratory factor analysis was seen in this way by some psychometric investigators, until its limitations became increasingly apparent (e.g., the existence of an infinite number of rotations of axes, all representing equally legitimate solutions statistically). To some of the same investigators, as well as to other investigators, confirmatory factor analysis or structural equation modeling may have come to seem to be a panacea, although these methods, too, have their limitations, such as reliance on individual differences. Today, some scientists view neural imaging methods as a panacea. Some psychologists are busy compiling mental atlases that link certain areas of the brain to certain aspects of cognitive processing, although they are often oblivious to the functional relations between the two and are sometimes making these links in the absence of an adequate theoretical foundation (see Sternberg, 2000). The truth is that no method will provide a panacea: Different methods have different advantages and disadvantages, and, by using multiple methods, one capitalizes on the strengths of the methods while helping to minimize the effects of their weaknesses.

Norms

Norms of a field may also lead to methodological fixation. Some years ago, Robert J. Sternberg submitted an article to one of the most prestigious psychological journals available. He was asked to revise the article, replacing regression analyses of the phenomenon under investigation with analyses of variance. The request was odd because the two methods of analysis gave equivalent information (see Cohen & Cohen, 1983). But the norm of the journal was use of analysis of variance reporting. Fields, journals, and other collectivities develop norms that to the members of those collectivities may seem perfectly reasonable and even beyond question. These norms may become presuppositions of behavior that are accepted in a rather mindless way (Langer, 1997). The norms may lead investigators to do things in a certain way, not because it is the best way, but, rather, because it comes to be perceived as the only way or the only way worth pursuing.

In Sum

Unified psychology, then, means giving up on single operations in favor of multiple converging operations. Such work requires either that individuals be trained in a wider variety of methodologies than they currently are trained in or else that they work in teams having members with various kinds of expertise (see Sternberg & Grigorenko, 1999).

Ultimately, the converging operations and perspectives that are brought to bear on a problem can and generally should go even beyond those of psychology. Investigations of many psychological phenomena can be enriched by the ideas of other disciplines, such as biology, anthropology, neuroscience, and so forth (Woodward & Devonis, 1993). For example, psychologists can enrich their perspectives of child rearing by understanding how people in other cultures rear children, or they can broaden their perspectives on aggressive behavior by taking into account what is considered to be aggressive in the first place in one culture versus another.

Multidisciplinary, Integrated Study of Psychological Phenomena

Field fixation can be as damaging to the understanding of psychological phenomena as is methodological fixation. Psychology is divided into areas such as biological psychology, clinical psychology, cognitive psychology, developmental psychology, industrial and organizational psychology, social psychology, personality psychology, and so forth. Departments often organize the specializations of their professors in this way, graduate programs are usually structured in this way, jobs are typically advertised in this way. This organization of the field, departments, graduate programs, and jobs represents a suboptimal organization of the field. It encourages division rather than unification.

Preserving the Status Quo

Several factors play a role in maintaining the current suboptimal organization of psychology.

Tradition

First and foremost, this method of organization is the way things have been done for a long time. When a system of organization is entrenched, people tend to accept it as a given. For example, most psychology departments have chairpersons, but members of those departments probably do not spend a lot of time questioning whether they should have chairpersons—they just accept this system of organization. Of course, new fields within psychology come and go. For example, the fields of evolutionary psychology and health psychology are relative newcomers to the roster of fields of psychology. They will either become part of the standard organization of the field or slowly disappear.

Vested Interest

Second, once a discipline such as psychology has been organized in a certain way, people in the discipline acquire a vested interest in maintaining that organization, much as people gain a vested interest in maintaining any system that seemingly has worked for them in the past. For example, most cognitive psychologists were trained as cognitive psychologists, and personality psychologists as personality psychologists. Were the field suddenly to reorganize, current scholars and practitioners might find themselves without the kind of knowledge base and even the socially organized field of inquiry that would allow them to continue to function successfully.

The Need to Specialize

Third, no one can specialize in everything. Students of psychology need to specialize in some way, and structuring psychology in terms of fields has been viewed as a sensible way to define specializations. Thus, someone who specializes in social psychology will be expected to know about a series of related phenomena such as impression formation, attribution, and stereotyping. Someone who specializes in cognitive psychology will be expected to know about a set of related phenomena such as perception, memory, and thinking. Successively greater levels of specialization ultimately may be encouraged; for example, a cognitive psychologist may pursue a very specific line of inquiry, such as cognitive approaches to memory, to implicit memory, or to the use of priming methodology in studying implicit memory.

Reasons to Change

We believe that the current organization of the field is distinctly suboptimal and even maladaptive. We have several reasons for this belief.

The Field Could Be Organized Better to Understand Psychological Phenomena

Examples of psychological phenomena include memory, intelligence, dyslexia, attachment, creativity, prejudice, and amnesia, among others. None of these phenomena are best studied within a specialized field of psychology.

For example, although memory can be investigated as a cognitive phenomenon, it can and should be studied through the techniques of a number of other fields.

These fields include biological psychology and cognitive neuroscience (e.g., in attempts to find out where in the brain memories are stored), clinical psychology (e.g., in the conflict over repressed memories), social psychology (e.g., in preferential memory for self-referential memories), and behavioral genetics (e.g., in the heritability of memory characteristics), to name just some of the relevant fields. Someone studying memory through only one approach or set of techniques will understand only part of the phenomenon.

Similarly, extraversion can be and has been studied from personality, differential, biological, cognitive, social, cultural, and other points of view. Someone studying extraversion from only one of these points of view—for example, personality—almost certainly will understand the phenomenon only in a narrow way, in terms of, say, extraversion as a trait, without fully appreciating the role of biological or cognitive processes or of culture, for that matter.

The same argument can be applied to virtually any psychological phenomenon. By subsuming psychological phenomena under fields of psychology, the discipline encourages a narrow view rather than a broad approach to understanding psychological phenomena.

Organizing by Fields Can Isolate Individuals Who Study the Same Phenomena

For example, two individuals within a psychology department may both study attachment, but if one is in personality psychology and another in developmental psychology, they may have little interaction. This is because in a typical department, students and professors are located next to—and attend the same meetings and read the same journals as—others in their field regardless of the phenomena being studied.

The Current Organization May Create False Oppositions Between Individuals or Groups Studying Phenomena from Different Vantage Points

Here is an example: Individuals studying memory from a cognitive perspective may never quite understand the work of those studying memory from a clinical standpoint. This can lead to a sense of hostility toward the viewpoints of those who do not understand their (preferred) way of studying memory. Or individuals studying love from social psychological versus clinical points of view may (and sometimes do) see themselves in opposition, as though there were a uniquely correct approach to studying a psychological phenomenon.

The Current System Tends to Marginalize Psychological Phenomena That Fall Outside the Boundaries of a Specific Field

For example, psychological phenomena such as imagination, motivation, or emotion may tend to be ignored in a department if they are not seen as part of the core of a field. This also extends to the people studying such phenomena, who may have difficulty getting hired because hiring is often done by area, and the people studying phenomena at the interface of fields of psychology may be perceived as not fitting neatly into any one area. In turn, faculty in a given area may not want to hire such people if they feel that their area will not get the full benefit of a slot or that such individuals will not contribute adequately to graduate (or even undergraduate) training in that so-called core field.

Research May Tilt Toward Issues to Which a Limited Set of Tools May Be Applied

The current system essentially equips students with a set of tools (e.g., the methods of developmental psychology, or cognitive neuroscience, or social psychology, or mathematical psychology). Instead of allowing students to be driven by substantive issues, the system encourages students to search for a phenomenon for which they can use their tools, much in the way a carpenter might seek objects for which he or she can use a hammer.

The Current System Can Discourage New Ways of Studying Problems

If someone wishes to educate students in terms of the existing boundaries of fields, he or she will encounter few problems. But if he or she wants to cross those boundaries, other faculty may worry that the individual students will not be properly trained in a field, may have trouble getting a job, or may not fit into the departmental structure. In truth, they may be justified in all these concerns.

The Traditional Disciplinary Approach of Largely Subsuming Psychological Phenomena Under Fields of Study Rather Than the Other Way Around Leads Psychologists to Confuse Aspects of Phenomena with the Phenomena as a Whole

This confusion is analogous to the use of synecdoche in speech, in which one substitutes a part for a whole (e.g., *crown* for *kingdom*). However, unlike poets or other writers, psychologists are unaware of their use of this device. The psychologists believe they are studying the whole phenomenon when, in fact, they are studying only a small part of it.

Consider the well-worn parable of the blind men each touching a different part of the elephant and each being convinced that he is touching a different animal. In psychology, the situation is like always studying the same part of a phenomenon and thinking that this part tells you all you need to know to understand the whole phenomenon. Consider two examples.

In the study of human intelligence, psychometricians may keep discovering a "general factor" and thus become convinced that the general factor largely explains intelligence. Biological psychologists may find a spot or two in the brain that light up during the fMRI or PET-scan analysis of the commission of cognitive tasks and become convinced that these parts of the brain fully explain intelligence. Cultural psychologists may find wide cultural differences in notions of the nature of intelligence and become convinced that intelligence is best explained simply as a cultural invention. Each psychologist touches a different part of the metaphorical elephant and becomes convinced that part represents the whole (and fairly simple) animal.

As a second example, attention deficit hyperactivity disorder (ADHD) has genetic, neuropsychological, cognitive, educational, social, and cultural aspects. Some of the debate in the field of ADHD has come to be over whether the origins of ADHD are genetic, neuropsychological, cognitive, educational, social, or cultural. This ongoing, fruitless debate is unlikely to end until scientists are trained in each other's fields and paradigms so that they will understand that learning disabilities, like other psychological phenomena, need to be understood from all of these perspectives, not just one. Of course, the same argument applies to many other psychological phenomena, such as emotions, consciousness, motivation, mental disorders, perception, memory, creativity, and so forth.

A Phenomenon-Based Proposal

In general, scientists who are not well trained in one another's techniques are likely to be suspicious of others' techniques and of the conclusions drawn from them. These scientists probably will continue to do research within their own paradigm, which keeps supporting their views and thereby reinforces their confidence that they are right and that those who adhere to a paradigm from some other field are misguided.

We believe that a more sensible and psychologically justifiable way of organizing psychology as a discipline and in departments and graduate study is in terms of psychological phenomena—which are not arbitrary—rather than so-called fields of psychology—which largely are arbitrary. Under this approach, an individual might choose to specialize in a set of related phenomena, such as learning and memory, stereotyping and prejudice, or motivation and emotion, and then study the phenomena of interest from multiple points of view. The individual thus would reach a fuller understanding of the phenomena being studied because he or she would not be limited by a set of assumptions or methods drawn from only one field of psychology.

Our proposal carries with it a number of advantages that are largely complementary to the disadvantages of the field-based approach that currently dominates the discipline. People might very well end up specializing in several related psychological phenomena, but they would understand these phenomena broadly rather than narrowly, which is certainly an advantage if their goal is comprehensive psychological understanding. Psychology would be less susceptible to tendencies that field-based organization encourages: narrowness, isolation, false oppositions, marginalization, largely method-driven rather than phenomenon-driven approaches to research, discouragement of new ways of approaching psychological phenomena, and confusion of the part with the whole.

In Sum

Unified psychology, then, means giving up a single disciplinary approach in favor of an integrated multidisciplinary approach in which problems rather than subdisciplines become the key basis for the study of psychology. One chooses a particular disciplinary approach because it is useful in studying a psychological phenomenon rather than choosing a particular psychological problem because it happens to fall within the subdiscipline in terms of which one defines oneself.

The Approach of Unified Psychology

The history of psychology may be viewed as the history of a sequence of failed paradigms. The paradigms failed not because they were wrong—paradigms are not right or wrong (Kuhn, 1970)—but rather because they provided only incomplete perspectives on the problems to which they were applied. Almost every introductory-psychology student learns how structuralism gained in popularity, only eventually to fall when its weaknesses were appreciated. The student learns as well how functionalism, associationism, and a host of other "–isms" have come and gone, with each generation of researchers hoping that their –ism will somehow be the last. At best, the sequence of paradigms has represented a dialectical progression (Hegel, 1807/ 1931; see discussion in Sternberg, 1999), with new paradigms synthesizing the best aspects of older ones. At worst, one failed –ism has simply replaced another without any signs of learning on the part of its adherents that this paradigm, too, shall pass. Of course, in each of these generations, many scholars have believed that they have at last found the answer, oblivious to the fact that they have merely repeated a pattern of the past.

When Robert J. Sternberg was in graduate school, he asked his graduate advisor about work the advisor had done previously on mathematical models of learning theory. The advisor, Gordon Bower, remarked that he had trouble remembering why he thought earlier that the questions the models addressed were so important. Such is how paradigms come and go. They go not when they are proven wrong but when they run out of steam, fail to account for new empirical results, or fail to provide the means to answer the questions that investigators in a given period of time most want to answer (see Kuhn, 1970, for a detailed discussion of the evolution of paradigms).

If one considers a basic psychological phenomenon, such as learning, one realizes that it can be studied in terms of an evolutionary paradigm, a brain-based biological paradigm, a cognitive paradigm, a behaviorist paradigm, a psychoanalytic paradigm, a genetic–epistemological paradigm, and so forth. There is no one correct perspective. Each perspective presents a different way of understanding the problem of learning.

Some Potential Objections to the Endeavor of Unified Psychology

Of course, there are potential objections to the concept of unified psychology. Consider some of them as well as possible responses.

The Discipline of Psychology Already Is Unified; the Call for a Unified Psychology Attacks a Straw Person

We see relatively little unification in the field at the present. The large majority of journals are specialized. Some that are not in theory are in practice accepting only articles in which the authors use certain accepted paradigms or methodologies. Granting panels often accept grant proposals in much the same way, although, of course, there are exceptions. Conventions or sections of conventions often are specialized. Courses often are taught in a disunified way, with topics presented in isolation from each other. For the most part, jobs are advertised in terms of fields of specialization, and promotions may depend on convincing referees within a narrow field of specialization that one is truly a member of the in-group of that field and that one is an important contributor to it. Even within broad-based organizations, such as the American Psychological Association, it has proven difficult to unify special interests, and many groups have split off precisely because of the difficulty of keeping the field unified and the view of some that such unification is not important.

The Discipline Already Has a Field of General Psychology, Which Is the Same as Unified Psychology

In today's world, general psychology is not the same as unified psychology. General psychology encompasses various fields of psychology but does not necessarily unify them. General psychology texts often cover a variety of topics in psychology without unifying them at all. For example, learning and memory typically are covered in separate chapters, despite their obvious relationship. General psychology is embracing but not necessarily unifying. But to the extent one wishes to redefine general psychology as unifying and not just embracing the many aspects that constitute psychology, we would be happy to view this form of general psychology as being the same as our proposed unified psychology.

Even If Unified Psychology Is Not the Same as General Psychology, There Is Nothing New in the Concept

At some level, we agree. Unified psychology represents a goal toward which many people have strived ever since psychology's earliest days. But not so many people have achieved it, and we suspect that as the field becomes more specialized, fewer and fewer people will. The term unified psychology, at worst, may help provide a rubric for a pretheoretical stance that many scientists and practitioners will find fits them better than rubrics that force adherence to paradigms or methodologies that are in themselves incomplete. To the extent that psychologists use a term to motivate what they do, we believe the term serves a valuable purpose. Thinking of oneself as, say, a social psychologist or a personality psychologist may guide what one studies and how one studies it. Thinking of oneself as a unified psychologist may do the same.

The Term *Unified Psychology* Is a Misnomer, Because One Has Substituted Divisions by Phenomena for Divisions by Fields

One perhaps could argue that the term *unified* never would apply unless one looked at something solely as a gestalt—as a single, indivisible entity. We disagree with this point of view, because even that indivisible entity would be a part of some greater whole, which in turn would be a part of some greater whole, and soon one would lapse into infinite regress. Unification is always with respect to something. When we use the term *unified,* we use it with respect to what currently constitutes the subdisciplines of psychology. We make no claim that our proposal is unified with respect to everything, a claim we believe, in any case, would be meaningless.

The Direction of the Discipline Is Toward Specialization, Not Integration: Needed in Training Are Specialists Who Can Do Precise Scientific Work, Not Generalists or Even Dilettantes Who, However Useful They Might Have Been in Psychology's Prescientific Days, No Longer Advance the Discipline

We have argued elsewhere (Sternberg & Grigorenko, 1999) that dilettantism is and always has been useful to the discipline of psychology. But unified psychology goes beyond dilettantism and is not contrary to specialization. Today, people of course need some kind of specialization. However, there is a narrow form of specialization and a broad form. Narrow specialization involves looking at a problem with tunnel vision and knowing only a narrow range of techniques to apply in solving that problem. In broad specialization, one may look at a fairly specific problem but do so with open eyes and with the benefit of the many problem-solving techniques a multidisciplinary approach leaves at one's disposal. Any phenomenon, no matter how specialized, can be studied in such a way. The value of such study is the message that unified psychology conveys.

The Proposal Is Inconvenient and Even Impractical

In the near term, our proposal would be inconvenient because it is inconsistent with an entrenched system that extends to departmental organization, graduate and even undergraduate education, job offerings, and the like. It also is inconvenient simply because this is not the way people currently in the field have been trained, and people tend to value systems that have worked for them in the past and that are likely to work for them in the future without disturbing their world. We believe or, at least, hope that the inconvenience of a new system would be outweighed by the ultimate benefit to the field that the proposed system would offer.

Training Under the New System Would Take Too Long

Some might view the kind of training we propose as taking longer than traditional training, but we see no reason to believe this is so. What would change is not so much how long one spends in training but how one spends the time one is in training. Truly, training in psychology is lifelong, and no matter what kind of graduate training one receives, one always needs to be learning in order to stay on top of a field, however that field is defined. Good training does not end with a diploma but, in some respects, merely changes in form with the diploma.

In Solving One Kind of Problem of Suboptimal Divisions, the New System Introduces Others

One could argue that the new system introduces new problems that are not so different from the ones it is supposed to solve. For example, psychological phenomena are mutually interdependent. Thus, studying such phenomena in depth still would give one only a limited picture of them. For example, interpersonal attraction may depend on personality, attitudes, early experience, and so forth. We believe this objection is mistaken, however. The comprehensive study of any phenomenon, such as interpersonal attraction, always has brought and always will bring to bear multiple perspectives on the multiple factors that contribute to the phenomenon. We view such interdependence not as a problem for but as an advantage of our approach.

In Sum

Unified psychology, then, means giving up a single paradigm in favor of the use of whatever paradigm may help shed light on a problem. Multiple paradigms can contribute to the understanding of a single psychological phenomenon, whereas locking oneself into any single paradigm reduces one's ability to fully grasp the phenomenon of interest.

Some Implications of the Unified-Psychology View

The unified-psychology perspective has several implications for modern-day work in psychology. Here are a few of them.

Psychology Will Only Fragment if Psychologists Wish It to

Gardner (1992) argued that psychology is undergoing a process of fragmentation and that eventually it may become a much smaller field, with much of what is currently classified as psychology being subsumed by disciplines such as cognitive science or cognitive neuroscience. Not everyone agrees with this assessment. However, psychology is more likely to fragment if people accept new fields as somehow providing the final questions or answers that old ones lacked. For example, researchers in the field of cognitive science have much to gain from studying the contexts of behavior, the social psychology of cognitive processes, links between cognition and emotion (or personality), and so forth. The new panaceas are no better than the old ones. Psychology needs all its parts—integrated in a unified way.

Students of psychology need to be trained in general psychology as well as in specializations and other fields of inquiry (e.g., biology, philosophy, anthropology, sociology, and statistics). However, general psychology is not tantamount to unified psychology. It is not enough to have all the disciplines of psychology under one big roof. The disciplines need to be synthesized with respect to paradigms, theories, and methods (see also Kalmar & Sternberg, 1988).

New Movements Will Soon Fail if They Are Not Unified

In our view, current thinking often inadvertently repeats the mistakes of prior thinking. For example, we are very optimistic about the development of positive psychology

(Seligman & Csikszentmihalyi, 2000). But looking only at the positive side of phenomena is likely to be as restrictive as looking only at the negative side. Ultimately, psychologists have to learn, as they have in the past, that a synthesis is needed to integrate a thesis and its antithesis. Neuroscientific approaches to cognition are proving to be quite useful, and the overwhelming number of jobs being offered in the cognitive neuroscience area suggests that this trend has taken hold across many departments of psychology. But cognitive neuroscience, like any other approach, answers some questions but not others. It is probably less useful than traditional cognitive approaches, for example, in suggesting to teachers how they can improve student learning. Teachers can benefit from knowing about the hazards of massed versus distributed practice or of retroactive and proactive interference. It is less clear how they can benefit, at this time, from knowing the part of the brain in which performance on a particular cognitive task is localized. Eventually, they may well be able to benefit. In the meantime, new approaches will continue to emerge, and they will have in common with current and past approaches that they answer some questions well, other questions poorly, and still other questions not at all.

We must admit to one fact: Unified movements will eventually fail too, in a sense. No movement lasts forever. However, what a unified movement is in the best position to do is to plant the seeds for its successors. For example, a unified approach to prejudice will reveal what questions cannot be answered with any available paradigms or methods and will help force psychologists to think of new ways to answer the questions that are recalcitrant under any available approach.

The Field of Psychology Is Not Well Set Up for the Propagation of Unified Psychology

Psychology departments are typically organized by fields. Graduate study is typically organized by fields. Often, many members of a given field within a given department share a common paradigm or methodological approach. Many awards and prizes within the field of psychology are organized by fields. Journals and granting organizations often divide themselves up by fields. Even divisions of the American Psychological Association are organized, to a large extent, by fields. There inevitably will be substantial vested interest in maintaining current systems for organizing old knowledge, discovering new knowledge, and propagating both kinds of knowledge. Therefore, we do not expect many immediate converts and suspect we will hear in the near future many reasons why the current system is the best system. People who profit from a system rarely wish to give it up! Eventually, of course, we hope that there will be many converts to the notion of unified psychology and that they, too, will wish to maintain their views. They will have one advantage, perhaps, over some others: They may be flexible enough to synthesize the new views with their existing old ones.

One of the Biggest Problems Is That People May Think They Practice Unified Psychology When in Fact They Do Not

Virtually everyone wishes to see him- or herself as open-minded and, moreover, as someone who is not locked into any one stifling way of doing things. Therefore, many people may believe they already practice unified psychology. But the organizational issues described above with respect to the field of psychology make it unlikely that this is the case. The field of psychology currently is organized, as we have discussed, to promote the individual disciplines much more than the unified study of phenomena. Indeed, examples abound of how work that falls or people who fall between the cracks can suffer. The people without a specialization recognized in the current system of psychology may find themselves locked out of jobs, journals, grants, prizes, and other aspects of the meager reward system psychology has to offer. Some people may well be termed *eclectic* for their use of a variety of ideas or techniques, but they may not sufficiently synthesize them to truly be unified psychologists. At the same time, some scholars may well practice unified psychology, and, of course, we hope they will diffuse their perspective to many others as well.

It is easy to become a unified psychologist. One need adhere to no particular set of methods, to no particular field, and to no particular paradigm. Indeed, the first step is precisely adhering to none of the above. We hope that many psychologists might find such a nonrestrictive way of thinking attractive. If any or all wish to view unified psychology as old wine in new bottles, we remind them that, so often, old wines are the best of all but that old bottles—sometimes with lead in their foil or corks that have rotted—usually are not the best. So we will be very happy if, after all, some decide that unified psychology is a vintage old wine in a new and better bottle. And we will be even happier if people drink of it.

References

Allport, G. W. (1929). The composition of political attitudes. *American Journal of Sociology, 35,* 220–238.

Anastasi, A. (1990, August). *Are there unifying trends in the psychologies of 1990?* Invited address presented at the 98th Annual Convention of the American Psychological Association, Boston, MA.

Baldwin, J. M. (1902). *Development and evolution.* New York: Macmillan.

Baldwin, J. M. (1906). *Social and ethical interpretations in mental development: A study in social psychology.* New York: Macmillan. (Original work published 1897)

Berlin, I. (1953). *The hedgehog and the fox.* New York: Simon & Schuster.

Bevan, W. (1982). A sermon of sorts in three plus parts. *American Psychologist, 37,* 1303–1322.

Bevan, W. (1991). Contemporary psychology: A tour inside the onion. *American Psychologist, 46,* 475–483.

Bevan, W. (1994). Plain truths and home cooking: Thoughts on the making and remaking of psychology. *American Psychologist, 49,* 505–509.

Brody, N. (2000). History of theories and measurements of intelligence. In R. J. Sternberg (Ed.), *Handbook of intelligence* (pp. 16–33). New York: Cambridge University Press.

Bronfenbrenner, U. (1979). *The ecology of human development.* Cambridge, MA: Harvard University Press.

Bronfenbrenner, U., & Morris, P. A. (1998). The ecology of developmental processes. In W. Damon (Series Ed.) & R. M. Lerner (Vol. Ed.), *Handbook of child psychology* (5th ed., Vol. 1, pp. 993–1028). New York: Wiley.

Cairns, R. B. (1998). The making of developmental psychology. In W. Damon (Series Ed.) & R. B. Lerner (Vol. Ed.), *Handbook of child psychology* (5th ed., Vol. 1, pp. 25–105). New York: Wiley.

Carroll, J. B. (1982). The measurement of intelligence. In R. J. Sternberg (Ed.), *Handbook of human intelligence* (pp. 29–120). New York: Cambridge University Press.

Carroll, J. B. (1993). *Human cognitive abilities: A survey of factor-analytic studies.* New York: Cambridge University Press.

Cohen, J., & Cohen, P. (1983). *Applied multiple regression/correlation analysis for the behavioral sciences* (2nd ed.). Hillsdale, NJ: Erlbaum.

Cooper, L. A., & Regan, D. T. (1982). Attention, perception, and intelligence. In R. J. Sternberg (Ed.), *Handbook of human intelligence* (pp. 123–169). New York: Cambridge University Press.

Deary, I. J. (2000). Simple information processing. In R. J. Sternberg (Ed.), *Handbook of intelligence* (pp. 267–284). New York: Cambridge University Press.

DeGroot, A. D. (1989, April). *Unifying psychology: Its preconditions.* Address presented at the Fourth International Congress of the International Association of Theoretical Psychology, Amsterdam, The Netherlands.

Dovidio, J. F., & Gaertner, S. L. (2000). Aversive racism and selection decisions: 1989 and 1999. *Psychological Science, 11,* 315–319.

Dovidio, J. F., Kawakami, K., Johnson, C., Johnson, B., & Howard, A. (1997). On the nature of prejudice: Automatic and controlled processes. *Journal of Experimental Social Psychology, 33,* 510–540.

Estes, W. K. (1982). Learning, memory, and intelligence. In R. J. Sternberg (Ed.), *Handbook of intelligence* (pp. 170–224). New York: Cambridge University Press.

Fowler, R. D. (1990). The core discipline. *American Psychologist, 45,* 1–6.

Gardner, H. (1983). *Frames of mind: The theory of multiple intelligences.* New York: Basic Books.

Gardner, H. (1992). Scientific psychology: Should we bury it or praise it? *New Ideas in Psychology, 10,* 179–190.

Gardner, H. (1999). *Intelligence reframed: Multiple intelligences for the 21st century.* New York: Basic Books.

Garner, W. R., Hake, H. W., & Erikson, C. W. (1956). Operationism and the concept of perception. *Psychological Review, 63,* 149–159.

Green, C. D. (1992). Is unified positivism the answer to psychology's disunity? *American Psychologist, 47,* 1057–1058.

Greenwald, A. G., & Banaji, M. R. (1995). Implicit social cognition: Attitudes, self-esteem, and stereotypes. *Psychological Review, 102,* 4–27.

Greenwald, A. G., Banaji, M. R., Rudman, L. A., Famham, S. D., Nosek, B. A., & Rosier, M. (2000). Prologue to a unified theory of attitudes, stereotypes, and self-concept. In J. P. Forgas (Ed.), *Feeling and thinking: The role of affect in social cognition* (pp. 308–330). New York: Cambridge University Press.

Greenwald, A. G., McGhee, D. E., & Schwartz, J. L. K. (1998). Measuring individual differences in implicit cognition: The implicit association test. *Journal of Personality and Social Psychology, 74,* 1464–1480.

Guilford, J. P. (1967). *The nature of human intelligence.* New York: McGraw-Hill.

Hegel, G. W. F. (1931). *The phenomenology of the mind* (J. D. Baillie, Trans.; 2nd ed.). London: Allen & Unwin. (Original work published 1807)

Kalmar, D. A., & Sternberg, R. J. (1988). Theory knitting: An integrative approach to theory development. *Philosophical Psychology, 1,* 153–170.

Kendler, H. H. (1970). The unity of psychology. *Canadian Psychologist, 11,* 30–47.

Kendler, H. H. (1987). A good divorce is better than a bad marriage. In A. W. Staats & L. P. Mos (Eds.), *Annals of theoretical psychology* (Vol. 5, pp. 55–89). New York: Plenum.

Kimble, G. A. (1989). Psychology from the standpoint of a generalist. *American Psychologist, 44,* 491–499.

Kimble, G. A. (1994). A frame of reference for psychology. *American Psychologist, 49,* 510–519.

Koch, S. (1981). The nature and limits of psychological knowledge: Lessons of a century qua "science." *American Psychologist, 36,* 257–269.

Krech, D. (1970). Epilogue. In J. R. Royce (Ed.), *Toward unification in psychology: The first Banff Conference on Theoretical Psychology* (pp. 297–301). Toronto, Ontario, Canada: University of Toronto Press.

Kuhn, T. S. (1970). *The structure of scientific revolutions* (2nd ed.). Chicago: University of Chicago Press.

Kuhn, T. S. (1991, November). *The problem with the historical philosophy of science* [The Robert and Maurine Rothschild Distinguished Lecture]. Address presented to a meeting of the History of Science Department, Harvard University, Cambridge, MA.

Kukla, A. (1992). Unification as a goal for psychology. *American Psychologist, 47,* 1054–1055.

Kuo, Z.-Y. (1967). *The dynamics of behavior development.* New York: Random House.

Kuo, Z.-Y. (1976). *The dynamics of behavior development: An epigenetic view.* New York: Plenum.

Laboratory of Comparative Human Cognition. (1983). Culture and cognitive development. In P. Mussen (Series Ed.) & W. Kessen (Vol. Ed.), *Handbook of child psychology* (4th ed., Vol. 1, pp. 295–356). New York: Wiley.

Langer, E. J. (1997). *The power of mindful learning.* Needham Heights, MA: Addison-Wesley.

Larson, G. E., Haier, R. J., LaCasse, L., & Hazen, K. (1995). Evaluation of a "mental effort" hypothesis for correlations between cortical metabolism and intelligence. *Intelligence, 21,* 267–278.

Leary, D. E. (2001). One big idea, one ultimate concern: Sigmund Koch's critique of psychology and hope for the future. *American Psychologist, 56,* 425–432.

Lerner, R. M. (1998). Theories of human development: Contemporary perspectives. In W. Damon (Series Ed.) & R. M. Lerner (Vol. Ed.), *Handbook of child psychology* (5th ed., Vol. 1, pp. 1–24). New York: Wiley.

Lohman, D. F. (2000). Complex information processing and intelligence. In R. J. Sternberg (Ed.), *Handbook of intelligence* (pp. 285–340). New York: Cambridge University Press.

MacIntyre, R. B. (1985). Psychology's fragmentation and suggested remedies. *International Newsletter of Paradigmatic Psychology, 1,* 20–21.

Mackintosh, N. J. (1998). *IQ and human intelligence.* Oxford, England: Oxford University Press.

MacLullich, A. M. J., Seckl, J. R., Starr, J. M., & Deary, I. J. (1998). The biology of intelligence: From association to mechanism. *Intelligence, 26,* 63–73.

Magnusson, D. (2000). The individual as the organizing principle in psychological inquiry: A holistic approach. In L. R. Bergman, R. B. Cairns, L.-G. Nilsson, & L. Nystedt (Eds.), *Developmental science and the holistic approach* (pp. 33–47). Mahwah, NJ: Erlbaum.

Maher, B. A. (1985). Underpinnings of today's chaotic diversity. *International Newsletter of Paradigmatic Psychology, 1,* 17–19.

McNally, R. J. (1992). Disunity in psychology: Chaos or speciation? *American Psychologist, 47,* 1054.

Messer, S. B. (1988). Philosophical obstacles to unification of psychology. *International Newsletter of Uninomic Psychology, 5,* 22–24.

Royce, J. R. (Ed.). (1970). *Toward unification in psychology: The first Banff Conference on Theoretical Psychology.* Toronto, Ontario, Canada: University of Toronto Press.

Rychlak, J. F. (1988). Unification through understanding and tolerance of opposition. *International Newsletter of Uninomic Psychology, 5,* 113–115.

Sameroff, A. J. (1983). Developmental systems: Contexts and evolution. In P. H. Mussen (Series Ed.) & W. Kessen (Vol. Ed.), *Handbook of child psychology* (4th ed., Vol. 1, pp. 237–294). New York: Wiley.

Sameroff, A. J., & Bartko, W. T. (1998). Political and scientific models of development. In D. Pushkar, W. M. Bukowski, A. E. Schwartzman, D. M. Stack, & D. R. White (Eds.), *Improving competence across the lifespan* (pp. 177–192). New York: Plenum.

Schneirla, T. C. (1957). The concept of development in comparative psychology. In D. B. Harris (Ed.), *The concept of development* (pp. 78–108). Minneapolis: University of Minnesota Press.

Scott, T. R. (1991). A personal view of the future of psychology departments. *American Psychologist, 46,* 975–976.

Seligman, M. E. P., & Csikszentmihalyi, M. (2000). Positive psychology: An introduction. *American Psychologist, 55,* 5–14.

Serpell, R. (2000). Intelligence and culture. In R. J. Sternberg (Ed.), *Handbook of intelligence* (pp. 549–580). New York: Cambridge University Press.

Sherif, M., Harvey, L. J., White, B. J., Hood, W. R., & Sherif, C. W. (1988). *The Robber's Cave experiment: Intergroup conflict and cooperation.* Middletown, CT: Wesleyan University Press. (Original work published 1961)

Spearman, C. (1927). *The abilities of man.* London: Macmillan.

Staats, A. W. (1983). *Psychology's crisis of disunity: Philosophy and method for a unified science.* New York: Praeger.

Staats, A. W. (1991). Unified positivism and unification psychology: Fad or new field? *American Psychologist, 46,* 899–912.

Staats, A. W. (1993). Separatism with unification. In H. V. Rappard, P. J. Van Strien, L. P. Mos, & W. J. Baker (Eds.), *Annals of theoretical psychology* (Vol. 9, pp. 155–164). New York: Plenum.

Staats, A. W. (1999). Unifying psychology requires new infrastructure, theory, method, and a research agenda. *Review of General Psychology, 3,* 3–13.

Sternberg, R. J. (Ed.). (1982). *Handbook of human intelligence.* New York: Cambridge University Press.

Sternberg, R. J. (1985). *Beyond IQ: A triarchic theory of human intelligence.* New York: Cambridge University Press.

Sternberg, R. J. (1990). *Metaphors of mind: Conceptions of the nature of intelligence.* New York: Cambridge University Press.

Sternberg, R. J. (1997). *Successful intelligence.* New York: Plume.

Sternberg, R. J. (1999). A dialectical basis for understanding the study of cognition. In R. J. Sternberg (Ed.), *The nature of cognition* (pp. 51–78). Cambridge, MA: MIT Press.

Sternberg, R. J. (Ed.). (2000). *Handbook of intelligence.* New York: Cambridge University Press.

Sternberg, R. J., & Grigorenko, E. L. (1999). In praise of dilettantism. *APS Observer, 12*(5), 37–38.

Sternberg, R. J., & Grigorenko, E. L. (2001). The misorganization of psychology. *APS Observer, 14*(1), 1, 20.

Sternberg, R. J., Grigorenko, E. L., Ferrari, M., & Clinkenbeard, P. (1999). A triarchic analysis of an aptitude-treatment interaction. *European Journal of Psychological Assessment, 15,* 1–11.

Thelen, E. (1992). Development as a dynamic system. *Current Directions in Psychological Science, 1,* 189–193.

Thelen, E., & Smith, L. B. (1994). A *dynamic systems approach to the development of cognition and action.* Cambridge, MA: MIT Press.

Thelen, E., & Smith, L. B. (1998). Dynamic systems theories. In W. Damon (Series Ed.) & R. M. Lerner (Vol. Ed.), *Handbook of child psychology* (5th ed., Vol. 1, pp. 563–634). New York: Wiley.

Thurstone, L. L. (1938). *Primary mental abilities.* Chicago: University of Chicago Press.

Vernon, P. A. (1997). Behavioral genetic and biological approaches to intelligence. In H. Nyborg (Ed.), *The scientific study of human nature: Tribute to Hans J. Eysenck at eighty* (pp. 240–258). Oxford, England: Pergamon/Elsevier Science.

Vernon, P. A., Wickett, J. C., Bazana, P. G., & Stelmack, R. M. (2000). The neuropsychology and psychophysiology of human intelligence. In R. J. Sternberg (Ed.), *Handbook of intelligence* (pp. 245–264). New York: Cambridge University Press.

Viney, W. (1989). The cyclops and the twelve-eyed toad: William James and the unity-disunity problem in psychology. *American Psychologist, 44,* 1261–1265.

Wapner, S., & Demick, J. (1989). A holistic, developmental systems approach to person-environment functioning. *International Newsletter of Uninomic Psychology, 8,* 15–30.

Wertheimer, M. (1988). Obstacles to the integration of competing theories in psychology. *Philosophical Psychology, 1,* 131–137.

Woodward, W. R., & Devonis, D. (1993). Toward a new understanding of scientific change: Applying interfield theory to the history of psychology. In H. V. Rappard, P. J. Van Strien, L. P. Mos, & W. J. Baker (Eds.), *Annals of theoretical psychology* (Vol. 9, pp. 87–123). New York: Plenum.

Fads in Psychology: What We Can Do

17

Robert J. Sternberg

When I was about 12, there was a period of time when anyone who was anyone—at least in my age group—danced the limbo. Not to know and more important, not to do the limbo was to be consigned to, well, limbo. Within a brief period of time, the limbo itself had gone into limbo, and except for occasional brief resurgences, it came and went like so many other fads, making very little long-term difference to anyone.

Fads, of course, are not limited to the limbo, nor to hula hoops and yo-yos; nor are they limited to the minds of children, as citizen-band radios and enormous tail fins have shown. We find them in science, too. Science, in general, and psychology, in particular, are as susceptible to fads as is any other domain. Some of these fads are presumably relatively harmless. But many others can cause more harm, consuming time, money, and even careers as people pursue blind alleys to dead ends, and as research funds and journal space are consumed by them.

Recognizing Fads

The problem is that while we are immersed in a fad, it is difficult to recognize the fad for what it is. Are there signs as to what's a fad and what's a worthwhile scientific endeavor? I believe that there are a number of signs of a fad, none of which is necessary or sufficient in itself, but which, in combination, constitute a prototype for a fad. Obviously, they are not the only signs, but perhaps they are representative ones.

Often, we see during a fad a sudden surge of interest that seems to appear out of almost nowhere, with little or no intellectual history to the research enterprise, or a kind of functional autonomy of the enterprise from its intellectual history. Accompanying this surge is a frenzy to produce results, driven by external pressure to work on the research problem or approach. The research is usually largely extrinsically motivated by factors such as availability of grant funding or quick publications. The research enterprise seems shallow, and avoids deep underlying questions. Indeed, the work is more likely to be task- or technique-driven than to be question-driven.

Costs of Fads

So we have fads in psychology. Why should we even care? After all, what harm did the hula craze or the yo-yo frenzy really cause? They gave children something to do, they helped the companies that made them, they provided jobs, and they probably improved the gross national product. Perhaps fads in science are even a good thing.

They're not, because scientific work that is merely faddish, like the revolution of a hula hoop or the throw of a yo-yo, just leads us back to where we started. If fads were cost-free, there would be no point to worrying about them. They're not. Fads cost lost time and energy. They often lead to futile research efforts with little of substance to show for much effort. Funding may be taken away from more important work, at the same time that publication of fad-driven articles may drive out publication of more substantial articles. Even worse, hiring may come to be based on following fads rather than on potential long-term contributions. At the same time, careers of those who do not follow the fads may be derailed. Talented people, seeing what is happening, may turn away from what they see as a fad-driven field of dubious reputation. Those who pursue the field may be trained in ways that quickly become irrelevant. Lectures and texts come to be crammed with material that is here today, gone tomorrow, so that students are ill-prepared for serious work in the field.

What We Can Do About Fads

If we wish to steer research toward being motivated by fundamental theories and questions rather than by the fad of the hour, what can we do? I believe there are things that we can do, and that we could do right now if we set our minds to them. We can insist on question-driven research, and choose and evaluate research topics based on their importance rather than on their faddishness. We can investigate the intellectual history of the research we do. And we can go for long-term payoffs in research, pressuring funding agencies to fund projects for long-term scientific merit rather than for short-term programmatic fit to a going fad.

Fads aren't going to disappear. It seems to be human nature to create them. But no one need mindlessly follow them. As scientists, as psychologists, we can do better.

APA Is a Diamond in the Rough 18

Robert J. Sternberg

Last night I ate dinner with a distinguished psychologist who told me he had "given up" on APA. "Why?" I asked. He hesitated for a moment, taken aback, perhaps, that anyone would actually ask him to justify his stance. He claimed that APA did little or nothing for the group with which he identified. I rattled off several things APA had, in fact, done recently for the group. Indeed, *no* organization does more for *all* groups in psychology than APA. He admitted he had to reconsider his stance. Like many others who have "given up" on APA, he really had not thought his position through. APA had a lot more to offer than he and others often realize.

This is not to say that I (or others) have always been thrilled with all aspects of APA. Quite the contrary. But one should not give up on an organization, anymore than one would give up on a significant other, because one has been dissatisfied at times. Have we really become such a profession or organization of "quitters"?

When I was in college, I was quite dissatisfied with my own country, and, in particular, with its involvement in what seemed to me to be a senseless war in Vietnam. I did not "quit" the United States. Like many others, I fought for change, and eventually America left its senseless involvement in Vietnam behind. Perhaps the United States even learned a few lessons in the process. Since that time, I have had other dissatisfactions with my country, and again have worked to change what I did not like. I feel

469

the same about APA. I am a member of many psychological organizations. But APA is the home organization for all psychologists of all persuasions. Just as citizens of a country can work to change what they do not like in the country, APA members can work to change anything they may not like about APA.

Organizational Modifiability

I am not saying that one should never give up on an organization. But whether one should give up in the face of dissatisfaction depends on the kind of organization with which one is dealing. I have proposed a theory of organizational modifiability (Sternberg, 2002) that can be useful in providing guidance regarding which organizations to stay with and which ones to quit. If an organization is largely unmodifiable, then it may not be worth staying with it because it has little or no hope for a better future. According to the theory, three factors underlie organizational modifiability: the organization's willingness to change, the organization's willingness to appear to change, and the organization's views regarding its quality (its "self-efficacy"). I refer to the theory as a "mineralogical" theory because each of eight possible (*yes* or *no*) values on each of these three factors is metaphorically viewed in terms of a different mineral. For example, a "rusted iron" organization is one that is unwilling to change, unwilling to appear to change, and that views itself as inefficacious. Like rusted iron, such an organization is literally falling apart on itself. It is truly hopeless. As another example, a "granite" organization is one that is unwilling to change, unwilling to appear to change, but that views itself as wholly efficacious. Such an organization views itself as attractive, but it is as hardened and unyielding as granite. The most promising type of organization is a "diamond in the rough" organization—one that is willing to change, willing to appear to change, and is self-efficacious.

Change at APA

APA is a diamond in the rough. It is willing to change. For example, the APA CEO Search Committee, of which I was co-chair, recommended and the APA Council of Representatives approved with no dissenting votes the appointment of the first African American CEO in the history of the organization. APA is willing to appear to change. For example, Past-president Phil Zimbardo, President-elect Diane E. Halpern, and I have formed a task force on governance that is right now evaluating the entire governance structure of APA. Is APA self-efficacious? Well, that's up to you. If enough people "give up" on APA, it won't be. APA is trying to do more for *all* groups as resources allow. Giving up becomes a self-fulfilling prophecy that can doom any organization. But if you work for APA and, when necessary, work to change APA, it will be a highly self-efficacious organization—a diamond in the rough of which we all can be proud. Whether it is or not is up to you.

APA is my first professional home. I invite you to make it yours.

Reference

Sternberg, R. J. (2002). Effecting organizational change: A "mineralogical theory" of organizational modifiability. *Consulting Psychology Journal: Practice and Research, 54*, 147–156.

Producing Tomorrow's Leaders—in Psychology and Everything Else

19

Robert J. Sternberg

What is the biggest problem facing the United States—and the world? Is it (a) education, (b) poverty, (c) crime, (d) warfare, (e) hunger, (f) women's right or nonright to choose whether to give birth, or what?

In this essay, I will argue that the greatest problem is none of these. It is *leadership*. Why? Because leaders decide where to put the priorities for solving problems, including all of the problems listed.

If leadership is so important, what is its status in psychology? Marginal, at best. Most psychology departments do not have courses on leadership. Courses are much more likely to be in business schools, or, occasionally, in education schools with a specialty in educational administration. Moreover, most of the research being done on leadership now is being done in business schools, not in psychology departments. Leadership has become a marginalized field, despite its importance. Enron, WorldCom, Global Crossing, Arthur Andersen, Adelphia—the list of leadership fiascoes goes on and on. These are cases of major ethical violations. But there are many kinds of bad leadership. Kellerman (2004) listed seven kinds of bad leadership, which she sees as resulting from incompetence, rigidity, intemperance, callousness, corruption, insularity, or evil. Worse, Lipman-Blumen (2004) has argued that people actually seek out bad leaders, believing that they will somehow provide them with the answers or the certainties that they cannot achieve for themselves.

The purpose of *Psi Chi*, historically, has not been merely to recognize high levels of achievement in psychology. To do that, it would merely have to recognize good students without any programmatic events to supplement that recognition. Rather, the purpose has been to identify the best students and then to develop the skills and attitudes that are conducive to leadership. If *Psi Chi*, or any other organization, wishes to develop skills and attitudes underlying good leadership, what skills and attitudes must it help develop? I have argued that effective leaders in any field possess high levels of WICS—wisdom, intelligence, and creativity, synthesized. Underlying WICS is the notion that leadership is a decision. People decide to lead, and to be good, or bad, leaders. Let's consider the synthesis of the three attributes of WICS, starting at the end, with creativity.

Creativity

Creativity reflects the skills and attitudes involved in generating ideas that are novel, high in quality, and appropriate to the task at hand. We have viewed creative people as those who are willing to defy the crowd (Sternberg & Lubart, 1995). Some of the greatest psychologists of modern times are those who have been willing to defy the crowd in psychology (Sternberg, 2003a). In this view, creative people are like good stock pickers—they formulate ideas whose value others may not see at first, and then they persuade others to accept their ideas. Eventually, they move on to the next idea. We refer to this process as "buying low and selling high in the world of ideas."

The first step toward leadership is having creative ideas. When organizations select leaders, they typically want someone who can solve preexisting problems that have defied solution as well as someone who can solve the unexpected challenges that lie ahead—in other words, someone who can see old problems in new ways and new problems with fresh perspectives. But organizations do not always choose new leaders in a way that maximizes creativity. For example, when leaders are chosen by committees composed of individuals already in the organization, those individuals may be conservative and choose someone who fits into already existing organizational cultural norms and perspectives. When leaders are chosen by election, voters may be more persuaded by effective rhetoric than by a coherent vision for a new future. Thus, in the end, people who are chosen for leadership roles may not always be the most creative ones under consideration. Moreover, there are different ways in which they can be creative (Sternberg, Kaufman, & Pretz, 2003).

Leaders of organizations can be creative in different ways.

- *Replicators* do more or less what the previous leaders did and for the same reason.
- *Redefiners* do more or less what the previous leaders did, but give different reasons for doing what they are doing.
- *Forward incrementers* move the organization forward in the same direction that it was going before and in relatively small steps.
- *Advance forward incrementers* move the organization forward in the same direction that it was going before but in relatively large steps.

- *Redirectors* take organizations from where they are into new directions.
- *Reinitiators* essentially reinvent organizations; they start over from scratch.
- *Synthesizers* try to find a direction that represents an integration of a number of different trends within the organization.

No one way of being creative is all-around "best." What is best for a given organization depends on the situation in which the organization finds itself. But to truly be a creative leader, one must have certain mind-sets that promote creative leadership. These are (Sternberg & Lubart, 1995):

- *Willingness to see problems in new ways.* Often leaders and followers alike get stuck in old ways of seeing things.
- *Willingness to scrutinize decisions.* No matter how creative someone is, the individual will sometimes have ideas that are either conceptually bad, or that just do not work. Creative leaders ask tough questions about ideas—their own and others'—and then they act on their scrutiny of these ideas.
- *Willingness to sell ideas.* Creative ideas do not sell themselves. Leaders have to sell them. The more the ideas defy conventional ways of doing things, the harder it is to sell the creative ideas.
- *Willingness to surmount obstacles.* Creative people and creative ideas always encounter obstacles. Sometimes, these obstacles seem overwhelming. The question then is whether the individual is willing to persevere to overcome the obstacles.
- *Willingness to use but also to set aside knowledge.* Knowledge can either help or hinder creativity. On the one hand, one cannot go beyond existing ideas without knowing what those ideas are. On the other hand, knowledge can lead to entrenchment so that one has trouble seeing things in new ways. One's knowledge can lead to tunnel vision.
- *Willingness to take sensible risks.* Creativity almost always involves risk-taking. The more an idea defies the crowd, the riskier it is. The creative individual is willing to risk.
- *Willingness to tolerate ambiguity.* There may be long periods of time in which the parameters or consequences of a creative idea are not clear. One must be willing to tolerate ambiguity long enough to fulfill the realization of the idea.
- *Self-efficacy.* To be creative, one needs to believe in one's own ability to be creative. Such belief is especially important when others do not believe in one.
- *Willingness to grow.* Creative people are willing to grow and to go beyond past ideas. They do not get stuck on an idea and then stay with it forever.
- *Courage.* Defying the crowd ultimately requires the courage to go one's own way, even in the face of resistance.

In our research on creativity, we have found that creativity can be measured successfully through having people produce creative products (Lubart & Sternberg, 1995; Sternberg & Lubart, 1995); that creative people do tend to be more risk-taking than less creative ones (Lubart & Sternberg, 1995; Sternberg & Lubart, 1995); and that creative people are better able to think in novel, nonentrenched ways than are less creative people (Sternberg, 1982; Sternberg & Gastel, 1989a, 1989b).

Successful Intelligence

Successful intelligence is one's skill in setting and meeting one's own goals in life, given the cultural context in which one lives. One is successfully intelligent by virtue of recognizing one's own strengths and capitalizing on them, and recognizing one's own weaknesses and correcting or compensating for them. Successful intelligence operates on the basis of three kinds of abilities: creative ability to generate ideas, analytical ability to make sure the ideas are good ideas, and practical abilities to ensure that the ideas work in practice and that one is able to convince others of their value.

Leadership can fail, or at least become less effective, as a result of a lack of any of these three skills. The creative part of intelligence refers specifically to creative abilities, and not to the whole of creativity discussed in the previous section. Analytical abilities are the types measured by conventional tests of intelligence and, to a lesser extent, by tests of academic skills. These abilities are needed to analyze problems and critique potential solutions. Practical abilities are used to ensure that ideas are capable of being implemented, and to persuade people of the value of these ideas. The key point here is that leaders need to be able to sell their ideas. At the time I am writing this, two countries—France and the Netherlands—recently voted down in separate referenda a new European Constitution that their leaders supported. The leaders failed to sell the followers on their ideas, and hence, the ideas were torpedoed.

Our research (e.g., Sternberg, Forsythe, et al., 2000) suggests that academic and practical intelligence are, largely, different things. In other words, someone can have a great deal of school smarts, but not so much common sense, and vice versa. Even people who study intelligence, who may be high in academic intelligence, are not necessarily high in common sense!

The implication of this fact is that our society may be somewhat dysfunctional when it comes to recognizing superior leadership potential. The society very heavily relies on the use of tests. In order to make one's way up the society—toward more education, toward better education, and toward higher-paying, more-responsible jobs—it helps greatly if one performs well on standardized tests. If one does not perform well, it often is difficult to gain access to the routes that lead to success and privilege. But if our claim is correct, the society may be reinforcing those with academic intelligence to an extent that is unwarranted, as practical skills do not always go hand-in-hand with academic ones.

In this view, the society should be testing abilities in broader ways that identify all of successful intelligence, not just a part of it. We have attempted such measurements in our own work on the Rainbow Project and the University of Michigan Business School Project (Sternberg, The Rainbow Project Collaborators, & University of Michigan Business School Project Collaborators, 2004). In the former, we have found that including tests of creative and practical intelligence as well as of academic intelligence can roughly double— at least for our sample—prediction of freshman-year grades, and substantially reduce differences in scores between members of diverse ethnic groups.

Wisdom

Wisdom is defined as one's use of one's intelligence, creativity, and knowledge for a common good, over the long and short terms, as guided by values, through a balance among one's own, other people's, and higher interests (such as community or global ones). In essence then, wise people are ones who use their abilities to further a common good (Sternberg, 1998, 2003b, 2004a). Wisdom can be measured in a variety of ways, such as by giving people life problems, asking them to solve those problems, and then scoring their responses in terms of the extent to which the responses adhere to the tenets of some theory of wisdom (Baltes & Staudinger, 2000).

Over time, Baltes and his colleagues (e.g., Baltes, Smith, & Staudinger, 1992; Baltes & Staudinger, 1993) have collected a wide range of data showing the empirical utility of the proposed theoretical and measurement approaches to wisdom. For example, Staudinger, Lopez, and Baltes (1997) found that measures of intelligence and personality as well as their interface overlap with, but are nonidentical to, measures of wisdom in terms of constructs measured. Staudinger, Smith, and Baltes (1992) showed that human-services professionals outperformed a control group on wisdom-related tasks. In a further set of studies, Staudinger and Baltes (1996) found that performance settings that were ecologically relevant to the lives of their participants and that provided for actual or "virtual" interaction of minds increased wisdom-related performance substantially.

People can be intelligent, and even successfully intelligent, but foolish. Josef Stalin, Adolph Hitler, and Mao Tse-tung all were, no doubt, smart. They also were responsible, individually and collectively, for many millions of deaths. Many smart leaders behave in foolish ways. They commit fallacies in their thinking. What are the kinds of fallacies they commit?

The unrealistic optimism fallacy. This fallacy occurs when one believes one is so smart or powerful that it is pointless to worry about the outcomes, and especially the long-term ones, of what one does because everything will come out all right in the end—there is nothing to worry about, given one's brains or power. If one simply acts, the outcome will be fine. Clinton tended to repeat behavior that, first as Governor and then as President, was likely to come to a bad end. He seemed not to worry about it.

The egocentrism fallacy. This fallacy arises when one comes to think that one's own interests are the only ones that are important. One starts to ignore one's responsibilities to other people or to institutions. Sometimes, people in positions of responsibility may start off with good intentions, but then become corrupted by the power they wield and their seeming unaccountability to others for it. A prime minister, for example, might use his office in part or even primarily to escape prosecution, as has appeared to happen in some European countries in recent years.

The omniscience fallacy. This fallacy results from having available at one's disposal essentially any knowledge one might want that is, in fact, knowable. With a phone call, a powerful leader can have almost any kind of knowledge made available to him or her. At the same time, people look up to the powerful leader as extremely knowledgeable or even close to all-knowing. The powerful leader may then come to believe that he or she really is all-knowing. So may his or her staff, as illustrated by Janis (1972) in his analysis of victims of groupthink. In case after case, brilliant government officials made the most foolish of decisions, in part because they believed they knew much more than they did. They did not know what they did not know. For example, John F. Kennedy's invasion of the Bay of Pigs in Cuba was based on faulty intelligence; so was the invasion of Iraq under George W. Bush.

The omnipotence fallacy. This fallacy results from the extreme power one wields, or believes one wields. The result is overextension, and often, abuse of power. Sometimes, leaders create internal or external enemies in order to demand more power for themselves to deal with the supposed enemies (Sternberg, 2004b). In the United States, the central government has arrogated more power than has been the case for any government in recent history on the grounds of alleged terrorist threats. In Zimbabwe, Robert Mugabe has turned one group against another, as has Hugo Chavez, each with what appears to be the similar goal of greatly expanding and maintaining his own power.

The invulnerability fallacy. This fallacy derives from the presence of the illusion of complete protection, such as might be provided by a large staff. People and especially leaders may seem to have many friends ready to protect them at a moment's notice. The leaders may shield themselves from individuals who are anything less than sycophantic.

Synthesis

Effective leaders exhibit a synthesis of three kinds of skills and attitudes. They use creativity to produce novel ideas, academic/analytical intelligence and attitudes to discern if they are good ideas, practical intelligence to make their ideas work and to get others to listen to them, and wisdom to ensure that their ideas promote a common good.

Although psychologists have been at the forefront in developing ideas about creativity (see Antonakis, Cianciolo, & Sternberg, 2004), they have been rather chary about putting their ideas about leadership into practice. Undergraduate and even graduate psychology students typically are taught little or nothing about leadership at all. And when they are, they are not typically shown how they can put to use what they have learned to become leaders themselves, in the field of psychology, or anywhere else either. It is time to practice what we preach. First, we should teach all undergraduates basic theories and research findings regarding leadership. Second, we should show them how to use ideas about leadership in their own lives, especially in but not limited to their work in psychology. Third, we should ourselves role model what we teach, so that our students can become the future leaders of tomorrow.

Ultimately, the view here is that people decide for leadership. Some years ago, I was asked if I wanted to run for President of the American Psychological Association. My first reaction was not to do it: I did not feel that I was extraverted enough. But the more I thought about it, the more I thought I had a useful mission for the organization—unity. My goal was to unify a diverse and sometimes fractious organization. So I decided on a plan. I would act the role of someone running for APA President. I would do what such a person would do, knowing that I was no such person. After enacting the role for a few months, I became that person. I forgot I was acting. I decided for leadership. So can you.

References

Antonakis, J., Cianciolo, A. T., & Sternberg, R. J. (Eds.). (2004). *The nature of leadership.* Thousand Oaks, CA: Sage.

Baltes, P. B., Smith, J., & Staudinger, U. (1992). Wisdom and successful aging. In T. B. Sonderegger (Ed.), *Psychology and aging* (pp. 123–167). Lincoln, NE: University of Nebraska Press.

Baltes, P. B., & Staudinger, U. M. (1993). The search for a psychology of wisdom. *Current Directions in Psychological Science, 2,* 75–80.

Baltes, P. B., & Staudinger, U. M. (2000). Wisdom: A metaheuristic (pragmatic) to orchestrate mind and virtue toward excellence. *American Psychologist, 55,* 122–135.

Janis, I. L. (1972). *Victims of groupthink.* Boston: Houghton Mifflin.

Kellerman, B. (2004). *Bad leadership.* Cambridge, MA: Harvard Business School Press.

Lipman-Blumen, J. (2004). *The allure of toxic leaders: Why we follow destructive bosses and corrupt politicians—and how we can survive them.* New York: Oxford University Press.

Lubart, T. I., & Sternberg, R. J. (1995). An investment approach to creativity: Theory and data. In S. M. Smith, T. B. Ward, & R. A. Finke (Eds.), *The creative cognition approach* (pp. 269–302). Cambridge, MA: MIT Press.

Staudinger, U. M., & Baltes, P. M. (1996). Interactive minds: A facilitative setting for wisdom-related performance? *Journal of Personality and Social Psychology, 71,* 746–762.

Staudinger, U. M., Lopez, D. F., & Baltes, P. B. (1997). The psychometric location of wisdom-related performance: Intelligence, personality, and more? *Personality & Social Psychology Bulletin, 23,* 1200–1214.

Staudinger, U. M., Smith, J., & Baltes, P. B. (1992). Wisdom-related knowledge in life review task: Age differences and the role of professional specialization. *Psychology and Aging, 7,* 271–281.

Sternberg, R. J. (1982). Nonentrenchment in the assessment of intellectual giftedness. *Gifted Child Quarterly, 26,* 63–67.

Sternberg, R. J. (1998). A balance theory of wisdom. *Review of General Psychology, 2,* 347–365.

Sternberg, R. J. (Ed.). (2003a). *Psychologists defying the crowd: Stories of those who battled the establishment and won.* Washington, DC: American Psychological Association.

Sternberg, R. J. (2003b). *Wisdom, intelligence, and creativity synthesized.* New York: Cambridge University Press.

Sternberg, R. J. (2004a). What is wisdom and how can we develop it? *Annals of the American Academy of Political and Social Science, 591,* 164–174.

Sternberg, R. J. (2004b). Why smart people can be so foolish. *European Psychologist, 9*(3), 145–150.

Sternberg, R. J., Forsythe, G. B., Hedlund, J., Horvath, J., Snook, S., Williams, W. M., Wagner, R. K., & Grigorenko, E. L. (2000). *Practical intelligence in everyday life.* New York: Cambridge University Press.

Sternberg, R. J., & Gastel, J. (1989a). Coping with novelty in human intelligence: An empirical investigation. *Intelligence, 13,* 187–197.

Sternberg, R. J., & Gastel, J. (1989b). If dancers ate their shoes: Inductive reasoning with factual and counterfactual premises. *Memory and Cognition, 17,* 1–10.

Sternberg, R. J., Kaufman, J. C., & Pretz, J. E. (2003). A propulsion model of creative leadership. *Leadership Quarterly, 14,* 455–473.

Sternberg, R. J., & Lubart, T. I. (1995). *Defying the crowd: Cultivating creativity in a culture of conformity.* New York: Free Press.

Sternberg, R. J., The Rainbow Project Collaborators, & University of Michigan Business School Project Collaborators. (2004). Theory based university admissions testing for a new millennium. *Educational Psychologist, 39,* 185–198.

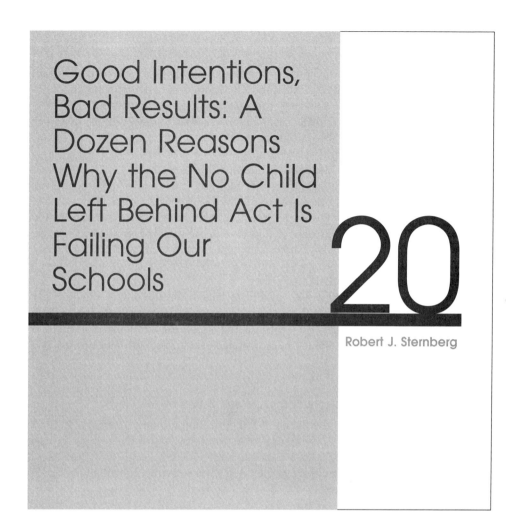

Good Intentions, Bad Results: A Dozen Reasons Why the No Child Left Behind Act Is Failing Our Schools

20

Robert J. Sternberg

The federal No Child Left Behind Act mandates national testing in our nation's schools in order to assess the quality of those schools. It was a well-intentioned piece of legislation passed by Congress to improve education. The Act recognized the need for accountability in schools, as well as for educational practice to be based on scientifically rigorous educational research. But it is having and will continue to have the opposite effect. The reason is that it flies in the face of much of what we know about the science of education. Here are a dozen reasons why the act is failing:

No accountability for standards of accountability. *The New York Times* recently reported that schools are in a state of chaos regarding how they are doing academically. State standards may show the schools to be excelling, while under the No Child Left Behind law, they are failing. The problem? There is no clear standard of accountability for the standards of accountability. The standards in the law, despite all the hoopla, are largely arbitrary and potentially even punitive. So schools are being held accountable to standards that meet no standard of accountability.

Penalizing schools with children from diverse backgrounds. We would like to believe that schools are exclusively responsible for the learning of pupils. But years of research have shown that, for better or worse, one of the best predictors, if not the best predictor, of achievement in a school is the socioeconomic status of the parents.

Schools with children of lower socioeconomic status will be at a disadvantage in almost any rigid standard of accountability. The same will be true for schools with many children for whom English is a second language.

Penalizing schools with children with diverse learning skills. Schools that have many children with learning disabilities or other diverse learning needs will almost inevitably fare poorly in a rigid accountability system that expects to have a single yardstick for all students. So these schools, too, will be penalized.

Encouraging cheating. Because the stakes for high scores are so high, schools are inadvertently encouraged to "fudge" the data, give children answers to tests, or make various attempts to exclude children from testing who, according to the Act, should be tested. The result is that schools are now under the same pressure students feel in high-stakes testing, and act similarly. They have started to cheat. There are many ways to cheat. For example, one is purposely to exclude scores of children with special needs and thereby fudge the data.

Encouraging schools to promote dropping out. Ironically, the "No Child" law inadvertently encourages schools to encourage their weaker students to drop out. In this way, those students' test scores will not reduce scores for the school. Student dropouts among low scorers actually have been increasing, arguably as a direct result of the legislation.

The assumption that what matters is what students know rather than how they use it. The tests assessing achievement under the No Child Left Behind Act largely measure knowledge rather than how knowledge is used. As a result, the emphasis in schools regresses to that of the drill-and-kill education of many years ago. That is, schools are starting again to emphasize rote learning instead of meaningful understanding and use of the knowledge students learn.

The assumption that knowledge of the three R's is supreme. Schooling is emphasizing more and more the traditional three R's of reading, writing, and arithmetic. There is nothing wrong with the three R's. But they are not all that matters to a sound education. Children, more and more, are being deprived of learning in art, music, history and social sciences, physical education, special programs for the gifted, and the like. In general, anything that might enrich children's education in a way that would make the children knowledgeable as well as wise and ready to make complex decisions in today's complex world is largely gone.

The assumption that good science should be politically guided. The Act specifies that educational practice be guided by good, rigorous science. But what is good science? The current administration, to an unprecedented degree, has decided to play an active role in deciding what it means by "good science." Some of the science thus supported may indeed be good science. But science has always proceeded best when it is left totally independent of the political process, and when competing schools of thought are left to slug it out on the scientific battlefield free of political influence or interference.

The view that conventional tests are some kind of panacea for the nation's educational woes. Relatively few countries in the world use the kinds of multiple-choice and short-answer tests that are so popular in the United States. They believe that such tests can measure only superficial levels of knowledge. There is nothing wrong, in principle, when these tests are used in conjunction with other kinds of tests. But when used alone, they trivialize the testing of children's skills, leading to an advantage for children who are skilled in the kinds of questions that appear on the tests.

Turning our schools into test-preparation courses. Our schools have become, to a large extent, test-preparation courses. At one time we worried that high schools were becoming test-preparation courses for college-entrance tests. Now schools at all levels are enduring the same fate. Worse, scores on one test often do not transfer to another test, so that schools are teaching very specific skills that will be of relatively little use outside the statewide testing program that has promoted them.

Insufficient funding. The No Child Left Behind Act is essentially an unfunded mandate from the federal government. The federal government is now piling up record deficits and is unlikely to put in the money the Act would need to succeed in any form. But states are also in the red. So we find ourselves, as a nation, stuck with an act that no one can afford but that the states are required to enact.

Dividing rather than unifying the world of education. The Act, originally passed with bipartisan support, no longer has the support of many Democrats and some Republicans. Moreover, it does not have the support of many of the nation's schools that are being forced to adhere to it. Forcing standards on schools dreamed up by politicians never has been, and never will be, the right way to create the best education for our children.

In sum, No Child Left Behind is an Act used to produce the nation's educational report card. But it, itself, receives a failing grade. Schools are being straitjacketed in attaining what is best for our children, and straitjackets cannot produce the kind of flourishing education system our children need and deserve.

Does the nation need a national educational reform Act? One could debate the merits of any such legislation. But if the United States is to have such an Act, here are some guidelines for what it should look like:

- All major stakeholders should have a role in formulating it, to ensure buy-in from all those who will be affected. To unify the world of education, a new act must be formulated in a totally consultative way, rather than be imposed from above.
- The Act should have a clear rationale for its standards of accountability.
- Any mandates of the act should be fully funded.
- The Act should recognize that different schools face very different situations with regard to the skills and knowledge base of the student body, level of parental support, funding, educational resources, experience of the teaching staff, and many other variables. These variables must be taken into account in generating expectations for schools.
- The Act should have as its priority rewarding success rather than punishing perceived failure. It should not be perceived primarily as punitive.
- The Act should recognize the wide range of student accomplishments that are important for success in school and in life—the three R's, but also progress in fields such as the natural and social sciences, the arts (including musical and dramatic ones), and athletics, among other things.
- The Act should recognize that achievement is not just about what one knows, but about how one analyzes what one knows, creatively goes beyond what one knows, and applies what one knows in practice.
- The Act should recognize that the best testing uses a variety of different kinds of assessments, including conventional assessments as well as assessments that emphasize performances and portfolios.

■ The Act should indeed stress the importance of science to the practice of education, but scientists alone should decide what constitutes good science. And we must recognize that science is not prepared at this moment to provide answers to all of the problems schools and the teachers in them face.

Most important, schools should be places that optimize education—that provide each student with the best possible education. They should not become test-preparation centers.

Index